Lecture Notes in Computer Science   14746

Founding Editors

Gerhard Goos
Juris Hartmanis

Editorial Board Members

Elisa Bertino, *Purdue University, West Lafayette, IN, USA*
Wen Gao, *Peking University, Beijing, China*
Bernhard Steffen, *TU Dortmund University, Dortmund, Germany*
Moti Yung, *Columbia University, New York, NY, USA*

The series Lecture Notes in Computer Science (LNCS), including its subseries Lecture Notes in Artificial Intelligence (LNAI) and Lecture Notes in Bioinformatics (LNBI), has established itself as a medium for the publication of new developments in computer science and information technology research, teaching, and education.

LNCS enjoys close cooperation with the computer science R & D community, the series counts many renowned academics among its volume editors and paper authors, and collaborates with prestigious societies. Its mission is to serve this international community by providing an invaluable service, mainly focused on the publication of conference and workshop proceedings and postproceedings. LNCS commenced publication in 1973.

Jurlind Budurushi · Oksana Kulyk · Sarah Allen ·
Theo Diamandis · Ariah Klages-Mundt ·
Andrea Bracciali · Geoffrey Goodell ·
Shin'ichiro Matsuo
Editors

Financial Cryptography and Data Security

FC 2024 International Workshops

Voting, DeFI, WTSC, CoDecFin
Willemstad, Curaçao, March 4–8, 2024
Revised Selected Papers

Editors
Jurlind Budurushi
Baden-Württemberg Cooperative State University Karlsruhe
Karlsruhe, Germany

Sarah Allen
Cornell Tech
New York, NY, USA

Ariah Klages-Mundt
Superluminal Labs
London, UK

Geoffrey Goodell
University College London
London, UK

Oksana Kulyk
IT University of Copenhagen
Copenhagen, Denmark

Theo Diamandis
Massachusetts Institute of Technology
Cambridge, MA, USA

Andrea Bracciali
University of Turin
Turin, Italy

Shin'ichiro Matsuo
Virginia Tech/Georgetown University
Arlington, VA, USA

ISSN 0302-9743　　　　　　ISSN 1611-3349　(electronic)
Lecture Notes in Computer Science
ISBN 978-3-031-69230-7　　ISBN 978-3-031-69231-4　(eBook)
https://doi.org/10.1007/978-3-031-69231-4

© International Financial Cryptography Association 2025
Chapter "Systematic User Evaluation of a Second Device Based Cast-as-Intended Verifiability Approach" is licensed under the terms of the Creative Commons Attribution 4.0 International License (http://creativecommons.org/licenses/by/4.0/). For further details see license information in the chapter.

This work is subject to copyright. All rights are solely and exclusively licensed by the Publisher, whether the whole or part of the material is concerned, specifically the rights of translation, reprinting, reuse of illustrations, recitation, broadcasting, reproduction on microfilms or in any other physical way, and transmission or information storage and retrieval, electronic adaptation, computer software, or by similar or dissimilar methodology now known or hereafter developed.
The use of general descriptive names, registered names, trademarks, service marks, etc. in this publication does not imply, even in the absence of a specific statement, that such names are exempt from the relevant protective laws and regulations and therefore free for general use.
The publisher, the authors and the editors are safe to assume that the advice and information in this book are believed to be true and accurate at the date of publication. Neither the publisher nor the authors or the editors give a warranty, expressed or implied, with respect to the material contained herein or for any errors or omissions that may have been made. The publisher remains neutral with regard to jurisdictional claims in published maps and institutional affiliations.

This Springer imprint is published by the registered company Springer Nature Switzerland AG
The registered company address is: Gewerbestrasse 11, 6330 Cham, Switzerland

If disposing of this product, please recycle the paper.

VOTING 2024 Preface

These proceedings collect the papers accepted at the 9th Workshop on Advances in Secure Electronic Voting (Voting 2024; http://fc24.ifca.ai/voting/), associated with the Financial Cryptography and Data Security 2024 conference (FC 2024). The Voting workshop was held on March 8, 2024.

This year's workshop received 13 submissions, of which 5 were accepted for publication. Thanks to the generous efforts of the PC, each paper received two reviews per submission in a double-blind process, providing constructive feedback to authors, followed by PC discussion where appropriate. We are grateful to our Program Committee for their time and effort.

We express our sincere gratitude to all those who submitted their work, the Program Committee for their careful work, and all those who participated in the workshop. We are grateful to Ray Hirschfeld and IFCA for organizing the event logistics and to the FC chairs and steering committee for their continued support of the Voting workshop.

May 2024

Jurlind Budurushi
Oksana Kulyk

Voting 2024 Organization

Program Chairs

Jurlind Budurushi	Baden-Württemberg Cooperative State University Karlsruhe, Germany
Oksana Kulyk	IT University of Copenhagen, Denmark

Program Committee

Roberto Araujo	Universidade Federal do Pará, Brazil
Josh Benaloh	Microsoft Research, USA
Matthew Bernhard	University of Michigan, USA
Jurlind Budurushi	Baden-Württemberg Cooperative State University Karlsruhe, Germany
Jeremy Clark	Concordia University, Canada
Costantin Catalin Dragan	University of Surrey, UK
Aleksander Essex	Western University, Canada
Tamara Finogina	Polytechnic University of Catalonia, Spain
Kristian Gjøsteen	Norwegian University of Science and Technology, Norway
Rolf Haenni	Bern University of Applied Sciences, Switzerland
Thomas Heines	Queensland University of Technology, Australia
Oksana Kulyk	IT University of Copenhagen, Denmark
Johannes Mueller	University of Luxembourg, Luxembourg
Olivier Pereira	UCLouvain, Belgium
Daniel Rausch	University of Stuttgart, Germany
Peter Roenne	University of Luxembourg, Luxembourg
Peter Y. A. Ryan	University of Luxembourg, Luxembourg
Carsten Schuermann	IT University of Copenhagen, Denmark
Philip Stark	University of California, Berkeley, USA
Vanessa Teague	Thinking Cybersecurity, Australia

DeFi 2024 Preface

These proceedings collect the papers accepted at the Fourth Workshop on Decentralized Finance (DeFi 2024, https://fc24.ifca.ai/defi/), held in association with the Financial Cryptography and Data Security 2024 conference (FC 2024) on March 8, 2024.

The focus of the DeFi workshop series is decentralized finance, a blockchain powered peer-to-peer financial system. This fourth version of the workshop again sought to solicit contributions from both academia and industry which focused on addressing fundamental, timely, and important questions at the center of DeFi.

The workshop received 32 submissions, of which 12 were accepted either as a short paper (5) or as a talk (7). All of the short papers and a subset of the talks, as précis, appear in these proceedings. Overall, the organizers were impressed by the quality of submissions received and were delighted by the strong attendance and lively discussion during the workshop.

The Organizing Committee would like to extend sincere thanks to all those who submitted their work, the Program Committee for their careful work, and all those who participated in the workshop. In addition, we would like to extend our thanks to Rafael Hirschfeld for all his support.

April 2024

Sarah Allen
Theo Diamandis
Ariah Klages-Mundt

DeFi 2024 Organization

Program Chairs

Sarah Allen — Flashbots, IC3
Theo Diamandis — Massachusetts Institute of Technology and Bain Capital Crypto
Ariah Klages-Mundt — Cornell University

Program Committee

Cuneyt Akcora	University of Central Florida
Guillermo Angeris	Bain Capital Crypto
Maryam Bahrani	a16z crypto
James Chiang	Aarhus University
Tarun Chitra	Gauntlet
Jeremy Clark	Concordia University
Matheus Ferreira	University of Virginia
Pranav Garimidi	a16z crypto
Khaled Grira	Block Analitica
Dominik Harz	Interlay
Ruizhe Jia	Columbia University
Mahimna Kelkar	Cornell University
Kshitij Kulkarni	UC Berkeley
Jiasun Li	George Mason University
Patrick McCorry	Arbitrum
Jason Milionis	Columbia University
Barnabe Monnot	Ethereum Foundation
Mahsa Moosavi	Offchain Labs/Concordia University
Daniel Moroz	Harvard University
Andreas Park	University of Toronto
Julien Prat	Polytechnic Institute of Paris
Palina Tolmach	Runtime Verification
Sam Werner	ICL
Alexei Zamyatin	Interlay
Fan Zhang	Yale University

WTSC 2024 Preface

These proceedings collect the papers accepted at the *Eighth Workshop on Trusted Smart Contracts (WTSC24* - http://fc24.ifca.ai/wtsc/*)*, associated to the Financial Cryptography and Data Security 2024 international conference (FC 2024). WTSC 2024 was hosted again on the beautiful island of Curaçao.

The WTSC series' main focus is on *smart contracts*, i.e. self-enforcing agreements in the form of executable programs, and other *decentralised applications* that interoperate with (possibly specialised) blockchain systems. These technologies have introduced unanswered and challenging research questions, as well as new and decentralised business models and use cases. Multidisciplinary and multifactorial aspects affect correctness, safety, privacy, authentication, efficiency, sustainability, resilience, and trust in smart contracts and decentralised applications.

The WTSC series aims to address the scientific foundations of Trusted Smart Contract engineering and their applications, i.e., the development of contracts and applications that enjoy some verifiable "correctness" properties, and to discuss open problems, proposed solutions, and the vision of future developments amongst a research community that is growing around these themes. This community includes users, practitioners, industry, institutions, and academia. Over the years, the number of theoretical problems and applications have increased, which is shown by the wide set of topics that are discussed at WTSC. The multidisciplinary Programme Committee of this eighth edition of WTSC comprised members from companies, universities, and research institutions from several countries worldwide. The association to FC 2024 provided, once again, an ideal context for running our workshop.

This year WTSC received twelve submissions by about thirty-five authors. Given the high quality of submission, five papers were finally accepted after double-blind peer review, with an average of four reviews per paper, some followed by discussion, providing constructive feedback to the authors of all submitted papers. We want to commend the generous effort by the PC. Revised papers after the discussion at the workshop are collected in the present volume.

Accepted papers analysed the current state of the art of smart contracts and their development. Key recent developments addressed by papers and discussed at the workshop included Layer-2 protocols, supporting Zero-Knowledge technology, models of smart contract computation, scam detection models, and on-chain execution cost models.

The fruitful collaboration with the Workshop on Coordination of Decentralized Finance (CoDecFin 2024) series this year provided two jointly invited speakers, both respected scientists in the community who gave very well-received speeches on timely and salient topics: *Inside Arbitrum,* by Ed Felten, Co-Founder and Chief Scientist, Offchain Labs/Arbitrum; and *On Privacy and Governance* by Fabian Schär, University of Basel.

Once again, WTSC 2024's chairs would like to thank everyone for their effort and valuable contributions: authors, program committee members, reviewers, and participants; as well as the support by IFCA, the FC 2024 committee, and our two generous sponsors: Riv Capital, the main sponsor, and HyperCycle, the gold sponsor; and Ray Hirschfeld for the usual exceptional organisation and coordination of the whole FC event.

May 2024

Andrea Bracciali
Geoffrey Goodell
WTSC24 Chairs
WTSC24 was supported by

WTSC 2024 Organization

Program Committee

Monika di Angelo	Vienna University of Technology, Austria
Igor Artamonov	Emerald, USA
Daniel Augot	Inria, France
Fadi Barbara	University of Turin, Italy
Massimo Bartoletti	University of Cagliari, Italy
Stefano Bistarelli	University of Perugia, Italy
Christina Boura	Versailles SQT Univ., France
Andrea Bracciali	University of Turin, Italy
Daniel Broby	Ulster University, UK
Martin Chapman	King's College London, UK
Nicola Dimitri	University of Siena, Italy
Josselin Feist	Trail of Bits, USA
Oliver Giudice	Banca d'Italia, Italy
Davide Grossi	University of Groningen, Netherlands
Geoffrey Goodell	UCL, UK
Yoichi Hirai	BedRock Systems GmbH, Germany
Michela Iezzi	Banca d'Italia, Italy
Ioannis Kounelis	Joint Research Centre, European Commission, Italy
Pascal Lafourcade	University of Clermont Auvergne, France
Enrique Larraia	nChain, USA
Andrew Lewis-Pye	London School of Economics, UK
Akaki Mamageishvili	Offchain Labs, Switzerland
Carsten Maple	University of Warwick, UK
Carla Mascia	Hub Innovazione Trentino, Italy
Neil McLaren	ConsenSys, UK
Patrick McCorry	Pisa Research, UK
Sihem Mesnager	University of Paris VIII, France
Bud Mishra	NYU, USA
Alex Norta	Tallinn University of Technology, Estonia
Akira Otsuka	Institute of Information Security, Japan
Federico Pintore	University of Trento, Italy
Massimiliano Sala	University of Trento, Italy
Jason Teutsch	Truebit, USA
Philip Wadler	University of Edinburgh, UK

Yilei Wang	Hong Kong Polytechnic University, China
Tim Weingärtner	Lucerne University, Switzerland
Santiago Zanella-Beguelin	Microsoft, UK
Dionysis Zindros	Stanford University, USA

CoDecFin 2024 Preface

These proceedings collect the papers accepted at the *Fifth Workshop on Coordination of Decentralized Finance (CoDecFin* - http://fc24.ifca.ai/codecfin/*)* associated to the Financial Cryptography and Data Security 2024 international conference (FC 2024). This year was the third opportunity to have an in-person workshop after the pandemic, and it was brilliant to have the opportunity to meet colleagues in person and exchange ideas with them during the conference and the workshop. Nonetheless, we were able to offer technical support to a number of speakers that could not yet travel to Curacao and allow them to present their contributions on-line.

The main purpose of the series of Workshops on Coordination of Decentralized Finance (CoDecFin) is to discuss multi-disciplinary issues regarding technologies and operations of decentralized finance based on permissionless blockchain.

From an academic point of view, security and privacy protection are among the leading research streams. The Financial Cryptography conference discusses these research challenges. On the other hand, other stakeholders than cryptographers and blockchain engineers have different interests in these characteristics of blockchain technology. For example, regulators face difficulty in tracing transactions in terms of anti-money laundering (AML) against privacy-enhancing crypto-assets. Another example is consumer protection in the case of cyberattacks on crypto-asset custodians. Blockchain business entities sometimes start their business before the technology has matured, but the technology and operations are not transparent to regulators and consumers. The main problem is a lack of communication among stakeholders of the decentralized finance ecosystem. G20 discussed the issue of insufficient communication among stakeholders in 2019. It concluded that there is an essential need to have a multi-stakeholder discussion among engineers, regulators, business entities, and operators based on the neutrality of academia.

The CoDecFin workshop was initiated in 2020 to facilitate such multi-stakeholder discussion in a neutral academic environment. The goals of CoDecFin are to have a common understanding of technology and regulatory goals and discuss essential issues of blockchain technology with all stakeholders mentioned above. It is a fantastic series of academic workshops especially because we can involve regulators and engineers in the discussion at the Financial Cryptography conference.

This year, we had four sessions: Keynote, (1) Economics and Consensus, (2) Wallet and Credentials, (3) Regulations and Standards, and (4) Joint Keynote session with WTSC 2024.

This year's edition of CoDecFin received fifteen submissions by about fifty authors. Given the high quality of the submissions, nine papers were accepted after double-blind peer reviews. Thanks to the generous effort by the PC, each paper received three reviews, providing constructive feedback to authors, followed by PC discussion where appropriate. Revised papers after the discussion at the workshop are collected in the present volume. CoDecFin also hosted, jointly with the 8th Workshop on Trusted Smart Contracts (WTSC 2024), a joint keynote session.

CoDecFin 2024's chair and program committee members would like to thank everyone for their usual effort and valuable contributions: authors, reviewers, and participants, as well as the support by IFCA, FC 2024 committees, and Ray Hirschfeld for the usual exceptional organization and coordination of the event.

June 2024

Shin'ichiro Matsuo
CoDecFin 24 Chair

CoDecFin 2024 Organization

Program Committee Members

Julien Bringer	Kallistech, France
Feng Chen	University of British Columbia, Canada
Victor Garcia	Universitat Oberta de Catalunya, Spain
Joaquin Garcia-Alfaro	Télécom SudParis, France
Carole House (Chair of the Technology Advisory Group at CFTC)	Georgetown University, France
Shin'ichiro Matsuo (Chair)	Virginia Tech/Georgetown University, USA
Kanta Matsuura	University of Tokyo, Japan
Steven Nam	Stanford Journal of Blockchain Law & Policy, USA
Jarek Nabrzyski	University of Notre Dame, USA
Roman Danziger Pavlov	SafeStead Inc., Canada
Robert Schwentker	DLT Education and BSafe.network, USA
Yonatan Sompolinsky	Hebrew University of Jerusalem, DAGlabs, Israel
Ryosuke Ushida	JFSA, Japan
Robert Wardrop	University of Cambridge Judge Business School, UK
Aaron Wright	Cardozo Law School, USA
Anton Yemelyanov	Base58 Association, Canada

Contents

9th Workshop on Advances in Secure Electronic Voting Schemes (Voting 2024)

RLAs for 2-Seat STV Elections: Revisited 3
    Michelle Blom, Peter J. Stuckey, Vanessa Teague, and Damjan Vukcevic

Efficient Weighting Schemes for Auditing Instant-Runoff Voting Elections 18
    Alexander Ek, Philip B. Stark, Peter J. Stuckey, and Damjan Vukcevic

Systematic User Evaluation of a Second Device Based Cast-as-Intended Verifiability Approach 33
    Tobias Hilt, Benjamin Berens, Tomasz Truderung, Margarita Udovychenko, Stephan Neumann, and Melanie Volkamer

On the Applicability of STARKs to Counted-as-Collected Verification in Existing Homomorphic E-Voting Systems 50
    Max Harrison and Thomas Haines

"You Shall Not Abstain!" A Formal Study of Forced Participation 66
    Wojciech Jamroga, Peter B. Roenne, Yan Kim, and Peter Y. A. Ryan

4th Workshop on Decentralized Finance (DeFI 2024)

Transaction Fee Mechanism Design with Active Block Producers 85
    Maryam Bahrani, Pranav Garimidi, and Tim Roughgarden

Transaction Ordering Auctions 91
    Christoph Schlegel

An Analysis of Fixed-Spread Liquidation Lending in DeFi 105
    Ciamac Moallemi and Utkarsh Patange

Structural Advantages for Integrated Builders in MEV-Boost 128
    Mallesh Pai and Max Resnick

8th Workshop on Trusted Smart Contracts (WTSC 2024)

EIP-4844 Economics and Rollup Strategies 135
    Davide Crapis, Edward W. Felten, and Akaki Mamageishvili

Message-Passing in the Extended UTxO Ledger 150
  Polina Vinogradova and Orestis Melkonian

ZeroAuction: Zero-Deposit Sealed-Bid Auction via Delayed Execution 170
  Haoqian Zhang, Michelle Yeo, Vero Estrada-Galiñanes, and Bryan Ford

Scam Token Detection Based on Static Analysis Before Contract
Deployment 189
  Taichi Igarashi and Kanta Matsuura

A Comparative Gas Cost Analysis of Proxy and Diamond Patterns in EVM
Blockchains for Trusted Smart Contract Engineering 207
  Anto Benedetti, Tiphaine Henry, and Sara Tucci-Piergiovanni

5th Workshop on Coordination of Decentralized Finance (CoDecFin 2024)

IZPR: Instant Zero Knowledge Proof of Reserve 225
  Trevor Conley, Nilsso Diaz, Diego Espada, Alvin Kuruvilla,
  Stenton Mayne, and Xiang Fu

A New Approach to Estimating Bitcoin Production Cost 240
  Go Yamamoto

Ethereum Proof-of-Stake Consensus Layer: Participation
and Decentralization 253
  Dominic Grandjean, Lioba Heimbach, and Roger Wattenhofer

Short Paper: The PoW Landscape in the Aftermath of The Merge 281
  Lucianna Kiffer, Sophia Skorik, Yann Vonlanthen, and Roger Wattenhofer

Accountable Wallet: A Comprehensive Framework for Proving
the Multifaceted Legitimacy of Wallet 293
  Masato Yamanaka, Mitchell Travers, and Ken Katayama

Reconstitution of NFTs Based on a Game Theory Model 313
  Jiahui Shao, Maochao Xu, Rui Fang, Xiaoxiao Hu, Weidong Shi,
  and Dana Alsagheer

Regulatory Implications of MEV Mitigations 335
  Yan Ji and James Grimmelmann

Towards Regulation of Brazilian Blockchain Utilization 364
  Marjori Klinczak, Jose Simao de Paula Pinto, and Egon Wildauer

An Analysis and Proposal on Standardization and R&D Strategies
to Promote Responsible Development of Digital Asset 371
   Takaya Sugino, Masato Yamanaka, and Carole House

Author Index 389

9th Workshop on Advances in Secure Electronic Voting Schemes (Voting 2024)

RLAs for 2-Seat STV Elections: Revisited

Michelle Blom[1(✉)], Peter J. Stuckey[2], Vanessa Teague[3], and Damjan Vukcevic[4]

[1] School of Computing and Information Systems, University of Melbourne, Parkville, Australia
michelle.blom@unimelb.edu.au
[2] Department of Data Science and AI, Monash University, Clayton, Australia
[3] Thinking Cybersecurity Pty. Ltd., Melbourne, Australia
[4] Department of Econometrics and Business Statistics, Monash University, Clayton, Australia

Abstract. Single Transferable Vote (STV) elections are a principled approach to electing multiple candidates in a single election. Each ballot has a starting value of 1, and a candidate is elected if they gather a total vote value more than a defined quota. Votes over the quota have their value reduced by a *transfer value* so as to remove the quota, and are passed to the next candidate on the ballot. Risk-limiting audits (RLAs) are a statistically sound approach to election auditing which guarantees that failure to detect an error in the result is bounded by a limit. A first approach to RLAs for 2-seat STV elections has been defined. In this paper we show how we can improve this approach by reasoning about lower bounds on transfer values, and how we can extend the approach to *partially* audit an election, if the method does not support a full audit.

1 Introduction

Single Transferable Vote (STV) elections are widely used around the world for multiple candidate contests. Risk-limiting audits (RLAs) are very complex for STV elections. Prior work has demonstrated that RLAs for some 2-seat STV elections, where at least one candidate has more than quota's worth of votes on their first preferences, are possible [1]. This existing work proposed two approaches for undertaking RLAs for 2-seat STV. The first tackles the case where this *first-round winner criterion* is satisfied, while the second presents a general method that applies when it does not. The latter method was generally not successful in forming an audit to verify the correctness of both winners.

This paper presents an improved method for 2-seat STV RLAs where the contest satisfies the first-round winner criterion. This new method is able to form audits for a greater number of contests, and reduces the expected sample sizes needed for these audits by 15 to 19% across the contests considered in our evaluation. The original method introduced assertions for (i) verifying that

---

This work was partially supported by the Australian Research Council: Discovery Project DP220101012, OPTIMA ITTC IC200100009.

the first winner achieved a quota on their first preferences, (ii) verifying an upper bound on the transfer value of this first winner, and (iii) using this upper bound, verifying that the second winner could not have possibly lost to any of the reported losers. We improve this method by introducing a new assertion that verifies a non-trivial *lower bound* on this first winner's transfer value, and using both bounds to fine tune the assertions formed in (iii). We additionally show how contests that perform a preliminary batch-elimination prior to electing any candidates can be audited using this scheme.

A full RLA, verifying the correctness of both winners, may not be possible for a given 2-seat contest. It may be desirable to perform some kind of audit to verify some aspects of the reported outcome. We show how the 'general' method can be re-framed as a five-stage process that forms a *partial* RLA. This process aims to establish (i) a subset of candidates as definite losers, and (ii) a subset of candidates as definite winners. The remaining candidates are *possible* winners. The first three stages of this revised general method are drawn from the work of [1]. In this paper we add a fourth stage that looks for opportunities to reduce the expected sample size of the partial audit. The final stage summarises what aspects of the reported outcome are verified by the audit, and which are not.

The remainder of this paper is structured as follows. Section 2 describes the variant of STV that we consider, and assertion-based RLAs. Three sections follow that consider different election scenarios and how to audit them: Sect. 3 covers auditing of batch elimination, Sect. 4 covers the improved *first-round winner* method and an evaluation against the existing approach, and Sect. 5 shows how we can partially audit elections where no candidate has a quota on first preferences. We conclude in Sect. 6.

2 Preliminaries

We consider a variant of STV, modelled on how STV is typically implemented in the United States. We describe this variant in Sect. 2.1.

We define an STV election as per Definition 1. We define a ballot b as a sequence of candidates π, listed in order of preference (most popular first), without duplicates but without necessarily including all candidates. We use list notation (e.g., $\pi = [c_1, c_2, c_3, c_4]$). The notation $\text{first}(\pi) = \pi(1)$ denotes the first item (candidate) in sequence π.

Definition 1 (STV Election). *An STV election E is a tuple $E = (\mathcal{C}, \mathcal{B}, \mathcal{Q}, N)$ where $\mathcal{C}$ is a set of candidates, $\mathcal{B}$ the multiset of ballots cast[1], $\mathcal{Q}$ the election quota (the number of votes a candidate must attain to win a seat—usually the Droop quota—Eq. 1), and N the number of seats to be filled.*

$$\mathcal{Q} = \left\lfloor \frac{|\mathcal{B}|}{N+1} \right\rfloor + 1 \tag{1}$$

---

[1] A multiset allows for the inclusion of duplicate items.

Table 1. An STV election, stating the number of ballots cast with each listed ranking over candidates c_1 to c_5. The quota, and first-preference tallies are listed.

Ranking	Count	Ranking	Count
$[c_1, c_3]$	8,001	$[c_3, c_4]$	5,000
$[c_1]$	1,000	$[c_4, c_1, c_2]$	3,950
$[c_2, c_3, c_4]$	3,000	$[c_5, c_2]$	50
Total			21,001

$N = 2$
$\mathcal{Q} = 7,001$
$t_{c_1,1} = 9,001 \qquad t_{c_4,1} = 3,950$
$t_{c_2,1} = 3,000 \qquad t_{c_5,1} = 50$
$t_{c_3,1} = 5,000$

Definition 2. *Projection* $\sigma_\mathcal{S}(\pi)$ *We define the projection of a sequence π onto a set $\mathcal{S}$ as the largest subsequence of π that contains only elements of $\mathcal{S}$. (The elements keep their relative order in π.) For example: $\sigma_{\{c_2,c_3\}}([c_1, c_2, c_4, c_3]) = [c_2, c_3]$ and $\sigma_{\{c_2,c_3,c_4,c_5\}}([c_6, c_4, c_7, c_2, c_1]) = [c_4, c_2]$.*

The tabulation of STV elections proceeds in rounds (see Sect. 2.1). Initially, all candidates are awarded the ballots on which they are the first ranked candidate. We call a candidate c's tally at this stage their *first-preference tally*, denoted $t_{c,1}$. We use $t_{c,r}$ to denote a candidate's tally at the start of round r of tabulation. In the election of Table 1, candidates c_1 to c_5 have first-preference tallies of 9001, 3000, 5000, 3950, and 50 votes, respectively.

2.1 'US' Style STV

Each ballot cast in the election starts with a value of 1. In any given round of tabulation, if no candidate's tally is equal to or above the election's quota, the candidate with the smallest tally is eliminated. All the ballots in the eliminated candidate's tally are redistributed to the next most preferred *eligible* candidate on the ballot. These ballots are transferred at their current value. At any stage where ballots are distributed from one candidate to another, the only candidates that are eligible to receive votes are those that have not yet been eliminated or elected to a seat, and who have less than a quota's worth of votes in their tally.

Eliminations proceed as described above until at least one candidate's tally equals or exceeds the election's quota. At this stage, these candidates are elected to a seat. These candidates will be elected to a seat in order of their *surplus*. For each such candidate, we define their *surplus* as the difference between their current tally and the quota. The ballots sitting in the tally pile of this candidate are *reweighted* and distributed to the next most preferred eligible candidate on the ballot. For a candidate c, elected to a seat in round r of tabulation, we define the *transfer value* τ_c used to reweight the ballots in their tally as shown in Eq. 2, where $t_{c,r}$ denotes the tally of c at the start of round r.

$$\tau_c = \frac{t_{c,r} - \mathcal{Q}}{t_{c,r}} \qquad (2)$$

For a ballot $b \in \mathcal{B}$, whose current value is $v_{b,r}$, its new value when it leaves the tally pile of candidate c upon their election to a seat becomes $\tau_c\, v_{b,r}$.

Tabulation proceeds by seating candidates whose tally reaches or exceeds a quota and distributing their votes to eligible candidates, and eliminating candidates when no candidate has a quota. This process continues until either all seats have been filled, or the number of candidates still standing equals the number of seats left to be filled. These remaining candidates are then elected.

Consider the election in Table 1. The quota is 7001 votes. Candidate c_1 has a quota on first preferences, and is elected to the first seat. Their transfer value is $\tau = (9001 - 7001)/9001 = 0.222$. The 8,001 $[c_1, c_3]$ ballots are given to candidate c_3, adding 1,776.222 votes to c_3's tally. The 1,000 $[c_1]$ ballots become *exhausted*. Candidate c_3 now has 6,776.222 votes. As no candidate has a quota's worth of votes, the candidate with the smallest tally is eliminated. Here, this is candidate c_5 on 50 votes. These 50 ballots are given to c_2 at their current value of 1. Candidate c_2 now has 3,050 votes. Still no candidate has a quota's worth of votes. Candidate c_2 is eliminated next. The 50 $[c_5, c_2]$ ballots become exhausted, and the 3,000 $[c_2, c_3, c_4]$ ballots are given to c_3, who now has 9,776.222 votes. Candidate c_3 has achieved a quota, and is elected to the second seat.

Batch Elimination. We also consider a variation of the above process in which a batch elimination step is first performed. We first determine if there are any candidates for which there is no mathematical possibility for them to win. For each candidate, we compute the number of ballots on which they are ranked, and compare this tally to the tally of the N candidates with the highest first-preference tally. Consider the election in Table 1. The two candidates with the highest first-preference tallies are c_1 on 8,001 votes, and c_3 on 5,000 votes. Candidate c_5 is ranked on 50 ballots. Candidates c_2 and c_4 are ranked on 7,000 and 11,950 ballots, respectively. There is no possibility for c_5 to win, so they are eliminated in the first round, and their 50 $[c_5, c_2]$ ballots are given to c_2.

Tabulation then proceeds as described above. Candidate c_1 is elected, giving c_3 1,776.2 votes and a tally of 6,776.2. Candidate c_2 is eliminated, giving 3,000 votes to c_3. Candidate c_3 is elected to the second seat on a tally of 9,776.2.

2.2 Assertion-Based Approaches to Risk-Limiting Audits

SHANGRLA [3] provides a general framework for RLAs, using *assertions* as 'building blocks'. An *assertion* is a statement about the full set of ballots in an election. These are typically expressed as an inequality about some property that would be consistent with a particular election outcome. An example of an assertion is "Alice received more votes than Bob". In the SHANGRLA framework, we need to design a set of assertions such that, if they are all true, they imply that the reported winner really won the election. To conduct an audit, we statistically test each assertion using general statistical methods that form part of the framework. Assertions need to have a specific mathematical form to fit into the framework. In general, any linear combination of tallies (counts of different types of ballots) can be converted into a SHANGRLA assertion [2]. All of the assertions we develop in this paper are of this form.

Table 2. Assertions verifying the batch elimination of the UWIs and Nikiforakis in the 2021 BoE election in Minneapolis, Minnesota, and their sample sizes.

Assertion	Sample Size
AG(S. Brandt, UWIs)	20
AG(S. Pree-Stinson, UWIs)	35
AG(S. Brandt, K. Nikiforakis)	27
AG(S. Pree-Stinson, K. Nikiforakis)	69
Total cost:	69

3 Context: Batch Elimination First

We first consider how we can verify, in an RLA, that the candidates eliminated as part of an initial batch elimination did indeed have no mathematical possibility of winning. To do so, we use the existing AG assertion of Blom *et al.* [1].

AG(w, l) Verifies that candidate w always has a higher tally than l by showing that w's first-preference tally is higher than the maximum tally l could achieve while w is still standing: $t_{w,1} > |\{b : b \in \mathcal{B}, \text{first}\left(\sigma_{\{w,l\}}(b)\right) = l\}|$.

For a US-STV election $E = (\mathcal{C}, \mathcal{B}, \mathcal{Q}, N)$, let $Top = \{c_1, \ldots, c_N\} \subset \mathcal{C}$ denote the N candidates with the highest first-preference tallies, and $Batch \subset \mathcal{C}$ the set of batch eliminated candidates. We verify that candidate $c \in Batch$ cannot win by showing that $\mathsf{AG}(c_i, c)$ for all $c_i \in Top$.

Example 1. We consider the 2021 Board of Estimates and Taxation election in Minneapolis, Minnesota. This two-seat STV election involved four candidates – S. Brandt, S. Pree-Stinson, P. Salica, and K. Nikiforakis – and a number of undeclared write-ins (UWIs). The first-preference tallies were 42672 votes for S. Brandt, 25597 votes for S. Pree-Stinson, 20786 votes for P. Salica, 5815 votes for K. Nikiforakis and 755 votes for UWIs. The quota or election threshold was 31876, and out of 145337 ballots, 49712 of these were invalid. The UWIs and K. Nikiforakis were eliminated in the first round with too few mentions to have a mathematical possibility of winning. S. Brandt was then elected, P. Salica was eliminated, leaving S. Pree-Stinson as the second winner. We verify this batch elimination in an RLA with the assertions shown in Table 2, alongside the expected number of ballots required to audit them.[2] □

Example 2. Batch Elimination First can change the result of an election. Consider the two-seat STV with candidates $\{w, a, b, c_1, c_2, c_3, c_4, c_5\}$ and ballots $[w] : 15001, [a] : 6875, [b] : 3125, [c_1, w, b] : 1000, [c_2, w, b] : 1000, [c_3, w, b] : 1000, [c_4, w, b] : 1000, [c_5, w, b] : 1000$. The Droop Quota is 10001. Without batch elimination we give a seat to w, then all the votes for w exhaust; then each of the c_i are eliminated leaving tallies $a : 6825$ and $b : 8125$, and finally b is seated.

---

[2] For all sample size estimations, we assume a risk limit of 10%, an error rate of 2 overstatements per 1000 ballots, and the ALPHA risk function of SHANGRLA [3].

With a batch elimination all of $c_1, \ldots, c_5$ are eliminated first, none of them has enough mentions to beat w, a, or b. Then w gets a seat with 20001 votes in its tally and each of its surviving votes are transferred at value 0.5. The tallies for a and b are then $a : 6875$ and $b : 5625$, so finally a is seated. □

4 Context: First Round Winner

Let $E = (\mathcal{C}, \mathcal{B}, \mathcal{Q}, N = 2)$ denote a US-STV election with winners $w_1, w_2 \in W$ in which candidate w_1 is elected to the first seat, in the first round of tabulation (i.e., $t_{w_1,1} \geq \mathcal{Q}$), after any batch elimination has taken place.

Prior Work: In the approach of [1], an IQ assertion is formed to verify that w_1 has a quota on their first preferences, $\mathsf{IQ}(w_1)$. They then establish an estimated upper bound, $\overline{\tau}_{w_1}$, on the transfer value of ballots from w_1 using an assertion of the form $\mathsf{UT}(w_1, \overline{\tau}_{w_1})$. Using this upper bound they create assertions to show that w_2 will always have a higher tally than all other candidates using NL assertions. The method continues to increase the transfer value upper bound $\overline{\tau}_{w_1}$, until the sample size of the resulting audit increases, or $\overline{\tau}_{w_1}$ reaches $2/3$ (the maximum transfer value in a 2 seat STV election).

New Approach: We vary this approach by introducing additional types of assertions to reduce the expected sample sizes required in an audit. The assertions (beyond AG) we use are (starred assertions are new):

$\mathsf{IQ}(c)$ Verifies that candidate c's first-preference tally is equal to or greater than a quota: $t_{c,1} \geq \mathcal{Q}$.
$\mathsf{UT}(c, \overline{\tau}_c)$ Assumes that candidate c has been elected on their first preferences, and verifies that the transfer value for c is less than $\overline{\tau}_c$: $t_{c,1} < \mathcal{Q}/(1 - \overline{\tau}_c)$.
$\mathsf{LT}(c, \underline{\tau}_c)$ Assumes that c has been elected on their first preferences, and verifies that the transfer value for c is greater than $\underline{\tau}_c$: $t_{c,1} > \mathcal{Q}/(1 - \underline{\tau}_c)$.
$\mathsf{AG}^*(w, l, W, \underline{\tau}, \overline{\tau})$ An extension of the AG assertion [1]. The assertion shows that candidate w will always have higher tally than candidate l in the context where the candidates in W have already been elected to a seat with lower and upper bounds on their transfer values $\underline{\tau}$ and $\overline{\tau}$.

The assertion compares the minimum tally of candidate w in this context, with the maximum tally of l. In the original AG assertion [1], the minimum tally of w consists only of those ballots on which w is ranked first. The AG^* assertion retains this and adds further counts to this minimum tally by including contributions from some ballots where w is not ranked first. Specifically, for all ballots b where $\text{first}(\sigma_{\mathcal{C}-W}(b)) = w$, we reduce them in value by taking a product of transfer value lower bounds for the candidates in W that precede w in its ranking, and add these to w's minimum tally.[3]

---

[3] In the actual election, there is a scenario where candidate w does not get these ballots in their vote count: if w is our next winner after those in W. In such a case, w will be a winner, and thus we can ignore it since the context where we use these assertions is precisely to show that w is a winner.

For each ballot $b \in \mathcal{B}$, we define its contribution to the minimum tally of w, and the maximum tally of l, as follows.

$$C_{min}^{\mathsf{AG}^*}(b, w, W, \underline{\tau}, \overline{\tau}) = \begin{cases} 1 & \text{first}(b) = w \\ \prod_{k \in W'} \underline{\tau}_k & \text{first}(\sigma_{\mathcal{C}-W}(b)) = w \\ & \text{and } W' = \{c \in W : c \text{ precedes } w \text{ in } b\} \\ 0 & \text{otherwise} \end{cases}$$

$$C_{max}^{\mathsf{AG}^*}(b, l, W, \underline{\tau}, \overline{\tau}) = \begin{cases} 0 & l \text{ does not occur in } b \\ 0 & w \text{ appears before } l \text{ in } b \\ \mathsf{maxt}(b, l, W, \overline{\tau}) & \text{first}(b) \in W \\ 1 & \text{otherwise} \end{cases}$$

where $\mathsf{maxt}(b, l, W, \overline{\tau}) = \max\{\overline{\tau}_c : c \in W \text{ precedes } l \text{ in } b\}$. We define the minimum tally of w, $t1_w^{min}$, and the maximum tally of l, $t1_l^{max}$, as follows:

$$t1_w^{min} = \sum_{b \in \mathcal{B}} C_{min}^{\mathsf{AG}^*}(b, w, W, \underline{\tau}, \overline{\tau}) \qquad (3)$$

$$t1_l^{max} = \sum_{b \in \mathcal{B}} C_{max}^{\mathsf{AG}^*}(b, l, W, \underline{\tau}, \overline{\tau}) \qquad (4)$$

We say that $\mathsf{AG}^*(w, l, W, \underline{\tau}, \overline{\tau})$ iff $t1_w^{min} > t1_l^{max}$. Note $\mathsf{AG}(w, l) \equiv \mathsf{AG}^*(w, l, \emptyset, \_, \_)$.

NL$^*(w, l, W, \underline{\tau}, \overline{\tau}, G^*, O^*)$ An extension of the NL assertion [1]. Establishes that candidate w will always have a higher tally than candidate l under the assumptions that: (i) the candidates in W *have already been seated*, with lower and upper bounds on their transfer values $\underline{\tau}$ and $\overline{\tau}$; (ii) G^* denotes the candidates $g \in \mathcal{C}$ for which $\mathsf{AG}^*(g, l, W, \underline{\tau}, \overline{\tau})$ holds; and (iii) O^* the candidates $o \in \mathcal{C}$ for which $\mathsf{AG}^*(w, o, W, \underline{\tau}, \overline{\tau})$ holds. This contrasts with the assumptions underlying the original NL assertion, which only assumes that the candidates W are seated *at some point*. The assertion compares the minimum tally of w, in this context, against the maximum tally of l.

We define w's minimum tally at a point at which they could be eliminated, where it is assumed that O^* have been prior eliminated. This minimum tally includes all ballots b where $\text{first}(\sigma_{\mathcal{C}-O^*}(b)) = w$, at value 1, and all ballots b where $\text{first}(\sigma_{\mathcal{C}-W}(b)) = w$, at a reduced value. For the maximum tally of l, we include all ballots on which l precedes w in their ranking, or l appears and w does not, excluding those on which a candidate $g \in G^*$ precedes l. For each ballot $b \in \mathcal{B}$, we define its contribution to the minimum tally of w, and the maximum tally of l, as follows.

$$C_{min}^{\mathsf{NL}^*}(b, w, W, \underline{\tau}, \overline{\tau}, O^*) = \begin{cases} 1 & \text{first}(\sigma_{\mathcal{C}-O^*}(b)) = w \\ \prod_{k \in W'} \underline{\tau}_k & \text{first}(\sigma_{\mathcal{C}-W}(b)) = w \\ & \text{and } W' = \{c \in W : c \text{ precedes } w \text{ in } b\} \\ 0 & \text{otherwise} \end{cases}$$

$$C^{\mathsf{NL}^*}_{max}(b,l,W,\underline{\tau},\overline{\tau},G^*) = \begin{cases} 0 & l \text{ does not occur in } b \\ 0 & w \text{ appears before } l \text{ in } b \\ 0 & \text{a } g \in G^* \text{ appears before } l \text{ in } b \\ \mathsf{maxt}(b,l,W,\overline{\tau}) & \mathsf{first}(b) \in W \\ 1 & \text{otherwise} \end{cases}$$

We define the minimum tally of w, $t2_w^{min}$, and the maximum tally of l, $t2_l^{max}$, as follows:

$$t2_w^{min} = \sum_{b \in \mathcal{B}} C^{\mathsf{NL}^*}_{min}(b, w, W, \underline{\tau}, \overline{\tau}, O^*) \tag{5}$$

$$t2_l^{max} = \sum_{b \in \mathcal{B}} C^{\mathsf{NL}^*}_{max}(b, l, W, \underline{\tau}, \overline{\tau}, G^*) \tag{6}$$

We say that $\mathsf{NL}^*(w, l, W, \underline{\tau}, \overline{\tau}, G^*, O^*)$ iff $t2_w^{min} > t2_l^{max}$.

Figure 1 outlines the procedure used to generate the assertions $\mathcal{A}$ of our new RLA for two-seat STV elections satisfying the first-round winner criterion. The prior approach [1] involved a single loop in which an upper bound on the first winner transfer value was incremented, and a candidate audit formed for each of these potential values for this upper bound. The original AG assertions were computed prior to this loop, as they did not take into account upper or lower bounds on the first winner's transfer value. Our new approach involves two loops – the outer loop (steps 5–34) over potential values for the lower bound on the first winner's transfer value, $\underline{\tau}_{w_1}$, and the inner loop (steps 10–29) over potential values for the upper bound on the first winner's transfer value, $\overline{\tau}_{w_1}$. For each candidate value of $\underline{\tau}_{w_1}$, the inner loop searches for a value for $\overline{\tau}_{w_1}$ that results in the cheapest audit. The outer loop searches for a value for $\underline{\tau}_{w_1}$ for which the inner loop yields the cheapest overall audit. As per Blom *et al.* [1], the first assertion we create is $\mathsf{IQ}(w_1)$ to verify that our first winner, w_1, does indeed achieve a quota on their first preferences (step 1). Where a group elimination has taken place, and our resulting election satisfies the first-round winner criterion, the $\mathsf{IQ}(w_1)$ assertion verifies that w_1 has a quota on the basis of their first-preference tally *and* any votes distributed to them from the group eliminated candidates.

AG* assertions, which are used to help us form the NL* assertions required to show that w_2 beats all of the original losers, are formed inside the inner loop (step 14), allowing us to take advantage of both lower and upper bounds on the first winner's transfer value. When forming each NL*, we add an AG* to our audit only if it allows us to reduce the expected ASN of the NL* we are trying to form, and where the ASN of the NL* without the AG* is higher than that of the AG* itself. In this way, we do not add AG* assertions to our audit where their benefit, in terms of making a NL* easier to audit, is outweighed by their cost.

Note that if our final audit contains an AG* and NL* with the same winner and loser, we remove the NL* from our audit as it is redundant.

Example 3. Consider again the 2021 Board and Estimates and Taxation election (Minneapolis, Minnesota). Example 1 presents the first stage of an RLA for this election, identifying the assertions required to check that the two batch eliminated candidates did not have a mathematical possibility of winning. After the distribution of these eliminated candidates' ballots, we have a three candidate election that satisfies the first winner criterion.

S. Brandt is elected at this stage, with two remaining candidates (S. Pree-Stinson and P. Salica) vying for the second seat. Using the algorithm in Fig. 1, we form the assertion IQ($S.Brandt$). The ASN for this assertion is 34 ballots.

We then enter the outer loop at step 5 with a lower bound on S. Brandt's transfer value set to 0. (Where $\underline{\tau}_{w_1}$ is 0 we actually do not compute the associated LT* assertion as it is not necessary). Then, starting with an upper bound on S. Brandt's transfer value set to his actual transfer value plus δ (with $\delta = 0.05$), we enter the inner loop of the algorithm in Fig. 1 at step 10. The UT assertion required to show that S. Brandt's transfer value is less than, in this case, 0.3311, has an ASN of 131 ballots. AG* assertions are computed (step 14), and the NL* assertion required to show that S. Pree-Stinson never loses to P. Salica in the context where S. Brandt is seated first (steps 16 to 24). The NL* assertion has an ASN of 402 ballots. (In this case, none of the AG* assertions were found to be helpful in reducing the margin of this NL* assertion, and $\mathbf{AG'} \leftarrow \emptyset$ in step 22). At this stage, we have an RLA for the election that costs 402 ballots. The inner loop is repeated, with the upper bound on S. Brandt's transfer value set to 0.3811. The required UT assertion now costs 60 ballots. However, when proceeding to create the NL* assertion required to show that S. Pree-Stinson never loses to P. Salica, the assertion now costs 628 ballots. The new candidate configuration for our RLA is more costly, at 628 ballots, than the previous one, at 402 ballots. So, we break out of our inner loop at step 29.

We repeat our outer loop, with the lower bound on S. Brandt's transfer value now 0.1406 (or half of his actual transfer value, as per step 33). The LT* assertion required to show that his transfer value is greater than this lower bound has an ASN of 59 ballots. We enter the inner loop at step 5 with the upper bound on S. Brandt's transfer value again set to 0.3311. The ASN of the UT assertion for this bound is, as before, 131 ballots. After proceeding through steps 14–24, we form an NL* assertion to show that S. Pree-Stinson never loses to P. Salica that now costs 247 ballots (again, we opt not to make use of any computed AG* assertions). We now have a configuration for our audit that costs 247 ballots in total. When incrementing $\overline{\tau}$ for S. Brant to 0.3811, we do not improve upon this ASN (in fact, it will increase to 285). We break out of the inner loop at step 29.

The outer loop will be repeated with $\underline{\tau}$ for S. Brandt increased to 0.1906. The required LT* assertion for this bound will cost 87 ballots. By working through the inner loop, as before, we are able to find an audit configuration costing 217 ballots. Repeating the outer loop again with $\underline{\tau}$ for S. Brandt increased to 0.2406 gives us an audit costing 194 ballots. The LT* assertion will cost 184 ballots in this audit, the UT 131 ballots, and the required NL* 194 ballots. Incrementing $\underline{\tau}$ for S. Brandt again to 0.2906, in step 33, puts us beyond his actual transfer value of 0.2811. The outer loop condition fails, and we finish with an audit costing 194 ballots. This audit contains the assertions listed in Table 3. □

1    $iq \leftarrow \mathsf{IQ}(w_1)$ ▷ Form assertion to verify that w_1 has a quota on first preferences
2    $\underline{\tau}_{w_1} \leftarrow 0$ ▷ Lower bound on transfer value for first winner w_1
3    $ASN \leftarrow \infty$ ▷ ASN of our audit
4    $\mathcal{A} \leftarrow \emptyset$ ▷ Assertions in our audit
5   **while** $\underline{\tau}_{w_1} < \tau_{w_1}$ **do** ▷ τ_{w_1} is the reported transfer value for w_1
6       $lt \leftarrow \mathsf{LT}^*(w_1, \underline{\tau}_{w_1})$ ▷ Form LT^* assertion, denoted lt.
7       $\overline{\tau}_{w_1} \leftarrow \underline{\tau}_{w_1} + \delta$ ▷ Upper bound on transfer value for first winner w_1
8       $\mathcal{A}' \leftarrow \emptyset$
9       $ASN' \leftarrow ASN$
10   **while** $\overline{\tau}_{w_1} < 2/3$ **do**
11          $ut \leftarrow \mathsf{UT}(w_1, \overline{\tau}_{w_1})$ ▷ Form UT assertion, denoted ut.
12          $\mathcal{A}'' \leftarrow \{lt, ut, iq\}$
13          $ASN'' \leftarrow \max(lt.ASN, ut.ASN, iq.ASN)$

             ▷ Compute AG^* assertions between w_2 and each $l \in losers$, and
                between each $l, l' \in losers$ such that $l \neq l'$
14          $\boldsymbol{AG} \leftarrow [\mathsf{AG}^*(c, l, [w_1], [\underline{\tau}_{w_1}], [\overline{\tau}_{w_1}]) \,|\, \forall c \in losers \cup \{w_2\}, l \in losers, c \neq l]$
15          $O^* \leftarrow [c \,|\, \mathsf{AG}^*(w_2, c, [w_1], [\underline{\tau}_{w_1}], [\overline{\tau}_{w_1}]) \in \boldsymbol{AG}]$

             ▷ Find NL^* assertions to show that w_2 never loses to each $l \in losers$
16   **for each** $l \in losers$ **do**
17             $G^* \leftarrow [c \,|\, \mathsf{AG}^*(c, l, [w_1], [\underline{\tau}_{w_1}], [\overline{\tau}_{w_1}]) \in \boldsymbol{AG}]$
18             $t2_{w_2}^{min} \leftarrow \sum_{b \in \mathcal{B}} C_{min}^{\mathsf{NL}^*}(b, w_2, [w_1], [\underline{\tau}_{w_1}], [\overline{\tau}_{w_1}], O^*)$ (Equation 5)
19             $t2_{l}^{max} \leftarrow \sum_{b \in \mathcal{B}} C_{max}^{\mathsf{NL}^*}(b, l, [w_1], [\underline{\tau}_{w_1}], [\overline{\tau}_{w_1}], G^*)$ (Equation 6)
20   **if** $t2_{w_2}^{min} > t2_{l}^{max}$ **then**
21                $nl \leftarrow \mathsf{NL}^*(w_2, l, [w_1], [\underline{\tau}_{w_1}], [\overline{\tau}_{w_1}], G^*, O^*)$
22                $\boldsymbol{AG}' \leftarrow \mathsf{AG}^*$ assertions between w_2 and $o \in O^*$, and between
                    $g \in G^*$ and l, that were *used to reduce* the ASN of nl
23                $\mathcal{A}'' \leftarrow \mathcal{A}'' \cup \{nl\} \cup \boldsymbol{AG}'$
24                $ASN'' \leftarrow \max(ASN'', nl.ASN, a.ASN \; \forall a \in \boldsymbol{AG}')$

25   **if** $ASN'' < ASN'$ **then**
26             $\mathcal{A}' \leftarrow \mathcal{A}''$
27             $ASN' \leftarrow ASN''$
28             $\overline{\tau}_{w_1} \leftarrow \overline{\tau}_{w_1} + \delta$
29   **else break**
30   **if** $ASN' < ASN$ **then**
31          $\mathcal{A} \leftarrow \mathcal{A}'$
32          $ASN \leftarrow ASN'$
33          $\underline{\tau}_{w_1} \leftarrow \underline{\tau}_{w_1} + \delta$ if $\underline{\tau}_{w_1} > 0$ and $\frac{\tau_{w_1}}{2}$ otherwise
34   **else break**

Fig. 1. Algorithm for generating assertions $\mathcal{A}$ for the revised RLA of a two-seat STV election satisfying the first-round winner criterion. The two reported winners of the election are w_1 and w_2, and *losers* denotes the remaining candidates. Given an assertion, a, we use the notation "$a.ASN$" to denote its ASN.

Table 3. Assertions verifying the election of S. Brandt and S. Pree-Stinson in the 2021 BoE election in Minneapolis, Minnesota, and their sample sizes.

Assertion	ASN	Assertion	ASN
Batch elimination		Election of S. Brandt and S. Pree-Stinson	
AG(S. Brandt, UWIs)	20	IQ(S. Brandt)	34
AG(S. Pree-Stinson, UWIs)	35	LT*(S. Brandt, 0.2406)	184
AG(S. Brandt, K. Nikiforakis)	27	UT(S. Brandt, 0.3311)	131
AG(S. Pree-Stinson, K. Nikiforakis)	69	NL*(S. Brandt, P. Salica, ...)	194
Total cost:			194

4.1 Evaluation

We contrast the expected cost (ASN) of our new two-seat STV RLA (for elections satisfying the first-round winner criterion) relative to the existing method [1]. For sample size estimations, we use a risk limit of 10%, an expected error rate of 2 overstatements per 1000 ballots, and the ALPHA risk function of SHANGRLA [3]. For the algorithm shown in Fig. 1, we use a value of 0.05 for δ. Table 4 contrasts the expected sample sizes required by our 2-seat STV RLAs across a set of real 2-seat STV instances–four BoE elections held in Minneapolis, Minnesota between 2009 and 2021, and four elections held as part of the Australian Senate election in 2016 and 2019–and a series of US and Australian (NSW) IRV elections re-imagined as 2-seat STV contests. All these instances satisfy the first-round winner criterion. Selected instances from the full set of 92 NSW Legislative Assembly (NSW-LA) elections, and 23 US IRV elections, are shown in Table 4.

Across the full set of 92 NSW-LA elections (re-imagined as 2-seat STV), no RLA could be formed using the prior approach [1] for 8 instances. With the new method, four of these instances become auditable–although in one case, Lismore, the cost is still quite high at 2180 ballots. Across the remaining 84 instances, the new approach reduces required sample sizes by 15% on average. Across the full set of 23 US IRV elections (re-imagined as 2-seat STV), no RLA could be formed for six instances using the prior approach [1]. Using the new approach, three of these instances become auditable, with sample sizes of 3925, 350, and 166, as shown in Table 4. Again, the new method reduces sample sizes for the remaining 17 elections by 15% on average. For the Australian Senate and Minneapolis STV elections, the new method reduces required sample sizes by 19%, on average.

5 Scenario: General Method

The *general method* of Blom et al. [1] describes how we can form an RLA for a 2-seat STV election where no candidate has a quota on their first preferences. We do not, in this paper, present an improvement to this approach–in the sense of enabling audits for instances that we could not previously audit. We do, however, show how we can adapt the method to perform *partial* audits of elections where a full RLA, verifying both winners, is not possible. The experiments of

Table 4. ASNs for our 2 seat STV RLAs, comparing the original method of [1] against the revised method. All instances satisfy the first-round winner criterion. Where the revised method improves on the original, ASNs are in bold.

Instance	$|\mathcal{C}|$	$|\mathcal{B}|$	$\mathcal{Q}$	ASN Prior RLA	ASN New RLA
MN BoE 2009	7	32086	10696	191	**100**
MN BoE 2013	5	48855	16286	33	**31**
MN BoE 2017	4	69694	23232	23	23
MN BoE 2021	5	95625	31876	402	**194**
AU Senate'16 ACT	22	254767	84923	77	**58**
AU Senate'19 ACT	17	270231	90078	131	**98**
AU Senate'16 NT	19	102027	34010	60	60
AU Senate'19 NT	18	105027	35010	58	58
US IRV elections re-imagined as 2 seat STV					
MN Mayor 2013	36	79415	26472	73	73
Aspen'09 Mayor	5	2528	843	43	**41**
Berkeley'10 D1 CC	5	5700	1901	60	**29**
Oakland'10 D4 CC	8	20994	6999	82	**64**
Oakland'10 Mayor	11	119607	39870	–	**3925**
Oakland'10 D6 CC	4	12911	4304	–	**350**
Pierce'08 CE	5	299132	99711	–	**166**
NSW'19 Legislative Assembly elections re-imagined as 2 seat STV					
Ballina	6	50127	16710	66	66
Bathurst	6	50833	16945	81	**57**
Clarence	6	49355	16452	147	**84**
Coffs Harbour	8	47333	15778	1225	**515**
Cootamundra	6	47448	15817	–	–
Heffron	5	50010	16671	1778	**211**
Holsworthy	6	48244	16082	20	20
Ku-ring-gai	6	48730	16244	202	**99**
Lake Macquarie	6	50082	16695	129	**73**
Lane Cove	6	50941	16981	132	**109**
Lismore	7	48145	16049	–	**2180**
Manly	6	48316	16106	363	**150**
Newcastle	8	50319	16774	214	**173**
North Shore	9	47774	15925	470	**184**
Northern Tablelands	4	48678	16227	–	**143**
Oxley	5	48540	16181	98	**80**
Pittwater	8	49119	16374	163	**110**
Summer Hill	6	48785	16262	–	**110**
Tamworth	6	50578	16860	–	**129**
Vaucluse	7	46023	15342	–	**325**
Wallsend	5	51351	17118	149	**83**
Willoughby	8	47857	15953	–	–
Wollondilly	8	50989	16997	120	**88**
Wollongong	7	51435	17146	205	**123**

Blom et al. [1] demonstrate that forming full RLAs for this class of 2-seat STV elections is challenging, and generally not possible with existing methods.

A partial RLA can be used to verify *some* aspects of the election outcome. For example, that some reported losers did indeed lose, and that one of the reported winners did indeed win. In this paper, we reframe the general method into five stages. We still use the original assertion types, AG and NL, as we are not assuming that one or more candidates have been *previously* seated. Stages 1, 2, and 3 are present in the general method of Blom et al. [1]. Stages 4 and 5 are introduced in this paper to (i) describe how we can form a partial RLA for a 2-seat STV election when a full RLA cannot be formed (Stage 5) and (ii) reduce the required sample size of the resulting partial or full RLA (Stage 4).

1. **Form AG Assertions** For each pair of candidates $c, c' \in \mathcal{C}$, we determine whether we can form the assertion $\mathsf{AG}(c, c')$. We keep track of each AG that we can form, and its cost.
2. **Rule out candidates (find Definite Losers)** We use the AG assertions that we formed in Stage 1 to determine whether some candidates definitely lost the election. All candidates $c \in \mathcal{C}$ for which there exists *at least two* other candidates $c', c'' \in \mathcal{C} - \{c\}$ such that $\mathsf{AG}(c', c)$ and $\mathsf{AG}(c'', c)$ *definitely lost* the election. We denote this set of candidates DL, and the set of AG assertions required to show that these candidates definitely lost as $\mathcal{A}_{DL}$. This set will contain two AG assertions for each definite loser. The maximum sample size required to audit any assertion in this set is denoted the Stage 2 sample size.
3. **Rule out alternate winner pairs** We consider all pairs of candidates from the set $\mathcal{C} - DL$, excluding the pair of reported winners, as potential alternate winner outcomes. We follow the approach of Blom et al. [1], and attempt to rule out each of these alternate winner pairs with an NL assertion. For a pair (c_1, c_2), we first assume that c_1 is seated *at some point*, and look for another candidate c' that never loses to c_2 in this context:

$$\mathsf{NL}(c', c_2, [c_1], G, O)$$

where G is the set of candidates g for which $\mathsf{AG}(g, c_2)$ and O the candidates o for which $\mathsf{AG}(c', o)$. We compare the cost of this NL assertion with one formed when we assume that c_2 is seated at some point, and look for a c' that never loses to c_1:

$$\mathsf{NL}(c', c_1, [c_2], G, O)$$

where G is the set of candidates g for which $\mathsf{AG}(g, c_1)$ and O the candidates o for which $\mathsf{AG}(c', o)$. The cheapest NL, assuming we are able to form at least one, is used to rule out the outcome of c_1 and c_2 winning together. We denote the set of assertions used to rule out candidate pairs in this stage, $\mathcal{A}_3$. This set includes the formed NL assertions and any AG assertion used to reduce the margin of those NL assertions. The maximum sample size required to audit an assertion in this set the Stage 3 sample size.

4. **Reduce audit sample size** Ruling out a candidate c in Stage 2, by looking for two other candidates who tallies are always greater than c, may be unnecessarily costly. We may have been able to rule out all alternate winner pairs involving c with cheaper NL assertions in Stage 3.

   While the Stage 2 sample size is higher than that of Stage 3, we take the current 'most difficult to rule out' candidate in DL, d. Let ASN_d^2 denote the sample size required to rule out d as a potential winner in Stage 2. We form a set of alternate winner pairs by pairing d with all candidates in $\mathcal{C} - DL$. We perform the Stage 3 process over this new pair set. If the sample size required to rule out these pairs, ASN_d^3, is less than ASN_d^2, we:
   (a) Remove the assertions formed in Stage 2 to rule out d from $\mathcal{A}_{DL}$;
   (b) Add the new assertions formed to rule out all alternate winner pairs involving d to $\mathcal{A}_3$;
   (c) Update the Stage 2 sample size, excluding the cost of ruling out d;
   (d) Update the Stage 3 sample size to include ASN_d^3; and,
   (e) Remove d from DL.

   If $ASN_d^3 \geq ASN_d^2$, or we could not rule out the new set of alternate winner pairs, we do not change our audit and move to Stage 5. Otherwise, we take the next most difficult to rule out candidate in DL, and repeat Stage 4.

5. **Summarise what can (and cannot) be audited** If we have been able to rule out each alternate winner pair with an NL, we have a full RLA. This RLA contains the assertions in $\mathcal{A}_{DL}$ and $\mathcal{A}_3$. If we were not able to rule out every alternate winner pair, we consider whether the ones we could rule out imply that some additional candidates definitely lost or definitely won. Let Rem denote the set of alternate winner pairs that we could not rule out.
   – **Definite Winners** If there is a candidate c present in *every* remaining pair in Rem, we add this candidate to a set DW.
   – **Definite Losers** Includes all candidates in DL (Stage 2) and any $c \in \mathcal{C} - DL$ (excluding the reported winners) that is not present in any of the alternate winner pairs in Rem. Each such c is added to DL.
   – **Potential Winners** All candidates in the set $\mathcal{C} - DL$ are potential winners. These are reported losers and winners whose elimination or election we could not verify.

   Our partial RLA contains the assertions in the set $\mathcal{A}_{DL} \cup \mathcal{A}_3$ and can be used to establish that the candidates in the set DL definitely lost, and that the candidates in the set DW definitely won.

Example 4. Consider the 2022 Australian Senate election for ACT, a 2-seat STV election that does not satisfy the first-round winner criterion. The quota for this election was 95073. None of the 23 candidates have a quota on their first preferences. GALLAGHER won her seat after the elimination of 11 candidates. After a further 9 candidates were eliminated, POCOCK won the second seat. In Stage 1, we can form 44 AG assertions with ASNs ranging from 14 to 1141. In Stage 2, we use some of these AGs to mark 16 candidates as *definite losers*. The maximum ASN of the assertions we use in this stage is 775. In Stage 3, there are 20 alternate winner pairs that we can form with the remaining 7 candidates.

We are able to rule out all but three of these with NL assertions, requiring a sample size of 420 ballots. The most expensive candidate to rule out as a winner in Stage 2 requires a sample of 775 ballots. In Stage 4, we take this 'expensive to rule out candidate', d, and rule out all alternate winner pairs involving d with NL assertions instead. These NL assertions have a maximum ASN of 47 ballots. Our overall audit cost reduces to 420 ballots. Our Stage 5 summary indicates that we can show that GALLAGHER correctly won, and that four of the remaining 22 candidates, including POCOCK, are potential winners. □

We have collected data for 587 3-4 seat STV elections taking place in 2017 and 2022 to elect local councillors in Scotland. These elections involve 3 to 13 candidates. When viewed as 2-seat STV elections, 428 of these instances involve an elimination in the first round. A full RLA can be formed for 68 of these 428 instances. For this set of 68 instances, performing Stage 4 reduces required sample sizes by 58% on average for 20 elections of the 68 (reductions range from 5% to 97%), and makes no difference on required sample size for the remaining 48. For the 360/428 instances for which a full RLA could not be formed, performing Stage 4 reduces the required sample size of the partial RLA in 122/360 of these instances (by 49% on average, from 2% to 99%).

6 Concluding Remarks

Auditing STV elections is a challenging problem, but one of very real interest given the common use of STV throughout the world. The main challenge arises as ballots can change their value across tabulation. In this paper we have shown how reasoning about both lower and upper bounds on transfer values may improve our ability to audit 2-seat STV elections. The revisions substantially reduce the number of ballots expected to be required to audit an election, and in some cases makes it possible to audit an election that the previous method [1] could not. We also show how to effectively audit batch elimination, as well as partially audit elections where no candidate gets a quota initially. While significant advances are still required to get to the point of auditing large Australian Senate elections, STV elections with 6 seats and over 100 candidates and say 4 million ballots, the new techniques we develop here help us on the path to this goal.

References

1. Blom, M., Stuckey, P.J., Teague, V., Vukcevic, D.: A first approach to risk-limiting audits for single transferable vote elections. In: Workshop on Advances in Secure Elections VOTING 2022 (2022)
2. Blom, M., et al.: Assertion-based approaches to auditing complex elections, with application to party-list proportional elections. In: Krimmer, R., et al. (eds.) E-Vote-ID 2021. LNCS, vol. 12900, pp. 47–62. Springer, Cham (2021). https://doi.org/10.1007/978-3-030-86942-7_4
3. Stark, P.B.: Sets of half-average nulls generate risk-limiting audits: SHANGRLA. In: Bernhard, M., et al. (eds.) FC 2020. LNCS, vol. 12063, pp. 319–336. Springer, Cham (2020). https://doi.org/10.1007/978-3-030-54455-3_23

Efficient Weighting Schemes for Auditing Instant-Runoff Voting Elections

Alexander Ek[1], Philip B. Stark[2], Peter J. Stuckey[3], and Damjan Vukcevic[1(✉)]

[1] Department of Econometrics and Business Statistics, Monash University, Clayton, Australia
damjan.vukcevic@monash.edu
[2] Department of Statistics, University of California, Berkeley, CA, USA
[3] Department of Data Science and AI, Monash University, Clayton, Australia

Abstract. Various risk-limiting audit (RLA) methods have been developed for instant-runoff voting (IRV) elections. A recent method, AWAIRE, is the first efficient approach that can take advantage of, but does not require, cast vote records (CVRs). AWAIRE involves adaptively weighted averages of test statistics, essentially "learning" an effective set of hypotheses to test. However, the initial paper on AWAIRE only examined a few weighting schemes and parameter settings.

We explore schemes and settings more extensively, to identify and recommend efficient choices for practice. We focus on the case where CVRs are not available, assessing performance using simulations based on real election data.

The most effective schemes are often those that place most or all of the weight on the apparent "best" hypotheses based on already seen data. Conversely, the optimal tuning parameters tended to vary based on the election margin. Nonetheless, we quantify the performance trade-offs for different choices across varying election margins, aiding in selecting the most desirable trade-off if a default option is needed.

A limitation of the current AWAIRE implementation is its restriction to a small number of candidates—up to six in previous implementations. One path to a more computationally efficient implementation would be to use lazy evaluation and avoid considering all possible hypotheses. Our findings suggest that such an approach could be done without substantially compromising statistical performance.

1 Introduction

Elections are crucial to democracy. Ensuring that elections truly reflect the preferences of the population should be a cornerstone of democratic governance. While there are many forms of elections, *ranked-choice* or *preferential* voting allows voters to express preferences among some or all candidates, rather than simply voting for a single candidate. Instant-runoff voting (IRV) is used in elections in many countries, including Australia, Ireland, and the USA.

Authors listed alphabetically.

© International Financial Cryptography Association 2025
J. Budurushi et al. (Eds.): FC 2024 Workshops, LNCS 14746, pp. 18–32, 2025.
https://doi.org/10.1007/978-3-031-69231-4_2

While ranked-choice voting captures more of the preferences of voters, assuring that their preferences are followed requires ensuring that the reported *outcome* of an election is correct, that is the reported winner of the election is the winner if we followed the election process correctly on the correct set of ballots. Risk-limiting audits (RLAs) are a way of checking that a reported election outcome is correct. As opposed to other auditing methods, RLAs guarantee with some minimum probability that they will correct an incorrect reported outcome of an election, and never alter a correct outcome. The *risk limit*, denoted by α, is the maximum chance that a wrong outcome will not be corrected.

The first RLA approach to auditing IRV elections, RAIRE [4], makes use of a digitised record of the votes in the election (the *cast vote records* (CVRs)) to generate a set of "assertions" that, if true, imply that the reported winner really won. These assertions are currently used in the SHANGRLA framework for RLAs [9], and have been used to audit actual elections [3]. More recently, an alternative approach to RLAs for IRV elections that does not require CVRs, AWAIRE [7], was published. AWAIRE has the advantage that many IRV elections are tabulated by hand,[1] and no digitised record of the ballots is actually made, so RAIRE is not applicable in these circumstances. While RAIRE commits to a set of assertions to check before the audit starts, AWAIRE adapts to the voter preferences observed in the audit sample as the audit progresses, identifying a sufficient set of assertions that are efficient to test statistically. AWAIRE is also more resilient than RAIRE when the reported outcome is correct but the digitised vote records lead to an erroneous elimination order.

AWAIRE uses a *weighting scheme* to adapt the assertions it will concentrate on as the audit progresses, and more and more observations of ballots are seen. In the original AWAIRE paper [7], the authors consider a few simple weighting schemes and a single default choice of parameters used for ALPHA [10], the statistical test used to test whether assertions are correct (within a statistical limit on the acceptable chance of error). In this paper we:

- Expand upon AWAIRE by investigating more weighting schemes and exploring how the margin of victory affects which weighting scheme is best.
- Investigate the effect of ALPHA tuning parameters on audit efficiency.

2 Auditing IRV Contests Using AWAIRE

2.1 Instant-Runoff Voting (IRV)

In an IRV contest, voters write on their ballot an ordering of (possibly a subset of) the candidates based on the voter's preference.

The votes are tabulated as follows: Initially, each ballot counts as a single vote for its first-choice candidate on that ballot. The candidate with the fewest first-choice votes is eliminated, while the others remain in the race. Every ballot that ranked the eliminated candidate first is now instead counted as a vote for

---

[1] Most, but not all, lower house elections in Australia are hand-counted IRV contests.

its second choice, i.e., it becomes a vote for the top-ranked candidate remaining in the race. This process continues until only one candidate remains, the winner. As a ballot need not list every candidate, if at any point there are only eliminated candidates listed on a ballot, then the ballot is *exhausted* and no longer contributes any votes. The above tabulating process leads to an *elimination order*: the order in which candidates are eliminated, with the last candidate in the order being the winner.

In order to audit an IRV election we need to show that it would be unlikely that any candidate other than the reported winner actually won.

2.2 The AWAIRE Framework

AWAIRE is an RLA method for IRV elections that does not require an electronic record of the votes on each ballot (CVRs) to proceed. In brief:

- AWAIRE tracks every elimination order that yields a winner other than the reported winner; we refer to these orders as *alt-order(s)*. If there is sufficiently strong evidence (based on a pre-specified risk limit) that no alt-order is correct, then the audit stops without a full hand count and AWAIRE concludes that the reported winner really won.
- Each alt-order is characterised by a set of *requirements*: necessary conditions for that elimination order to be correct. If the data refutes at least one requirement for each alt-order, then the reported outcome is confirmed.
- A *test supermartingale* is constructed for each requirement. A test supermartingale is also constructed for each alt-order, by defining each new term as a (predictable) convex combination of the terms in the test supermartingales for each requirement in the alt-order.
- As the audit progresses, the convex combination for each alt-order is updated to give more weight to the test supermartingales that are giving the strongest evidence that their corresponding requirements are false.
- The audit stops when the test supermartingale for every alt-order exceeds $1/\alpha$, or when every ballot has been inspected and the correct outcome is known.
- The process described above has risk limit α.

2.3 Test Supermartingales

A supermartingale is a mathematical model of a gambler's fortune in a sequence of wagers that are fair or biased against the gambler. Specifically, a supermartingale is a stochastic process $(M_t)_{t \in \mathbb{N}}$ (e.g., fortune after t bets) with respect to another stochastic process $(X_t)_{t \in \mathbb{N}}$ (e.g., a series of t coin flips that we bet on), where the conditional expected value of the next observation, given all past observations, is not greater than the current observation; that is, $\mathbb{E}(M_t \mid X_1, \ldots, X_{t-1}) \leqslant M_{t-1}$.

A test statistic that is a nonnegative supermartingale starting at 1 when a hypothesis is true can be used to test that hypothesis. We call such a process a *test supermartingale* for the hypothesis. By Ville's inequality [11], which generalises Markov's inequality to nonnegative supermartingales, the chance that a test supermartingale ever exceeds $1/\alpha$ is at most α if the null hypothesis is true. Hence, rejecting the null hypothesis when $M_t \geq 1/\alpha$ for some time t is a level α test of the hypothesis.

In words, suppose that a gambler starts with a fortune of $1 and is not allowed to go into debt. The gambler bets on a sequence of games. The chance that the gambler's fortune ever gets to $\$1/\alpha$ is at most α if the games are fair or biased against the gambler. If the gambler succeeds in amassing a fortune of, say, $1,000, then that is quite strong evidence that some of the games had odds that were favorable to the gambler—that the games were not all fair or sub-fair. Had the games all been fair or sub-fair, the chance of reaching a fortune of $1,000 would be at most $1/1000 = 0.001$.

2.4 Hypotheses and Requirements

The process of auditing an IRV contest can be expressed as a collection of hypothesis tests. In the AWAIRE framework, we try to reject each alt-order. For an election with k candidates, there are $m = k! - (k-1)!$ alt-orders. Let H_0^j denote the hypothesis that the jth alt-order is correct. Then, to conclude that the reported winner really won without the audit becoming a full hand count, we need to reject the composite null hypothesis

$$H_0 = H_0^1 \cup \cdots \cup H_0^m.$$

To reject an alt-order in the AWAIRE framework, we need to reject one or more of its *requirements*, relations that must hold for the alt-order to hold (i.e., they are necessary and sufficient for alt-order i to be correct). Hence, if we can reject one requirement with risk α, then we can reject the alt-order with risk α. We must reject

$$H_0^i = R_i^1 \cap R_i^2 \cap \cdots \cap R_i^{r_i},$$

where $R_i^1, R_i^2, \ldots, R_i^{r_i}$ are the requirements of alt-order i.

In IRV, each requirement is comprised of so-called *directly beats* assertions. The assertion $\mathbf{DB}(i, j, \mathcal{S})$, where $\mathcal{S} \supseteq \{i, j\}$, holds if candidate i has more votes than candidate j, given that only the candidates in $\mathcal{S} \supseteq \{i, j\}$ have not been eliminated. If the assertion is true, then it means that j cannot be the next eliminated candidate (as j would be eliminated before i) if only the candidates $\mathcal{S}$ remain standing. For more details about the assertions and how to build test supermartingales for individual assertions, we refer the reader to [7].[2]

At each time t, a ballot is drawn without replacement. Every ballot is encoded (via an *assorter*, see [9]) as either evidence against (value 1), for (value 0), or neutral to (value $1/2$) a requirement being true. Each requirement can be expressed as the hypothesis that the mean of a list of encoded ballots is less than $1/2$. We test the requirement using the ALPHA test supermartingale [10].

---

[2] An understanding of these details is not necessary for the current paper.

ALPHA involves specifying a function that can be thought of as a running estimate of the population of assorter. One such function, shrinkTrunc(), has two tuning parameters, η_0, which can be thought of as an initial estimate of the true assorter mean for the ballots, and d, which can be thought of as how much emphasis we put on η_0 (higher values) or how eagerly we learn from the sample (lower values). In this paper we explore the effect of those parameters on audit sample sizes. Other parameters of ALPHA were set to the same values used by [7].

3 Weighting Schemes

In the AWAIRE framework, the assorter associated with each requirement r from some alt-order[3] is applied to the sample (at time ℓ), forming the list of values $(X_t^r)_{t=1}^{\ell}$. Let $M_{r,\ell}$ be the test supermartingale for requirement r evaluated at time ℓ, which can be written as a product of increments:

$$M_{r,\ell} := \prod_{t=0}^{\ell} m_{r,t},$$

where $m_{r,0} = 1$ denotes the starting value and $m_{r,t}$ reflects how X_t^r impacts the cumulative evidence that requirement r is false. For example $m_{r,t} < 1$ means that X_t^r gives no evidence that r is false; $m_{r,t} > 1$ means that X_t^r gives evidence that r is false. Because $M_{r,\ell}$ is a test supermartingale,

$$\mathbb{E}(m_{r,t} \mid (X_\ell^r)_{\ell=0}^{t-1}) \leqslant 1, \qquad (1)$$

if r is true. These supermartingales are referred to as *base* test supermartingales.

3.1 Intersection Test Martingales

Each alt-order has an *intersection* test supermartingale, which measures the cumulative evidence for that alt-order being the true elimination order. To correct for multiplicity, the intersection test supermartingale uses a weighted average of its base test supermartingales.

Specifically, let the weights at time t be $\{w_{r,t}\}_{r=1}^{r_i}$. These can depend on the data collected up to time $t-1$, but not on any later data. Using those weights, the intersection test supermartingale is a product of weighted combinations of the terms of the base test supermartingales:

$$M_\ell := \prod_{t=1}^{\ell} \frac{\sum_{r=1}^{r_i} w_{r,t} m_{r,t}}{\sum_{r=1}^{r_i} w_{r,t}}, \quad \ell = 0, 1, \ldots,$$

with $M_0 := 1$.

The base test supermartingales for requirements that are false tend to grow with t. We explore how to make M_ℓ grow quickly by choosing efficient weighting schemes.

---
[3] The details in this section are analogous for every alt-order.

3.2 Previous Schemes

The original AWAIRE paper [7] investigates a number of schemes for weight selection:

Linear. Proportional to previous value, $w_{r,t} := M_{r,t-1}$.
Quadratic. Proportional to the square of the previous value, $w_{r,t} := M_{r,t-1}^2$.
Largest. Take only the largest base supermartingale(s) and ignore the rest, $w_{r,t} := 1$ if $r \in \arg\max_{r'} M_{r',t-1}$; otherwise, $w_{r,t} := 0$.

Experiments in [7] found **Largest** to be the most robust choice. But there are many more weighting schemes possible, and indeed a single weighting scheme may not be the best for different IRV elections.

3.3 New Schemes: Variants of Previous Schemes

We introduce several new weighting schemes usable within AWAIRE to try to generate intersection test supermartingales that grow quickly. The schemes in the previous subsection are *myopic*: they only look at the previous value of the base supermartingales. This makes them inefficient when two or more base test supermartingales frequently swap leadership positions. Below we examine more complex weighting schemes, many of which look back at the test supermartingale values of the last i steps:

LargestCount(i) Put all weight on the base test supermartingale that was largest most often in the previous i draws. This is a less myopic version of **Largest**.

LargestMean(i) Put all weight on the base test supermartingale whose mean in the last i draws was largest. Again this is a less myopic version of **Largest** that also takes into account the magnitude of the difference between different requirements.

Linear+ Same as Linear, but if at least one base test supermartingale is greater than 1 at step $t-1$, put weight 0 on all base test supermartingales that are less than 1. This attempts to remove from consideration requirements that appear to be compatible with the data.

LinearCount(i) Put weight in linear proportion to how many times each requirement has been the largest looking back i steps. This is fairer version of **LargestCount** that spreads its bets on requirements that have been largest.

LinearMean(i) Taking the moving average value of each requirement looking back i steps, put weight in linear proportion to their means. This is a less myopic version of **Linear**.

Quadratic+ Same as Quadratic, adapted in an analogous way to Linear+.

3.4 New Schemes: Portfolio Algorithms

There is a large literature on *portfolio algorithms*, which aim to maximise the growth of wealth in a stock market by selecting a portfolio of stocks. This involves selecting how to split some starting capital into amounts to invest in each stock and how to re-invest the capital each period. Our weighting schemes fit this paradigm, with the base test supermartingales representing individual stocks and the weights corresponding to the fraction of the current fortune invested in each stock in each time period. Any portfolio algorithm that only uses information about previous stock prices yields a weighting scheme that could be used with AWAIRE.

We attempted to test a variety of portfolio algorithms, but the vast majority of papers describing such algorithms do not include software. The most comprehensive collection of software we found was at:

https://github.com/Marigold/universal-portfolios

We tried to use these, but the only scheme that ran successfully was:

ONS(δ) "Online Newton Step" with tuning parameter δ [1]. This is a family of weighting schemes coming from investment portfolio management.

The other algorithms either did not apply to our problem or crashed due to floating point overflow. Even ONS(δ) sometimes crashed for $\delta = 0.66, 1$, and sometimes 2. Thus, we analyse ONS with $\delta > 2$.

Previous work has shown that (under suitable conditions) the optimal portfolio is a *constant rebalanced portfolio* [2,5], where at each timestep the fraction of the current capital invested in a given stock is constant over time. The optimal allocation, however, can only be determined in hindsight.

A class of portfolio algorithms that are asymptotically optimal are *F-weighted portfolios*, also known as *universal portfolios* [6]. However, they often perform poorly for small sample sizes and do not necessarily have computationally efficient implementations [8]. Nevertheless, they might inspire better weighting schemes; we discuss some ideas in Sect. 5.

3.5 Software

Our software implementation of the new weighting schemes, along with the AWAIRE implementation, is available at: https://github.com/aekh/awaire.

4 Analyses and Results

4.1 Data

We used the same NSW 2015 Legislative Assembly election data as in the AWAIRE paper [7], consisting of 71 contests with 6 or fewer candidates.[4] Experiments showed that the relative performance of the weighting schemes and various tuning parameters for ALPHA depend on the margin of victory. To understand these differences more clearly, we partitioned the dataset into four categories based on the margin of victory:

Huge. Margins of 10% and above. (41 contests)
Large. Margins in the range 4–10%. (19 contests)

---

[4] https://github.com/michelleblom/margin-irv.

Medium. Margins in the range 1.5–4%. (7 contests)
Small. Margins less than 1.5%. (4 contests)

4.2 Initial Comparison of Weighting Schemes

First, let's compare the weighting schemes we have listed above. We will use the $d = 50$ and $\eta_0 = 0.52$ as was used in previous AWAIRE paper. We will refer to this as *the previous default*. We used a risk limit of 5%. See Fig. 1 for results. For each weighting scheme, we ran 500 simulated audits for each contest. First we calculated statistics across all simulated audits in each of the four margin categories.

Figure 1 indicates that Quadratic+, LargestCount(5), LinearCount(7), and the previously introduced Largest are consistently best while also performing somewhat differently across the four categories. The following sections concentrate on those weighting schemes.

4.3 Tuning Parameters for shrinkTrunc() in ALPHA

The purpose of these experiments is twofold: first, to understand what the best tuning parameters are for ALPHA when dealing with IRV contests; second, to ensure that the evaluation of the weighting schemes is somewhat decoupled from the choice of underlying test supermartingale.

We used $\eta_0 \in \{0.505, 0.51, 0.52, 0.54\}$ and $d \in \{10, 50, 100, 200, 500, 1000\}$. For time reasons, for these experiments we used a subset of the contests consisting of 3 elections per margin category: (a) the contest with the smallest margin, (b) the contest with the largest margin, and (c) a contest in the middle (rounded to smaller margin if no true middle).

Figure 2 shows the results from these experiments. There was no single best choice of tuning parameters, but $\eta_0 = 0.51$ and $d = 200$ were reasonable defaults. Selecting η_0 and d involves trade-offs in performance across contests. For example, with $\eta_0 = 0.51$, increasing d improved efficiency for Small-margin elections but decreased efficiency for the Huge-margin category. The default choice balances efficiency across the categories by slightly prioritising good performance for Large and Medium at the expense of Small and Huge. Our reasoning is as follows:

– Audits for Huge-margin contests will generally only need small sample sizes, thus increasing the number of samples by a relatively large percentage has low absolute cost.
– Audits of contests with very small margins may require sampling fractions so large that a full hand count is more efficient.

4.4 Detailed Comparison of Selected Weighting Schemes

From the results in Fig. 2, we see two types of patterns: either the difference between the weighting schemes is barely discernable, or Quadratic+ differs

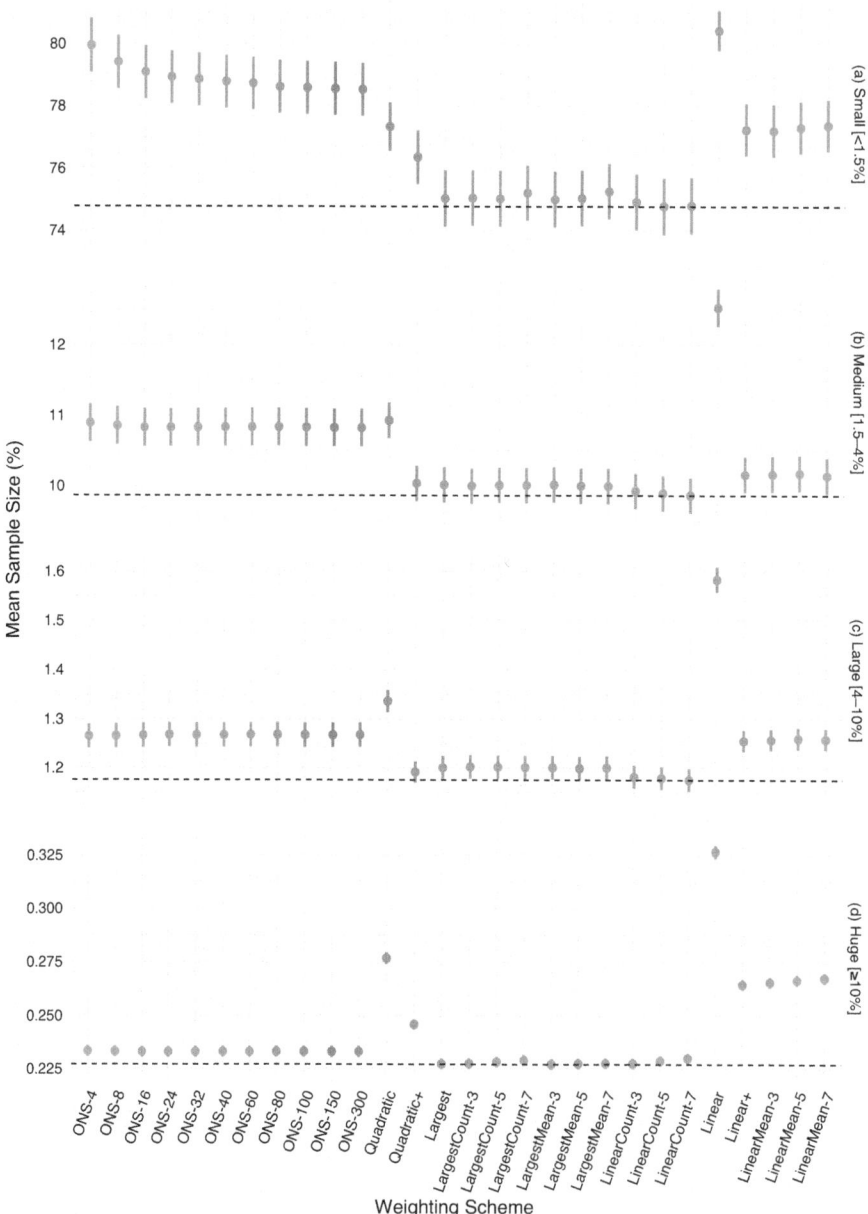

Fig. 1. Mean sample size (as a percentage of the total ballots in each contest; ±2 standard errors) across all simulated audits in each of the margin categories (rows). The vertical gridlines in panels (a)–(d) correspond respectively to approximately 500, 150, 25 and 10 ballots. The dashed lines show the best mean sample size achieved within each panel.

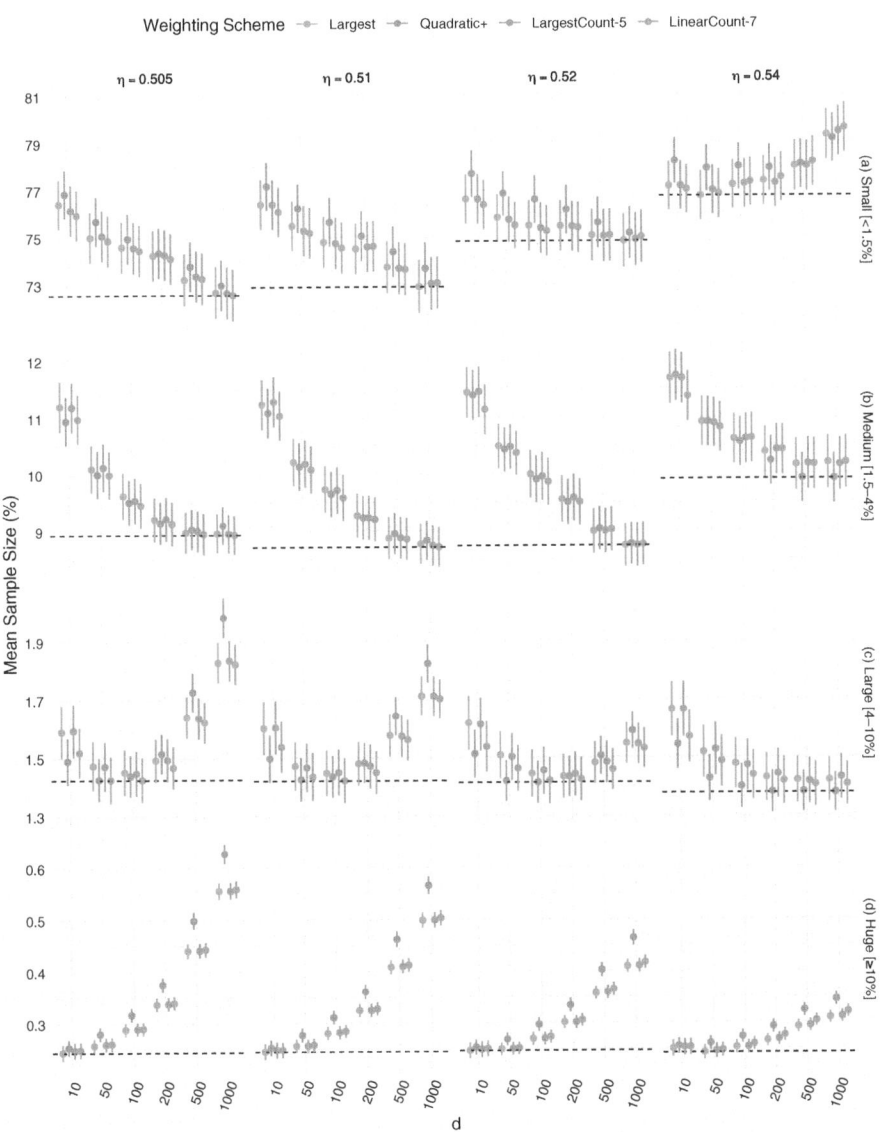

Fig. 2. Mean sample size (as a percentage of the total ballots in each contest; ±2 standard errors) across all simulated audits in each of the margin categories (rows) and settings for `shrinkTrunc()` (η_0 across columns and d on the x-axis). Three contests were selected to represent each category, see Sect. 4.3 for details. The dashed lines show the best mean sample size achieved within each panel.

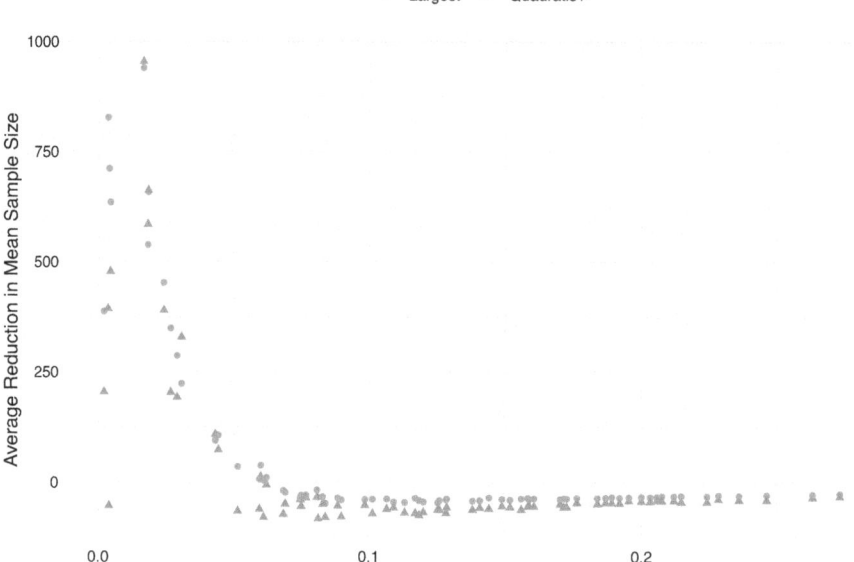

Fig. 3. Average reduction in mean sample size for two default choices compared to the previous default choice. Each point represents a single contest (averaged over 500 simulated audits). The margin (x-axis) is shown as a proportion out the total ballots in each contest.

clearly from the others (performing either better or worse). Since the other three methods performed so similarly, we recommend using Largest because of its simplicity (it only requires storing values from 1 draw in the past). Therefore, we selected only Quadratic+ and Largest for further comparisons.

In this section, we will compare their performance with $\eta_0 = 0.51$ and $d = 200$ (as selected in Sect. 4.3) against Largest with $\eta_0 = 0.52$ and $d = 50$ (the default in [7]). We used all contests with 6 or fewer candidates for the comparison.

Figure 3 shows the average reduction in the mean sample size, plotted against the margin of each contest. The Largest and Quadratic+ schemes both perform similarly. There is a substantial reduction in sampling effort for elections with small-to-medium margins, and a very slight increase for large-to-huge margins. Figure 4 compares the average reduction in mean sample size for the two new default choices in more detail. For the majority of contests, the Largest scheme is slightly better than Quadratic+.

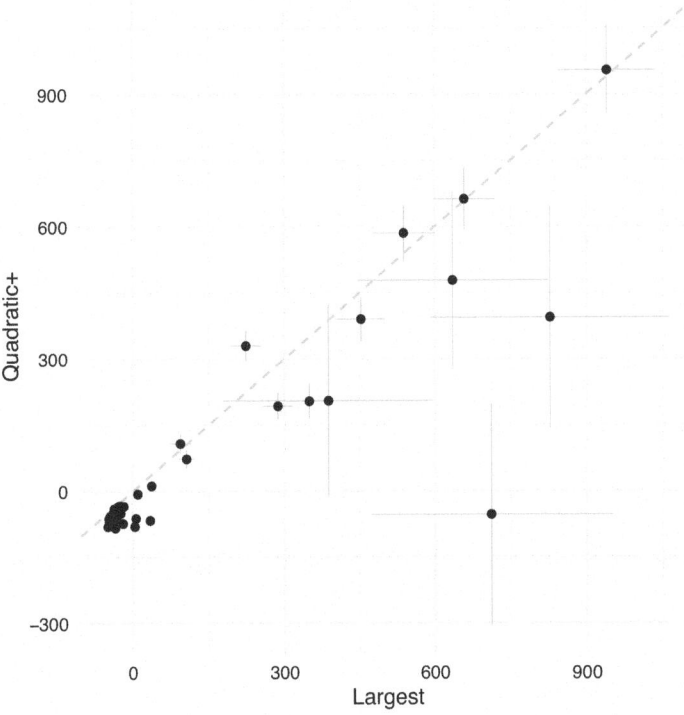

Fig. 4. Average reduction in mean sample size for our two default choices; now ±1 standard error in both directions. Each point represents a single contest (averaged over 500 simulated audits). The majority of points are on the right-hand side of the diagonal, indicating a larger average reduction when using Largest as compared to Quadratic+.

5 Improving Weighting Schemes Using More Sophisticated Portfolio Approaches

As discussed earlier in Sect. 3.4, previous theoretical work has shown that the optimal weighting scheme will be a constant rebalanced portfolio, for a set of weights that can only be determined in hindsight.

We conjecture that for typical elections, the optimal set of weights concentrates on a single requirement, and perhaps sometimes across a small number of requirements (when some base test supermartingales frequently swap leadership positions).

It would be interesting to explore this conjecture by approximating the optimal constant rebalanced weighting scheme using some kind of optimisation algorithm with the full set of ballots. If the conjecture is true, then it would explain why Largest and similar schemes often performed well in our comparisons. In elections where the conjecture is false, it would be worth exploring some more complex schemes.

The class of F-weighted portfolio algorithms is natural to consider based on asymptotic results, although we note that their short-run performance and computational complexity are typically poor.

The Linear scheme is in fact an F-weighted portfolio algorithm, for a rather restrictive choice of the distribution F; see Theorem 1 below. Most of the other schemes, including Largest, are not in that class because they can change zero weights to non-zero weights over time (not possible with an F-weighted algorithm). However, these schemes might be able to be approximated by an F-weighted algorithm, by "rounding off" weights that are very close to 0 or 1.

This suggests that we could work with more complex F-weighted portfolio algorithms if we approximate them appropriately. For example, consider the "general universal portfolio" by Cover [6], which creates an F that places positive mass on every face of a simplex. We could mimic this in a more heuristic and computationally efficient way by greedily grouping only the best base martingales together and optimising the weight amongst them with a general F. Such a calculation would require applying possible weights (within the group) across the full history every time the weights are updated, which is more demanding than our current schemes, but it might be feasible for a small group of requirements.

Theorem 1. *Linear is an F-weighted portfolio algorithm.*

Proof. Consider a set of requirements R_i. Let $\boldsymbol{b} := (b_1, b_2, \ldots, b_{r_i})$ be a vector of nonnegative weights for the base test supermartingales for the r_i requirements in this set. Let $M_t(\boldsymbol{b})$ be the intersection test supermartingale obtained using the weight vector $\boldsymbol{b}$ at each time step (a constant rebalanced portfolio).

An *F-weighted portfolio* updates the weights at each time step using a performance-weighted average of constant rebalanced portfolios and an initial distribution F across possible weight vectors:

$$\boldsymbol{b}_t = \frac{\int \boldsymbol{b} M_{t-1}(\boldsymbol{b}) F(\boldsymbol{b}) \, d\boldsymbol{b}}{\int M_{t-1}(\boldsymbol{b}) F(\boldsymbol{b}) \, d\boldsymbol{b}}.$$

Let $\boldsymbol{b}_r = (0, 0, \ldots, 1, \ldots, 0)$, consisting of a weight 1 for the rth component and 0 for all others. Using these weights yields the base test supermartingale for requirement r. In other words, $M_t(\boldsymbol{b}_r) = M_{r,t}$.

Consider a distribution F that places mass on all vectors $\boldsymbol{b}_r$, and zero probability elsewhere: $F(\boldsymbol{b}) = 1/r_i \sum_{r=1}^{r_i} \delta_{\boldsymbol{b}_r}(\boldsymbol{b})$, where δ is the Dirac delta function. We show that this produces the Linear weighting scheme:

$$\boldsymbol{b}_t = \frac{\int \boldsymbol{b} M_{t-1}(\boldsymbol{b}) 1/r_i \sum_{r=1}^{r_i} \delta_{\boldsymbol{b}_r}(\boldsymbol{b}) \, d\boldsymbol{b}}{\int M_{t-1}(\boldsymbol{b}) 1/r_i \sum_{r=1}^{r_i} \delta_{\boldsymbol{b}_r}(\boldsymbol{b}) \, d\boldsymbol{b}} = \frac{\sum_{r=1}^{r_i} \boldsymbol{b}_r M_{t-1}(\boldsymbol{b}_r)}{\sum_{r=1}^{r_i} M_{t-1}(\boldsymbol{b}_r)} = \frac{\sum_{r=1}^{r_i} \boldsymbol{b}_r M_{r,t-1}}{\sum_{r=1}^{r_i} M_{r,t-1}}.$$

This is precisely the weight vector for the Linear scheme ($w_{r,t} := M_{r,t-1}$). □

6 Discussion

AWAIRE has many adjustable parameters including tuning parameters in the base ALPHA test supermartingales and the adaptive selection of weights in combining the base test supermartingales. We explored an extensive range of weighting schemes and of tuning parameters for shrinkTrunc() in ALPHA, providing a deeper understanding of the trade-offs. We provided recommendations for default choices of the parameters in shrinkTrunc() for ALPHA and the adaptive weights.

This work focused on auditing IRV contests when the election reports a winner but does not report the interpretation of individual ballot cards (CVRs). [7] shows that reliable CVRs, if they are available, can make AWAIRE more efficient. In some jurisdictions, CVRs are not available but some information about the election count is, such as round-by-round vote tallies. It might be possible to use such tallies to tune AWAIRE parameters. For example, the last-round margin is often the margin of the contest as a whole, or at least provides an upper bound. This could be used to set η_0 to a useful default value specific for that contest, rather than simply using our default choice.

For any specific alt-order, the requirements will have a range of assorter margins, each with a different optimal tuning for ALPHA. Absent any information (such as CVRs) to tune the tests individually, we proposed a default value of η_0 to use for all requirements. Large values of d will make ALPHA adapt very slowly to the data, which will be helpful for some requirements but reduce efficiency for others, as illustrated in Fig. 3.

Our work has useful implications for a "lazy" implementation of AWAIRE that decreases the computational burden. Essentially, only schemes that have sparse weights (such as Largest) are feasible. The fact that Largest and its variants were among the best schemes suggests that a lazy implementation should not incur a large penalty in statistical performance. The major challenge will be to ensure that a good requirement is found early on in any lazy algorithm, but once that is done the audit should perform competitively without needing to explore for more requirements.

It was difficult to find many practically useful software implementations of existing portfolio algorithms. That limited how many we could include in our comparison. However, many portfolio algorithms are known to be either computationally inefficient, or only asymptotically optimal but perform poorly for small time horizons; thus, they would not fare well in our comparisons anyway. It may be the case that some existing algorithms would perform better than all of the ones we have tried thus far. Future work can explore implementing any algorithms that are expected to be computationally efficient and also perform well on short time horizons.

There may be a theoretically best weighting scheme that could be determined from the complete set of ballots (i.e., "in hindsight"). Future work could investigate optimal weighting and ways to approximate it efficiently and adaptively in practice.

It would be interesting to see to what extent the theoretically best schemes place nearly all of their weight on only a few requirements. We suspect this might be the case, given how well the Largest scheme performs in our comparisons.

Acknowledgements. We thank Michelle Blom and Vanessa Teague for helpful discussions and suggestions. This work was supported by the Australian Research Council (Discovery Project DP220101012, OPTIMA ITTC IC200100009) and the U.S. National Science Foundation (SaTC 2228884).

References

1. Agarwal, A., Hazan, E., Kale, S., Schapire, R.E.: Algorithms for portfolio management based on the Newton method. In: Proceedings of the 23rd International Conference on Machine Learning, ICML 2006, pp. 9–16. Association for Computing Machinery, New York (2006). https://doi.org/10.1145/1143844.1143846
2. Algoet, P.H., Cover, T.M.: Asymptotic optimality and asymptotic equipartition properties of log-optimum investment. Ann. Probab. **16**(2), 876–898 (1988). https://doi.org/10.1214/aop/1176991793
3. Blom, M., et al.: You can do RLAs for IRV. In: Proceedings of E-Vote-ID 2020. TalTech Press (2020). Preprint: arXiv:2004.00235
4. Blom, M., Stuckey, P.J., Teague, V.: RAIRE: risk-limiting audits for IRV elections. arXiv:1903.08804. Preliminary version appeared in Electronic Voting (E-Vote-ID 2018). LNCS, vol. 11143. Springer, Cham (2019)
5. Breiman, L.: Optimal gambling systems for favorable games. In: Proceedings of the Fourth Berkeley Symposium on Mathematical Statistics and Probability, Volume 1: Contributions to the Theory of Statistics, vol. 4, pp. 65–79. University of California Press (1961). https://projecteuclid.org/proceedings/berkeley-symposium-on-mathematical-statistics-and-probability/Proceedings-of-the-Fourth-Berkeley-Symposium-on-Mathematical-Statistics-and/Chapter/Optimal-Gambling-Systems-for-Favorable-Games/bsmsp/1200512159
6. Cover, T.M.: Universal portfolios. Math. Financ. **1**(1), 1–29 (1991). https://doi.org/10.1111/j.1467-9965.1991.tb00002.x
7. Ek, A., Stark, P.B., Stuckey, P.J., Vukcevic, D.: Adaptively weighted audits of instant-runoff voting elections: AWAIRE. In: Volkamer, M., et al. (eds.) E-Vote-ID 2023. LNCS, vol. 14230, pp. 35–51. Springer, Cham (2023). https://doi.org/10.1007/978-3-031-43756-4_3. Preprint: arXiv:2307.10972
8. Kalai, A.T., Vempala, S.: Efficient algorithms for universal portfolios. J. Mach. Learn. Res. **3**, 423–440 (2002). https://www.jmlr.org/papers/v3/kalai02a.html
9. Stark, P.B.: Sets of half-average nulls generate risk-limiting audits: SHANGRLA. In: Bernhard, M., et al. (eds.) FC 2020. LNCS, vol. 12063, pp. 319–336. Springer, Cham (2020). https://doi.org/10.1007/978-3-030-54455-3_23. Preprint: arXiv:1911.10035
10. Stark, P.B.: ALPHA: audit that learns from previously hand-audited ballots. Ann. Appl. Stat. **17**(1), 641–679 (2023)
11. Ville, J.: Etude critique de la notion de collectif. No. 3 in Monographies des Probabilites, Gauthier-Villars, Paris (1939)

Systematic User Evaluation of a Second Device Based Cast-as-Intended Verifiability Approach

Tobias Hilt[1]([✉]), Benjamin Berens[1], Tomasz Truderung[2], Margarita Udovychenko[2], Stephan Neumann[3], and Melanie Volkamer[1]

[1] Karlsruhe Institute for Technology, Karlsruhe, Germany
{tobias.hilt,benjamin.berens,melanie.volkamer}@kit.edu
[2] POLYAS GmbH, Kassel, Germany
{t.truderung,m.udovychenko}@polyas.com
[3] Saarbrücken, Germany
stephan@stephanneumann.it

Abstract. End-to-end verifiable e-voting schemes enhance the verifiability of individual votes during the election process. Specifically, methods for cast-as-intended verifiability empower voters to confirm that their cast votes have not been manipulated by the voting client. There are mainly three approaches to implement cast-as-intended verifiability in remote e-voting systems: (1) return-code based, (2) challenge-based and (3) second-device-approach. To investigate the usability, perceived trustworthiness and manipulation effectiveness for the second-device-approach, we conducted a user study with 133 participants. The results are similar to those from related work investigating the other two approaches.

Keywords: Cast-as-intended verifiability · Second-Device approach · User Study · Manipulation Detection Efficacy

1 Introduction

Elections are the bedrock of modern democracies. In an era of increasing digitalization, governments have adopted electronic solutions in various areas, and elections are no exception. Switzerland [23] and Estonia [8] stand out as notable examples, allowing voters to exercise their right to vote in national elections through remote e-voting channels. France has recently (re)joined this trend, allowing citizens living abroad to vote online in the 2022 legislative elections, after the introduction of an online channel for the 2012 election and it being halted in the 2017 election due to security concerns [6]. Germany has also made progress in this area, introducing an online voting channel in last year's social security elections (being the third-largest nation wide German election) in addition to the traditional postal voting channel [12].

The adoption of remote e-voting offers clear advantages as a voting channel. For example, it simplifies the voting process for citizens living abroad and increases the efficiency and accuracy of the counting process. However, it is important to recognize that the integration of technology introduces the risk of deliberate manipulation of votes [10]. To mitigate this risk and increase the likelihood of detecting such tampering, security measures similar to election audit procedures for paper-based voting systems are essential. This includes verifying that: (1) the voting client accurately encoded the vote as intended by the voter (cast-as-intended verifiability), (2) the vote recorded by the voting system corresponds to the cast vote (recorded-as-cast verifiability), and (3) the recorded vote is accurately included in the final election result (tallied-as-recorded verifiability).

Our focus is on cast-as-intended verifiability, for which there are primarily three approaches: the Benaloh Challenge, Return-Codes, and the second-device approach. However, only the first two have undergone extensive user studies, assessing their general usability and effectiveness in detecting vote manipulations. This research focuses on investigating the usability, manipulation detection efficacy and perceived trustworthiness of the third approach, commonly known as the second-device approach. This approach is for example employed in Estonian national elections and was used in the GI-Election 2023[1].

We conducted a user study using an actual system implementing this approach with 133 participants. The study had two phases, in which each participant had to cast their vote once. The first phase was used to assess usability and simultaneously served as a deception, since participants were informed that their provided usability feedback on the voting system would be (at least partly) implemented for them to reassess in the second phase of the study. In reality, the second phase examined manipulation detection efficacy for two types of manipulation in addition to perceived trustworthiness.

Our results, encompassing both general usability and manipulation effectiveness, are compared with findings from related studies on the other two approaches. Of particular note is the manipulation detection efficacy of the two manipulation types closely matching the results reported in comparable studies. Trustworthiness of the system was perceived neutral, while high usability was attributed.

2 Background and Related Work

2.1 Cast-as-Intended Verifiability in Remote Electronic Voting

The term "E-Voting" describes the process of casting one's vote with the help of an electronic device, which can range from automated teller machines to complex remote electronic voting systems. The focus of this research is on remote electronic voting systems. One important aspect about remote electronic voting systems is the possibility to check that one's vote was cast-as-intended. There are mainly three approaches to implement cast-as-intended verifiability in remote electronic voting systems: (1) Using the Benaloh Challenge introduced in [4], (2) Providing so called return codes after the vote is cast as required in Switzerland

---

[1] GI = Gesellschaft für Informatik; https://gi.de, Last accessed 15.02.24.

and e.g. proposed in [9] which voters are supposed to compare with the codes provided on their code sheet send to them via postal mail before the election, (3) Enabling voters after having cast their vote to use a second device with an independent verifying application to check if their vote cast as intended. This approach is for instance applied in Estonia since 2013 (see e.g. [11] for a detailed description).

2.2 User Studies in Remote Electronic Voting

In the general context of electronic voting there have been made several user studies such as [26], examining Prêt á Voter [22], but as the system we used is based on remote electronic voting our focus is on user studies that are comparable to our approach. From the before mentioned three approaches to implement cast-as-intended verifiability in remote electronic voting systems, the first two approaches have been extensively evaluated with respect to their usability and usability improvements have been proposed and evaluated - e.g. the Benaloh Challenge has been studied in [1,20] and the return code approach in [15,17]. A comparative user study of both approaches was conducted in [14]. In [18], all three cast-as-intended verifiability approaches were compared regarding their manipulation detection efficacy in a user study. The third approach has received comparatively less attention; however, recent studies, such as the one conducted by [13], have delved into this area. In their research, the authors used semi-structured interviews to explore Estonian i-Voters' understanding of the cast-as-intended verifiability implemented in the Estonian i-Voting protocol.

3 System Description: Vote Casting and Cast-as-Intended Verifiability

The cast-as-intended verifiability mechanism considered in this paper is based on the use of a second device performing the corresponding cast-as-intended verifiability mechanism. There are two commonly used realizations of such a mechanism, e.g. a web application or a native mobile application. For this user study, our focus is on the web application as we consider it difficult to find participants who are going to install an app on their mobile phones just for such a study.

From the voter's point of view the voting process is divided into two parts (see Fig. 1).

1st Device. The voter authenticates themselves at the voting system, using the credentials they received[2]. Upon successful authentication the voter is greeted and the ballot is displayed. The voter selects and confirms their choice. After that the vote is cast and the voter is presented a confirmation page (see Fig. 2),

---

[2] In this study, these credentials were provided in the form of a role-card, containing the voter-ID and an election invitation letter, containing the password.

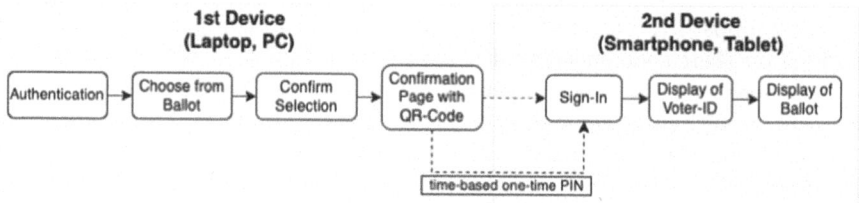

Fig. 1. Simplified Vote Casting and Verifying Process

including a QR code that can be used to perform cast-as-intended verifiability with a second device[3]. In addition this page displays a time-based one-time PIN, which is needed for authenticating at the web application. The PIN is refreshed every 30 s to deter vote selling and prevent voters from easily sharing their cast vote.

Fig. 2. Confirmation page of the voting system with the QR code and time-based one-time PIN

2nd Device. In order to perform cast-as-intended verifiability, which is optional, voters must scan the QR code with a suitable device (i.e. a smartphone or tablet). After scanning the QR code the voter is transferred to the web application, hosted by an independent provider[4], where they must authenticate using the

---

[3] The interfaces are inspired by the interfaces used by the Polyas company in their verifiable voting system. We improved the language and design based on our usability expertise.

[4] In our study we simulated the host to be OSCE (Organization for Security and Co-operation in Europe), while we hosted the web application on our own servers.

time-based one-time PIN, that is currently displayed on the confirmation page on the first device.

The details of the system used are described in [19], giving information why the following cast-as-intended verifiability specific security properties are provided.

Election Integrity. Election integrity wrt. cast-as-intended is ensured under the following assumptions: (1) voters actually verify their vote and check if both their displayed voter-ID and selection matches; (2) one of the devices (the primary voting device or the second device) is not corrupted; (3) either the voting-system or at least one of the verification mechanisms (if there are more than one) used by the voter to verify are not corrupt.

Ballot Privacy. For ballot privacy, the voter needs to trust the second device, as it learns the voter's choice (which it displays to the voter).

4 Methodology

4.1 Recruitment, Ethics and Data Protection

Recruitment. Participants needed to be 18 years or older and be fluent in German, in order to be recruited. Additionally, only participants using a PC or laptop were allowed, as we wanted to minimize the possibility of participants being unable to verify their vote with a second device due to them participating with their smartphone.

Ethics. We coordinated the process alongside the ethical guidelines and received approval by the ethical committee of the KIT (Karlsruhe Institute for Technology). Participants were granted a compensation of 3€ (Second phase: 4€), which was calculated using the approximate study time multiplied by the minimum wage in Germany. We offered participants to abort the study after debriefing and still receive the money, which none of them did.

Data Protection In cooperation with the data protection officer of our university, we created information about the usage of collected data, conforming to recent GDPR, which we presented to participants at the beginning of the study to inform participants about their rights and the usage of their collected data.

4.2 Research Questions

As already pointed out in Sect. 2 there has been limited work done to examine usability of remote electronic voting systems with cast-as-intended verifiability utilizing a second device. Thus, we try to contribute by answering the following research questions:

RQ1: *How usable do voters perceive a remote electronic voting system with cast-as-intended verifiability utilizing a second device?*

RQ2: *What is the manipulation detection efficacy of voters using a remote electronic voting system with cast-as-intended verifiability utilizing a second device?*

RQ3: *How trustworthy do voters perceive a remote electronic voting system with cast-as-intended verifiability utilizing a second device?*

To answer these questions we designed an extensive, two phase user study, which is explained in the following subsections.

4.3 Study Procedure

The study consisted of two phases. Phase one focused on perceived usability, while phase two examined manipulation detection efficacy and perceived trustworthiness. As participants were told the study was solely about perceived usability and that in the second phase they would have to reassess a reworked system, phase one also served as deception. All supplementary material used is attainable in the Appendix A.

Phase 1. The most important processes of phase one are illustrated in Fig. 3 and explained below.

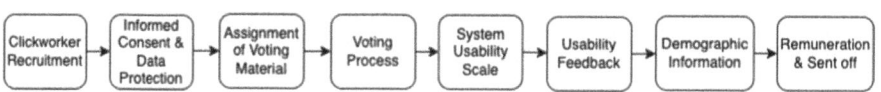

Fig. 3. Structure of Phase 1

Clickworker Recruiting. Participants were exclusively recruited with the online panel "clickworker"[5], from which participants were transferred to the online questionnaire[6].

Informed Consent & Data Protection. Starting the online questionnaire participants were presented the informed consent form and the data protection regulation.

---

[5] https://www.clickworker.de, Last accessed 14.12.2023.
[6] https://www.soscisurvey.de, Last accessed 14.12.2023.

Assignment of Voting Material. Participants received a role card, including their personal identifier and the choice they should vote for in this election. They also received an invitation letter to the election, which contained the voting rules, the password needed for authentication, the link to a report website, in case they experience problems during the election and brief paragraph encouraging voters to verify their vote. For this research, we chose to replicate the European Parliament election scenario. In addition, we chose to simulate the letter as if it came from the Federal Returning Officer. Within this simulated letter, a brief paragraph was included to encourage voters to actively verify their votes. We could have used a straightforward informational approach, but this would likely have not motivated many participants, as seen in the German Social Election [12]. Our decision to create a unique paragraph was influenced by research demonstrating that simply providing information about this verification feature does not increase the rate at which voters engage in verification [24]. Based on research from [21], we developed the following text, which includes both an analogy and a norm cue to further motivate voters (translated from German):

> By verifying, attempts of manipulation can be detected, which are usually uncovered in a classic election with the help of independent election observers. [**Analogy**]
> Voters who want to protect democracy should therefore use their second device to check whether their vote was correctly transmitted to the digital ballot box. [**Norm**]

Voting Process. The voting process followed the logic explained in Fig. 1, from Sect. 3. The voting system was hosted by POLYAS[7], while the verification web application was hosted by our institute (Karlsruhe Institute for Technology).

System Usability Score. To objectively assess the perceived usability of the voting process we utilized the system usability scale [5], in the German version[8].

Usability Feedback. As part of the deception we asked participants open-ended questions about perceived usability.

Demographic Information. Participants were asked their age and gender.

Remuneration & Sent-off. Participants were thanked for participating, paid and reminded, that the second would start two weeks later.

---

[7] www.polyas.de, last accessed 20.02.2024.
[8] https://community.sap.com/t5/additional-blogs-by-sap/system-usability-scale-jetzt-auch-auf-deutsch/ba-p/13487686, last accessed 16.02.2024.

Phase 2. Two weeks after the completion of phase one the second phase started. Eligible for this phase were only the participants from phase one that actually participated in the election and verified their vote ($n = 133$)[9]. The general structure of this phase is illustrated in Fig. 4 and the processes that differ from phase one are explained below.

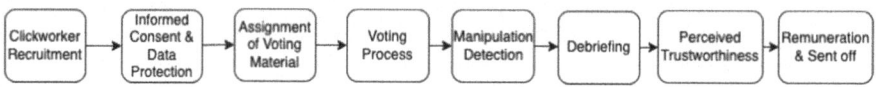

Fig. 4. Structure of Phase 2

Voting Process. Participants were assigned to one of two voting systems based on the ID assigned in their role card, with each system subject to manipulation. In the event that participants detected tampering they had different reporting options, which are explained in Subsect. 4.4. The voting process for the two types of manipulations and their respective viable reporting options is illustrated in Fig. 5.

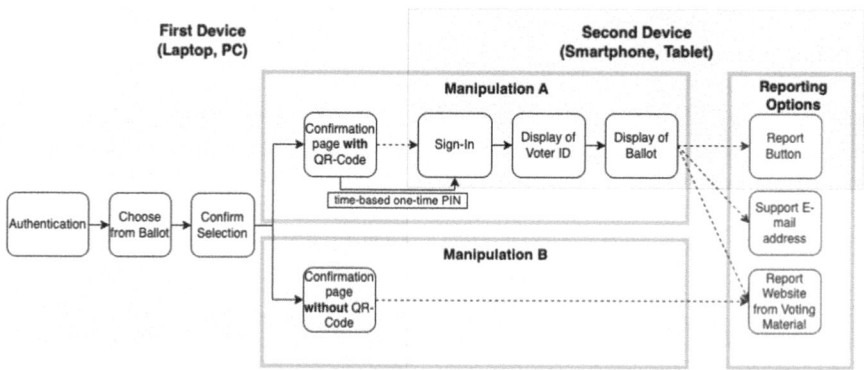

Fig. 5. Simplified Voting Process in Phase 2

Manipulation Detection. Upon completion of the voting process, participants were asked an open-ended question to determine if they observed any anomalies. If they responded in the affirmative, they were then asked about the nature of the irregularities they observed and whether they took the initiative to report them.

---

[9] We confirmed this by providing an anonymised list of IDs to the online survey. This ensured that only Clickworkers whose IDs were on the list were able to participate.

Debriefing. Based on the version of the voting system they experienced and the detection status of the manipulation, participants received a customized debriefing explaining the actual purpose of the study.

Perceived Trustworthiness. After the debriefing, participants were asked to mark their perceived trustworthiness of the remote electronic voting system on a Likert scale from one to five.

4.4 Type of Manipulation

We investigated two potential attack vectors applicable to remote electronic voting systems with cast-as-intended verifiability, inspired by those manipulation types examined by related work. First, we simulated a scenario in which a malicious voting device manipulated the vote without the voter's knowledge. Specifically, the voting application was configured to change the vote cast from "CDU" to "SPD", which are both German parties. Detection of this manipulation is possible if the voter chooses to verify his vote with a second (honest) device. In this case the voter has several secure reporting mechanisms available, including using the dedicated button within the verifying application, accessing the reporting website linked from the invitation letter, or reporting the problem using the dedicated support email addresses from the verification web application. Henceforth, this manipulation scenario is referred to as ***MT-A*** *(= Manipulation Type A: Vote Tampering Manipulation)*.

We also simulated a scenario in which, the voting system itself has malicious intent, by manipulating the interface, making it impossible for the voter to verify their vote. We modified the system to withhold the display of a QR code at the end of the voting process, preventing voters from verifying their votes. The voter should refrain from using the support email address provided by the voting interface, as the platform lacks integrity. Consequently, in this scenario, the only viable option is to report using the reporting website from the election invitation letter. This form of manipulation is referred to as ***MT-B*** *(= Manipulation Type B: Verification Prevention Manipulation)*.

4.5 Pre-study

A pre-study involving 20 participants was conducted to assess system functionality and connectivity. Insights from the pre-study led to adjustments in the logic governing credential assignment, ensuring reliable payment for participants completing the online questionnaire. Minor modifications were also made to the voting material, such as aligning the voting period in the election invitation letter with the date specified in the role card.

5 Results

5.1 Demographic Information

A total of 176 participants were initially recruited, with 43 excluded due to data pruning (non-human answers or answers from participants that did not vote and just clicked through the survey[10]). The final sample for phase one consisted of 133 participants. Among them, 90 identified as male, 43 as female[11], and the majority held a university degree ($n = 64$). For phase two, 85 participants returned, of which 79 successfully participated. Exclusions were made for those who did not vote ($n = 4$), provided insufficient responses, as in blank spaces, ($n = 1$), or aborted the survey ($n = 1$). The remaining 79 participants included 50 men and 29 women.

5.2 *RQ1:* Perceived Usability

To evaluate the perceived usability, we employed the System Usability Scale (SUS), a standardized scale utilized for evaluating the perceived usability across various products [5]. The scale ranges from 0 to a maximum of 100 points, with higher values indicating better subjective usability. In order to assess the actual perceived usability, we chose to survey participants during phase one, where they experienced the unaltered system. Outliers that were 1.5 times the interquartile range over the third quartile or below the first quartile were excluded, as proposed by the IQR-method to prune data [7]. In total, three outlier were excluded. The average SUS score among the remaining participants was 78.92 ($sd = 14.26$), indicative of good usability [3]

5.3 *RQ2:* Manipulation Detection Efficiency

When assessing whether participants detected the manipulation, we included two factors: (1) the response to a question in the online questionnaire and (2) the usage of the reporting system. Regarding (1), the online questionnaire contained the question "Did you notice anything unusual during the election?". If participants responded in the affirmative and their answer contained a clear relation to one of the manipulation types, their response was categorized as "Detected", otherwise as "Not detected". For (2) all responses to the reporting system (i.e., the report website and support mail address, see Sect. 4.4) were inspected and categorized by two members of the research team. After a final discussion about the responses and their categorization a percentage agreement of 97.47% was reached. As before, responses were categorized as "Detected" and "Not detected". If one of the factors was categorized as "Detected", the responding participant was categorized as having detected the manipulation.

---

[10] Detected by comparing the IDs from the voting system with the corresponding survey ID.

[11] Note: It was possible to state "other" or "prefer not to state" but none of the participants did so.

Table 1. Amount of participants that detected the manipulation for both manipulation types.

	Detected	Not Detected
MT-A	40 (96%)	2 (4%)
MT-B	9 (24%)	28 (76%)
Total	49 (62%)	30 (38%)

Table 1 gives an overview of the manipulation detection efficacy, showing the overal detection rate at 62%. MT-A was detected far more often than MT-B (96% vs. 24%). A Fisher-exact confirmed the difference to be statistical significant (OR = 0.0174, 95% CI = [0.00172, 0.0877], $p < 0.001$). To determine whether gender has a statistical impact on the manipulation detection efficacy, we performed a CHI-squared test, which proves, that gender has no effect $X^2(1, N = 79) = 0.060793$, $p = 0.8052$. As not every age group had a minimum of five participants who detected the manipulation and five who did not detect it, a Fisher-exact test was conducted. The results indicate that age also had no significant effect on manipulation detection efficiency ($p = 0.8597$).

5.4 RQ3:Perceived Trustworthiness

After debriefing participants about the actual purpose of the study, they were requested to assess the trustworthiness of the remote electronic voting system by indicating their level of trust on a Likert scale ranging from one ("Not Trustworthy at all") to five ("Very Trustworthy"). On average, participants exhibited a neutral stance toward trustworthiness with a slight inclination towards positive perceived trustworthiness (3.15, $sd = 1.25$), as illustrated in Table 2.

Table 2. Distribution of participants' perceived trustworthiness based on manipulation type and whether or not they detected the manipulation.

Perceived Trustworthiness	Overall		MT-A		MT-B	
	Detected	Not Detected	Detected	Not Detected	Detected	Not Detected
Not Trustworthy at all (= 1)	16.3%	6.7%	17.5%	0%	11.1%	7.2%
Not Trustworthy (= 2)	16.3%	20%	15%	0%	22.2%	21.4%
Neutral (= 3)	26.5%	26.7%	27.5%	0%	22.2%	28.6%
Trustworthy (= 4)	28.6%	26.7%	27.5%	50%	33.3%	25%
Very Trustworthy (= 5)	12.2%	20%	12.5%	50%	11.1%	17.8%
Mean Rating	3.04	3.33	3.03	4.5	3.11	3.25
	3.15		3.09		3.22	

Participants that did not detect the manipulation expressed a slightly higher level of perceived trustworthiness (3.33, $sd = 1.21$) compared to those that did (3.04, $sd = 1.27$). A Fisher-exact test confirmed this marginal difference not to be statistically significant ($p = 0.7063$).

Participants from $MT\text{-}B$ rated the system similar (3.22 $sd = 1.2$) to participants from $MT\text{-}A$ (3.09 $sd = 1.3$), indicating that manipulation type has no statistical impact on perceived trustworthiness. A Fisher-exact test confirmed this presumption ($p = 0.7886$).

6 Discussion

6.1 Perceived Usability

In terms of usability (i.e. the SUS scores) the second device approach we used in this study performed similar to the other approaches from related work. Whereas the approaches from related work scored SUS-scores between 73 and 85, participants from our study attributed the approach a score of 79, describing "good usability". The comparison to related studies remains difficult as we used an actual voting system, while all of them used mock-up systems. Table 3 gives an overview of the archieved SUS scores.

6.2 Manipulation Detection Efficacy

As previously mentioned the comparison to the related work is difficult, especially with regards to manipulation detection efficacy due to several reasons: (1) the study design, (2) the instructions provided to the participants and (3) the note or request to participants to verify their vote, greatly differ from study to study. Another potential factor of influence is the presumption all of the other studies made in which they determined, that participants should see the voting system for the first time, when they were objected to the manipulation, as for that point in time no e-Voting was available for the participants in the real world (all these studies were conducted in Germany).

Table 3 also shows the detection rates from the various studies[12]. In the following we mainly focus on the user studies based on the return code based and second device approach, as these approaches have already been implemented in actual elections.

Overall $MT\text{-}A$ was detected in 100% of cases in several studies based on the return-code based approach. The detection efficacy for $MT\text{-}B$ is always much lower compared to $MT\text{-}A$, as also shown in Kulyk et al.'s study [16]. Ultimately the detection efficacy for $MT\text{-}B$ is far better in return-code based approaches compared to the second device approach. This difference is potentially explained by the used approaches: Inherent to the return-code based approach is the voters expectation to receive something back after casting the vote, hence the name "return-code". Part of the voting process, as described in the voting material, is the verification. In contrast in the second device approach, the voter **can** (but does not need to), perform cast-as-intended verifiability. As the cast-as-intended

---

[12] Note, the comparison only provides some hints as the study designs are different in detail. Future work should investigate in a comparative study considering both manipulation types.

Table 3. Overview of User Studies examining the detection rate of different manipulation types. *The authors made improvements to the systems/materials. We only included the improved versions.

Source	cast-as-intended Verifiability Approach	SUS	Manipulation Type	Detection Efficacy
[25]*	Return-Code	82	MT-A	41%
[17]*	Return-Code	85	MT-A	100%
[16]*	Return-Code	81	MT-A	100%
			MT-B	43%
[18]	Return-Code	85	MT-A	100%
	Challenge	73		28%
	Second Device	85		64%
[14]	Return-Code	-	MT-A	100%
	Challenge			77%
[24]*	Return-Code	-	MT-B	71%
This study	Second Device	79	MT-A	96%
			MT-B	24%

verifiability-step is performed after casting the vote, it may be that voters are already mentally finished with the voting process, that they are more likely to not detect something missing, i.e. the QR code to perform cast-as-intended verifiability.

There is only one previous paper [18] which studied the manipulation detection rate for the second device approach (for MT-A only). Their detection rate was 64% and ours 96%. The improved detection rate may be explained by the fact that participants in our study had already used the honest system before and were therefore more likely to detect the manipulation.

6.3 Perceived Trustworthiness

The well reported usability may also have influenced perceived trustworthiness, as trustworthiness is often attributed to usable systems [2]. Although no statistical effects based on manipulation detection, gender, age, or manipulation type could be determined, the sequencing of the manipulation detection questions, debriefing, and subsequent trustworthiness assessment may have influenced participants' perceptions due to increased awareness of manipulation risks. Those who suspected manipulation may have rated trustworthiness differently than those who suspected error or did not notice anything unusual prior to the debriefing. This potential post hoc bias should be acknowledged, and future research should examine the effect of the debriefing sequence on trustworthiness ratings. It is important to assess perceived trustworthiness both before and after debriefing to understand potential changes influenced by participants' awareness of manipulation risks.

6.4 Limitation

By explicitly informing participants of the study's focus on usability, there is a potential bias. Participants may have paid more attention to the usability aspects and may have overlooked the introduced manipulation. Additionally, by instructing voters how to vote their ability to detect the manipulation may have been reduced as it is more likely to detect if a personal choice (with a potential emotional connection) to a party is changed compared to a random one, that was assigned to them. The study did not comprehensively address all possible MT-Attempts. For example, we used a web-based application to reduce the burden on participants. However, this introduces an additional attack vector not covered in our study, similar to *MT-B*. In this scenario, adversaries could redirect participants to a spoofed web application that displays a fake ballot, which contains the vote the voter intended to cast. Detecting this manipulation would require voters to examine the URL of the QR code to ensure that it redirects to the legitimate web application. Another potential attack vector we did not examine is the clash attack. In this scenario, the vote is altered, but during cast-as-intended verifiability with the second machine, the voter is presented with a different ballot containing the originally intended vote. Detecting this tampering could involve asking the voter to confirm that the ballot presented on the second machine is in fact their own, typically accomplished by comparing voter IDs. However, implementing this in our study was challenging because participants were assigned new voter IDs that they had never seen before, as opposed to a real-world scenario where voter IDs are familiar (e.g., social security number or ID card number). Both of these attack vectors warrant investigation in future research. We only offered the verification application from one provider whereas in a real election voters should have the option to choose from several providers. The process of categorizing participants answers into "Detected" and "Not detected" also forms a limitation. While participants correctly identified changes in their votes or the absence of a QR code for cast-as-intended verifiability, they typically described these instances as errors, revealing a potential disconnect in perception, e.g., "My vote was wrong" (Participant 65) or "Confusingly, I did not receive a QR code" (Participant 31).

7 Conclusion

We evaluated the second device based cast-as-intended verifiability approach which has not been thoroughly investigated, yet but is used in actual elections. We conducted a two-phase user study. Phase one focused on perceived usability, while phase two examined the effectiveness of two types of manipulation detection and perceived trustworthiness. Thus, first phase was also used as deception for the second phase. Moreover with the two phases, we were able simulate that participants knew the system already when studying the manipulation detection. We found that the second device approach performed similarly in terms of both perceived usability and manipulation detection compared to existing user studies that primarily examined the return code-based approach. Furthermore, we found a similarity between the two: in both approaches, voters showed difficulty in detecting *MT-B*, where the voting system does not allow the voter to perform cast-as-intended verifiability. In comparison to user studies from the return-code based approach, we perform slightly worse but using return-code based approach is also not feasible for all kind of elections, as the process becomes more complex with larger elections, especially visually impaired people. Consequently, in the future one should decide on a case by case basis which approach to choose.

Acknowledgments. This work was funded by the Topic Engineering Secure Systems, subtopic 46.23.01 Methods for Engineering Secure Systems, of the Helmholtz Association (HGF) and supported by KASTEL Security Research Labs, Karlsruhe.

A Appendix

All supplementary material used for the study, as well as the structure of the online questionaire is attainable at https://doi.org/10.35097/1934.

References

1. Acemyan, C.Z., Kortum, P., Byrne, M.D., Wallach, D.S.: Usability of voter verifiable, end-to-end voting systems: baseline data for Helios, Prêt à Voter, and Scantegrity II. USENIX J. Election Technol. Syst. **2**(3), 26–56 (2014)
2. Acemyan, C.Z., Kortum, P.: The relationship between trust and usability in systems. Proc. Hum. Factors Ergon. Soc. Annu. Meet. **56**(1), 1842–1846 (2012)
3. Bangor, A., Kortum, P.T., Miller, J.T.: Determining what individual SUS scores mean: adding an adjective rating scale. J. Usability Stud. **4**(3), 114–123 (2009)
4. Benaloh, J.: Simple verifiable elections. In: Electronic Voting Technology Workshop, EVT 2006. USENIX Association, Berkeley (2006)
5. Brooke, J.: SUS-a quick and dirty usability scale. Usability Eval. Ind. **189**(194), 4–7 (1996)
6. Cortier, V., Gaudry, P., Glondu, S., Ruhault, S.: French 2022 legislatives elections: a verifiability experiment. In: Accepted for: International Joint Conference on Electronic Voting (E-VOTE-ID) (2023)
7. Dodge, Y.: Exploratory data analysis. In: Dodge, Y. (ed.) The Concise Encyclopedia of Statistics, pp. 192–194. Springer, New York (2008). https://doi.org/10.1007/978-0-387-32833-1_136
8. Estonian National Electoral Committee: Statistics about Internet Voting in Estonia (2015). https://www.valimised.ee/en/archive/statistics-about-internet-voting-estonia
9. Galindo, D., Guasch, S., Puiggalí, J.: 2015 Neuchâtel's cast-as-intended verification mechanism. In: Haenni, R., Koenig, R.E., Wikström, D. (eds.) VOTELID 2015. LNCS, vol. 9269, pp. 3–18. Springer, Cham (2015). https://doi.org/10.1007/978-3-319-22270-7_1
10. Halderman, J.A., Teague, V.: The new south wales ivote system: security failures and verification flaws in a live online election. CoRR abs/1504.05646 (2015)
11. Heiberg, S., Willemson, J.: Verifiable Internet Voting in Estonia. In: 6th International Conference on Electronic Voting, Verifying the Vote (EVOTE), pp. 1–8. IEEE (2014)

12. Hilt, T., Kulyk, O., Volkamer, M.: German social elections 2023: an overview and first analysis. In: Accepted for: International Joint Conference on Electronic Voting (E-VOTE-ID) (2023)
13. Hilt, T., Sein, K., Mällo, T., Villemson, J., Volkamer, M.: Voter perception of cast-as-intended verifiability in the estonian i-vote protocol. In: Accepted for: International Joint Conference on Electronic Voting (E-VOTE-ID) (2023)
14. Kulyk, O., Henzel, J., Renaud, K., Volkamer, M.: Comparing "challenge-based" and "code-based" internet voting verification implementations. In: Lamas, D., Loizides, F., Nacke, L., Petrie, H., Winckler, M., Zaphiris, P. (eds.) INTERACT 2019. LNCS, vol. 11746, pp. 519–538. Springer, Cham (2019). https://doi.org/10.1007/978-3-030-29381-9_32
15. Kulyk, O., Ludwig, J., Volkamer, M., Koenig, R.E., Locher, P.: Usable verifiable secrecy-preserving E-voting. In: 6th International Joint Conference on Electronic Voting (E-Vote-ID). University of Tartu Press (2021)
16. Kulyk, O., Volkamer, M., Müller, M., Renaud, K.: Towards improving the efficacy of code-based verification in internet voting. In: Bernhard, M., et al. (eds.) FC 2020. LNCS, vol. 12063, pp. 291–309. Springer, Cham (2020). https://doi.org/10.1007/978-3-030-54455-3_21
17. Marky, K., Zimmermann, V., Funk, M., Daubert, J., Bleck, K., Mühlhäuser, M.: Improving the usability and UX of the swiss internet voting interface. In: ACM CHI (2020)
18. Marky, K., Zollinger, M.L., Roenne, P., Ryan, P.Y., Grube, T., Kunze, K.: Investigating usability and user experience of individually verifiable internet voting schemes. ACM Trans. Comput.-Hum. Interact **28**(5) (2021)
19. Müller, J., Truderung, T.: CAISED: a protocol for cast-as-intended verifiability with a second device. In: Volkamer, M., et al. (eds.) E-Vote-ID 2023. LNCS, vol. 14230, pp. 123–139. Springer, Cham (2023). https://doi.org/10.1007/978-3-031-43756-4_8
20. Neumann, S., Olembo, M.M., Renaud, K., Volkamer, M.: Helios verification: to alleviate, or to nominate: is that the question, or shall we have both? In: Kő, A., Francesconi, E. (eds.) EGOVIS 2014. LNCS, vol. 8650, pp. 246–260. Springer, Cham (2014). https://doi.org/10.1007/978-3-319-10178-1_20
21. Olembo, M.M., Renaud, K., Bartsch, S., Volkamer, M.: Voter, what message will motivate you to verify your vote. In: USEC. Internet Society (2014)
22. Ryan, P.Y.A., Teague, V.: Pretty good democracy. In: Christianson, B., Malcolm, J.A., Matyáš, V., Roe, M. (eds.) Security Protocols 2009. LNCS, vol. 7028, pp. 111–130. Springer, Heidelberg (2013). https://doi.org/10.1007/978-3-642-36213-2_15
23. Serdult, U., Germann, M., Mendez, F., Portenier, A., Wellig, C.: Fifteen years of internet voting in Switzerland. In: ICEDEG, pp. 126–132. IEEE (2015)
24. Thürwächter, P.T., Volkamer, M., Kulyk, O.: Individual verifiability with return codes: manipulation detection efficacy. In: Krimmer, R., Volkamer, M., Duenas-Cid, D., Rønne, P., Germann, M. (eds.) E-Vote-ID 2022. LNCS, vol. 13553, pp. 139–156. Springer, Cham (2022). https://doi.org/10.1007/978-3-031-15911-4_9
25. Volkamer, M., Kulyk, O., Ludwig, J., Fuhrberg, N.: Increasing security without decreasing usability: comparison of various verifiable voting systems. In: Eighteenth Symposium on Usable Privacy and Security (SOUPS 2022), Boston, MA. USENIX Association (2022)
26. Winckler, M., et al.: Assessing the usability of open verifiable e-voting systems: a trial with the system Prêt à voter. In: ICE-GOV, pp. 281–296 (2009)

Open Access This chapter is licensed under the terms of the Creative Commons Attribution 4.0 International License (http://creativecommons.org/licenses/by/4.0/), which permits use, sharing, adaptation, distribution and reproduction in any medium or format, as long as you give appropriate credit to the original author(s) and the source, provide a link to the Creative Commons license and indicate if changes were made.

The images or other third party material in this chapter are included in the chapter's Creative Commons license, unless indicated otherwise in a credit line to the material. If material is not included in the chapter's Creative Commons license and your intended use is not permitted by statutory regulation or exceeds the permitted use, you will need to obtain permission directly from the copyright holder.

On the Applicability of STARKs to Counted-as-Collected Verification in Existing Homomorphic E-Voting Systems

Max Harrison and Thomas Haines

Australian National University, Canberra, Australia
thomas.haines@anu.edu.au

Abstract. Scalable Transparent ARguments of Knowledge (STARKs) are a kind of succinct zero-knowledge proof which do NOT require trusting any party to generate a Common Reference String (CRS). In this work, we examine the applicability of STARKs to improving Counted-as-Collected verification in the homomorphically tallied elections. In particular we are interested in using STARKs to allow very efficient tally verification while providing everlasting privacy to the information made available for public verification. This work provides a useful reference for the computational and verifiability trade-offs of using STARKs.

1 Introduction

A slew of various electronic voting protocols and systems (Helios, STAR-Vote, Belenios, ElectionGuard, etc.) follow a general approach pioneered by Benaloh and Yung [BY86] that utilises homomorphic encryption to preserve privacy while maintaining the verifiability of these systems. In this general approach, voters submit additively homomorphic ciphertexts which are then composed into an output ciphertext representing the vote tally. This output ciphertext can then be decrypted to reveal the vote tally, all while the underlying votes are never exposed and remain secure in their encrypted form. This approach preserves the privacy of voters while also maintaining verifiability of the voting protocol.

The exact verification procedure differs between voting systems but in general the verifier checks zero-knowledge proofs to ensure the (encrypted) ballots are well formed and then homomorphically combines these checking that the accumulated ciphertext decrypts to the claimed result, with the aid of more zero-knowledge proofs; optionally, the verifier may also check that the ballots came from valid voters by checking digital signatures or the like.

The intuition behind the approach we evaluate is that we get the tallier, or a third-party, to produce a STARK proof which says that all the evidence is valid with respect to the normal verification procedure; the verifier then checks the STARK proof rather than original evidence. We enhance this approach by committing (within a Merkle tree) to the original verification data in constant

---

T. Haines—The recipient of an Australian Research Council Australian Discovery Early Career Award (project number DE220100595).

size which reduces the data required to verify dramatically; the statement proved by the STARK proof is then that the prover can open the commitment to values which satisfy the normal verification procedure.

1.1 Limitations of the Existing Approaches

On a per ballot basis the standard homomorphic tally approach is fairly efficient, at least for simple elections, but the cost of verification grows linearly in the number of ballots cast which quickly become prohibitive. In our running example of a referendum with 2^{24} voters (roughly the number of eligible voters in the Australian 2023 Voice referendum) the verification time is approximately 77 core-days and the size of the inputs to the verification is roughly 38 GB; these values will be explained in Sect. 3. While these values are certainly manageable they do pose a hurdle to the idealised world where each voter checks the election result for themselves.

In addition to the computational costs of verification, many Governments have been hesitant to release the data required for verification even when it existed; examples of this include the Estonian IVXV system [oE], the Swiss Post system [Swi21], and iVote system as used in New South Wales and Western Australia. While this hesitation is certainly multifaceted the privacy risk of doing so is certainly a significant part of the equation; for example, the lack of randomness in ballot generation [Gjø16] in the Norwegian system would have been much more disastrous if these ballots were published. Ideally, we like a system where the information released for verification perfectly hid the individual ballots à la everlasting privacy [HMMP23].

1.2 STARKs

There has been an orthogonal thread of research and development in cryptographic proof schemes within the last decade, enabling the construction of *succinct* ZK proofs - these novel proof schemes enable the construction and verification of ZK proofs in radically shorter time frames and data sizes. A prominent example of such a system is one introduced by [BSBHR18]: STARKs (Scalable Transparent ARguments of Knowledge) are a proof-of-computation scheme that have a number of attractive properties relevant to the development of e-voting systems. They are fully transparent, meaning they do NOT rely on any complex trusted setup ceremonies. They rely on very few cryptographic assumptions and are very modular to any specific implementation. STARKs are also highly parallelisable, allowing huge workloads to be distributed efficiently. Crucially, the STARK-constructed succinct ZK proofs are very efficient to both generate and verify, with verification time and proof size sublinear in the size of input data.

1.3 STARKs for Counted-as-Collected

There are many places in an electronic voting protocol where one might consider using STARKS, or Zero-Knowledge Succinct Non-Interactive Argument of

Knowledge (SNARKs) if one is willing to accept the trust assumption; to our knowledge all other previous works considered SNARKs but STARKs could be used instead at an increased computational cost. Huber et al. [HKK+22] use them to prove that an election result (the outcome of the social choice function) is correct with regards to commitments to votes. Both Sheikhi et al. [SGS23] and Devillez et al. [DPP22] use it as part of ballot validity proofs. We, however, are interested in the applicability of STARKs to enhance existing homomorphically tallied election systems by increasing the efficiency and privacy of checking that the election result is correct with regards to the collected ballots (Counted-as-collected), and optionally eligibility verification as well.

While STARKs immediately fix the computational-time issue for the verifier they do not immediately fix the issue with verification input size since we would still need to send all the encrypted votes; we address this issue by committing to all the encrypted votes in a Merkle tree and sending the root of the tree along with the STARK proof, see Sect. 2 for details. In addition, there is no guarantee that the prover can produce the proofs for the statements we care about within the time-frame of an election. Our analysis shows that primary constraint on the prover, at least on the current state-of-the-art implementations, is not the execution time but rather the availability of Random Access Memory (RAM); we address this limitation by producing proofs which prove that batches of votes are: well formed, come from valid voters, and are correctly homomorphically accumulated. The homomorphically accumulated ciphertexts from each batch are then themselves combined and verifiable decrypted.

One of the advantage of using a Merkle tree is that we can provide logarithmic sized proofs of inclusion to voters that their ballot is among those tallied. In the specific instance we evaluated, which used digital signatures, this is not necessary since the fact that one of ballots has a signature valid with respect to the voter's public key serves to prove inclusion. However, in many cases digital signature are not used and the ability to prove Collected-as-Cast in sublinear time and space is important to the overall efficiency of the system; we note that care must be taken to ensure all internal nodes of the Merkle tree are perfectly hiding if this approach is taken and everlasting privacy is desired.

Our construction reduces the amount of time and data required to verify an election result by l orders of magnitude, at the cost of increasing the required RAM of the talliers by l orders of magnitude. Our construction hides the verification information behind a perfectly hiding commitment: a computationally unbounded adversary cannot extract any more information about individual votes than what is revealed by the vote result. We also present evaluation data for an example implementation of the protocol to practically characterise the asymptotic behaviour of the protocol in both proving and verification.

1.4 Contribution

We believe the approach we evaluate is essentially the obvious way to use STARKs in the context of existing homomorphically tallied voting systems; in that sense, we consider this work's primary contribution to be carefully presenting and evaluating this approach rather than the approach itself. The only downside of the approach we evaluate, that we are aware of, is the marked increase in difficulty in building an independent verifier; we note that this could be mitigated by having some verifiers directly verify the original proofs though we would need to trust those verifiers for everlasting privacy.

- We formalise a construction which reduces the amount of data and time required to verify by l orders of magnitude at the cost increasing the RAM the bulletin board needs by l orders of magnitude.
- The construction hides the verification information behind a perfectly hiding commitment so that even an unconstrained adversary cannot recover the individual votes being each commitment.
- The construction also allows proofs of collected-as-cast which are logarithmic in the number of voters.
- We characterise the asymptotic behaviour of both the prover and the verifier.

In our running example a tallier machine with ~6TB RAM (relatively cheap in the context of modern data centres), reduces the verification time from approximately 77 core-days for a naive execution of the verification procedure to a projected time of 2.57 core-minutes. In addition, it reduces the sizes of the inputs from the naive 37.92GB to a total proof size of 1.54 GB, being the collective size of the STARK proofs for each batch.

Our evaluation code can download from the following link
https://github.com/gerlion/STARKs_for_Homomorphic_Tallying.

2 Construction

For completeness we present a somewhat simplified protocol demonstrating the technique; this construction is not intended to be a contribution and is essentially [CGS97] with some small modifications. The e-voting protocol consists of the following participants:

- the election authority EA.
- the set of voters $V_1, \ldots, V_n$.
- the set of talliers $T_1, \ldots, T_m$.

The protocol requires some form of communication between the participants. We model this (following [CPP13]) through two append-only *bulletin boards*: the public bulletin board $\mathcal{PB}$ and the secret bulletin board $\mathcal{SB}$. All participants can read from and publish to the public bulletin board $\mathcal{PB}$. We assume the content of the secret bulletin board $\mathcal{SB}$ is only able to be read by the talliers $T_1, \ldots, T_m$, but anyone can write to the board $\mathcal{SB}$ via a private (but not anonymous) channel.[1]

---

[1] i.e. an outside observer can store the *metadata* of the channel but not the actual correspondence *data*. This corresponds to the assumptions made in the literature for *practical* everlasting privacy. We have practical constructions to realise such channels long-term, e.g. post-quantum TLS [SSW20].

The election authority EA is responsible for setting up the election (date, set of candidates, voting methods, etc.). The election authority EA provides the following election public information: the candidate list, the list of eligible voters' signature public keys, the list of valid talliers' signature public keys, and the public voting parameters. We assume that the authority EA has a valid signature public key pk_{EA} known to all participants.

The voters interact with the authority EA to register for an election. They publish their ballot information to $\mathcal{SB}$. The talliers are responsible for tallying the results - they read the ballot from the $\mathcal{SB}$, verify voter signatures and the ballot correctness proofs, compute the tally and commitment values, and publish the resulting tally, commitment values, and STARK proofs to the $\mathcal{PB}$.

For the election scheme, PK denotes the public ElGamal encryption key and sk denotes the secret decryption key such that $PK = sk \cdot G$, note we are using multiplicative notation since ElGamal will be defined over an elliptic curve in our evaluation. The secret key sk is jointly generated by the talliers using standard techniques, we denote sk_j as the jth share of the secret key.

2.1 Cryptographic Primitives

The proposed e-voting protocol is composed of several cryptographic *primitives* and relies on several *proof systems*.

Definition 1 (ElGamal Encryption Scheme). *The **ElGamal encryption scheme** is a triple of PPT algorithms defined as follows:*

- KeyGenE$(\lambda) \to (\mathcal{P}, K, sk)$: *on input of security parameter λ, it derives the encryption parameters $\mathcal{P} = (\mathcal{G}, q, g)$, chooses the secret key $sk \in \mathbb{Z}_q$, and computes the public key $K = sk \cdot G \in \mathcal{G}$, where $sk \cdot G$ denotes the generator element $G \in \mathcal{G}$ composed with itself sk times. The parameters $\mathcal{P}$ contains a cyclic group $\mathcal{G}$ of prime order q generated by G with group composition $\circ$, and $\mathbb{Z}_q$ is the additive subgroup of integers modulo q.*
- Enc$(\mathcal{P}, m, K) \to (\alpha, \beta)$: *on input of a message $m \in \mathcal{G}$ and public key $K \in \mathcal{G}$, it chooses $r \in \mathbb{Z}_q$ and computes $(\alpha, \beta) = (r \cdot G, m \circ (r \cdot K))$.*
- Dec$(\mathcal{P}, (\alpha, \beta), sk) \to m$: *on input a ciphertext (α, β) and secret key sk, it computes $m = \beta \circ (-sk \cdot \alpha) = (m \circ (r \cdot K)) \circ ((r - sk) \cdot G)$.*

Definition 2 (Digital Signature Scheme). *A **digital signature scheme** $\mathcal{S}$ is a triple of PPT algorithms defined over a (finite) message space $\mathcal{M}$ and a signature space Σ as follows:*

- KeyGenS$(\lambda) \to (sk, pk)$: *on input of security parameter λ, it chooses a signature key pair (sk, pk).*
- Sign$(m, sk) \to \sigma$: *on input a message $m \in \mathcal{M}$ and a signing key sk, it outputs a signature $\sigma \in \Sigma$.*
- VerifyS$(\sigma, m, pk) \to 0/1$: *on input a signature σ, message m, and verification key pk, it outputs 1 if it accepts the signature and 0 otherwise.*

We require that for a validly generated key pair $(sk, pk) \leftarrow \text{KeyGenS}(\lambda)$ and for any message $m \in \mathcal{M}$, a valid signature $\sigma \leftarrow \text{Sign}(m, sk)$ must be accepted:

$$\Pr[\text{VerifyS}(\sigma, m, pk) = 1] = 1$$

The signature scheme used by the protocol should be secure: participants in the scheme should be convinced that the respective parties actually authored any published information in order for verification to be valid.

Authenticated Data Structures. An authenticated data structure (ADS) allows a party to compute a short hash $H(L)$ of some sequence $L = (x_1, \ldots, x_n)$ so that the party can:

1. prove properties (e.g. membership and non-membership) of L with respect to $H(L)$.
2. *commit* to the sequence L, i.e. another party can receive $H(L)$ and know that the committing party cannot change the sequence L without changing $H(L)$.

An ADS scheme can be seen as an extension of the more general *commitment scheme*[2].

Definition 3 (ADS Scheme). *An **authenticated data structure scheme** $\mathcal{D}$ is a quadruple of PT algorithms defined over some input element space $\mathcal{X}$ as follows:*

- SetupA$(\lambda) \to \mathcal{AP}$: *on input of security parameter λ, it derives commitment parameters $\mathcal{AP}$ including a description of some collision-resistant hash function $H : \mathcal{X} \to \mathcal{Y}$ where the input to H can either be single element in $\mathcal{X}$ or a pair of elements in $\mathcal{Y}$.*
- Commit$(\mathcal{AP}, L) \to r$: *on input of commitment parameters $\mathcal{AP}$ and some list of elements $L = (x_1, \ldots, x_n) \in \mathcal{X}^n$, it derives a commitment value $r \in \mathcal{Y}$.*
- Open$(\mathcal{AP}, i, x, L) \to \phi$: *on input of commitment parameters $\mathcal{AP}$, an index $1 \leq i \leq n$, an element $x \in \mathcal{X}$, and a list $L \in \mathcal{X}^n$, it outputs a membership proof ϕ that $x = x_i$ for $L = (x_1, \ldots, x_n)$.*
- VerifyA$(\mathcal{AP}, i, x, r, \phi) \to 0/1$: *on input of commitment parameters $\mathcal{AP}$, an index $1 \leq i \leq n$, an element $x \in \mathcal{X}$, a commitment value $r \in \mathcal{Y}$, and a membership proof ϕ, it outputs 1 if it accepts the proof and 0 otherwise.*

For any sequence $L \in \mathcal{X}^n$ with a commitment value $r \leftarrow \text{Commit}(\mathcal{AP}, L)$ and any element $x_i \in L$, a valid membership proof $\phi \leftarrow \text{Open}(\mathcal{AP}, i, x, L)$ must be accepted:

$$\Pr[\text{VerifyA}(\mathcal{AP}, i, x, r, \phi) = 1] = 1$$

It should be hard for a party to commit to some sequence and be able to prove false properties about that sequence.

---

[2] In a commitment scheme, a party commits to a general message m instead of committing to a sequence L. We can view the ADS scheme as a commitment scheme with the additional functionality of proving some desired properties about the committed message.

NIZK Ballot Correctness Proofs. To maintain voter privacy, the protocol aggregates voter ballots in their encrypted form. This is susceptible to voters encrypting non-valid plaintext votes: if a voter encrypts $m' = 100 \cdot G$ and submits this to a simple referendum (where valid votes are either 0 or 1) this could unfairly impact the final vote result. We thus want to able to form proofs of *ballot correctness* that $m \in \{0 \cdot G, 1 \cdot G\}$, but in such a way that we do not reveal the underlying vote value. This is achieved through a NIZK proof system $\Phi = (\text{ProveB}, \text{VerifyB})$ where the two PPT algorithms are defined as follows:

- ProveB$(v, (\alpha, \beta), PK) \to \pi$: on input of a vote v, an ElGamal ciphertext (α, β), and an encryption public key PK, it outputs a NIZK **ballot correctness** proof π.
- VerifyB$(\pi, (\alpha, \beta), PK) \to 0/1$: on input of a NIZK ballot correctness proof π, a ciphertext (α, β), and an encryption public key PK, it outputs 1 if it accepts the proof and 0 otherwise.

A *valid* proof $\pi \leftarrow \text{ProveB}(v, (\alpha, \beta), PK)$ is one for which the vote v is a valid value for the respective election, the ciphertext (α, β) hides v, and the public key PK is the one used to encrypt (α, β). The NIZK proof system used by the protocol should be sound: only valid proofs (with overwhelming probability) should be accepted by VerifyB.

2.2 Definition of the Protocol

We first explicitly specify a relation R proved by the STARK framework in the protocol. For ciphertext c, NIZK ballot correctness proof π, signature σ, voter public signature key pk, and public encryption key PK, define the predicate p to accept valid signature and proof tuples, i.e.

$$p(c, \pi, \sigma, pk, PK) = \begin{cases} 1 & \text{if } [\text{VerifyS}((c, \pi), \sigma, pk) = 1] \wedge [\text{VerifyB}(\pi, c, PK) = 1] \\ 0 & \text{otherwise} \end{cases}$$

Then for private witness $\omega = (pk_1, \ldots, pk_n, c_1, \ldots, c_n, \eta)$ where

- $pk_1, \ldots, pk_n$ is the list of voter public keys.
- $c_1, \ldots, c_n$ is the list of voter ciphertexts.
- $\eta \in \mathbb{Z}_q$ is the secret hiding value.

and public inputs $\rho = (r_p, r'_c, C)$ where

- r_p is the commitment value to the list of voter public keys.
- r'_c is the product of the commitment value to the list of voter ciphertexts and the secret hiding value η.
- C is the product ciphertext of the voter ciphertexts.

define the relation R over public encryption key PK by the following conjunction:

$$R(\rho, \omega) : [r_p = \mathrm{Commit}(pk_1, \ldots, pk_n)]$$
$$\bigwedge [r'_c = \mathrm{Commit}(c_1, \ldots, c_n) \cdot \eta]$$
$$\bigwedge \left[\bigwedge_{i=1}^{n} p(c_i, \pi_i, \sigma_i, pk_i, PK) \right] \bigwedge \left[C = \prod_{i=1}^{n} c_i \right]$$

The protocol (see Fig. 1) is then defined in terms of four functions, i.e. $EP = (\mathrm{SETUP}, \mathrm{VOTE}, \mathrm{TALLY}, \mathrm{EXTRACT})$ and proceeds in five phases: *Setup, Voting, Tallying, Result, Verification*. The functions are specified as follows:

- SETUP$(\lambda, l, l') \rightarrow (\mathcal{PP}, SK, m_{EA}, \sigma_{EA})$ - on input a security parameter λ, list of voter public signature keys $l = \{pk_1, \ldots, pk_n\}$, and list of tallier public signature keys $l' = \{pk'_1, \ldots, pk'_m\}$:
  1. generates the public parameters $\mathcal{PP} = (\mathcal{P}, \mathcal{AP}, \mathcal{SP}, PK)$ where $\mathcal{AP} \leftarrow$ SetupA(λ), $\mathcal{SP} \leftarrow$ SetupT(λ), $(\mathcal{P}, PK, SK) \leftarrow$ KeyGenE(λ).
  2. for the parameter message $m_{EA} = (\mathcal{PP}, l, l')$, produces a signature $\sigma_{EA} \leftarrow$ Sign(m_{EA}, sk_{EA}).
- VOTE$(v, pk, m_{EA}, \sigma_{EA}) \rightarrow (m_v, \sigma_v)$ - on input a vote value v, a voter private signature key sk, and a parameter message-signature pair (m_{EA}, σ_{EA}):
  1. attempts to verify the message VerifyS$(m_{EA}, \sigma_{EA}, pk_{EA}) \rightarrow 0/1$. On success it extracts the public parameters $\mathcal{PP}$, and halts on failure.
  2. encrypts the vote into a ciphertext $c \leftarrow$ Enc(v, PK).
  3. produces a NIZK proof of ballot correctness $\pi \leftarrow$ ProveB(v, c, PK).
  4. for the ballot message $m_v = (c, \pi)$, produces a signature $\sigma_v \leftarrow$ Sign(m_b, sk).
- TALLY$(m_{EA}, \sigma_{EA}, M_v, \Sigma_v, pk', SK_j) \rightarrow (m_t, \sigma_t)$ - on input a parameter message-signature pair (m_{EA}, σ_{EA}), a set of voter ballots $M_b = \{m_{v1}, \ldots, m_{vn}\}$ with signatures $\Sigma_v = \{\sigma_{v1}, \ldots, \sigma_{vn}\}$, a tallier public signature key pk', and a portion of the secret decryption key SK_j:
  1. verify both the parameter message VerifyS$(m_{EA}, \sigma_{EA}, pk_{EA}) \rightarrow 0/1$ and the voter ballots VerifyS$(m_{vi}, \sigma_{vi}, pk_i) \rightarrow 0/1$ together with NIZK correctness proofs VerifyB$(\pi_i, c_i, PK) \rightarrow 0/1$. For any ballots which fail either the signature or proof check reject the ballot.
  2. takes the product of all verified ciphertexts $C_j = \prod_{i=1}^{n} c_i$.
  3. computes commitment values $r_p \leftarrow$ Commit$(pk_1, \ldots, pk_n)$, $r_c \leftarrow$ Commit$(c_1, \ldots, c_n)$ for the included ballots.
  4. composes the ciphertext commitment r_c with a random hiding value $\eta \in \mathbb{Z}_q$ to obtain the output commitment value $r'_c = \eta \cdot r_c$.
  5. produces a STARK proof $\psi_j \leftarrow$ ProveT$(\tau_j, \rho_j, \omega_j)$ for public inputs $\rho_j = (r_p, r'_c, C_j)$, private witness $\omega_j = (pk_1, \ldots, pk_n, c_1, \ldots, c_n, m)$, and computational trace τ_j asserts the relation $R(\rho, \omega)$.
  6. decrypts the vote result C_j into the partial plaintext Γ_j with the portion of the secret key $\Gamma_j \leftarrow$ Dec(Γ_j, SK_j).
  7. for the message $m_t = (\psi, \rho, \Gamma_j)$, produces the signature $\sigma_t \leftarrow$ Sign(m_t, sk').
- EXTRACT$(M_t, \Sigma_t) \rightarrow (\Gamma, \sigma_C)$ - on input a set of potential tally messages $M_t = \{m_{t1}, \ldots, m_{tm}\}$ with corresponding signatures $\Sigma_t = \{\sigma_{t1}, \ldots, \sigma_{tn}\}$:

1. attempts to verify the tally messages $\text{VerifyS}((\psi_j, \rho_j, \Gamma_j), \sigma_j, pk'_j) \to 0/1$ and verify the STARK proofs $\text{VerifyT}(\psi_j, \rho_j) \to 0/1$. If fewer than k tally messages succeed both checks, it halts execution.
2. aggregates the partial results $\Gamma_1, \ldots, \Gamma_m$ into the final result $\Gamma = \prod_{j=1}^{m} \Gamma'_j$.
3. produces the signature $\sigma_C \leftarrow \text{Sign}(\Gamma, sk_{EA})$.

The relation R is equivalent to the computational integrity of the function TALLY on input-output pair (ω, ρ): if the relation R holds then c is the valid product of the input ciphertexts, r_p and r'_c are valid commitment values, and each ciphertext is proven to be correct and from a valid public key.

Assuming that the used signature scheme is secure, the ADS scheme is secure, binding, and hiding, and the non-interactive proof systems used by the protocol are both sound and zero-knowledge, we intend the protocol to have:

- privacy against an efficient adversary, with access to the ballot ciphertexts.
- everlasting privacy against a computationally unbounded adversary with access to only published information and communication metadata.
- efficient collected-as-cast verification through the ADS membership proofs.
- efficient counted-as-cast verification through the STARK proofs.

3 Evaluation

This section discusses the details of an example implementation of the protocol, presents the collected performance data and projects it to larger inputs, and compares the resulting data to a naive verification of an election.

3.1 Implementation Details

The implementation is primarily written in Cairo0 [GPR21]. The Cairo runner is given the implementation program and voting input data ω, and outputs a compiled Cairo program and public inputs ρ. The compiled Cairo program, private witness ω, and public inputs ρ are passed to a STARK prover outputting a STARK proof ψ. The proof ψ and public inputs ρ can then be passed to a STARK verifier for verification of results. The implementation instantiates the protocol's cryptographic primitives using:

- **Elliptic Curve:** the STARK elliptic curve [Sta23a].
- **Hash Function:** the Pedersen hash function [HBHW22, Section 5.4.1.7].
- **Digital Signature Scheme:** the Elliptic Curve Digital Signature Algorithm (ECDSA) [JMV01].
- **ADS Scheme:** Functionality is provided either using Merkle trees or hash chains. The presented performance data is collected using Merkle trees. If the hash function used to construct a Merkle tree is collision resistant, the Merkle tree ADS scheme is provably secure [BS23, Theorem 8.8].
- **NIZK Proofs:** NIZK proofs of ballot correctness are implemented according to the ElectionGuard (Version 2.0.0) specification [BN23].

The Protocol
(*Setup Phase*) To setup an election, EA performs the following steps:
1: Aggregates $l = \{pk_1, \ldots, pk_n\}$ and $l' = \{pk'_1, \ldots, pk'_m\}$.
2: Generates $(PK, SK, m_{EA}, \sigma_{EA}) \leftarrow \text{SETUP}(\lambda, l, l')$.
3: Chooses a threshold tuple (k, m) and distributes PK_j to $T_1, \ldots, T_m$.
4: Writes (m_{EA}, σ_{EA}) to $\mathcal{PB}$.
(*Voting Phase*) To cast a vote v_i, the voter V_i with public key pk_i performs the following steps:
1: Reads a potential message-signature pair m_{EA}, σ_{EA} from $\mathcal{PB}$.
2: Generates $(m_{vi}, \sigma_{vi}) \leftarrow \text{VOTE}(v_i, pk_i, m_{EA}, \sigma_{EA})$. If execution is halted due to a failed
signature, restart at step 1.
3: Writes (m_{vi}, σ_{vi}) to $\mathcal{SB}$ via a private channel.
(*Tallying Phase*) To produce a partial vote result Γ_j, the tallier T_j with public key pk'_j performs the following steps:
1: Reads a potential message-signature pair m_{EA}, σ_{EA} from $\mathcal{PB}$.
2: Reads the set of submitted message-signature pairs M_v, Σ_v from $\mathcal{SB}$.
3: Generates $(m_t, \sigma_t) \leftarrow \text{TALLY}(m_{EA}, \sigma_{EA}, M_v, \Sigma_v, pk', SK_j)$. If execution is halted due to a
failed parameter message signature, restart at step 1.
4: Writes (m_t, σ_t) to $\mathcal{PB}$.
(*Result Phase*) To announce an election result Γ, EA performs the following steps:
1: Reads the set of submitted tallier message-signature pairs M_t, Σ_t from $\mathcal{PB}$.
2: Generates $(\Gamma, \sigma_C) \leftarrow \text{EXTRACT}(M_t, \Sigma_t)$. If execution is halted due to
too many failed signatures, restart at step 1.
3: Writes (Γ, σ_C) to $\mathcal{PB}$.
(*Verification Phase*) To verify a result, each voter V_i can optionally perform the following steps:
1: Query the tallier T_j for the membership proof $\phi_j \leftarrow \text{Open}(i, c_i, \omega)$. The voter V_i can then
verify this proof $\text{VerifyA}(i, c_i, r'_c) \to 0/1$.
2: Verify the signature of the announced election result $\text{VerifyS}(\Gamma, \sigma_C, pk_{EA}) \to 0/1$.
3: Verify the set of submitted tallier message-signature pairs M_t, Σ_t from $\mathcal{PB}$,
i.e. $\text{VerifyS}((\psi_j, \rho_j, \Gamma_j), \sigma_j, pk'_j) \to 0/1$.
4: Verify the set of submitted STARK proofs $\psi_1, \ldots, \psi_m$ by $\text{VerifyT}(\psi_j, \rho_j) \to 0/1$.

Fig. 1. Protocol Summary

– **Commitment Scheme:** Pedersen commitments [Ped91]; standard measures need to be taken to ensure the commitments are binding [HLPT20].

The group points of the STARK elliptic curve over the Cairo field provides the finite cyclic group used for ElGamal. The StarkWare STONE prover and verifier [Sta23b] is used to provide the STARK functionality. The STONE prover supports multithreading, so the implementation is easily able to take advantage of parallelism to reduce the proving time for higher core CPUs. The main limitation of the implementation is the amount of system memory required by the STONE prover.

3.2 Performance Data

Default STONE proof & prover parameters were used to produce STARK proofs at an estimated security level of 128 bits. There is a tradeoff in these parameters between proof security, proof size, proving time, and memory usage. Much more aggressive memory optimisations are possible at the cost of proving time and vice versa. The evaluation data was collected on the following machine:

Evaluation Machine Specifications

- CPU: AMD Ryzen 3 2200G - 4 cores, 4 threads @ 3.5 GHz
- RAM: 16 GB DDR4 - 2400 MT/s
- Operating System: Fedora Linux 38 (Workstation Edition) x86_64

We are limited in data collection by the system memory requirements: an input of 2^7 votes would have a minimum memory requirement for proving of $(2 \cdot 32 \cdot 2^{23} \cdot 27) \approx 14.5\,\text{GB}$, which cannot be run on the evaluation machine. We are thus limited to lengths of inputs up to 2^6 votes. We present implementation timing data is in Table 1, and the implementation memory data is in Table 2. Actual measured observations are stated in black, and projected values for larger inputs are presented in red. Projections are simplified versions of the proven theoretical asymptotic behaviour for STARKs: verification time and proof size are modelled logarithmically in the number of votes, whereas runner time, proving time, and peak memory usage are modelled linearly. This is likely slightly optimistic but presents a useful contextualisation of the asymptotic behaviour.

Due to the parallelism of the STONE prover, proving time is measured in *core-minutes* (core-min): the total amount of time measured for all assigned cores. This can be divided by the number of CPU cores assigned to a workload to yield the actual proving time - e.g. a proving time of 6.46 core-minutes is equivalent to a proving time of 1.62 minutes on the 4-core evaluation machine's CPU. Verification time is also measured in core-seconds.

We see the two main draw of STARKs in the performance data: verification time remains practically constant for all sizes of inputs, and proof size grows at an exponentially slower rate as compared to the sizes of the inputs. This comes at the cost of a linear increase in the amount of system memory required by the

Table 1. Implementation timing data. Projections in red.

Input Votes	Runner (min)	Proving (core-min)	Verification (core-s)
4	0.08	1.77	0.18
8	0.14	3.23	0.16
16	0.26	6.46	0.17
32	0.50	12.91	0.17
64	0.98	26.25	0.22
128	1.93	52.35	0.23
256	3.84	104.73	0.24
512	7.65	209.49	0.25
1024	15.28	419.01	0.27
2048	30.53	838.04	0.28
4096	61.03	1676.10	0.29
8192	122.04	3352.22	0.31
16384	244.06	6704.46	0.33
32768	488.09	13408.94	0.34

Table 2. Implementation memory data. Projections in red.

Input Votes	Inputs Size (MB)	Proof Size (MB)	Peak RAM (GB)
4	0.009	1.009	0.72
8	0.018	1.062	1.38
16	0.037	1.148	2.82
32	0.073	1.317	5.50
64	0.145	1.620	11.00
128	0.290	1.824	21.96
256	0.579	1.972	43.88
512	1.158	2.120	87.73
1024	2.315	2.267	175.41
2048	4.629	2.415	350.79
4096	9.258	2.563	701.53
8192	18.516	2.711	1403.03
16384	37.031	2.855	2803.02
32768	74.062	3.004	5612.01

talliers. We can mitigate this memory requirement by some degree by configuring the prover parameters (at the cost of increasing the proving time), but we are fundamentally limited by the minimum lower bound memory requirement. Proving time represents the majority of the computational workload, but is likely fairly trivial for a server-grade machine that is able to readily exploit the prover's parallelism. We can handle larger tallies by running the protocol on batches of the input votes and combining each batch's results. This comes at the cost of a linear increase in verification time and proof size in the number of batches, but still allows protocol verification efficiency with orders of magnitude smaller than the naive verification. This results in even very large elections exhibiting significant reductions in the amount of time and size of the data required to verify when compared to naive verification.

We can exhibit this through a direct comparison between naive recomputation and the proposed protocol, see Table 3. As the EC point exponentiations represent the majority of the computational workload involved in the naive recomputation, we can form a estimated lower bound on the naive verification time for a given size of input votes: we simply take the product of the time taken for EC point exponentiations per vote and the number of input votes.

We present simple measurements taken for EC point exponentiations on the evaluation machine in Table 3. This allows us to construct direct comparisons between naive recomputation for verification and the proposed protocol: we present projected log-log plots comparing the verification times and proof sizes of the proposed protocol and the lower bounds of naive verification in Fig. 2, assuming that the protocol is performed by a tallier who has access to 6TB of RAM (which can be acquired relatively cheaply in modern data centres).

We can give a concrete comparison for a real-life example: for a referendum of 2^{24} voters (roughly the number of eligible voters in the Australian 2023 Voice referendum) our implementation on the assumed tallier machine would batch this into about 2^9 batches of the proposed protocol; *note that the batches only include validity and accumulation, decryption is still only done once on a ciphertext which accumulates all batches*. This reduces the verification time from the naive recomputation's lower bound of approximately 77 **core-days** to a projected time of 2.57 **core-minutes** for the proposed protocol, and reduces the sizes of the inputs from the naive 37.92 GB to a total proof size of 1.54 GB.

Table 3. Measurements on the evaluation machine for naive estimation.

Measurement	Value
Time for 1024 EC point exponentiations:	36.899 (core-s)
Time per EC point exponentiation:	0.036 (core-s)
Number of exponentiations per input vote:	11
Time of exponentiations per input vote:	0.396 (core-s)

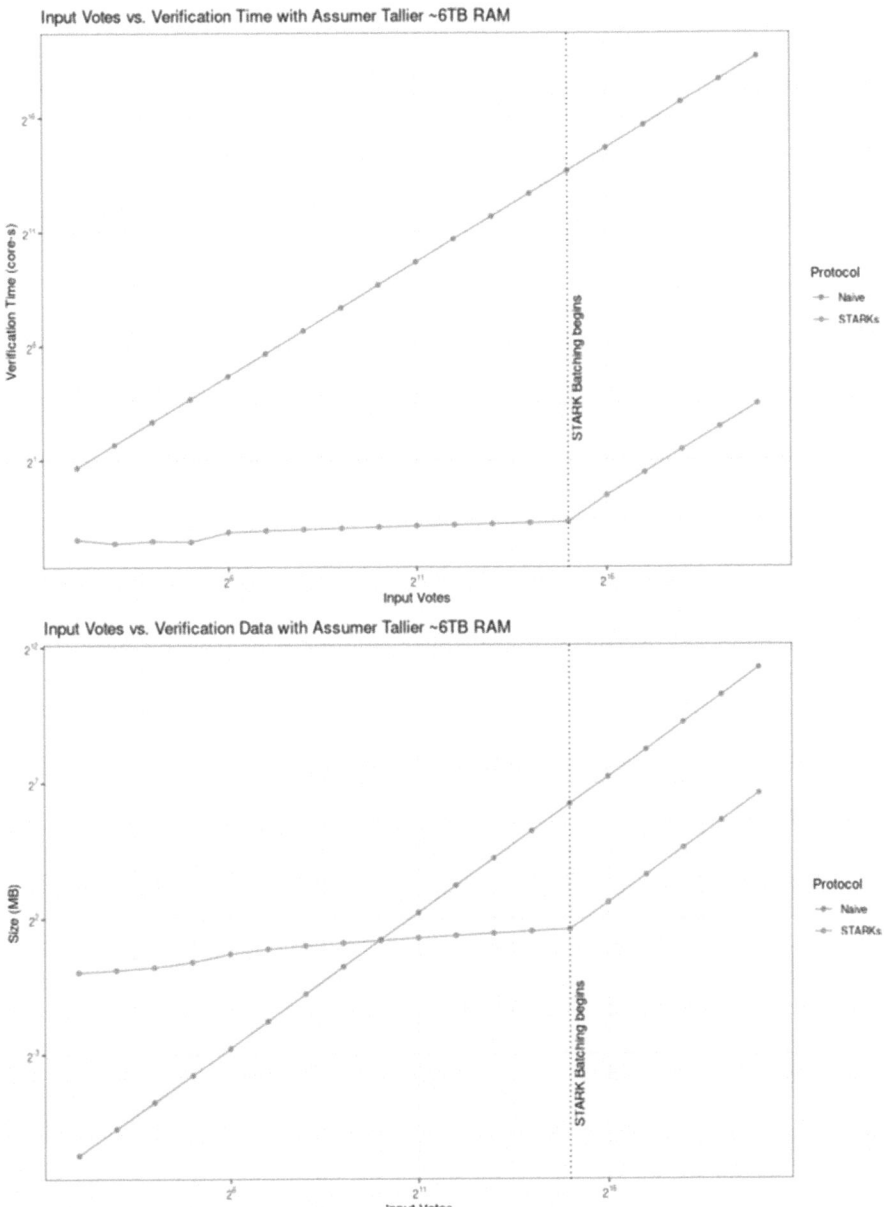

Fig. 2. Double logarithm plots of projected verification time and data with an assumed tallier of ∼6 TB RAM

4 Conclusion

We hope to have convinced the reader that STARKs provide very interesting trade-offs for homomorphically tallied voting systems. The advantage confers large reductions in several metrics for verification in practice, dramatically decreasing the level of necessary computational resources to verify a given result - enabling election verification on consumer-grade hardware (e.g. laptops and smartphones). This empowers voters to be able to verify an election result independently, increasing trust in the overall democratic process; the main downside of the approach appears to be the increased difficult in implementing a fully independent verifier. The approach is ultimately limited by the computational resources that the talliers have access to (both in computing power and system memory), but this is assuaged by the fact that this role would likely be performed by a set of server-grade machines. Our key takeaways are as follows:

Prover Effort The proving time does not appear to become prohibitive even if we consider large elections, particularly since the prover parallelises very efficiently. However, the RAM required quickly becomes a constraint. In some cases this can efficiently be dealt with by proving the normal verification procedure in batches; however, this technique does not seem to generalise easily beyond homomorphically tallied elections.

Verifier Effort The verifier's computational time is not constant as might have been hoped for due to the requirement of batching the prover. However, the many orders of magnitude which is practicality achievable is enough make the verifiers work attractively small. The amount of data which needs to be sent to prover can be made very small for homomorphically tallied elections.

4.1 Future Work: Mix-Net Based Systems

Adapting the approach for *mix-net* based systems would provide support for ranked voting elections or systems supporting write-ins. Based on our analysis we would expect the prover time to increase compared to homomorphic tallied elections by the same factor the normal verification procedure time is increased. However, the issue of batching the mixing would result in a significant loss of privacy; finding a batching method for mix-net verification which does not incur a privacy penalty would be of great use.

The attractiveness of STARKs for mix-nets compared to homomorphic tallying is limited by the normal inclusion of all the ballots in plaintext in the tally; the number of ballots is linear in the number of voters which limits the size advantage of STARKs; there doesn't seem to be anyway to compress this in general without also proving the correction execution of the underlying voting methods' social choice function on the plaintext ballots.

References

[BN23] Benaloh, J., Naehrig, M.: Electionguard design specification (version 2.0.0). Technical report, Microsoft Research (2023)

[BS23] Boneh, D., Shoup, V.: A graduate course in applied cryptography. Version 0.6 (2023)

[BSBHR18] Ben-Sasson, E., Bentov, I., Horesh, Y., Riabzev, M.: Scalable, transparent, and post-quantum secure computational integrity. Cryptology ePrint Archive **46** (2018)

[BY86] Benaloh, J.C., Yung, M.: Distributing the power of a government to enhance the privacy of voters (extended abstract). In: PODC, pp. 52–62. ACM (1986)

[CGS97] Cramer, R., Gennaro, R., Schoenmakers, B.: A secure and optimally efficient multi-authority election scheme. Eur. Trans. Telecommun. **8**(5), 481–490 (1997)

[CPP13] Cuvelier, É., Pereira, O., Peters, T.: Election verifiability or ballot privacy: do we need to choose? In: Crampton, J., Jajodia, S., Mayes, K. (eds.) ESORICS 2013. LNCS, vol. 8134, pp. 481–498. Springer, Heidelberg (2013). https://doi.org/10.1007/978-3-642-40203-6_27

[DPP22] Devillez, H., Pereira, O., Peters, T.: How to verifiably encrypt many bits for an election? In: Atluri, V., Di Pietro, R., Jensen, C.D., Meng, W. (eds.) ESORICS 2022, vol. 13555, pp. 653–671. Springer, Heidelberg (2022). https://doi.org/10.1007/978-3-031-17146-8_32

[Gjø16] Gjøsteen, K.: Real-world electronic voting: design, analysis and deployment. In: Chapter E-voting in Norway, p. 103. CRC Press, Boca Raton (2016)

[GPR21] Goldberg, L., Papini, S., Riabzev, M.: Cairo - a turing-complete stark-friendly cpu architecture. Cryptology ePrint Archive 1063 (2021)

[HBHW22] Hopwood, D., Bowe, S., Hornby, T., Wilcox, N.: Zcash protocol specification 2022.3.8 [nu5]. Technical report, Electric Coin Company (2022)

[HKK+22] Huber, N., et al.: Publicly tally-hiding verifiable e-voting. In: CCS, pp. 1443–1457. ACM (2022)

[HLPT20] Haines, T., Lewis, S.J., Pereira, O., Teague, V.: How not to prove your election outcome. In: IEEE Symposium on Security and Privacy, pp. 644–660. IEEE (2020)

[HMMP23] Haines, T., Mosaheb, R., Müller, J., Pryvalov, I.: Sok: secure e-voting with everlasting privacy. Proc. Priv. Enhancing Technol. **2023**(1), 279–293 (2023)

[JMV01] Johnson, D., Menezes, A., Vanstone, S.: The elliptic curve digital signature algorithm (ECDSA). Int. J. Inf. Secur. **1**, 36–63 (2001)

[oE] State Electoral Office of Estonia. Ivxv online voting system. https://github.com/vvk-ehk/ivxv

[Ped91] Pedersen, T.P.: Non-interactive and information-theoretic secure verifiable secret sharing. In: Feigenbaum, J. (ed.) CRYPTO 1991. LNCS, vol. 576, pp. 129–140. Springer, Heidelberg (1992). https://doi.org/10.1007/3-540-46766-1_9

[SGS23] Sheikhi, M., Giustolisi, R., Schürmann, C.: Receipt-free electronic voting from zk-snark. In: SECRYPT, pp. 254–266. SCITEPRESS (2023)

[SSW20] Schwabe, P., Stebila, D., Wiggers, T.: Post-quantum tls without handshake signatures. Cryptology ePrint Archive 534 (2020)

[Sta23a] StarkEx. STARK curve (2023). https://docs.starkware.co/starkex/crypto/stark-curve.html. Accessed 12 Oct 2023

[Sta23b] StarkWare. Stone prover (2023). https://github.com/starkware-libs/stone-prover. Accessed 12 Oct 2023

[Swi21] Swiss Post. Swiss post voting system (2021). https://evoting-community.post.ch/

"You Shall Not Abstain!" A Formal Study of Forced Participation

Wojciech Jamroga[1,2], Peter B. Roenne[1], Yan Kim[1(✉)], and Peter Y. A. Ryan[1]

[1] Interdisciplinary Centre for Security, Reliability, and Trust, SnT,
University of Luxembourg, Esch-sur-Alzette, Luxembourg
{peter.roenne,yan.kim,peter.ryan}@uni.lu
[2] Institute of Computer Science, Polish Academy of Science, Warsaw, Poland
w.jamroga@ipipan.waw.pl

Abstract. In this paper we revisit the idea of participation privacy in secure voting, i.e., when public data does not reveal whether a given voter participated in the election. This is an important property, especially when defining coercion-resistance preventing forced abstention attacks, and it is frequently mentioned as one of the main necessary conditions. However, what has been largely overlooked in the secure voting literature, is the idea of preventing forced participation attacks, i.e., where a voter is forced, or more subtly feels forced, to participate in an election. Whereas a high participation rate might seem like a desirable democratic property, there are cases when a part of the society wants to boycott the vote, e.g., in order to express its disapproval, or to prevent the proposed legislation. We logically formalise the idea of resistance to forced participation and, perhaps surprisingly, show that it is to some extent dual to forced abstention resistance. We also give intuitive examples of systems that satisfy one, but not the other.

Keywords: formal methods · voting · coercion-resistance · receipt-freeness · participation privacy

1 Introduction

In this paper, we revisit the notion of participation privacy in elections. This is a property that can be desirable for several reasons. For example, in Germany and Switzerland it is required that the fact of having voted (or not) must be private. This was also a motivation for the design of the participation-private KTV-Helios scheme [41]. In terms of coercion-resistance, this is an important property especially when wanting to guard against forced abstention attacks where the coercer prevents a voter from casting a vote. The point is that *forced abstention resistance* is a quite separate property from being able to equivocate the content of a ballot to a coercer. Several methods have been developed to achieve this. Firstly, the voting scheme can be designed so that public ballots cannot be directly attributed to a voter, e.g. by using anonymous vote casting channels as in the JCJ scheme [35]. Secondly, obfuscating ballots can be used to hide real ballots, see e.g. [41]. Thirdly, some systems even refrain from publishing ballots – as it is the case in the Estonian voting system. However, the latter solution fails in providing universal verifiability (especially for eligibility verifiability), a security property which is intuitively at odds with the participation privacy.

What we point out in this paper, is that it has been largely overlooked in the secure voting literature that besides forced abstention resistance, it can also be important to guard against *forced participation* attacks, where the coercer forces the voter to participate in the election, or more subtly the voter feels forced to participate.

A high participation rate might at the first glance seem like a desirable democratic property. Some electoral systems even have mandatory election participation to increase the turnout. Others directly flag people who voted, e.g., providing 'I voted' stickers. However, there are important cases where a part of the electorate wants to boycott an election, e.g., in order to express its disapproval, or to prevent the proposed legislation if certain levels of participation are mandatory.

We demonstrate that the methods used to achieve participation privacy, and especially forced *abstention* resistance, do not necessarily imply forced *participation* resistance, and vice versa. We also formally define these properties in the strategic logic $\mathbf{ALT}^*$, which allows us to derive relations between the privacy notions, thus laying a foundation for future work on the topic.

Structure of the Paper. We first present the motivating scenario from the Polish parliamentary election and referendum of 2023 in Sect. 2. Next, in Sect. 3, we introduce the structures and the logical formalism used to represent multi-agent systems and reason about agents' strategic abilities. We also provide an example of how certain privacy-type properties (such as coercion-resistance and receipt-freeness) can be formally translated into corresponding logical formulae. Then, in Sect. 4, we consider several voting protocols and mechanisms that are designed to provide participation privacy and the corresponding variants of coercion-resistance. We determine whether the proposed measures are vulnerable to forced participation attacks (and thus susceptible to coercion), and study their relation with forced abstention- and forced-participation resistance. In Sect. 5, we discuss the related work. Finally, Sect. 6 provides a summary, concluding remarks, and plans for future work.

2 Motivating Scenario: Polish Election and Referendum '23

On 15 October 2023, the latest Polish parliamentary election were held. Together with the election, a referendum took place. It asked four questions in the form of yes/no approval of: selling state properties to foreign entities, increasing the retirement age, dismantling of the barrier along Polish-Belarus border, and admission of thousands of illegal immigrants from Middle East and Africa (sic!) [66].

The organization of the referendum gave rise to a number of controversies (e.g., vague questions, lack of clear guidelines for electoral commissions). It was also argued that the questions were designed in a way that guarantees nearly unanimous outcome, and thus feign an appearance of massive public support for the ruling party. Importantly, the Polish constitution specifies that if the turnout in a referendum exceeds 50% of the eligible voters, its outcome is legally binding (whatever that would actually mean in case of such ambiguous questions). Moreover, invalid votes *are* included in the turnout. Because of that, opposition representatives were concerned that the results of the referendum could be used to undermine the outcome of the parliamentary election in case the opposition wins majority in the parliament [24,54]. Consequently, the opposition leaders encouraged the voters to boycott the referendum, so that the required 50% turnout would not be reached.

Outcome. The referendum ended with a turnout 40.91% with almost unanimous answer "NO" to all four questions: 96.49%, 94.61%, 96.04%, 96.79% respectively [58]. In accordance with the Constitution of Poland, the National Election Commission (NEC) concluded the result to be not binding [56]. The turnout in the parliamentary election was 74,38%, the highest in the Polish post-1989 history [57]. Thus, nearly half of the election participants refused to take and cast their referendum ballots. While the ruling party obtained the highest support, the coalition of center-left opposition parties won a majority in the new parliament.

Privacy and Coercion-Resistance. According to the legislation [59], the voters checking in at a polling station were issued two election ballots (one for the lower, and one for the upper chamber of the parliament), as well as one referendum ballot. A voter could refuse to collect a ballot (or ballots). In that case, the electoral commission official handling the registration noted the fact in the voters' register [26]. Since the register was open to see by everybody on the local commission (as well as the members of the superior electoral commissions), the voter's participation (or abstention) could be only considered semi-private. This was even more problematic in smaller – especially rural – constituencies, where most families had a friend or a relative on the local commission. Thus, voters who wanted to boycott the referendum were potentially vulnerable to coercion, e.g., by a dominating family member [67].

Interestingly, the Polish story has an additional, subtle twist. Voters who refused to take the referendum ballot could be, with very high probability, assumed to have voted for the centre-left opposition in the parliamentary election. Thus, the voter's active abstention in the referendum leaks information about the same voter's vote in the election. Reportedly, that posed a significant dilemma for many voters in rural areas (where right-wing sympathies prevail). If they wanted to vote without exposing their center/left preferences, they could either vote for the opposition in the election but participate in the referendum against their wish, or abstain from voting in both the election and the referendum [32]. In consequence, the voter was put in a "voting Nelson hold" that combined forced participation (in the referendum) with forced abstention (in the election).

3 Formal Definitions

Intuitively, privacy is about the *ability* of the voter to prevent the exposure of sensitive information about their part in the election. Similarly, coercion resistance is closely related to the voter's ability to avoid coercion and choose the voting behaviour that expresses their preferences best. We will use standard models of multi-agent systems and the strategic logic **ATL*** to formalise the relevant aspects of the interaction.

3.1 Models of Multi-agent Interaction

Concurrent Game Structures [3,25,65]. An imperfect information *concurrent game structure* (CGS) is a tuple $M = \langle \text{Agt}, St, PV, L, Act, d, o, \{\sim_a \mid a \in \text{Agt}\}\rangle$, where:

- $\text{Agt} = \{1, \ldots, k\}$ is a non-empty finite set of agents,
- St is a finite non-empty set of states,
- PV is a set of atomic propositions,
- $L : St \mapsto \mathcal{P}(PV)$ is a labelling function,
- Act is a non-empty set of actions,
- $d : \text{Agt} \times St \mapsto \mathcal{P}(Act)$ denotes actions that are available for each agent in each state,
- $o : St \times Act^1 \times \ldots \times Act^k \mapsto St$ is a transition function that assigns the outcome state $q' = o(q, \alpha_1, \ldots, \alpha_k)$ to each state q and tuple of actions $\langle \alpha_1, \ldots, \alpha_k \rangle$, such that $\alpha_i \in d(i, q)$ for $i = 1, \ldots, k$,
- $\sim_a \subseteq St \times St$ is an (epistemic) equivalence relation for each $a \in \text{Agt}$.

Informally, whenever $q \sim_a q'$, the states q and q' are said to be indistinguishable to an agent a. Here, every CGS is assumed to be *uniform*, that is:

$$\forall_{q,q' \in St} (q \sim_a q' \Rightarrow d(a,q) = d(a,q'))$$

Strategies [3,65]. A (memoryless) *strategy* for agent $a \in \text{Agt}$ is function $\sigma_a : St \mapsto Act$ that prescribes every state with some available action, i.e., $\forall_{q \in St} \sigma_a(q) \in d(a,q)$. We assume strategies to be uniform, that is:

$$\forall_{q,q' \in St} (q \sim_a q' \Rightarrow \sigma_a(q) = \sigma_a(q'))$$

The set of all strategies for $a \in \text{Agt}$ is denoted by Σ_a^{ir}.[1]

A *collective strategy* for $A = \{a_1, \ldots, a_l\} \subseteq \text{Agt}$ is a tuple of corresponding (individual) strategies $\sigma_A = (\sigma_{a_1}, \ldots, \sigma_{a_l})$. The set of all such strategies is denoted by Σ_A^{ir}.

Paths [3,19]. An infinite sequence of states $\lambda = q_0 q_1 q_2 \ldots$ in CGS, where there is a transition connecting every q_i with q_{i+1}, is called a *path*. For a path λ and

---

[1] The lowercase letters "i" and "r" refer to imperfect information and imperfect recall respectively [65].

$i \geq 0$ by $\lambda[i]$ and $\lambda[i, \infty]$ we denote a state in i-th position and an infinite suffix starting from $\lambda[i]$ respectively.

The outcome $out(q, \sigma_A)$ returns a set of paths that can occur when agents in A execute σ_A starting from state q onward, that is $\lambda \in out(q, \sigma_A)$ iff:

(i) $\lambda[0] = q_0$, and
(ii) $\forall_{i \geq 0}. \exists_{\langle \alpha_1^i, \ldots, \alpha_k^i \rangle}. \forall_{a_j \in A} \left(\alpha_{a_j}^i = \sigma_{a_j}(\lambda[i]) \land \lambda[i+1] = o(\lambda[i], \alpha_1^i, \ldots, \alpha_k^i) \right).$

3.2 Alternating-Time Temporal Logic ATL*

To express system requirements and capture properties of interaction between agents, we will use alternating-time temporal logic **ATL*** [2,3,65].

Syntax. Given a finite set of agents Agt and a set of atomic propositions PV, the syntax of **ATL*** is defined by the following grammar:

$$\phi ::= p \mid \neg \phi \mid \phi \lor \phi \mid \langle\!\langle A \rangle\!\rangle \psi$$
$$\psi ::= \phi \mid \neg \psi \mid \psi \lor \psi \mid \mathrm{X} \psi \mid \psi \,\mathrm{U}\, \psi$$

where $p \in PV$ is an atomic proposition, $A \subseteq$ Agt is a subset of agents (called coalition), temporal operators "X" and "U" stand for *"in the next state"* and *"(strong) until"* respectively. Additional Boolean connectives and temporal operators can be derived in a standard way; in particular: $\mathrm{F}\psi \equiv \top \,\mathrm{U}\, \psi$ for *"now or sometime in the future"* and $\mathrm{G}\psi \equiv \neg \mathrm{F} \neg \psi$ for *"now and always in the future."*

Informally, formula $\langle\!\langle A \rangle\!\rangle \gamma$ says that the group of agents A can enforce the temporal property γ no matter how the other agents in Agt$\setminus A$ proceed.

Semantics. Given a CGS M, a state q and a path λ, the satisfaction relation $\models$ is inductively defined as follows:

$M, q \models p$ iff $q \in L(p)$,
$M, q \models \neg \phi$ iff $M, q \not\models \phi$,
$M, q \models \phi_1 \lor \phi_2$ iff $M, q \models \phi_1$ or $M, q \models \phi_2$,
$M, q \models \langle\!\langle A \rangle\!\rangle \psi$ iff $\exists \sigma_A \in \Sigma_A^{\mathrm{ir}} \; \forall_{\lambda \in out^{\mathrm{ir}}(q, \sigma_A)} \; M, \lambda \models \psi$,

$M, \lambda \models \phi$ iff $M, \lambda[0] \models \phi$,
$M, \lambda \models \neg \psi$ iff $M, \lambda \not\models \psi$,
$M, \lambda \models \psi_1 \lor \psi_2$ iff $M, \lambda \models \psi_1$ or $M, \lambda \models \psi_2$,
$M, \lambda \models \mathrm{X}\psi$ iff $M, \lambda[1, \infty] \models \psi$,
$M, \lambda \models \psi_1 \,\mathrm{U}\, \psi_2$ iff $\exists i \geq 0 \; M, \lambda[i, \infty] \models \psi_2$ and $\forall_{0 \leq j < i} \; M, \lambda[j, \infty] \models \psi_1$.

Thus, the semantics of the "sometime" and "always" modalities becomes:

$M, \lambda \models \mathrm{F}\psi$ iff $\exists i \geq 0 \; M, \lambda[i, \infty] \models \psi$,
$M, \lambda \models \mathrm{G}\psi$ iff $\forall i \geq 0 \; M, \lambda[i, \infty] \models \psi$.

The standard **ATL*** can be further extended to support reasoning about agents' knowledge. The epistemic formula $K_a\phi$ says that an agent $a \in \mathsf{Agt}$ *knows* that ϕ holds. Hence, the following rule is added to semantic:

$$M, q \models K_a\phi \quad \text{iff} \quad \forall_{q' \in St}(q \sim_a q' \Rightarrow M, q' \models \phi)$$

3.3 Expressing Privacy-Related Properties in ATL*

Let $Vot \subseteq \mathsf{Agt}$ be the set of eligible voter agents, $c \in \mathsf{Agt}$ a coercer, and Bal set of possible returned ballots, including a special case of "returning nothing". We use the following functions:

- $info : Bal \mapsto Data$ to extract information that was filled on a ballot;
- $vote : Bal \mapsto \mathcal{P}(Choice)$ to extract information on the selection made only, where $\mathcal{P}(Choice) \subsetneq Data$ and $Choice$ corresponds to relevant information (e.g., set of candidates for single choice voting);
- $vb, vv : Bal \mapsto \{\top, \bot\}$ for ballot and vote validity respectively; the intuition is that a *ballot is valid*, if it was not damaged or completely destroyed, and a *vote is valid* if it was cast with a valid ballot that was also duly filled.

There could be many ways of completing the ballot form (including adding some satellite data), and adding extra notes on the ballot will normally lead to invalidation of the vote, i.e. $\forall_{b \in Bal}(info(b) \neq vote(b) \Rightarrow vv(b) = \bot)$.

In what follows we consider some $v, v' \in Vot \setminus \{c\}$, s.t. $v \neq v'$, $v^* \in Vot$, $a \in \mathsf{Agt} \setminus \{v^*\}$, $a^* \in \mathsf{Agt}$, $i, j \in Bal$, s.t. $i \neq j$, and $x, y \in \mathcal{P}(Choice)$, s.t. $x \neq y$.

The atomic proposition $recor_{v^*, i}$ asserts that a ballot $i \in Bal$ was recorded for voter $v^* \in Vot$, $cast_{v^*, i}$ asserts that a voter $v^* \in Vot$ cast a ballot $i \in Bal$, and $voted_{v^*, x}$ asserts that a voter $v^* \in Vot$ cast some ballot with $x \in \mathcal{P}(Choice)$ selected.[2] Depending on the system, a different set of assumptions and corresponding logical implications and equivalences over aforementioned propositions can be made (Fig. 1). For example:

- in systems, where voter casts a single vote maximally one vote per voter can be recorded: $\forall_{v^*, i}(recor_{v^*, i} \Rightarrow \bigwedge_j \neg recor_{v^*, j})$,
- in systems, where voters are allowed to re-vote, effectively overwriting the previously cast votes: $\forall_{v^*, i, j}(recor_{v^*, i} \wedge recor_{v^*, j} \Rightarrow \neg vv(i) \vee \neg vv(j))$,
- in traditional paper-based voting system, where cast-as-intended is provided by design: $\forall_{v^*, b}(cast_{v^*, b} \wedge vote(b) = x \iff voted_{v^*, x})$.

---

[2] The subtle difference between $voted_{v^*, x}$ and $cast_{v^*, i}$ is that $x \in \mathcal{P}(Choice)$ only indicates the relevant selections (e.g., it would not capture the presence of any "hidden" marks), whereas $i \in Bal$ can represent any possible ballot along with all the information that can be derived from it.

Note also that we formalise coercion resistance as the ability of the voter to *effect any* election choice. Thus, we do not need to represent the *intention* of the voter; it suffices to reason solely about the voter's possible choices.

Additionally, we introduce dual abstract propositions $abst_{v^*}$ and prt_{v^*} denoting voter's genuine abstention and participation in the voting itself. Note that prt_{v^*} alone does not necessarily imply the vote from v^* would count towards a turnout. The exact definition and method for computing a turnout will depend on the legislation; moreover, in many cases (e.g., re-voting) it cannot be inferred from a single ballot alone, and the corresponding turnout function must be defined over a multi-set of returned ballots.

Fig. 1. Naturally derived implications for considered coalitions.

The paper [68] reviews various definitions for receipt-freeness and coercion-resistance properties, and provides their logical transcriptions with a focus on strategic aspects. The relevant properties (excluding those using the belief operator) are presented below with their original labels:

RF1a. $\bigwedge_{v,v',x} \neg \langle\!\langle v \rangle\!\rangle \ \mathrm{F}\,(voted_{v,x} \wedge K_{v'} voted_{v,x})$

RF1b. $\bigwedge_{v^*,a,x} \neg \langle\!\langle v \rangle\!\rangle \ \mathrm{F}\,(voted_{v,x} \wedge K_a voted_{v,x})$

RF2. $\bigwedge_{v,x} \neg \langle\!\langle v \rangle\!\rangle \ \mathrm{F}\,(voted_{v,x} \wedge K_c voted_{v,x})$

RF3. $\bigwedge_{v,x} \neg \langle\!\langle c,v \rangle\!\rangle \ \mathrm{F}\,(voted_{v,x} \wedge K_c voted_{v,x})$

RF5. $\bigwedge_{v,x} \neg \langle\!\langle c,v \rangle\!\rangle \ \mathrm{F}\,(voted_{v,x} \wedge K_c voted_{v,x})$

RF6. $\bigwedge_{v^*,a,x} \neg \langle\!\langle v \rangle\!\rangle \ \mathrm{F}\,(voted_{v,x} \wedge K_a voted_{v,x})$

CR2a. $\bigwedge_{v,x} \neg \langle\!\langle c,v \rangle\!\rangle \ \mathrm{F}\,(voted_{v,x} \wedge K_c voted_{v,x})$

CR2b. $\bigwedge_{v,x} \neg \langle\!\langle c,v \rangle\!\rangle \ \mathrm{F}\,(voted_{v,x} \wedge (\bigvee_y K_c \neg voted_{v,y}))$

CR3. $\bigwedge_{v,x,y} \langle\!\langle v \rangle\!\rangle \ \mathrm{F}\,(voted_{v,x} \wedge \mathrm{G} \neg K_c \neg voted_{v,y})$

For instance, property **RF2** says that the voter v has no strategy such that eventually v has voted for candidate x and the coercer knows that, however we might choose the actual values of v and x.

The transcription of properties **RF5** and **CR2a** is identical with that of **RF3**, and **RF6** with **RF1b**, and thus written in grey.

3.4 Resistance to Forced Participation and Forced Abstention

Following the approach of [68], we formalise the properties of forced participation resistance (**FPR**) and forced abstention resistance (**FAR**) as:

FPR. $\bigwedge_{v^*,a} \neg \langle\!\langle v^*,a \rangle\!\rangle \ \mathrm{F}\,(prt_{v^*} \wedge K_a \neg abst_{v^*})$

FAR. $\bigwedge_{v^*,a} \neg \langle\!\langle v^*,a \rangle\!\rangle \ \mathrm{G}\,(abst_{v^*} \wedge K_a \neg prt_{v^*})$

Thus, **FPR** says that there is no collective strategy for the voter v^* and another voter a which ensures that, eventually, v^* has participated in the election and a knows that v^* has not abstained. Similarly, **FAR** says that there is no collective strategy for the voter v^* and another voter a to make sure that v^* consistently abstains and a consistently knows that v^* has not participated.

Remark 1. Note that quantifiers over voters often exclude the coercer, i.e., range over $Vot \setminus \{c\}$. Depending on the context, this might make a significant difference. A notable example is Selene voting system [61], where the coercer being a voter himself would possess a knowledge of his own tracker, and then it is possible that a voter, who wishes to fake his vote, happens to point to the coercer's tracker.

Furthermore, we formalise the notion of *public participation privacy* by:

PPP. $\bigwedge_{v^*,a} \neg \langle\!\langle \varnothing \rangle\!\rangle \, \mathrm{F}\, (K_a \neg prt_{v^*} \lor K_a \neg abst_{v^*})$

Theorem 1. *(i) **FPR** $\Rightarrow$ **PPP** and (ii) **FAR** $\Rightarrow$ **PPP**.*

Proof. Follows directly from the facts that $K_a \varphi \Rightarrow \varphi$ for any $a \in \mathrm{Agt}$, and $\langle\!\langle \varnothing \rangle\!\rangle \varphi \Rightarrow \langle\!\langle A \rangle\!\rangle \varphi$ for any $A \subseteq \mathrm{Agt}$.

Thus, **PPP** is a necessary condition for both **FPR** and **FAR**.

4 Protocols and Examples

In this section, we discuss several example protocols that, in varying degrees, provide resistance to forced abstention and/or forced participation coercion.

4.1 Indelible Ink

Applying an indelible ink (usually by dipping the forefinger of a voter) is designed to prevent double-voting. According to [21,42], one of the earliest adoptions of election inking was in India back in 1960–1980s. This method provides abstention-privacy (in the simplest case, one could simply dip their finger into a bottle of writing ink) but lacks participation-privacy, which opens up possibilities to coercion and may sometimes even undermine the voter's safety.

We found reports of ink compound being smuggled [70], disenfranchisement attacks when voters were forced or tricked into having their finger marked by malicious third-party [7,33], disinformation attacks aimed to weaken public confidence in integrity of the results, threats (both to inked and non-inked voters) [21,33], and post-election violence towards those who had their finger marked [37]. We refer the interested reader to [21,22] for more details and an evidence study.

As a counter-measure to potential exposure of the voter's participation, some countries deploy an invisible ink, such that a special UV LED is needed to check the mark [22,49]. While it does not guarantee complete participation-privacy, it might be seen as its weaker variant under certain assumptions. However, it is notable that with different inking methods, the risks of forced abstention and forced participation attacks appear to have inverse relationship.

Interestingly, [33] describes a case of voters refusing to cast a vote immediately after getting an ink-mark. Depending on the legal constraints, this might be a viable response to forced-participation coercion.

4.2 KTV-Helios

The KTV Helios scheme is designed to have participation privacy [41]. Here the voter casts ballots each encrypting a number. The actual chosen candidate will be the sum of all of these numbers. Others can cast ballots too on behalf of the voter, but without knowing the voter's secret key these ballots will have to be encryptions of zero and thus do not affect the overall vote. The point of these obfuscating ballots is to give the voter plausible deniability: Even if the voter casts a ballot together with the coercer, he or she can update the result by casting another corrective vote, but claim it was an obfuscating ballot from another voter. We have here assumed a coercer model where the voter always casts ballots oneself, and thus knows the corresponding number, i.e., an over-the-shoulder coercer model.

In this model, we also have forced abstention resistance because the voter can cast a vote and plausibly claim it was an obfuscating vote. Interestingly, it might also provide forced participation resistance since – even if the voter first casts a valid vote together with the coercer – he or she can later correct the sum back to zero using a corrective ballot, and claim it was an obfuscation ballot from someone else.

Interestingly, there is a small asymmetry between the two notions in this scheme. If a voter should not vote at all, there is a small probability that no obfuscating votes are cast on behalf of that voter, hence making abstention clear. That is, even without interaction between the voter and the coercer, we have a small probability of leaking the abstention, whereas if the voter participated it would never be provable without interaction between the voter and coercer.

4.3 Estonian E-Voting System

The Estonian system allows to verify ballots directly via the random coins used in the ballot construction. However, to achieve a level of coercion-resistance the system allows for the last-vote-counts re-voting. This kind of a voting system enables forced abstention resistance, since the voter might cast a ballot without telling the coercer. On the other hand, the voter can prove participation by casting a ballot and verifying this together with the coercer, thus we do not achieve forced participation resistance.

4.4 S&P 2024

A recent scheme with vote updating [23] from S&P 2024 is also based on the over-the-shoulder coercion model. Here obfuscating votes are cast by the election authority and these will override votes cast together with a coercer, if the voter has already cast a vote on their own. Due to the obfuscation, this does provide forced abstention resistance in the constrained coercer model of [23]. However, if the coercer casts the very first ballot together with the voter, then this will be a valid ballot which can only be overwritten by other valid ballots. Hence, the scheme does not obtain forced participation resistance.

4.5 JCJ

In the JCJ voting protocol [35] a voter uses secret credentials to cast votes. A coercer is simply presented with a fake credential, and could even try to vote on his own, however ballots with invalid credentials will not be counted. Assuming the tally procedure does not leak, this allows us to achieve resistance against both forced abstention and forced participation attacks.

Yet, as pointed out in [14,20], the public deduplication process might leak important information. Let us e.g. say that the coercer knows that all voters vote twice, but the coerced voter does not know this. Thus, if the coercer sees a vote in the deduplication phase only appearing once, he knows it came from the coerced voter. In consequence, the scheme does not have forced abstention resistance. On the other hand, we could still have forced participation resistance because the voter might simply refrain from casting a vote with the real credential.

4.6 Opt-Out Schemes

Depending on the legislation, a general method striving to achieve forced participation resistance is to include an additional (opt-out) checkbox for "do not participate" on ballots.

The point is that if the scheme already provides coercion-resistance including forced abstention resistance then the coerced voter can cast a ballot and choose this option while being able to deny it to the coercer. Thus in this case forced abstention resistance can help to provide forced participation resistance. However, this option might also be used by a coercer to launch a forced abstention attack, so we again see a duality between the two properties here.

5 Related Work

The related work can be divided into two strands. On the one hand, various flavours of privacy and coercion-resistance have been defined and discussed in the literature. On the other hand, some authors have attempted to capture those properties in modal logics of time, knowledge, and/or strategies. The second strand includes also attempts at automated verification by theorem proving or model checking, based on such formalisations.

Receipt-Freeness and Coercion Resistance. Over the years, the properties of *ballot secrecy, receipt-freeness, coercion resistance,* and *voter-verifiability* were recognized as important for an election to work properly. In particular, [8] introduced receipt freeness as a required property for avoiding coercion in e-voting systems. It was later extended in [52] by considering different levels of voter-control for the coercers, and different levels of collusion between coercer and other parties in the election, and further in [55]. [35] introduced coercion resistance as the property of being receipt free, plus resisting against randomization, forced abstention and simulation attacks. Moreover, significant progress has been made in the development of coercion-resistant voting systems, especially in combination with various forms of vote verifiability [13,62], cf. for instance [12,60,61,63].

Formal definitions of vote privacy, and receipt freeness and coercion resistance in various process calculi were proposed and discussed in [5,15–18,45,53] introduced a simulation based definition for coercion resistance, see also [51] for a survey. Several works such as [1,4,40,46–48,64,69] have developed weaker, more practical, or more efficient ways to realize the assumptions for achieving of receipt freeness and coercion resistance (without introducing new definitions).

Specification of Voting Properties in Modal Logics of Time, Knowledge, and/or Strategies. [6,34,44] have used epistemic logic to express the property of coercion resistance in elections. More sophisticated formalisations, based on temporal or temporal-epistemic specifications, were used in [10,50,71], combined with verification through automated theorem proving, and in [9] together with verification by model checking. Formalizations in strategic-epistemic logic were proposed in [27,29–31,36,43,68], often with experimental verification of integrity and security requirements for a given voting protocol.

In a related line of work, modal logics of strategies, time, and knowledge were used to specify correctness of contract signing and non-repudiation protocols [11, 28,38,39].

6 Conclusions

We have introduced the notion of forced participation attacks and defined formally forced participation resistance and forced abstention resistance, along with public participation privacy.

We highlight the internal strain between the first two properties by demonstrating several protocols which satisfy resistance to forced abstention but not to forced participation or vice versa.

Acknowledgments. This research has been supported by NCBR Poland and FNR Luxembourg under the PolLux/FNR-CORE project SpaceVote (POLLUX-XI/14/SpaceVote/2023 and C22/IS/17232062/SpaceVote) and the FNR-CORE project PABLO (C21/IS/16326754/PABLO). For the purpose of open access, and in fulfilment of the obligations arising from the grant agreement, the authors have applied CC BY 4.0 license to any Author Accepted Manuscript version arising from this submission.

References

1. Aditya, R., Lee, B., Boyd, C., Dawson, E.: An efficient mixnet-based voting scheme providing receipt-freeness. In: Katsikas, S., Lopez, J., Pernul, G. (eds.) TrustBus 2004. LNCS, vol. 3184, pp. 152–161. Springer, Heidelberg (2004). https://doi.org/10.1007/978-3-540-30079-3_16
2. Alur, R., Henzinger, T.A., Kupferman, O.: Alternating-time temporal logic. In: Proceedings of the 38th Annual Symposium on Foundations of Computer Science (FOCS), pp. 100–109. IEEE Computer Society Press (1997)
3. Alur, R., Henzinger, T.A., Kupferman, O.: Alternating-time temporal logic. J. ACM **49**, 672–713 (2002). https://doi.org/10.1145/585265.585270
4. Araújo, R., Ben Rajeb, N., Robbana, R., Traoré, J., Youssfi, S.: Towards practical and secure coercion-resistant electronic elections. In: Heng, S.-H., Wright, R.N., Goi, B.-M. (eds.) CANS 2010. LNCS, vol. 6467, pp. 278–297. Springer, Heidelberg (2010). https://doi.org/10.1007/978-3-642-17619-7_20
5. Backes, M., Hritcu, C., Maffei, M.: Automated verification of remote electronic voting protocols in the applied pi-calculus. In: IEEE 21st Computer Security Foundations Symposium, CSF 2008, pp. 195–209. IEEE (2008)
6. Baskar, A., Ramanujam, R., Suresh, S.: Knowledge-based modelling of voting protocols. In: Proceedings of the 11th Conference on Theoretical Aspects of Rationality and Knowledge, pp. 62–71. ACM (2007)
7. BBC News: Tsvangirai rejects 'sham' ballot (2008). http://news.bbc.co.uk/2/hi/africa/7478399.stm
8. Benaloh, J., Tuinstra, D.: Receipt-free secret-ballot elections. In: Proceedings of the Twenty-Sixth Annual ACM Symposium on Theory of Computing, pp. 544–553. ACM (1994)
9. Boureanu, I., Jones, A.V., Lomuscio, A.: Automatic verification of epistemic specifications under convergent equational theories. In: Proceedings of International Joint Conference on Autonomous Agents and Multiagent Systems (AAMAS), pp. 1141–1148 (2012)
10. Bruni, A., Drewsen, E., Schürmann, C.: Towards a mechanized proof of selene receipt-freeness and vote-privacy. In: Krimmer, R., Volkamer, M., Braun Binder, N., Kersting, N., Pereira, O., Schürmann, C. (eds.) E-Vote-ID 2017. LNCS, vol. 10615, pp. 110–126. Springer, Cham (2017). https://doi.org/10.1007/978-3-319-68687-5_7
11. Chadha, R., Kremer, S., Scedrov, A.: Formal analysis of multiparty contract signing. J. Autom. Reason. **36**(1–2), 39–83 (2006)
12. Chaum, D., Ryan, P.Y.A., Schneider, S.: A practical voter-verifiable election scheme. In: di Vimercati, S.C., Syverson, P., Gollmann, D. (eds.) ESORICS 2005. LNCS, vol. 3679, pp. 118–139. Springer, Heidelberg (2005). https://doi.org/10.1007/11555827_8
13. Cortier, V., Galindo, D., Küsters, R., Müller, J., Truderung, T.: SoK: verifiability notions for e-voting protocols. In: IEEE Symposium on Security and Privacy, pp. 779–798 (2016). https://doi.org/10.1109/SP.2016.52
14. Cortier, V., Gaudry, P., Yang, Q.: Is the JCJ voting system really coercion-resistant? Cryptology ePrint Archive (2022)
15. Delaune, S., Kremer, S., Ryan, M.: Coercion-resistance and receipt-freeness in electronic voting. In: 19th IEEE Computer Security Foundations Workshop, pp. 12–pp. IEEE (2006)

16. Delaune, S., Kremer, S., Ryan, M.: Verifying privacy-type properties of electronic voting protocols: a taster. In: Chaum, D., et al. (eds.) Towards Trustworthy Elections. LNCS, vol. 6000, pp. 289–309. Springer, Heidelberg (2010). https://doi.org/10.1007/978-3-642-12980-3_18
17. Delaune, S., Kremer, S., Ryan, M.D.: Receipt-freeness: formal definition and fault attacks. In: Proceedings of the Workshop Frontiers in Electronic Elections (FEE 2005), Milan, Italy. Citeseer (2005)
18. Dreier, J., Lafourcade, P., Lakhnech, Y.: A formal taxonomy of privacy in voting protocols. In: 2012 IEEE International Conference on Communications (ICC), pp. 6710–6715. IEEE (2012)
19. Emerson, E.: Temporal and modal logic. In: van Leeuwen, J. (ed.) Handbook of Theoretical Computer Science, vol. B, pp. 995–1072. Elsevier (1990)
20. Estaji, E., Haines, T., Gjøsteen, K., Rønne, P.B., Ryan, P.Y.A., Soroush, N.: Revisiting practical and usable coercion-resistant remote e-voting. In: Krimmer, R., et al. (eds.) E-Vote-ID 2020. LNCS, vol. 12455, pp. 50–66. Springer, Cham (2020). https://doi.org/10.1007/978-3-030-60347-2_4
21. Ferree, K.E., Jung, D.F., Dowd, R.A., Gibson, C.C.: Election ink and turnout in a partial democracy. Br. J. Polit. Sci. **50**(3), 1175–1191 (2020)
22. Gerhard, A.S.H., Atic, M., Letic, P., Erben, P.: Indelible Ink in Elections. White paper, IFES (2009). https://web.archive.org/web/20191108205514/https://www.ifes.org/sites/default/files/ifes_gerhard_atic_letic_erben_white_paper_indelible_ink_in_elections_may_2019.pdf
23. Giustolisi, R., Garjan, M.S., Schuermann, C.: Thwarting last-minute voter coercion. Cryptology ePrint Archive (2023)
24. Żaneta Gotowalska-Wróblewska: Jak nie brać udziału w referendum? [how not to take part in the referendum?] (2023). https://wiadomosci.wp.pl/nie-chcesz-wziac-udzialu-w-referendum-oto-co-powinienes-zrobic-6950661018536768a
25. van der Hoek, W., Wooldridge, M.: Cooperation, knowledge and time: alternating-time temporal epistemic logic and its applications. Stud. Logica **75**(1), 125–157 (2003)
26. Horbaczewski, R.: Sad najwyższy odpowiedział, czy bedzie osobny spis wyborców na referendu (2023). https://www.prawo.pl/samorzad/odnotowanie-niepobrania-karty-referendalnej-przez-komisje,523420.html
27. Jamroga, W., Knapik, M., Kurpiewski, D.: Model checking the SELENE E-voting protocol in multi-agent logics. In: Krimmer, R., et al. (eds.) E-Vote-ID 2018. LNCS, vol. 11143, pp. 100–116. Springer, Cham (2018). https://doi.org/10.1007/978-3-030-00419-4_7
28. Jamroga, W., Mauw, S., Melissen, M.: Fairness in non-repudiation protocols. In: Meadows, C., Fernandez-Gago, C. (eds.) STM 2011. LNCS, vol. 7170, pp. 122–139. Springer, Heidelberg (2012). https://doi.org/10.1007/978-3-642-29963-6_10
29. Jamroga, W., Kim, Y.: Practical model reductions for verification of multi-agent systems. In: Proceedings of the Thirty-Second International Joint Conference on Artificial Intelligence, IJCAI, pp. 7135–7139. ijcai.org (2023). https://doi.org/10.24963/IJCAI.2023/834
30. Jamroga, W., Kim, Y., Kurpiewski, D., Ryan, P.Y.A.: Towards model checking of voting protocols in UPPAAL. In: Krimmer, R., et al. (eds.) E-Vote-ID 2020. LNCS, vol. 12455, pp. 129–146. Springer, Cham (2020). https://doi.org/10.1007/978-3-030-60347-2_9
31. Jamroga, W., Kurpiewski, D., Malvone, V.: Natural strategic abilities in voting protocols. In: Groß, T., Viganò, L. (eds.) STAST 2020. LNCS, vol. 12812, pp. 45–62. Springer, Cham (2021). https://doi.org/10.1007/978-3-030-79318-0_3

32. Jaros, J.: Wieś boi sie bojkotu referendum. To bedzie tajemnica poliszynela [The countryside is afraid to boycott the referendum. It will be an open secret] (2023). https://kalisz.wyborcza.pl/kalisz/7,181359,30197487,tajemnica-wyborcza-fikcja-podczas-referendum-kobiety-o-przedwyborczych.html
33. Jha, P.S.: What a tiny spot of ink can mean. World Press Rev. **49**(12) (2002). https://www.worldpress.org/Asia/801.cfm
34. Jonker, H.L., Pieters, W.: Receipt-freeness as a special case of anonymity in epistemic logic. In: Proceedings of IAVoSS Workshop On Trustworthy Elections (WOTE 2006). Robinson College (2006)
35. Juels, A., Catalano, D., Jakobsson, M.: Coercion-resistant electronic elections. In: Proceedings of the 2005 ACM Workshop on Privacy in the Electronic Society, pp. 61–70. ACM (2005)
36. Kim, Y., Jamroga, W., Ryan, P.Y.A.: Verification of the socio-technical aspects of voting: the case of the Polish postal vote 2020. In: Proceedings of STAST (2022, to appear). https://arxiv.org/abs/2210.10694
37. King, L.: Taliban cut off Afghan voters' ink-stained fingers, election observers say. Los Angeles Times (2009). https://www.latimes.com/archives/la-xpm-2009-aug-23-fg-afghan-election23-story.html
38. Kremer, S., Raskin, J.: Game analysis of abuse-free contract signing. In: Proceedings of the 15th IEEE Computer Security Foundations Workshop (CSFW 2002), pp. 206–220. IEEE Computer Society Press (2002). https://doi.org/10.1109/CSFW.2002.1021817
39. Kremer, S., Raskin, J.F.: A game-based verification of non-repudiation and fair exchange protocols. J. Comput. Secur. **11**(3) (2003). https://doi.org/10.1007/3-540-44685-0_37
40. Ku, W.C., Ho, C.M.: An e-voting scheme against bribe and coercion. In: IEEE International Conference on e-Technology, e-Commerce and e-Service, EEE 2004, pp. 113–116. IEEE (2004)
41. Kulyk, O., Teague, V., Volkamer, M.: Extending helios towards private eligibility verifiability. In: Haenni, R., Koenig, R.E., Wikström, D. (eds.) VOTELID 2015. LNCS, vol. 9269, pp. 57–73. Springer, Cham (2015). https://doi.org/10.1007/978-3-319-22270-7_4
42. Kumar, R.K.: The business of 'black-marking' voters. The Hindu (2004). https://web.archive.org/web/20040412223708/http://www.hindu.com/2004/03/17/stories/2004031700571300.htm
43. Kurpiewski, D., et al.: Verification of multi-agent properties in electronic voting: a case study. In: Advances in Modal Logic, pp. 531–556. College Publications (2022)
44. Kusters, R., Truderung, T.: An epistemic approach to coercion-resistance for electronic voting protocols. In: 2009 30th IEEE Symposium on Security and Privacy, pp. 251–266. IEEE (2009)
45. Küsters, R., Truderung, T., Vogt, A.: A game-based definition of coercion-resistance and its applications. In: Proceedings of the 2010 23rd IEEE Computer Security Foundations Symposium, pp. 122–136. IEEE Computer Society (2010)
46. Lee, B., Kim, K.: Receipt-free electronic voting scheme with a tamper-resistant randomizer. In: Lee, P.J., Lim, C.H. (eds.) ICISC 2002. LNCS, vol. 2587, pp. 389–406. Springer, Heidelberg (2003). https://doi.org/10.1007/3-540-36552-4_27
47. Lee, B., Boyd, C., Dawson, E., Kim, K., Yang, J., Yoo, S.: Providing receipt-freeness in mixnet-based voting protocols. In: Lim, J.-I., Lee, D.-H. (eds.) ICISC 2003. LNCS, vol. 2971, pp. 245–258. Springer, Heidelberg (2004). https://doi.org/10.1007/978-3-540-24691-6_19

48. Magkos, E., Burmester, M., Chrissikopoulos, V.: Receipt-freeness in large-scale elections without untappable channels. In: Schmid, B., Stanoevska-Slabeva, K., Tschammer, V. (eds.) I3E 2001. IIFIP, vol. 74, pp. 683–693. Springer, Boston, MA (2002). https://doi.org/10.1007/0-306-47009-8_50
49. Mascol Technologies: Invisible election ink. https://www.election-ink.co.uk/
50. Meier, S., Schmidt, B., Cremers, C., Basin, D.: The TAMARIN prover for the symbolic analysis of security protocols. In: Sharygina, N., Veith, H. (eds.) CAV 2013. LNCS, vol. 8044, pp. 696–701. Springer, Heidelberg (2013). https://doi.org/10.1007/978-3-642-39799-8_48
51. Meng, B.: A critical review of receipt-freeness and coercion-resistance. Inf. Technol. J. **8**(7), 934–964 (2009)
52. Michels, M., Horster, P.: Some remarks on a receipt-free and universally verifiable mix-type voting scheme. In: Kim, K., Matsumoto, T. (eds.) ASIACRYPT 1996. LNCS, vol. 1163, pp. 125–132. Springer, Heidelberg (1996). https://doi.org/10.1007/BFb0034841
53. Moran, T., Naor, M.: Receipt-free universally-verifiable voting with everlasting privacy. In: Dwork, C. (ed.) CRYPTO 2006. LNCS, vol. 4117, pp. 373–392. Springer, Heidelberg (2006). https://doi.org/10.1007/11818175_22
54. Notes from Poland: Exit poll: Polish government's referendum invalidated by low turnout (2023). https://notesfrompoland.com/2023/10/15/exit-poll-polish-governments-referendum-invalidated-by-low-turnout/
55. Okamoto, T.: Receipt-free electronic voting schemes for large scale elections. In: Christianson, B., Crispo, B., Lomas, M., Roe, M. (eds.) Security Protocols 1997. LNCS, vol. 1361, pp. 25–35. Springer, Heidelberg (1998). https://doi.org/10.1007/BFb0028157
56. Państwowa Komisja Wyborcza [National Electoral Commission]: Obwieszczenie państwowej komisji wyborczej z dnia 17 października 2023 r. o wynikach głosowania i wyniku referendum przeprowadzonego w dniu 15 października 2023 r. (2023). https://isap.sejm.gov.pl/isap.nsf/DocDetails.xsp?id=WDU19970780483
57. Państwowa Komisja Wyborcza [National Electoral Commission]: Turnout in 2023 elections for sejm (2023). https://wybory.gov.pl/sejmsenat2023/en/frekwencja/pl
58. Państwowa Komisja Wyborcza [National Electoral Commission]: Turnout in nationwide referendum 2023 (2023). https://referendum.gov.pl/referendum2023/en/frekwencja/pl
59. Państwowa Komisja Wyborcza [National Electoral Commission]: Uchwała nr 211/2023 pkw z dnia 25 września 2023 r. w sprawie wytycznych dla obwodowych komisji wyborczych dotyczacych zadań i trybu przygotowania oraz przeprowadzenia głosowania w obwodach głosowania utworzonych w kraju w wyborach do sejmu rzeczypospolitej polskiej i do senatu rzeczypospolitej polskiej oraz w referendum ogólnokrajowym zarzadzonych na dzień 15 października 2023 r. (2023). https://pkw.gov.pl/prawo-wyborcze/uchwaly-pkw/2023-r/uchwala-nr-2112023-pkw-z-dnia-25-wrzesnia-2023-r-w-sprawie-wytycznych-dla-obwodowych-komisji-wyborcz
60. Ryan, P.Y.A.: The computer ate my vote. In: Boca, P., Bowen, J., Siddiqi, J. (eds.) Formal Methods: State of the Art and New Directions, pp. 147–184. Springer, London (2010). https://doi.org/10.1007/978-1-84882-736-3_5
61. Ryan, P.Y.A., Rønne, P.B., Iovino, V.: Selene: voting with transparent verifiability and coercion-mitigation. In: Clark, J., Meiklejohn, S., Ryan, P.Y.A., Wallach, D., Brenner, M., Rohloff, K. (eds.) FC 2016. LNCS, vol. 9604, pp. 176–192. Springer, Heidelberg (2016). https://doi.org/10.1007/978-3-662-53357-4_12

62. Ryan, P.Y.A., Schneider, S.A., Teague, V.: End-to-end verifiability in voting systems, from theory to practice. IEEE Secur. Priv. **13**(3), 59–62 (2015). https://doi.org/10.1109/MSP.2015.54
63. Ryan, P.Y.A., Teague, V.: Pretty good democracy. In: Christianson, B., Malcolm, J.A., Matyáš, V., Roe, M. (eds.) Security Protocols 2009. LNCS, vol. 7028, pp. 111–130. Springer, Heidelberg (2013). https://doi.org/10.1007/978-3-642-36213-2_15
64. Schläpfer, M., Haenni, R., Koenig, R., Spycher, O.: Efficient vote authorization in coercion-resistant internet voting. In: Kiayias, A., Lipmaa, H. (eds.) Vote-ID 2011. LNCS, vol. 7187, pp. 71–88. Springer, Heidelberg (2012). https://doi.org/10.1007/978-3-642-32747-6_5
65. Schobbens, P.Y.: Alternating-time logic with imperfect recall. Electron. Notes Theor. Comput. Sci. **85**(2), 82–93 (2004)
66. Sejm Rzeczypospolitej Polskiej [Parliament of the Republic of Poland]: Uchwała sejmu rzeczypospolitej polskiej z dnia 17 sierpnia 2023 r. o zarzadzeniu referendum ogólnokrajowego w sprawach o szczególnym znaczeniu dla państwa (2023). https://isap.sejm.gov.pl/isap.nsf/download.xsp/WDU20230001636/O/D20231636.pdf
67. Sitnicka, D.: Najważniejsze sa wybory, referendum jest drugorzedne. podpowiadamy, jak je bezpiecznie zbojkotować (2023). https://oko.press/referendum-bojkot-glosowanie
68. Tabatabaei, M., Jamroga, W., Ryan, P.Y.A.: Expressing receipt-freeness and coercion-resistance in logics of strategic ability: preliminary attempt. In: Proceedings of the 1st International Workshop on AI for Privacy and Security, PrAISe@ECAI 2016, pp. 1:1–1:8. ACM (2016). https://doi.org/10.1145/2970030.2970039
69. Weber, S.G., Araujo, R., Buchmann, J.: On coercion-resistant electronic elections with linear work. In: The Second International Conference on Availability, Reliability and Security, ARES 2007, pp. 908–916. IEEE (2007)
70. Wong, R.: Ink washout. The Star (2008). https://web.archive.org/web/20080430202643/http://www.thestar.com.my/election/story.asp?file=%2F2008%2F3%2F5%2Felection2008%2F20540844&sec=Election2008&focus=1
71. Zollinger, M., Rønne, P.B., Ryan, P.Y.A.: Mechanized proofs of verifiability and privacy in a paper-based e-voting scheme. In: Proceedings of 5th Workshop on Advances in Secure Electronic Voting (2020)

4th Workshop on Decentralized Finance (DeFI 2024)

Transaction Fee Mechanism Design with Active Block Producers

Maryam Bahrani[1], Pranav Garimidi[1(✉)], and Tim Roughgarden[1,2]

[1] a16z Crypto, Menlo Park, USA
{mbahrani,pgarimidi,troughgarden}@a16z.com
[2] Columbia University, New York, USA

Abstract. The incentive-compatibility properties of blockchain transaction fee mechanisms have been investigated with *passive* block producers that are motivated purely by the net rewards earned at the consensus layer. This work introduces a model of *active* block producers that have their own private valuations for blocks (representing, for example, additional value derived from the application layer). The block producer surplus in our model can be interpreted as one of the more common colloquial meanings of the term "MEV." The main results of this work show that transaction fee mechanism design is fundamentally more difficult with active block producers than with passive ones: with active block producers, no non-trivial or approximately welfare-maximizing transaction fee mechanism can be incentive-compatible for both users and block producers. These results can be interpreted as a mathematical justification for the current interest in augmenting transaction fee mechanisms with additional components such as order flow auctions, block producer competition, trusted hardware, or cryptographic techniques.

1 Introduction

1.1 Transaction Fee Mechanisms for Allocating Blockspace

Blockchain protocols such as Bitcoin and Ethereum process transactions submitted by users, with each transaction advancing the "state" of the protocol. Such protocols have finite processing power, so when demand for transaction processing exceeds the available supply, a strict subset of the submitted transactions must be chosen for processing. The component of a blockchain protocol responsible for choosing the transactions to process and what to charge for them is called its *transaction fee mechanism (TFM)*.

Previous academic work on TFM design has focused on the game-theoretic properties of different designs, such as incentive-compatibility from the perspective of users (ideally, with a user motivated to bid its true value for the execution of its transaction), of block producers (ideally, with a block producer motivated to select transactions to process as suggested by the TFM), and of cartels of

---

T. Roughgarden—Author's research at Columbia University supported in part by NSF awards CCF-2006737 and CNS-2212745.

users and/or block producers. Discussing incentive-compatibility requires defining utility functions for the relevant participants. In most previous works on TFM design (and in this work), users are modeled as having a private value for transaction inclusion and a quasi-linear utility function (i.e., value enjoyed minus price paid). In previous work—and, crucially, unlike in this work—a block producer was modeled as *passive*, meaning its utility function was the net reward earned (canonically, the unburned portion of the transaction fees paid by users, possibly plus a block reward).

While this model is a natural one for the initial investigation of the basic properties of TFMs, it effectively assumes that block producers are unaware of or unconcerned with the semantics of the transactions that they process.

1.2 MEV and Active Block Producers

It is now commonly accepted that, there are unavoidable interactions between the consensus layer (block producers) and the application layer (users), specifically with block producers deriving value from the application layer that depends on which transactions they choose to process (and in which order), colloquially known as "MEV". For a canonical example, consider a transaction executing a trade on an automated market maker (AMM). The trade might move the spot price of the AMM out of line with external markets and thereby give the block producer an arbitrage opportunity to include its own "backrunning" transaction immediately after the submitted trade transaction.

The first goal of this work is to generalize the existing models of TFM design in the minimal way that accommodates *active* block producers, meaning block producers with a utility function that depends on both the transactions in a block (and their order) and the net fees earned. Specifically, the block producer will have its own private valuation which is an abstract function of the block that it publishes. We then assume that a block producer acts to maximize its *block producer surplus (BPS)*, meaning its private value for the published block plus any additional profits (or losses) from fees (or burns). Our model captures, in particular, canonical on-chain DeFi opportunities such as arbitrage and liquidation opportunities, but a block producer's valuation can reflect arbitrary preferences, perhaps derived also from off-chain activities (e.g., a bet with a friend) or subjective considerations.

In this work, we treat a block producer as a single entity that publishes a block based on the transactions that it is aware of. This would be an accurate model of block production until a few years ago. More recently block production has evolved into a more complex process, typically involving "searchers" (who identify opportunities for extraction from the application layer), "builders" (who assemble such opportunities into a valid block), and "proposers" (who participate directly in the blockchain protocol and make the final choice of the published block). One interpretation of a block producer in our model is as a vertically integrated searcher, builder, and proposer.

2   Overview of Results

Our starting point is the model for transaction fee mechanism design defined in [22]. In this model, each user has a private valuation for the inclusion of a transaction in a block, and submits a bid along with its transaction. As in [22], we consider TFMs that choose the included transactions and payments based solely on the bids of the pending transactions. A block producer publishes any block that it wants, subject to feasibility (e.g., with the total size of the included transactions respecting some maximum block size). A TFM is said to be *dominant-strategy incentive-compatible (DSIC)* if every user has a dominant (i.e., always-optimal) bidding strategy. The DSIC property is often associated with a good "user experience (UX)," in the sense that each user has an obvious optimal bid. In [22], a TFM was said to be *incentive-compatible for myopic miners (MMIC)* if it expects a block producer to publish a block that maximizes the net fees earned (at the consensus layer). Here, we introduce an analogous definition that accommodates active block producers: We call a TFM *incentive-compatible for block producers (BPIC)* if it expects a block producer to publish a block that maximizes its private valuation plus the net fees earned. An ideal TFM would satisfy, among other properties, both DSIC and BPIC.

This work shows that TFM design is fundamentally more difficult with active block producers than with passive ones. Our first result is that, with active block producers, *no* non-trivial TFM satisfies both DSIC and BPIC, where "non-trivial" means that users must at least in some cases pay a nonzero amount for transaction inclusion.

Theorem 1 (Main Impossibility Result). *If the TFM $(\mathbf{x}, \mathbf{p}, \mathbf{q})$ is DSIC with bidding strategy σ and BPIC with active block producers, then the payment rule $\mathbf{p}$ is identically zero on the range of σ.*

While with passive block producers the EIP-1559 mechanism of Buterin et al. [5] is non-trivial and satisfies DSIC and BPIC provided the mechanism's base fee is not excessively low [22], with an active block producer it is no longer DSIC. Intuitively, a user a user might be motivated to underbid in the hopes of an effective subsidy by the block producer (who may include the transaction anyways, if it derives outside value from it). Theorem 1 shows that this breakdown in incentive-compatibility is not a failure of EIP-1559 per se, but rather stems from a fundamental obstacle to TFM design with active block producers.

Our second main result shows that TFMs that do not charge non-zero transaction fees—and in particular (by Theorem 1), TFMs that are both DSIC and BPIC—cannot provide any meaningful welfare-maximization guarantees.

Theorem 2 (Impossibility of Non-Trivial Welfare Guarantees). *Let $(\mathbf{x}, \mathbf{p}, \mathbf{q})$ denote a TFM that is BPIC and DSIC with bidding strategy σ. For every approximation factor $\rho > 0$, there exists a BP valuation v_{BP}, BP blockset $\mathcal{B}$, block $B^* \in \mathcal{B}$, and transactions with corresponding user valuations $\mathbf{v}$ such that*

$$W(B) \leq \rho \cdot W(B^*),$$

where $B = \mathbf{x}(\sigma(\mathbf{v}), v_{BP}, \mathcal{B})$.

Intuitively, the issue is the lack of alignment between the preferences of users and of the block producer: If a block producer earns no transaction fees from any block, it might choose a block with non-zero private value but only very low-value transactions over one with no private value but very high-value transactions.

Impossibility results like Theorems 1 and 2 are meant to guide rather than discourage further work on the problem, by highlighting the paths forward along which positive progress might be made. In fact, these results can be interpreted as a mathematical justification for the community's current interest in augmenting transaction fee mechanisms with additional components such as order flow auctions (e.g., [18]), block producer competition (e.g., [10]), trusted hardware (e.g., [14]), or cryptographic techniques (e.g., [6]).

3 Related Work

Defining MEV. Daian et al. [9] introduced the notion of miner/maximal extractable value. They defined MEV as the value that miners or validators could obtain by manipulating the transactions in a block. Since this work there have been many follow-up works attempting to formalize MEV and analyze its effects in both theory and practice. Attempts to give exact theoretical characterizations of MEV appear in [2,4,19,23]. Several empirical papers study the impact and magnitude of MEV using heuristics applied to on-chain data [20,21,25]. Another line of work [3,16,17] studies MEV in specific contexts, such as for arbitrage in AMMs, in which it is possible to characterize how much MEV can be realized from certain transactions. We argue that our definition of BPS captures, in a precise way and in a concrete economic model, one of the more common meanings of the term "MEV."

General TFM Literature. The model in this work is closest to the one used by Roughgarden [22] to analyze (with passive block producers) the economic properties of the EIP-1559 mechanism [5], the TFM used currently in the Ethereum blockchain. There have also been several follow-up works to [22] that use similar models. Chung and Shi [8] proved impossibility results showing that the incentive-compatible guarantees of the EIP-1559 mechanism are in some sense optimal. Several works slightly modify this setting in attempt to circumvent this impossibility result [8,15,24,26,27].

Credible Mechanisms. A more distantly related line of work involves mechanism design in the presence of strategic auctioneers. Akbarpour and Li [1] introduce the notion of *credible* mechanisms, where any profitable deviations by the auctioneer can be detected by at least one user. While similar in spirit to BPIC as introduced here, there are several important differences. For example, the theory of credible mechanisms assumes fully private communication between bidders and the auctioneer and no communication among bidders, whereas TFM bids are commonly collected from a public mempool. There is also a line of follow-up work that takes advantage of cryptographic primitives to build credible auctions on the blockchain [7,11–13].

References

1. Akbarpour, M., Li, S.: Credible auctions: a trilemma. Econometrica **88**(2), 425–467 (2020)
2. Babel, K., Daian, P., Kelkar, M., Juels, A.: Clockwork finance: automated analysis of economic security in smart contracts. In: IEEE Symposium on Security and Privacy, pp. 2499–2516 (2023)
3. Bartoletti, M., Chiang, J.H., Lluch-Lafuente, A.: Maximizing extractable value from automated market makers. In: Eyal, I., Garay, J.A. (eds.) FC 2022. LNCS, vol. 13411, pp. 3–19. Springer, Cham (2022). https://doi.org/10.1007/978-3-031-18283-9_1
4. Bartoletti, M., Zunino, R.: A theoretical basis for blockchain extractable value. CoRR abs/2302.02154 (2023)
5. Buterin, V., Conner, E., Dudley, R., Slipper, M., Norden, I., Bakhta, A.: EIP-1559: fee market change for ETH 1.0 chain (2019). https://github.com/ethereum/EIPs/blob/master/EIPS/eip-1559.md
6. Charbonneau, J.: Encrypted mempools (2023). https://joncharbonneau.substack.com/p/encrypted-mempools
7. Chitra, T., Ferreira, M.V.X., Kulkarni, K.: Credible, optimal auctions via blockchains. arXiv preprint arXiv:2301.12532 (2023)
8. Chung, H., Shi, E.: Foundations of transaction fee mechanism design. In: Proceedings of the 2023 Annual ACM-SIAM Symposium on Discrete Algorithms (SODA), pp. 3856–3899. SIAM (2023)
9. Daian, P., et al.: Flash boys 2.0: frontrunning in decentralized exchanges, miner extractable value, and consensus instability. In: 2020 IEEE Symposium on Security and Privacy, SP 2020, San Francisco, CA, USA, 18–21 May 2020, pp. 910–927. IEEE (2020)
10. Domothy: Burning MEV through block proposer auctions (2022). https://ethresear.ch/t/burning-mev-through-block-proposer-auctions/14029
11. Essaidi, M., Ferreira, M.V.X., Weinberg, S.M.: Credible, strategyproof, optimal, and bounded expected-round single-item auctions for all distributions. In: Proceedings of the 13th Innovations in Theoretical Computer Science Conference (ITCS) (2022)
12. Ferreira, M.V.X., Parkes, D.C.: Credible decentralized exchange design via verifiable sequencing rules. In: Proceedings of the 55th Annual ACM Symposium on Theory of Computing, pp. 723–736 (2023)
13. Ferreira, M.V.X., Weinberg, S.M.: Credible, truthful, and two-round (optimal) auctions via cryptographic commitments. In: Proceedings of the 21st ACM Conference on Economics and Computation, pp. 683–712 (2020)
14. Flashbots: The Future of MEV is SUAVE (2022). https://writings.flashbots.net/the-future-of-mev-is-suave/
15. Gafni, Y., Yaish, A.: Greedy transaction fee mechanisms for (non-) myopic miners. arXiv preprint arXiv:2210.07793 (2022)
16. Heimbach, L., Wattenhofer, R.: Eliminating sandwich attacks with the help of game theory. In: Suga, Y., Sakurai, K., Ding, X., Sako, K. (eds.) ASIA CCS 2022: ACM Asia Conference on Computer and Communications Security, Nagasaki, Japan, 30 May 2022–3 June 2022, pp. 153–167. ACM (2022)
17. Kulkarni, K., Diamandis, T., Chitra, T.: Towards a theory of maximal extractable value I: constant function market makers. CoRR abs/2207.11835 (2022)

18. Miller, R.: MEV-Share: programmably private orderflow to share MEV with users (2023). https://collective.flashbots.net/t/mev-share-programmably-private-orderflow-to-share-mev-with-users/1264
19. Obadia, A., Salles, A., Sankar, L., Chitra, T., Chellani, V., Daian, P.: Unity is strength: a formalization of cross-domain maximal extractable value. CoRR abs/2112.01472 (2021)
20. Qin, K., Zhou, L., Gervais, A.: Quantifying blockchain extractable value: How dark is the forest? In: 43rd IEEE Symposium on Security and Privacy, SP 2022, San Francisco, CA, USA, 22–26 May 2022, pp. 198–214. IEEE (2022)
21. Qin, K., Zhou, L., Livshits, B., Gervais, A.: Attacking the DeFi ecosystem with flash loans for fun and profit. In: Borisov, N., Diaz, C. (eds.) FC 2021. LNCS, vol. 12674, pp. 3–32. Springer, Heidelberg (2021). https://doi.org/10.1007/978-3-662-64322-8_1
22. Roughgarden, T.: Transaction fee mechanism design. ACM SIGecom Exchanges **19**(1), 52–55 (2021). https://arxiv.org/abs/2106.01340
23. Salles, A.: On the formalization of MEV (2021). https://collective.flashbots.net/t/on-the-formalization-of-mev/879
24. Shi, E., Chung, H., Wu, K.: What can cryptography do for decentralized mechanism design. arXiv preprint arXiv:2209.14462 (2022)
25. Torres, C.F., Camino, R., State, R.: Frontrunner jones and the raiders of the dark forest: an empirical study of frontrunning on the Ethereum blockchain. In: Bailey, M., Greenstadt, R. (eds.) 30th USENIX Security Symposium, USENIX Security 2021, 11–13 August 2021, pp. 1343–1359. USENIX Association (2021)
26. Wu, K., Shi, E., Chung, H.: Maximizing miner revenue in transaction fee mechanism design. In: Guruswami, V. (ed.) 15th Innovations in Theoretical Computer Science Conference, ITCS 2024, 30 January to 2 February 2024, Berkeley, CA, USA. LIPIcs, vol. 287, pp. 98:1–98:23. Schloss Dagstuhl - Leibniz-Zentrum für Informatik (2024)
27. Zhao, Z., Chen, X., Zhou, Y.: Bayesian-Nash-incentive-compatible mechanism for blockchain transaction fee allocation. arXiv preprint arXiv:2209.13099 (2022)

Transaction Ordering Auctions

Christoph Schlegel(✉)

Flashbots, George Town, Cayman Islands
`christoph@flashbots.net`

Abstract. We study equilibrium investment into bidding and latency reduction for different sequencing policies. For a batch auction design, we observe that bidders shade bids according to the likelihood that competing bidders land in the current batch. Moreover, in equilibrium, in the ex-ante investment stage before the auction, bidders invest into latency until they make zero profit in expectation. We compare the batch auction design to continuous time bidding policies (time boost) and observe that (depending on the choice of parameters) they obtain similar revenue and welfare guarantees.

1 Introduction

Various transaction ordering policies for roll-up sequencers, exchanges or L1 blockchains have been proposed. The following categories seem to cover the available options well:

- *First Come First Serve* orders transactions by time stamp of arrival at whatever server orders the transactions. Questions of decentralized implementation aside, this policy seems appealing and intuitive to many. It is the go-to policy in traditional finance and hence users are used to interacting with it. FCFS appeals to basic intuitions about fairness [4,5]. But there is also an efficiency argument to be made: FCFS provides an incentive to incorporate new external information quickly into the state of the system.
- *Bidding Based Ordering*: Orders are processed in batches or blocks. Transactions within a batch interval are ordered according to a function of the attached bids. The function can (hypothetically) be arbitrarily complex: we could order transactions by bid, we could auction individual slots in the batch, or even allow combinatorial bidding where users express preferences over the entire content of the block. Also the "bid" can sometimes be interpreted broadly, for example in Ethereum block building, the bid could contain the amount of MEV the user allows the block builder to extract from them.
- *Random ordering or other "shuffling" protocols*: Randomness [3], if implementable, is a means to achieve ex-ante fairness when ranking transactions. In a different direction, verifiable sequencing rules [1] are designed to make it detectable if a sequencer deviates from the rule.
- *Hybrid policies*: The above policies can be mixed and matched. For example, FCFS can be implemented with discrete buckets where orders within a bucket

are ordered randomly. A recent proposal [6], orders transactions by a scoring rule called "time boost" that scores transactions by a combination of time stamps and bids.

While these policies look very different from each other, a substantial aspect of all of them is that they organize a contest for earlier transaction execution among those users that care about it (CEX-DEX arb traders, liquidators, etc.). The term contest here has the usual meaning from economics: users exert effort (investing in latency, spending money on bidding, spamming your server with transactions) to produce a signal (a timestamp, a bid, a set of transactions IDs) and based on these signals, we decide which transactions to include and in which order (and therefore decide who wins the different contests).

The framing as a contest is helpful, in so far as it gives us an indication of what it means to choose a transaction ordering policy: we organize a contest among users and users maximize whatever signal maximizes their chances of winning the contest. Thus, we need to decide on what dimension we want them to compete: latency investment, expenditure on bidding, the number of transaction requests you receive, increasing entropy, a mixture of all of them, etc.?

In the following, I want to focus on the first two categories of transaction ordering policies, time stamp and bidding based policies, and hybrid policies mixing between the first two categories. This is because these policies have an implicit or explicit focus on efficiency (broadly understood) which is desirable. A maybe under-appreciated aspect of bidding-based policies is that they do not eliminate latency competition completely. Even in a pure batch auction, there still is an advantage for low latency bidders when approaching the end of the batch. This has for example been documented [2] in Ethereum block building, where searchers specialized in CEX-DEX arbitrage need low latency to be competitive in "top of block" MEV.

Following this observation, I analyze the equilibrium bidding and equilibrium latency investment of bidders interacting with a batch auction policy and derive the equilibrium welfare and revenue achieved. In comparison to an analysis that does not take latency into consideration, we observe further bid shading in equilibrium. Bidders lower their bids as a function of the odds of being included in the current batch. As a second step, I analyze the (ex-ante) latency investment decisions of the bidders interacting with a batch auction. It turns out that in equilibrium bidders will engage in a race to the bottom where all expected profits from participating in the batch auction is compete away through latency investment so that bidders break even in expectation. The analysis is carried out for a first price winner-pay auction. However, the analysis also carries over to other pricing rules such as an all-pay auction which frequently occurs in practice. The analysis of the batch auction is applicable to several different situations relevant in practice, such as the competition for the top of block slot in L1 blockchains or to L2 sequencers using a batch auction design.

Besides batch auctions, alternative "continuous" bidding policies [6] have been suggested. In these policies, transactions are ordered by time stamp, but bidders can additionally improve their position by bidding. As a second contribution, I also analyze the equilibrium bidding behavior in this kind of market design and compare efficiency and revenue to the batch auction case. The comparison depends on the choice of parameters, the length of the batch in the batch auction versus the maximal time advantage that can be obtained by bidding. However, choosing the parameters comparably, the two design perform very similarly.

Some disclaimers: The following analysis is purely economic. I abstract away from questions of consensus and implementation and assume that the policies considered can be implemented, because they are run by a trusted centralized sequencer or because we know how to decentralize these policies in a satisfying way. I abstract away from incentive compatibility problems (MEV extraction, censoring etc.) on the side of the party that implements the transaction ordering policy and assume that the policies are implemented as stated.

2 Equilibrium Analysis of Bidding and Latency Investment

The starting point of my analysis is a bidding and/or latency race between two bidders, who each want their transaction to be executed before the other bidder's transaction (I would expect similar results to hold for more than two bidders). A typical situation that triggers such race could, for example, be an arbitrage opportunity arising through a price discrepancy between an off-chain CEX and an on-chain DEX. Another typical example would be a competition for executing a liquidation. While there are other MEV games played in reality, where bidders have more complicated preferences over transactions orderings than just about how two transactions are ordered relative to each other, these atomic contest for earlier inclusion constitute a large fraction of trading activity on most platforms. Moreover, many other strategies contain an element of it, as it might be a necessary part of the execution of a more complicated trade.

I assume that the value of earlier execution can be different for the two bidders, for example they could have different amounts of liquidity deployed on different platforms so that they can extract different amounts of value from an arb. However, both of the two bidders should have a non-negative value for having their transaction be executed first. The situation is a race between the two bidders in the sense that the bidder, whose transaction is included later, cannot extract any value.

I assume that there are two sources of uncertainty for the two bidders:

1. The bidders are uncertain about the competitor's value of winning.
2. The bidders are uncertain about each others' latency. Timestamps are uncertain and random but correlated with (ex-ante) latency investment decisions.

2.1 Batch Auctions

In a batch auction, all transactions arriving within a pre-specified time window (according to some time stamping scheme) are ordered according to their

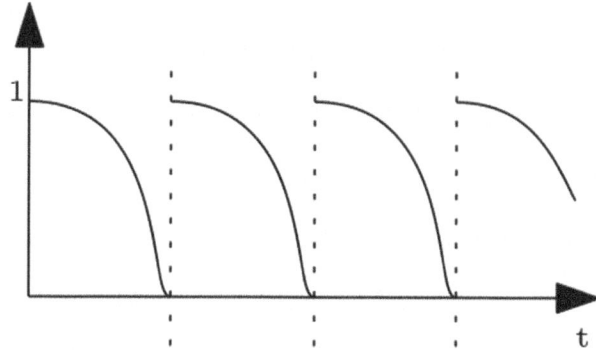

Fig. 1. Probability T_i of inclusion in the current batch. Dotted lines indicate batch cut-offs.

attached bid, with the highest bid transaction being executed first (if feasible), the second highest bid transaction second (if feasible) etc. A bid cut-off (or reserve price) can be used to bound the total number of transactions being included. A variety of payment rules can be used. In the following, I assume that the competition between the two bidders follow a first price auction format with two possible interpretations: 1) the payment rule is pay-as-you bid, but the capacity is bounded so that the lower bid transaction is not executed 2) the lower bid transaction is reverted if it does not land in the higher slot. Qualitatively very similar results would also hold for an all-pay batch auction, see Remark 2.

For the analysis I normalize time so that bidding happens during a unit time interval $[0, 1]$. The timing is as follows:

1. An arbitrage opportunity arrives uniformly at random in the unit interval. When the arbitrage opportunity occurs, bidders learn their valuations. A player i has a valuation v_i to have his transaction included first, where v_i is distributed according to $F_i(x)$.
2. Bidders send a bid for inclusion. Depending on their latency and time of observing the arb, their bid gets included in the current or in the next batch.
3. At the end of the batch, bids are evaluated according to a first price auction. The higher bid transaction is executed and pays the attached bid.

Assume that there are two bidders with valuations v_1 and v_2, distributed, for simplicity, i.i.d. uniform on the unit interval. Qualitatively, the analysis carries over to non-uniform valuations. The assumption of independent valuations models the case where there is heterogeneity between the two bidders, while the common component in valuations is known with certainty.

Assume that bidder i has probability of $T_i(\tau)$ of submitting a bid at time $0 \leq \tau \leq 1$ which is included in the current batch and probability $1 - T_i(\tau)$ of being included in a later batch (Fig. 1).

We can interpret $T_i(\tau)$ either as objective probabilities or as bidders' (subjective) beliefs. I don't make any particular assumption on T_i other than that

$1 - T_i(\tau)$ is a differentiable CDF, so that $T_i(0) = 1$ and $T_i(1) = 0$. It is straightforward to calculate equilibrium bidding strategies, both for 1) the situation where each bidder is certain about whether or not their own bid gets included in the batch but uncertain about the competitor's bid, and for 2) the situation where bidders are uncertain about their own bid and the competitor's bid.

Proposition 1. *The symmetric equilibrium bidding strategy in the batch auction is*
$$b(v) = \frac{v^2}{2(v + \frac{1-T(\tau)}{T(\tau)})},$$
which gives a payoff of
$$\Pi(\tau) = \tfrac{1}{2} - \tfrac{1}{3}T(\tau).$$

Proof. For the case that for bidder i the arb realizes at τ, he knows that he can make into the batch and his valuation is v_i, his optimal bid solves
$$\max_{0 \leq b_i \leq 1} (v_i - b_i)(T_j(\tau)Pr_{v_j \sim F_j}[b_i \geq b_j(v_j)] + (1 - T_j(\tau))),$$

i.e. bidder i wins if the other bidder lands in the same batch but i bids higher (which happens with probability $(T_j(\tau)Pr_{v_j \sim F_j}[b_i \geq b_j(v_j)])$ or the other bidder lands in a later batch (which happens with probability $1 - T_j(\tau)$). Taking first order conditions and assuming that we are in a symmetric equilibrium so that $Pr[b_i \geq b_j] = Pr[v_i \geq v_j] = F(v_i)$, we get:

$$\frac{(v_i - b_i(v_i))f(v_i)T_j(\tau)}{b'_i(v_i)} - (T_j(\tau)F(v_i) + (1 - T_j(\tau))) = 0,$$

where $b_i(v)$ is the optimal bid as a function of the valuation and $b'_i(v)$ its derivative. Solving the differential equation obtained from the first order condition with the boundary condition $b_i(0) = 0$ (if the bidder has no value for the arb he doesn't bid), we get the equilibrium bidding strategy:

$$b(v) = \frac{v^2}{2(v + \frac{1-T(\tau)}{T(\tau)})}.$$

To calculate the equilibrium pay-off we integrate over the value distribution:
$$\Pi(\tau) = \int_0^1 (v_i - b_i)(T(\tau)F_j(v_i) + (1 - T(\tau)))dv_i$$
$$= \int_0^1 (v_i - \frac{v^2}{2(v + \frac{1-T(\tau)}{T(\tau)})})(T(\tau)v_i + (1 - T(\tau)))dv_i = \tfrac{1}{2} - \tfrac{1}{3}T(\tau).$$

□

Remark 1. Similarly, we can derive the optimal bid, if bidders are uncertain not only about the competitor's but also their own bid making it into the current batch. In that case, bidder i's bid solves

$$\max_{0 \le b_i \le 1} (v_i - b_i)((T_i(\tau)T_j(\tau) + (1 - T_i(\tau))(1 - T_j(\tau)))Pr_{v_j \sim F_j}[b_i \ge b_j(v_j)] + T_i(\tau)(1 - T_j(\tau))).$$

By the same kind of calculation, the equilibrium bidding strategy for the symmetric case is:

$$b(v) = \frac{v^2}{2(v + \frac{T(\tau)(1-T(\tau))}{T(\tau)^2 + (1-T(\tau))^2})}.$$

Remark 2. Similarly, we can derive the optimal bid for an all-pay version of the batch auction. In that case, bidder i's bid solves

$$\max_{0 \le b_i \le 1} v_i((T_i(\tau)T_j(\tau) + (1-T_i(\tau))(1-T_j(\tau)))Pr_{v_j \sim F_j}[b_i \ge b_j(v_j)] + T_i(\tau)(1-T_j(\tau))) - b_i.$$

By the same kind of calculation, the equilibrium bidding strategy for the symmetric case is:

$$b(v) = \frac{v^2}{2} T(\tau).$$

We can make the following observations about equilibrium bidding:

Remark 3. In equilibrium,

1. bids are lower than in a standard first price auction,
2. bidders shade bids according to the odds $\frac{1-T(\tau)}{T(\tau)}$ that the competitor gets included in a later batch,
3. the payoffs for bidders are higher than in a standard first price auction,
4. the revenue for the auctioneer is lower.

2.2 Ex-ante Latency Investment for Batch Auctions

Next let us look at the latency investment game induced by the batch auction design. Assume that prior to bidding, bidders invest in latency reduction. The bidders do not know the arrival time and the value of the arb when making the investment decision. The investment is therefore at the ex-ante stage. When making their investment decision, the bidders only know the expected ex-ante profit from the auction as analyzed above. Assume that it costs $C(\Delta)$ for a user to invest into latency so that he can send messages with delay Δ. We assume that

1. it is impossible to send arbitrarily fast messages, $\lim_{\Delta \to 0} C(\Delta) = \infty$,
2. it is possible without any additional investment into latency to send a bid at the beginning of the batch that is included in the batch, $C(1) = 0$,
3. lower latency is more expensive than higher latency, i.e. $C(\Delta)$ is strictly decreasing,
4. there is increasing marginal cost of a marginal time advantage, i.e. C is convex.

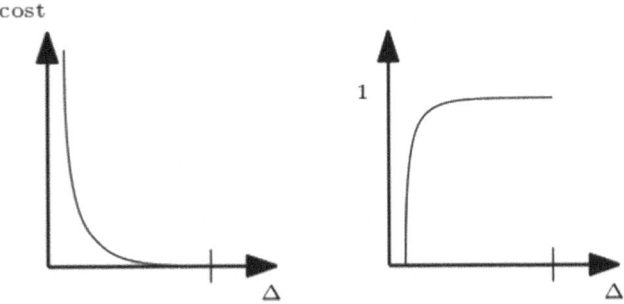

Fig. 2. Cost of latency and the implied equilibrium latency distribution (prob that latency is smaller than Δ.

Suppose that bidder i invests into latency with delay Δ_i so that he is able to bid on all arbs arriving up to time $1 - \Delta_i$. Assuming uniform arrivals of arbs, defining the probability that bidder j has delay at most Δ_j by $\sigma_j(\Delta_j)$, bidder i's profit of investing into latency to obtain a delay of Δ_i is (see the analysis in the previous section) (Fig. 2):

$$\int_0^{1-\Delta_i} (\tfrac{1}{2} - \tfrac{1}{3}T(\tau))d\tau - C(\Delta_i) = \int_{\Delta_i}^1 (\tfrac{1}{2} - \tfrac{1}{3}\sigma_j(\Delta))d\Delta - C(\Delta_i).$$

From this we can construct a symmetric equilibrium of the investment game. The proofs of all subsequent propositions and observations are in the appendix.

Proposition 2. *There is a symmetric equilibrium of the ex-ante investment game with mixed strategy*

$$\sigma(\Delta) = 3/2 + 3C'(\Delta),$$

in which bidders make 0 profit on average.

Ex-ante investment into latency leads to zero average profit for bidders in equilibrium: The ex-ante expected gains from bidding in the batch auction are equal to the cost of latency investment of the bidder independently of the cost function.

Finally, we are interested in the expected value of the latency difference $\Delta := |\Delta_2 - \Delta_1|$ induced by the latency investment. This quantity is relevant for the welfare and revenue guarantees of the batch auction. We have

$$E_\sigma[|\Delta|] = E_\sigma[\max\{\Delta_1, \Delta_2\}] - E_\sigma[\min\{\Delta_1, \Delta_2\}]$$

$$= \int_{\underline{\Delta}}^{\overline{\Delta}} 2\Delta\sigma'(\Delta)\sigma(\Delta)d\Delta - \int_{\underline{\Delta}}^{\overline{\Delta}} 2\Delta\sigma'(\Delta)(1 - \sigma(\Delta))d\Delta$$

$$= \int_{\underline{\Delta}}^{\overline{\Delta}} 2\Delta\sigma'(\Delta)(2\sigma(\Delta) - 1)d\Delta = \int_{\underline{\Delta}}^{\overline{\Delta}} 6\Delta C''(\Delta)(2 + 6C'(\Delta))d\Delta$$

Example 1. Consider a cost function of the form $C(\Delta) = c/\Delta$. Then $C'(\Delta) = -c/\Delta^2$ and $C''(\Delta) = 2c/\Delta^3$. We get the strategy:

$$\sigma(\Delta) = 3/2 - 3c/\Delta^2$$

for $\sqrt{2c} < \Delta < \sqrt{6c}$. Then the average latency difference is given by the expectation of the absolute value of $\Delta := \Delta_2 - \Delta_1$,

$$E[|\Delta|] \approx 0.3203 * \sqrt{c}$$

Accordingly, the average welfare gap to optimal bidding is $0.16016\sqrt{c}$ and the average revenue is $1/3 - 0.10677 * \sqrt{c}$.

2.3 Hybrid Policies: Time Boost

[6] describe a hybrid transaction ordering policy that orders transaction by time stamp of arrival at the (centralized) sequencer, but allows bidders to get a time boost by paying an additional fee. The time boost for paying a fee of F is

$$\pi = \frac{gF}{F+c},$$

with parameters g and c, and transactions are ordered by the score

$$\pi - t$$

where t is the timestamp of arrival of a bid at the sequencer and π is the time boost. The parameters have the following interpretation: Parameter g gives the maximal time boost, a user can get from bidding. In particular, transactions finalize after waiting g. Parameter c is the marginal cost per unit of time (normalized by g). The auction is all-pay: Bidders need to pay the time boost fee no matter how transactions are ordered.

Let us again consider the scenario where arb opportunities appear uniformly at random on a time interval and assume that the arb is only good for the earlier transaction. If a bidder has a lower score he will get a payout of zero, but still needs to pay.

The analysis of time boost is more complex than the previous analysis for the batch auction, since now the precise time stamps of the two bidders matter and not only whether the time stamp is before the batch cut-off or not. Thus, making the same analysis as previously, where the values and time stamps of the bidder follows some distribution is generally intractable. However, we can analyze the case where the value of the arb to the other bidder is uncertain, but the time stamps are certain.[1] This simplification is not innocent, but it is a reasonable approximation of reality when bidders interact repeatedly and can

---

[1] The other extreme case, where the value of the arb is commonly known by the bidders, but the time stamps are uncertain, is also tractable to analyse, see [7] for an analysis.

estimate the expected time stamp of the competitor with very good accuracy. For simplicity, I consider a linear approximation for the boost formula:

$$F = \frac{c\pi}{g-\pi} \approx \frac{c\pi}{g}.$$

For a reasonably large boost parameter, e.g. $g = 10$ when $c = 1$ the marginal cost $\frac{cg}{(g-\pi)^2}$ (which is relevant for deriving optimal bidding policies) is approximated very well by c/g and we can expect to get qualitatively very similar results for the true boost formula, as long as g is sufficiently large. In the following, I assume $g \geq c$. The equilibrium analysis now follows an all-pay auction with a head start for the lower latency bidder.

Proposition 3. *The equilibrium signaling strategies in time boost are*

$$\pi_1 = \begin{cases} \frac{gv_1^2}{2c} - \frac{\Delta}{2}, & \text{if } v_1 \geq \sqrt{\frac{c}{g}\Delta}, \\ 0 & \text{if } v_1 < \sqrt{\frac{c}{g}\Delta}, \end{cases}$$

and

$$\pi_2 = \begin{cases} \frac{gv_2^2}{2c} + \frac{\Delta}{2}, & \text{if } v_2 \geq \sqrt{\frac{c}{g}\Delta}, \\ 0 & \text{if } v_2 < \sqrt{\frac{c}{g}\Delta}, \end{cases}$$

Remark 4. The Arbitrum proposal considers an all-pay auction format where bids are not reverted if the other bidder obtains a higher score. While the choice of the all pay auction format is caused by technical requirements (the sequencer is agnostic about the content of the transactions and cannot in- or exclude them based on un-observable characteristics), it is still interesting to check what would happen in the Arbitrum proposal if the payment rule is a standard first price auction. By a completely analogous calculation, we obtain:

$$\pi_1 = \begin{cases} \frac{gv_1}{2c} - \frac{\Delta}{2}, & \text{if } v_1 \geq \frac{c}{g}\Delta, \\ 0 & \text{if } v_1 < \frac{c}{g}\Delta, \end{cases}$$

and

$$\pi_2 = \begin{cases} \frac{gv_2}{2c} + \frac{\Delta}{2}, & \text{if } v_2 \geq \frac{c}{g}\Delta, \\ 0 & \text{if } v_2 < \frac{c}{g}\Delta, \end{cases}$$

An immediate implication of the previous calculations is that the parameter c in the time boost formula should be selected small to increase participation and revenue. In a similar way, the maximal time boost g should be selected large. However, the latter comes with trade-offs, as finalization of bids is slower. I comment on these parameter choices and compare the performance in the next section.

2.4 Comparing Batch Auctions and Time Boost

It is instructive to compare the relative performance of the two auction formats. To make the batch auction comparable to the time boost proposal, I assume that if neither of the two bidders make it into the batch because they have too high latency, then their orders are both processed in the next batch. We can then look into the equilibrium in either model as a function of the realized difference in latency $\Delta := |\Delta_2 - \Delta_1|$ between the two bidders where Δ_i is the delay of bidder i when sending a bid to the sequencer.

First, let us look at allocative efficiency: how likely is it that the higher valuation bidder wins the race? In the batch auction this can only happen if the two bidders end in different batches and the faster bidder has the lower valuation which happens with probability $\Delta/2$. Under time boost, this can only happen, if the slower bidder refrains from bidding (which in our equilibrium happens if his valuation is below the threshold $u := \sqrt{\frac{c}{g}\Delta}$) while having a higher valuation. This leads to the following observation:

Observation 1. *Under the batch auction design, the likelihood that the high valuation bidder loses is half the latency difference $\frac{\Delta}{2}$.*

Under the time boost design, the likelihood is half the cost of compensating for the latency difference $\frac{c}{g}\frac{\Delta}{2}$.

The likelihood of the higher valuation bidder winning is higher under time boost if and only if the marginal cost of bidding is small $\frac{c}{g} \leq 1$.

Next let us look at the welfare loss relative to the first best where the item is always allocated to the higher valuation bidder: under which design is this welfare gap larger? In the first best, the surplus is the expectation of the maximum of the two valuations which is 2/3 for the i.i.d. uniform case.

Observation 2. *Under the batch auction design, the welfare gap to the optimum is $\Delta/6$.*

Under the time boost design, the welfare gap is $\frac{1}{6}(\frac{c}{g}\Delta)^{3/2}$.

The welfare gap is smaller with time boost, if and only if the marginal cost of bidding is small $\frac{c}{g} \leq 1/\sqrt[3]{\Delta}$.

Next let's look at bidding revenue for the auctioneer. The ex-ante revenue from bidding is the sum of payments received.

Observation 3. *Under the batch auction design, the revenue is $(1 - \Delta)/3$.*

Under the time boost design, the revenue is $(1 - (\frac{c}{g}\Delta)^{3/2})/3$.

The revenue is higher under time boost if and only if the marginal cost of bidding is small $\frac{c}{g} \leq 1/\sqrt[3]{\Delta}$.

For the previous comparison, note that I have normalized the size of batches to 1, whereas the g parameter, which plays a similar role as the batch size, is allowed to be larger than 1. To get an intuition what happens with variable batch size, note that if a unit time interval is subdivided into two batches while there is still one arb per unit of time, then the likelihood that the lower valuation bidder wins the race doubles. Similarly, the welfare gap grows and the revenue decreases in the number of batches. Thus, choosing larger batches has a qualitatively very similar effect as choosing a larger maximal time boost g.

3 Conclusion

The previous analysis is stylized but has immediate implications for economic design: While latency competition is much less severe for the batch auction than in a FCFS design, there are still advantages of low latency bidding. Towards the end of a batch, bidders with a faster connection can underbid relative to optimal bidding in a standard first price auction, since there is a substantial likelihood that slower competitors do not make it into the current batch. This has an adverse effect on efficiency and revenue. Moreover, the equilibrium analysis predicts that all profits of the bidders are competed away through latency investment by the bidders in the ex-ante stage before the actual bidding.

If the time boost design is implemented, special attention should be put on the choice of parameters. Choosing the marginal cost of bidding too high is detectable in equilibrium. In that case we can predict little use of time boost bidding (no bidding rather than producing low signals) and the parameters should be adjusted.

A Proof of Proposition 2

Proof. By symmetry, $\sigma(\Delta) := \sigma_1(\Delta) = \sigma_2(\Delta)$ which describes the (mixed) strategy of each bidder. Since we are in an equilibrium, it has to be the case that the profit is constant on the support of σ, i.e. for each $\Delta \in [\underline{\Delta}, \overline{\Delta}]$ we need

$$\frac{\partial}{\partial \Delta} \left(\int_\Delta^1 (\tfrac{1}{2} - \tfrac{1}{3}\sigma(\Delta))d\Delta - C(\Delta) \right) = 0 \Rightarrow -\tfrac{1}{2} + \tfrac{1}{3}\sigma(\Delta) - C'(\Delta) = 0$$

We obtain the mixed strategy:

$$\sigma(\Delta) = 3/2 + 3C'(\Delta).$$

The support of σ is obtained by setting the above formula equal to 0 resp. 1 which gives $C'(\underline{\Delta}) = -1/2$ and $C'(\overline{\Delta}) = -1/6$.

Substituting the strategy into the expression for the profit, we see that bidders make zero average profit

$$\int_{\Delta_i}^1 (\tfrac{1}{2} - \tfrac{1}{3}\sigma(\Delta))d\Delta - C(\Delta_i) = \int_{\Delta_i}^1 -C'(\Delta)d\Delta - C(\Delta_i) = C(\Delta_i) - C(\Delta_i) = 0.$$

□

B Proof of Proposition 3

Proof. First I solve the model when the bidders have the same latency and produce the same timestamp. Then this is just a standard all pay auction. Each bidder solves

$$\max_{\pi} v_i Pr_{v_j \sim F_j}[\pi \geq \pi_j(v_j)] - \tfrac{c}{g}\pi,$$

where $\pi_2(v_2)$ is bidder j's time boost bid as a function of his valuation.

Assuming differentiability of the equilibrium bidding functions, equilibrium bidding is characterized by the first order condition:

$$\frac{v_i f_j(v_i)}{\pi'_i(v_i)} - \frac{c}{g} = 0$$

Solving the differential equation obtained from the first order condition with the boundary condition $\pi_i(0) = 0$ (if the bidders are symmetric, both start bidding at the zero valuation), we get (for uniformly distributed valuations):

$$\pi(v) = \frac{gv^2}{2c}$$

In the case that there is a latency difference Δ, bidder 1 solves

$$\max_{\pi} v_1 Pr_{v_2 \sim F_2}[\pi + \Delta \geq \pi_2(v_2)] - \tfrac{c}{g}\pi = v_1 F_2[v_2(\pi + \Delta)] - \tfrac{c}{g}\pi,$$

and $v_j(\pi)$ is the inverse of π_j (assuming that we are in a separating equilibrium such that such inverse exists). Similarly bidder 2 solves

$$\max_{\pi} v_2 Pr_{v_1 \sim F_1}[\pi - \Delta \geq \pi_1(v_1)] - \tfrac{c}{g}\pi = v_2 F_1[v_1(\pi - \Delta)] - \tfrac{c}{g}\pi.$$

I use the following approach to construct an equilibrium for the asymmetric case. The equilibrium strategies are obtained by subtracting a constant term from the optimal strategy in the symmetric case for the first bidder

$$\pi_1(v) = \frac{gv_1^2}{2c} - K_1 \Leftrightarrow v_1(\pi) = \sqrt{\frac{2c(\pi + K_1)}{g}}$$

and adding a constant term for the second bidder

$$\pi_2(v) = \frac{gv_2^2}{2c} + K_2 \Leftrightarrow v_2(\pi) = \sqrt{\frac{2c(\pi - K_2)}{g}}$$

The first order condition for the first bidder is

$$v_1 v'_2(\pi + \Delta) - c/g = v_1 \sqrt{\frac{c}{2g(\pi + \Delta - K_2)}} - c/g = 0 \Rightarrow \Delta = K_1 + K_2$$

and for the second bidder is

$$v_2 v_1'(\pi - \Delta) - c/g = v_1\sqrt{\frac{c}{2g(\pi - \Delta + K_1)}} - c/g = 0 \Rightarrow \Delta = K_1 + K_2.$$

There should be a smallest threshold u such that bidders only bid if their valuation is above the threshold: $v_i \geq u$. To guarantee continuity of the expected payout at $v_1 = u$, the faster bidder should bid $\pi_1 = 0$ at $v_1 = u$ to obtain an expected payout of u^2. In that case:

$$K_1 = gu^2/(2c) \text{ and } K_2 = \Delta - gu^2/(2c)$$

To guarantee continuity of the expected payout at $v_2 = u$, the weak bidder should be indifferent between bidding and not bidding at the threshold:

$$u^2/2 - c\pi_2(u)/g = 0 \Rightarrow K_2 = gu^2/(2c) = K_1.$$

Therefore: $K_1 = K_2 = \Delta/2$ and $u = \sqrt{c\Delta/g}$. We get the equilibrium bidding strategies.

C Calculations for Sect. 2.3

C.1 Derivation of Welfare Loss (Observation 2)

Assume w.l.o.g. $\Delta_1 \leq \Delta_2$ in the following calculations. For the batch auction design we have an expected surplus of:

$$\Delta E[v_1] + (1-\Delta)E[\max\{v_1, v_2\}] = \Delta/2 + (1-\Delta)\tfrac{2}{3} = 2/3 - \Delta/6.$$

For the time boost auction we have an expected surplus of:

$$Pr[v_2 \leq u]E[v_1] + Pr[v_1 \leq u \leq v_2]E[v_2 | v_2 \geq u]$$
$$+ Pr[v_1 \geq u, v_2 \geq u]E[\max\{v_1, v_2\} | v_1 \geq u, v_2 \geq u]$$
$$= u/2 + u(1-u)\tfrac{1+u}{2} + (1-u)^2 \tfrac{u+2}{3} = 2/3 - \tfrac{u^3}{6} = 2/3 - \tfrac{1}{6}(\tfrac{c}{g}\Delta)^{3/2}$$

$\square$

C.2 Derivation of Revenue (Observation 3)

For the batch-auction design, bidders bid as in a standard first price auction if they expect the other bidder to land in the same batch, and 0 otherwise (or the minimal bid/fee if there is one). A standard first price auction has an expected revenue of $1/3$. Thus the expected revenue is $(1-\Delta)/3$. Under time boost, given the equilibrium derived previously, the expected payment for the faster bidder is

$$Pr[v_1 \geq u]E[\tfrac{v_1^2 - u^2}{2} | v_1 \geq u] = 1/6 - u^2/2 + u^3/3,$$

and that for the slower bidder is

$$Pr[v_2 \geq u]E[\tfrac{v_2^2+u^2}{2}|v_2 \geq u] = 1/6 + u^2/2 - 2u^3/3.$$

Therefore the sum of the two is

$$(1-u^3)/3 = (1-(\tfrac{c}{g}\Delta)^{3/2})/3.$$

References

1. Ferreira, M.V.X., Parkes, D.C.: Credible decentralized exchange design via verifiable sequencing rules. In: Proceedings of the 55th Annual ACM Symposium on Theory of Computing, pp. 723–736 (2023)
2. Gupta, T., Pai, M.M., Resnick, M.: The centralizing effects of private order flow on proposer-builder separation. In: Bonneau, J., Weinberg, S.M. (eds.) 5th Conference on Advances in Financial Technologies (AFT 2023). Leibniz International Proceedings in Informatics (LIPIcs), vol. 282, pp. 20:1–20:15. Schloss Dagstuhl – Leibniz-Zentrum für Informatik, Dagstuhl, Germany (2023)
3. Kavousi, A., Le, D.V., Jovanovic, P., Danezis, G.: BlindPerm: efficient MEV mitigation with an encrypted mempool and permutation. IACR Cryptology ePrint Archive, p. 1061 (2023). https://eprint.iacr.org/2023/1061
4. Kelkar, M., Deb, S., Long, S., Juels, A., Kannan, S.: Themis: fast, strong order-fairness in Byzantine consensus. Cryptology ePrint Archive (2021)
5. Kursawe, K.: Wendy, the good little fairness widget: Achieving order fairness for blockchains. In: Proceedings of the 2nd ACM Conference on Advances in Financial Technologies, pp. 25–36 (2020)
6. Mamageishvili, A., Kelkar, M., Schlegel, J.C., Felten, E.W.: Buying time: latency racing vs. bidding for transaction ordering. In: Bonneau, J., Weinberg, S.M. (eds.) 5th Conference on Advances in Financial Technologies (AFT 2023). Leibniz International Proceedings in Informatics (LIPIcs), vol. 282, pp. 23:1–23:22. Schloss Dagstuhl – Leibniz-Zentrum für Informatik, Dagstuhl, Germany (2023)
7. Mamageishvili, A., Schlegel, J.C.: Shared sequencing and latency competition as a noisy contest. arXiv preprint arXiv:2310.02390 (2023)

An Analysis of Fixed-Spread Liquidation Lending in DeFi

Ciamac Moallemi and Utkarsh Patange(✉)

Columbia Business School, New York, USA
uspatange@gmail.com

Abstract. We model and analyze fixed spread liquidation in DeFi lending as implemented by popular pooled lending protocols such as AAVE, JustLend, and Compound. Empirically, we observe that over 70% of liquidations occur in the absence of any downward price jumps. Then, considering who monitors their loan with an exponentially distributed horizon, we compute the liquidation cost incurred in closed form as a function of the monitoring frequency. We compare this cost against liquidation data obtained from AAVE protocol V2, and observe a match with our model assuming the borrowers monitor their loans 3–4 times more often than they interact with the pool. Such borrowers must balance the financing cost against the likelihood of liquidation. We compute the optimal health factor in this situation assuming a financing rate for the collateral. Empirically, we observe that borrowers are far more conservative compared to our model predictions indicating a very low financing and opportunity cost.

Keywords: DeFi · Lending · Liquidations

1 Introduction

Lending is one of core functions of finance. In traditional as well as decentralized finance, the lenders are protected from counter-party risk through over-collateralization: the practice of using an asset valued more than the lent amount as a guarantee against the loan being repaid. In this paper, we model and study collateralized lending in decentralized finance (DeFi) as it is practiced by the most popular DeFi lending platforms today. In particular, three lending platforms (AAVE, JustLend, and Compound Finance) contribute $10.76 billion in total value locked (TVL) of the $14.73 billion TVL in DeFi lending platforms as of June 8, 2023. All three platforms use a protocol similar to the one we study here.

DeFi lending is most commonly implemented through lending pools (for example, the AAVE V2 lending pool). Users deposit their cryptocurrency tokens in the pool to earn interest. These deposits are lent by the platform to other users. To borrow, a user needs to have sufficient collateral available in their account to support their debt. A user can use multiple assets as collateral against their

---

We thank anonymous reviewers for suggestions that helped improve our paper.

loan, which in turn, can also consist of multiple cryptocurrencies. A user continues to earn interest on their collateral assets even after borrowing against them. The interest rates charged by the platform, and those earned by the depositors depend on the utilization of the pool, and can change with the supply and demand of the particular cryptocurrencies. In the present work, we shall assume constant interest rates. We shall also assume that the collateral and the debt each consist of a single asset. We formalize our model and assumptions in Sect. 2.

Any collateralized lending protocol needs a mechanism to sell the collateral and repay the loan if the collateral value drops. In DeFi, this is handled by incentivizing third-party liquidators. These liquidators repay a fraction of the loan, and in return receive collateral in a larger amount. Because the liquidators receive payment from the borrower's collateral, a rational borrower always has an incentive to prevent liquidations. In particular, a rational borrower who continuously monitors their debt and collateral value would repay part of their loan if the collateral value drops to a certain threshold, possibly by using a flashloan to free up and sell some of the collateral, instead of letting the loan be liquidated and allowing liquidators to receive some of the collateral. Thus, the loan would never get liquidated if the price process is continuous, and the borrower monitors the loan continuously. However, in practice, loans do get liquidated, suggesting either that the price process has jumps or that the borrowers do not monitor their loans. In Sect. 4.3, we establish that a vast majority of liquidations occur when there was no downward jump in the price process in the preceding hour. Therefore, in this paper, we shall consider a "passive" borrower—one who is unable to monitor the state of their loan continuously—who takes out the loan but does not track the loan state until a later time.

Such a borrower can either face a high risk of liquidation, or deposit a large amount of collateral and weather the resulting opportunity cost. We consider the problem of balancing these trade-offs in Sect. 3. In Sect. 4, we use data to validate our model by comparing observed liquidation costs to model prediction, and the borrowers' health factors with our model optima. We leave all figures and tables for the Appendix.

Our goal is to use tools from quantitative finance, namely the risk neutral pricing framework of the Black-Scholes model, in order to better guide usage and design of these lending protocols. As such, throughout the paper, we assume a continuous price process.[1] In this setting, we make the following contributions:

1. We compute the cost of liquidation for a passive borrower and compute optimal quantity of the collateral that balances the cost of capital against the liquidation cost. Our results provide guidance to borrowers regarding the trade-offs between different levels of collateralization based on the volatility in the asset and the borrower's monitoring frequency and cost of capital.
2. Empirically, we observe that a vast majority of liquidations occur in time periods in which the null hypothesis of price continuity cannot be rejected.

---

[1] In practice, the smart contracts rely on price oracles that update the prices at discrete time instances. We instead assume a continuously updating oracle in addition to a continuous price process.

3. We compute the average liquidation costs borne by the borrowers for different health factors and compare with model predictions, and observe a match assuming the loans are monitored three to four times more often than the frequency at which borrowers interact with the pool.
4. We compare the health factors maintained by the borrowers with the model optima and observe that the borrowers are far more conservative compared to model predictions indicating a very low opportunity cost/financing cost for maintaining the health factors.

Related Papers. With growing interest in DeFi protocols, there have been quite a few recent papers that study DeFi lending. A large number of these papers study the inherent fragility of these protocols. [3] systematize the knowledge about lending pools and formally model user interactions with such pools. Using this model, they are able to analyze the vulnerabilities in the lending platforms. [20] study liquidations in such lending protocols from an empirical standpoint. They consider potentials to abuse the existing system and hurt the borrower, and suggest an alternative liquidation mechanism. [17] observe an inherent systemic fragility in the DeFi lending markets when there is price impact to trading. This stems from liquidators selling the collateral and thereby, moving the prices further, causing cascading liquidations of other loans. [23] also study such liquidation spirals, and recommend changes to existing liquidation protocols to prevent their harmful effects. [19] propose a new financial instrument called a "reversible call option" to mitigate liquidations, and potentially strengthen the market.

Other related papers focus on the ways attackers can take advantage of this fragility, and suggest methods to address them. [25] systematize the knowledge about attacks on DeFi protocols in general. [8] present a novel governance attack strategy that would have allowed an attacker to steal 0.5bn USD worth of collateral, and mint an unlimited supply of DAI tokens. [10] argue for redundancy in program logic to minimize severity and frequency of DeFi attacks and provide a novel algorithm to implement it for smart contracts. [6] present a framework for analyzing risk in fixed-spread lending protocols and show that the liquidation incentive, which is necessary to keep loans solvent, also acts as an incentive for the liquidators to manipulate prices and cause liquidations of loans having a health factor close to one.

Closer to this work are papers that model and analyze the design and usage of DeFi lending platforms. [12] evaluate the economic security of the Compound protocol. [9] empirically examine the data on interest rates, lending pool utilization, and conduct a liquidity study of the markets for DAI, ETH and USDC across AAVE, Compound and dYdX. [2] formally analyze lending pools using a statistical analyzer and show how such an analysis can be used to find threshold and reward parameters that reduce the risk of unrecoverable loans. [21] investigate how the Compound protocol is used by its users, and identify systemic risk arising from such usage. [24] develop an evaluation model for DeFi lending protocols that can be used by participants to decide which protocol to use.

There are also papers that use lending protocols as a tool to design other applications, and analyze them. [13] study non-custodial stablecoins that arise from lending markets, and suggest design improvements for their long-term stability. [14] develop a stochastic model to study such non-custodial stablecoins. [5] suggest allowing liquidity provider (LP) shares on constant function market makers to be borrowed to improve capital efficiency for LPs.

2 Model

A DeFi loan is a contract between a borrower and a lender. Under the contract, the borrower, at time $t = 0$, borrows V_0 units of currency $\mathcal{C}$ (numéraire) against N_0 units of asset (collateral) $\mathcal{B}$. Both the borrowed amount and the collateral accrue interest with time at constant rates γ_V and γ_C respectively. At time t, the loan amount V_t and the collateral amount N_t evolve so that $dV_t = V_t \gamma_V \, dt$, $dN_t = N_t \gamma_C \, dt$. Note here that both the loan and the collateral accrue interest. The lending platform is able to pay this interest to the depositors because it rehypothecates the collateral as a loan to other borrowers. The borrow rate and deposit rate (sometimes known as the "supply" rate) are determined by the supply and demand of the respective assets, and are important tools the platform employs to balance supply and demand of each asset. The risks a platform faces due to this practice is out of the scope of this paper.

Let the spot price of the collateral $\mathcal{B}$ be p_t. We assume p_t evolves as per the Black-Scholes model. The price process evolves stochastically and has continuous sample paths. Specifically, consider a filtered probability space $\left(\Omega, \mathcal{F}, (\mathcal{F}_t)_{t \geq 0}, \mathbb{Q}\right)$ satisfying the usual conditions. We assume the price of the collateral, p_t, to be an Itô process on this space given by a geometric Brownian motion, i.e., $dp_t = \mu p_t \, dt + \sigma p_t \, dB_t$, where B_t is the standard Brownian motion, μ is the expected rate of return and σ is the return volatility. We also assume that $\mathbb{Q}$ is a risk-neutral measure. In other words, $\mu = r$, the risk-free rate.

The total value of the collateral in the loan at time t is given by $N_t p_t$. While the loan is unpaid, the borrower does not have access to their collateral, and so as long as $V_t < N_t p_t$, the borrower has an incentive to pay back the loan and free up the collateral since the value of the collateral exceeds the value of the loan. Let T be the first time at the borrower observes the loan after its origination. We call T the monitoring horizon. The idea is that when the loan is originated, the borrower must decide the level of collateralization, and is unable to adjust the collateral over the interval $(0, T)$. At time T, the borrower again observes the state of the market and the state of the loan, and can revisit this decision.

The lender is exposed to the market risk of the collateral. As is common with collateralized loans, this is addressed by over collateralization. This is implemented by defining a borrowing capacity, c_t, for the borrower given by $c_t := N_t p_t \ell$, where $\ell \in (0, 1)$ is known as the liquidation threshold. Similar to loans in traditional finance, the lender can conclude that the borrower has defaulted once $c_t < V_t$ and liquidate the collateral. Having a borrowing capacity less than the value of the collateral, thus, gives the lender some respite from the market risk associated with the collateral. The assets used in DeFi, however, are much more volatile than those in traditional finance and thus further safeguards are desirable.

These safeguards are implemented by paying a third party, known as a liquidator, to liquidate some fraction of the loan once $c_t < V_t$. The ratio $h_t := c_t/V_t$ is called the *health factor*, and the loan is said to be unhealthy if $h_t < 1$. The liquidators are paid in the collateral, and thus assume the market risk. To prevent the borrower from losing too much of their collateral, the fraction of the loan a liquidator can liquidate is bounded above by $F \in (0,1)$, known as the *close factor*. Formally, the loan evolves as per the following steps:

1. The borrower starts the loan knowing contract parameters ℓ, F, λ, and the interest rates γ_C, γ_V.
2. At time t, if $c_t < V_t$, a liquidator is allowed to liquidate the unhealthy loan as follows:
   (a) The liquidator decides on a fraction $f \in (0, F)$ to liquidate, and pays $V_t f$ to the lender. The contract pays back the same value in collateral priced at $p_t/(1+\lambda)$. The fraction f is said to be the "factor of liquidation". If $f = F$, we say that it is a "close-factor liquidation".
   (b) The loan now has debt $V_{t+dt} = V_t(1-f)$ and collateral $\tilde{N}_{t+dt} = N_t - V_t f(1+\lambda)/p_t$.

Note that the liquidator receives amount $V_t f(1+\lambda)/p_t$ in collateral, and earns a profit of $\lambda V_t f$ if it can be sold at price p_t. This mechanism is thus referred to as *fixed spread liquidation*, λ being called the "liquidation spread". Collectively, we call F, ℓ, and λ as the contract parameters.

In the rest of the paper, we find it convenient to work with the health factor h_t, instead of working with the price. In particular, applying Itô's lemma, we can see that $\log(h_t)$ satisfies the stochastic differential equation $d\log(h_t) = \tilde{\mu}\,dt + \sigma\,dB_t$, where $\tilde{\mu} := r + \gamma_C - \gamma_V - \sigma^2/2$. In other words, $h_t = h_0 \exp(\sigma B_t + \tilde{\mu} t)$. Note that we assume that the liquidator can buy or sell arbitrary quantities of the asset without moving the price.

3 Cost of Liquidation

We assume the following condition is satisfied by the contract parameters.

Assumption 1 (Collateral Sufficiency). $\ell(1+\lambda) < 1$.

We observe in Appendix A that this condition implies full recovery of the loan.

Let $\tau_1 := \inf\{t > 0 : h_t \leq 1\}$, denote the stopping time when the loan becomes available for liquidation. As discussed previously, because of sample path continuity, we have $h_{\tau_1} = 1$. At time τ_1, the liquidator removes collateral worth $\lambda V_{\tau_1} F$ by performing a close-factor liquidation. The loan then continues with debt amount $V_{\tau_1}(1-F)$ and health factor $\tilde{H}(1,F)$. This new loan is subject to the same liquidation risk and we can thus use a recursive formulation to compute the total cost of liquidation of the original loan. To make the calculations tractable, we shall assume that the monitoring horizon is exponentially distributed with rate ν. Due to the memoryless property of the exponential distribution, the cost of further liquidations is independent of the time passed. We can thus write the expected present value of the cost of liquidation as follows:

$$p_q(V,h)$$
$$= \mathbb{E}_\mathbb{Q} \left[e^{-r\tau_1} \left(\lambda V e^{\gamma_V \tau_1} F + p_q \left(e^{\gamma_V \tau_1} V(1-F), \tilde{H}(1,F) \right) \right) \mathbb{1}(\tau_1 \leq T) \mid h_0 = h \right], \tag{1}$$

where, $\tilde{H}(1,F)$ is the health factor immediately after liquidation, given by Eq. (4). Before we can compute the above, we need some assumptions on the rate ν. In particular, we observe that, if there is no liquidation, the expected value of the debt amount after the monitoring horizon is given by

$$\mathbb{E}\left[e^{\gamma_V T} V\right] = \begin{cases} \frac{\nu}{\nu - \gamma_V}, & \nu - \gamma_V > 0 \\ \infty, & \nu - \gamma_V \leq 0. \end{cases}$$

To avoid the debt amount (similarly the collateral) diverging to infinity, we shall make the following assumptions about the monitoring frequency ν.

Assumption 2. $\nu > \gamma_V, \nu > \gamma_C$.

In practice (cf. Table 1), we find that extreme parameter values are required for Assumption 2 to be violated. Consider the following example.

Example 1. Let $\gamma_V = 30.0\%, \gamma_C = 25.0\%$ be the annualized interest rates. Then we need $\nu < 0.3$ for Assumption 2 to be violated. This is equivalent to the average monitoring horizon being over 3 years.

Note that the interest rates γ_V, γ_C in Example 1 are unusually high, making the divergence possible, and even then only when the monitoring horizon is very large in expectation as well. We can now prove the following theorem.

Theorem 1. *If monitoring horizon T is distributed exponentially with parameter ν that satisfies Assumption 2, then the borrower's expected discounted liquidation cost up to time T is given by*

$$p_q(V,h) = \lambda V F h^{-\kappa} \left(1 - \frac{1-F}{\tilde{H}(1,F)^\kappa} \right)^{-1},$$

where,

$$\kappa := \left(\sqrt{\tilde{\mu}^2 + 2\sigma^2(\nu + r - \gamma_V)} + \tilde{\mu} \right) / \sigma^2.$$

For convenience, we define $\pi(h) := p_q(V,h)/V$, to be the normalized expected discounted liquidation cost. Table 1 lists the values of contract parameters in various popular lending pools. As mentioned earlier, we observe that $r > \gamma_V > \gamma_C$ in all lending pools, except for Compound III. Thus, Assumption 2 is satisfied for any $\nu > 0$ in these pools. Example 1 shows that ν needs to be unrealistically

Table 1. Values of contract parameters in leading lending platforms on Ethereum Mainnet assuming a loan of USDC against collateral of WETH. All rates are annualized, and all values are current as of Nov 30, 2023. Compound III does not pay any interest on the deposit being used as collateral.

Parameter	Aave V2	Aave V3	Compound III	JustLend
Liquidation threshold (ℓ)	86%	83%	93%	75%
Liquidation spread (λ)	4.5%	5%	3%	8%
Close factor (F)	50%	50%	100%	50%
Deposit rate (γ_C)	1.03%	1.84%	0.0%	0.72%
Borrow rate (γ_V)	5.06%	13.58%	2.86%	3.80%

small for it to be violated with Compound III parameters. We discuss the cost function in further detail in Sect. 4.1. We now consider a control problem where the borrower decides on an initial health factor for the loan. It costs the borrower αh to get a loan with health factor h per unit debt, for some $\alpha > 0$. Here, α determines the financing cost the borrower faces. The borrower aims to minimize the total cost along with the expected payment to the liquidator. In other words, the borrower faces the optimization problem of minimizing $C(h) := \alpha h + \pi(h)$ for $h \geq 1$. We can prove the following theorem.

Theorem 2. *Under the assumptions of Theorem 1, the optimal health factor is*

$$h^* = \max\left\{1, \left(\kappa \lambda F \alpha^{-1} / \left(1 - \frac{1-F}{\tilde{H}(1,F)^\kappa}\right)\right)^{\frac{1}{1+\kappa}}\right\}. \qquad (2)$$

We discuss the optimal health factor in further detail in Sect. 4.1.

4 Empirical Analysis

4.1 Comparative Statics

Cost Function. First, we consider the liquidation cost function $\pi(h) = p_q(V,h)/V$. It is instructive to write $\pi(h)$ as an infinite sum.

$$\pi(h) = \frac{\lambda F}{h^\kappa}\left(1 + \frac{1-F}{\tilde{H}(1,F)^\kappa} + \frac{(1-F)^2}{\tilde{H}(1,F)^{2\kappa}} + \ldots\right). \qquad (3)$$

Here, nth term in the sum can be interpreted as the expected cost from the nth liquidation. We can see that the cost decreases as κ increases. We would like to see how the cost changes with the horizon rate ν, and the volatility σ. Clearly, κ increases with ν. After some algebra, we can also see that, as long as $\nu + r - \gamma_V > 0$ as guaranteed by Assumption 2, κ decreases with σ. We now fix the contract parameters to their real world values. We use AAVE V2 lending pool to get our contract parameters because as of this writing, it is the lending pool with the highest TVL. For the risk-free rate, we use the 1 month yield curve rate published by US Treasury, which as of this writing is 5.56%. Fixing these parameters, we plot the normalized liquidation cost function, $\pi(h)$ against h for

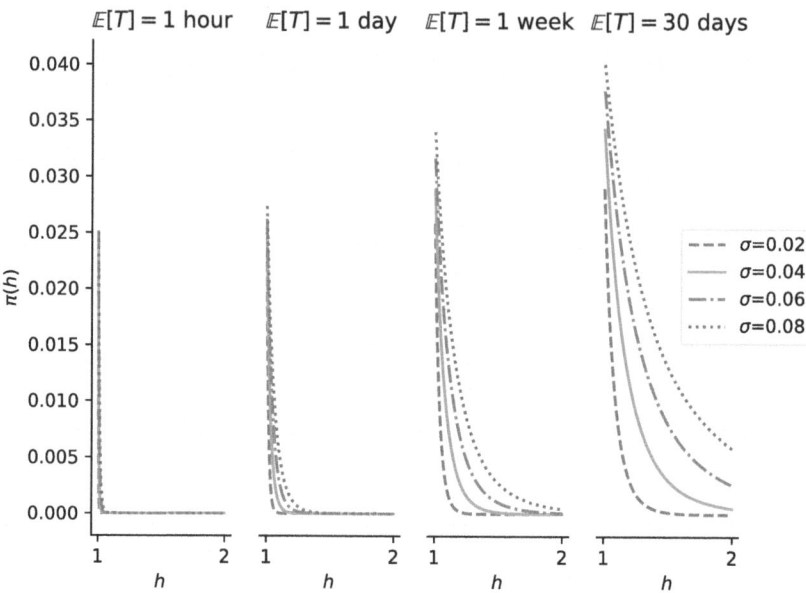

Fig. 1. Normalized expected discounted cost of liquidation against initial health factor for different values of volatility σ (daily) and expected horizon length.

different values of σ and $\mathbb{E}[T] = 1/\nu$ in Fig. 1. Here, both T and σ are in daily units. The figure shows that $\pi(h) = p_q(V, h)/V$ is a decreasing function of h, which is to be expected since it increases the likelihood of the first liquidation. We see that as volatility increases, the risk of liquidation increases, and hence so does the liquidation cost when everything else is held fixed. We also see that the cost decreases as expected horizon length decreases, and the borrower pays back the loan in a shorter length of time in expectation. Furthermore, as the expected horizon length decreases (ν increases), the curves for different σ come closer indicating that the effect of volatility on the expected cost of liquidation decreases as the horizon becomes shorter in expectation.

Optimal Health Factor. Now, we would also like to know how h^* changes with $\mathbb{E}[T]$, σ, and other variables of interest. To that end, we fix all parameters from Table 1 and vary the expected length of monitoring horizon, the liquidation spread, and the financing rate in Figs. 2, 3a, and 3b respectively for different values of σ. For all figures, the default financing rate is assumed to be the same as the risk-free rate, and the default expected monitoring horizon is assumed to be 1 day. Based on the financing rate, we set

$$\alpha = \frac{r'}{\ell(\nu - r')},$$

so that αh represents the expected cost of capital borne by the borrower in the monitoring horizon. Here r' is the financing rate. This is because getting a loan of V_0 amount and obtaining a health factor h requires one to deposit total collateral worth $N_0 b_0 = hV_0/\ell$. The cost of financing this amount of collateral with rate r' is given by,

$$\mathbb{E}\left[e^{r'T}\frac{hV_0}{\ell} - \frac{hV_0}{\ell}\right] = \frac{r'hV_0}{\ell(\nu - r')}.$$

Note that we assume $r' < \nu$ since otherwise, the cost of capital would diverge to ∞.

We see from Fig. 2 that the borrower needs to start with a larger initial health factor if the asset is more volatile or if the monitoring horizon is longer. This is because in both cases the loan is more likely to get liquidated. We also observe that the rate of increase in the optimal health factor is larger when the asset has a larger volatility.

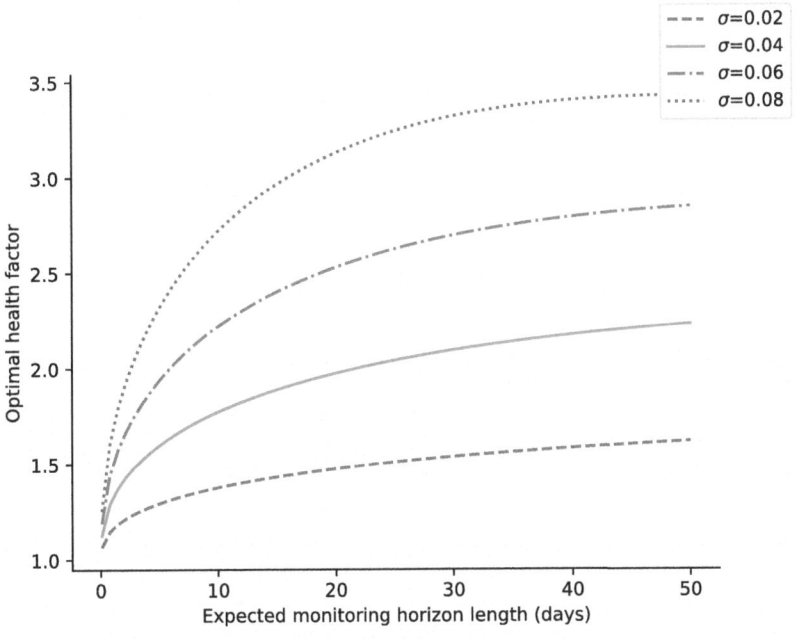

Fig. 2. h^* vs $\mathbb{E}[T]$

Figure 3a shows that the optimal health factor increases with the liquidation spread, and that this increase is steeper for a more volatile asset. This is because the borrower loses more in each liquidation when the spread is large, and the probability of such a liquidation increases with σ.

Figure 3b shows that the optimal health factor decreases with the financing rate since it costs more to obtain the necessary capital to get a loan with any given health factor. This decline is also steeper for riskier assets. This is because the optimal health factor of a riskier asset is larger than that of a less risky asset

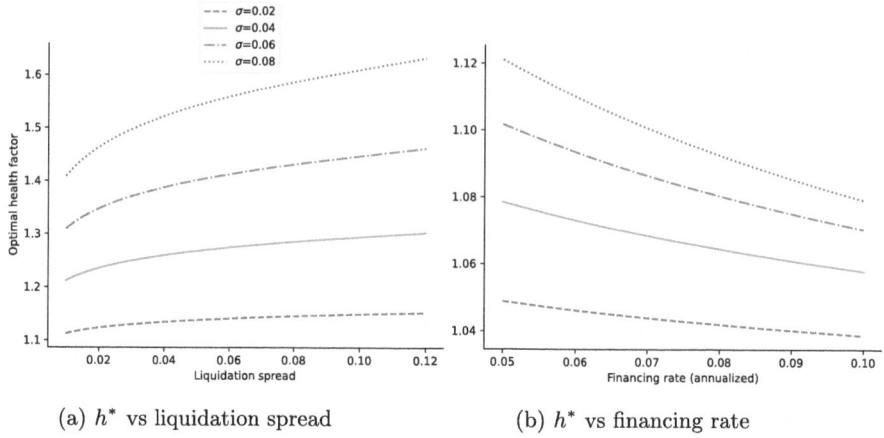

(a) h^* vs liquidation spread (b) h^* vs financing rate

Fig. 3. h^* vs liquidation threshold and financing rate.

to begin with, and so the incremental cost due to rising financing rate is higher for a risky asset held in a loan at an optimal health factor.

4.2 Data

We get lending data from AAVE V2 lending pool on Ethereum Mainnet [1], risk free interest rates from US treasury daily par yield curve rates for 1 month maturity [22], and minutely prices from Binance Public Data [4]. All data spans from March 15, 2021 through Jan 31, 2024.

From the lending pool, we fetch all deposit, borrow, repay and withdraw events, and filter them so that only users that have borrowed USDC against a collateral of WETH remain. For each event, we ensure that this condition is satisfied for two consecutive blocks: the block in which the event occurred (current block), and the immediately preceding block (prior block). For these two blocks, we get user health factors. We also get user's debt, collateral amount, borrow rates, and the pool's liquidation threshold and liquidation spread for the current block. We further filter this data to remove rows with a debt less than 100 USDC, or a health factor less than 1. We call this the health-factors table. This table has 28,876 rows.

For all the users in the health-factors table, we separately fetch all their interactions with the pool. These may include setting or unsetting one of their deposits as collateral for their loan, borrowing or depositing currencies other than USDC or WETH, etc. We use this data to figure out the lifetime of a loan and the average time elapsed between user interactions with the lending pool when a particular loan was active. Lifetime of a loan is defined to be from the first block with a non-zero debt to the last block with a non-zero debt. We assign each distinct loan a unique loan id. We call this the user-interactions table. We then join this table with the health factors table by figuring out the loan id from the block number of the current block, so that each row in the health factor table has the loan id, as well as the average intervention time.

From Binance, we get the minutely candles of WETH-USDC prices. Unfortunately, these prices are not available for the entire period as of this writing. Notably, they are missing for the period between September 29, 2022 through March 12, 2023. We use WETH-USDT prices as a proxy for this period. We verify that for the period where both prices are available, the difference between the two is always less than 10%, and is less than 0.2% in 95% of the times. We resample this data to a 15 min frequency and compute daily volatility for each calendar day, and use it to compute expected liquidation costs and the optimal health factors on that day.

From US Treasury, we get the daily par yield curve rates for 1 month maturity. We use this rate as the risk free rate on that day. These rates are not published on weekends. We use the most recent available rates as proxy for the rates on days on which they are unavailable.

We also get liquidation data from the lending pool. This consists of all loans that covered a USDC debt by grabbing a WETH collateral. For each liquidation, we get the debt liquidated, and the block number. This liquidation table has 1,213 rows. We use this table to compute the liquidation costs between user interactions in the following way: for each user interaction in the user-interaction table, we discount and add up the liquidated amount until the next interaction on that same loan. For discounting, we use the risk-free rate at the interaction time. For interactions that are common between the user-interaction and health-factor tables, we get the liquidated debt. We multiply this by the liquidation spread and divide by the debt in the current block to get the empirical liquidation cost function $\hat{\pi}(h)$.

To summarize, we have the following tables:

1. `health-factors`: Containing health factors immediately before and after a deposit/withdraw/borrow/repay event. Also contains borrow and deposit interest rates, debt and collateral amounts, liquidation cost and loan id.
2. `prices`: Contains WETH-USDC prices at 15 min intervals. Also contains daily return volatility.
3. `liquidations`: For each liquidation event, contains the amount of debt repaid.
4. `user-interactions`: Each lending pool transaction for each user in health-factors table.
5. `interest-rates`: daily risk-free rates.

4.3 Why Do Liquidations Occur?

A rational borrower who observes that their loan is close to being liquidated would never allow such a liquidation. They could instead get a flashloan, repay part of their debt, free up and sell some collateral, and repay the flash-loan. Since we observe liquidations, one of two things must be happening:

1. The price process has downward "jumps", leading to liquidations.
2. Users do not monitor their loans at all times.

In this section, we validate our hypothesis that the majority of liquidations occur due to users not monitoring their loans. To do this, we construct a hypothesis test to detect jumps in the price process. First, we resample our price process to a period Δt. Let the price at hour t be p_t. We have for each t:

H0: There is no jump from $t - \Delta t$ to t.
H1: There is a jump from $t - \Delta t$ to t.

To conduct this test, we need an estimate of the volatility at time $t - \Delta t$, and we use returns from n preceding periods to compute it. This methodology is described by [16]. Specifically, we compute the returns $r_t = \log(p_t/p_{t-1})$, and the realized bipower variation in the past twenty periods. We obtain a square root and scale it by $\sqrt{\pi/2}$ to get an estimate of volatility $\sigma_{t-1}^{(j)}$ that is robust to jumps. Formally,

$$\sigma_{t-1}^{(j)} = \sqrt{\frac{\pi}{18 \cdot 2} \sum_{i=1}^{18} |r_{t-i} r_{t-i-1}|}$$

We then compute the t-statistic $s_t = r_t/\sigma_{t-1}^{(j)}$. If $|s_t| > 1.96$, we refute the null hypothesis at a 95% confidence level. If $s_t > 1.96$, we say that there was an upward jump, and if $s_t < -1.96$, we say that there was a downward jump at time t.

Thus, we identify the specific hours in which downward jumps occur. For each liquidation in the `liquidations` table, we check whether it occurred in an hour with a downward jump. That is, if the liquidation happened at time $t^{(l)}$, we find i such that $t_i < t^{(l)} \leq t_{i+1}$, and check if there was a downward jump at hour t_{i+1}. Table 2 summarizes the results that show a vast majority of liquidations occurring in time periods without any downward jumps.

Table 2. The fraction of liquidations occurring in periods without downward jumps computed for different period lengths, and different window sizes.

Δt	$n = 20$	$n = 30$	$n = 40$	$n = 50$	$n = 60$
30 min	0.81	0.81	0.82	0.81	0.79
1 h	0.78	0.77	0.79	0.79	0.79
2 h	0.77	0.76	0.77	0.76	0.79
12 h	0.69	0.71	0.71	0.70	0.70
1 day	0.72	0.73	0.75	0.75	0.75

4.4 Empirical Liquidation Cost

Now, we compute the empirical liquidation cost and compare it with our closed form. To get the expected liquidation cost for a loan k at time t using our closed form, we need the following parameters: $h = h^{(k,t)}, F = F^{(t)}, \ell = \ell^{(t)}, \lambda =$

$\lambda^{(t)}, \gamma_C = \gamma_C^{(k,t)}, \gamma_V = \gamma_V^{(k,t)}, r = r^{(t)}, \sigma = \sigma^{(t)}, \nu = \nu^{(k)}$. All of these except for $\nu^{(k)}$ can be found from the health-factors and the prices tables. Unfortunately, there is no way for us to determine the average monitoring frequency ν for a user. Instead, we use the average interaction frequency $\hat{\nu}$, which is a lower bound on ν. Assuming that users monitor more frequently than $\hat{\nu}$, we expect to overestimate the liquidation costs when we use the closed form to compute them.

To compute the empirical liquidation costs, we divide the health-factors table into twenty bins, so that each bin contains an equal number of rows. We then compute an average liquidation cost, as well as the average of the expected liquidation cost for each bin. Figure 4 shows the plot of these two costs against the centers of the health factor bins. As we can see, the liquidation cost is indeed overestimated due to our usage of $\hat{\nu}$ instead of ν. However, if we assume that the monitoring frequency is three or four times the intervention frequency, then the two costs match in most bins. Note that to compute this, we discarded the few ($< 5\%$) cases where the liquidation took place at a health factor less than one. We also discarded the last two health factor bins since they did not have any liquidations. We note a mismatch in the very first bin, and Fig. 5, which shows the medians of intervention intervals for the same health factor bins, explains the reason: The intervention interval in the first bin is small (=0.25 days), indicating a monitoring frequency of 12–16 times a day. The fact that oracle updates are hourly can not be ignored when computing the liquidation cost for this bin, and this is the reason our model overestimates the cost.

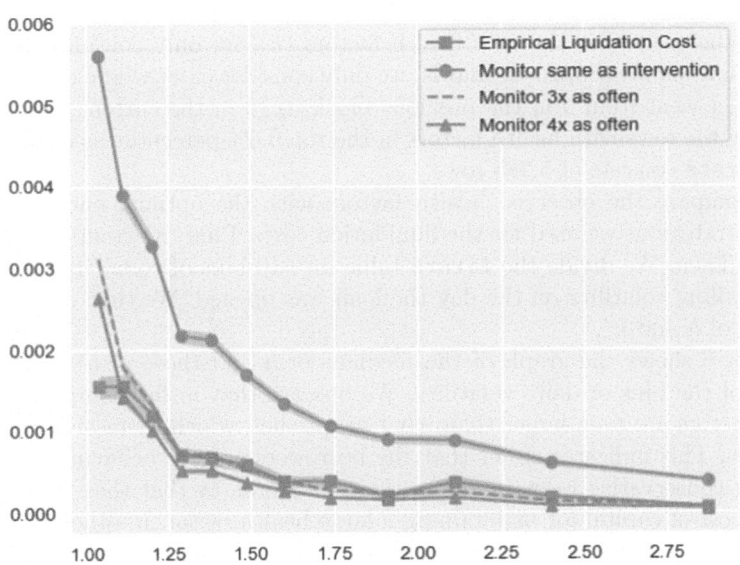

Fig. 4. The empirical and expected liquidation cost versus health factor.

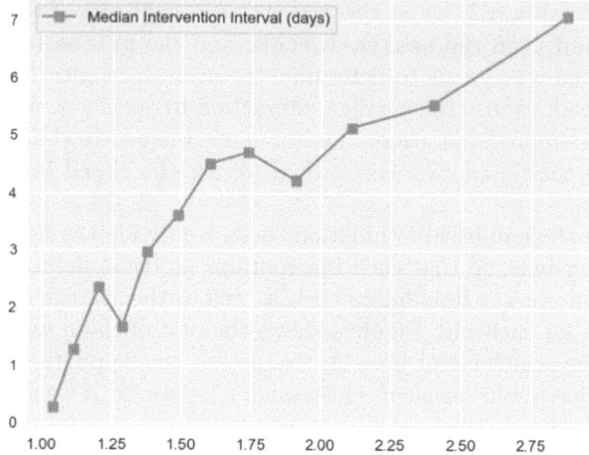

Fig. 5. Medians of intervention intervals in each health factor bin.

4.5 Observed Health Factors

We now turn to our empirical findings. As before, we use the intervention frequency $\hat{\nu}$ in lieu of the monitoring frequency ν. We therefore expect to overestimate the optimal health factors. Let our estimates be $\hat{h}^*$. Another parameter we need is the financing rate. We use the borrow rate for the collateral (WETH) as the financing rate r'. We are interested in knowing how $\hat{h}^*$ compare with those held by the users. For the user health factors ($\hat{h}$), we only consider the times when a new loan was opened, that is, we only consider cases where debt amount of the user went from 0 in the previous block to ¿0 in the current block. After removing the rows with health factors in the top 0.5% percentile as outliers, this table firsts consists of 5,285 rows.

To compare the observed health factors with the optimal ones, we use a similar strategy as we used for the liquidation costs. First, we compute $\hat{h}^*$ using Eq. (2). Then, We divide the firsts table into 10 bins of equal sizes based on the prevailing volatility on the day the loan was opened. We then compute the medians of $\hat{h}$ and $\hat{h}^*$.

Figure 6 shows the graph of the medians of $\hat{h}$ and those of $\hat{h}^*$ against the centers of the bins of daily volatility. We observe that in fact, empirically, the health factors are even larger than what we predict, which themselves are overestimates. This indicates either that the borrowers are not behaving optimally, by being conservative in maintaining their collateral, or that they face a much smaller cost of capital for maintaining a large health factor. In other words, the parameter α in the optimization problem is small compared to the liquidation costs. We can compute the implied α from observed health factors. Figure 7 shows the histogram of this implied α in log scale after removing the bottom 5% percentiles. From this, α indeed appears to be very small compared to liquidation costs.

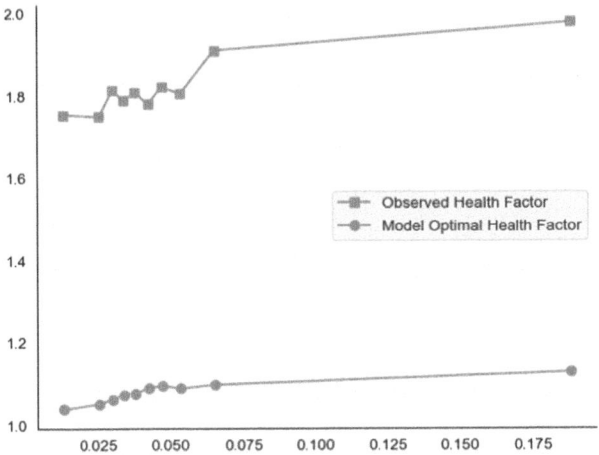

Fig. 6. Medians of Empirical and Optimal health factors versus volatility

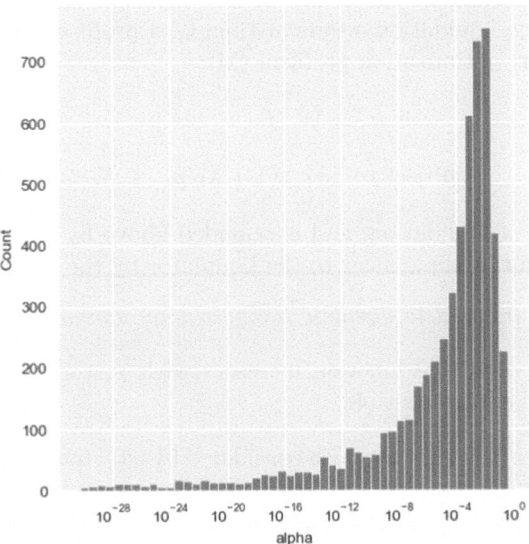

Fig. 7. Histogram of implied α, the weight given to the cost of capital.

At first glance, it appears that even though $\hat{h} > \hat{h}^*$, they both follow a similar trend. We formalize this by doing a regression analysis. We regress $\hat{h}$ against $\hat{h}^*$. Formally, we estimate the model $\hat{h} = \beta_1 \hat{h}^*$. On performing OLS regression, we get $\beta_1 = 2.221$. The standard error and the t-value in the coefficient is 0.031 and 72.379 respectively. This indicates a trend of users increasing their health factors in response to market conditions.

A Contract Parameters and Lender Recovery

First, we establish what effect a liquidation has on the health of a loan. Clearly, it would be desirable to the borrower and the lender that the loan becomes healthier after liquidation. Lemma 1 establishes such a condition. We note that this condition was also observed by [20] and [23].

Lemma 1. *If $h_t > \ell(1+\lambda)$, then the health factor improves upon any liquidation.*

Proof. Let $\tilde{H}(h_t, f)$ denote the post-liquidation health factor when a loan having a health factor $h_t \leq 1$ is liquidated at factor f. We have,

$$\tilde{H}(h_t, f) := \frac{p_t \ell}{V_t(1-f)} \left(N_t - \frac{fV_t(1+\lambda)}{p_t} \right) = \frac{h_t - f(1+\lambda)\ell}{1-f}. \quad (4)$$

Then, we have,

$$\tilde{H}(h_t, f) > h_t \iff h_t > \ell(1+\lambda).$$

Let us now consider liquidator incentives and establish their optimal behavior. Assuming that the liquidation occurs at time t_0, a profit-maximizing liquidator faces the following optimization problem (M):

$$\max_{0 \leq f \leq F} \lambda V_{t_0} f \quad (5)$$

$$\text{subject to} \quad V_{t_0} f(1+\lambda)/p_{t_0} \leq N_{t_0}. \quad (6)$$

Here, f is factor of liquidation, and is bounded above by the close factor. The constraint (6) limits the payment to the liquidator by the available collateral.

Lemma 2. *It is optimal to liquidate the maximum amount possible.*

Proof. Since the objective function increases with f, the profit is maximized when f is set as large as possible.

Optimal liquidator behavior was also considered by [20], but their setting allowed for jumps in the price process, and thus health factors could become strictly less than 1 at the time of liquidation. Consequently, their setting allowed for multiple successive liquidations on the same loan, which would not be possible here.

We now assume that there are a large number of liquidators competing to liquidate unhealthy loans. Due to Lemma 2, this means that an unhealthy loan gets liquidated as soon as its health factor drops to 1. We are now ready to prove that whenever the "collateral sufficiency" condition (Assumption 1) is satisfied, the lender is able to recover the loan.

Theorem 3. *If the collateral sufficiency condition is satisfied, then*

1. *$h_t \geq 1$ for all t.*
2. *Lender never loses any money, and*
3. *Each liquidation takes place at the close factor.*

Proof. For part 1, it suffices to prove that each time there is a liquidation, the health factor becomes larger than 1. To that end, suppose that the first liquidation takes place at time t. Then, $\ell(1+\lambda) < 1 = h_t$, and hence by Lemma 1, the post-liquidation health factor is greater than 1. Combined with the fact that the initial health-factor is greater than 1, the liquidators have an incentive to liquidate, and that the prices are continuous, we get the result.

For part 2, we note that as long as $N_t p_t > V_t$, the borrower has no endogenous incentive to default. This is equivalent to the condition that $h_t > \ell$. Since $\ell < 1$, it is always satisfied due to part 1.

For part 3, we note that constraint (6) is redundant due to our assumption, i.e., it is satisfied by any $f \in [0, F]$. To see this, we observe that

$$\frac{N_{t_0} p_{t_0}}{V_{t_0}(1+\lambda)} = \frac{h_{t_0}}{\ell(1+\lambda)},$$

$$= \frac{1}{\ell(1+\lambda)}, \qquad (h_{t_0} = h_{\tau_1} = 1)$$

$$\geq 1. \qquad \text{(due to the assumption.)}$$

Thus, constraint (6) is satisfied by any $f \leq F \leq 1$. The maximum allowable factor of liquidation as prescribed by Lemma 2 then must be the close factor.

B Proof of Theorem 1

Proof. First, we note by a sample path argument that $p_q(\alpha V, h) = \alpha p_q(V, h)$ for $\alpha \geq 0$. This is because, in any sample path, keeping h constant, multiplying V by α results in each payoff to the liquidator being multiplied by α. Thus, we can rewrite Eq. (1) as

$$p_q(V, h) = (1 - F) p_q(V, \tilde{H}(1, F)) E_1(h) + \lambda V F E_1(h),$$

where,

$$E_1(h) = \mathbb{E}_\mathbb{Q} \left[e^{(\gamma_V - r)\tau_1} \mathbb{1}(\tau_1 \leq T) \mid h_0 = h \right].$$

We observe that,

$$E_1(h) = \mathbb{E}_\mathbb{Q} \left[e^{(\gamma_V - r - \nu)\tau_1} \mathbb{1}(\tau_1 < \infty) \mid h_0 = h \right],$$

by conditioning the expectation on τ_1 and applying tower law. Define

$$X_t(h) := \frac{\log(h_0) - \log(h_t)}{\sigma}, \qquad (7)$$

$$= (-B_t) + \left(-\frac{\tilde{\mu}}{\sigma}\right) t,$$

$$\stackrel{d}{=} B_t + ct,$$

where $c := -\frac{\tilde{\mu}}{\sigma}$, and consider again the expression,

$$E_1(h) = \mathbb{E}_\mathbb{Q}\left[e^{(\gamma_V - r - \nu)\tau_1}\mathbb{1}(\tau_1 < \infty) \mid h_0 = h\right].$$

We can redefine τ_1 to be the first hitting time of the drifted Brownian motion to the level $a := \frac{\log(h_0)}{\sigma} > 0$. By Girsanov Theorem, the process X_t is a standard Brownian motion on $0 \leq t \leq \tau_1$ under measure $\tilde{\mathbb{Q}}$, where

$$\frac{d\tilde{\mathbb{Q}}}{d\mathbb{Q}} = \exp\left(-cB_{\tau_1} - c^2\tau_1/2\right).$$

Denoting by $\mathbb{E}_{\tilde{Q}}$ the expectation with respect to measure $\tilde{\mathbb{Q}}$, we can write,

$$E_1(h) = \mathbb{E}_{\tilde{Q}}\left[\exp\left(B_{\tau'_a}c + \frac{c^2}{2}\tau'_a + (\gamma_V - r - \nu)\tau'_a\right)\mathbb{1}(\tau'_a < \infty) \mid h_0 = h\right]$$

$$= \mathbb{E}_{\tilde{Q}}\left[\exp\left(X_{\tau'_a}c - \frac{c^2}{2}\tau'_a + (\gamma_V - r - \nu)\tau'_a\right)\mathbb{1}(\tau'_a < \infty) \mid h_0 = h\right]$$

$$= e^{ac}\mathbb{E}_{\tilde{Q}}\left[\exp\left(\left(-\frac{c^2}{2} + \gamma_V - r - \nu\right)\tau'_a\right)\mathbb{1}(\tau'_a < \infty) \mid h_0 = h\right],$$

where τ'_a is the hitting time of a standard Brownian motion (X_t under measure $\tilde{\mathbb{Q}}$) to the level $a > 0$. Since τ'_a is not integrable, and finite with probability 1, $E_1(h)$ is infinite whenever,

$$-\frac{c^2}{2} + \gamma_V - r - \nu > 0$$
$$\iff \tilde{\mu}^2 + 2\sigma^2(\nu + r - \gamma_V) < 0.$$

Note that due to Assumption 2, we have

$$\tilde{\mu}^2 + 2\sigma^2(\nu + r - \gamma_V) > 0.$$

Now, we can use the fact that,

$$M_t = \exp\left(\eta X_t - \eta^2 t/2\right),$$

is a Martingale for $\eta \in \mathbb{R}$ with respect to $(\mathcal{F}_t)_{t \geq 0}$ under the measure $\tilde{\mathbb{Q}}$ to prove that,

$$\mathbb{E}_{\tilde{Q}}\left[\exp\left(-\frac{\eta^2}{2}\tau'_a\right)\right] = \exp\left(-|\eta|a\right). \tag{8}$$

Then, we get that,

$$E_1(h) = e^{ac}e^{-a\sqrt{c^2 + 2(\nu + r - \gamma_V)}}$$
$$= h^{-\kappa}.$$

To summarize, we have

$$E_1(h) = \begin{cases} h^{-\kappa}, & (\tilde{\mu}+\sigma^2)^2 + 2\sigma^2(\nu-\gamma_C) \geq 0, \\ \infty, & (\tilde{\mu}+\sigma^2)^2 + 2\sigma^2(\nu-\gamma_C) < 0. \end{cases} \quad (9)$$

Finally, we have

$$p_q(V,h) = h^{-\kappa}\left(\lambda V F + (1-F)p_q(V,\tilde{H}(1,F))\right),$$

$$\implies p_q(V,\tilde{H}(1,F)) = \tilde{H}(1,F)^{-\kappa}\left(\lambda V F + (1-F)p_q(V,\tilde{H}(1,F))\right),$$

$$\implies p_q(V,\tilde{H}(1,F)) = \frac{\lambda V F \tilde{H}(1,F)^{-\kappa}}{\left(1 - (1-F)\tilde{H}(1,F)^{-\kappa}\right)},$$

$$\implies p_q(V,h) = \frac{\lambda V F}{h^\kappa \left(1 - \frac{1-F}{\tilde{H}(1,F)^\kappa}\right)}.$$

C Proof of Theorem 2

Proof. We note that the function $C(h)$ is convex and therefore, apply first order conditions to get the maxima. We further note that if the maxima is less than 1, then the cost functions is increasing beyond 1, and $h=1$ is optimal feasible.

D Price Manipulation

We consider the case of *predatory borrowing*, where an agent can manipulates the price of an asset in the spot market so as to inflate the value borrow against it at the inflated value. The agent can then walk away with the borrowed amount. First, we need to model price impact. For this, we use the very general model introduced by [11]. Let $B(p,q)$ denote the expected price of trade when quantity $q > 0$ is bought in the market at the starting price p. After the trade, let the expected final price be denoted by $U(p,q) \geq p$. Now consider the following sequence of events: (1) a borrower buys quantity q of an asset at starting price p, and moves it up; (2) then, the borrower uses the asset as collateral and borrows against it. To maximize their profits, the needs to find $q > 0$ that maximizes $qU(p,q)\ell - qB(p,q)$. In this scenario, we can prove the following theorem.

Theorem 4. *The above strategy is profitable in expectation to the borrower for some q only if $\ell > \min_q B(p,q)/U(p,q)$.*

Proof. We can rewrite the profit of the borrower as

$$qU(p,q)\left(\ell - \frac{B(p,q)}{U(p,q)}\right).$$

This is positive for some q if and only if

$$\ell > \min_q \frac{B(p,q)}{U(p,q)}.$$

Theorem 4 does not assume anything about the buying process, but only about the price evolution as a function of the quantity being bought. In fact, we can microfound the functions B and U by assuming that the quantity q is traded over a finite interval $[0, t]$ and that the price process follows a price impact function. As an example, consider the model proposed by [7] (the Gatheral model). This is the simplest model in that the price process follows a random walk and its drift is influenced by the trades. We need only consider the expected price process. According to this model, if the price at time 0 is p_0, and the asset is bought at a determinstic rate ν_t, then the price evolves as per the following equation:

$$\mathbb{E}[p_t] = p_0 + \int_0^t f(\nu_s) G(t-s) \, ds \tag{10}$$

where $f(\nu_t)$ represents the immediate impact of trading at rate ν_t and the transience function $G(\tau)$ represents decay of that price impact after time τ.

Corollary 1. *Under the Gatheral model, if $f : \mathbb{R} \to \mathbb{R}$ is an increasing continuous surjective function, and $G : \mathbb{R}^+ \to \mathbb{R}^+$ is a decreasing continuous function such that $G(0) = 1$, then a predatory borrowing attack with a constant purchase rate is profitable in expectation for some purchase rate if*

$$\ell > \int_0^T tG(T-t) \, dt \Big/ \left(T \int_0^T G(T-t) \, dt \right).$$

Proof. The last term in Eq. (10) signifies the noise due to external market participants. For this discussion, we only consider the effect of price impact in expectation, and so ignore this term. Let the constant rate of trading by the borrower be ν. In this scenario, we have $q = \nu T$, the average trading price is given by

$$B(p_0, q) = \frac{\int_0^T \nu p_t \, dt}{\nu T} = \frac{p_0 T + f(\nu) \int_0^T \int_0^t G(t-s) \, ds \, dt}{T}$$
$$= p_0 + f(\nu) \int_0^T \frac{(T-t) G(t)}{T} \, dt,$$

and the final price is given by,

$$U(p_0, q) = p_T = p_0 + f(\nu) \int_0^T G(T-t) \, dt.$$

Finally, we have,

$$\min_{q=\nu T} \frac{B(p_0, q)}{U(p_0, q)} = \min_{\nu} \frac{p_0 + f(\nu) \int_0^T \frac{(T-t)G(t)}{T} \, dt}{p_0 + f(\nu) \int_0^T G(T-t) \, dt}$$
$$= \frac{\int_0^T t G(T-t) \, dt}{T \int_0^T G(T-t) \, dt}.$$

Thus, the Gatheral model allows for the predatory borrowing attack if

$$\ell > \frac{\int_0^T tG(T-t)dt}{T\int_0^T G(T-t)dt}.$$

We note that the existence of a profitable rate of purchase does not depend on the price impact function, but only on the decay function. How large the rate should be for profitability does, however, depend on the price impact function.

We now consider specific examples of the impact and transience functions.

Example 2. The canonical functional form of the transience function $G(\tau)$ as proposed by [7] is $G(\tau) = \tau^{-\gamma}$. In this case we need $\ell > 1/(2-\gamma)$ for the existence of a constant purchase rate that would be profitable to the borrower. Note that such a purchase rate can be high and might require access to a large amount of capital. This result can be used by lending pool designers to decide contract parameters. For example, if the price impact is known to follow the Gatheral model with $G(\tau) = \tau^{-0.4}$, as suggested by [7], then the designers should ensure that $\ell < 0.625$ to disallow such an attack.

Example 3. Another interesting possibility is that $G(\tau) = e^{-\rho \tau}$ for some $\rho > 0$ as suggested by [18]. In this scenario, we need $\ell > 1 + \frac{1}{e^{\rho T}-1} - \frac{1}{\rho T}$. We can also get a similar, but more complicated result when G is exponential. Picking a suitable T is necessary in this case. We note that the borrower needs to be able to sustain trading at a constant rate for the entire time horizon T, and so the designer need to not worry about T being arbitrarily large. For example, if ρ is estimated to be 0.5 per day, and we set $T = 1$ day, then $\ell < 0.541$ disallows the predatory borrowing attack. With the same ρ, $T = 0.5$ days require that $\ell < 0.521$.

Example 4. When ℓ satisfies the condition in Theorem 4, we can use our model to compute the quantity needed for such an attack. For example, let $\ell = 0.93$ as seen in Compound III. Suppose that the price impact function follows the square-root law, which is widely used in practice (see [15]). For simplicity, suppose that buying is instantaneous and that the price impact is permanent ($G(\tau) = 1$). To compute the transaction cost, we use the square-root model as calibrated by [15]. In this model, we have

$$B(p,q) = p + 1.208 \cdot 10^{-3} p\sigma\sqrt{q/V},$$

where σ is the daily returns volatility and V is the daily traded volume of the asset. This model corresponds to the price update function

$$U(p,q) = p + 1.812 \cdot 10^{-3} p\sigma\sqrt{q/V}.$$

Now suppose we have $\ell = 0.93$ as in Compound III. For attacker profitability, we need to find q such that $\ell U(p,q) > B(p,q)$. Taking $p = 2000$ for a WETH-USDC loan and solving, we find that q needs to be larger than $34 \cdot 10^{12}$ times the daily traded volume for this attack to be profitable to the attacker. Such an attack does not seem feasible in practice. However, this example illustrates the utility of our methodology.

References

1. AAVE: Aave v2 lending pool. https://docs.aave.com/developers/v/2.0/. Accessed 08 Dec 2023
2. Bartoletti, M., Chiang, J., Junttila, T., Lluch Lafuente, A., Mirelli, M., Vandin, A.: Formal analysis of lending pools in decentralized finance. In: Margaria, T., Steffen, B. (eds.) ISoLA 2022. LNCS, vol. 13703, pp. 335–355. Springer, Cham (2022). https://doi.org/10.1007/978-3-031-19759-8_21
3. Bartoletti, M., Chiang, J.H., Lafuente, A.L.: SoK: lending pools in decentralized finance. In: Bernhard, M., et al. (eds.) FC 2021. LNCS, vol. 12676, pp. 553–578. Springer, Heidelberg (2021). https://doi.org/10.1007/978-3-662-63958-0_40
4. Binance: Binance public data. https://github.com/binance/binance-public-data. Accessed 08 Dec 2023
5. Chitra, T., Angeris, G., Evans, A., Kao, H.T.: A note on borrowing constant function market maker shares. In: DeFi 2022 - Proceedings of the 2022 ACM CCS Workshop on Decentralized Finance and Security, co-located with CCS 2022, pp. 55–61. Association for Computing Machinery, Inc (2022). https://doi.org/10.1145/3560832.3564260
6. Cohen, S.N., Sabate-Vidales, M., Szpruch, L., Gontier Delaunay, M.: The paradox of adversarial liquidation in decentralised lending. SSRN Electron. J. (2023). https://doi.org/10.2139/ssrn.4540333. https://papers.ssrn.com/abstract=4540333
7. Gatheral, J.: No-dynamic-arbitrage and market impact. Quant. Finan. **10**(7), 749–759 (2010). https://doi.org/10.1080/14697680903373692. https://www.tandfonline.com/action/journalInformation?journalCode=rquf20
8. Gudgeon, L., Perez, D., Harz, D., Livshits, B., Gervais, A.: The decentralized financial crisis. In: Proceedings - 2020 Crypto Valley Conference on Blockchain Technology, CVCBT 2020, pp. 1–15. Institute of Electrical and Electronics Engineers Inc. (2020). https://doi.org/10.1109/CVCBT50464.2020.00005
9. Gudgeon, L., Werner, S., Perez, D., Knottenbelt, W.J.: DeFi protocols for loanable funds: interest rates, liquidity and market efficiency. In: AFT 2020 - Proceedings of the 2nd ACM Conference on Advances in Financial Technologies, pp. 92–112. Association for Computing Machinery, Inc (2020). https://doi.org/10.1145/3419614.3423254. https://arxiv.org/abs/2006.13922v3
10. Gudgeon, L.J.F.: On the brink of a second financial system: modelling and mitigating risk in decentralised finance (2023). https://doi.org/10.25560/106325. http://spiral.imperial.ac.uk/handle/10044/1/106325
11. Huberman, G., Stanzl, W.: Price manipulation and quasi-arbitrage. Econometrica **72**(4), 1247–1275 (2004). https://doi.org/10.1111/j.1468-0262.2004.00531.x. http://www.econometricsociety.org/
12. Kao, H.T., Chitra, T., Chiang, R., Morrow Gauntlet, J.: An Analysis of the Market Risk to Participants in the Compound Protocol (2019). https://scfab.github.io/2020/FAB2020_p5.pdf
13. Klages-Mundt, A., Minca, A.: (In)Stability for the Blockchain: Deleveraging Spirals and Stablecoin Attacks. Cryptoeconomic Systems (2021). https://doi.org/10.21428/58320208.e46b7b81. http://arxiv.org/abs/1906.02152
14. Klages-Mundt, A., Minca, A.: While stability lasts: a stochastic model of noncustodial stablecoins. Math. Finan. **32**(4), 943–981 (2022). https://doi.org/10.1111/mafi.12357. https://onlinelibrary.wiley.com/doi/full/10.1111/mafi.12357
15. Kyle, A.S., Obizhaeva, A.A.: Market microstructure invariance: empirical hypotheses. Econometrica **84**(4), 1345–1404 (2016). http://www.jstor.org/stable/43866470

16. Lee, S.S., Mykland, P.A.: Jumps in financial markets: a new nonparametric test and jump dynamics. Rev. Finan. Stud. **21**(6), 2535–2563 (2007). https://doi.org/10.1093/rfs/hhm056
17. Lehar, A., Parlour, C.A.: Systemic fragility in decentralized markets. SSRN Electron. J. **2022** (2022). https://doi.org/10.2139/ssrn.4164833
18. Obizhaeva, A.A., Wang, J.: Optimal trading strategy and supply/demand dynamics. In: American Finance Association Meetings (2006). https://doi.org/10.1016/j.finmar.2012.09.001. https://papers.ssrn.com/sol3/papers.cfm?abstract_id=686168
19. Qin, K., Ernstberger, J., Zhou, L.: Mitigating decentralized finance liquidations with reversible call options. In: Proceedings of Financial Cryptography and Data Security (2023). https://ifca.ai/fc23/preproceedings/168.pdf
20. Qin, K., Zhou, L., Gamito, P., Jovanovic, P., Gervais, A.: An empirical study of DeFi liquidations: incentives, risks, and instabilities. In: Proceedings of the ACM SIGCOMM Internet Measurement Conference, IMC, pp. 336–350 (2021). https://doi.org/10.1145/3487552.3487811
21. Saengchote, K.: Decentralized lending and its users: insights from compound. J. Int. Finan. Markets Inst. Money **87** (2023). https://doi.org/10.1016/j.intfin.2023.101807. https://etherscan.io/address/0xdac17f958d2ee523a2206206994597c13d831ec7#writeContract
22. US Department of Treasury: Daily treasury par yield curve rates. https://home.treasury.gov/resource-center/data-chart-center/interest-rates/TextView?type=daily_treasury_yield_curve&field_tdr_date_value_month=202312. Accessed 08 Dec 2023
23. Warmuz, J., Chaudhary, A., Pinna, D.: Toxic Liquidation Spirals (2022). http://arxiv.org/abs/2212.07306
24. Yang, S., Cui, W.: An evaluation system for defi lending protocols (2023). https://arxiv.org/abs/2303.01022
25. Zhou, L., et al.: SoK: decentralized finance (DeFi) attacks. In: Proceedings - IEEE Symposium on Security and Privacy, vol. 2023-May, pp. 2444–2461 (2023). https://doi.org/10.1109/SP46215.2023.10179435. https://arxiv.org/abs/2101.08778v6

Structural Advantages for Integrated Builders in MEV-Boost

Mallesh Pai[1,2](✉) and Max Resnick[2]

[1] Rice University, Houston, TX 77005, USA
mallesh.pai@rice.edu
[2] Special Mechanisms Group, Consensys Inc., Fort Worth, USA
http://www.mechanism.org

Abstract. Currently, over 90% of Ethereum blocks are built using MEV-Boost, an auction that allows validators to sell their block-building power to builders who compete in an open English auction in each slot. A majority of these are produced by integrated builders, operated by trading firms, began to overtake many of the neutral builders. Outside of the integrated builder teams, little is known about which advantages integration confers beyond latency and how latency advantages distort on-chain trading. This paper explores these poorly understood advantages. We make two contributions. First, we point out that integrated builders are able to bid truthfully in their own bundle merge and then decide how much profit to take later in the final stages of the PBS auction when more information is available, making the auction for them look closer to a second-price auction while independent searchers are stuck in a first-price auction. Second, we find that latency disadvantages convey a winner's curse on slow bidders when underlying values depend on a stochastic price process that change as bids are submitted.

Keywords: First-price auction · Second-price auction · Latency Advantage · Common Value Auction

1 Introduction

Nominally, new Ethereum blocks are produced by ordinary validators who, having been temporarily anointed as the *proposer* by the protocol, gather transactions from the mempool and pack them together into the most valuable block they can produce. In practice, over 90 percent of proposers elect to outsource the building of the block by auctioning it off to the highest bidder through MEV-Boost [8]. The bidders in this auction are called *builders*. As the name suggests, builders specialize in building valuable blocks, by any means necessary. [1] revealed that several builders integrate with their own trading shops in order to more effectively capture CEX/DEX arbitrage. These 'HFT' builders or integrated builders win far more blocks when the CEX price was volatile in the time since the preceding slot (when there was more CEX/DEX arbitrage available) relative to when the price was stable, confirming that these builders have a significant advantage in extracting CEX/DEX arbitrage. But why does integration confer such a sizable advantage? In this paper we propose two simple models to show how the latency advantage plays out in auction settings.

We first consider a private values environment. This is the case, for example, if bidders' values come purely from the associated tips of the transactions in their block: the fact that other builders have a different value just reflects the fact that they constructed a different block. The second model considers a common-value setting. This, for example, is the case for a top-of-block CEX/DEX arb (i.e., where the competition is for the right to trading with an AMM pool on-chain, using information from a continuous time CEX).[1] In this case latency advantages manifest as an information advantage, i.e., the ability to bid later in the auction. The basic upshot of our results is that in either case, integrated/ low-latency bidders are advantaged. Our results therefore provide additional reasons for the rise of integrated builders (originally documented in [1]).

2 Private Values

There are $n = n_A + n_B$ builders in the PBS auction. Of these n_A are integrated builders and n_B are independent/non-integrated builders. In this section we assume independent private values: every integrated builder has a value that is drawn from a distribution with CDF F_A and density f_A, and every non-integrated builder has a value drawn from a distribution with CDF F_B and density f_B. All draws are independent. We consider the following hybrid auction: there is a single item for sale. All bidders simultaneously submit bids. The highest bidder wins the item but if the winner is an integrated builder, then they pay the next-highest bid, whereas if the winner is instead an independent builder, they pay their own bid. In short, the integrated builders compete in, what is in their view, a second-price auction while the non-integrated builders compete in a first-price auction.

Lemma 1. *From the point of view of the non-integrated builders, the auction is equivalent to a first-price auction of n_B agents where there is a random, secret reserve price distributed according to the CDF $F_A^{n_A}$.*

Let $\sigma(\cdot)$ denote bidding strategy of the non-integrated buyers, i.e., a bidder of value v bids $\sigma(v)$, a strictly increasing function. Then we must have:

Lemma 2. *The symmetric Bayes-Nash equilibrium among non-integrated bidders $\sigma(\cdot)$ solves:*

$$\sigma(v) = v - \frac{\int_0^v F_B^{n_B-1}(t) F_A^{n_A}(\sigma(t)) dt}{F_B^{n_B-1}(v) F_A^{n_A}(\sigma(v))}. \tag{1}$$

---

[1] Such arbs are a major source of AMM liquidity provider (LP) losses, see e.g. [4,5] for theoretical foundations and [6] for some estimates.

2.1 Analytical Solutions

To see analytical solutions assume that $n_B = 1$ and that F_A is the uniform distribution on $[0,1]$, i.e., $F_A(t) = t \iff t \in [0,1]$. So in this case, we have that:

Proposition 1. *If there is a single non-integrated builder, it bids $\frac{n_A}{n_A+1}$ of its value in the auction. As a result its equilibrium surplus in the auction is:* $S(v) = \left(\frac{n_A}{n_A+1}\right)^{n_A} \frac{v^{n_A+1}}{n_A+1}$ *whereas if this bidder was also integrated its surplus in the auction would be* $S(v) = \frac{v^{n_A+1}}{n_A+1}$. *In other words being the sole non-integrated builder costs it a fraction $\left(\frac{n_A}{n_A+1}\right)^{n_A}$ of its surplus relative to if it had been an integrated builder.*

Now let's suppose that $n_B = n$ for $n > 1$. In this case, we can conclude that:

Proposition 2. *The equilibrium bids of the n non-integrated bidders as a function of their value, $\sigma_n(v)$, satisfies $\frac{n_A}{n_A+1} v \leq \sigma_n(v) \leq v$.*

It follows straightforwardly, by an analogous appeal to revenue equivalence, that each of these non-integrated bidders still has a lower expected surplus than if they were bidding truthfully.

3 Common Values

We now consider a setting where the object for sale has a common value, i.e. the value of the object is the same regardless who eventually wins. This may be the case if the object for sale is the top slot of a block, designated as e.g. a CEX-DEX arb or a DeFi liquidation. The realized value would then be the same regardless of who wins it. Such a common value model was proposed in [3].

We consider the case of two kinds of bidders as before, fast bidders and slow bidder. The slow bidders bid at time 0, at which time the present value of the object is v_0. The process follows a martingale, i.e., we assume that t seconds after this the process is worth $v_t = (\exp m_t) v_0$ where $m_t \sim N(\mu t, \frac{\sigma^2}{2} t)$ and $\mu = -\frac{\sigma^2}{2}$. In particular the latter implies that $\mathbb{E}[v_{t+\delta}|v_t] = v_t$ for any $t, \delta \geq 0$.

Proposition 3. *In the auction described above, the slow bidders always bid 0 and the fast bidder always wins.*

3.1 The PBS Candlestick

Validators are not required to call the block exactly at the start of the slot [7], network delays are never a certainty, and clock synchronization can vary between validators. What this means is that, in practice, a speed advantage may not manifest itself deterministically. A slow bidder may simply have fewer opportunities to update their bid in the PBS auction (as a result of their speed, or lack thereof). We model this as a candlestick auction.[2] To capture the speed advantage of the fast bidder, we consider the following simplified model: (1) The slow bidders submit sealed bids at time 0, (2) The fast bidder has an option to bid at time Δ with probability $p \in [0, 1]$. We assume there are at least two slow bidders. This model is a simplified version of a "revision game" as originally proposed in [2]. Slow bidders can submit a first bid, but then the fast bidder has a stochastic opportunity to revise their bid, while the slow bidder does not have such an opportunity.

Proposition 4. *The winning slow bidder in the period 0 auction bids the largest $b_0^S \in [0, v_0]$ solving: $(1-p)(v_0 - b_0^S) + pP(v_\Delta < b_0^S)(E(v_\Delta | v_\Delta < b_0^S) - b_0^S) = 0$. They win the item with probability $pP(v_\Delta < b_0^S) + (1-p)$.*

Therefore, stochastic opportunities for the fast bidder to outbid the slow bidder lessens the adverse selection faced by the latter, and therefore allow for positive bids and positive probability of winning for the fast bidder.

4 Conclusion

As has been documented in multiple venues, the builder market in Ethereum increasingly favors integrated builder-searchers. A priori, one might think that there is no reason for searchers to integrate with builders, and indeed that competitive searchers might be better served focusing on searching and simply letting builders compete for their orders. While it is understood that integration confers and advantage to integrated builders relative to non-integrated builders, little is understood about exactly how. This paper sheds a first light on how latency advantages play out in an auction setting, both in the case of private value and common values. We leave to future work quantifying the source of the advantage, i.e., additional time to construct blocks etc. versus advantages in the auction.

Acknowledgement. We thank Davide Crapis, Julian Ma, Barnabè Monnot, Alex Nezlobin and Thomas Thiery for helpful comments and suggestions.

Disclosure of Interests. The authors are both employees at Consensys Inc.

References

1. Gupta, T., Pai, M.M., Resnick, M.: The centralizing effects of private order flow on proposer-builder separation (2023)
2. Kamada, Y., Kandori, M.: Revision games. Econometrica **88**(4), 1599–1630 (2020)
3. Ma, J.: A dynamic auction model for pbs. In: MEV Workshop SBC (2023)
4. Milionis, J., Moallemi, C.C., Roughgarden, T.: Automated market making and arbitrage profits in the presence of fees. arXiv preprint arXiv:2305.14604 (2023)

---

[2] A candlestick auction is one where bids are accepted until a (real-world) candle runs out, or some other stochastic process terminates. This was intended to ensure that no one could know exactly when the auction would end and make a last-second bid.

5. Milionis, J., Moallemi, C.C., Roughgarden, T., Zhang, A.L.: Automated market making and loss-versus-rebalancing. arXiv preprint arXiv:2208.06046 (2022)
6. Milionis, J., Moallemi, C.C., Roughgarden, T., Zhang, A.L.: Quantifying loss in automated market makers. In: Proceedings of the 2022 ACM CCS Workshop on Decentralized Finance and Security, pp. 71–74 (2022)
7. Schwarz-Schilling, C., Saleh, F., Thiery, T., Pan, J., Shah, N., Monnot, B.: Time is money: strategic timing games in proof-of-stake protocols (2023)
8. Wahrstätter, A., Zhou, L., Qin, K., Svetinovic, D., Gervais, A.: Time to bribe: measuring block construction market. arXiv preprint arXiv:2305.16468 (2023)

8th Workshop on Trusted Smart Contracts (WTSC 2024)

EIP-4844 Economics and Rollup Strategies

Davide Crapis[1], Edward W. Felten[2], and Akaki Mamageishvili[2](✉)

[1] Ethereum Foundation, Zug, Switzerland
[2] Offchain Labs, Princeton, USA
amamageishvili@offchainlabs.com

Abstract. We study the economics of the Ethereum improvement proposal 4844 and its effect on rollups' data posting strategies. Rollups' cost consists of two parts: data posting and delay. In the new proposal, the data posting cost corresponds to a blob posting cost and is fixed in each block, no matter how much of the blob is utilized by the rollup. The tradeoff is clear: the rollup prefers to post a full blob, but if its transaction arrival rate is low, filling up a blob space causes too large delay cost. The first result of the paper shows that if a rollup transaction arrival rate is too low, it prefers to use the regular blockspace market for data posting, as it offers a more flexible cost structure. Second, we show that shared blob posting is not always beneficial for participating rollups and change in the aggregate blob posting cost in the equilibrium depends on the types of participating rollups. In the end, we discuss blob cost-sharing rules from an axiomatic angle.

1 Introduction

Ethereum improvement proposal (EIP) numbered 4844, dubbed as EIP-4844, is meant to create a cheaper and more efficient calldata posting service on the Ethereum main chain, sometimes called layer one (L1). Such posting service is primarily interesting for rollups, that serve a purpose to scale the main chain by moving execution to them. The goal is to facilitate the Ethereum ecosystem move to rollups. Today, the largest optimistic and ZK rollups offer fees that are 3–50x lower than Ethereum main chain. This EIP and follow-ups will further reduce costs of transacting on rollups by providing extra space, thus creating strong incentives for users to switch to using rollups and enabling new applications that can borrow Ethereum main chain security at a much lower cost.

In this project, we study the economics of the proposal. We refer to the market created by EIP-4844 as the data market and the gas market of the Ethereum mainnet as the main market. In particular, we look at the trade-offs faced by rollups that are adopting the new service:

(1) When should a rollup use the data market versus the main market for sending data to L1?
(2) Is there a substantial efficiency gain in aggregating data from multiple rollups and what happens to the data market fees?

(3) When would rollups decide to aggregate and what is the optimal cost-sharing scheme?

In what follows we set up an economic model of aggregate rollup demand that we use to study the above questions. We make simplifying assumptions that allow us to obtain a crisp characterization of optimal rollup data posting strategies. In particular, we consider a continuous-time model in a large market with many rollups.

We model the cost of rollups as a sum of two parts. The first part of the cost is observable, it is a data posting cost. The second is delay cost. For some applications delay of L1 finality is not crucial. However, many applications built on top of rollups need fast L1 finality for their liveness and some even include it in their security model. The goal of the rollup is to minimize overall costs per transaction, as the per-transaction costs are what users incur and care about when using rollups. The proposal is to create a new market for posting *blobs*, 127 KB large data chunks that Ethereum validators will keep for certain amount of time. In our setting, the blob posting price is calculated in the equilibrium state endogenously, depending on the demand for data market. The main market price per gas is assumed to be fixed for simplicity. The promise of dynamic pricing mechanism for base fees governing L1 (EIP-1559) is that equilibrium price for gas is found quickly. This property holds at least on sufficiently long intervals. The assumption is introduced for the simplicity of the analysis and for obtaining closed form solutions. However, it does not change the nature of most of the results qualitatively to assume a variable price. The rollups decide between using either of the two technologies for transaction-relevant data posting, that is, both markets are perfect substitutes for each other[1]. We show that if the demand for blob posting is high, it drives smaller rollups to use the main market data posting strategy. We identify conditions when posting data on the main market is better for the rollup than posting blobs. In the second part of the paper, the joint blob posting option for two (or more) rollups is studied. Depending on the type of rollups that decide to post a shared blob, the price of the blob in the equilibrium can change in both directions, up or down. We derive bounds on the increase or decrease of the blob price in relative terms. If the shared blob posting is profitable, the rollups can join in doing so. We study cost-sharing rules from the axiomatic angle, by employing the Nash bargaining solution concept from the economic theory. In particular, we show that if both rollups were using data market, in the joint blob posting large rollup has to pay less than a proportional cost of the joint blob. On the other hand, it always pays more than half of the joint blob cost and the improvement of the large rollup is always less than the improvement of the small rollup.

1.1 Related Literature

In [5], the authors study how under the EIP-1559 dynamic fee mechanism the gas usage converges to the target usage over time. This theoretical and empirical

---
[1] Using both markets interchangeably is technologically feasible.

observation is a cornerstone of our modeling of the equilibrium state. [4] proposes a dynamic posted-price mechanism-which uses not only block utilization but also observable bids from past blocks to compute a posted price for subsequent blocks, they study the stability and welfare optimality of the proposed policy in a steady state. In [3], the authors argue that different resource types should be independently priced, as converting all resources in one unit and pricing it uniformly is economically inefficient. EIP-4844 can be seen as the first step towards fixing the economic inefficiencies of pricing different types of resources together. [1] provides a definition and empirical analysis of the upcoming EIP-4844 fee market, which introduces data gas on the Ethereum blockchain and a data gas pricing mechanism modeled after the fee update mechanism of EIP-1559. [2] studies optimal dynamic pricing method for multiple resources, with uncertain future demand flow and statistical dependencies between resource demands. In [6] the authors provide a rollup data batch posting strategy, in the context of a single independent rollup, and in the absence of a dedicated market for data. They analyze trade-offs between price and time that are similar in nature to the ones faced here in the presence of a dual market and multiple rollups.

2 Continuous-Time Model

In this section, we outline modeling assumptions and derive initial results on the rollup behavior in the presence of two potential markets. We make the following list of assumptions:

- Delay cost of a transaction is aD, where D is the delay, in time units, experienced by the transaction (a time when a transaction was posted in a batch or blob to L1, minus time when it arrived to L2 sequencer), and $a > 0$ is a positive constant.
- L1 gas price is G, which is treated as a constant.
- The base cost of a batch- or blob-posting transaction on L1 is $P_0 G$. Here P_0 indicates the size of the metadata associated with the rollup transaction containing a batch/blob.
- The cost of posting a blob on L1 is $P_0 G + B$, where B will be set later to a market-clearing price. The latter is interpreted as the minimum price for which no more than three blobs are posted per time unit on average.
- The cost of posting a batch of n transactions on L1 is $(P_0 + P_1 n)G$.

The target number of blobs per Ethereum block is denoted by k^2. We treat time as continuous so that a blob can be posted at any time. Conceptually, a "time unit" can be thought of as one L1 block time, but in this model, we will allow blobs to be posted "in between" L1 blocks. Suppose there are rollups with transaction arrival rates $R_1, R_2, ..., R_n$ and they are sorted in decreasing rates, $R_i \geq R_{i+1}$ for any $i \in \{1, ..., n-1\}$. The goal of a rollup is to minimize cost per transaction. The latter is obtained by dividing the total cost by the total

---
[2] Initially set to 2 and currently set to 3.

number of transactions in the blob and paid by rollup users. The justification of this approach is that even though some transactions arrive earlier than others, their arrival time can be assumed to be uniformly random. This payment rule corresponds to users paying average costs, and therefore, satisfies some fairness properties.

3 Analysis

In this section, we obtain results on the tradeoff between using data and main markets. First, we show the following:

Proposition 1. *There is a threshold n^*, such that for any $i > n^*$, a rollup i uses the direct on L1 posting strategy.*

Proof. Let us determine the optimal strategy for a single rollup, assuming the prices on both the data market and on L1 are fixed. There are two strategies any rollup could use: (1) posting blobs or (2) posting directly on L1. The rollup finds a strategy that minimizes the cost within each of these strategies separately and then selects the strategy that has a lower cost.

First, consider a blob-posting strategy. Suppose a rollup with generic rate R posts a blob every time t. Then, a blob contains Rt transactions, with the total cost (posting cost plus delay cost) of

$$T_B(t) := P_0 G + B + \int_0^t aR\tau d\tau = P_0 G + B + \frac{aRt^2}{2}. \quad (1)$$

The cost per transaction is:

$$Tr_B(t) := \frac{T_B(t)}{Rt} = \frac{P_0 G + B}{Rt} + \frac{at}{2}. \quad (2)$$

By the first order condition (FOC), $Tr_B(t)$ is minimized when

$$t_B := t = \sqrt{\frac{2(P_0 G + B)}{aR}}. \quad (3)$$

Plugging t_B obtained above in (2), gives that the cost per transaction is

$$Tr_B(t) = \frac{P_0 G + B}{R}\sqrt{\frac{aR}{2(P_0 G + B)}} + \frac{1}{2}\sqrt{\frac{2(P_0 G + B)a}{R}} = \sqrt{\frac{2(P_0 G + B)a}{R}} = at_B,$$

and the number of transactions per blob is $C_B := Rt_B = \sqrt{\frac{2(P_0 G + B)R}{a}}$.

Next, we consider an L1-posting strategy. Suppose a rollup posts a batch every time t, with Rt transactions per batch. Similarly to the calculation of the cost in (1), the total cost of a batch is

$$T_E(t) := (P_0 + RtP_1)G + \frac{aRt^2}{2}, \quad (4)$$

and the cost per transaction is

$$Tr_E(t) := \frac{P_0 G}{Rt} + P_1 G + \frac{at}{2}. \tag{5}$$

By the FOC, this is minimized when $t = \sqrt{2P_0 G/(aR)}$. Plugging the above value in (5) gives that the cost per transaction is:

$$Tr_E = \frac{P_0 G}{R}\sqrt{\frac{aR}{2P_0 G}} + P_1 G + \frac{a}{2}\sqrt{\frac{2P_0 G}{aR}} = \sqrt{\frac{2P_0 G a}{R}} + P_1 G,$$

and the number of transactions per batch is $Rt = \sqrt{2P_0 GR/a}$.

Now, we focus on the indifference condition between posting blobs and posting on L1. That is, we solve for the value of B that makes the rollup indifferent between the two strategies. For this, set costs per transaction in both cases equal:

$$\sqrt{\frac{2(P_0 G + B)a}{R}} = P_1 G + \sqrt{\frac{2P_0 G a}{R}}.$$

Multiplying both sides by $\sqrt{R/(2a)}$ and squaring gives $P_0 G + B = (\sqrt{R/2a}P_1 G + \sqrt{P_0 G})^2$, or equivalently

$$B + P_0 G = \frac{RP_1^2 G^2}{2a} + 2P_1 G\sqrt{\frac{RP_0 G}{2a}} + P_0 G.$$

Canceling terms, we get

$$B = \frac{RP_1^2 G^2}{2a} + 2P_1 G\sqrt{\frac{RP_0 G}{2a}}. \tag{6}$$

For any finite G and $B > 0$, there are two scenarios. First, there is an index n^* such that in (6), the right-hand side is lower than the left-hand side, therefore, the rollup prefers to use a main market posting strategy, a contradiction. Second, if such an index does not exist, then we set the threshold equal to n. This finishes the proof of the proposition. □

Next, we demonstrate how to calculate the equilibrium price B and the threshold in Proposition 1. For simplicity, suppose that $P_0 = 0$. Then, the time between posting for rollup i is $t_i = \sqrt{\frac{2B}{aR_i}}$. The algorithm proceeds in two steps:

- Step 1. Initialization: To hit the target of k blobs per time unit, we require that

$$k = \sum_{i=1}^{n} \frac{1}{t_i} = \sum_{i=0}^{n} \frac{\sqrt{aR_i}}{\sqrt{2B}}.$$

Solving B gives:

$$B = \frac{a(\sum_{i=1}^{n}\sqrt{R_i})^2}{2k^2}. \tag{7}$$

Let $\sum_{i=1}^{n}\sqrt{R_i} =: R$ is a positive real number. Plugging this value in (6), gives the initial value on m such that for a rollup with rate R_m, LHS of (6) is larger than RHS of (6).

- Step 2. In the loop, we increase m initialized in the previous step by one, calculate new equilibrium price B with a set of rollups $\{1, 2, ..., n\}$, as long as the LHS of (6) is smaller than the RHS. Once we find a value of k, for which LHS is higher than the RHS, we output B and $n^* = m$, as an answer.

Note that the condition in Step 2 may never be satisfied. In this case, n^* is set to n. Intuitively, the calculation of B in the initialization step assumes that all rollups use a blob posting strategy. However, it might be that some rollups under this price will not use a blob posting strategy, that is, it is an overestimation of the price. The second step fixes this potential overestimation by first excluding all small rollups and adding them one by one.

Example 1. Consider an example in which rates drop exponentially, that is, suppose $R_i = \frac{R_{i-1}}{2}$ for any $i \in \{1, ..., n\}$.

Assume that G is very large, that is, all rollups use a blob posting strategy. To hit the target of k blobs per time unit, we require that:

$$k = \sum_{i=0}^{n} \frac{1}{t_i} = \sqrt{\frac{aR_0}{2B}} \sum_{i=0}^{n} (\sqrt{2})^{-i} \approx \sqrt{\frac{aR_0}{2B}} \frac{\sqrt{2}}{\sqrt{2}-1} = \sqrt{\frac{aR_0}{B}} \frac{1}{\sqrt{2}-1}.$$

The approximation is taken by assuming a large enough value of n. We get an equivalent condition $k(\sqrt{2}-1) \approx \sqrt{aR_0/B}$. Solving for B gives:

$$B \approx \frac{aR_0}{k^2(3-2\sqrt{2})}.$$

For $k = 2$, an initial EIP-4844 target number of blobs per block, $B \approx 1.46 aR_0$, and the time between posting for rollups is $1.71, 2.42, 3.42, ...$ For $k = 3$, a current EIP-4844 target, $B \approx 0.65 aR_0$, and the time between posting for rollups is $1.14, 1.62, 2.27, ...$

4 Joining Chains

Suppose two rollups join forces in posting blobs. There are three different type of profiles of these rollups in the equilibrium derived above. In the first, both rollups use blob posting technology. In the second, one rollup uses blob posting technology, while the other uses the main market to post the data. In the third, both rollups use the main market for posting the data. In this section, we analyze what happens with the equilibrium price of the blob in these different scenarios and derive a cost-sharing scheme that satisfies certain reasonable properties. Let B^N denote the new price in the equilibrium after two rollups join in posting blobs.

Case 1: In this case, both rollups post the blobs in the initial equilibrium state. We obtain that the blob price in the new equilibrium state decreases, because of the blob price formula (7). In the following, we show a result of how large this decrease can be.

Proposition 2. B^N satisfies the following inequalities: $B \geq B^N \geq B/2$.

Proof. Assume that the two rollups joining in the blob posting are indexed i and j. Then, B can be rewritten as $B = c(\sqrt{R_i} + \sqrt{R_j} + t)^2$ and $B^N = c(\sqrt{R_i + R_j} + t)^2$, where $c = \frac{1}{2k^2}$ and $t = \sum_{k \neq i,j} \sqrt{R_k}$. $B \geq B^N$ is equivalent to $\sqrt{R_i} + \sqrt{R_j} \geq \sqrt{R_i + R_j}$, that trivially holds for any $R_i, R_j > 0$. The second inequality, $B^N \geq B^N/2$, is equivalent to $\sqrt{2}\sqrt{R_1 + R_2} \geq \sqrt{R_1} + \sqrt{R_2}$. The latter is equivalent to $(R_1 - R_2)^2 \geq 0$, which holds trivially.

From the proof above we see that the equality in $B^N = B/2$ holds if and only if there are only two rollups and their transaction rates are equal. For obtaining the corner solution, it is also implicitly assumed that no other rollup joins the blob posting strategy, in the new state with a lower price.

Case 2: In this case, one rollup posts blobs, and the other posts on the main market in the initial arrangement. Joining blob posting pushes the price of the blob posting up, assuming that no rollup stops using blob posting technology. In the following, we derive an upper bound on the price increase.

Proposition 3. B^N satisfies the following inequalities: $2B \geq B^N \geq B$.

Proof. Assume that the rollup that posts blobs is indexed i, that is, its transaction rate is R_i and the rollup that posts calldata at the main market has a transaction rate R. Then, the old blob price in the equilibrium is equal to $B = c(\sqrt{R_i} + t)^2$, where $c = \frac{1}{2k^2}$ and $t = \sum_{k \neq i} \sqrt{R_k}$. The new price, on the other hand, is equal to $B^N = c(\sqrt{R_i + R} + t)^2$. It is obvious that $B^N \geq B$, since no rollup stops using blob posting strategy. $2B \geq B^N$ is equivalent to $\sqrt{2}(\sqrt{R_i} + t) \geq \sqrt{R_i + R} + t$. It is sufficient to show that $\sqrt{2}\sqrt{R_i} \geq \sqrt{R_i + R}$, equivalent to $R_i \geq R$. The latter holds because the rollup with transaction rate R_i posts blobs in the equilibrium and has a higher transaction rate than the rollup with R rate, posting on the main market.

Case 3: In this case, both rollups use the main market for posting the data in the initial setting. Assume they join in posting blobs and no rollup stops using blob posting technology. Then, the new blob price B^N in the equilibrium increases. We obtain the following upper bound on the increase.

Proposition 4. B^N satisfies the following inequalities: $2B \geq B^N \geq B$.

Proof. The proof is similar to the proof of Proposition 3. Two rollups with transaction rates R^1 and R^2 that were posting their data in the main market, can reach a level that is almost $2R_1$. In fact, as long as $R^1 + R^2 \geq R_1$, the rollup with rate R_1 would not post blobs in the new equilibrium, a contradiction with the assumption. This gives an upper bound of $2B$ on the new equilibrium price.

4.1 Cost Sharing

Suppose there are two chains, with transaction arrival rates $R_L = R$, from now on referred to as large rollup, and $R_S = Rf$, referred to as small rollup. $0 < f < 1$ is a real number. Assume $P_0 = 0$, that is, there are no metadata costs. We use the same model as above. Let Tr_L and Tr_S denote costs per transaction of large and small rollups, respectively, C_L and C_S denote the total number of transactions posted by large and small rollups separately.

In the following, for the illustration of calculating these parameters above, in this and the next subsections, we assume that both rollups use a blob posting strategy. If the big chain is the only one using the blob space and it posts every t_L time, then optimal posting time is $t_L = \sqrt{2B/(aR)}$, with a cost per transaction of $Tr_L = \sqrt{2Ba/R}$ and the total number of transactions in blob $C_L = \sqrt{2BR/a}$.

For the small chain only, we have optimal posting time $t_S = \sqrt{2B/(aRf)}$, with a cost per transaction of $Tr_S = \sqrt{2Ba/(Rf)}$ and the total number of transaction in the blob is $C_S = \sqrt{2BRf/a}$.

If the two chains post their blobs separately, the small chain has a higher per transaction cost, by a factor of $1/\sqrt{f}$ per transaction, since $t_S/t_R = 1/\sqrt{f}$. Because the large chain has more transactions, it pays more overall, by a factor of $1/\sqrt{f}$.

A joint blob is also posted so that it minimizes cost per transaction. This is a Pareto efficient approach, as otherwise, both rollups could agree to deviate to the optimal strategy and share added value in any way. Based on the analysis in the proof of proposition, a joint blob is posted every $t_J = \sqrt{\frac{2B^N}{(1+f)aR}}$. The total cost per blob is:

$$B^N + \frac{a(1+f)R}{2} \cdot \frac{2B^N}{(1+f)aR} = 2B^N.$$

In all three cases, the total cost per blob is equal to 2 times the blob price. A cost per transaction of $Tr_J = \sqrt{2B^N a/(R(1+f))}$ and the total number of transaction in the blob is $C_J = \sqrt{2B^N R(1+f)/a}$.

First, note that if $Tr_J > Tr_L$, the rollups will not join in posting blobs together, as it is not profitable for a large rollup. Therefore, an interesting case is when $Tr_J < Tr_L \leq Tr_S$. In Propositions 2, 3 and 4, we obtained that $2B \geq B^N \geq B/2$. That is, the relation between Tr_J and Tr_L can be arbitrary. We discuss a suitable cost-sharing rule in the next section.

4.2 The Nash Bargaining Solution

In this section, we take an axiomatic approach to the cost-sharing rule between rollups that decide to post blobs together. One such approach is suggested by the Nash Bargaining solution. First, we introduce the required notation and then reduce the cost-sharing rule to solving the Nash Bargaining problem. Let A denote the set of all possible bargaining outcomes. In particular, $D \in A$ is the outcome if no agreement can be reached. In our setting, A is interpreted as a set of cost-sharing options between two rollups, while D is interpreted as a case when rollups post their blobs separately. The utility (payoff) function of agent i is given by $u_i : A \to \mathbb{R}$. We consider linear utility functions, in particular. Let S denote the set of all possible utilities (payoffs):

$$S = \{(s_1, s_2) \mid s_1 = u_1(a), s_2 = u_2(a), a \in A\}.$$

Let $s := (s_1, s_2)$. Further, let $d = (d_1, d_2) = (u_1(D), u_2(D))$ be the utility vector if no agreement could be reached (threat point). Two Requirements on S to have a characterization: 1) There exists $s \in S$ with $s_i > d_i$ $\forall i$, and 2) S is compact and convex. Our set satisfies these properties, as we will see later. Then, define $S' = \{s \mid s_i \geq d_i \ \forall i\} \subseteq S$. Let $H(S)$ denote the set of *Pareto-optimal* outcomes. *Pareto-optimal* (or *Pareto-efficient*) means that there is no other outcome that makes one player better off without making another player worse off. In our case, this means that rollups pay completely for the blob posting cost and do not overpay. Now, we are in the position to define a Nash Bargaining Solution.

Definition 1. *A* **bargaining solution** *is a rule that assigns a solution vector $f(S, d) \in S$ to every bargaining problem $B = (S, d)$.*

Let $f_i(S, d)$ denote the i-component of $f(S, d)$. That is: $f(S, d) = (f_1(S, d), f_2(S, d))$. We have the following 4 axioms.

Axiom 1 (Invariance of Utility Scaling). *If there are two bargaining situations $B = (S, d)$ and $\bar{B} = (\bar{S}, \bar{d})$ with $\bar{S} = \{\alpha_1 s_1 + \beta_1, \alpha_2 s_2 + \beta_2 : s \in S\}$ and $\bar{d}_i = \alpha_i d_i + \beta_i \ \forall i$, where $\alpha_1, \alpha_2 > 0$. Then, for the solution, the following holds: $f_i(\bar{S}, \bar{d}) = \alpha_i f_i(S, d) + \beta_i \ \forall i$.*

The axiom states that if we change the way we measure utility when we construct a bargaining problem but keep new utility scales decision-theoretically equivalent to the old ones, then the bargaining solution in utility-allocation space changes in the same way, so that it still corresponds to the same real outcome.

Axiom 2 (Pareto Optimality). *If $f(S, d)$ is a solution to $B = (S, d)$, then $f(S, d) \in H(S)$.*

The axiom states that there is no other feasible allocation that is better than the solution for one player and not worse than the solution for the other player. For the next axiom, we need a definition:

Definition 2. *A game is called symmetric if two conditions hold: (1) $d_1 = d_2$, and (2) $(s_1, s_2) \in S$, then $(s_2, s_1) \in S$.*

Axiom 3 (Symmetry). *If (S, d) is symmetric, then the solution is also symmetric, i.e. $f_1(S, d) = f_2(S, d)$.*

The axiom states that, if the positions of players 1 and 2 are completely symmetric in the bargaining problem, then the solution also treats them symmetrically.

Axiom 4 (Independence of Irrelevant Alternatives). *Let (S,d) and (T,d) be two bargaining situations with $S \subset T$ and $f(T,d) \in S$, then $f(T,d) = f(S,d)$.*

The axiom states that eliminating feasible alternatives (other than the threat point) that would not have been chosen does not affect the result.

Theorem 1 ([7]). *There is a unique bargaining solution, f^N, satisfying the four axioms above and it has the following representation for every two-person bargaining problem:*

$$f^N(S,d) = \arg \max_{s \in H(S)} (s_1 - d_1)(s_2 - d_2) = s^*. \tag{8}$$

The expression $(s_1-d_1)(s_2-d_2)$ is called the Nash Product. Suppose the large rollup is indexed by 1 and the small rollup is indexed by 2. The disagreement point in our setting is $(d_1, d_2) = (Tr_L, Tr_S)$. Assuming that posting a joint blob is profitable, that is, $Tr_J < Tr_L$, the rollups need to decide how to share the new blob price B^N. Suppose the large rollup pays B_1 and the small rollup pays B_2, with $B_1, B_2 \geq 0$. Then, we can redefine their per-transaction costs, which define points (s_1, s_2) in the payoff set. This defines a two-dimensional space. However, note that because of the Pareto efficiency, $B_1 + B_2 = B$ holds, since underpaying is not an option, and overpaying is not efficient. Therefore, we are down to 1 dimensional space, as $B_1 \in [0, B^N]$ defines it fully.

The number of large and small rollup transactions in the blob are denoted by $C_{J,L}$ and $C_{J,S}$, respectively. Since their rate ratio is $\frac{1}{f}$, we have $C_{J,L} = \frac{C_J}{1+f}$ and $C_{J,S} = \frac{C_J f}{1+f}$, so that they sum up to C_S. Let $d_{J,L}$ and $d_{J,S}$ denote the total delay costs of the large and small rollups, respectively. Then $d_{J,L} = \frac{aRt_J^2}{2}$ and $d_{J,S} = \frac{aRft_J^2}{2}$. Having settled all necessary parameters, we proceed to calculate s_1 and s_2 values for given B_1. s_1 is calculated as $s_1 = \frac{B_1 + d_{J,L}}{C_{J,L}}$ and s_2 is calculated as $s_2 = \frac{B^N - B_1 + d_{J,S}}{C_{J,S}}$. Plugging in s_1 and s_2 in (8), and simplification by getting rid of constant denominators gives the following optimization problem:

$$\arg \max_{B_1} (B_1 + d_{J,L} - C_{J,L} Tr_L)(B^N - B_1 + d_{J,S} - C_{J,S} Tr_S). \tag{9}$$

Since (10) is a negative quadratic polynomial in B_1, we solve the optimal value by the first order condition with respect to B_1:

$$B_1 = (B^N + d_{J,S} - d_{J,L} - C_{J,S} Tr_S + C_{J,L} Tr_L)/2. \tag{10}$$

The solution of (10) directly gives a sharing rule for a blob cost and also determines per transaction costs for both rollups. Note that it is only a function of f, and therefore, the contract between the rollups can be easily automated. The axiomatic approach of this section can be easily generalized to $m > 2$ rollups, by taking a Nash product over m rollups $(s_1-d_1)(s_2-d_2)\cdot...\cdot(s_m-d_m)$. However, the optimization problem at hand can be much harder to solve, as it is $m-1$ dimensional. The number of dimensions comes from $m-1$ rollups' contributions towards the final blob cost. The last rollup contribution is determined by the contributions of the rest.

First, we show a structural result that will come in handy later. The result is similar to the one in Proposition 2, in that we lower bound the new equilibrium price in terms of the original equilibrium price B, and a parameter f.

Lemma 1. $\frac{B^N}{B} \geq \frac{1+f}{(1+\sqrt{f})^2}$.

Proof. Similar to the proof of Proposition 2, the ratio between B^N and B is minimized if there are only two rollups posting blobs. Then, in this case, by (7) we have that $B^N/B = \frac{\sqrt{R+Rf}}{(R+\sqrt{Rf})^2} = \frac{1+f}{(1+\sqrt{f})^2}$, which finishes the proof.

Next, we show that the Nash bargaining outcome the large rollup to pay, is always an internal value:

Proposition 5. $B_1 \in (0, B^N)$ for any $f < 1$.

Proof. Plugging all values in the formula of B_1 gives:

$$B_1 = 0.5(B^N + \frac{aRf}{2}\frac{2B^N}{a(1+f)R} - \frac{aR}{2}\frac{2B^N}{a(1+f)R} - \frac{f}{1+f}\sqrt{\frac{2B^N(1+f)R}{a}}\sqrt{\frac{2Ba}{Rf}} + \frac{1}{f+1}\sqrt{\frac{2B^N(1+f)R}{a}}\sqrt{\frac{2Ba}{R}}).$$

Simplifying gives:

$$B_1 = (B^N \frac{f}{1+f} + \sqrt{B^N B}(\sqrt{\frac{1}{1+f}} - \sqrt{\frac{f}{1+f}})). \tag{11}$$

Then, $B_1 < B^N$ is equivalent to:

$$B(1+f)(1-\sqrt{f})^2 < B^N.$$

Note that the condition in the Lemma 1 readily implies the condition above, which finishes the proof of the proposition.

Note that B_1 does not depend on R and a, see (11), but only on blob prices and f, as claimed earlier. To get an intuition of the parameters above, in the following, we consider an example. Let Tr_{J,L,B_1} and Tr_{J,S,B_1} denote effective per transaction costs after fixing the amount large rollup pays for the blob price, B_1. The following holds:

$$Tr_{J,L,B_1} = (B_1 + d_{J,L})/C_{J,L} \text{ and } Tr_{J,S,B_1} = (B^N - B_1 + d_{J,S})/C_{J,S}. \tag{12}$$

Let the rollup $X \in \{L, S\}$ improvement is denoted by

$$I_{X,B_1} := (Tr_X - Tr_{J,X,B_1})/Tr_X = 1 - Tr_{J,X,B_1}/Tr_X,$$

and the proportional payment of the large rollup $B_1^{pr} := \frac{B^N}{1+f}$.

Example 2. Suppose $R = B = a = 1$ and $f = 0.25$. That is, a small rollup has 4 times less traffic than a large rollup. Then, in the case of large rollup posting blobs alone, parameters are equal $t_L = Tr_L = C_L = \sqrt{2} \approx 1.41$. Parameters of the small rollup posting alone: $t_S = Tr_S = \sqrt{8} \approx 2.82$ and $C_L = \sqrt{0.5} \approx 0.71$. The joint posting parameters are: $t_J = Tr_J = \sqrt{2 \cdot 0.81/1.25} \approx 1.14$ and $C_J = \sqrt{2.5 \cdot 0.81} \approx 1.42$. Large rollup includes $C_{J,L} = \frac{1.42}{1.25} \approx 1.138$ transactions in the joint blob, small rollup includes $C_{J,S} \approx 0.285$ transactions. Large rollup total delay is $d_{J,L} \approx 1.14^2/2 = 0.65$ and small rollup delay is $d_{J,S} = 0.25 d_{J,L} \approx 0.16$. Finally, we plug in all parameters in the calculation of the large rollup share in the Nash bargaining solution (10):

$$B_1 \approx (0.81 + 0.16 - 0.65 - 0.285 \cdot 2.82 + 1.138 \cdot 1.41)/2 \approx 0.564.$$

Then, the small rollup pays $B_2 \approx 0.15$. Note that they do not share the total price 0.81 proportionally, which would result in the large rollup paying $B_1^{pr} = 0.81 \cdot \frac{4}{5} = 0.648$. Plugging in all values, we obtain $Tr_{J,L,B_1} = (0.56 + 0.65)/1.138 \approx 1.07$ and $Tr_{J,S,B_1} = (0.15 + 0.16)/0.28 \approx 1.43$. That is, the large rollup improvement is $I_{L,B_1} \approx 24.7\%$, while the small rollup improvement is $I_{S,B_1} \approx 49.4\%$. Note that the large rollup improvement of the per-transaction cost is smaller than the improvement of the small rollup.

Observations obtained in the example above are more general, which we show in the following propositions. First, we show that the Nash bargaining outcome for the large rollup is less than the proportional payment to the blob price:

Proposition 6. $B_1 \leq B_1^{pr}$ *for any* $f < 1$.

Proof. $B_1 < B^{pr} = \frac{B^N}{1+f}$ from (11) is equivalent to

$$\sqrt{\frac{B^N B}{1+f}}(1 - \sqrt{f}) < \frac{B^N(1-f)}{1+f}, \quad (13)$$

which is on its own equivalent to $B < \frac{(1+\sqrt{f})^2}{1+f} B^N$. This condition is exactly the condition in the Lemma 1, which finishes the proof of the proposition.

Next, we obtain a lower bound on the Nash bargaining outcome. Namely, we show the following:

Proposition 7. $B_1 \geq B^N/2$ *for any* $f < 1$.

Proof. The condition $B_1 \geq B^N/2$ is equivalent to

$$\sqrt{B^N B}\frac{1 - \sqrt{f}}{\sqrt{1+f}} \geq \frac{1-f}{2(1+f)} B^N,$$

which after simplification becomes:

$$\frac{B^N}{B} \leq 4(1+f)(1+\sqrt{f})^2.$$

The right-hand side of the above inequality is decreasing in f and achieves its minimum value 2 when $f = 1$. By Proposition 2, we know that $B \geq B^N$, which finishes the proof.

That is, the large rollup never pays less than half of the new blob price, which is fair.

Last, we show that the large rollup improvement in the Nash bargaining outcome is less than the small rollup improvement.

Proposition 8. $I_{L,B_1} \leq I_{S,B_1}$ for any $f < 1$.

Proof. The condition is equivalent to:

$$B^N \frac{(1+\sqrt{f})f}{1+f} + \sqrt{B^N B}(1+\sqrt{f})(\sqrt{\frac{1}{1+f}} - \sqrt{\frac{f}{1+f}}) \geq \frac{B^N}{1+f}(f\sqrt{f}-1) + B^N\sqrt{f}. \tag{14}$$

Further simplification gives:

$$\frac{2}{1+f} + \sqrt{\frac{B}{B^N}}\frac{1-f}{\sqrt{f+1}} - B^N\sqrt{f} \geq 0.$$

Let $p := \sqrt{B/B^N}$. We show that the function

$$h(f) := \frac{2}{1+f} + p\frac{1-f}{\sqrt{1+f}} - \sqrt{f}$$

is decreasing in f on the interval $[0, 1]$ for any $p > 0$. Note that $dh(f)/df < 0$ for any $f > 0$. Since $h(1) = 0$, we get the proof of the proposition.

The intuition is simple: a small rollup has much more room to improve than a large rollup. Note that the result holds *unconditionally* regarding the equilibrium prices B and B^N. Since we consider only Pareto-efficient solutions, the result, in particular, implies that a Nash bargaining solution favors the small rollup compared to the "fair" blob cost-sharing rule, which improves both rollup per-transaction costs equally. The latter favors the large rollup to a high extent: the rollups pay almost equally even if $f = 0.25$.

In this section, we assumed that the two rollups engaged in the joint blob posting were the ones that initially were posting blobs. This in particular gives a lower bound on the new equilibrium price, derived in the Lemma 1, and is used in the proofs of Propositions 5 and 6. If one or both rollups were using the main market, then the propositions would be automatically satisfied, as the new equilibrium price goes up.

5 Extensions

In this section, we discuss two natural extensions of the baseline model. In the first extension, the blob size is limited. Suppose there is the maximum blob size

U, so that for any rollup, $Rt \leq U$, or equivalently, the posting time t is upper bounded by U/R. Intuitively, adding an upper bound on the blob size causes the blob price in the equilibrium to increase, compared to the baseline model. The reason is that with the upper bound the rollups produce blobs even faster. To figure out rollup optimum posting time in the case of using the data market, we again solve the optimal time of posting using the first-order condition and compare the blob size with the upper bound U. If the obtained size is larger than the upper bound, then we take the size to be U and adjust the posting time accordingly. If on the other hand, the optimal size is smaller than the upper bound, the rollup keeps the same optimal strategy. Calculating the main market posting time is done exactly as in the main model, therefore, deciding on the posting strategy given equilibrium price is trivial. Calculating the equilibrium price is also easy.

Shared blob posting stays the same if the aggregate demand does not cross the threshold, and cost-sharing does not need modification as well. If one of the participating rollups reaches the threshold size itself and the other one does not, then it has more bargaining power, as it saves only on the delay cost. However, if both rollups reach the threshold themselves, cost-sharing becomes more intricate. Both rollups save only on the delay cost, and therefore, large rollup has lower bargaining power over a small rollup, compared to the baseline model.

In the second extension, rollups have compression technology. It is natural to assume that compression technology is monotonic, that is, the compression factor is increasing in the data size. Then, the existence of compression, in general, favors bigger rollups as well, since they generate enough transaction data to compress efficiently faster than smaller rollups do. In the case of shared blob posting, this advantage should be compensated. The Nash bargaining outcome guarantees such compensation since the per-transaction cost in the disagreement point for the small rollup will be low because of compression, as the joint blob posting does not let the small rollup use compression to full extent.

6 Conclusions and Future Work

We introduced a simple economic model to analyze EIP-4844 and its effects on rollups to decrease L1 data costs. In the proposed model, large enough rollups use a new market for posting their data to L1, while the rest continue using the original market. Moreover, we studied sharing blob posting and cost-sharing rules. First, we outlined conditions when sharing is profitable for both rollups and then described an axiomatic approach to the blob-posting cost-sharing rule. The are many interesting future research avenues: (a) optimal strategy in an oligopolistic market with relevant strategic interaction between rollups; (b) strategic consumers and endogenous main market equilibrium price – we can extend the above model with demand growth to study questions about the equilibrium structure of demand; (c) finally, using agent-based simulation, we can numerically test the theoretical results obtained above in an environment that closely represents the actual Ethereum market and proposed data market with dynamic transaction fee adjustment. For example, we can model discrete block time and compression technology of rollups. This would allow us to validate our results and provide insights into practical rollup posting policies/services as well as L1 fee market design.

References

1. Crapis, D.: Eip-4844 fee market analysis (2023). https://ethresear.ch/t/eip-4844-fee-market-analysis/15078
2. Crapis, D., Moallemi, C.C., Wang, S.: Optimal dynamic fees for blockchain resources. CoRR arxiv:2309.12735 (2023)
3. Diamandis, T., Evans, A., Chitra, T., Angeris, G.: Dynamic pricing for non-fungible resources. CoRR arxiv:2208.07919 (2022). https://doi.org/10.48550/arXiv.2208.07919,
4. Ferreira, M.V.X., Moroz, D.J., Parkes, D.C., Stern, M.: Dynamic posted-price mechanisms for the blockchain transaction-fee market. In: Baldimtsi, F., Roughgarden, T. (eds.) AFT 2021: 3rd ACM Conference on Advances in Financial Technologies, Arlington, Virginia, USA, 26–28 September 2021, pp. 86–99. ACM (2021). https://doi.org/10.1145/3479722.3480991,
5. Leonardos, S., Reijsbergen, D., Monnot, B., Piliouras, G.: Optimality despite chaos in fee markets. CoRR arxiv:2212.07175 (2022)
6. Mamageishvili, A., Felten, E.W.: Efficient Rollup batch posting strategy on Base Layer. CoRR arxiv:2212.10337 (2022). https://doi.org/10.48550/arXiv.2212.10337
7. Nash Jr, J.F.: The bargaining problem. Econometrica: J. Econ. Soc. 155–162 (1950)

Message-Passing in the Extended UTxO Ledger

Polina Vinogradova[1]($\boxtimes$) and Orestis Melkonian[2]

[1] Input Output, Canada (IOG), Ottawa, Canada
polina.vinogradova@iohk.io
[2] Input Output, United Kingdom (IOG), Kirkwall, UK
orestis.melkonian@iohk.io

Abstract. A notable problem faced by developers of smart contracts running on an extended UTxO (EUTxO) ledger is *double satisfaction*: interacting contracts that make payouts may validate with insufficient payments made to some recipients. In this work, we formalize the notion of a stateful contract constraint being vulnerable to double satisfaction. Next, we formalize interaction among scripts and stateful contracts via *message-passing*, consisting of a specification and an implementation of a stateful distributed message-passing contract, together with a proof of the integrity of its implementation. Messages specify sender and receiver outputs, as well as the data and assets being communicated, which are recorded on the ledger in the form of special NFT tokens distributed across UTxO entries that also contain the sent assets. We give two applications of our design by considering a message: (1) as a record of a successful script computation, akin to memoization, and (2) as a mechanism for asynchronous structured contracts communication that enables a principled separation of contract communication from its computation. Building on this application of message-passing, we present a result stating that making payouts from stateful contracts using message-passing is not vulnerable to double satisfaction.

Keywords: Blockchain · Ledger · UTxO · EUTxO · Smart contract · Formal verification · Small-step operational semantics · Message-passing · Double satisfaction · Simulation relation

1 Introduction

Message-passing is the standard for communicating data and assets between contracts in account-based ledgers [3,14,26]. An alternative to the account-based ledger model is the EUTxO (extended UTxO) ledger model, implemented by platforms such as Cardano [7,16] and Ergo [10]. It is a smart contract- (or *script*-) enabled UTxO-based ledger model, where user-defined script code is used to specify conditions a transaction must satisfy to be permitted to spend a UTxO entry or mint a token. Communication between scripts in EUTxO-based ledgers follows a different architecture than for account-based models. A script may require that another script executes successfully within the same transaction.

Script interaction and communication is implemented using these kinds of *script dependencies*, as well as other constraints on the script-executing transaction.

Relying on unstructured, ad-hoc communication among EUTxO scripts presents some challenges, in particular, in terms of amenability to formal verification. For example, in order for a stateful contract to make progress, in addition to executing scripts implementing the contract, it may be necessary to run arbitrary collections of scripts on which the contract update depends (either directly or via a sequence of dependencies). Another challenge is tracking the flow of assets and data, including marking certain quantities of assets or data as "from" a particular contract (e.g. a payout to a specific address), or "to" a particular contract (e.g. a pay-in from an address). Asset flow tracking is a special case of the more general *double satisfaction problem* (DSP).

The DSP may occur when multiple scripts within the same transaction share a constraint satisfied by the transaction. Problematic occurrences of DS are due to the lack of a mechanism to associate the fulfillment of a constraint with the script imposing said constraint. For example, a payout is made only once, satisfying two scripts, each of which was expecting a separate payout. Because many contracts make payouts, this is a widely discussed problem in EUTxO programming. In Sect. 3, we present a formalization of the DSP, which has not previously been formalized.

Previous work presents principled approaches to building stateful contracts in the EUTxO ledger model, such as the constraint-emitting machine design pattern [6], as well as the more general structured contract framework (SCF) [22]. These have been mechanized in the Agda proof assistant [20] and provide the conceptual basis for the actual specification of the Cardano ledger specification [7,16], which is formulated with small-step semantics and is also mechanized in Agda [15].

We present an EUTxO layer-2 implementation of *asynchronous message-passing* as a principled approach to communication among individual scripts and the stateful contracts they implement. Our message-passing architecture is a stateful contract constructed as an instance of the structured contract framework.

The state of the message-passing contract is a set of messages. On the ledger, a special NFT token encodes a single message in the contract state, and individual message tokens are distributed across distinct UTxO entries. Each message specifies *sender* and *recipient* UTxO entries, which are authenticated at the time of minting (burning, resp.) of the message token. The message token specifies the data being sent, and must be placed in a UTxO also containing the assets being sent. Any script is able to interface with the message-passing contract so long as (i) the user input to the script can be decoded as a list of messages being produced and consumed, and (ii) the contract ensures the minting and burning of the message NFTs corresponding to the messages it sends or receives.

Our decentralized stateful contract design constitutes a way to interpret the notion of message-passing communication on an EUTxO ledger. The scripts implementing this design facilitate concurrent updates to asset token balances on the ledger that exist independently of a shared database. We argue that the message-passing approach to script and stateful contract communication addresses some of the challenges of writing scripts to run on an EUTxO ledger. To that end, we present two use cases of message-passing together with formal specification and verification of properties related to the integrity of their behaviour. We demonstrate how expressing payouts as messages from a stateful contract can resolve the DSP for payouts. The main contributions of this work are:

(i) formalization of the double satisfaction problem (Sect. 3);
(ii) specification and implementation of a message-passing structured contract (Sect. 4);
(iii) an application of the message-passing contract for memoization, including proven properties of its behaviour (Sect. 5.1);
(iv) an application of the message-passing contract as a means of asynchronous communication of data and assets between structured contracts, which serves as an alternative to communication via ad-hoc dependencies. We formalize properties of this application, including resilience of payout messages to the DSP (Sect. 5.2).

We note that an extended version of this paper, containing additional results, proofs, pseudocode, and examples, is available at[1].

2 Background

2.1 The EUTxO Ledger Model

First, we give an overview of the semantics we use for our contract and ledger specifications, introduced in prior work [4,6,22], but included here for the sake of self-containment.

Ledger Types. For the purposes of self-containment, we include a description of EUTxO ledger model types. We note and justify the (minimal) changes we introduce to the existing model in the description. The types of booleans, natural numbers, and integers are denoted by $\mathbb{B}$, $\mathbb{N}$, and $\mathbb{Z}$, respectively. The type $\mathsf{Ix} := \mathbb{N}$ is used for indexing, e.g. of elements in a list. The type $\mathsf{Slot} := \mathbb{N}$ is used to indicate blockchain time.

The ledger state consists of a UTxO set, which is a collection of unspent outputs, each associated with a unique identifier. An output is a triple $(a, v, d) \in$ Output, where $a \in$ Script is the address of the output, $v \in$ Value is the collection of assets at this address, and $d \in$ Datum is data specified by the user at the time of constructing the transaction which creates this output (we give more details on these three types below). The type of the UTxO set is $\mathsf{UTxO} := \mathtt{OutputRef} \mapsto$ Output, which is a finite key-value map with unique keys of type $\mathtt{OutputRef}$. We denote a single element in a finite key-value map u (such as the UTxO set) by $i \mapsto o \in u$. An output reference $(tx, ix) \in \mathtt{OutputRef} := \mathsf{Tx} \times \mathsf{Ix}$ pointing to an

---

[1] https://fc24.ifca.ai/wtsc/WTSC24_2.pdf.

output o in a UTxO set consists of the transaction tx, which added $(tx, ix) \mapsto o$ to the UTxO set, and the index ix, which is the position of output o in the list of outputs of tx.

The type Value is used to represent bundles of multiple kinds of assets Each type of asset in the bundle $v \in$ Value has a unique asset ID, $a \in$ AssetID := Policy × TokenName, which identifies a class of fungible tokens. Associated to the asset ID of each type of asset in a bundle is a a quantity $q \in$ Quantity := $\mathbb{Z}$, specifying the amount of the asset with the given ID in v. When v contains 0 of a given asset type, its asset ID is not included in v. An asset bundle containing one kind of asset with asset ID (policy, tokenName) of quantity one is denoted by { policy $\mapsto$ {tokenName $\mapsto$ 1} }.

An asset with ID (p, t) has the minting (and burning) policy $p \in$ Policy := Script. When an asset under this policy is minted or burned, the policy script is executed to determine whether the transaction is allowed to perform this action. The token name t is specified by the user at the time of constructing the minting transaction. It is used to differentiate between assets under the same policy. Unlike previous work [4,22], where the token name is a string, we take TokenName := Data. Value forms a group under addition (+) with a zero element (0) and a partial order ($\leq$) [5].

A script $s \in$ Script is a piece of user-defined code that is executed as part of transaction validation, applied to specific inputs. Script code is stateless and produces a boolean output. Scripts are executed as part transaction validation to check that a transaction is permitted to do the action with which the script is associated. Scripts are used to specify permissions for two kinds of actions: spending an output (these are referred to as "validators", or sometimes the "address" of the output), and minting or burning tokens (these are called minting policies).

We denote script application by $[\![\_]\!]$, followed by the script arguments. At the time of evaluation, the arguments supplied to a script consist of transaction data (of the transaction executing it), as well as the data about the specific action for which the script specifies permission (i.e. the output being spent, or the tokens being minted under the policy). An extra piece of data $d \in$ Redeemer, associated with the particular action being validated, is specified by the user at the time transaction construction.

On-chain data of variable type, including Datum, Redeemer, and TokenName, are all type synonyms for Data; for the sake of brevity, we will omit explicit calls to the corresponding encoding/decoding functions as these will be obvious from the types involved, so any time a value is used as Data presupposes that decoding is successful.

Updates to the ledger state are specified in the form of a Tx (transaction) data structure. A transaction $tx \in$ Tx contains (i) a set of *inputs*, each containing an output reference, an output, and the associated redeemer, (ii) a list of outputs, which get entered into the UTxO set with the appropriately generated output references, (iii) a pair of slot numbers representing the validity interval of the transaction, (iv) a Value being minted by the transaction, (v) a redeemer for each of the minting policies being executed, and (vi) the set of (public) keys that signed the transaction, alongside their signatures.

Small-Step Specifications. We formulate the transitions of ledgers and contracts in the form of small-step operational semantics [21], as exemplified by the official specification of the Cardano ledger [7,16]. In our specifications and contract implementation pseudocode, we follow standard set-theory notation, and clarify any non-standard notation usage alongside it.

A transition relation $\mathsf{TRANS} \subseteq (\mathsf{Env} \times \mathsf{State} \times \mathsf{Input} \times \mathsf{State})$ is a collection of 4-tuples. A member $(env,\ s,\ i,\ s')$ of this relation is also denoted by :

$$env \vdash s \xrightarrow{i} s'$$

The variable $env \in \mathsf{Env}$ is the environment of the state transition, $s \in \mathsf{State}$ is the starting state, $i \in \mathsf{Input}$ is the input, and $s' \in \mathsf{State}$ is the end state. The system TRANS is a labelled transition system. For a given transition $(env,\ s,\ i,\ s') \in \mathsf{TRANS}$, the pair $(env,\ i)$ of an environment and an input make up the *label* of this transition from s to s'. Conventionally [7], env is block-level data, such as blockchain time, whereas i is specified by the user, e.g. a transaction.

Ledger Transition Semantics. The ledger semantics on top of which we build the results of this paper are found in existing work [4,6,22], but we include them here for self-containment and in order to introduce appropriate notation. The ledger transition system is given by the subset $\mathsf{LEDGER} \subseteq \mathsf{Slot} \times \mathsf{UTxO} \times \mathsf{Tx} \times \mathsf{UTxO}$. Membership in this subset is specified by a single transition rule `ApplyTx`, which ensures that $(slot,\ utxo,\ tx,\ utxo') \in \mathsf{LEDGER}$ whenever `checkTx`$(slot,\ utxo,\ tx) = \mathsf{True}$, and $utxo'$ is given by $(\{\ i \mapsto o \in utxo\ |\ i \notin tx.\mathtt{outputRefs}\ \}) \cup tx.\mathtt{outputs}$. Here, the notation $\mathtt{r}.f$ represents accessing a (named) field f of a record $\mathtt{r}$. This is expressed in rule APPLYTX below, where any unbound variables are implicitly considered as universally quantified.

$$\textsc{ApplyTx}\frac{utxo' := (\{\ i \mapsto o \in utxo\ |\ i \notin tx.\mathtt{outputRefs}\ \}) \cup tx.\mathtt{outputs} \quad \mathtt{checkTx}\,(slot,\ utxo,\ tx)}{slot \vdash (utxo) \xrightarrow{ledgertx} ((utxo'))}$$

The function $\mathtt{checkTx} : \mathsf{Slot} \times \mathsf{UTxO} \times \mathsf{Tx} \to \mathbb{B}$ checks the predicates which are consistent with the EUTxO model on which this work builds [4,22]. This includes executing all required validator and minting policy scripts with the appropriate inputs. The projection $tx.\mathtt{outputRefs}$ returns a UTxO set containing an entry $k \mapsto o$ for each input i of tx, where the key of the entry is the output reference k of i, and its value is the output o of i. The value $utxo'$ is calculated by removing the UTxO entries in $utxo$ corresponding to those in $tx.\mathtt{outputRefs}$, and adding the entries constructed by tx, see [22] for details.

2.2 Structured Contracts

The structured contract framework [22] is a formalism for specifying and demonstrating the integrity of the implementation of a stateful contract on LEDGER.

We give the definition here for self-containment and in order to introduce the appropriate notation. A structured contract includes a small-steps semantics specification, as well as a ledger representation of its state and input. The ledger representation is a pair of functions: one which computes the contract state from a given UTxO state (or fails), and another which computes the input to the contract for a given transaction.

For a given valid LEDGER step, the representation functions must compute a valid step in the structured contract specification given that the starting UTxO state corresponds to a contract state. This integrity constraint is expressed as a proof obligation for the instantiation of a structured contract. This design guarantees that no invalid contract state updates are ever possible on the ledger.

Suppose $\mathsf{STRUC} \subseteq (\{\star\} \times \mathsf{State} \times \mathsf{Input} \times \mathsf{State})$ is a small-step transition system. Let $\pi : \mathsf{UTxO} \to \mathsf{State} \cup \{\star\}$ and $\pi_{\mathsf{Tx}} : \mathsf{Tx} \to \mathsf{Input}$ be functions such that :

$$\frac{\pi\, u \neq \star \quad e \vdash (u)\mathit{ledger}\mathsf{t}(u')}{(\pi\, u' \neq \star) \;\wedge\; \star \vdash (\pi\, u)\mathit{struc}\pi_{\mathsf{Tx}}\, t((\pi\, u'))}$$

The triple $(\mathsf{STRUC}, \pi, \pi_{\mathsf{Tx}})$ is called a *structured contract*, and we denote it by $(\mathsf{STRUC}, \pi, \pi_{\mathsf{Tx}}) \succeq \mathsf{LEDGER}$. Note that π is function with an output that is a *maybe* type, $\mathsf{State} \cup \{\star\}$, where $\{\star\}$ is a singleton. When $\pi\, u = \star$, there is no contract state corresponding to the ledger state u. The block-level data is never exposed to user-defined scripts in this model, so that the context of a structured contract is necessarily $\star \in \{\star\}$.

3 The Problem of Double Satisfaction

In the EUTxO model, scripts place constraints on the transactions executing them. *Multiple scripts* may place the *same constraint* on the data of a given transaction. The issue with certain undesirable instances of this situation is called the *double satisfaction problem* (DSP). The DSP has been discussed in Plutus documentation,[2] and in the context of contract audits,[3,4] but has not yet been formally analyzed.

The DSP applies to scripts and structured contracts that require transactions to make payouts, so it is frequently encountered in EUTxO script programming. A *naive* payout is a constraint of the form "the transaction must include an output containing value v, with address a". When two structured contract implementations both place such a constraint on a transaction, it may be satisfied by a single transaction output $(a, v, \_)$, resulting in insufficient payment made to

---

[2] https://plutus.readthedocs.io/en/latest/reference/writing-scripts/common-weaknesses/double-satisfaction.html.
[3] https://medium.com/@vacuumlabs_auditing/cardano-vulnerabilities-1-double-satisfaction-219f1bc9665e.
[4] https://github.com/tweag/tweag-audit-reports/blob/main/Marlowe-2023-03.pdf.

a. Note here that we use the notation _ to represent a term whose value is not relevant to the computation in which it appears.

To formalize this kind of vulnerability, let us assume that all systems discussed in this section are deterministic (i.e. have exactly one end state for each pair of input and start state), and define the following function, which returns all pairs of states in all valid transitions of a given structured contract STRUC :

$$\text{s STRUC} = \{\ (s, s')\ |\ \exists\, i,\ (\star, s, i, s') \in \text{STRUC}\ \}$$

Definition (Transition Constraint). A *constraint* of a transition system STRUC is a subset $C \subseteq \{\star\} \times \text{State} \times \text{Input} \times \text{State}$ such that $\text{STRUC} \subseteq C$.

Definition (Double Satisfaction). A structured contract $(\pi, \pi_{\text{Tx}}, \text{STRUC})$ is *vulnerable to double satisfaction* with respect to a constraint C whenever there exists another contract $(\pi, \pi_{\text{Tx}}, \text{STRUC}')$, with $\text{STRUC} \subseteq \text{STRUC}'$ and s STRUC = s STRUC$'$, such that $\text{STRUC}' \cap C \subsetneq \text{STRUC}'$.

Example (TOGGLE with Extra Constraint). Consider a $(\pi, \pi_{\text{Tx}}, \text{TOGGLE})$ contract, with State := $\mathbb{B}$ (i.e. Boolean), and Input := (toggle $\cup$ $\{\star\}$) $\times$ Interval[Slot].

$$\text{NoOp}\frac{}{\vdash (x)\,TOGGLE(\star,\_)(x)} \qquad \text{Toggle}\frac{5 \leq j < k \leq 9}{\vdash (x)\,Toggle(toggle,[j,k])((\neg\,x))}$$

We define a contract TOGGLE$'$ by removing $5 \leq j < k \leq 9$ from rule Toggle, assume it has the same projections π, π_{Tx} as TOGGLE, and define the constraint

$$C(\star, \_, (t, [j, k]), \_) := (t = \text{toggle}) \Rightarrow (5 \leq j < k \leq 9)$$

The contracts TOGGLE$'$ and TOGGLE transition between the same states: s TOGGLE = s TOGGLE$' = x \mapsto x,\ x \mapsto \neg\, x$. Note that TOGGLE = TOGGLE$' \cap$ C $\subsetneq$ TOGGLE$'$, hence TOGGLE is vulnerable to DS with respect to C.

Discussion. Vulnerability to the DSP comes from the lack of association of some property of transaction data with a *specific structured contract* (or script implementing it) that requires this property to hold. Our DS definition formalizes the association between a transaction property and a contract by defining a property to be associated with a contract only in the case when the a property can be expressed as a predicate on the contract state update. Thus, any property not expressible as a property of a contract state update is vulnerable to DS.

This defines a broad class of constraints that are vulnerable to DS, but for which this vulnerability may not necessarily be problematic. The preceeding example demonstrates an unproblematic constraint, C, which only requires that a toggle action happens at a particular time interval. It is possible that multiple contracts require that some other action be performed in that same time interval simultaneously.

The onus is on the structured contract author to determine for which constraints placed on the transaction by the contract double satisfaction vulnerability is a problem. Then, changes must be made to the contract to ensure that the vulnerability is removed. A general approach to mitigating arbitrary instances of DSP vulnerability is outside the scope of this work, however, in Sect. 6, we propose a solution to the DSP for payouts. A similar approach can be taken for DSP vulnerability for pay-ins. It is possible to define classes of contracts that are never vulnerable to DS. See the extended version of this work for a proof of the following lemma:

Lemma (DS-Free Contracts). A deterministic structured contract $(\pi, \pi_{\mathsf{Tx}}, \mathsf{STRUC})$ is not vulnerable to double satisfaction with respect to any constraint whenever for any (s, i), there exists an s' such that $(\star, s, i, s') \in \mathsf{STRUC}$.

DSP Mitigation. An existing heuristic for addressing the DSP is to include a constraint in the implementing script(s) that forces them to fail if *any other scripts* are being run by the transaction. This effectively mitigates negative consequences of potential vulnerabilities of the given contract's constraints to the DSP. This is likely not a practical solution in many cases, however, as it is too restrictive. We note that, like the above example, this constraint is not on the contract state update, but rather, on the transaction. This means that it is itself vulnerable to DS. However, vulnerability of this constraint to DS will likely not be deemed to be a problem by script authors, as the purpose of introducing it is to mitigate the negative consequences of other constraints' vulnerabilities.

4 Message-Passing in EUTxO

Conceptually, a message is data sent from a sender to a recipient [1]. In our design, a message is a data structure of type Msg encoded on the ledger in a specific way. It also includes a sender, receiver, and some data or assets. The content of $m \in \mathsf{Msg}$ is encoded as the TokenName of an NFT with the minting policy msgsTT. It is encoded as such in order to maintain certain guarantees about the message's integrity, which are ensured by the NFT minting policy. A message $m \in \mathsf{Msg}$ consists of the following fields:

(i) an output reference inUTxO : OutputRef. An output with this reference must be spent when the message token is minted;
(ii) an index msgIx : Ix. It is used to uniquely identify a message whenever multiple messages are produced in association with spending a single UTxO entry;
(iii) an output msgTo : Output. It is an output that must be spent to validate the consumption of the message *by that recipient* (such an output may not be unique);
(iv) an output msgFrom : Output. It is an output that must be spent to validate production of the message *by that sender*. Specifically, the entry $m.\mathtt{inUTxO} \mapsto m.\mathtt{msgFrom}$ must be spent;

(v) a value msgValue : Value. It specifies the assets being sent. When a message is minted and placed in an output, this output must *also* contain these assets;
(vi) data msgData : Data. It is the data being sent via this message.

Each message requires a unique identifier to enable some of the applications we present later. Here, we use an approach based on the thread token mechanism to ensure NFT uniqueness [4]. This mechanism requires that the thread token's minting policy checks that a particular output reference is spent from the UTxO by the minting transaction, and exactly one token is minted under this policy. To uniquely identify a message NFT we use the output reference inUTxO, together with the message index msgIx. Duplication of unique identifiers is forbidden by the implementing scripts.

Sending a list of messages is done by submitting a transaction that (i) **mints** the NFTs encoding each of the messages, and (ii) for each message, spends the sender output with a redeemer containing the list of messages "from" that output. For an output to receive a list of messages, a transaction must spend the outputs containing the messages, and **burn** the message tokens. It must also spend the receiver output, and supply it with a redeemer containing the messages it is receiving.

The state of the message-passing contract is given by a set of messages, with State$_{\mathsf{MSGS}}$:= Msg, which represents messages that have been sent, but not yet received. Here, Msg denotes the set of all subsets of Msg. The input is the whole transaction, with Input$_{\mathsf{MSGS}}$:= Tx. The MSGS transition system specifies the rules for sending and receiving messages, see Fig. 1.

The function

$$\mathsf{msgTkn}\ msg := \{\ \mathsf{msgsTT} \mapsto \{\ msg \mapsto 1\ \}\ \}$$

encodes a message as a message token, recording the message data as its token name, and msgsTT as its minting policy. According to this policy, each message token minted by a transaction must be placed into a UTxO entry locked by a special validator, msgsVal, which only checks that any message token in that UTxO entry is burned. The message token minting policy msgsTT performs the same checks and assignments (1, 3, 5, 6, 7) that are in the MSGS specification in Fig. 1, with the notable exception of checking the non-duplication of existing messages, as required by (2). This cannot be checked explicitly by msgsTT because it cannot inspect the global set of existing messages under this policy, and must instead be proved as a consequence of the generation of the message's unique identifier. The type of the decoded redeemer for both msgsTT and msgsVal is $\{\star\}$, as they are not used in the implementation.

The notation $[a1; ...; ak] : [A]$ represents a list of type A, with concatenation denoted by $+\!\!+$. The predicate _#_ takes two lists, returning True if they are disjoint, and [f a | $a \leftarrow as$] denotes list comprehension. The contracts msgsTT and msgsVal implementing the MSGS specification are given in Figs. 4 and 3.

The projection function π_{Msg} returns, for a given $utxo$, all messages encoded in the message tokens that exist in the UTxO set. It returns $\star$ when one or more

$$\text{PROCESS} \frac{\begin{array}{c}
\text{(1) construct a list of messages encoded in redeemers} \\
sndMsgs := [\,(msg, i) \mid i \leftarrow tx.\text{inputs}, (sr, msg) \leftarrow (i.\text{redeemer}), sr = \text{send}\,] \\
rcvMsgs := [\,(msg, i) \mid i \leftarrow tx.\text{inputs}, (sr, msg) \leftarrow (i.\text{redeemer}), sr = \text{receive}\,] \\
\\
\text{(2) check that no new messages are duplicates} \\
[\,\text{getMsgRef}\, m \mid (\_, m) \leftarrow newOuts\,] \mathbin{\#} [\,\text{getMsgRef}\, m \mid (\_, m) \leftarrow usedInputs\,] \\
\mathbin{\#} [\,\text{getMsgRef}\, m \mid m \leftarrow msgs\,] \\
\\
\text{(3) compute the set of message token-containing outputs being created} \\
newOuts := \{\,(o, msg) \mid o \in tx.\text{outputs}, \text{msgTkn}\, msg \subseteq o.\text{value}\,\} \\
\\
\text{(4) check that all the messages are correctly constructed : correct sender output,} \\
\text{sender has correct redeemer, output reference is spent, one message per output,} \\
\text{output containing message token has correct validator and sufficient value} \\
\forall\, (o, msg) \in newOuts,\, (msg, (msg.\text{inUTxO}, msg.\text{msgFrom},\_)) \in sndMsgs \\
\land\, \{\, t \subseteq o.\text{value} \mid \text{dom}\, t = \{\text{msgsTT}\}\,\} = \text{msgTkn}\, msg \\
\land\, o.\text{validator} = \text{msgsVal} \land o.\text{value} \geq msg.\text{msgValue} \\
\\
\text{(5) compute the set of message token-containing outputs being spent} \\
usedInputs := \{\,(i, msg) \mid i \in tx.\text{inputs}, \text{msgTkn}\, msg \subseteq i.\text{output.value}\,\} \\
\\
\text{(6) check that all messages are correctly consumed :} \\
\text{the receiver output is correct, input has correct redeemer, and message exists} \\
\forall\, (i, msg) \in usedInputs,\, (msg, (\_, msg.\text{msgTo},\_)) \in rcvMsgs \land msg \in msgs \\
\\
\text{(7) check minting and burning of message tokens :} \\
\Sigma_{(\_,msg) \in newOuts}\, \text{msgTkn}\, msg + \Sigma_{(\_,msg) \in usedInputs}\, (-1) * (\text{msgTkn}\, msg) \\
= \{\,\text{msgsTT} \mapsto tkns \in tx.\text{mint}\,\}
\end{array}}{\star \vdash (\,msgs\,) \xrightarrow[\text{MSGS}]{tx} \left(\begin{array}{c} (msgs \setminus [\,m \mid (\_, m) \leftarrow usedInputs\,]) \\ \cup [\,m \mid (\_, m) \leftarrow newOuts\,] \end{array}\right)}$$

Fig. 1. Specification of the MSGS transition

messages have been duplicated or outputs incorrectly generated in the $utxo$. This is guaranteed by `msgOutsOK`, see Fig. 2 for the details.

$$\pi_{\text{Msg}}\, utxo := \begin{cases} \{\, m \mid \_ \mapsto o \in utxo, \text{msgTkn}\, m \subseteq o.\text{value}\} & \text{if } \texttt{msgOutsOK}\, utxo \\ \star & \text{otherwise} \end{cases}$$

We give a proof sketch of the simulation relation between LEDGER and MSGS in the extended version of this paper. Recall that this relation ensures the integrity of the implementation, i.e. that the implementation of MSGS via the msgsTT and msgsVal scripts only allows ledger updates that are mapped to *valid* MSGS transitions (by the π and π_{Tx} projections).

5 Message-Passing Use Cases

In this section we discuss applications of the message-passing structured contract.

5.1 Memoization

There may be strict resource use constraints that apply to executing code on a blockchain. It may not be possible for a transaction to run the code of a large contract in its entirety. It may be desirable to divide such code into less memory- and CPU-intensive functions whose outputs are pre-computed for use by an aggregate function. A script may not trust values pre-computed off-chain, so a proof that a value was correctly computed on-chain is required. In this section we describe a technique for constructing such proofs using the MSGS contract. It is similar to a specific kind of caching called *memoization* [12], which is also how we refer to our approach.

Consider a function myFunction : MyInType $\to$ MyOutType which performs some computation. We define a script checkMyFunction (Fig. 5a), which wraps the computation done by myFunction. This script mints a message token with data (*fIn*, *fOut*), such that myFunction *fIn* = *fOut*, and a script useMyFunction (Fig. 5b) that can consume a message with the redeemer [(receive, m)] when m is addressed to an output locked by useMyFunction, and is sent by an output locked by checkMyFunction. This message serves as a proof that myFunction *fIn* = *fOut*, so, useMyFunction can perform a computation checkStuff relying on the fact that myFunction *fIn* = *fOut*. Note that msgTo is not constrained by this contract, so that the generated message can be addressed to any recipient.

We give the result that formalizes the use of message-passing to prove that myFunction *fIn* = *fOut*.

Lemma (Verified Input-Output Pairs). For any $(s, u, tx, u') \in$ LEDGER, with $\pi\, u \neq \star$ and $(i, (\text{useMyFunction}, v, d), r) \in tx.\texttt{inputs}$, such that

$$[(\text{receive, } m)] = r$$
$$(\textit{fIn, fOut}) = m.\texttt{msgData}$$
$$m.\texttt{msgFrom} = (\text{checkMyFunction, \_, \_})$$

necessarily myFunction *fIn* = *fOut*, and $m.\texttt{msgTo} = (\text{useMyFunction}, v, d)$. For a proof sketch, see the extended version of the paper. Note here that the memoization approach we presented can be viewed as a kind of *untrusted oracle*. The computation done to produce the memoized input-output pair cannot be falsified, so that no trust is required to make use of it.

5.2 Contracts Using Message-Passing

Stateful contract interaction, or communication, in the EUTxO model is implemented via dependencies [4]. A *dependency* of a script c is a constraint requiring that another script c' must be executed within the same transaction, possibly with specific arguments. Using the MSGS contract to implement communication between contracts reduces ad-hoc reliance on arbitrary script dependencies, and makes contract interaction more principled and amenable to formal verification.

Message-Passing in the Extended UTxO Ledger   161

We say that stateful contracts *use message-passing* when they require the production or consumption of messages to or from scripts implementing the contract. We formalize this notion in this section. Note that due to space constraints, we omit several interesting results about contracts using message-passing, as well as a detailed example of a contract that makes payouts via messages, all of which can be found in the extended version of this work.

Message-passing specification is closely integrated with ledger semantics, and inspects the scripts, redeemers, and datums of the input transaction. Because of this, a message-passing contract must also inspect these in order to correctly construct a message. So, a state projection function for a contract that uses message-passing includes the UTxO entry relevant to the contract state, in full. The contract input is the complete transaction.

Suppose that $F : \text{Output} \mapsto \mathbb{B}$ is a constraint on outputs, and $c : \text{UTxO} \to \mathbb{B}$ is a constraint on a valid UTxO state. The contract denoted by $(\pi_{\text{Fc}}, \pi_{\text{Tx}}, \text{STRUC})$ is a structured contract with

$$\text{State} := \{ i \mapsto o \in u \mid u \in \text{UTxO}, F\, o \}$$

$$\pi_{\text{Fc}}\, u := \begin{cases} \{ i \mapsto o \in u \mid F\, o \} & \text{if } c\, u \\ \star & \text{otherwise} \end{cases}$$

$$\pi_{\text{Tx}} := \text{id}$$

We can combine STRUC and MSGS to construct the structured contract $\text{STRUC}_{\text{MSGS}}$,

$$\pi_{\text{State}-M}\, u := \begin{cases} (\pi_{\text{Fc}}\, u, \pi_{\text{Msg}}\, u) & \text{if } \pi_{\text{Fc}}\, u \neq \star \neq \pi_{\text{Msg}}\, u \\ \star & \text{otherwise} \end{cases}$$

$$\pi_{\text{Tx}-M} := \text{id}_{\text{Tx}}$$
$$\text{STRUC}_{\text{MSGS}} := \{ (\star, (s, m), tx, (s', m')) \mid (\star, s, tx, s') \in \text{STRUC}, (\star, m, tx, m') \in \text{MSGS} \}$$

We call this contract *message-augmentation* of STRUC. We define the following functions that filter messages sent or received by STRUC :

$$\texttt{getFromSTRUCmsgs}\; msgs := \{\, m \mid m \in msgs,\, F\,(m.\texttt{msgFrom})\, \}$$
$$\texttt{getToSTRUCmsgs}\; msgs := \{\, m \mid m \in msgs,\, F\,(m.\texttt{msgTo})\, \}$$

Definition (Uses Message-Passing). We say that STRUC *uses message-passing* whenever the set defined by

$$\texttt{getMSGS}\,(\star, (s, m), tx, (s'm')) := \texttt{getFromSTRUCmsgs}\,(m' \backslash m) \cup \texttt{getToSTRUCmsgs}\,(m \backslash m')$$

is non-empty for some $(\star, (s, m), tx, (s'm')) \in \text{STRUC}_{\text{MSGS}}$.

We define the set of *payouts* in the step $(\star, (s, m), tx, (s'm')) \in \text{STRUC}_{\text{MSGS}}$ by

$$\texttt{getPayouts}\,(\star, (s, m), tx, (s'm')) := \{ msg \in \texttt{getFromSTRUCmsgs}\,(m' \setminus m) \mid\\ msg.\texttt{msgValue} > 0 \wedge \neg\, (F\,(msg.\texttt{msgTo})) \}$$

Whenever this set is necessarily non-empty for some step in $\mathsf{STRUC_{MSGS}}$, we say that it *makes payouts with messages*.

Discussion A contract is said to use message-passing whenever there is a step in $\mathsf{STRUC_{MSGS}}$ that requires the production or consumption of a non-empty set of messages to or from STRUC. Some computation performed by contracts implementing STRUC may be contingent on receiving a specific message. For example, accepting a payment message sent by another contract.

Contracts that use message-passing share common features that are both necessary and sufficient for a script c implementing the contract to be able to interface with the message-passing contract: (i) the script's redeemer must decode to a list of sent/received messages, and (ii) the script must ensure that the corresponding messages are included in the transaction's mint field.

For a given step $(\star, s, t, s') \in \mathsf{STRUC}$, we refer to the messages sent and received by outputs that make up s, i.e. those filtered by F, as a script's *communication*. Calculating s' for the given (s,t) is the STRUC contract's computation. STRUC may still include arbitrary dependencies on scripts implementing contracts other than MSGS. Specifying when a contract has no non-message dependencies is important for determining when it is guaranteed to be able to progress. This is, however, the subject of future work.

6 Messages as Payouts

A *payout* is a message that is from STRUC, but not addressed to STRUC, and specifies a sent value greater than zero. The function that returns all the payouts for a given contract, `getPayouts`, is a function of the start and end MSGS states *only*. Consider a transition $(\star, (s, m), tx, (s'm')) \in \mathsf{STRUC_{MSGS}}$. To guarantee that a message-payout msg is made whenever rule $R \subseteq \mathsf{STRUC_{MSGS}}$ applies, R must ensure that (i) $msg \in m' \setminus m$, (ii) `msgValue` $msg > 0$, and (iii) msg must be *from* an output locked by some script c implementing STRUC. The script c implementing this constraint of STRUC should instead include the constraint `msgTkn` $msg \in tx.$`mint`. For a detailed example of making payouts via messages, see the extended version of this work. Making payouts in this way has an advantage over the naive approach to payouts.

MSGS Payouts and Double Satisfaction. In Sect. 3 we present a naive approach to payouts. This approach is vulnerable to DS, since the constraint requiring a payout to be made is expressed as a function the input transaction, rather than the state. Naive payout outputs can be produced and consumed by any valid transaction at any time, independently of the state update of any contract. Without a mechanism to *associate a payout with its sender*, is not possible to include naive payouts in a contract's state.

Intuitively, making payouts via messages provides such a mechanism by ensuring that the sender of the payout is recorded in the message token, and that the message token has a unique identifier. Formally, since making payouts via messages can be expressed as a predicate on a the start and end MSGS states, rather than on the input transaction, constraints on message payouts are not vulnerable to DS for a message-enhanced contract. We can express this as follows (see Appendix A for the proof):

Lemma (MSGS-payouts and DS). Suppose $(\pi_{\mathsf{F},\mathsf{c}}, \pi_{\mathsf{Tx}}, \mathsf{STRUC})$ is a structured contract, and $\mathsf{STRUC}_{\mathsf{MSGS}}$ is its message-enhanced version. Let $\mathsf{C} \supset \mathsf{STRUC}_{\mathsf{MSGS}}$ be a constraint expressible in terms of some predicate C' on the set of payout messages,

$$\mathsf{C}\ (\star, (s,m), tx, (s'm')) := \mathsf{C}\text{'}\ (\texttt{getPayouts}_{\mathsf{STRUC}}\ (\star, (s,m), tx, (s', m')))$$

Then, the contract $\mathsf{STRUC}_{\mathsf{MSGS}}$ is not vulnerable to DS with respect to C.

7 Discussion

7.1 Related Work

Message-passing is the backbone of distributed computing [1,8]. The π-calculus process calculus has been developed to formalize message-passing between processes in distributed computing scenarios [17]. We conjecture that it may be possible to apply this formalism to message-passing between structured contracts.

The UTxO ledger model introduced by Bitcoin [18], as well as EUTxO ledger implementations [10], are themselves message-passing schemes, wherein a transaction is a message to a script. Our scheme reinterprets messages in a way that allows them to have a single verified sender output, and a receiver that is also an output. The contract MSGS can be viewed as a kind of linear sub-ledger within LEDGER, which can be used as a tool in specification and verification of properties of communicating contracts.

In account-based ledgers [3,14,26], (synchronous) message-passing is the default mode of communication between contracts. The Scilla programming language [25], with its emphasis on separating communication from computation for stateful contracts on the Zilliqa ledger [26], inspired this work. Even though Scilla was developed for the account-based ledger model, the communicating automata structure it uses to model contracts may be useful in describing message-passing structured contracts as well.

Existing work on rigs [9], which are cryptographic data structures that provide integrity-at-a-distance, presents an approach to maintaining data integrity across potentially multiple state-managing machines. Aspects of this approach are similar in spirit to the thread-token technique we use to uniquely identify messages and ensure non-duplication of message tokens on the ledger; both are based on temporal and causal dependencies of operations on one another.

A version of asynchronous, but centralized, message-passing is implemented in the ERC-20 Ethereum contract for fungible tokens [11]. The ERC-20 design is primarily for asset transfers, whereas ours can be used to communicate authenticated data as well. Implementing message-passing via a centralized data-storage contract such as ERC-20 on an EUTxO ledger would significantly increase contention over UTxO entries between message-passing transactions, and therefore reduce concurrency.

Formalization of blockchain and ledger functionality forms a foundation for rigorous reasoning about smart contracts security, discussed in the detailed overview [24]. Mathematical models of EUTxO and UTxO ledgers and smart contracts on those ledgers, including ours, often specify a simplified version of actual implementations [2,4,6,13,19,23].

7.2 Future Work

The scheme we presented in Fig. 1 is such that the outputs that must be spent in order to consume a given message are fully specified (via the msgTo field of the message), including their scripts, values, and datums. In future work, this constraint could be relaxed for a more permissive and versatile system design. A *time of expiry* can be added to the message structure and used to specify a time after which a message can be consumed under different constraints. Changing the type of the message-passing redeemer from a list of messages to a list of messages (for communication) together with some extra data (for computation) can allow a given script to more easily engage in both computation and communication as a result of applying a transaction.

In this work, we did not specify trace-based properties of LEDGER or any structured contract STRUC. This topic, in general, is the subject of future work. Of particular interest are structured contracts that can be guaranteed to take a step without the need for executing "external" scripts, i.e. ones other than those used to implement that contract. It may be unrealistic for a contract to always take a step without *any* external contracts validating, e.g. running a script which locks funds used for paying into the contract. However, it seems feasible to limit a structured contract's dependencies to message-passing only. Formalizing and proving properties about this class of structured contracts in the future is of interest.

In the future, we intend to mechanize this contract and its applications in Agda, building upon the formal EUTxO ledger model [6] and structured contracts framework [22]. To achieve the goal of integrating our work into the more realistic mechanization of the Cardano ledger [15], and eventually implement it on the platform, some adjustments to our design may be required.

7.3 Conclusion

Principled approaches to implementing and reasoning about the behavior of stateful smart contracts in the EUTxO ledger model have already been formalized in existing work. However, such models do not include any special provisions for analyzing communication among contracts. In this work, we focus on formalizing communication of data and assets among scripts as well as the stateful contracts they implement. We first formalize a common problem in contract interaction—the double satisfaction problem, which has to do with a single transaction satisfying the constraints of multiple scripts it executes. We demonstrate how a single pay-out made by a transaction in the case where a payment *per executed script* was expected may constitute an instance of the DS formalism we presented.

We define what a message data structure is in the context of an EUTxO ledger—a unique identifier associated with the data and assets being sent, as well as its sender and receiver outputs. We then define how to use the ledger asset-minting mechanism to encode messages as tokens which appear in the UTxO set. Messages are sent and received asynchronously, tracked by a distributed structured contract MSGS. A proof of correctness of its implementation guarantees that minted message tokens specify verified sender, receiver, data, and come with appropriate amounts of sent assets.

To give examples of formal reasoning about the message-passing contract and its applications, we present two use cases. The first is a variation on memoization, wherein message tokens specifying input-output pairs of a particular computation serve as proof artefacts of its correctness. The second formalizes the idea of structured contract communication via message-passing. We formalize when a message constitutes a "payout" from a contract, and then demonstrate how expressing payouts as messages can address vulnerability to the DSP in the case of payouts. The necessity of executing the MSGS-implementing scripts (which may require fee payment) whenever messages are sent and received is a limitation of our design.

Acknowledgments. We would like to thank Manuel Chakravarty for providing inspiration for this work, by being one of the first proponents of the message-passing idiom for concurrency in the EUTxO model. We would also like to thank Philip Wadler for useful discussions.

A Proofs

Proof of Lemma (MSGS-payouts and DS). Suppose that $(\pi_{F,c}, \pi_{Tx}, \text{STRUC}')$ is another (more permissive) structured contract, with $\text{STRUC}_{\text{MSGS}} \subseteq \text{STRUC}'_{\text{MSGS}}$, and s $\text{STRUC}_{\text{MSGS}}$ = s $\text{STRUC}'_{\text{MSGS}}$. For any $(\star, (s, m), tx, (s', m')) \in \text{STRUC}'_{\text{MSGS}}$, by definition,

$\text{getPayouts}_{\text{STRUC}'}(\star, (s, m), tx, (s', m')) =$
$\{\, ms \in m' \setminus m \mid F\,(ms.\texttt{msgFrom}) \land ms.\texttt{msgValue} > 0 \land \neg\,(F\,(ms.\texttt{msgTo}))\,\}$

which depends only on F (which is the same for STRUC and STRUC'), and $m'\setminus m$. Now, by the assumed preconditions on STRUC', for any $(\star, (s, m), tx, (s', m')) \in \text{STRUC}'_{\text{MSGS}}$, we can find $(\star, (s, m), tx', (s', m')) \in \text{STRUC}_{\text{MSGS}} \subseteq \text{STRUC}'_{\text{MSGS}}$. Then,

$$\begin{aligned}
\texttt{C}\,(\star, (s, m), tx, (s'm')) &= \texttt{C'}\,(\text{getPayouts}_{\text{STRUC}'}(\star, (s, m), tx, (s', m'))) \\
&= \texttt{C'}\,(\text{getPayouts}_{\text{STRUC}}(\star, (s, m), tx', (s', m'))) \\
&= \texttt{C}\,(\star, (s, m), tx', (s'm'))
\end{aligned}$$

Therefore, any transition in $\text{STRUC}'_{\text{MSGS}}$ must also satisfy C. We get that $\text{STRUC}'_{\text{MSGS}} \cap \texttt{C} = \text{STRUC}'_{\text{MSGS}}$, meaning that $\text{STRUC}_{\text{MSGS}}$ is not vulnerable to DS with respect to such a C.

B Pseudocode

$\mathsf{msgOutsOK} : \mathsf{UTxO} \to \mathbb{B}$
$\mathsf{msgOutsOK}\ utxo :=$
$\quad\quad\forall\ (i \mapsto o) \in utxo, \{\ \mathsf{msgsTT} \mapsto \{m \mapsto q\}\} \subseteq o.\mathsf{value} \Rightarrow$
$\quad\quad\quad (q = 1)$
$\quad\quad\quad \wedge\ (m \neq \star)\ \wedge\ (m.\mathsf{inUTxO} \mapsto \_\ \notin utxo)$
$\quad\quad\quad \wedge\ [\![\mathsf{msgsTT}]\!]\ (\star, (i.\mathsf{id}, \mathsf{msgsTT}))$
$\quad\quad\quad \wedge\ \forall (i' \mapsto o') \in utxo, i \neq i',\ \{\ \mathsf{msgsTT} \mapsto \{m \mapsto \_\}\} \notin o'.\mathsf{value}$
$\quad\wedge\ \forall\ (tx, ix) \mapsto o\ \in\ utxo,\ \forall\ i \in tx.\mathsf{inputs},$
$\quad\quad\quad [\![i.\mathsf{output.validator}]\!]\ (i.\mathsf{output.datum},\ i.\mathsf{redeemer},\ (tx, i))$
$\quad\quad\quad \wedge\ (ix \mapsto o) \in tx.\mathsf{outputs}$

$\quad\mathsf{SR} := \{\mathsf{send}, \mathsf{receive}\}$
$\quad$ *Tag specifying whether message is being sent or received*

$\mathsf{getMsgRef} : \mathsf{Msg} \to (\mathsf{OutputRef}, \mathsf{Ix})$
$\mathsf{getMsgRef}\ msg := (msg.\mathsf{inUTxO},\ msg.\mathsf{msgIx})$
$\quad$ *Returns unique message identifier*

Fig. 2. Projections and auxiliary MSGS functions

$\mathsf{msgsTT} := \mathsf{msgsTT}'\ \mathsf{msgsVal}$

$[\![\mathsf{msgsVal}]\!]\ (\_,\ \_,\ (tx, i)) :=$
$\quad \forall\ msg \in \{\{\ m\ |\ \mathsf{msgsTT}'\ (i.\mathsf{output.validator}) \mapsto \{\ m \mapsto 1\}\} \subseteq i.\mathsf{output.value}\ \},$
$\quad \{\ \mathsf{msgsTT}'\ (i.\mathsf{output.validator}) \mapsto \{msg \mapsto -1\}\} \subseteq tx.\mathsf{mint}$

Fig. 3. Minting policy and validator for UTxO containing message tokens

msgsTT′ : Script → Script

⟦msgsTT′ mv⟧ (_, (tx, pid)) := ∀ msg, { pid ↦ {msg ↦ _} } ⊆ tx.mint,

[getMsgRef m | (_, m) ← newOuts] # [getMsgRef m | (_, m) ← usedInputs]

∧ ∀ (o, msg) ∈ newOuts,

  (msg, (msg.inUTxO, msg.msgFrom, _)) ∈ sndMsgs

  ∧ { t ⊆ o.value | dom t = {pid} } = msgTkn msg

  ∧ o.validator = mv ∧ o.value ≥ msg.msgValue

∧ ∀ (i, msg) ∈ usedInputs, (msg, (_, msg.msgTo, _)) ∈ rcvMsgs

∧ $\Sigma_{(\_,msg) \in newOuts}$ msgTkn msg + $\Sigma_{(\_,msg) \in usedInputs}$ (−1) ∗ (msgTkn msg) =

{pid ↦ $tkns$ ∈ tx.mint }

where

msgTkn msg := { pid ↦ {msg ↦ 1} }

sndMsgs := [(msg, i) | i ← tx.inputs, (sr, msg) ← i.redeemer, sr = send]

rcvMsgs := [(msg, i) | i ← tx.inputs, (sr, msg) ← i.redeemer, sr = receive]

newOuts := { (o, msg) | o ∈ tx.outputs, msgTkn msg ⊆ o.value }

usedInputs := { (i, msg) | i ∈ tx.inputs tx, msgTkn msg ⊆ i.output.value }

Fig. 4. Minting policy constructor for message tokens

⟦checkMyFunction⟧ (_, r, (tx, i)) :=
  m.inUTxO = i.outputRef
  ∧ m.msgFrom = i.output
  ∧ m.msgValue = 0
  ∧ msgTkn m ⊆ tx.mint
  ∧ myFunction fIn = $fOut$

where

[(send, m)] = r

(fIn, $fOut$) = m.msgData

⟦useMyFunction⟧ (d, r, (tx, i)) :=
  (m.msgFrom = (checkMyFunction, _, _)
  ∧ m.msgTo = i.output
  ∧ (−1) ∗ (msgTkn m) ⊆ tx.mint
  ∧ checkStuff d r (tx, i) (fIn, $fOut$))
  ∨ checkOtherStuff d r (tx, i)

where

[(receive, m)] = r

(fIn, $fOut$) = m.msgData

(a) Script minting message token.   (b) Script using the memoized output.

Fig. 5. Scripts for memoizing the output of myFunction.

References

1. Andrews, G.: Foundations of Multithreaded, Parallel, and Distributed Programming. Addison-Wesley, Boston (1999)
2. Bartoletti, M., Bracciali, A., Lepore, C., Scalas, A., Zunino, R.: A formal model of Algorand smart contracts (2021)
3. Buterin, V.: Ethereum: a next-generation smart contract and decentralized application platform (2014). https://ethereum.org/en/whitepaper/

4. Chakravarty, M.M.T., et al.: Native custom tokens in the extended UTXO model. In: Margaria, T., Steffen, B. (eds.) ISoLA 2020. LNCS, vol. 12478, pp. 89–111. Springer, Cham (2020). https://doi.org/10.1007/978-3-030-61467-6_7
5. Chakravarty, M.M.T., et al.: $UTXO_{ma}$: UTXO with multi-asset support. In: Margaria, T., Steffen, B. (eds.) ISoLA 2020. LNCS, vol. 12478, pp. 112–130. Springer, Cham (2020). https://doi.org/10.1007/978-3-030-61467-6_8
6. Chakravarty, M.M.T., Chapman, J., MacKenzie, K., Melkonian, O., Peyton Jones, M., Wadler, P.: The extended UTXO model. In: Bernhard, M., et al. (eds.) FC 2020. LNCS, vol. 12063, pp. 525–539. Springer, Cham (2020). https://doi.org/10.1007/978-3-030-54455-3_37
7. Corduan, J., Güdemann, M., Vinogradova, P.: A formal specification of the Cardano ledger (2019). https://github.com/input-output-hk/cardano-ledger/releases/latest/download/shelley-ledger.pdf
8. Coulouris, G., Dollimore, J., Kindberg, T.: Distributed Systems: Concepts and Design (International Computer Science). Addison-Wesley Longman, Amsterdam (2005)
9. Coward, K., Toliver, D.R.: Simple rigs hold fast (2022)
10. Ergo Team: Ergo: A Resilient Platform For ContractualMoney (2019). https://whitepaper.io/document/753/ergo-1-whitepaper
11. Ethereum Team: ERC-20 TOKEN STANDARD (2023). https://ethereum.org/en/developers/docs/standards/tokens/erc-20
12. Field, A., Harrison, P.: Functional Programming. International computer science series, Addison-Wesley (1988). https://books.google.ca/books?id=nYtQAAAAMAAJ
13. Gabbay, M.J.: Algebras of UTxO blockchains. Math. Struct. Comput. Sci. **31**(9), 1034–1089 (2021). https://doi.org/10.1017/S0960129521000438
14. Goodman, L.: Tezos-a self-amending crypto-ledger (white paper) (2014). https://tezos.com/whitepaper.pdf
15. Knispel, A., et al.: Formal specification of the Cardano blockchain ledger, mechanized in Agda (2024). https://omelkonian.github.io/data/publications/cardano-ledger.pdf
16. Knispel, A., Vinogradova, P.: A Formal Specification of the Cardano Ledger integrating Plutus Core (2021). https://github.com/input-output-hk/cardano-ledger/releases/latest/download/alonzo-ledger.pdf
17. Milner, R.: Communicating and Mobile Systems: The Pi-Calculus. Cambridge University Press, Cambridge (1999)
18. Nakamoto, S.: Bitcoin: A Peer-to-Peer Electronic Cash System (2008). https://bitcoin.org/en/bitcoin-paper
19. Nester, C.: A foundation for ledger structures. In: Anceaume, E., Bisière, C., Bouvard, M., Bramas, Q., Casamatta, C. (eds.) 2nd International Conference on Blockchain Economics, Security and Protocols, Tokenomics 2020, Toulouse, France, 26–27 October 2020. OASIcs, vol. 82, pp. 7:1–7:13. Schloss Dagstuhl - Leibniz-Zentrum für Informatik (2020). https://doi.org/10.4230/OASICS.TOKENOMICS.2020.7
20. Norell, U.: Dependently typed programming in agda. In: Koopman, P., Plasmeijer, R., Swierstra, D. (eds.) AFP 2008. LNCS, vol. 5832, pp. 230–266. Springer, Heidelberg (2009). https://doi.org/10.1007/978-3-642-04652-0_5
21. Plotkin, G.: A structural approach to operational semantics. J. Log. Algebr. Program. **60–61**, 17–139 (2004). https://doi.org/10.1016/j.jlap.2004.05.001
22. Vinogradova, P., et al.: Structured contracts in the EUTxO ledger model (2024). https://fmbc.gitlab.io/2024/files/FMBC2024.pdf

23. Rupić, K., Rožić, L., Derek, A.: Mechanized formal model of bitcoin's blockchain validation procedures. In: Bernardo, B., Marmsoler, D. (eds.) 2nd Workshop on Formal Methods for Blockchains (FMBC 2020). Open Access Series in Informatics (OASIcs), vol. 84, pp. 7:1–7:14. Schloss Dagstuhl – Leibniz-Zentrum für Informatik, Dagstuhl, Germany (2020). https://doi.org/10.4230/OASIcs.FMBC.2020.7. https://drops.dagstuhl.de/entities/document/10.4230/OASIcs.FMBC.2020.7
24. Sánchez, C., Schneider, G., Leucker, M.: Reliable smart contracts: state-of-the-art, applications, challenges and future directions. In: Margaria, T., Steffen, B. (eds.) ISoLA 2018. LNCS, vol. 11247, pp. 275–279. Springer, Cham (2018). https://doi.org/10.1007/978-3-030-03427-6_21
25. Sergey, I., Nagaraj, V., Johannsen, J., Kumar, A., Trunov, A., Hao, K.C.G.: Safer smart contract programming with Scilla. Proc. ACM Program. Lang. **3**(OOPSLA), 185 (2019)
26. Team, T.Z.: The ZILLIQA Technical Whitepaper (2017). https://docs.zilliqa.com/whitepaper.pdf

ZeroAuction: Zero-Deposit Sealed-Bid Auction via Delayed Execution

Haoqian Zhang[1], Michelle Yeo[2], Vero Estrada-Galiñanes[1], and Bryan Ford[1]([✉])

[1] École Polytechnique Fédérale de Lausanne, Lausanne, Switzerland
{haoqian.zhang,vero.estrada,bryan.ford}@epfl.ch
[2] National University of Singapore, Singapore, Singapore
mxyeo@nus.edu.sg

Abstract. Auctions, a long-standing method of trading goods and services, are a promising use case for decentralized finance. However, due to the inherent transparency property of blockchains, current sealed-bid auction implementations on smart contracts requires a bidder to send at least two transactions to the underlying blockchain: a bidder must first commit their bid in the first transaction during the bidding period and reveal their bid in the second transaction once the revealing period starts. In addition, the smart contract often requires a deposit to incentivize bidders to reveal their bids, rendering unnecessary financial burdens and risks to bidders. We address these drawbacks by enforcing delayed execution in the blockchain execution layer to all transactions. In short, the blockchain only accepts encrypted transactions, and when the blockchain has finalized an encrypted transaction, the consensus group decrypts and executes it. This architecture enables ZeroAuction, a sealed-bid auction smart contract with zero deposit requirement. ZeroAuction relies on the blockchain enhanced with delayed execution to hide and bind the bids within the encrypted transactions and, after a delay period, reveals them automatically by decrypting and executing the transactions. Because a bidder only needs to interact with the blockchain once instead of two times to participate in the auction, ZeroAuction significantly reduces the latency overhead along with eliminating the deposit requirement.

Keywords: Commit-and-Reveal · Auction · Blockchain · Decentralized Finance

1 Introduction

The auction, an ancient way of negotiating the exchange of goods and services, enters the world of blockchains and decentralized finance powered by general smart contracts [27]. While the blockchain provides an ideal platform for open auctions in which every bidder can observe others' bids during the bidding period, it is notably challenging to implement sealed-bid auctions due to the inherent transparent property of blockchains.

A sealed-bid auction should hide the bids during the bidding phase, bind them so they can not be modified, and reveal the bids during the revealing phase. To implement a sealed-bids auction under a transparent blockchain, auctioneers often rely on a commit-and-reveal approach in which a bidder first sends a commit transaction which contains the hash of their bid during the bidding phase, and the bidder propagates the reveal transaction to disclose their bid once the bidding phase is over. Although this simple approach hides the bids, bidders can choose not to pay if they win. In addition, it allows bidders to only reveal the bids that financially benefit them, *e.g.*, by committing multiple bids, but only revealing the smallest one that can win the auction. Altogether, these types of misbehaviour negatively impact the *fairness* of the protocol. To financially discourage these actions, a sealed-bid auction smart contract often requires a deposit from bidders during the bidding phase and returns the deposit when a bidder honestly finishes the auction. Section 2 provides an example of such a smart contract simplified from previous work [5,16,17].

However, this approach still has several drawbacks: (a) a bidder needs to interact with the blockchain for at least two rounds causing excessive latency overhead; (b) the smart contract needs to store the commitment of each bid leading to unnecessary storage overhead; (c) the smart contract requires deposits to incentivize the bidders to reveal their bids even for a bidder who only wants to bid a little, rendering avoidable financial burdens; (d) as the smart contract keeps the deposit, there are security risks of the deposits, such as the DAO attack [18]; (e) it is challenging for the auctioneer to decide the required deposit [23]; (f) bidders can choose never to reveal their bids; (g) due to a network congestion event [15] or deliberate denial-of-service (DoS) attack [10], the blockchain might fail to include the revealed transaction; (h) the number of auctions in which a bidder can participate is limited by the deposit requirement.

To overcome these drawbacks, we adopt *delayed execution* [29], a feature embedded in the blockchain architecture. When executing transactions under delayed execution, consensus nodes must execute all transactions with a global delay time parameter, and consensus nodes should not observe the content of any transaction during the delay time period to ensure the effectiveness of the delay execution; thus, the blockchain has to accept the encrypted transactions and the decryption and execution of the transaction can only happen after the delay. A blockchain enhanced with delayed execution enables the optimization of the commit-and-reveal scheme because the underlying blockchain, rather than users, handles the bid reveals.

In reality, a recipient should only accept a transaction once the blockchain finalizes the transaction after T block confirmations to mitigate double-spending attacks. For example, Ethereum requires 64 block confirmations (2 epochs) for a transaction to be finalized [11]. Our delayed execution adopts the same delay time parameter as the required T block confirmations for all transactions so that the blockchain executes and finalizes a transaction at the same time after a T block delay, and the delayed execution does not increase the transaction latency.

We demonstrate ZeroAuction, a sealed-bid auction smart contract with *zero* deposit requirement under our delayed execution. In ZeroAuction, a bidder only needs to send one transaction in which the bidder pays for their bid if it is the current highest bid. The blockchain under delayed execution automatically hides transactions; thus, bids are private during the bidding phase. When entering the revealing phase, the blockchain executes the transactions one by one, charging the current highest bid while returning other funds. Because a bidder only needs to send one transaction instead of two to participate in the auction, ZeroAuction reduces the latency for bidders by half and eliminates the deposit requirement. We present ZeroAuction in detail in Sect. 3.

We stress that ZeroAuction mitigates the drawbacks mentioned above: (a) a bidder only needs to interact with the blockchain once instead of two, significantly reducing the latency overhead; (b) ZeroAuction does not need to store the bids commitment from bidders in the smart contract; (c)-(e) ZeroAuction eliminates the deposit requirement; (f)-(g) the blockchain guarantees the revealing of all bids regardless of the bidders' behaviors and network environment; (h) a bidder can use the same funds to bid in multiple auctions, as there is no deposit requirement. To our knowledge, our solution is the first blockchain-based sealed-bid auction solution without a deposit requirement. However, we note that these advantages also come with an associated cost: auctioneers can not set up their preferred bidding period for more than the fixed global delayed time.

Previously, F3B utilized the idea of delayed execution to mitigate front-running attacks with a negligible latency overhead [29]. Tuxedo uses delayed execution to scale computations on blockchains [9]. This paper demonstrates the potential of delayed execution from the point of optimizing sealed-bid auction smart contracts.

Finally, we discuss a number of promising approaches for implementing delayed execution. We conclude that the threshold encryption method achieves the best trade-off within the existing toolbox in terms of achieving the properties of delayed execution, providing compatibility with existing blockchains, and inducing a reasonable latency overhead [19,29].

2 Preliminaries

In this section, we briefly introduce the properties of a sealed-bid auction, the commit-and-reveal scheme with a sealed-bid auction example and the delayed execution abstraction.

2.1 Sealed-Bid Auction Properties

We require a sealed-bid auction smart contract to satisfy at least the following properties (formal definitions in Appendix A):

- **Hiding:** No bidder knows the bid of any other bidder during the bidding period.
- **Binding:** A bidder can not change their bid once the blockchain finalizes the bidding transaction.
- **Revealing:** All the sealed bids will be revealed during the revealing period.

Algorithm 1: Commit-and-reveal auction smart contract

1 **Init** *Upon creating the auction smart contract*:
2   Set d as required deposit for the auction
3     $highest \leftarrow 0$, $winner \leftarrow \varnothing$, $hash \leftarrow []$
4
5 **Bid** *Upon receiving i's commitment c_i first time in bidding period*:
6   Assert(i transfers d)
7     $hash[i] \leftarrow c_i$
8
9 **Reveal** *Upon receiving i's bid b_i and salt r_i first time in revealing period*:
10   Assert(Hash(b_i, r_i) = $hash[i]$)
11   Assert($b_i \leq d$)
12   **if** $b_i > highest$ **then**
13   Distribute $highest$ to $winner$ when $winner \neq \varnothing$;
14   Distribute $d - b_i$ to i
15         $highest \leftarrow b_i$
16         $winner \leftarrow i$
17   **else**
18   Distribute d to i;
19   **end**

- **Non-malleability:** No bidder can alter any encrypted bid from others into another form such that the plaintext of the altered encrypted bid is related to the original bid.

The non-malleability property ensures that simply observing one bidder's encrypted bid does not give another bidder an unfair advantage, for example, to prevent a malicious bidder from altering an existing bid's ciphertext to bid 1 coin more than the value in the encrypted bid. Specifically, we consider the notion of NM-CPA security commonly used in the context of sealed-bid auctions [6,7,20]. Intuitively, NM-CPA security states that the plaintext decryptions of encrypted bids produced by an adversarial bidder must be indistinguishable.

To illustrate the benefit of delayed execution, we did not consider the posterior privacy property, which hides the losing bids from the public. We note that additional cryptographic tools like Zero-Knowledge Proofs (ZKP) or Multi-Party Computation (MPC) are needed for sealed-bid auctions ensuring the posterior privacy property [3,12,13].

2.2 Commit-and-Reveal Smart Contract for Sealed-Bid Auction

Algorithm 1 illustrates implementing a commit-and-reveal smart contract simplified from real-world examples on the blockchain for a sealed-bid auction [5,16,17]. The smart contract contains two phases: (a) the bidding phase (**Bid** function), where each bidder submits their hidden bid commitment. This implements the commit stage of the commit-and-reveal scheme. (b) the revealing phase (**Reveal** function), where every bidder reveals his bid and the contract determines the winning bidder. This implements the reveal stage of the commit-and-reveal scheme.

In the bidding phase, bidders submit their hidden bid commitment c_i, and to ensure that bidders have enough funds to pay for what they bid, each bidder needs to transfer a deposit d. For simplicity, the contract requires any bid must be equal or smaller than the required deposit[1]. The array *hash* stores the commitments for all bidders.

In the revealing phase, each bidder submits their bid b_i and random salt r_i. The smart contract first checks that the hash of the bid and salt is identical to the commitment c_i sent in the bidding phase. If the hash is not equal to the hash of c_i, the function terminates with the bidder losing their deposit. Otherwise, if b_i is the current highest bid, the contract keeps b_i of the bidder's deposit and returns the remainder $d - b_i$ portion of the deposit to the ith bidder and the fund of the previous *winner*, if any. If b_i is not the current highest bid, the contract returns all his deposit d. When all bidders reveal their bids, the contract determines the *winner*, which is the bidder who submitted the highest bid and can pay for their bid.

This commit-and-reveal auction smart contract can satisfy the hiding, binding, and non-malleability properties, but it only partially satisfies the revealing property. The hiding and binding property directly follows from the underlying cryptographic commitment scheme. The non-malleability property may or may not be satisfied depending on the underlying commitment scheme (*i.e.*, whether the commitments are non-malleable [8]). Finally, the revealing property is enforced by fact that the deposit held by the smart contract is larger than the bids as well as the check done by the smart contract (Line 10) to ensure that the smart contract will slash the deposit if bidders do not reveal their bids or reveal an incorrect bid. Therefore, rational bidders will choose to reveal their bids during the reveal phase. Nevertheless, this revealing guarantee *does not hold* for malicious bidders.

We note, however, that this contract has several notable drawbacks:

(a) Each bidder has to interact with the blockchain for two rounds, increasing the latency overhead.
(b) The contract needs to store the bid commitment for each bidder, which increases the storage overhead.
(c) The deposit acts as an additional financial threshold for participating in the auction. Even a bidder who only wants to bid a small amount of funds could have to pay a high deposit to even participate in the auction.
(d) As the smart contract keeps the deposit, the deposits are exposed to security risks, such as the DAO attack [18].
(e) The auctioneer must set up the required deposit as an upper bound for all bids. Determining a minimal upper bound is extremely difficult when initi-

---

[1] By allowing a bidder to bid more than his deposit, they may choose not to pay for their bid at a cost of losing his deposit.

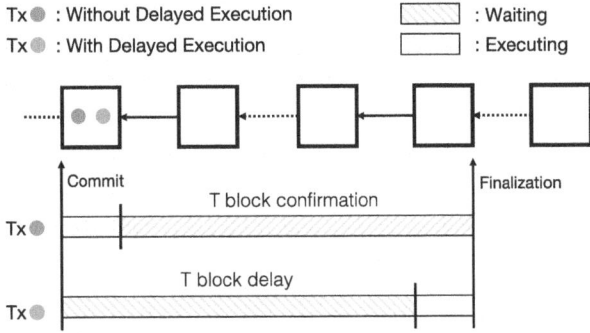

Fig. 1. In a blockchain without delayed execution, the consensus nodes execute the blue transaction upon its commitment, but recipients must wait for T block confirmation until its finalization. In the blockchain with delayed execution, the consensus nodes first wait for a T block delay before decrypting and executing the green transaction when the blockchain finalizes the transaction. Both transactions have the same finalization time; thus, the delayed execution does not increase transaction latency. (Color figure online)

ating the contract as it relies on external knowledge of bidders' preferences and solvency status [23].

(f) Users can choose never to reveal their bids. In particular, unless we impose stronger assumptions on the adversarial model of the users in the system (e.g., deposit slashing with only rational users, which would make it irrational to withhold revealing of bids), there is no guarantee that Algorithm 1 can implement a commit-and-reveal smart contract with revealing property.

(g) The revealed bid might be missed due to network congestion [15] or a deliberate denial-of-service (DoS) attack [10], violating the revealing property.

(h) The deposit requirement limits the number of auctions in which a bidder can participate, as the coins used in the deposit for one auction cannot be used as a deposit for another auction.

2.3 Delayed Execution Abstraction

A delayed execution is an abstraction on the execution layer to ensure blockchains execute transactions with a delay [9,29]. We require that consensus nodes must execute all transactions with a fixed delay time. Furthermore, consensus nodes should not observe the content of any transaction during the delayed period to ensure the effectiveness of the delay execution. Hence, the blockchain has to accept *encrypted transactions*, and the decryption and execution of the transactions can only happen after the delay.

We formally define an abstraction of a delayed execution protocol on an underlying blockchain as follows:

Definition 1 (Delayed Execution Abstraction). *A delayed execution abstraction Π of some other protocol Π' is a tuple $(T_0, T, T', \Pi', (\text{Enc}, \text{Dec}))$ where*

$\infty > T' > T > 0$, T_0 is the time of execution of Π', and (Enc, Dec) are the encryption and decryption functions of a committing encryption scheme. Π takes the same inputs as Π' and encrypts the inputs using Enc. Π ensures that its outputs are the same as Π', and that any decryption of encrypted ciphertexts and outputs occur before $T_0 + T$ w.p. ϵ for some negligible $\epsilon > 0$ and after $T_0 + T'$ w.p. 1.

In the context of blockchains, Π' could refer to the execution of transactions or smart contracts running on the blockchain. For instance, Π' can be an open auction smart contract, and T_0 would denote the block's height in the blockchain containing the committed smart contract. The T parameter represents the delay time in blocks to delay the transaction outputs. T' denotes the upper bound on the execution time of Π, i.e., the time it takes to obtain the outputs of Π' considering the delay time and the execution time of the underlying protocol Π'.

Choosing Confirmation Time as Delay Time: Although transactions are delayed as ciphertexts, we can choose a specific delay time so that adding delayed execution does not increase the transaction latency of the underlying blockchain. In practice, we note that all blockchains require recipients to wait for certain number of block confirmations before accepting a transaction to mitigate double-spending attacks. For instance, Ethereum requires 64 block confirmations (2 epochs) for a transaction to be finalized [11]. Without loss of generality, we assume that our underlying blockchain requires T block confirmation[2] to finalize a transaction into the blockchain. If we adopt the same T for the delayed time, the blockchain with delayed execution can finalize a transaction at the same time as the underlying blockchain. Figure 1 illustrates this process: in the underlying blockchain without delayed execution, the consensus nodes immediately execute the blue transaction upon its commitment, but then recipients must wait for T block confirmation until its finalization. In contrast, for the blockchain with delayed execution, the consensus nodes first wait for the T block delay before decrypting and executing the green transaction when the blockchain finalizes the transaction. Therefore, both transactions have the same finalization time, and the delayed execution with a T block delay does not increase transaction latency.

3 Auction Smart Contract with Delayed Execution

This section introduces ZeroAuction, an auction smart contract under the delayed execution, with a pseudocode and running examples. We argue how ZeroAuction satisfies the properties of the sealed-bid auction informally and show how ZeroAuction can overcome the drawbacks mentioned in Sect. 2.

3.1 Pseudocode

Algorithm 2 describes the ZeroAuction smart contract. When the auctioneer creates the smart contract, the consensus nodes run the **Init** function, which

---

[2] T can be 1 for the blockchains with instant finalization.

Algorithm 2: ZeroAuction smart contract with delayed execution

```
1  Init Upon creating the auction smart contract:
2  |   highest ← 0, winner ← ∅
3
4  Bid Upon receiving i's bid b_i in the bidding period:
5  |   if b_i > highest then
6  |   |   Assert(i transfers b_i)
7  |   |   Distribute highest to winner when winner ≠ ∅;
8  |   |   highest ← b_i
9  |   |   winner ← i
10 |   end
```

initializes two valuables: *highest*, which indicates the value of the current highest bid, and *winner*, which records the current winner of the auction. During the biding period, each bidder can submit his bid by calling **Bid** function, which encapsulates both commit and reveal phases. The function checks whether this bid is more than the current *highest*. If so, the smart contract asks the bidder to transfer the amount of his bid to itself, refunds the current *winner*, and finally update the current *highest* and *winner*. If not, the bidder loses the auction.

3.2 Under the Delayed Execution Environment

ZeroAuction, as presented in Algorithm 2, implements an open auction, as none of the bids are hidden. However, it becomes a sealed-bid auction when employed in a delayed execution environment. Bidders submit their bids within the delay time, so the delayed execution guarantees hiding the bids during the bidding period and revealing them during the revealing period.

Requirements: We require the delay time in the delayed execution to be the same as the confirmation time T of the underlying blockchain. Thus, when the blockchain with delayed execution decrypts and executes the transaction, it also finalizes the transaction without extra latency overhead. We also require the bidding time in any sealed-bid auction to be $\leq T$. Observe that a bidding time of more than T reveals the plaintext of encrypted bids submitted at the start of the bidding period to other bidders before the bidding period is over. We further demand that the blockchain delay executes all transactions by T time, including non-auction transactions, such as transfer transactions. This requirement ensures that no user can make quick transfers to another account during the auction to affect the outcome of the auction, given information revealed about others' bids during the revealing period.

Non-malleability: To guarantee the non-malleability property of the auction, a bidder first encrypts their transaction using a symmetric non-malleable encryption scheme, and the delayed execution ensures the release of the symmetric key

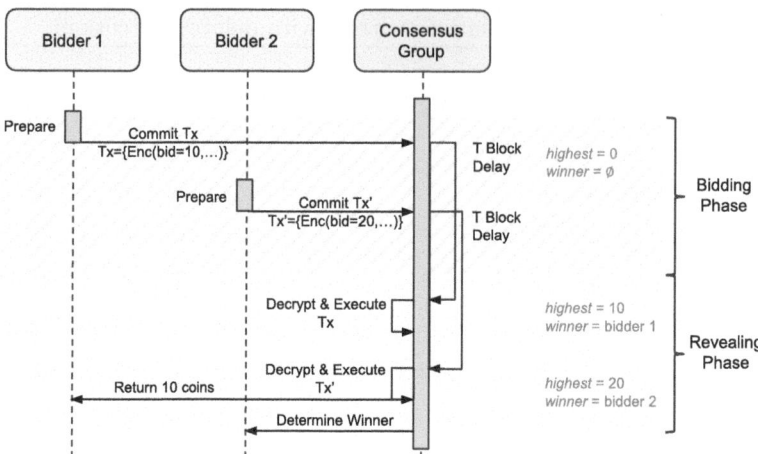

Fig. 2. A running example with two bidders. Both bidders commit their encrypted transactions to the blockchain during the bidding phase. After T block delay of each transaction, the consensus group decrypts and executes the transaction. At the end of the execution phase, the smart contract can determine the final auction winner.

after the delay so that consensus nodes can decrypt and execute the transaction. Specifically, when committing a ZeroAuction contract under delayed execution, participating bidders first need to encrypt their entire original signed transaction (which contains their bid) under a symmetric CPA-secure encryption scheme (*e.g.*, block cipher with CBC mode of operation) and then append a strongly-unforgeable message authentication code (MAC) onto the resulting ciphertext. This encrypt-then-MAC composition is NM-CPA secure under these assumptions on the encryption scheme and MAC [2]. Next, bidders also further encrypt all relevant keys used to encrypt-then-MAC their bid transaction under the delayed execution (further discussion in Sect. 4.1) and send the encrypted symmetric keys as well as the encrypted transactions to the blockchain. Finally, the delayed execution decrypts and releases the symmetric keys after T blocks so that consensus nodes can decrypt and execute the transaction.

3.3 Single Auction Running Examples

This subsection provides examples with two bidders under the delayed execution with T as the global delayed parameter. For simplicity, we assume the bidding period is T in this example. We logically create two phases: the first T blocks as the bidding phase and the second T blocks as the revealing phase.

Two Successful Bids: In the first example, we demonstrate two legitimate bidders, presented in Fig. 2. Assuming there are two bidders, bidder 1 and bidder 2, with their bids being 10 and 20 coins, respectively. We further assume they have enough cryptocurrency in their account balances to support their bids if they win. During the bidding phase, both bidders must seal and hide their bids by encrypting their signed transactions. We assume that both bidders prepare their encrypted transactions, and the blockchain successfully commits them, with bidder 1's transaction ordered before that of bidder 2.

T blocks after committing the encrypted transactions on the blockchain, consensus nodes begin to decrypt and execute the transactions. Upon executing bidder 1's transaction, the value *highest* is 0, and bidder 1's bid is more than *highest*; thus, the following things happen: (a) Bidder 1 needs to transfer 10 coins to the smart contract, (b) *highest* updates to 10, (c) *winner* changes to bidder 1. Upon executing bidder 2's transaction, the value *highest* is 10 and, bidder 2's bid is more than *highest*; thus, the following things happen: (a) Bidder 2 needs to transfer 20 coins to the smart contract, (b) Bidder 1 receives the refund of 10 coins from the smart contract, (c) *highest* updates to 20, (d) *winner* changes to bidder 2. At the end of the revealing phase, the blockchain has executed all the bidding transactions. The value *winner* records bidder 2 as the auction's final winner, and bidder 2 has already paid for what he bids.

One Failed Bid: In the second example, we assume that bidder 2 does not have enough balance to support his bid. The procedure is the same as before until the blockchain executes the bidder 2's transaction. However, as bidder 2 does not have enough balance to transfer 20 coins to the smart contract, the transaction failed in the assertion, and consensus nodes then revert and discard the transaction. At the end of the revealing phase, we can be sure that bidder 1 is the final winner, and bidder 1 has already paid what he bids.

3.4 Auction with Transfer Transactions

As the consensus nodes cannot verify the transaction until its decryption and execution, the bidder could submit a bid with a value that is more than their balance during the bidding period. If the bidder wants to make the bidding transaction valid, they can make transactions to transfer more coins to their balance. However, the bidder must commit the transfer transaction before the commitment of the bidding transaction so that the blockchain executes the transfer transaction before the bidding transaction, as the blockchain delays all transactions by T blocks. In contrast, if, by the time of the execution, the bidder still does not have enough funds, the bidding transaction will fail as in line 6 of Algorithm 2.

When the revealing phase starts, the bidder can observe the bids from other bidders and accordingly make a transfer transaction to change their balance. However, we argue that the bidder can not benefit from it. Because the blockchain delays all transactions by T blocks, it will execute the transfer transaction committed during the revealing phase after the execution of the bidding transaction. Thus, the transfer transaction does not affect the auction.

3.5 Multiple Auctions

Because ZeroAuction does not need deposit, a bidder can use the same funds to participate in multiple auctions. For example, suppose there are two auctions, with auction A happening before auction B. A bidder thus can bid all their funds for both auctions. If the bidder wins auction A, they will not have enough funds to support their bid for auction B; thus, auction B fails the assertion (Line 6). If the bidder does not win auction A, they can still use the same funds for auction B. The blockchain delaying all transactions guarantees that, even though the bidder's available fund for auction B may change because of auction A, such change happens without knowing any of the bids in auction B.

3.6 ZeroAuction Properties

We informally reason how the ZeroAuction achieves the sealed-bid auction properties. **Correctness:** After all executions, *winner* is the bidder who submits the highest bid with the ability to pay; Hence, *winner* is the legitimate winner of the auction. **Hiding:** As all transactions submitted during the bidding period are encrypted, no entity can observe the bids. **Binding:** Once the blockchain finalizes the bidding transaction, the consensus nodes firmly writes the transaction into the blockchain; thus, no entity can change the bid. **Revealing:** The blockchain guarantees the revealing of the bids during the revealing period. **Non-malleability:** As the encrypt-then-MAC composition used in our delayed execution is NM-CPA secure [2], no bidder can benefit from copying and changing other bidders' ciphertexts. We formally prove these properties in Sect. 5.

We acknowledge that ZeroAuction only achieves a weak version of binding in that a bidder can bid more than they have without consequence. We stress, however, that this is a feature and not a bug of ZeroAuction. In doing so, we eliminate the deposit requirement and allow a bidder to participate in multiple auctions using the same funds. Additionally, although the balance of the bidder may change before the execution of their bidding transaction and consequently alter the result of the auction due to the transactions committed before the bidding transaction, we note that such behavior only happens without the knowledge of other revealed bids due to all transactions being delayed for the same T blocks.

In addition, ZeroAuction addresses the drawbacks mentioned in Sect. 2:

(a) Each bidder only needs to interact with the blockchain once only during the bidding period (see **Bid** function in Algorithm 2), decreasing the latency overhead.
(b) ZeroAuction does not need to store bid commitments from each bidder as in the array of hashed commitments (*hash*) in Algorithm 1, reducing the storage overhead.
(c)–(e) ZeroAuction does not require any deposit; hence, ZeroAuction mitigates the security risk of the deposited funds and relieves the auctioneer from determining the deposit amount.

(f)–(g) The blockchain guarantees the revealing of bids regardless of the bidders' behaviors and network environment.

(h) As ZeroAuction does not require a deposit, a bidder can participate in multiple auctions using the same fund.

However, achieving those advantages brings an inflexibility: ZeroAuction cannot have a bidding period of more than T blocks.

4 Discussion

In this section, we discuss possible implementations of the delayed execution methods and apply the delayed execution to optimize all the commit-and-reveal smart contracts.

4.1 Possible Encryption Methods for Delayed Execution

There are multiple approaches to implement a delayed execution. This subsection briefly discusses those approaches and argues that threshold encryption, though imperfect, is the best approach to implement delayed execution within the existing toolbox.

Encryption and Decryption by a Centralized Authority: A centralized authority can help to reveal the transaction. When committing a transaction to the blockchain, a user first encrypts the transaction with a symmetric key and then uses the public key of the centralized authority to encrypt this symmetric key. After the delay, the centralized authority reveals the symmetric key. However, this approach brings the single-point-of-failure issue to the system that the centralized authority might be malicious or offline.

Time-Lock Puzzle: Alternatively, a user can use a time-lock puzzle to blind the transaction. For example, blockchain can use a verifiable delay function [4,21] to implement a proof-of-elapsed-time, and consensus nodes have to compute the function to decrypt the transaction. However, it is still an open challenge to link the computational time to real-time, and the variance of the solving time can pose a security issue to delayed execution, *e.g.*, a lucky node solves the puzzle fast, thus observing the bid during the bidding period.

Trusted Execution Environment: Instead of trusting an authority, we can utilize a trusted execution environment achieved by hardware, such as Intel SGX [28]. The hardware guarantees the delayed execution of transactions. Nevertheless, this method is subject to a single point of failure or compromise [22,25].

Threshold Encryption: Instead of relying on a centralized authority, we can rely on a group of nodes to decrypt a transaction. Specifically, t out of n nodes can decrypt the transaction after the delay. However, $t-1$ out of n can not reveal anything about the transaction, even if they collude. While it is natural to deploy this method for a permissioned blockchain, it is unclear how to offer compatibility to a proof-of-work blockchain without changing its security assumption. In addition, running threshold decryption increases the overhead of the underlying blockchain system.

In conclusion, each method has its pros and cons, and none of the methods are entirely satisfactory. We hope that as scientific research advances in this domain, better methods will emerge. Nevertheless, from a practical perspective within the existing toolbox, we argue that the threshold encryption method achieves the properties of the delayed execution (guaranteed by its security assumption), provides maximum compatibility to various blockchain systems' security assumptions (not relying on any centralized component), and demonstrates a reasonable latency delay [19,29]. We note that existing work F3B uses delayed execution based on threshold encryption to mitigate front-running attacks, and its threshold encryption component only induces a negligible (0.026%) increase in transaction latency on Ethereum [29], demonstrating that the threshold encryption solution is practical in real-world scenarios.

4.2 Optimizing Other Commit-and-Reveal Smart Contracts

Although we only discuss optimizing the sealed-bid auction example under the delayed execution, such a technique can generally be applied in other smart contract on blockchains relying on the commit-and-reveal scheme, such as voting, quizzes, random number generations, and games. In general, a user no longer needs to interact with the blockchain for two rounds to commit and reveal the value, but the blockchain, by default, hides and reveals the value (and the entire transaction). Thereby, other commit-and-reveal smart contracts can benefit in many ways similar to ZeroAuction: (a) reducing the latency cost that a user only writes data to the blockchain once; (b) preventing the output bias that a user may choose not to reveal his value in the traditional commit-and-reveal approach; (c) eliminating the deposit requirement in the committing phase, as the blockchain guarantees the revealing of the secret value. We leave the proof and demonstration of this generalization as future work.

5 Analysis of Delayed Execution

In this section, we formally show that ZeroAuction achieves all the necessary properties of a sealed-bid auction. For ease of exposition, we defer the formal definition of a commit-and-reveal scheme as well as the non-malleability property in Appendix A.

Let Π be a delayed execution abstraction with delay parameter T and execution time upper bound T' of a ZeroAuction protocol Π' for a single bid. Recall that T_0 is the time of execution of the underlying protocol Π'.

Theorem 1. Π is ϵ_1-hiding in the time period $[T_0, T_0 + T]$, ϵ_2-binding, and T'-revealing for $\epsilon_1, \epsilon_2 > 0$, ϵ_1, ϵ_2 negligible, and finite $T' > 0$.

Proof. Recall that the ZeroAuction protocol Π' does not alter the input bid in any form and the output of Π' is simply the input bid.

We first show that Π is ϵ_1-hiding for the duration $[T_0, T_0 + T]$. Let m be the input of Π' (the bid). Π runs $\mathsf{Enc}(m, r) = c$ for input m and some random value r. As $(\mathsf{Enc}, \mathsf{Dec})$ is CPA secure, and decryption of c only occurs before time $T_0 + T$ w.p. ϵ, the probability ϵ_1 that the message m can be retrieved from the ciphertext c during the time interval $[T_0, T_0 + T]$ is $\epsilon_1 < \epsilon + \epsilon'$ where ϵ' is the probability of a PPT adversary breaking the underlying encryption scheme. Since ϵ and ϵ' are both negligible, ϵ_1 is also negligible.

We now show that Π is ϵ_2-binding. Since $(\mathsf{Enc}, \mathsf{Dec})$ is a committing encryption scheme, for any distinct m, m', $\mathbb{P}[\mathsf{Dec}(\mathsf{Enc}(m)) = m'] < \epsilon_2$ for some negligible ϵ_2. Thus Π is ϵ_2-binding.

Finally, we show that Π is T'-revealing. From Definition 1, Π outputs the same outputs as Π' almost surely within T' time from the execution of Π for finite T'. Thus, Π is T'-revealing. □

Theorem 2. Π with a CPA secure symmetric ecryption scheme and strongly unforgeable MAC is NM-CPA secure.

Proof. Follows as per Theorem 4.4 in [2].

Theorem 3. Π satisfies all 4 sealed-bid auction properties.

Proof. Follows directly as a consequence of Theorems 1 and 2.

6 Related Work

Many papers have proposed to implement sealed-bid auctions on blockchains. Depending on who reveals the bids, we can classify the sealed-bid auction designs into two types: relying on bidders or a trusted third party(*e.g.*, an auctioneer) or group.

For the auction designs relying on bidders to reveal the bids [5,16,17] (similar to our commit-and-reveal design in Sect. 2.2), the bidders must first commit their bids and then reveal them, with two rounds of interactions with the blockchain causing excessive latency overhead. Further, such design requires to incentivize bidders to reveal their bids.

A trusted third party(group) can help to reveal the bids. Galal and Youssef proposed a sealed-bid auction that relies on an auctioneer to determine the winner with verifiability using zero-knowledge proofs (ZKP) [12,13]. Nevertheless, it still requires bidders to interact with the blockchain for two rounds. Strain utilizes the two-party computation to compare pairs of bids and uses ZKP to prove the outcome is correct [3]. However, its complexity grows as bidders increase, and it is too costly to use on the Ethereum blockchain. Trustee [14] relies on Intel SGX [28] to implement a sealed-bid auction while reducing the gas cost on Ethereum. However, it brings the concerns of a single point of failure or compromise. Riggs uses time-based cryptography on the application layer to achieve a non-interactive auction, but the high gas cost makes it not practical on Ethereum [24].

We propose ZeroAuction to demonstrate how delayed execution optimizes sealed-bid auction smart contracts. Unlike previous work, a bidder does not need a deposit to participate in the auctions and only needs to interact with the blockchain once. However, our solution has an upper bound of possible bidding duration.

Limited works have explored the delayed execution on blockchains. Tuxedo uses delayed execution to scale computations on blockchains [9]. F3B utilizes delayed execution to mitigate front-running attacks with a negligible latency overhead and addresses the spamming and incentive issues when a blockchain adopts the delayed execution [29].

7 Conclusion

In this paper, we first introduce a technique that delay executes transactions on the blockchain and also outline a protocol named ZeroAuction that demonstrates the utility of our delay execution technique to sealed-bid auctions. We show that if the delay time is the same as the confirmation time of the underlying blockchain, delay executing transactions does not increase transaction latency. Further, we demonstrate that when executing ZeroAuction under delayed execution, bidders do not need a deposit and only require one round of interaction with the blockchain to participate in a sealed-bid auction. However, our solution brings a major inflexibility: the bidding period can be at most the global delay time.

A Cryptographic Primitives and Definitions

A.1 Commit-and-Reveal Scheme

A commit-and-reveal scheme is a pair of algorithms (Commit, Reveal) run between two parties S and R in two stages, where the sender S wants to commit a message m to the receiver R. In the following, we adapt the notation and definition of commitment scheme from previous work [26]. Both parties receive a security parameter (1^n) as input. In the commit stage, Commit(m, r) takes as a plaintext message m from a message space $\mathcal{M}$, a random string r, and outputs a commitment string c. In the reveal stage, Reveal(c, r, m^*) takes as input a commitment string c, randomness r and an auxiliary parameter m^{*}[3]. The sender S

---

[3] We use m^* as a placeholder for auxiliary information that S might have to send R depending on how the commit-and-reveal scheme is actually implemented. For instance, in hash-based commitment schemes m^* would be the message that S committed to in the commit stage.

sends a single message m^* as well as r to R and R either outputs m and accepts or rejects.

In the context of sealed-bid auctions, we require a commit-and-reveal scheme to satisfy 3 additional properties: ϵ_1-hiding, ϵ_2-cryptographic binding, and τ-revealing for positive but negligible values of ϵ_1 and ϵ_2, and some $\tau > 0$. We define these properties as follows:

Definition 2 (ϵ-hiding). *Let $\Pi = ($Commit, Reveal$)$ be a commit-and-reveal scheme. Let us define the following game played between PPT R and honest S during the commit stage of the commit-and-reveal protocol.*

- *R chooses $m_0, m_1 \in \mathcal{M}$ and gives m_0, m_1 to S*
- *S runs $c_0 \leftarrow$ Commit(m_0, r_0) and $c_1 \leftarrow$ Commit(m_1, r_1)*
- *S samples a random bit $b \xleftarrow{\$} \{0,1\}$ and gives c_b to R*
- *R outputs a guess bit b'*

We say Π is ϵ-hiding if $\forall\ m_0, m_1$, $\mathbb{P}[b' = b] < \frac{1}{2} - \epsilon$ for some $\epsilon > 0$.

The ϵ-hiding property of commit-and-reveal schemes in the context of sealed-bid auctions guarantee that once a bid is committed, any adversary can only uncover the bid with negligible probability during the commit stage. This guarantees that the *bids are hidden from others during the bidding period*.

Definition 3 (ϵ-binding). *Let $\Pi = ($Commit, Reveal$)$ be a commit-and-reveal scheme. We say Π is ϵ-cryptographic binding if for all PPT S, S succeeds in the following game with honest R with negligible probability.*

- *S produces a commitment c during the commit stage of Π*
- *S outputs two distinct messages m_0, m_1 such that for both $b = 0$ and $b = 1$, R on input (c, r_b, m^*) accepts and outputs m_b.*

The ϵ-binding property of commit-and-reveal schemes in the context of sealed-bid auctions guarantee that once a bid is committed, the commitment can only open to two different messages with negligible probability. This ensures that *committed bids cannot be modified*.

Definition 4 (τ-revealing). *Let $\tau > 0$ be some time parameter, S, R PPT, and $\Pi = ($Commit, Reveal$)$ be a commit-and-reveal scheme. We say Π is τ-revealing if for all $m \in \mathcal{M}$, S and honest R running Reveal(Commit$(m,r), r, m^*)$ results in R accepting and outputting m in time at most τ.*

We are interested in commit-and-reveal schemes that satisfy the τ-revealing property for finite τ. This ensures that all committed bids will be revealed during the revealing period, and guarantees that *participants cannot selectively and indefinitely withhold bids*.

A.2 NM-CPA Security

Init
$k \xleftarrow{\$} \mathcal{K}; b \xleftarrow{\$} \{0,1\}; S \leftarrow \emptyset$

LR(m_0, m_1)
if pdec then $C \leftarrow \bot$
else $C \xleftarrow{\$} Enc(k, m_b); S \leftarrow S \cup \{C\}$
return C

Enc(m)
$C \xleftarrow{\$} Enc(k, m)$
return C

Dec*(C^*)
pdec $\leftarrow$ true
for $i \in [|C^*|]$:
  if $C^*[i] \in S$ then $M^*[i] \leftarrow \bot$
  else $M^*[i] \leftarrow Dec(k, C^*[i])$
return M^*

Finalise(d)
Return $(d = b)$

Fig. 3. NM-CPA security game $\Gamma^{\text{nm-cpa}}$ for symmetric key encryption schemes

We use the definition of NM-CPA security for symmetric encryption schemes from [2], which we will reiterate here for completeness. NM-CPA security is defined via the following game $\Gamma^{\text{nm-cpa}}$ (refer to Fig. 3). The game begins with the initialization step that chooses a symmetric encryption key k randomly from some keyspace $\mathcal{K}$, as well as a fixed random bit b. The adversary is allowed access to a special left-or-right (LR) encryption oracle that takes in a pair of messages (m_0, m_1) and always encrypts the left (m_0) or the right (m_1) message depending on the choice of b [1]. In parallel, the adversary also has access to a one-time-use decryption oracle Dec^* which takes as input a vector of ciphertexts and outputs the plaintext decryption of each ciphertext. After querying Dec^*, the adversary does not have access anymore to the LR oracle; however, it continues to have access to the plaintext encryption oracle Enc. Finally, the adversary outputs a guess bit d, and we say the adversary wins the game (output of game is 1) if $d = b$. For any adversary $\mathcal{A}$, we define the advantage of the adversary to be the following: $Adv^{\text{nm-cpa}}(\mathcal{A}) = 2 \cdot \mathbb{P}[\Gamma^{\text{nm-cpa}} \text{ outputs } 1] - 1$.

NM-CPA security is shown by comparing the advantage of the adversary in the NM-CPA security game to an adversary with the same resources in another game and then using a known security reduction to show NM-CPA security. We omit the details in this write-up for clarity of exposition, but we refer the interested reader to [2] for a thorough overview.

References

1. Bellare, M., Desai, A., Jokipii, E., Rogaway, P.: A concrete security treatment of symmetric encryption. In: FOCS, pp. 394–403. IEEE Computer Society (1997)
2. Bellare, M., Namprempre, C.: Authenticated encryption: relations among notions and analysis of the generic composition paradigm. J. Cryptol. **21**(4), 469–491 (2008)

3. Blass, E.-O., Kerschbaum, F.: Strain: a secure auction for blockchains. In: Lopez, J., Zhou, J., Soriano, M. (eds.) ESORICS 2018. LNCS, vol. 11098, pp. 87–110. Springer, Cham (2018). https://doi.org/10.1007/978-3-319-99073-6_5
4. Boneh, D., Bonneau, J., Bünz, B., Fisch, B.: Verifiable delay functions. In: Shacham, H., Boldyreva, A. (eds.) CRYPTO 2018. LNCS, vol. 10991, pp. 757–788. Springer, Cham (2018). https://doi.org/10.1007/978-3-319-96884-1_25
5. Chen, B., Li, X., Xiang, T., Wang, P.: Sbrac: blockchain-based sealed-bid auction with bidding price privacy and public verifiability. J. Inf. Secur. Appl. **65**, 103082 (2022)
6. Choi, S.G., Dachman-Soled, D., Malkin, T., Wee, H.: A black-box construction of non-malleable encryption from semantically secure encryption. J. Cryptol. **31**(1), 172–201 (2018)
7. Coretti, S., Dodis, Y., Tackmann, B., Venturi, D.: Non-malleable encryption: Simpler, shorter, stronger. IACR Cryptol. ePrint Arch. 772 (2015)
8. Di Crescenzo, G., Katz, J., Ostrovsky, R., Smith, A.: Efficient and non-interactive non-malleable commitment. In: Pfitzmann, B. (ed.) EUROCRYPT 2001. LNCS, vol. 2045, pp. 40–59. Springer, Heidelberg (2001). https://doi.org/10.1007/3-540-44987-6_4
9. Das, S., Awathare, N., Ren, L., Ribeiro, V.J., Bellur, U.: Better late than never; scaling computation in blockchains by delaying execution. arXiv preprint arXiv:2005.11791 (2020)
10. Eskandari, S., Moosavi, S., Clark, J.: SoK: transparent dishonesty: front-running attacks on blockchain. In: Bracciali, A., Clark, J., Pintore, F., Rønne, P.B., Sala, M. (eds.) FC 2019. LNCS, vol. 11599, pp. 170–189. Springer, Cham (2020). https://doi.org/10.1007/978-3-030-43725-1_13
11. Gasper (2022). https://ethereum.org/en/developers/docs/consensus-mechanisms/pos/gasper/. Accessed 03 Oct 2022
12. Galal, H.S., Youssef, A.M.: Succinctly verifiable sealed-bid auction smart contract. In: Garcia-Alfaro, J., Herrera-Joancomartí, J., Livraga, G., Rios, R. (eds.) DPM/CBT -2018. LNCS, vol. 11025, pp. 3–19. Springer, Cham (2018). https://doi.org/10.1007/978-3-030-00305-0_1
13. Galal, H.S., Youssef, A.M.: Verifiable sealed-bid auction on the ethereum blockchain. In: Zohar, A., Eyal, I., Teague, V., Clark, J., Bracciali, A., Pintore, F., Sala, M. (eds.) FC 2018. LNCS, vol. 10958, pp. 265–278. Springer, Heidelberg (2019). https://doi.org/10.1007/978-3-662-58820-8_18
14. Galal, H.S., Youssef, A.M.: Trustee: full privacy preserving vickrey auction on top of ethereum. In: Bracciali, A., Clark, J., Pintore, F., Rønne, P.B., Sala, M. (eds.) FC 2019. LNCS, vol. 11599, pp. 190–207. Springer, Cham (2020). https://doi.org/10.1007/978-3-030-43725-1_14
15. Kharif, O.: Cryptokitties mania overwhelms ethereum network's processing (2017). https://www.bloomberg.com/news/articles/2017-12-04/cryptokitties-quickly-becomes-most-widely-used-ethereum-app
16. Król, M., Sonnino, A., Tasiopoulos, A., Psaras, I., Rivière, E.: Pastrami: privacy-preserving, auditable, scalable & trustworthy auctions for multiple items. In: Proceedings of the 21st International Middleware Conference, pp. 296–310 (2020)
17. Lu, G., Zhang, Y., Lu, Z., Shao, J., Wei, G.: Blockchain-based sealed-bid domain name auction protocol. In: Chen, B., Huang, X. (eds.) AC3 2021. LNICST, vol. 386, pp. 25–38. Springer, Cham (2021). https://doi.org/10.1007/978-3-030-80851-8_3
18. Mehar, M.I., et al.: Understanding a revolutionary and flawed grand experiment in blockchain: the dao attack. J. Cases Inf. Technol. (JCIT) **21**(1), 19–32 (2019)

19. Momeni, P.: Fairblock: preventing blockchain front-running with minimal overheads. Master's thesis, University of Waterloo (2022)
20. Pass, R., Shelat, A., Vaikuntanathan, V.: Relations among notions of non-malleability for encryption. In: Kurosawa, K. (ed.) ASIACRYPT 2007. LNCS, vol. 4833, pp. 519–535. Springer, Heidelberg (2007). https://doi.org/10.1007/978-3-540-76900-2_32
21. Pietrzak, K.: Simple verifiable delay functions. In: ITCS. LIPIcs, vol. 124, pp. 60:1–60:15. Schloss Dagstuhl - Leibniz-Zentrum für Informatik (2019)
22. Ragab, H., Milburn, A., Razavi, K., Bos, H., Giuffrida, C.: Crosstalk: speculative data leaks across cores are real. In: 2021 IEEE Symposium on Security and Privacy (SP), pp. 1852–1867. IEEE (2021)
23. Schwartzbach, N.I.: Deposit schemes for incentivizing behavior in finite games of perfect information. CoRR arxiv:2107.08748 (2021)
24. Tyagi, N., Arun, A., Freitag, C., Wahby, R., Bonneau, J., Mazières, D.: Riggs: decentralized sealed-bid auctions. In: Proceedings of the 2023 ACM SIGSAC Conference on Computer and Communications Security, pp. 1227–1241 (2023)
25. Van Bulck, J., et al.: Foreshadow: extracting the keys to the intel SGX kingdom with transient Out-of-Order execution. In: 27th USENIX Security Symposium (USENIX Security 18), pp. 991–1008 (2018)
26. Wee, H.: One-way permutations, interactive hashing and statistically hiding commitments. In: Vadhan, S.P. (ed.) TCC 2007. LNCS, vol. 4392, pp. 419–433. Springer, Heidelberg (2007). https://doi.org/10.1007/978-3-540-70936-7_23
27. Wood, G., et al.: Ethereum: a secure decentralised generalised transaction ledger. Ethereum Project Yellow Paper **151**(2014), 1–32 (2014)
28. Xing, B.C., Shanahan, M., Leslie-Hurd, R.: Intel® software guard extensions (intel® SGX) software support for dynamic memory allocation inside an enclave. In: Proceedings of the Hardware and Architectural Support for Security and Privacy 2016, pp. 1–9 (2016)
29. Zhang, H., Merino, L.H., Qu, Z., Bastankhah, M., Estrada-Galiñanes, V., Ford, B.: F3B: a low-overhead blockchain architecture with per-transaction front-running protection. In: Bonneau, J., Weinberg, S.M. (eds.) 5th Conference on Advances in Financial Technologies (AFT 2023). Leibniz International Proceedings in Informatics (LIPIcs), vol. 282, pp. 3:1–3:23. Schloss Dagstuhl – Leibniz-Zentrum für Informatik, Dagstuhl (2023). https://doi.org/10.4230/LIPIcs.AFT.2023.3, https://drops.dagstuhl.de/opus/volltexte/2023/19192

Scam Token Detection Based on Static Analysis Before Contract Deployment

Taichi Igarashi[1,2](✉) and Kanta Matsuura[2]

[1] Fast Retailing, Tokyo, Japan
taichi.igarashi@fastretailing.com
[2] The University of Tokyo, Tokyo, Japan
kanta@iis.u-tokyo.ac.jp

Abstract. In recent years, the number of crimes using smart contracts has increased. In particular, fraud using tokens, such as rug-pull, has become an ignorable issue in the field of decentralized finance because a lot of users have been scammed. Therefore, constructing a detection system for scam tokens is an urgent need. Existing methods are based on machine learning, and they use transaction and liquidity data as features. However, they cannot completely remove the risk of being scammed because these features can be extracted after scam tokens are deployed to blockchain. In this paper, we propose a scam token detection system based on static analysis. In order to detect scam tokens before deployment, we utilize code-based data, such as bytecodes and opcodes, because they can be obtained before contract deployment. Since N-gram includes information regarding the order of code sequences and scam tokens have the specific order of code-based data, we adopt N-gram of them as features. Furthermore, for the purpose of achieving a high detection performance, each feature is categorized into a scam-oriented feature or benign-oriented one to make differences in the values of feature vectors between scam and benign token. Our results show the effectiveness of code-based data for detection by achieving a higher F1-score compared to the methods in another field of fraud detection in Ethereum based on code-based data. In addition, we also confirmed that the position of effective code for detection is near the start position of runtime code in our experiments.

Keywords: Ethereum · Smart contract · Token · Fraud · Scam token

1 Introduction

Today, a lot of services and applications using blockchain have been developed, and especially in Ethereum, various kinds of services have been realized by smart contract, which is the computer program interpreted by the Ethereum Virtual Machine (EVM). Some of these services utilize their original token to activate transactions because token enables users to trade their assets.

Thanks to the standard of token in Ethereum called ERC (Ethereum Request for Comments) [1], users who want to use the original token in their service easily develop their token by using this standard, and their token can be traded with other token which is developed by using the same ERC standard.

However, a lot of frauds using tokens have occurred in these days. As an ample, rug pull is now prevalent in Decentralized Finance (DeFi). Rug pull is a malicious maneuver where scammers create a new token and promote it to investors, only to abruptly abandon the project after they steal a lot of cryptocurrency from investors. In this fraud, the token issued by scammers, which is called "scam token" in the rest of this paper, seems to be benign but is craftily created to trick investors. For example, except the scammer who creates a scam token, users can only buy it but cannot sell it due to the crafty implementation. In this meaning, a scam token has no value for investors. Users can easily be scammed because scammers usually sell scam tokens by combining social engineering techniques. Today, the number of scam tokens has grown rapidly, as shown in the report of Solidus [2]. 125,084 scam tokens were found in 2022 whereas the number was 1,548 in 2020. This fact shows that there exists a high possibility that a lot of users encounter this type of scam, and it has become one of the big issues that cannot be ignored in recent years. Thus, detecting and reducing the number of scam tokens deployed to blockchain is important. In order to emphasize the meaning that "token" is one kind of smart contract, the word "token" is described as "token contract" in the rest of this paper.

Existing researches on fraud detection in Ethereum are categorized into three types: detection of fraudulent accounts, Ponzi scheme detection, and scam token contract detection. In the field of detecting fraudulent accounts, most researchers focus on identifying users who commit fraud, especially phishing scams. These methods are mainly based on transaction data extracted from blockchain. For detection, they construct a transaction network and create features for machine learning (ML) by applying an embedding method to the network. Ponzi scheme is one of the investment frauds. Scammers aim to go bankrupt at the appropriate time to obtain a lot of cryptocurrency from investors. To achieve their goal, they have to continue to collect a lot of investment, and at the same time, they also pay one part of the new users' investment to existing investors on the pretense of paying a dividend. Combining social engineering with the smart contracts in which Ponzi scheme logic is incorporated, this type of fraud has occurred in Ethereum recently. Existing researches for detecting Ponzi schemes focus on the transaction data regarding trade of cryptocurrency, or the presence of Ponzi scheme logic in the smart contract. On the contrary to the above two kinds of scams, few researches about scam token contract detection have been proposed. Since existing researches in this field are usually based on transaction and liquidity data, which are extracted after token contracts are deployed to blockchain, there exists a high possibility that users are actually scammed even when their detection systems are applied to blockchain. Therefore, detecting scam token contracts before deployment is desirable.

In order to overcome the above issues, we propose a scam token contract detection system based on static analysis. Unlike transaction and liquidity data, code-based data, such as bytecodes and opcodes, can be obtained before the deployment of token contracts to blockchain. Thus, our method can detect it before users are actually scammed. The contributions of this paper are as follows:

1. To the best of our knowledge, our method is the first detection method of scam token contracts based on code-based data.
2. Our experimental results show the effectiveness of code-based data, realizing to detect scam token contracts before deployment to blockchain.
3. From our experiments, we confirmed that the position of the effective code for detection is near the beginning of the runtime code of token contracts.

The rest of this paper is constructed as follows. Related work of fraud in Ethereum is introduced in Sect. 2. Proposed scheme is described in Sect. 3. Evaluation results are shown in Sect. 4. Limitations and future work are described in Sect. 5. Finally, the conclusion of this paper is presented in Sect. 6.

2 Related Work

In this section, we review studies related to the solutions against fraud in Ethereum. Though our main goal is to detect scam token contracts, there exist only a few researches directly on such detection to the best of our knowledge. Thus, we expand the range of surveys to find an effective way for detection and seek the requirements that the detection system should achieve by identifying overall shortcomings in this field.

2.1 Fraudulent Account Detection

Ibrahim et al. [5] utilize effective features selected from transaction data, such as token names and the amount of ether that fraudulent accounts send and receive. In their experiment, they realized 98.77% accuracy as the best by using random forest, decision tree, and K-Nearest Neighbor (KNN). Though this method achieves high accuracy, the dataset used in their experiment is imbalanced such that the number of scam tokens is much less than that of benign tokens. Wen et al. [6] make a transaction network from the transaction and address data of phishing accounts and their neighbor nodes. They apply the transaction network-based features to some ML algorithms, such as Support Vector Machine (SVM), KNN, and AdaBoost. In particular, 92.76% accuracy was recorded when using AdaBoost. Although the above methods adopt relatively simple ML algorithms, Duan et al. [7] proposed a new embedding algorithm and Graph Convolutional Network (GCN) model suited for transaction network. Experimental results show that their new embedding algorithm and GCN model recorded better detection performance compared to existing embedding methods and GCN models, and achieved 94.6% accuracy.

2.2 Ponzi Scheme Detection

Wang et al. [9] proposed a detection method of the smart contract in which Ponzi scheme logic is incorporated, which is denoted as Ponzi smart contract. They utilize N-gram of opcode sequences as features for ML. One of the merits of adopting opcode sequences is that they include information of the order of calling function, which is generally effective in analyzing computer programs such as smart contracts. Due to the specific logic of Ponzi scheme, the order of function is considered to be important information. Thus, to focus on opcode sequences is totally reasonable. However, methods using code-based data are highly influenced by the code-reuse problem, which makes it difficult to distinguish between benign and malicious smart contracts when they have similar codes. Fan et al. [10] make a graph representing the deals between users and contracts from transaction data and generate topological features of the graph. Their method used multiple ML models to detect Ponzi smart contracts, and achieved a high F1-score with 0.946 especially when using XGBoost. However, their method cannot completely reduce the risk of being scammed because transaction data can be extracted only after smart contracts are deployed to blockchain. Aljofey et al. [11] utilized both transaction and opcodes data of contracts to make features, and achieved 0.888 F1-score. Although they use both transaction-based and code-based features, which are considered to be effective for identifying Ponzi smart contracts, their detection performance is at the same level with other methods.

2.3 Scam Token Contract Detection

Mazorra et al. [12] proposed a method of detecting scam token contracts. They used transaction and liquidity data of token contracts as features for XGBoost model, and recorded 99.36 % accuracy. However, Nguyen et al. [13] pointed out that they do not select effective features, and also multiple features include transaction data extracted after the scam actually happens. In order to overcome this problem, Nguyen et al. [13] utilized only the transaction data which are extracted before the scam occurs. They also achieved a 0.990 F1-score in their experiment. While these methods recorded a high detection performance, it is difficult to prevent radically the occurrence of frauds caused by deployed scam token contracts. Since rug-pull, which is a fraud using scam token contracts, is executed in a short time as shown in the previous research [14], detection systems have to also detect in a short time to prevent the fraud. In this situation, the methods based on transaction and liquidity data have to monitor all token contracts and wait until there is a sufficient amount of data regarding each token contract to decide precisely whether it is benign or fraudulent. However, considering practical use, it is not realistic to monitor all token contracts due to the large number of them which have been deployed to blockchain already.

2.4 Requirements

Due to the above reasons and a growing number of scam token contracts, detecting all of them deployed to blockchain has become a fairly challenging task. Thus, a method that can detect before deployment is required for the prevention of fraud. When we aim at creating such a method, the thing which has to be considered is decreasing False Positive Rate (FPR), which is the metrics representing the extent of how many benign token contracts are misclassified as scam token contracts. This is because the action of benign users will be restricted if this kind of misclassification occurs. Considering these things, it is necessary to achieve the two requirements below:

1. Due to an increasing number of scam token contracts, a method which can detect them before deployment is desirable.
2. For the purpose of not restricting the deployments of benign token contracts, the detection system should achieve a low FPR as possible.

3 Proposed Scheme

In order to satisfy the above requirements, we propose a scam token contract detection method based on static analysis. For the purpose of accomplishing the first requirement, namely preventing the deployment of scam token contracts, we focus on code-based data, such as bytecodes and opcodes. In general, smart contract code is interpreted by EVM before the deployment to blockchain. Thus, code-based data can be extracted before deployment, and is useful for achieving our goal. Thinking of code-based data, there exist three possible ways to generate features: using source codes, opcodes, and bytecodes. However, the source codes of most smart contracts are not available in Etherscan [8], which is the source of our datasets. On the contrary, we can obtain bytecodes from Etherscan, and also opcodes can be extracted by disassembling bytecodes. Though the effectiveness of opcodes for Ponzi scheme detection is demonstrated in [9], whether bytecodes are effective or not remains unclear. Therefore, we construct two detection methods, one is based on bytecodes, and the other is based on opcodes. Then, we compare the detection performance between them in order to find a more effective way.

To accomplish the second requirement, we design effective features from code-based data. As demonstrated in [9], N-gram is one of the effective features in the field of detecting malicious computer programs. N-grams are sets of words included in a given window whose size is N, and generally, this window is moved one word forward to compute them. Since N-gram includes information regarding the order of code, it is useful for static analysis of programs. Thus, we design N-gram-based features. Moreover, in order to make differences between scam and benign token contracts, we divide N-gram features into two types: scam-oriented N-gram, and benign-oriented N-gram. Each N-gram feature is classified into one of these classes by comparing the percentage of contracts with the N-gram feature between scam and benign token contracts. By adopting this strategy, a difference appears in the values of feature vectors between them.

In the following subsections, we describe the bytecode of smart contract used in proposed method, feature engineering, and system model of proposed method.

3.1 Bytecode of Smart Contract

The bytecode of smart contracts is mainly divided into two types: creation code and runtime code. Creation code is the specific code which deploys runtime code to blockchain. Unlike creation code, runtime code is actually stored in blockchain and defines the smart contract. What is the relation between them is that creation code has init code, which is responsible for mainly initializing the constructor, before runtime code. In other words, runtime code is a part of the creation code. Opcode is one part of assembly language obtained by disassembling bytecodes. In our method, we got opcodes by applying a disassembling tool [15] to bytecodes.

We extract only runtime code to detect scam token contracts. This is because the logic of token contracts is included in runtime code. Moreover, we can only extract runtime code in Etherscan because creation codes of most smart contracts are not provided. Therefore, we utilize only runtime code (Fig. 1).

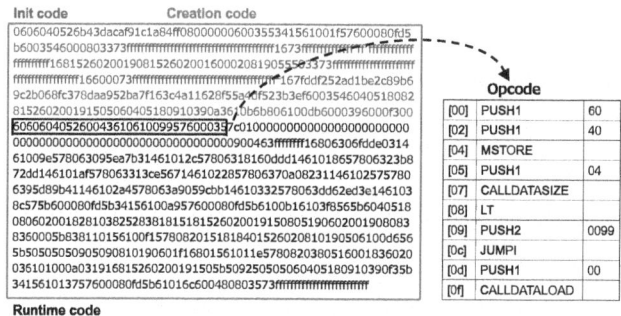

Fig. 1. Bytecode and opcode of smart contract

3.2 Feature Engineering

Proposed method adopts code-based data as features for scam token contract detection. We designed two types of features, bytecode-based features and opcode-based features, in order to find a more effective one.

The basic scheme to generate a feature vector of each sample is common between these two features: to make N-gram features. For the purpose of generating N-gram features of each sample, N-gram dictionary, which is a set of N-grams and represented as the set ND below, is created in the following steps. First of all, for each sample, code-based data (bytecodes or opcodes) are extracted. Then, N-grams of code-based data are created, and the union of them composes a set ND_i, when i is the index of the sample. Finally, when code-based data of all samples are extracted, ND is created as the union of ND_i. When using opcodes, ND is described as an opcode-based N-gram dictionary denoted by OND. In contrast, a bytecode-based N-gram dictionary is denoted by BND.

A feature vector of each sample is created on the basis of ND. In order to clarify the difference between scam and benign token contracts, each N-gram in ND is categorized into two types: scam-oriented N-gram and benign-oriented N-gram. Each scam-oriented N-gram in ND is selected when the percentage of scam token contracts with the N-gram is higher than that of benign token contracts, and vice versa. A feature vector of each sample is created on the basis of ND by assigning 1, -1, or 0 in accordance with the conditions below:

1. If an N-gram of ND is scam-oriented and is included in the sample, value 1 is assigned.
2. If an N-gram of ND is benign-oriented and is included in the sample, value -1 is assigned.
3. If an N-gram of ND is not included in the sample, value 0 is assigned.

In the case of using opcodes as features, however, hexadecimal digits are also obtained besides opcodes, which are the operands taken by the specific opcodes like "push" when converting bytecodes into opcodes. Some of these hexadecimal digits have meaningful information for detection because they may represent the specific address of EVM stack and storage, or signatures of functions. Therefore, besides the N-gram of opcodes, we also utilize these hexadecimal digits as features. For the purpose of using hexadecimal digits as features, a hexadecimal dictionary, represented as the set HD below, is also generated with the same series of the above procedure. The values of a feature vector of each sample based on HD are decided to be also 1, -1, or 0 by classifying each hexadecimal in HD into benign-oriented or scam-oriented. These series of procedures to make feature vectors are described in Appendix as pseudocode.

N-gram features are usually created on the basis of the frequency of each N-gram. However, in this strategy, the size of token contracts highly influences the detection performance because the bigger size of each token contract is, the more specific N-grams emerge in the token contract. Therefore, we assigned values on the basis of the existence of each N-gram to reduce such influence.

3.3 System Model

Figure 2 shows the system model and application place of proposed method. Proposed method firstly collects samples of token contracts from Etherscan [8]. Then, for each token contract, a feature is made using N-grams of code-based data (bytecodes, set of opcodes, and hexadecimal digits). Based on these features, the learning phase is executed by SVM model, which performs well in binary classification tasks. We used RBF kernel-based SVM, and a hyper-parameter C is set to 1.0. Using this model, whether each input sample is a scam token contract or not is decided. Though one of our goals is to realize high detection performance, we do not use other classifiers because selecting a better one is not our main goal, and also SVM is lightweight and has sufficient detection performance. Instead, our goal is to show the effectiveness of code-based data and find the position of effective data.

We assume that proposed method will be applied to Detection system 1 in Fig. 2, which tries to detect scam token contracts before they are deployed to blockchain. Aiming at realizing such a detection system, it needs to be integrated into client software or EVM because each contract deployment transaction is verified by validators. When each validator verifies such transaction, it executes the transaction on the client software and checks the occurrence of error in the calculation. Since the transaction has bytecodes of token contract, to decide whether it is a scam token or not can be realized in this validation process when our model is applied to client software or EVM. On the contrary, existing methods work as Detection system 2 in Fig. 2, which detects only scam token contracts which have been deployed to blockchain already, because they are based on transaction and liquidity data. Due to an increasing number of scam token contracts, to prevent the deployment is important besides to detect ones deployed to blockchain. Thanks to the use of code-based data, proposed method can prevent the deployment itself. Even if proposed method cannot detect some scam token contracts due to the misclassification, we can reduce the number of ones deployed to blockchain, meaning that the possibility for users of being scammed and the amount of work of Detection system 2 can be lower.

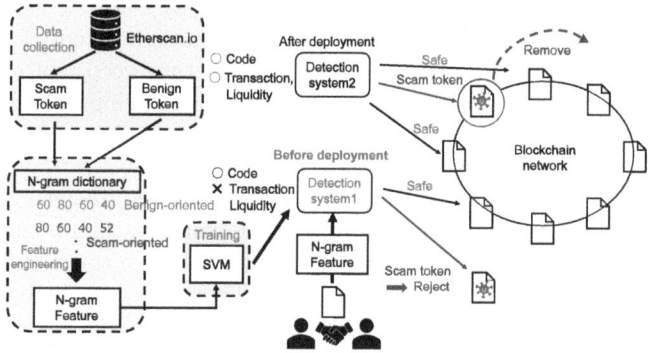

Fig. 2. System model and application place of proposed method

4 Evaluation

4.1 Dataset

Following the existing researches [12,13], our datasets of token contract samples were collected from Etherscan [8]. The number of scam token contracts is 1,259, whereas benign is 981. For each scam token contract sample, the label is provided as Phish/Hack by the Etherscan Token tracker. On the other hand, we collected benign token contracts by selecting reliable ones which are not labeled as Phish/Hack and have a lot of valid transactions. In the field of fraud detection based on supervised learning in Ethereum, it is common to use labels provided by Etherscan for evaluation. Thus, in our all experiments, we trust the labels from Etherscan. The ratio of train and test data is 7:3.

4.2 Evaluation Metrics

In order to evaluate proposed method, general metrics in classification tasks, such as accuracy, precision, recall, and F1-score are utilized in our experiments. In particular, F1-score is an important metric indicating the overall performance even when the dataset is imbalanced. Let TP, FN, TN, and FP denote the number of scam token samples classified correctly as "scam", the number of scam token samples misclassified as "benign", the number of benign token samples classified correctly as "benign", and the number of benign token samples misclassified as "scam". These metrics are calculated as

$$Accuracy = \frac{TP+TN}{TP+TN+FP+FN}, \quad Precision = \frac{TP}{TP+FP},$$

$$Recall = \frac{TP}{TP+FN}, \quad F1-score = 2 \cdot \frac{Precision \cdot Recall}{Precision + Recall}.$$

Furthermore, we also use FPR, which is the ratio of how many benign tokens are misclassified as "scam", for the second requirement. In contrast to the above metrics, the detection performance is well if FPR is low. FPR is defined as

$$FPR = \frac{FP}{FP+TN}.$$

4.3 Experiment

There exist three main goals of our experiments: demonstrating the effectiveness of code-based data, knowing the position of effective information in token contract code, and investigating the influence of fixing the length of bytecode. As a prerequisite, one of the shortcomings of using code-based data is that the detection performance is relatively low when there exists similar code between scam and benign token contracts. This problem is called code-reuse problem, and proposed method can be influenced by this problem because token contracts are generally created by imitating existing ones according to the report [16]. Thus, we aim at achieving the same level of detection performance with methods using code-based data in other scam detection fields on Ethereum. If proposed method records such a level, we can contribute to the field of scam token contract detection significantly in terms of reducing radically the risk of fraud and the amount of work to find deployed scam token contracts. At the same time, we also intended to know the position of effective information which makes a difference between scam and benign token contracts for developing future research. Besides these two goals, we also aim at knowing the effect when the length of the bytecode is fixed. This is because there exists a high possibility that a big difference can appear in the existence of N-gram, which is the basic of feature for proposed

Table 1. Detection performance when using all bytecodes

Features	Accuracy	Precision	Recall	F1-score	FPR[%]
Bytecode	0.906	0.942	0.883	0.911	6.56
Opcode	0.911	0.933	0.903	0.918	7.97

method, when all lengths of bytecodes are used. If the detection performance when using the fixed length of bytes is the same level or higher than that of when using all bytes, the former is better in terms of being not influenced by contract size and reducing computational complexity.

Considering the above three goals, we decided to conduct three kinds of experiments. In the first place, we evaluated detection performance when all lengths of bytecodes are used in order to demonstrate the effectiveness of code-based data. In the second place, for the purpose of knowing the position of effective information, detection performances when changing the position of bytecodes with a fixed length were measured. Finally, we investigated the influence of the length and position of bytecodes on detection performance by changing them based on the result of the second experiment.

Experiment Using All Bytes. In order to evaluate the effectiveness of code-based data for scam token contract detection, in this experiment, we utilized all lengths of bytecodes and evaluated the detection performances for each feature: bytecode-based, and opcode-based. For the purpose of reducing the number of dimensions and shortening the learning time, features are created by adopting 2-gram ($N = 2$) of code-based data. Table 1 shows the detection performance when using all lengths of bytecodes. As shown in Table 1, proposed method achieved more than 90% accuracy in both the situation using bytecode and opcode. Compared to [12], which uses transaction and liquidity data, the performance of proposed method is worse because they achieved 99.36% accuracy. However, compared to [9], which is the detection method of Ponzi smart contract focusing on opcode, proposed method outperforms their method in terms of recording a higher F1-score. We achieved 0.918 with opcode features whereas their method recorded 0.90 in their experiment. Furthermore, proposed method also surpasses [11], which is also the detection method of Ponzi smart contract based on various features composed of opcode, source code, and transaction data. This is because the F1-score of their method is at most 0.887 in their experiment, while proposed method achieved 0.918 with opcode features.

Considering the above results and one of our goals, which is achieving the same level of performance with methods which are based on code-based data in other fraud detection fields on Ethereum, the detection performance of proposed method is adequate. Therefore, we can conclude that code-based data, such as bytecode and opcode, are effective for scam token contract detection.

Investigation of the Position of Effective Bytes. In order to know the position of effective information, we conducted an experiment demonstrating the differences in performance when the position of the bytecode is changed. Before this experiment, we firstly checked the length of the bytecode for all samples.

Table 2 shows the bytecode length of all samples. As shown in Table 2, we found that about 88% of all samples have over 2048 bytes, and the length which the largest number of samples have is 4097-8192 bytes. Moreover, scam token contracts tend to have a shorter length of bytes compared to benign token contracts in our dataset. Considering these facts, there exists a possibility that the distinctive codes of scam token contracts are located near the initial position of runtime code. Therefore, to identify the position of effective information, we measured detection performances when changing the start position of extracted bytecodes on the assumption that effective information exists at most within the first 4096 bytes. Provided that the token contracts which do not have the bytecodes at the specified position are excluded. The length of extracted bytecodes is fixed to 128 bytes, and N is also set to 2. In addition, only bytecode-based feature is used because we do not aim at optimizing the detection performance but just knowing the position of effective bytecodes in this experiment.

Table 2. Bytecode length of all samples

Length [B]	Scam token	Benign token	Total
1–256	12	1	13
257–512	51	0	51
513–1024	131	13	144
1025–2048	20	44	64
2049–4096	285	224	509
4097–8192	550	412	962
8193–16384	178	235	413
16385–32768	32	52	84

Table 3 shows the detection performance when changing the position of bytecodes. From Table 3, the bytecodes at 129–256-th byte include the most effective information because the detection performance is the highest as they achieved 0.915 F1-score. This result is quite similar to that of when using all bytecodes shown in Table 1, furthermore, outperforms especially in precision, F1-score, and FPR. From this result, we can firstly say that selecting effective information is more important than using all bytes because a high detection performance was achieved without extracting long lengths of bytes. Moreover, the bytecodes up to 1024-th byte seem to have effective information compared to ones after 1024-th byte because all the case when using bytecodes in each of the eight categories up to 1024-th byte (1–128-th, 129–256-th, ..., 897–1024-th) achieved more than 0.880 F1-score, which is recorded when using bytecodes in only eight out of the other twenty-four categories after 1024-th byte. Therefore, we consider that the effective information for scam token contract detection exists near the start position of runtime code. Besides that, we also found some candidates for effective bytecodes. For example, the bytecodes at 3457–3584-th byte can be useful for accomplishing our purpose because not only F1-score is over 0.900 but also the fourth lowest FPR is recorded when using them. The bytecodes at the three categories, 1793–1920-th, 2177–2304-th, and 2561–2688-th byte, are also effective as they contribute to the top eight F1-score. The top eight categories in terms of F1-score are listed in Table 4.

Table 3. Detection performance when changing the position of bytecodes

Position	Accuracy	Precision	Recall	F1-score	FPR[%]
1–128	0.894	0.970	0.842	0.901	3.48
129–256	0.906	0.952	0.881	0.915	5.92
257–384	0.871	0.912	0.860	0.885	11.31
385–512	0.904	0.934	0.884	0.908	7.28
513–640	0.870	0.957	0.814	0.880	5.19
641–768	0.879	0.929	0.842	0.883	7.74
769–896	0.889	0.916	0.863	0.889	8.39
897–1024	0.883	0.920	0.854	0.886	8.36
1025–1152	0.872	0.912	0.853	0.881	10.41
1153–1280	0.842	0.901	0.782	0.837	9.28
1281–1408	0.845	0.904	0.773	0.833	8.25
1409–1536	0.860	0.918	0.797	0.853	7.43
1537–1664	0.869	0.941	0.789	0.858	5.02
1665–1792	0.865	0.943	0.789	0.859	5.26
1793–1920	0.887	0.948	0.839	0.890	5.51
1921–2048	0.880	0.942	0.825	0.880	5.78
2049–2176	0.881	0.955	0.815	0.879	4.35
2177–2304	0.890	0.937	0.843	0.887	6.01
2305–2432	0.879	0.953	0.826	0.885	5.26
2433–2560	0.865	0.927	0.820	0.870	7.87
2561–2688	0.884	0.920	0.871	0.895	9.84
2689–2816	0.880	0.934	0.842	0.886	7.29
2817–2944	0.876	0.960	0.807	0.877	4.07
2945–3072	0.863	0.934	0.785	0.853	5.69
3073–3200	0.847	0.873	0.812	0.841	11.79
3201–3328	0.870	0.976	0.778	0.866	2.24
3329–3456	0.863	0.919	0.797	0.853	7.11
3457–3584	0.903	0.963	0.844	0.900	3.51
3585–3712	0.869	0.931	0.814	0.868	6.91
3713–3840	0.845	0.956	0.737	0.833	3.70
3841–3968	0.880	0.927	0.830	0.876	6.82
3969–4096	0.873	0.971	0.765	0.856	2.23

Table 4. The top eight categories in terms of F1-score

1st	2nd	3rd	4th	5th	6th	7th	8th
129–256	385–512	1–128	3457–3584	2561–2688	1793–1920	769–896	2177–2304

Influence of Length and Position on Detection Performance. In order to know whether the detection performance is enough when the length and position of bytecodes are fixed, we conducted experiments based on the result of the second experiment on the two conditions below:

1. We compare the detection performances when changing the length of bytecodes extracted from the first 1024 bytes of runtime code, which includes relatively effective information demonstrated by the second experiment.
2. The detection performances when using the bytecodes in the top eight categories regarding F1-score in Table 3 are also checked in order to achieve a better performance of proposed method. Since some of these bytecodes are not included in the samples whose size is small, we also have to confirm if this condition is influenced by token contract size by checking the size of the misclassified samples.

If the performances of proposed method in these conditions are the same level or higher than that of when using all bytes, the formers are better because they are less influenced by token contract size and need lower computational complexity.

In the first place, we conducted an experiment on the first condition. In this experiment, we compared the result when N is set to 2 or 4 (2-gram or 4gram). Table 5 shows the detection performances when the length of bytecodes is changed within the first 1024 bytes. From Table 5, proposed method achieved 0.917 accuracy and 0.925 F1-score at the best when using 2-gram bytecodes features from 1024 bytes. Since this result is higher than that of the first experiment shown in Table 1, to fix the length of extracted bytecodes works positively with regard to being less influenced by token contract size and reducing computational complexity. Moreover, proposed method outperforms [9,11], which are the detection methods of Ponzi smart contract focusing on opcode, because each of their methods achieved 0.90 and 0.887 F1-score while the proposed method achieved 0.925. From Table 5, we also consider that the difference of N does not affect detection performances, especially when the length of bytecodes is enough to realize good performance. Though 4-gram was more effective when the length was short, the difference in detection performance between when using 2-gram and 4-gram did not become big as the increase of length. When the amount of information is not sufficient to detect, 4-gram can help increase them because it includes more information regarding the order of code-based data compared to 2-gram. However, this effect can be decreased as the amount of information becomes sufficient. Considering the above things and the influence of the number of dimensions on learning time, we consider that using 2-gram of code-based data is more efficient than using 4-gram.

Table 5. Detection performance when changing the length of bytecodes

Length [B]	Feature	2-gram					4-gram				
		Accuracy	Precision	Recall	F1-score	FPR [%]	Accuracy	Precision	Recall	F1-score	FPR[%]
16	bytecode	0.660	0.629	0.944	0.755	69.00	0.795	0.687	0.941	0.794	65.4
	opcode	0.644	0.619	0.963	0.754	77.01	0.676	0.655	0.885	0.753	58.92
32	bytecode	0.817	0.897	0.761	0.823	11.15	0.841	0.875	0.824	0.849	13.96
	opcode	0.751	0.889	0.655	0.754	11.39	0.810	0.860	0.769	0.812	14.38
64	bytecode	0.824	0.888	0.791	0.837	13.10	0.891	0.923	0.875	0.898	8.88
	opcode	0.821	0.882	0.801	0.840	15.00	0.830	0.913	0.781	0.842	10.25
128	bytecode	0.896	0.948	0.864	0.904	6.19	0.897	0.933	0.887	0.909	8.87
	opcode	0.872	0.916	0.855	0.884	10.45	0.882	0.938	0.847	0.890	7.14
256	bytecode	0.890	0.936	0.861	0.897	7.38	0.897	0.961	0.863	0.909	5.16
	opcode	0.884	0.948	0.836	0.889	5.67	0.872	0.886	0.882	0.884	14.00
512	bytecode	0.905	0.936	0.884	0.909	7.10	0.902	0.957	0.868	0.910	5.24
	opcode	0.885	0.907	0.874	0.890	10.13	0.905	0.935	0.890	0.912	7.71
1024	**bytecode**	**0.917**	**0.940**	**0.910**	**0.925**	**7.48**	0.915	0.931	0.913	0.922	8.20
	opcode	0.906	0.945	0.897	0.920	7.89	0.905	0.940	0.891	0.914	7.64

In order to seek better performance, we used the bytecodes in the top eight categories regarding F1-score shown in Table 4 instead of the first 1024 bytes, which includes the bytecodes in the four out of the top eight categories. From the experiment on the first condition, N is only set to 2 (2-gram) in this condition. We changed the number of bytecodes used as features within the top eight categories, and compared the results. Table 6 shows the detection performance when using the bytecodes in the top eight categories. This result shows that the highest detection performance is recorded when using bytecode-based features constructed from all the bytecodes in the top eight categories. We achieved 0.924 accuracy and 0.933 F1-score, which are the best performances of all our experiments. From Table 5 and Table 6, we can say that bytecode is slightly more effective than opcode in proposed methods. In regard to FPR, [11] achieved 2.14 % while proposed method recorded 6.67 %. This result seems to show that proposed method is inferior to their method for the purpose of achieving a low FPR, which is the second requirement. However, their dataset is highly imbalanced such that the number of benign contracts is 1,596 whereas only 308 scam contracts are used. Therefore, it is easier to learn the benign contracts in their experiments compared to our experiments. Moreover, we consider that the number of benign token contracts is not so many compared to that of scam token contracts in the real world. This is shown in [12,13], which are the methods of scam token contract detection, as [13] collected 23,871 scam token contracts and 1,830 benign contracts, and [12] collected 24,870 scam token contracts and only 674 benign contracts. Assuming that 1,880 benign token contracts, which is the largest number of them used in the researches of scam token contract detection, are generated within one year, we have to deal with only 0.334 false positives per day caused by the FPR of proposed method. Considering these facts, we can conclude that the FPR of proposed method is within an allowable range.

In order to know whether the result is influenced by the token contract size or not, we also checked the size of misclassified samples. We found that only 8.16 % of misclassified samples on the first condition do not have a part of bytecodes in the first 1024 bytes while 34.62 % of misclassified samples on the second condition do not include a part of bytecodes in the top eight categories. From these results, we can say that the detection performances are not highly influenced by the size of token contracts on both conditions because most of the misclassified samples have all the specified bytecodes. However, the method on the first condition, using the first 1024 bytes, is more immune to token contract size than that of on the second condition considering the percentage of misclassified samples which do not have a part of specified bytecodes. Therefore, the method using 2-gram of bytecodes extracted from the first 1024 bytes is the better choice when we aim at being independent of token contract size as possible.

Table 6. Detection performance when using the bytecodes in the top eight categories

Categories	bytecode					opcode				
	Accuracy	Precision	Recall	F1-score	FPR [%]	Accuracy	Precision	Recall	F1-score	FPR[%]
Top 2	0.894	0.926	0.879	0.902	8.67	0.899	0.934	0.886	0.909	8.36
Top 3	0.900	0.962	0.860	0.908	4.55	0.876	0.922	0.858	0.889	9.82
Top 4	0.915	0.934	0.905	0.919	7.35	0.879	0.926	0.854	0.889	8.84
Top 5	0.890	0.948	0.855	0.899	6.32	0.893	0.925	0.88	0.902	9.12
Top 6	0.896	0.926	0.880	0.902	8.52	0.900	0.943	0.889	0.915	8.30
Top 7	0.905	0.946	0.882	0.913	6.53	0.896	0.926	0.887	0.906	9.21
Top 8	**0.924**	**0.949**	**0.917**	**0.933**	**6.67**	0.911	0.933	0.903	0.918	7.98

5 Limitation and Future Work

Proposed method has some drawbacks. Firstly, the detection performance of proposed method is not sufficient as compared with that of the methods based on transaction and liquidity data. This is because our method is also influenced by code-reuse problem since code-based data are used as features. For not being influenced by this problem, we have to consider the more effective feature engineering technique to make a big difference between scam and benign token contracts. Secondly, the features of proposed method do not have interpretability for detection. Though we reveal the position of effective bytecodes for detecting scam token contracts, their specific functions or behaviors cannot be found in the proposed method. In order to know these things as a future work, the use of Control Flow Graph (CFG), which represents the control flow during the execution of token contracts and is constructed from opcode sequences, can be effective.

6 Conclusion

In this paper, we have proposed a scam token contract detection method based on static analysis. This is realized by using N-grams of code-based data, such as bytecodes and opcodes. Thanks to using code-based data, we realized the scam token contract detection before deployment. N-gram of code-based data and our feature engineering scheme also contribute to the relatively high F1-score and low FPR compared to the methods of other fields of fraud detection in Ethereum based on code-based data. Furthermore, we found that the effective bytecodes exist near the start position of runtime code in our experiment. In particular, proposed method recorded a high performance when using 1024 bytes from the start of runtime code.

Acknowledgement. We thank the anonymous referees for their valuable comments and helpful suggestions. This work was partially supported by JSPS KAKENHI Grant Number 22H03589, and JST CREST Grant Number JPMJCR22M1, Japan.

Appendix   Algorithm of Feature Engineering

Algorithm 1. Making dictionary
Input: All *Samples*
1: **for** $Sample_i$ in all *Samples* **do**
2:      Extract code-based data of $Sample_i$
3:      **if** code-based data are bytecodes **then**
4:          Make N-grams of bytecodes
5:          Create set BND_i, the union of all N-grams of bytecodes in $Sample_i$
6:      **else if** code-based data are opcodes **then**
7:          Divide opcodes data into opcodes and hexadecimal digits
8:          Make N-grams of opcode
9:          Create set OND_i, the union of all N-grams in opcodes in $Sample_i$
10:         Create set HD_i, the union of all hexadecimal digits in $Sample_i$
11:     **end if**
12: **end for**
13: Make BND, the union of all BND_i if code-based data are bytecodes.
14: Make OND and HD, the unions of all OND_i and HD_i if code-based data are opcodes.

Algorithm 2. Feature engineering

Input: Each *Sample*
1: Extract code-based data of *Sample*
2: **if** Code-based data are bytecodes **then**
3:     Make N-grams of bytecodes
4:     **for all** N-gram in *Sample* **do**
5:         **if** N-gram is in BND **then**
6:             **if** N-gram is scam-oriented N-gram **then**
7:                 Feature vector[index of the N-gram] = 1
8:             **else if** N-gram is benign-oriented N-gram **then**
9:                 Feature vector[index of the N-gram] = -1
10:             **end if**
11:         **else**
12:             Feature vector[index of the N-gram] = 0
13:         **end if**
14:     **end for**
15: **else if** Code-based data are opcodes **then**
16:     Divide opcode-data into opcodes and hexadecimal digits
17:     Execute the same procedure in line 3-14 replacing BND with OND to create opcode-based features
18:     Execute the same procedure in line 4-14 replacing N-gram and BND with hexadecimal digits and HD to create hexadecimal-based features
19: **end if**

References

1. Ethereum Improvement Proposals. ERC-20: Token Standard. [Online] Available: https://eips.ethereum.org/EIPS/eip-20 . Accessed 19 Sept 2023
2. Solidus Lab. The Rug Pull Report. [Online] Avaliable: https://www.soliduslabs.com/reports/rug-pull-report . Accessed 19 Sept 2023
3. Luu, L., Chu, D.H., Olicke, H., Saxena, P., Hobor, A.: Making smart contracts smarter. In: Proceedings of the 2016 ACM SIGSAC conference on computer and communications security, pp. 254-269 (2016)
4. Yuan, Q., Huang, B., Zhang, J., Wu, J., Zhang, H., Zhang, X.: Detecting phishing scams on ethereum based on transaction records. In: 2020 IEEE International Symposium on Circuits and Systems, pp. 1-5. IEEE (2022)
5. Ibrahim, R.F., Elian, A.M., Ababneh, M.: Illicit account detection in the ethereum blockchain using machine learning. In: Proceedings of 2021 International Conference on Information Technology, pp. 488-493 (2021)
6. Wen, H., Fang, J., Wu, J., Zheng, Z.: Transaction-based hidden strategies against general phishing detection framework on ethereum. In: Proceedings of IEEE International Symposium on Circuits and Systems, pp. 1–5 (2021)
7. Duan, X., Yan, B., Dong, A., Zhang, L., Yu, J.: Phishing frauds detection based on graph neural network on ethereum. In: International Conference on Wireless Algorithms, Systems, and Applications, Springer Nature Switzerland, pp. 351-363 (2022)
8. Etherscan. The Ethereum Blockchain Explorer. [Online] Available: https://etherscan.io . Accessed 19 Sept 2023

9. Wang, M., Huang, J.: Detecting ethereum ponzi schemes through opcode context analysis and oversampling-based adaboost algorithm. Comput. Syst. Sci. Eng. **47**(1), 1023–1042 (2023)
10. Fan, S., Fu, S., Luo, Y., Xu, H., Zhang, X., Xu, M.: Smart contract scams detection with topological data analysis on account interaction. In: Proceedings of the 31st ACM International Conference on Information and Knowledge Management, pp. 468-477 (2022)
11. Aljofey, A., Rasool, A., Jiang, Q., Qu, Q.: A feature-based robust method for abnormal contracts detection in ethereum blockchain. Electronics **11**(18), 2937 (2022)
12. Mazorra, B., Adan, V., Daza, V.: Do not rug on me: leveraging machine learning techniques for automated scam detection. Mathematics **10**, 1–24 (2022)
13. Nguyen, M.H., Dau, S.H., Li, X.: Rug-pull malicious token detection on blockchain using supervised learning with feature engineering. In: Proceedings of the 2023 Australasian Computer Science Week, pp. 72–81 (2023)
14. Xia, P., et al.: Demystifying Scam Tokens on Uniswap Decentralized Exchange. In: arXiv 2021, arXiv:2109.00229
15. pyevmasm. API Reference. [Online] Available: https://pyevmasm.readthedocs.io/en/latest/api.html . Accessed 19 Sept 2023
16. He, N., Wu, L., Wang, H., Guo, Y., Jiang, X.: Characterizing code clones in the ethereum smart contract ecosystem. In: Financial Cryptography and Data Security: 24th International Conference, FC 2020, 2020 Revised Selected Papers 24, pp. 654-675 (2020). Springer International Publishing

A Comparative Gas Cost Analysis of Proxy and Diamond Patterns in EVM Blockchains for Trusted Smart Contract Engineering

Anto Benedetti[1,2], Tiphaine Henry[1(✉)], and Sara Tucci-Piergiovanni[1]

[1] Université Paris-Saclay, CEA, List, 91120 Palaiseau, France
`tiphaine.henry@cea.fr`
[2] École Supérieure de Génie Informatique, Paris, France

Abstract. Blockchain applications are witnessing rapid evolution, necessitating the integration of upgradeable smart contracts. Software patterns have been proposed to summarize upgradeable smart contract best practices. However, research is missing on the comparison of these upgradeable smart contract patterns, especially regarding gas costs related to deployment and execution. This study aims to provide an in-depth analysis of gas costs associated with two prevalent upgradeable smart contract patterns: the proxy and diamond patterns. The proxy pattern utilizes a proxy pointing to a logic contract, while the diamond pattern enables a proxy to point to multiple logic contracts. A comparative analysis of gas costs for both patterns is conducted and compared to a traditional non-upgradeable smart contract. From this analysis, a theoretical contribution is derived in the form of two consolidated blockchain patterns and a corresponding decision model.

Keywords: Blockchain · Software Patterns · Upgradeable Smart Contracts · Proxy Pattern · Diamond Pattern

1 Introduction

Smart contracts are pivotal for orchestrating digital transactions in a reliable and secure manner in blockchain platforms [19]. Smart contracts are particularly important on Ethereum and similar blockchain platforms, where they are used in diverse areas including digital finance or industrial traceability.

As blockchain applications evolve, the need for smart contracts to be not only secure but also upgradeable becomes apparent [8]. In this context, a set of upgradeable smart contract patterns, including the proxy and diamond patterns, have surfaced to answer the lack of classical smart contracts' adaptability whose logic cannot be changed once deployed [22, 27]. The proxy pattern uses a proxy contract to delegate calls to an implementation contract, providing a flexible and upgradeable solution. The diamond pattern, introduced in EIP-2535, addresses concerns like contract size limitations and facilitates enhanced maintainability and versioning through multiple implementation contracts.

Research has focused on identifying upgradeable smart contracts pattern families, pointing towards proxy and diamond-based strategies [14,21,22,27]. However, the papers do not provide an in-depth analysis of the functional and non-functional properties of these patterns, nor gas costs behaviors. Hence, a research gap is identified regarding a thorough study of the proxy and diamond patterns, especially in terms of a gas costs analysis.

To address this issue, this paper aims to answer the following research questions: *(RQ1) How do the classic, proxy, and diamond patterns differ in terms of gas consumption, scalability, and ease of use?* And *(RQ2) What implications do these differences have for the development of blockchain applications, considering the traditional classic pattern as a baseline?*

In this paper, we contribute to the literature through a unified approach to compare gas costs in upgradeable smart contracts. We leverage this methodology to provide a comparative gas cost analysis of the proxy and diamond patterns in EVM blockchains, compared against a monolithic non-upgradeable smart contract, which is used as a baseline. Based on these results, we derive a theoretical contribution in the form of two smart contract patterns adhering to the Alexandrian form format following the standard proposed by Christopher Alexander [1]. These patterns include the results of our comparative analysis and contribute to the broader understanding of upgradeable smart contract patterns and their use in blockchain applications. Based on these patterns, a decision model for using these patterns is proposed, emphasizing functional and non-functional properties for each design decision.

The remainder of this paper is structured as follows. Section 2 introduces key concepts related to smart contracts and blockchain patterns, and Sect. 3 presents studies already made on linked concepts. Section 4 presents the method used to carry a comparative analysis on proxy versus diamond gas costs. Section 5 presents the results of the tests made on the different patterns. Section 6 leverages these findings to propose two consolidated proxy and diamond patterns as well as a decision model for using these patterns. Section 7 finally concludes the paper with a summary and a discussion of the results and some considerations for future work.

2 Background

2.1 Smart Contracts

A smart contract is a program hosted on a blockchain network [30]. When a smart contract executes, its updated state (or storage) is registered into a transaction. Then, that transaction is stored in the blockchain ledger making it immutable and tamper-proof [4]. More precisely, the final validated results are stored in a Merkle Patricia trie whose nodes correspond to an account or a smart contract. A smart contract comprises both variables and functions. Smart contract functions can execute arbitrary code, access the state of the variables and optionally update them. The default function's mutability gives the right to read and modify state variables. However, function mutability can be constrained to add more security when it comes to accessing these variables. On the one hand, a `pure` function cannot read nor modify the state of the contract; it is only used to compute a value, often using the parameters passed to it. On the other hand, a `view` function can read the state of the contract, but cannot modify it. Smart contracts are immutable, meaning that once deployed, they cannot be modified [7,31]. This is a security feature, as it prevents malicious actors from modifying the code, so that the contract can be trustable and unbreakable. However, this also means that if a bug is found in the code, it cannot be fixed, and the only solution is to deploy a new contract. Also, if a new feature is added to the contract, the only way to do it is to deploy a new contract. This is a problem for users, as they have to migrate to the new contract, and for developers, as they have to maintain multiple contracts. To address this issue, several patterns have emerged, which are discussed later in the paper [8,22].

2.2 Gas and Storage in the Ethereum Virtual Machine (EVM)

The EVM is a Turing-complete virtual machine that runs on every node of the Ethereum network and other EVM-based blockchains. It provides a secure and isolated environment for smart contract execution [16]. Gas is the unit of computation in the EVM, and every operation performed by the EVM has a gas cost associated with it [15]. The user pays this cost in the form of gas fees, to the miner/validator who executes the smart contract. It is the miner's incentive to execute the smart contract and record the results on the blockchain, but also a way to prevent spam and denial of service attacks. Storage in the EVM is linked to the concept of gas, as every operation involving storage whether it is writing new data or modifying existing data incurs a gas cost. This cost is proportional to the storage resources consumed, reflecting the principle that the more network resources (like memory and storage space) a transaction uses, the more it needs to compensate the network. Every smart contract has its own storage space, which is isolated and theoretically unlimited.

Smart contracts' storage utilizes a key-value store, with these key-value pairs referred to as storage slots. A key for a storage slot is determined by the index of the slot, which is numbered contiguously from 0 to $2^{256} - 1$. A value is a 32-byte (or 256-bit) word, also called an item. Data smaller than 32 bytes can be packed into a single slot, but if it is larger, the transaction is reverted [12]. Some types of data are stored in multiple slots, such as arrays and mappings which are stored in multiple contiguous slots [13]. Strings are also stored in multiple slots, where one slot stores the length of the string, and the other slots store each 32-byte chunk of the string [11]. A `struct`, which is a collection of variables, is stored in a single slot if it fits, otherwise, it is stored in multiple contiguous slots. The gas cost of writing to storage increases with the number of slots written to. This means that writing multiple variables, if they fit within a single slot, incurs the same gas cost as writing a single variable.

3 Related Work

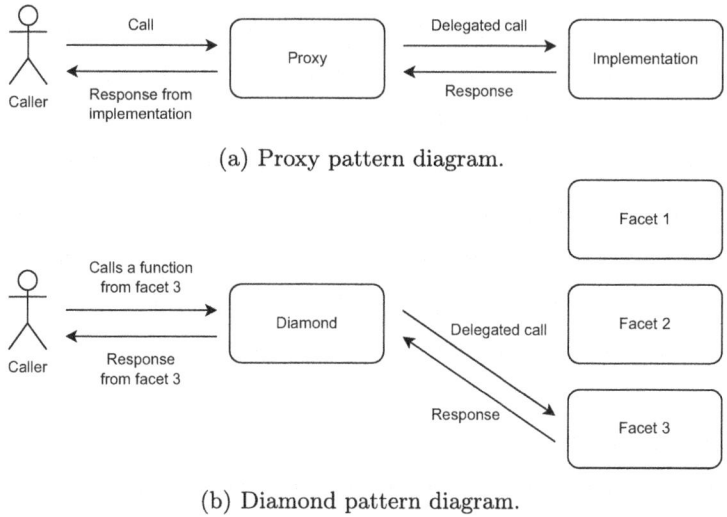

(a) Proxy pattern diagram.

(b) Diamond pattern diagram.

Fig. 1. Illustration of the Proxy and Diamond patterns

Software engineering patterns provide well-tested solutions for frequently encountered application development use cases [2]. Standardized formatting such as the Alexandrian Form Format systematically include for each pattern the description, the forces or tradeoffs at stake, the benefits and drawbacks, and their main applications. A family of patterns focusing on blockchain patterns has recently emerged in the literature [28,33]. The later include smart-contract related best practices such as upgradability patterns which refer to decentralized application maintenance strategies that can be applied for adding or updating features [8]. Two recurring upgradability patterns are identified in the literature, namely the proxy and diamond patterns [14,21,22,27].

The proxy pattern, pictured in Fig. 1a enables smart contract updates without changing the contract's address or requiring data migration [25]. It consists of two contracts, the user-interacted proxy and the logic-holding implementation. The proxy forwards calls to the implementation via delegated calls. Shared storage ensures that if the implementation is updated, the storage persists. To update the implementation, a new contract is deployed, and the proxy is directed to it, eliminating the need for user migration and preventing data loss. Compound, a key DeFi protocol, exemplifies this pattern through multiple upgrades, including Compound III[1].

The diamond pattern, depicted in Fig. 1b is a more upgradeable version of the proxy pattern. This pattern solves the maximum contract size problem, which

---
[1] https://compound.finance/.

is a limitation of the proxy pattern. Indeed, logic can be separated into small contracts referred to as facets. A main contract, referred to as the implementation or diamond contract, points at the different facets to retrieve the applicable logic. The diamond contract can be upgraded by adding, replacing or removing facets. The diamond pattern is used in a diverse array of projects, as documented in Nick Mudge's Awesome Diamonds repository [24]. For example, Aavegotchi, a Non-Fungible Token (NFT) based gaming protocol, employs a single diamond pattern with eight distinct facets[2].

A set of studies provide insight on upgradeable smart contract patterns. Kannengiesser et al. conduct a study on key smart contract development challenges across various distributed ledger technology (DLT) protocols, including Ethereum, Hyperledger, and EOSIO [19]. They highlight upgradability as a significant challenge and reference two upgradeable smart contract patterns, namely the diamond (referred to as the fa'ade pattern) pattern and the proxy pattern. However, the paper lacks an in-depth analysis of these patterns. Two papers identify the proxy pattern but do not detail the forces, advantages, drawbacks, or gas costs considerations of this pattern [14,21]. There is no mention of the diamond pattern. Two other works present a set of upgradeable smart contract patterns, including the proxy and diamond patterns [22,27]. However, the papers do not provide an in-depth analysis of the functional and non-functional properties of these patterns, nor gas costs behaviors. Additionally, it is to note that two studies focus on gas cost efficiency strategies in smart contracts development. Zarir et al.'s work focuses on transaction parameters rather than architectural design [34]. The study by Di et al. identifies smart contract coding metrics impacting gas costs [10]. However, it does not specifically focus on upgradeable smart contracts. These contracts possess unique functionalities like proxy pointers and proxy contract management. In summary, a research gap is identified regarding a thorough study of the proxy and diamond patterns. There is a lack of studies about gas costs analysis and formalization of the proxy and diamond patterns, especially using the Alexandrian form format.

4 Methodology

The methodology section of this paper details the approach employed for comparing the proxy and diamond patterns. This involves the definition of a baseline scenario and the development of a gas consumption evaluation test bench.

4.1 Protocol

Smart contract deployments are one of the most expensive operations in terms of gas costs. Therefore, assessing the deployment costs associated with various patterns is essential. Additionally, upgrades often necessitate deploying additional smart contracts, making it crucial to compare the deployment costs of each subsequent upgrade. The protocol leverages a file notarization scenario, a standard

---

[2] https://www.aavegotchi.com/.

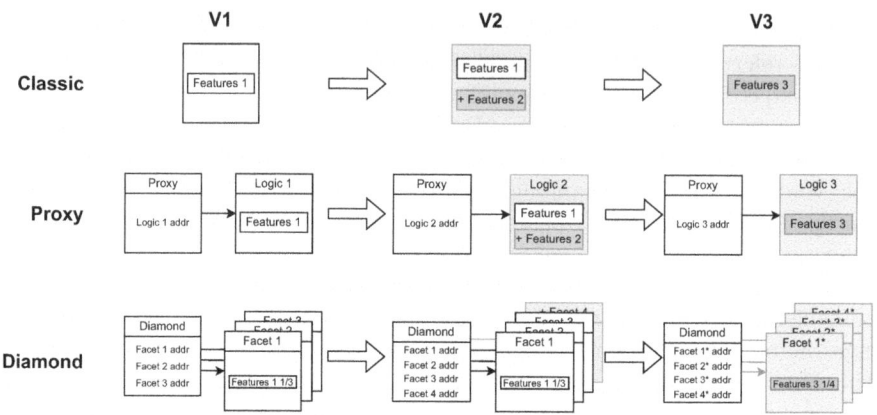

Fig. 2. Evolution of the notarization application across versions by patterns.

use of smart contracts to ensure the integrity of critical data such as diplomas or scientific workflows [5,9,20]. The scenario is implemented using the proxy and diamond patterns, as well as a reference monolithic non-upgradeable smart contract referred to as the classic pattern. For each pattern, the initial deployment of the notarization smart contract is referred to as version 1. The study then proceeds to two sequential upgrades of the application, a minor one (version 2) and a major one (version 3), to evaluate the gas costs. Features are added as updates are made. Figure 2 demonstrates the upgrades for each pattern. Then the analysis turns to comparing the average gas cost of each function, for seeing which pattern is the less gas intensive when it comes to execution. Each function is accompanied by a test case ran hundreds of times, to simulate real-world usage of this file notarization application over an extended period and to check the robustness of the code.

4.2 Implementation

The code is written in Solidity, the main language used to develop decentralized application on EVM blockchains. For the experiment, the Universal Upgradeable Proxy Standard (UUPS) proxy pattern is used because it is the recommended standard at the time of writing by OpenZeppelin [6]. For this study, the diamond pattern implemented by SolidState is used. It utilizes Nick Mudge's gas-efficient Diamond 2 model [23,29] in a plug-and-play fashion: the developer only needs to import the diamond made by SolidState without any configuration needed.

Version 1: Basic Notarization Application. In the first version of the notarization use case, files are represented by a mapping between their name and their hash. The logic encompasses several functions. The function addFile is designed to notarize a file on the blockchain and modifies the state of the contract. The getFileName function is a view function that returns the name of the file. Similarly, getFileHash is a view function that provides the hash of the file. Lastly, `compareHash` is a pure function for comparing two hashes passed as parameters; while this operation is ideally performed off-chain, it is included here to demonstrate the gas cost of a pure function.

Version 2: Updatable File. In case of file modifications, a function for updating it on the blockchain is needed. The second version of this notarization application contains the `updateFile` function, added on top of the previous version. This function updates the file hash of a notarized file and so modifies the state of the contract. This version can be seen as a minor update.

Version 3: Access Control. For security reasons, access control is mandatory, so that only the owner of a file can modify or delete it. This involves creating a `File` structure containing the owner's address, the hash of the file's contents, the creation timestamp and the last modification timestamp. The previous mapping is replaced by one between the file's name and its `File` structure instance. Then, the `addFile` and `updateFile` functions are modified to work with this new `File` structure, and access control is added, where the new logic smart contract ensures that the caller interacts only with his own files. This version can be seen as a major update.

4.3 Unit Tests

As mentioned in Sect. 4.1, each function has a unit test that is run hundreds of times (704 iterations for the addFile function across all unit tests of version 3, for example). It calls the function with random parameters (file name, hash, etc.) and checks that the result is correct. This is done to simulate real-world usage of this file notarization application. An expected result is computed before the function call, and the actual result is compared to it. In the `addFile` unit test, we expect the smart contract to add the file name and hash to its storage, using either the proxy or diamond pattern. The `updateFile` unit test should update the file hash in the contract's storage, while the `deleteFile` test ensures the file's removal. In the `compareHash` test, the outcome should be true for matching hashes and false otherwise. The `getFileName`, `getFileHash`, `getFileOwner`, `getFileCreatedAt`, and `getFileLastModifiedAt` unit tests respectively verify the return of the file's name, hash, owner address, creation timestamp, and last modification timestamp. Finally, the `getFileDetails` test checks for the return of all the previously mentioned file properties.

Testing each single function is important to ensure that the code is robust and that it does not break when upgrading the smart contract. These tests are also conducted to compare the gas costs across various patterns, specifically examining each type of function, including pure, view, and state-modifying functions. By testing pure functions, the gas costs of computations without storage access can be assessed and compared across patterns. View functions are tested to evaluate the gas costs of computations with storage access. Finally, state-modifying functions are tested to assess the gas costs of storage writes.

Smart contracts used for this study are developed using Foundry [17]. Foundry plays a critical role in this testing process by autonomously simulating an Ethereum Virtual Machine (EVM) blockchain environment. During test execution, it deploys the contracts and carries out the testing scenarios within this emulated setting, utilizing the default configuration of this local blockchain. The entire source code, tests and results here are available in the accompanying source code repository[3].

4.4 Results Retrieval

Through these unit tests, Foundry produces gas reports that provide insights into the gas consumption for each function, alongside the gas costs associated with deployment and the size of the contracts. The cost of function calls is quantified in gas units, and the contract size is measured in bytes.

These gas cost results for each function are derived by summing the gas costs associated with every operation performed within the function. Each operation, also known as opcode, has a fixed gas cost, which is the same for all patterns. Those instructions are described in the Ethereum Yellow Paper [31]. For example, the SLOAD opcode, which reads a value from storage, has a fixed cost of 100 for warm access, and 2100 gas for cold access. Then, the deployment cost is the sum of several components. First, the TRANSACTION opcode incurs 21,000 gas units, representing the base cost of every transaction on the EVM. Additionally, there is the CREATE opcode, costing 32,000 gas units, which is used for creating a new contract. Next, the cost related to the bytecode includes 4 times the number of 0 bytes and 16 times the number of non-zero bytes. Furthermore, 200 gas units are added for every byte of the contract's size. Finally, if a constructor function is present, its cost is also included in the deployment cost.

In addition, the framework furnishes complete stack traces of the calls, detailing the gas consumption for each operation. These traces are utilized to construct charts that capture the gas cost of each function call. This level of detail supplements gas reports, which typically provide only a summary of costs, including the minimum, average, median, and maximum values.

5 Evaluation

This section presents the gas costs evaluation of the proxy and diamond smart contract patterns, against a baseline built using the classic pattern in the context of an app deployment and upgrade[4].

5.1 Gas Cost During Smart Contract Deployment and Upgrades

The primary aim is to compare the gas costs during the deployment (version 1) and upgrades (version 2 and 3) of the file notarization application implemented

---

[3] https://anonymous.4open.science/r/proxy-diamond-patterns-gas-analysis.
[4] All results can be found here: https://anonymous.4open.science/r/proxy-diamond-patterns-gas-analysis/data.

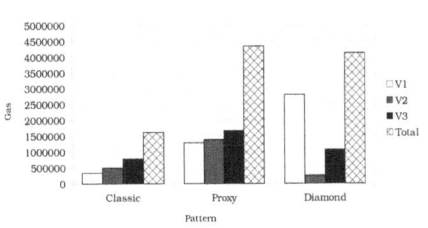
(a) Deployment cost by pattern and version.

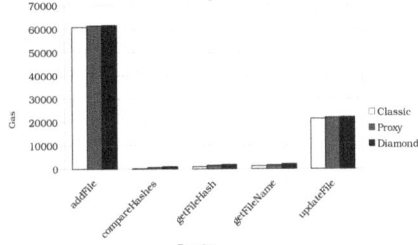
(b) Average function cost by pattern for version 2.

Fig. 3. Evaluation results

with the three different patterns. For the classic and proxy pattern, a new contract is deployed for each version. For the proxy, the proxy pointer is updated in the smart contract implementation. For the diamond pattern, in version 2, only facet is changed, and in version 3, all facets are changed.

Figure 3a presents the deployment costs, in gas units, of each version by pattern. The cost of deployment increases with each version, except for the diamond pattern, where the initial cost of deployment is significant. In all, the classic pattern requires just 1,614,545 units of gas, while the proxy and diamond patterns consume around 2.6 times as much, at 4,343,104 and 4,123,977 units of gas respectively. The classic pattern appears the most gas efficient. The increased consumption at deployment of the proxy and diamond patterns relates to the need to deploy more contracts compared to the classic pattern: two for the proxy pattern, and four for the diamond one.

5.2 Gas Cost During Smart Contract Execution

The analysis now shifts to comparing the average gas cost of functions to determine the most gas efficient execution pattern. Gas cost behaviors in versions 1 and 3 align with online gas reports. Notably, `addFile` and `updateFile` functions are the costliest, while remaining functions incur comparatively lower gas costs. Across the three patterns, the proxy and diamond patterns exhibit slightly higher expenses than the classic pattern. Notable cost discrepancies include `compareHashes` being significantly cheaper than `addFile` in the classic pattern. This difference is attributed to `addFile` requiring two storage writes while other functions mainly perform storage reads. The classic pattern avoids delegation to other contracts, unlike the proxy and diamond patterns, resulting in additional costs. Furthermore, incurring more operations when invoking a diamond adds to its expense compared to a proxy. Getters in the classic pattern involve state lookups, costing 2100 gas for cold storage loads, while `compareHashes` is a `pure` function, devoid of state lookups or modifications, resulting in lower gas costs.

In reviewing the data obtained from the comparative analyses, the deployment phase exhibits the most significant variation among the different patterns, primarily due to the fluctuating number of smart contracts deployed. For this metric, the diamond pattern is the cheapest, especially for minor upgrades. During execution, the gas costs are similar across patterns, though there is a marginal escalation in costs when transitioning from the classic architecture to the proxy pattern, and subsequently from the proxy to the diamond pattern. This increase in gas costs is due to the additional operations required to delegate calls to the logic contract(s) in the proxy and diamond patterns.

6 Discussion

This section summarizes and consolidates the proxy and diamond patterns following the Alexandrian form format proposed by C. Alexander [2]. A decision model is proposed to help developers choose between both patterns.

6.1 Proxy Pattern Outline

- **Summary:** The proxy pattern facilitates upgradability in smart contracts through a proxy contract pointing to the latest version of a logic contract.
- **Context:** A smart contract must be upgraded due to evolving requirements and potential improvements [7].
- **Problem:** Traditional smart contracts lack the ability to be updated without manual storage migration, posing challenges in addressing vulnerabilities, enhancing functionality, and adapting to changing circumstances.
- **Forces (tradeoffs):** The problem requires balancing the following forces: (i) *Immutability vs. Upgradability*. Smart contracts on blockchain platforms are traditionally immutable once deployed; (ii) *Gas Costs vs. Flexibility*. Minimizing gas costs while providing flexibility for contract upgrades; (iii) *Trust vs. Transparency*. Establishing trust in the upgrade process while maintaining transparency.
- **Solution:** The smart contract proxy pattern introduces a proxy contract as an intermediary layer. This proxy delegates calls to a logic contract, allowing seamless upgrades by deploying new logic contracts and updating the proxy to point to the latest version, hence allowing for dynamic updates.
- **Consequences:**
    - Benefits:
        * *Upgradability*. Allows upgrades without the need to change the contract address nor requiring data migration;
        * *Simplest Upgradeable Pattern*. The upgrade process consists in deploying a new logic contract and a proxy update pointing to it with a proxy administration function.
    - Drawbacks:
        * *Compatibility Maintenance*. Requires consistent function selectors and storage layouts;
        * *Limited Direct Function Visibility*. Logic functions visibility only accessible in the documentation;

* *Storage Collision.* It requires careful consideration of storage layout to avoid storage overlap between the proxy and the logic contract as if both contracts use the same storage slot, it can lead to data loss. A convention is to use namespaced storage layouts for naming struct holding storage variables [18].
  * *Function Selector Clash.* Different functions having the same selector can override each other [26]. This requires careful naming of function selectors as the Solidity compiler cannot detect function selector clashes between the proxy and logic contracts due to cross-contract interactions.
- **Related patterns:** Diamond pattern.
- **Known uses:** Two standardized implementations are proposed in the Ethereum Improvement Proposal *EIP-897* and in OpenZeppelin's smart contract development framework [3,22]. *Compound* and *USDC*, respectively a DeFi protocol and a stable coin, both implement the proxy pattern for upgrades.

6.2 Diamond Pattern Outline

- **Summary:** employing multiple implementation contracts to balance contract size, maintainability and versioning;
- **Context:** Need for a solution to improve maintainability in large contracts.
- **Problem:** Traditional approaches face challenges in managing contract size and versioning effectively.
- **Forces (tradeoffs):** The problem requires balancing the following forces: (i) *Contract Size vs. Modularity* Balancing the need for compact contract sizes with the demand for modular, well-organized code structures; (ii) *Maintainability vs. Simplicity* Achieving improved maintainability without introducing unnecessary complexity; (iii) *Scalability vs. Consistency* Scaling smart contract applications requires accommodating versioning and updates.
- **Solution:** The diamond pattern introduces a structure where a proxy can point to multiple logic contracts. It involves the deployment of all contracts (diamond and facets), retrieving facets function selectors, and leveraging both to implement a diamond cut.
- **Consequences:**
  * Benefits:
    * *Better upgradability.* Possibility to deploy smaller contracts during upgrades or updates to already deployed facets without requiring address change or data migration;
    * *Modularity.* Code reusable across multiple contracts. A facet can be used in multiple diamonds;
    * *Contract size.* Thanks to a modular structure, it can theoretically support an infinite number of facets. Therefore, the whole smart contract system has no size limit;
    * *Cheaper minor upgrades.* Most of the time, only one facet is updated, so only small contracts are deployed for low gas costs;

* *Shorter compilation time.* Only modified facets need to be compiled, so for the same logic code, the compilation time is shorter than for the classic pattern and proxy pattern.
 - Drawbacks:
   * *Implementation Complexity.* A more complex structure compared to the classic and proxy patterns, and a lack of supporting libraries.
   * *Complexity in managing multiple logic contracts.* Managing multiple logic contracts require careful consideration during upgrades. It requires developers to manage the diamond storage manually because of the multiple implementation contracts.
   * *Limited Direct Function Visibility.* Like the proxy pattern, users depend on documentation to identify callable functions.
   * *Storage collision risks* similarly to Proxy pattern
   * *Function selector clash* similarly to Proxy pattern
 - *Related patterns:* Proxy pattern.
 - *Known uses: Aavegotchi,* a NFT-based gaming protocol; *GeoWeb,* a dApp managing digital land property rights using NFTs.

6.3 Choosing Between the Proxy and Diamond Patterns

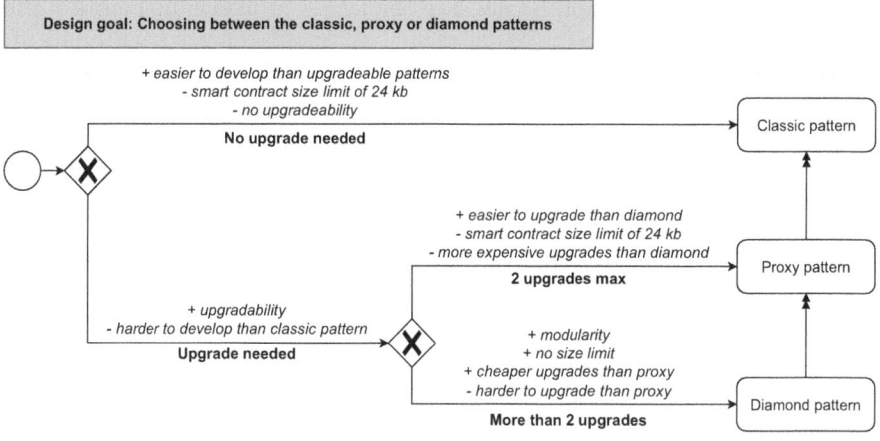

Fig. 4. Decision model for upgradeable smart contract pattern usage.

Figure 4 proposes a decision model to orient between a proxy or a diamond pattern in the design stage of an upgradeable smart contract. It follows the design goal decision model introduced by Xu where decisions are modeled using a logical BPMN flow [32]. More precisely, arrows, logical gateways, and functional and non-functional properties orient the decision path.

The choice of smart contract pattern largely depends on the need for upgradability. For scenarios without upgradability needs, the classic pattern is preferable due to its straightforward development process, relying on contract inheritance and library imports. However, upgrades in the classic pattern often involve complex and resource-intensive data migration. This pattern also poses challenges in communicating new contract addresses to users, potentially affecting the user experience. For extensive upgradeable features, the diamond pattern is recommended. Its modular nature allows for easy addition or removal of facets, reducing compilation time. However, it is less cost-effective initially compared to the proxy pattern and requires in-depth knowledge of smart contract storage and facet-library management. The proxy pattern is advised for limited code sizes or infrequent upgrades. It simplifies development and integrates easily with libraries like OpenZeppelin's. This pattern enhances upgradability by separating logic and state, reducing the need for data migration. But it offers less flexibility and modularity compared to the diamond pattern and demands careful consideration to maintain compatibility across versions.

In the end, while the classic pattern excels in execution ease, the proxy and diamond patterns provide a more manageable framework for upgrades, simplifying contract interactions for users during updates. The diamond pattern is more suitable for extensive upgrades, while the proxy pattern is recommended for limited upgrades and simpler development.

7 Conclusion

In conclusion, this comprehensive study delves into the intricacies of upgradeable smart contract design patterns'a critical facet of contemporary blockchain applications. The comparative analysis specifically focuses on the gas costs associated with deploying, using, and upgrading decentralized applications using two prominent upgradeable patterns: the proxy and diamond patterns.

Each pattern unfolds with distinct strengths and weaknesses, delineating its applicability across diverse scenarios. The classic pattern implies an unpractical and costly approach to smart contract upgrades because of the need of manual data migration. The proxy pattern offers the simplest solution for upgradability, but security concerns such as storage collisions and function selector clashes remain. This demands a developer's careful attention and thus results in a more challenging pattern to utilize. The diamond pattern is the most complex of the three, but it offers the most flexibility and maintainability thanks to its modularity. Moreover, the diamond pattern is the most gas efficient when it comes to doing more than two upgrades. This is because the diamond pattern does not need to deploy long contracts, but only small facets. Finally, this pattern is the most scalable because it does not have a contract size limit. Despite these considerations, real-world implementations in projects like Compound, USDC, GeoWeb, and Aavegotchi underline the use of the proxy and diamond patterns as facilitators for flexible, upgradeable, and scalable smart contracts.

To generalize these initial findings, the study advocates for extending experiments beyond the notarization scenario used as a comparison baseline for this paper. Essential to this endeavor is the necessity for additional experiments encompassing diverse blockchain networks and pattern libraries to extrapolate and validate the findings. For future work, a replication of the study on alternative upgradeable patterns would also provide a more comprehensive understanding of upgradeable smart contract patterns.

References

1. Alexander, C.: A pattern language: towns, buildings, construction. Oxford University Press (1977)
2. Alexander, C.: The timeless way of building, vol. 1. Oxford University Press, New york (1979)
3. Amri, S.A., Aniello, L., Sassone, V.: A review of upgradeable smart contract patterns based on openzeppelin technique. The Journal of The British Blockchain Association (2023)
4. Ayub, M., Saleem, T., Janjua, M., Ahmad, T.: Storage state analysis and extraction of ethereum blockchain smart contracts. ACM Transactions on Software Engineering and Methodology **32**(3), 1–32 (2023)
5. Badr, A., Rafferty, L., Mahmoud, Q.H., Elgazzar, K., Hung, P.C.: A permissioned blockchain-based system for verification of academic records. In: NTMS. IEEE (2019)
6. Barros, G., Gallagher, P.: Erc-1822: Universal upgradeable proxy standard (uups). https://eips.ethereum.org/EIPS/eip-1822 (2019-03-04). Accessed 4 Mar 2019
7. Buterin, V., et al.: Ethereum: a next generation smart contract and decentralized application platform (2013). URL {http://ethereum. org/ethereum. html} (2017)
8. Chen, J., Xia, X., Lo, D., Grundy, J., Yang, X.: Maintaining smart contracts on ethereum: Issues, techniques, and future challenges. arXiv preprint arXiv:2007.00286 (2020)
9. Coelho, R., Braga, R., David, J.M.N., Stroele, V., Campos, F., Dantas, M.: A blockchain-based architecture for trust in collaborative scientific experimentation. J. Grid Comput. **20**(4), 1–31 (2022)
10. Di Sorbo, A., Laudanna, S., Vacca, A., Visaggio, C.A., Canfora, G.: Profiling gas consumption in solidity smart contracts. J. Syst. Softw. (2022)
11. Docs, S.: Bytes and string. https://docs.soliditylang.org/en/latest/internals/layout_in_storage.html#bytes-and-string (2023-04-14), accessed: April 14, 2023
12. Docs, S.: Layout of state variables in storage, 14 Apr 2023. https://docs.soliditylang.org/en/latest/internals/layout_in_storage.html
13. Docs, S.: Mappings and dynamic arrays, 14 Apr 2023. https://docs.soliditylang.org/en/latest/internals/layout_in_storage.html#mappings-and-dynamic-arrays. Accessed 14 Apr 2023
14. Ebrahimi, A.M., Adams, B., Oliva, G.A., Hassan, A.E.: A large-scale exploratory study on the proxy pattern in ethereum. Preprint (2023)
15. Ethereum: Gas and fees. https://ethereum.org/en/developers/docs/gas/ (2023-07-19). Accessed 19 July 2023
16. Ethereum: Ethereum virtual machine (evm). https://ethereum.org/en/developers/docs/evm/ (2023-09-02). Accessed 2 Sep 2023
17. Foundry: Foundry book. https://book.getfoundry.sh/ (2023-11-22). Accessed 22 Nov 2023

18. Francisco Giordano, Hadrien Croubois, E.G., Lau, E.: Erc-7201: Namespaced storage layout. https://eips.ethereum.org/EIPS/eip-7201
19. Kannengießer, N., Lins, S., Sander, C., Winter, K., Frey, H., Sunyaev, A.: Challenges and common solutions in smart contract development. IEEE Trans. Software Eng. **48**(11), 4291–4318 (2021)
20. Leible, S., Schlager, S., Schubotz, M., Gipp, B.: A review on blockchain technology and blockchain projects fostering open science. Frontiers in Blockchain, p. 16 (2019)
21. Marchesi, L., Marchesi, M., Destefanis, G., Barabino, G., Tigano, D.: Design patterns for gas optimization in ethereum. In: 2020 IEEE International Workshop on Blockchain Oriented Software Engineering (IWBOSE), pp. 9–15. IEEE (2020)
22. Meisami, S., Bodell III, W.E.: A comprehensive survey of upgradeable smart contract patterns. arXiv preprint arXiv:2304.03405 (2023)
23. Mudge, N.: Diamond 2 hardhat implementation. https://github.com/mudgen/diamond-2-hardhat (2022-12-16). Accessed 16 Dec 2022
24. Mudge, N.: Awesome diamonds. https://github.com/mudgen/awesome-diamonds (2023-11-01). Accessed 1 Nov 2023
25. OpenZeppelin: Proxy patterns. https://blog.openzeppelin.com/proxy-patterns (2018-04-19). Accessed 19 April 2018
26. Palladino, P.: Malicious backdoors in ethereum proxies. https://medium.com/nomic-foundation-blog/malicious-backdoors-in-ethereum-proxies-62629adf3357 (2018-06-01)
27. Qasse, I., Hamdaqa, M., Jónsson, B.T.: Smart contract upgradeability on the ethereum blockchain platform: an exploratory study. arXiv:2304.06568 (2023)
28. Six, N., Herbaut, N., Salinesi, C.: Blockchain software patterns for the design of decentralized applications: a systematic literature review. Blockchain: Research and Applications **3**(2), 100061 (2022)
29. SolidState: Solidstate diamond. https://github.com/solidstate-network/solidstate-solidity/tree/master/contracts/proxy/diamond (2023-10-12). Accessed 12 Oct 2023
30. Szabo, N.: Formalizing and securing relationships on public networks. First monday (1997)
31. Wood, G., et al.: Ethereum: a secure decentralised generalised transaction ledger. Ethereum Project Yellow Paper **151**(2014), 1–32 (2014)
32. Xu, X., Bandara, H.D., Lu, Q., Weber, I., Bass, L., Zhu, L.: A decision model for choosing patterns in blockchain-based applications. In: ICSA. IEEE (2021)
33. Xu, X., Pautasso, C., Zhu, L., Lu, Q., Weber, I.: A pattern collection for blockchain-based applications. In: Proceedings of the 23rd European Conference on Pattern Languages of Programs, pp. 1–20 (2018)
34. Zarir, A.A., Oliva, G.A., Jiang, Z.M., Hassan, A.E.: Developing cost-effective blockchain-powered applications: a case study of the gas usage of smart contract transactions in the ethereum blockchain platform. TOSEM (2021)

5th Workshop on Coordination of Decentralized Finance (CoDecFin 2024)

IZPR: Instant Zero Knowledge Proof of Reserve

Trevor Conley[1], Nilsso Diaz[1], Diego Espada[1], Alvin Kuruvilla[1], Stenton Mayne[2], and Xiang Fu[1]

[1] Hofstra University, Hempstead, NY 11549, USA
{tconley1,ndiaz5,despada1,akuruvilla1}@pride.hofstra.edu,
Xiang.Fu@hofstra.edu
[2] Kn0x1y, Cape Town, South Africa
stentonian@kn0x1y.xyz
https://www.kn0x1y.xyz/

Abstract. We present a non-interactive and public verifier scheme that allows one to assert the asset of a financial organization *instantly* and *incrementally* in zero knowledge with high throughput. It is enabled by the recent breakthrough in lookup argument, where the prover cost can be independent of the lookup table size after a pre-processing step. We extend the cq protocol [21] and develop an aggregated non-membership proof for zero knowledge sets. Based on it, we design a non-intrusive protocol that works for pseudo-anonymous cryptocurrencies such as BTC. It has $O(n\log(n))$ prover complexity and $O(1)$ proof size, where n is the platform throughput (instead of anonymity set size). We implement and evaluate the protocol. Running on a 56-core server, it supports 1024 transactions per second.

Keywords: Proof of Reserve · Proof of Asset · Solvency · Zero Knowledge Proof · Lookup Argument

1 Introduction

First defined in Provisions [15], the zero knowledge (zk) proof-of-solvency (PoS) problem is to prove in zero knowledge that the *asset* of an organization is greater than its *liability*. Due to the volatility of financial market, we are interested in a variation called *instant zk-solvency* problem, i.e., to prove solvency of an organization instantly and incrementally, e.g., at a frequency of 1 Hz. This seems like a daunting task that requires very expensive computing resources. For instance, in [15] to generate and then verify a single zk-solvency proof for an anonymity set of $500k$ BTC addresses needs about 1 h. In our work, we use the entire 80 million BTC addresses as the anonymity set, and in fact it can be arbitrarily large. The key observation of our work is that *the ownership of an account needs to be proved only once*, and then the total asset can be proved incrementally. We assume that the registration and verification of liability is handled by frameworks such as DAPOL(+) [10,27], then we just need to focus on the instant zk-proof for asset only. In the rest of the paper we use terms "proof-of-reserve" and "proof-of-asset" (PoA) interchangeably. The "asset" ("reserve") here refers to the asset that is in control by the organization.

We consider pseudo-anonymous cryptocurrencies such as Ethereum and BTC where transaction details are public. Here, we abstract away platform specifics and use "account" to denote e.g., BTC wallet address and Ethereum account.[1] Let **S** represent the account set owned by an organization. At each transaction cycle, the market (or a trusted smart contract) discloses two vectors: (1) **a**: the list of all accounts that are involved in any transaction in the current cycle; and (2) Δ where each Δ_i represents the balance change of the i'th account in **a**. Let v be the total balance change for **a** ∩ **S**, and let $\mathbf{C_S}$ be the Pedersen commitment to **S**. We present a constant size zk-proof which convinces the verifier that a commitment $\mathbf{C}_v$ hides the valid value for v, given **a**, Δ, and $\mathbf{C_S}$. Since $\mathbf{C_S}$ does not disclose information of **S**, the incremental balance change of **S** is proved in zero knowledge.

The main challenge here is the concrete performance. We leverage the recent break-through in lookup arguments [21,22,24,26,31,36,37]. Built upon the cq protocol [21], we develop an aggregated non-membership proof for zero knowledge sets, i.e., to show that the intersection of two committed zk-sets is empty, which is used to demonstrate accumulated balance over **a** ∩ **S**. Because we leverage the pre-processed lookup arguments, the prover complexity is independent of the size of **S**. Let n denote the throughput of the platform, the prover cost is $O(n\log(n))$ field operations and a constant number of group multi-exponentiation of size $O(n)$. The verifier complexity and proof size are both $O(1)$. Concretely, running over a 56-core server at Google Cloud Computing, our protocol has throughput of 1024 transactions per second (TPS), which is half of Visa Network and 140 times faster than BTC. A second protocol works for privacy preserving cryptocurrencies such as Monero and ZeroCoin and we defer the details to an extended version of this paper.

2 Related Work

The earliest attempt of asset proof is [35] which is not zero knowledge. In [16], the solution depends on special TPM hardware. Provisions [15] provides a zk-solution to both the proof of reserve and liability problems, mainly relying on zk-Σ-protocols. Its prover and verifier complexity are both linear with the size of anonymity set, and it addresses pay-to-pubkey mode of BTC only. MProve(+) [17,19], Revelio [20], and Nummatus [18] each targets at a specific platform (e.g., Monero and Quisquis), and their design is tightly coupled with the platform (e.g.,

---

[1] Even though BTC uses UTXO and allows mixing, from a BTC transaction and its input, one can extract its sender/receiver BTC addresses and the change of balance for each address. In case no-reuse principle is practiced, a BTC address is regarded as a use-once account. In this case, to make our model work, an organization can pre-compute a fixed set of BTC addresses for future use, and periodically expand this set. We discuss its impact on the overall cost of the scheme in Sect. 5.1.

exploiting the ring signature in Monero). Their prover and verifier complexity are both linear. In [1], zk-SNARK and double discrete logarithm proofs (DDLOG) are combined to prove asset, where DDLOG is very expensive (e.g., costing over 2000 group elements for the proof of one coin). gOTzilla [3] employs MPC-in-the-head and 1-out-of-n oblivious transfer. It can handle anonymity set size of 80 million, but lacks non-interactiveness (i.e., it needs the verifier to be online with the prover).

Table 1. Comparison of Related Work. n: anonymity set size, t: blockchain throughput, m: number of accounts controlled by the organization. In practice, $t << n$, e.g., for BTC t is 7 and n is 80 million. Hashed: whether the scheme supports hash in generating account address. Complexity includes field operation cost. NI: non-interactive. The complexity of gOTzilla is for the case $m = 1$. We do not know if its proof size scales linearly or sub-linearly with m.

Scheme	Prover Work	Proof Size	Hashed	NI	Incremental
Provisions [15]	$O(n)$	$O(n)$	N	Y	N
MProve [17,19,20]	$O(n)$	$O(n)$	Y	Y	N
zkSNARK e.g. [30]	$O(n\log(n))$	$O(1)$	Y	Y	N
CompositeNIZK [1]	$O(n\log(n))$	$O(n)$	Y	Y	N
gOTzilla [3]	$O(n)$	$O(\log(n))$	Y	N	N
This Work	$O(t\log(t))$	$O(1)$	Y	Y	Y

In Table 1, we present a brief comparison of the asymptotic complexity of all the aforementioned related works. Compared with them, the proof size and verifier complexity of our protocol are $O(1)$. In addition, because the platform throughput (e.g., 7 for BTC, or 2000 in Visa network) is much smaller than the anonymity set size (e.g., 80 million for BTC), the concrete cost of prover work in our scheme is much smaller. None of the aforementioned related work is concretely efficient for supporting an incremental, non-interactive, public verifier, and instant zk-asset proof scheme for the scale of the throughput as presented in this paper. On the other hand, the protocol presented in this paper is only used for the incremental zk-proof, and its bootstrap process (see Sect. 4.1) needs to leverage the "classical" PoA technique. We provide an open-source implementation of our protocol.[2]

In the cryptocurrency industry, there is a recent increase of interest in PoS systems, after the FTX scandal. For instance, Binance provides a PoA system since late 2022 [4]. Its zk-protocol works only for proving liability, and its corporate holdings are manually verified by a third party auditor Mazar [14], who backed off in December 2023. The solution provided in this paper helps to rule out unreliable human factors and it provides *instant* asset report instead of monthly updates. OKX [29] provides a similar PoS system as Binance, where

---
[2] https://github.com/xfu2006/izpr

zkSTARK is used to assert user contribution to total liability. It differs in the verification of corporate holdings - OKX publishes all of its wallet addresses, hence losing privacy of its assets. Summa [34] takes a similar approach where the asset addresses are disclosed. More industrial efforts in PoA can be found in [9], and a comprehensive survey of academic work can be found in [11].

3 Preliminaries

3.1 Notations

We use **P** and **V** to denote the prover and the verifier. Let $\mathcal{G}$ be a generator of bilinear groups for security parameter λ, i.e., $(q, \mathbf{g}_1, \mathbf{g}_2, \mathbb{G}_1, \mathbb{G}_2, \mathbb{G}_T, e) \leftarrow \mathcal{G}(1^\lambda)$, where all groups have order q, and $\mathbf{g}_1$ ($\mathbf{g}_2$) the generator of $\mathbb{G}_1$ ($\mathbb{G}_2$). $e: \mathbb{G}_1 \times \mathbb{G}_2 \to \mathbb{G}_T$ is the bilinear map. Let $\mathbb{F}$ be the scalar field of $\mathbb{G}_1$. $s \xleftarrow{\$} \mathbb{F}$ represents sampling s uniformly from $\mathbb{F}$. We use n and N to denote the size of query and lookup tables. We assume the existence of n-th and N-th roots of unity so FFT is applicable. We follow the notations in Groth16 [25]. For instance, $\mathbf{g}_1{}^a \mathbf{g}_1{}^b$ is written as $[a]_1 + [b]_1$. We use $[n]$ to denote range $[1, n]$. A vector $\mathbf{t} \in \mathbb{F}^n$ is written as $(\mathbf{t}_1, \ldots, \mathbf{t}_n)$. $\mathbf{u} + \mathbf{v}$ denotes $(\mathbf{u}_1 + \mathbf{v}_1, \ldots, \mathbf{u}_n + \mathbf{v}_n)$, and $\alpha \mathbf{u}$ is $(\alpha \mathbf{u}_1, \ldots, \alpha \mathbf{u}_n)$. We use ω_n for the n'th root of unity, i.e., $(\omega_n)^n = 1$. We define $\mathbb{H}_n = \{\omega_n^1, \ldots, \omega_n^n\}$, and the corresponding set of Lagrange base polynomials is denoted as $\{L_{n,i}(X)\}_{i=1}^n$, where $L_{n,i}(\omega_n^i) = 1$ and $L_{n,i}(\omega_n^j) = 0$ for $j \neq i$. Given a multi-set S, its vanishing polynomial $z_S(X)$ is defined as $z_S(X) = \prod_{s \in S}(X - s)$. It is known that $z_{\mathbb{H}_n}(X) = X^n - 1$. Given $s \in \mathbb{F}$, its Pedersen commitment $\mathbf{C}_s$ is defined as $\mathbf{C}_s = [s]_1 + r[h]_1$ for a random r, where h is unknown to the prover.

Given $\mathbf{t} \in \mathbb{F}^n$, its encoding polynomial $t(X)$ is defined as a $n - 1$ degree polynomial: $t(X) = \sum_{i=1}^n \mathbf{t}_i L_{n,i}(X)$. We use the univariate zk-VPD scheme [38] to provide zk-vector commitment. Sample $r_t \in \mathbb{F}$, and the masked polynomial for $\mathbf{t}$ is defined as: $\hat{t}(X) = t(X) + r_t z_{\mathbb{H}_n}(X)$, and the vector commitment to $\mathbf{t}$ is: $\mathbf{C_t} = [\hat{t}(s)]_1$, where s is the trapdoor of a KZG commitment key [28]. Given a public point z, using the univariate port of the zk-VPD scheme, the prover can convince the verifier that a Pedersen commitment $\mathbf{C}_y$ hides a value $y = t(z)$ without disclosing y. Note that $\hat{t}(X)$ is also a 1-leaky masked polynomial of $t(X)$ [13, Sect. 3.6] (also in [8,23]), in the sense that running standard KZG opening proof for one evaluation of $\hat{t}(X)$ still keeps $\mathbf{t}$ zero knowledge. 2-leaky masking is similarly achieved by defining $\hat{t}(X)$ as $\hat{t}(X) = t(X) + (r_{t_1} X + r_{t_0}) z_{\mathbb{H}_n}(X)$. In summary, for any vector $\mathbf{u} \in \mathbb{F}^n$, we use $u(X)$, $\hat{u}(X)$, and $\mathbf{C_u}$ to denote its encoding polynomial, masked polynomial, and vector commitment.

We use the notation from [6] to specify zk-protocols. Consider Schnorr's DLOG as an example: $\pi_{\mathsf{DLOG}}(\mathbf{h})\{(x) : \mathbf{h} = [x]_1\}$. Here DLOG in π_{DLOG} is a mnemonic. ($\mathbf{h}$) is the public information. The tuple before ":" is the secret known by prover only, i.e., (x). Then the statement inside curly braces states the relation: the prover knows the secret discrete logarithm of $\mathbf{h}$.

3.2 Lookup Argument

Let $\mathbf{t} \in \mathbb{F}^n$ and $\mathbf{T} \in \mathbb{F}^N$, a lookup argument for $\mathbf{t} \hat{\subset} \mathbf{T}$ asserts that for each $i \in [n]$: $\mathbf{t}_i \in \mathbf{T}$. Note that both $\mathbf{t}$ and $\mathbf{T}$ may contain duplicates. We need a homomorphic and zero knowledge look-up argument, and a slight zk-enhancement of cq [21] satisfies our needs. The basic idea of cq is to pre-compute commitments of quotient polynomials in $O(N\log(N))$ time. Then for arbitrary query table $\mathbf{t}$ of size n, the prover work is $O(n\log(n))$, thus independent of N. We need to enhance cq so that it is zero knowledge. In our extension, we exploit bounded leaky-zk as in [12,13], and Schnorr style Σ-protocols as in [33]. We will present its full technical details in the extended version of this paper. Similar constructions for the zk-enhancement of cq can be found in two concurrent work: segment lookup [13] and matrix lookup [7]. We denote it as $\pi_{\text{ZK\_LOOKUP}}$, as shown below:

1. $(\mathsf{pk}, \mathsf{vk}) \leftarrow \mathtt{Setup}\,(N, \lambda)$: a trusted set-up given security parameter λ and lookup table size limit N, samples bilinear groups and generates the prover and verifier keys $(\mathsf{pk}, \mathsf{vk})$ for KZG.
2. $(\mathsf{aux}_\mathbf{T}, \mathbf{C_T}) \leftarrow \mathtt{Preprocess}(\mathbf{T}, \mathsf{pk})$: Given the lookup table $\mathbf{T}$, it generates $\mathsf{aux}_\mathbf{T}$ (the preprocessed information) and $\mathbf{C_T}$ (a commitment to $\mathbf{T}$).
3. $\pi \leftarrow \mathtt{Prove}(\mathsf{pk}, \mathsf{aux}_\mathbf{T}, \mathbf{T}, \mathbf{t})$: produces a zero knowledge proof π for $\mathbf{t} \hat{\subset} \mathbf{T}$.
4. $1/0 \leftarrow \mathtt{Verify}(\mathsf{vk}, \mathbf{C_T}, \mathbf{C_t}, \pi)$: checks that π is valid.
5. $\pi \leftarrow \mathtt{FoldProve}(\mathsf{pk}, \mathsf{aux}_\mathbf{U}, \mathbf{U}, \mathsf{aux}_\mathbf{V}, \mathbf{V}, \mathbf{u}, \mathbf{v}, \alpha)$: produces a zero knowledge proof π for $\mathbf{u} + \alpha\mathbf{v} \hat{\subset} \mathbf{U} + \alpha\mathbf{V}$.

Theorem 1. *Under the Q-DLOG assumption [21] in the Algebraic Group Model (AGM) and Random Oracle Model (ROM), $\pi_{\text{ZK\_LOOKUP}}$ is perfectly complete, computational knowledge sound, and zero knowledge.*

The proof generally follows the analysis of cq [21], and is similar to that of [7,13]. Our zk-cq implementation can be replaced by the one in [7], without impacting the rest of the protocol.

Based upon $\pi_{\text{ZK\_LOOKUP}}$, we develop $\pi_{\text{RANGE}}(\mathbf{C_a}, 2^B)$, a batched zk-range proof which asserts that $\mathbf{C_a}$ is a Pedersen vector commitment to $\mathbf{a} \in \mathbb{F}^n$, and each $\mathbf{a}_i$ in $\mathbf{a}$ is in range $[0, 2^B)$. It has $O(1)$ proof size and $O(n\log(n))$ prover complexity.

4 IZPR Protocol

4.1 Overview

We first provide a high level overview of the IZPR protocol. As the scheme is based upon cq, IZPR needs an one-time trusted setup to provide prover and verifier keys. It has two stages: a bootstrap stage and an incremental proof stage.
Bootstrap: the goal of the initial stage is to provide the proof for the ownership of accounts and the initial total balance. In the discussion below, we use "prover" to denote the organization who provides the asset proof.

The prover has the following secret information: (1) $\mathbf{s} \in \mathbb{F}^N$: secret keys. (2) $\mathbf{S} \in \mathbb{F}^N$: public accounts (e.g., for BTC each $\mathbf{S}_i = \mathsf{hash}(g^{\mathbf{s}_i})$ where g is a generator in curve secp256k1 and hash is a combination of SHA256 and RIPMD160). (3) $\mathbf{v} \in \mathbb{F}^N$: initial account balances for a specific timestamp ts, i.e., $\mathbf{v}_i$ is the asset value of $\mathbf{S}_i$.

Here, we specifically note that for the case when the organization practices the no-reuse principle of BTC address, the prover has to pre-compute sufficient private key/public account pairs for future use. If an account does not appear in the blockchain yet, its value is set to 0.

The verifier is provided with the following information: (1) the snapshot of the entire cryptocurrency platform at timestamp ts, which includes the list of all accounts and their balances. Usually a succinct commitment, e.g., the root of a Merkle tree of such information, is provided. We denote such succinct commitment as $\mathbf{C_T}$, and we use $(\mathbf{S}_i, \mathbf{d}_i) \in \mathbf{C_T}$ to indicate that the value of $\mathbf{S}_i$ in $\mathbf{C_T}$ is $\mathbf{d}_i$, and we use the notation $\mathbf{S}_i \notin \mathbf{C_T}$ for $\mathbf{S}_i$ does not appear in $\mathbf{C_T}$. (2) The information provided by the prover: $\mathbf{C_S}$: the Pedersen vector commitment to $\mathbf{S}$, and $\mathbf{C_\mathcal{I}}$: a Pedersen commitment to the initial asset value $\mathcal{I}$.

The goal of the prover is to convince the verifier that: the prover has the knowledge of $\mathbf{S}, \mathbf{d}, \mathbf{s}$ such that all of the following are true:

1. *Commitments Validity:* knowledge of $\mathbf{S}$ behind $\mathbf{C_S}$ and $\mathcal{I}$ behind $\mathbf{C_\mathcal{I}}$.
2. *Ownership:* knowledge of private keys $\mathbf{s}$, which generate accounts, e.g., for BTC: $\forall i \in [1, N] : \mathbf{S}_i = \mathsf{hash}(g^{\mathbf{s}_i})$.
3. *Account Existence:* $\forall i \in [1, N] : (\mathbf{S}_i \notin \mathbf{C_T} \land \mathbf{d}_i = 0) \lor (\mathbf{S}_i, \mathbf{d}_i) \in \mathbf{C_T}$.
4. *Initial Asset:* $\mathcal{I} = \sum_{i=1}^{N} \mathbf{d}_i$

Incremental Stage: At any time, the prover maintains a Pedersen commitment $\mathbf{C}_\mathcal{B}$ to the total balance $\mathcal{B}$ of all accounts. $\mathcal{B}$ can be kept as a secret depending on business needs. At the bootstrap, the prover has established that $\mathbf{C}_\mathcal{B} = \mathbf{C}_\mathcal{I}$. The prover also publishes $\mathbf{C_S}$.[3]

Then at each cycle (blockchain epoch), the prover executes a π_{IZPR} protocol (details in Sect. 4.3), based on the public information of the cryptocurrency platform, as shown in the following.

1. The cryptocurrency platform publishes the following information: (1) $\mathbf{a}$: the list of all accounts that are involved in any transaction in the current cycle; (2) $\mathbf{\Delta}$: the change of balance for each account in $\mathbf{a}$. Let p be the order of the scalar field $\mathbb{F}$ used. If the balance change is negative, e.g., $-c$, then it is represented as $p - c$ in $\mathbb{F}$. To reduce the verifier complexity, the Pedersen vector commitment to the above are provided and let them be: $\mathbf{C_a}$ and $\mathbf{C_\Delta}$.
2. The prover provides a constant-size proof π_{IZPR} which asserts that: given $\mathbf{C_S}$, $\mathbf{C_a}$, $\mathbf{C_\Delta}$, the total balance change for $\mathbf{a} \cap \mathbf{S}$ according to $\mathbf{\Delta}$ is a value v hiding in a Pedersen commitment $\mathbf{C}_v$. The $O(1)$ size proof is made public and can be verified non-interactively by any verifier.
3. The prover then updates $\mathbf{C}_\mathcal{B} \leftarrow \mathbf{C}_\mathcal{B} + \mathbf{C}_v$, leveraging the homomorphic property of Pedersen commitment.

---

[3] It is assumed that $\mathbf{S}$ is fixed. It is possible to periodically expand $\mathbf{S}$, which is briefly discussed in Sect. 5.1.

Assuming that $\mathbf{C}_\mathcal{L}$ commits to the total liability $\mathcal{L}$. $\mathbf{C}_\mathcal{B} - \mathbf{C}_\mathcal{L}$ commits to $\mathcal{B} - \mathcal{L}$. The zk-range proof to show $\mathcal{B} - \mathcal{L} > 0$ incurs trivial cost. Thus, the organization can prove its solvency without disclosing the total asset and liability value. In certain market situation, this might be desirable. With slight change, one can also prove that the secret total asset value $\mathcal{B}$ is 10% greater than total liability in zero knowledge, providing more assurance to clients of the organization.

In practice, the concern is the scalability of the scheme. We extend the cq protocol, and develop a number of constructions for realizing the IZPR scheme. The rest of this section delves into the technical details.

4.2 Positive-Negative Lookup

We first need an enhanced version of lookup argument. Given the secret query table $\mathbf{t}$, and a public lookup table $\mathbf{T}$, the goal is to assert that a Pedersen commitment $\mathbf{C_o}$ encodes a Boolean vector $\mathbf{o}$ such that $\mathbf{o}_i$ indicates whether $\mathbf{t}_i$ is contained in $\mathbf{T}$. We call it Zero Knowledge Positive-Negative Lookup argument ("zk-PN-Lookup" for short). The basic idea is straight-forward. Let $\mathbf{T}$ be sorted in ascending order. When $\mathbf{t}_i \notin \mathbf{T}$, we simply identify $\mathbf{T}_j$ and $\mathbf{T}_{j+1}$ s.t. $\mathbf{T}_j < \mathbf{t}_i < \mathbf{T}_{j+1}$.

Formally, we assume that all elements in lookup tables are in range $[0, 2^B)$, e.g., for BTC, B is 160. Given a private and sorted table $\mathbf{A} = \{\mathbf{A}_1 < ... < \mathbf{A}_{N-1}\}$ with all elements in range $(0, 2^B)$, define $\mathbf{T} = \{0, \mathbf{A}_1, ..., \mathbf{A}_{N-1}\}$, and $\mathbf{T}' = \{\mathbf{A}_1, ..., \mathbf{A}_{N-1}, 2^B\}$. We call $(\mathbf{T}, \mathbf{T}')$ the *sorted vector pair* for $\mathbf{A}$ with bound 2^B. Their relation can be proved with a separate zk-proof. Then $\pi_{\text{PN\_LOOKUP}}$ is defined below:

$\pi_{\text{PN\_LOOKUP}}(\mathbf{C_T}, \mathbf{C_{T'}}, \mathbf{C_t}, \mathbf{C_o}, B)\{(\mathbf{T}, \mathbf{T'}, \mathbf{t}, \mathbf{o}) :$
$\mathbf{C_t} = [\hat{t}(s)]_1 \land \mathbf{C_o} = [\hat{o}(s)]_1 \land \mathbf{C_T} = [\hat{T}(s)]_1 \land \mathbf{C_{T'}} = [\hat{T'}(s)]_1 \land$
$\forall i \in [n] : ((\mathbf{o}_i = 1 \land \exists j \text{ s.t. } \mathbf{T}_j = \mathbf{t}_i) \lor (\mathbf{o}_i = 0 \land \exists j \text{ s.t. } \mathbf{T}_j < \mathbf{t}_i < \mathbf{T'}_j))\}$

Figure 1 presents the details of the $\pi_{\text{PN\_LOOKUP}}$ protocol. We now explain its design idea and informally reason about its security.

There are two cases to cover: (1) $\mathbf{t}_i \notin \mathbf{T}$, i.e., there exists j s.t. $\mathbf{T}_j < \mathbf{t}_i < \mathbf{T'}_j$; and (2) $\mathbf{t}_i \in \mathbf{T}$, i.e., there exists a k s.t. $\mathbf{T}_k = \mathbf{t}_i$. The prover derives two private vectors $\mathbf{u}$ and $\mathbf{v}$ to assist the proof. Consider the following example.

Example 1. Let $\mathbf{T} = (0, 100, 200, 300)$ and $\mathbf{T'} = (100, 200, 300, 2^B)$. Let $\mathbf{t} = (100, 250)$, and the resulting $\mathbf{o} = (1, 0)$. To reason about the position of elements in $\mathbf{t}$, the prover computes in private: $\mathbf{u} = (100, 200)$ and $\mathbf{v} = (200, 300)$. Note that for each i: $(\mathbf{u}_i, \mathbf{v}_i)$ constitutes a pair of elements in $\mathbf{T}$ and $\mathbf{T'}$ of the same index. This property is proved via a folded lookup argument (steps 1–3 in Fig. 1): Given the vector commitments to $\mathbf{u}$ and $\mathbf{v}$, the prover samples a random challenge α and then the prover proves that each element of vector $\mathbf{u} + \alpha \mathbf{v}$ belongs to $\mathbf{T} + \alpha \mathbf{T'}$. Given α is random, the probability that the property being violated is negligible. Then the prover needs to argue that for each i: $\mathbf{u}_i \leq \mathbf{t}_i \leq \mathbf{v}_i$. This is accomplished using two batched zk-range proofs (step 5 in Fig. 1).

> 1. **P** computes **f** and **o** of size n for **t**:
>
> $$(\mathbf{f}_i, \mathbf{o}_i) = \begin{cases} (j,1) & \text{if } \exists j \text{ s.t. } \mathbf{T}_j = \mathbf{t}_i \\ (k,0) & \text{if } \exists k \text{ s.t. } \mathbf{T}_k < \mathbf{t}_i < \mathbf{T}'_k \end{cases}$$
>
> Then **P** computes $\mathbf{u} = (\mathbf{T}_{\mathbf{f}_i})_{i=1}^n$ and $\mathbf{v} = (\mathbf{T}'_{\mathbf{f}_i})_{i=1}^n$, and the vector commitments: $\mathbf{C_u}, \mathbf{C_v}, \mathbf{C_o}$. $\mathbf{P} \to \mathbf{V} : (\mathbf{C_u}, \mathbf{C_v}, \mathbf{C_o})$.
> 2. $\mathbf{V} : \alpha \xleftarrow{\$} \mathbb{F}$. $\mathbf{V} \to \mathbf{P} : \alpha$.
> 3. **P** computes $\pi \leftarrow \texttt{FoldProve}(\mathsf{pk}, \mathsf{aux}_\mathbf{T}, \mathbf{T}, \mathsf{aux}_{\mathbf{T}'}, \mathbf{T}', \mathbf{u}, \mathbf{v}, \alpha)$. $\mathbf{P} \to \mathbf{V} : \pi$.
> 4. **V** aborts if $\texttt{Verify}(\mathsf{vk}, \mathbf{C_T} + \alpha \mathbf{C_{T'}}, \mathbf{C_u} + \alpha \mathbf{C_v}, \pi)$ returns 0.
> 5. **P** and **V** run $\pi_{\text{RANGE}}(\mathbf{C_t} - \mathbf{C_u}, 2^B)$, and $\pi_{\text{RANGE}}(\mathbf{C_v} - \mathbf{C_t}, 2^B)$.
> 6. **P** shows **o** is a Boolean array by proving that there exists a $q_o(X)$ s.t.
>
> $$o(X)(o(X) - 1) = q_o(X) z_{\mathbb{H}_n}(X)$$
>
> 7. **P** proves $o(X)$ is correct. **P** computes $\mathbf{d} = \mathbf{t} - \mathbf{u}$ (note $\mathbf{C_t} - \mathbf{C_u}$ commits to **d**). Then **P** shows there are $q(X)$ and $v(X)$ s.t.
>
> $$o(X)d(X) + (1 - o(X))(v(X)d(X) - 1) = q(X) z_{\mathbb{H}_n}(X)$$
>
> Here $v(X)$ encodes the inverse of each $\mathbf{d}_i$ if it exists.

Fig. 1. PN-Lookup Argument

Next, in Step 6 of Fig. 1, the prover convinces the verifier that **o** is a Boolean array, i.e., for $i \in [n]$: $\mathbf{o}_i(\mathbf{o}_i - 1) = 0$, which enforces that $\mathbf{o}_i$ is either 1 or 0. Consider the encoding polynomial $o(X) = \sum_{i=1}^n \mathbf{o}_i L_{n,i}(X)$, based on the property of Lagrange base polynomials, we have for $i \in [n]$: $o(\omega_n^i) = \mathbf{o}_i$. Thus the prover needs show the existence of a polynomial $q_o(X)$ s.t. $o(X)(o(X)-1) = q_o(X) z_{\mathbb{H}_n}(X)$. The prover cannot disclose $o(X)$ or $q_o(X)$, instead, their masked polynomials are used, to preserve zero knowledge. Similarly, Step (7) in Fig. 1 proves that $o(X)$ encodes the correct information, i.e., when $\mathbf{t}_i \in \mathbf{T}$, $o(\omega_n^i) = 1$, otherwise $o(\omega_n^i) = 0$.

$\pi_{\text{PN\_LOOKUP}}$ immediately leads to an aggregated non-membership proof. Given a preprocessed $\mathbf{C_T}$, to prove that $\mathbf{t} \cap \mathbf{T} = \emptyset$ can be achieved by running $\pi_{\text{PN\_LOOKUP}}$ first and then showing that $\mathbf{C_o}$ is a Pedersen vector commitment to $(0)_{i=1}^n$. The prover complexity of $\pi_{\text{PN\_LOOKUP}}$ $O(n \log(n))$ and its verifier complexity is $O(1)$.

Using Fiat-Shamir transform, $\pi_{\text{PN\_LOOKUP}}$ can be converted into a non-interactive proof. We then have the following:

Lemma 1. *Under the Q-DLOG assumption in the AGM and ROM, $\pi_{\text{PN\_LOOKUP}}$ is perfectly complete, computational knowledge sound, and zero knowledge.*

4.3 π_{IZPR} Protocol

We now consider π_{IZPR}, the asset proof for pseudo-anonymous cryptocurrencies. It is *non-intrusive* in the sense that there is no change needed on the blockchain, or any participants who have no need for asserting assets. The protocol assumes that at the bootstrap step, the organization has provided the ownership proof for each account in **S**. Let **T** and **T**′ be the corresponding sorted vector pair for **S**. To verifier, only their commitments ($\mathbf{C_T}$ and $\mathbf{C_{T'}}$) are visible.

For each transaction cycle, the blockchain makes two vectors public: **a**: the list of accounts, and **Δ**, the corresponding balance change of each account in **a**. We use $[0, 2^B)$ as positive and $[|\mathbb{F}| - 2^B, |\mathbb{F}|)$ as negative values. Let $n = |\mathbf{a}|$,[4] and $N = |\mathbf{T}|$. Typically, the value of n is not large and determined by the throughput of the platform. For instance, BTC, ETH, Visa Network and NYSE operate at 7, 30, 1700, and 24000 TPS, respectively. In this work, we aim at accomplishing 1000 TPS, and set $n = 2048$ (assuming each transaction causing updates on two accounts) and $N = 8$ million. Define $\mathbf{C_a} = [a(s)]_1$ (without blinding factor) and similarly is $\mathbf{C_\Delta}$ defined. They are used only as succinct representation of **a** and **Δ** and need to be publicly computable (thus no hiding property is needed). On the other hand, $\mathbf{C_T}$ and $\mathbf{C_{T'}}$ are hiding.

Intuitively, π_{IZPR} states that $\mathbf{C}_v$ commits to a value v that is the sum of balance changes for all accounts that appear in the intersection of **S** and **a** as sets. It is formally defined below.

$$\pi_{\text{IZPR}}(B, \mathbf{C_T}, \mathbf{C_{T'}}, \mathbf{C_a}, \mathbf{C_\Delta}, \mathbf{C}_v)\{(\mathbf{T}, \mathbf{T'}, \mathbf{a}, \mathbf{\Delta}, v, r):$$
$$\mathbf{C}_v = [v]_1 + r[h]_1 \wedge v = \sum_{\mathbf{a}_j \in \mathbf{S} \cap \mathbf{a}} \Delta_j$$
$$\mathbf{C_a} = [a(s)]_1 \wedge \mathbf{C_\Delta} = [\Delta(s)]_1 \wedge \mathbf{C_T} = [\hat{T}(s)]_1 \wedge \mathbf{C_{T'}} = [\hat{T}'(s)]_1\}$$

The protocol is built upon $\pi_{\text{PN\_LOOKUP}}$, and the details are presented in Fig. 2. In the following we present its design idea and an informal analysis of its security.

(Steps 1–2): Given **a**, the prover first computes a Boolean vector **o** where each $\mathbf{o}_i$ indicates if $\mathbf{a}_i$ appears in **T**. Note that the validity of **o** is established in step 7. Then the prover defines an accumulator vector **u** s.t. $\mathbf{u}_1 = 0$ and its last element is the sum of all account balance changes, i.e., the value of v. Therefore, for $i \in [1, n-1]$, we have: $\mathbf{u}_{i+1} = \mathbf{u}_i + \mathbf{o}_i \Delta_i$, i.e., the Boolean $\mathbf{o}_i$ decides whether to include Δ_i in the sum. Let $u(X)$ be the encoding polynomial of vector **u**, we then have the following listed in Step 2:

$$u(X\omega_n) - u(X) - o(X)\Delta(X) = q(X)z_{\mathbb{H}_n}(X)/(X - \omega_n^n) \tag{1}$$

Here ω_n is the n'th root of unity, and the $u(X\omega_n)$ and $u(X)$ intuitively model the relation between $\mathbf{u}_{i+1}$ and $\mathbf{u}_i$. The last item $z_{\mathbb{H}_n}(X)/(X - \omega_n^n)$ expresses the range condition $[1, n-1]$, i.e., given that $z_{\mathbb{H}_n}(X) = \prod_{i=1}^{n}(X - \omega^i)$, the formula excludes the case $i = n$.

Note that for each vector, e.g., **u**, the commitment to its *masked* polynomial $\hat{u}(X)$ is sent to the verifier, for preserving zero knowledge.

(Steps 3–5) The verifier samples a random challenge t, and the prover uses KZG polynomial commitment to assert the evaluation of each related polynomial at point t (step 4), and then the verifier use these values to check Eq. 1 (step 5). Given that for each $i \in [n] : u(\omega_n^i) = \hat{u}(\omega_n^i)$, and by Schwartz-Zippel, the probability of failing soundness is negligible. Also note that since each polynomial is

---
[4] In the implementation $|\mathbf{a}| = |\mathbf{u}| - 1$.

---

1. **P** receives input: **S**, **a**, and **Δ**.
   V receives input: B, $\mathbf{C_a}$, $\mathbf{C_\Delta}$, $\mathbf{C_T}$, $\mathbf{C_{T'}}$, and $\mathbf{C}_v$.
2. **P** computes array $\mathbf{o}_i$ as shown in Figure 1, and v the accumulation of balance changes of $\mathbf{a} \cap \mathbf{S}$. Define polynomial $u(X)$ s.t.

   $$u(\omega_n^1) = 0$$
   $$u(\omega_n^n) = v$$
   $$u(X\omega_n) - u(X) - o(X)\Delta(X) = q(X)z_{\mathbb{H}_n}(X)/(X - \omega_n^n)$$

   P samples random openings and computes masked polynomials $\hat{u}(X)$, and $\hat{o}(X)$. In particular, make $\hat{u}(X)$ 2-leaky by:
   $\hat{u}(X) = u(X) + (r_{u_1}X + r_{u_0})z_{\mathbb{H}_n}(X)$. Define $\hat{\Delta}(X) = \Delta(X)$. Define
   $\hat{q}(X) = \frac{\hat{u}(X\omega_n) - \hat{u}(X) - \hat{o}(X)\hat{\Delta}(X)}{z_{\mathbb{H}_n}(X)/(X - \omega_n^n)}$. Compute $\mathbf{C_u} = [\hat{u}(s)]_1$, $\mathbf{C_o} = [\hat{o}(s)]_1$, and $\mathbf{C_q} = [\hat{q}(s)]_1$. $\mathbf{P} \to \mathbf{V} : (\mathbf{C_u}, \mathbf{C_q}, \mathbf{C_o})$.
3. **V** samples $t \xleftarrow{\$} \mathbb{F}$. $\mathbf{V} \to \mathbf{P} : t$.
4. **P** computes $t_{u2} = \hat{u}(t\omega_n)$, $t_u = \hat{u}(t)$, $t_o = \hat{o}(t)$, $t_\Delta = \hat{\Delta}(t)$, and $t_q = \hat{q}(t)$. **P** and **V** run standard KZG opening proof for them, where the last 4 can be batched. **P** and **V** run another KZG opening for $\hat{u}(\omega_n^1) = 0$.
5. **V** checks $t_{u2} - t_u - t_o t_\Delta = t_q(t^n - 1)/(t - \omega_n^n)$.
6. **P** and **V** engage in a univariate zk-VPD [38] opening proof to prove that $\mathbf{C}_v = [v]_1 + r_v[h]_1$ for some r_v and $u(\omega_n^n) = v$, but without disclosing the value of v.
7. **P** and **V** run $\pi_{\text{PN\_LOOKUP}}(\mathbf{C_T}, \mathbf{C_{T'}}, \mathbf{C_a}, \mathbf{C_o}, B)$.

Fig. 2. π_{IZPR} Protocol

involved in KZG evaluation proof for up to 2 times, and their masked polynomials have their degrees raised correspondingly, which preserves zero knowledge. The same technique is used in [8,23].

(Step 6) Finally, the prover needs to convince the verifier that $\mathbf{u}_n = v$, without disclosing the value of v. KZG cannot be used here, because it discloses the evaluation itself. Instead, we employ a univariate instantiation of the zk-VPD [38] scheme, which given the KZG commitment to a polynomial p, a point t and proves that a Pedersen commitment $\mathbf{C}$ hides the value of $p(t)$. This finally concludes the proof that $\mathbf{C}_v$ is a Pedersen commitment to the sum of balance changes of $\mathbf{a} \cap \mathbf{S}$.

Theorem 2. *Under the Q-DLOG assumption in AGM and ROM, π_{IZPR} is perfectly complete, computational knowledge sound, and zero knowledge. Its prover complexity is $O(|\mathbf{a}|\log(|\mathbf{a}|))$. Its verifier complexity and proof size are both $O(1)$.*

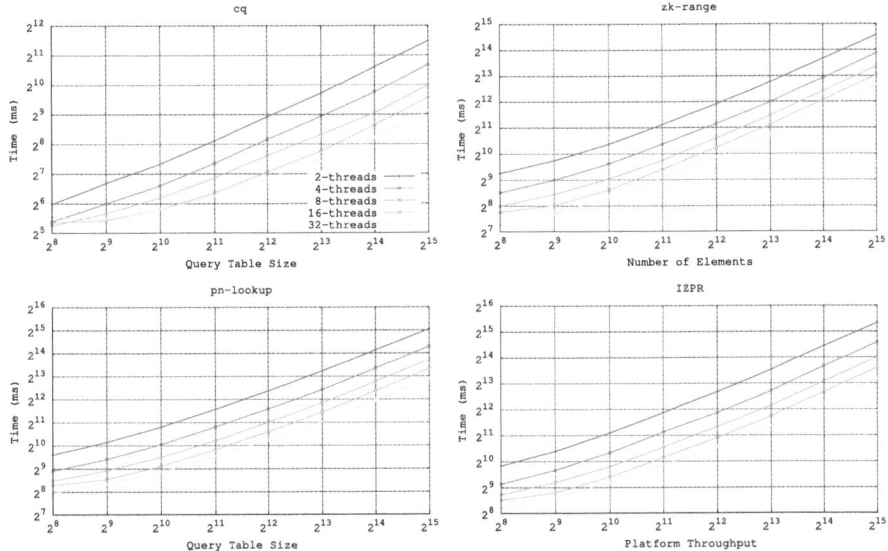

Fig. 3. Scalability of π_{IZPR}

5 Implementation and Evaluation

We implemented and evaluated π_{IZPR} over BLS12-381 (providing 128-bit security). Our implementation consists of 4600 lines of Rust, and is based on the arkworks library [2] (which provides parallelism via multi-threaded Rayon). Fig. 3 shows the scalability of the zk-cq protocol, the batched zk-range proof based on cq, the zk-pn-lookup protocol and the π_{IZPR} protocol. The evaluation data is collected over a GCP C2D instance with 56 cores, and the best performance is achieved at $2^{\lfloor \log(56) \rfloor} = 32$ threads. For the zk-range proof, we assert range $[0, 2^{160})$ and split each field element into 8 chunks of 20-bit numbers. Therefore given n elements in a batched zk-range proof, it results in a lookup argument for query table size of $16n$. The concrete prover cost of zk-range proof for processing $32k$ 160-bit field elements needs 6.46 s with 32 threads, equivalent to 24.76 bit/(thread,ms), which is faster than bullet range proof (e.g., 1621 ms for 32×64−bit range proofs in Table 2 [5]).[5]

The lookup table has 8 million entries (simulating an exchange owning 10% of existing BTC addresses). The one-time preprocessing for π_{IZPR} (mainly for the cq) takes 4 h.[6] The prover cost for 2048 account updates is 0.935 s (32-threads), and the verification cost is 45 ms (1-thread). Assuming that each transaction results in change of 2 accounts, this is equivalent to supporting TPS of 1024,

---

[5] For range proof, if cq is replaced by plookup [24] or logUp [26], or more recent Lasso [32], additional gain of performance can be achieved.

[6] The cost does not include the ownership proof for each BTC address.

which is half of the speed of Visa Network and 146 times of BTC. The proof size is 3.4 kb.

5.1 Discussion on Bootstrap Cost

There are many ways to realize the bootstrap process, which is out of the scope of this paper, as the bootstrap is orthogonal to the incremental proof protocol. We briefly describe a way to do the bootstrap using a ZK-SNARK[7] and then state the estimated cost.

The basic idea of the SNARK is to hide the organization's account set **S** inside a bigger, public set of accounts called the anonymity set, **S'**. Ownership of each account in **S** is proved via a signature, so the organization is expected to be able to produce a set of signatures **E** such that the mapping between **S** and **E** is a bijection. After verifying the signatures the SNARK calculates the sum of balances of **S**, and produces a commitment to this value. Finally, the SNARK produces the commitment $\mathbf{C_S}$, which is how it is linked to the IZPR protocol.

We have the following input signals to the SNARK:

1. pub **S'** (contains addresses & asset balances)
2. pvt **E**

The SNARK does these computations:

1. Verify each signature in **E** and check that it corresponds to exactly one account in **S'**
2. Sum up the balances for each account related to a signature in **E**, V
3. Create a commitment to V and output this as a public signal, $\mathbf{C}_V$
4. Create a commitment to **S** and output this as a public signal, $\mathbf{C_S}$

The verifier needs to check that each address and balance in the anonymity set are the same as found on the blockchain. They then need to check that the public signal $\mathbf{C_S}$ is the same as the one used in the IZPR protocol. To update the asset sum, the verifier can add the public signal $\mathbf{C}_V$ from the SNARK to the commitment $\mathbf{C}_v$ from IZPR.

There are some hurdles to overcome with the above SNARK. The first issue is the size of the anonymity set: since this is a public signal, it must form part of the proof, so the size of the proof is $O(|\mathbf{S'}|)$. If we would like to keep the proofs succinct then we can use a Merkle tree for the anonymity set. Instead of having **S'** as a public signal, we have only the root as a public signal, and then have Merkle proofs as private signals, which are verified inside the SNARK. Using a Merkle tree allows us to make our anonymity set very large without taking up too many constraints. Even if our anonymity set was 10^{15} it would only need 2× more constraints than if the set had 100M elements.

Another problem is the cost of verifying ECDSA signatures (the signature scheme for Bitcoin) inside a SNARK. The size of the secp256k1 base field is

---

[7] A full description of the design can be found here: https://hackmd.io/@JI2Ftqaw SzO-olUw-r48DQ/rJXtAeyLT.

greater than the native field sizes used for SNARKS, which means the values of coordinates for points on secp256k1 need to be stored using at least 2 SNARK field values. Basic operations like addition and multiplication thus become expensive. If we stick to the Circom ecosystem and use Groth16 as our proving system then the number of R1CS constraints to verify x ECDSA signatures is about $0.45x + 1$ (in millions of constraints)[8]. Given the current constraint limit of 256M (limited by largest available PTAU file) this means we are limited to about 600 signatures. We can get around this issue by using recursive SNARKs.

We can split up **S** into batches and input each batch into a different SNARK, which can be computed in parallel. We need a final SNARK to verify the proofs of the batches of SNARKS (this is the recursive step) and sum up the intermediate sums produced by each batch. With the current recursive implementation[9] the max number of signatures supported is about 6000, although this number can be increased using snarkpack.

Regarding computational cost, if we assume $|\mathbf{S}| = 6000$ then the computational time is dominated by proving key generation. This takes around 155 h on an EC2 m7g.8xlarge. The other expensive operation is compilation, which takes around 4 h. We need 3 m7g.8xlarge's to take advantage of the recursive and parallel nature of the design. The total USD cost is around $875. This amounts to about 0.14 US dollar for the initial asset proof per BTC address.

6 Conclusion

Based on the recent progress of lookup arguments, we develop a zero knowledge protocol for asserting the asset of an organization incrementally. The prover cost does not depend on the number of the accounts owned by an organization (which can be arbitrarily large), but on the *throughput* of the platform. With modest computing resources, the protocol can support regular business transaction systems at 2^{10} TPS. We foresee that with some light implementation efforts, e.g., leveraging MPI, the protocol can be further scaled.

Acknowledgment. We would like to thank Dr. Ariel Gabizon for the recommendation of appropriate lookup arguments for this work. We appreciate the constructive suggestions from the reviewers for improving this manuscript. This research is supported by an unrestricted research gift from Chan Zuckerberg Initiative, and a Hofstra SEAS FRDG grant. Trevor Conley is supported by the Hofstra SEAS AsPire'23 Summer Research Program, Fall'23 Stuart and Nancy Rabinowitz Honors College Research Assistant Program, and various student travel support resources from Hofstra University.

References

1. Agrawal, S., Ganesh, C., Mohassel, P.: Non-interactive zero-knowledge proofs for composite statements. In: CRYPTO, pp. 643–673 (2018)

---

[8] https://github.com/puma314/batch-ecdsa.
[9] https://github.com/silversixpence-crypto/zk-proof-of-assets.

2. arkworks contributors. `arkworks` zksnark ecosystem (2022)
3. Baldimtsi, F., Chatzigiannis, P., Gordon, S., Le, P., McVicker, D.: gOTzilla: Efficient disjunctive zero-knowledge proofs from MPC in the head, with application to proofs of asset in cryptocurrencies. PoPETs **4**, 229–249 (2022)
4. Binance: Improving crypto transparency with zero-knowledge proof (2023). https://academy.binance.com/en/articles/improving-crypto-transparency-with-zero-knowledge-proof
5. Bünz, B., Bootle, J., Boneh, D., Poelstra, A., Wuille, P., Maxwell, G.: Bulletproofs: short proofs for confidential transactions and more. In: SSP, pp. 315–334 (2018)
6. Camenisch, J., Stadler, M.: Efficient group signature schemes for large groups. In: Kaliski, B.S. (ed.) CRYPTO 1997. LNCS, vol. 1294, pp. 410–424. Springer, Heidelberg (1997). https://doi.org/10.1007/BFb0052252
7. Campanelli, M., Faonio, A., Fiore, D., Li, T., Lipmaa, H.: Lookup arguments: improvements, extensions and applications to zero-knowledge decision trees (2023). https://hal.science/hal-04234948/document
8. Campanelli, M., Faonio, A., Fiore, D., Querol, A., Rodríguez, H.: Lunar: a toolbox for more efficient universal and updatable zkSNARKs and commit-and-prove extensions. In: Tibouchi, M., Wang, H. (eds.) ASIACRYPT 2021. LNCS, vol. 13092, pp. 3–33. Springer, Cham (2021). https://doi.org/10.1007/978-3-030-92078-4_1
9. Carter, N.: Nic's PoR wall of fame (2023). https://niccarter.info/proof-of-reserves/
10. Chalkias, K., Lewi, K., Mohassel, P., Nikolaenko, V.: Distributed auditing proofs of liabilities. IACR Cryptology ePrint Archive (2020). https://eprint.iacr.org/2020/468
11. Chatzigiannis, P., Baldimtsi, F., Chalkias, K.: SoK: auditability and accountability in distributed payment systems. In: Sako, K., Tippenhauer, N.O. (eds.) ACNS 2021. LNCS, vol. 12727, pp. 311–337. Springer, Cham (2021). https://doi.org/10.1007/978-3-030-78375-4_13
12. Chiesa, A., Hu, Y., Maller, M., Mishra, P., Vesely, N., Ward, N.: Marlin: preprocessing zkSNARKs with universal and updatable SRS. In: Canteaut, A., Ishai, Y. (eds.) EUROCRYPT 2020. LNCS, vol. 12105, pp. 738–768. Springer, Cham (2020). https://doi.org/10.1007/978-3-030-45721-1_26
13. Choudhuri, A., Garg, S., Goel, A., Sekar, S., Sinha, R.: SublonK: sublinear prover plonk (2023). https://eprint.iacr.org/2023/902
14. CoinDesk: Binance's bitcoin reserves are overcollateralized, new report says (2023). https://www.coindesk.com/business/2022/12/07/binances-bitcoin-reserves-are-overcollateralized-says-audit
15. Dagher, G., Bünz, B., Bonneau, J., Clark, J., Boneh, D.: Provisions: privacy-preserving proofs of solvency for bitcoin exchanges. In: CCS, pp. 720–731 (2015)
16. Decker, C., Guthrie, J., Seidel, J., Wattenhofer, R.: Making bitcoin exchanges transparent. In: Pernul, G., Ryan, P.Y.A., Weippl, E. (eds.) ESORICS 2015. LNCS, vol. 9327, pp. 561–576. Springer, Cham (2015). https://doi.org/10.1007/978-3-319-24177-7_28
17. Dutta, A., Bagad, S., Vijayakumaran, S.: MProve+: privacy enhancing proof of reserves protocol for Monero. IEEE Trans. Inf. Forensics Secur. **16**, 3900–3915 (2021)
18. Dutta, A., Jana, A., Vijayakumaran, S.: Nummatus: a privacy preserving proof of reserves protocol for Quisquis. In: Hao, F., Ruj, S., Sen Gupta, S. (eds.) INDOCRYPT 2019. LNCS, vol. 11898, pp. 195–215. Springer, Cham (2019). https://doi.org/10.1007/978-3-030-35423-7_10

19. Dutta, A., Vijayakumaran, S.: MProve: a proof of reserves protocol for Monero exchanges. In: Euros&p Workshops, pp. 330–339 (2019)
20. Dutta, A., Vijayakumaran, S.: Revelio: a MimbleWimble proof of reserves protocol. In: CVCBT, pp. 7–11 (2021)
21. Eagen, L., Fiore, D., Gabizon, A.: cq: Cached quotients for fast lookups. IACR Cryptology ePrint Archive (2022). https://eprint.iacr.org/2022/1763
22. Gabizon, A., Khovratovich, D.: flookup: fractional decomposition-based lookups in quasi-linear time independent of table size. IACR Cryptology ePrint Archive (2022)
23. Gabizon, A., Williamson, Z., Ciobotaru, O.: PLONK: permutations over Lagrange-bases for Oecumenical noninteractive arguments of knowledge. IACR Cryptology ePrint Archive (2019). https://eprint.iacr.org/2019/953
24. Gabizon, A., Williamson, Z.J.: plookup: a simplified polynomial protocol for lookup tables. IACR Cryptology ePrint Archive (2020)
25. Groth, J.: On the size of pairing-based non-interactive arguments. In: Fischlin, M., Coron, J.-S. (eds.) EUROCRYPT 2016. LNCS, vol. 9666, pp. 305–326. Springer, Heidelberg (2016). https://doi.org/10.1007/978-3-662-49896-5_11
26. Habock, U.: Multivariate lookups based on logarithmic derivatives. IACR Cryptology ePrint Archive (2022)
27. Ji, Y., Chalkias, K.: Generalized proof of liabilities. In: CCS, pp. 3465–3486 (2021)
28. Kate, A., Zaverucha, G.M., Goldberg, I.: Constant-size commitments to polynomials and their applications. In: Abe, M. (ed.) ASIACRYPT 2010. LNCS, vol. 6477, pp. 177–194. Springer, Heidelberg (2010). https://doi.org/10.1007/978-3-642-17373-8_11
29. OKX: One year of proof of reserves (2023). https://www.okx.com/proof-of-reserves
30. Parno, B., Howell, J., Gentry, C., Raykova, M.: Pinocchio: nearly practical verifiable computation. In: SSP, pp. 238–252 (2013)
31. Posen, J., Kattis, A.: Caulk+: table-independent lookup arguments. IACR Cryptology ePrint Archive (2022)
32. Setty, S., Thaler, J., Wahby, R.: Unlocking the lookup singularity with lasso. IACR Cryptology ePrint Archive (2023). https://eprint.iacr.org/2023/1216
33. Srinivasan, S., Karantaidou, I., Baldimtsi, F., Papamanthou, C.: Batching, aggregation, and zero-knowledge proofs in bilinear accumulators. In: CCS, pp. 2719–2733 (2022)
34. summa-dev: Monorepo for Summa proof of solvency protocol (2023). https://github.com/summa-dev/summa-solvency
35. Wilcox, Z.: Proving your Bitcoin reserves (2014). https://bitcointalk.org/index.php?topic=595180.0
36. Zapico, A., Buterin, V., Khovratovich, D., Maller, M., Nitulescu, A., Simkin, M.: Caulk: lookup arguments in sublinear time. In: CCS, pp. 3121–3134 (2022)
37. Zapico, A., Gabizon, A., Khovratovich, D., Maller, M., Ràfols, C.: Baloo: nearly optimal Lookup Arguments. IACR Cryptology ePrint Archive (2022)
38. Zhang, Y., Genkin, D., Katz, J., Papadopoulos, D., Papamanthou, C.: A Zero-Knowledge Version of vSQL. IACR Cryptology ePrint Archive, vol. 2017, p. 1146 (2017)

A New Approach to Estimating Bitcoin Production Cost

Go Yamamoto[✉][iD]

NTT Digital, Inc., Tokyo, Japan
go.yamamoto.public@gmail.com

Abstract. Estimating Bitcoin production cost is a common concern for economists, financial engineers, environmental activists, investors, and regulators. The costs affect the robustness of the Bitcoin ecosystem, the sustainability of its energy consumption, and ultimately, the value of its assets. The existing estimation approach relies on estimating power consumption by analyzing the performance of mining hardware available in the market.

This paper proposes a new approach to estimating Bitcoin production cost, based on a behavioral model of miners instead of analyzing energy costs by surveying mining hardware profiles. We apply a theoretical model that derives the rational hash rate from a miner's risk tolerance to infer the production cost solely from changes in the Bitcoin price and the mining difficulty parameter. We present methods to generate a time series of estimated production costs using actual Bitcoin prices and difficulty parameters. The results show that the estimated production costs, using only Bitcoin prices and difficulty parameters, closely track the energy costs estimated from mining hardware profiles. This suggests that most miners behave rationally, as the model assumes, and that we have obtained an alternative method to estimate the cost of Bitcoin production.

1 Introduction

Estimating Bitcoin production cost is a common concern for economists, financial engineers, environmental activists, investors, and regulators. The costs affect the robustness of the Bitcoin ecosystem, the sustainability of its energy consumption, and, ultimately, the value of its assets. Traditional estimation approaches rely on estimating power consumption by analyzing the performance of mining hardware available on the market.

This paper introduces a new approach to estimating Bitcoin production cost without evaluating the energy cost. Previous theoretical studies allow us to calculate the rational hash rates for miners, given Bitcoin prices and production costs. We estimate Bitcoin production costs from the prices and the difficulty parameters by solving the formula in reverse. The resulting estimation persistently tracks the observed energy costs over ten years of historical data. This

---

The fundamental part of this study was completed while the author was with NTT Social Informatics Laboratories.

© International Financial Cryptography Association 2025
J. Budurushi et al. (Eds.): FC 2024 Workshops, LNCS 14746, pp. 240–252, 2025.
https://doi.org/10.1007/978-3-031-69231-4_16

convergence of theoretical results with real-world data suggests that most miners behave rationally, as the theory predicts, and that we have obtained a new method to estimate the cost of Bitcoin production.

So far, several issues have been identified with the method of estimating production cost by surveying the unit energy costs and the power consumption based on the performance data of mining hardware:

1. The costs paid by miners vary widely; it is unknown what proportion of Bitcoin's marginal production cost is accounted for by energy costs.
2. There is no significant way to verify that the estimated energy cost is sufficiently reasonable.
3. It is challenging to know in real-time how costs change as long as it uses methods that estimate the internal information of the miner.

The mainstream of conventional research on Bitcoin production costs appears to aim at mitigating these downsides. Related to the first issue, about the gap between production costs and energy costs, Song and Aste [7] argue that non-energy costs are ultimately proportional to energy costs. Skobelev [6], however, disagrees, explaining the need for a more accurate understanding of CAPEX and OPEX and attempting to capture more practical hardware profiles by studying Google search trends. Regarding the second issue, Song and Aste [7] looks at more accurate power costs considering regional disparities and a detailed understanding of hardware profiles. Hayes [5] examines the history of mining hardware profiles captured by the Bitcoin community and considers regression models that consider comparisons with Altcoins. The third issue does not seem to be approached by many academic projects. One standard and reliable power consumption survey is the CBECI index [3] maintained by the Cambridge Centre for Alternative Finance. They estimate the profile of mining hardware in the market by average, based on a hybrid top-down approach initially developed by Bevand [1]. The CBECI is available to the public and updated daily.

This paper contributes to solving these issues by introducing an independent source of cost estimation. Moreover, the new estimation method provides a more convenient and real-time solution.

The study in this paper proceeds as follows. First, we review the results of prior research on the rational hash rate according to the von Neumann-Morgenstern expected utility model, given information on Bitcoin prices and production costs. We then demonstrate that these results can be used to calculate the marginal costs per hash computation using only Bitcoin prices and difficulty parameters.

Next, we apply this theoretical result to historical data. The noisy behavior of Bitcoin prices hinders the estimation of hash computation costs using actual data. Therefore, we first remove outliers from the raw estimated data series using the standard IQR method and then eliminate the noise with an extended version of regression analysis. The marginal cost of one hash computation is thus estimated. Using this estimated hash computation cost, we obtain a new indicator for estimating Bitcoin production costs.

The indicator is highly correlated with the estimated energy cost of Bitcoin production using the CBECI. The correlation shows an R^2 score of about 0.9, which has persisted over the last ten years. Moreover, the regression analysis between the indicator and energy cost shows a clear trend in the residuals, varying over time spans from months to years. This suggests that the indicator contains more information than the power consumption alone. Indeed, we can observe that the estimated relationship between the indicator and power consumption data has changed significantly only on a few limited occasions over the past decade.

This suggests that the estimated production costs reveal a history of changes in the Bitcoin mining business's cost structure. In this paper, we focus on the scientific aspects and defer examining the consistency of this mathematical analysis with actual historical events. Future research should delve into the social, legal, and economic implications to provide a comprehensive understanding of the Bitcoin mining industry's evolution.

2 Marginal Production Cost of Bitcoin in Thoery

2.1 Model of Blockchain Mining and the Rational Hash Rates

We work with the following model of the PoW blockchain networks, such as Bitcoin, which simplifies and idealizes the reality concerning revenue, expense, and mining strategies of the miners, including mining pools. We explicitly model the mining pools of risk-sharing type only. Miner's contribution by the risk-free type policy is interpreted as the Mining Pool's purchase of hash rates.

We use the discrete-time model with time $t = 0, 1, 2, \cdots$ and employ the following parameters of the Blockchain Network processed in each period. Each period is L seconds and is very short, for example, milliseconds.

B Market price of the block reward. We assume transaction fees are negligible.
H Network hash rate.
τ Expected block interval. 10 minutes for Bitcoin.
δ The difficulty parameter.
D $2^{32}\delta/\tau$.
r Risk-free rate for period L. We assume $r > 0$.

We consider two types of agents. One is a Miner, and the other is a Mining Pool. We employ the following parameters for each Miner.

w Total wealth.
Q Hash rate generated by the Miner.
c Marginal cost of one hash computation, including depreciation.
M The aggregated hash rate of the Mining Pool the Miner contributes to.

Each Miner has wealth w and generates hash rate Q on its decision. It pays mining costs according to the hash rate and receives mining rewards by contributing the hash rate to a Mining Pool. The cost is cLQ for hash rate Q for L

seconds. A Miner receives a proportional reward of $B\frac{Q}{M}$ from the Mining Pool when the Mining Pool finds a new block.

Each miner is assumed to take risks according to the expected utility model with an isoelastic utility function. The isoelastic utility function is

$$W_\lambda(x) = \frac{x^{1-\lambda} - 1}{1 - \lambda}. \tag{1}$$

The miner has a risk aversion parameter $\lambda \in (0, \infty)$ that characterizes $W_\lambda(x)$ by the Arrow-Pratt measure of relative risk aversion $\lambda = \mathcal{A}(W_\lambda(x))$, where $\mathcal{A}(U(x)) = -x\frac{U''(x)}{U'(x)}$. A smaller λ indicates that miners are willing to take larger risks for the size of their investment capital.

We consider a group of Miners contributing to one Mining Pool with an aggregated hash rate of M. We assume that each Miner has a different parameter. Let the parameters of Miner i be hash rate Q_i, amount of investment capital w_i, risk aversion parameter λ_i, and the cost of computing a hash once c_i.

According to the analysis of the expected utility model for Bitcoin mining [8], the rational contribution chosen by each Miner i is

$$Q_i = \frac{(1+r)M}{\lambda_i B}\left(1 - \frac{(1+r)\tau c_i D}{B}\right) w_i. \tag{2}$$

In the following, let $B' = B/(1+r)$ for notational simplicity. B' is the present value of the block reward received L seconds later.

2.2 Estimating Marginal Cost of Hash Computation

Let $\eta_i = 1 - \frac{c_i \tau D}{B'}$. η_i is the expected operating margin for Miner since B is the revenue per block for the entire network, and τD is the expected number of hash calculations required by the entire network to mine one block, so $c_i \tau D$ is the expected cost of mining one block for that Miner.

Using Eq. (2), we obtain

$$B'\frac{Q_i}{M} = \eta_i \frac{w_i}{\lambda_i}. \tag{3}$$

Equation (3) describes how a Miner can determine the hash rate share in the Mining Pool by rational decision according to an isoelastic utility function.

Assume that all Miners participating in the Mining Pool determine the hash rates by Eq. (3). Then we have $\sum_i Q_i = M$, hence by summing Eq. (3) for i, we obtain

$$B' = \sum_i \eta_i v_i, \tag{4}$$

where we define $v_i = w_i/\lambda_i$. v_i can be interpreted as the effective amount of investment capital adjusted by the risk aversion parameter.

Assume that there are m such Mining Pools in total, and each Mining Pool satisfies Eq. (4) separately. Taking their sum, we get

$$mB' = \sum_k \eta_k v_k. \tag{5}$$

Here, the sum on the right-hand side is the total sum of all the Miners participating in those Mining Pools. Hence, we have

$$B' = \bar{w}\tilde{\eta}, \tag{6}$$

where we define

$$\tilde{\eta} = \frac{\sum_k \eta_k v_k}{\sum_k v_k} \tag{7}$$

and $\bar{w} = \frac{1}{m}\sum_k v_k$. $\bar{w}$ is the average of the sum of the adjusted amounts of investment capital for each Mining Pool. $\tilde{\eta}$ is the weighted average of the minor's operating margin on sales, weighted by the adjusted amount of investment capital.

$\tilde{\eta}$ satisfies

$$\tilde{\eta} = 1 - \frac{\tau D}{B'}\tilde{c}, \tag{8}$$

where $\tilde{c} = \frac{\sum_k c_k v_k}{\sum_k v_k}$. $\tilde{c}$ is the average cost per hash weighted by the adjusted amount of investment capital. Eq. (8) says that the average operating margin is equal to the total value minus the average operating cost ratio. Then, from Eqs. (6) and (8), we obtain

$$B' = \bar{w}\left(1 - \frac{\tau D}{B'}\tilde{c}\right). \tag{9}$$

We consider a situation in which Eq. (9) is satisfied from $t = n - d$ to $t = n$. Denote B and D at time $t = n - d$ as B_{n-d} and D_{n-d}, and at time $t = n$ as B_n and D_n. We consider a moderately short d and assume that $\bar{w}_n = \bar{w}_{n-d}$ and $\tilde{c}_n = \tilde{c}_{n-d}$. This assumption implies no significant difference in the amount of capital in the Mining Pool and no significant change in the average cost of the hash computation.

Then, we have $B'_{n-d} = \bar{w}_{n-d}(1 - \frac{\tau D_{n-d}}{B'_{n-d}}\tilde{c}_{n-d})$ and $B'_n = \bar{w}_n(1 - \frac{\tau D_n}{B'_n}\tilde{c}_n)$, therefore,

$$\frac{B'_{n-d}}{B'_n} = \frac{1 - \frac{\tau D_{n-d}}{B'_{n-d}}\tilde{c}_n}{1 - \frac{\tau D_n}{B'_n}\tilde{c}_n}.$$

By solving this equation for $\tilde{c}_n$, we have

$$\tau \tilde{c}_n = \frac{B'_n - B'_{n-d}}{D_{n-d}\frac{B_n}{B_{n-d}} - D_n\frac{B_{n-d}}{B_n}}. \tag{10}$$

Equation (10) implies that the marginal cost of one hash computation can be estimated from changes in the market price of Bitcoin and the difficulty parameter. It is considered that time series $\{\tau \tilde{c}_t D_t\}_t$ estimates the expected production cost of Bitcoin of one block reward.

3 Data Processing Methods for the Cost Estimation

The time series data of historical Bitcoin prices contains much noise. To estimate the cost of one hash computation using $\tilde{c}$ of Equation (10), we must process the data to extract the essential part of the data.

3.1 Removing Outliers

We first want to remove extremely large absolute values from the time series data given by the right-hand side of Eq. (10). Since the difference between two independent noise components appears in the denominator, a straightforward calculation of this equation applied to the historical Bitcoin price data reveals very large values with a certain probability. We use the IQR method, a standard method for removing such outliers.

IQR is defined as the difference between the first quartile of the data set (Q_1, the 25% point from the bottom of the data) and the third quartile (Q_3, the 25% point from the top of the data).

We set IQR $= Q_3 - Q_1$ and consider as outliers any value smaller than $Q_1 - 1.5 \cdot$ IQR or larger than $Q_3 + 1.5 \cdot$ IQR. The constant 1.5 is the standard constant by custom.

A time series of $\tau\tilde{c}$ of Eq. (10) after removing outliers using the IQR method is illustrated by the red plot in Fig. 1. Although the noise is still intense, a slowly changing trend can be observed for the changes by the time windows of months.

3.2 Local Regression Analysis

After removing the outliers, indicator $\tilde{c}$ mostly shows a time-series graph like the red plot in Fig. 1. Although the influence of noise caused by the stochastic Bitcoin price is still significant, looking at the graph's trend over the months, we can see that the local average value of the graph is changing slowly.

This section considers how to extract information about this trend somehow. For this purpose, we use a non-parametric model employing local regression analysis.

First, we may consider using simple regression analysis to remove the noise locally. For example, if we want to obtain an estimate of $\tilde{c}$ from January to December 2022, then we can draw a regression line in this window. If we run this calculation moving the window on the ten years of data, the regression line estimating $\tilde{c}$ changes slowly as the window moves. Then, we obtain the reasonable estimation of $\tilde{c}$ that changes continuously in ten years by "connecting" regression lines for each moving window to obtain a curve representing the estimation from the time series data. It is the basic idea of the LOWESS curve model, initially proposed by Cleveland [4].

We can calculate the LOWESS curve as follows. The time series data to be analyzed are weighted by a weight function, and then regression analysis is performed. Moving the weight function along the x-axis allows a curve that smoothly connects the regression lines for each window. There are several standard choices of weight functions, but here, we use the Cubic weight function according to the tradition. Namely,

$$w(x) = (1 - \left|\frac{x}{h}\right|^3)^3, \tag{11}$$

where h is the window size, and $w(x) = 0$ when $|x| > h$.

A moderate choice of h is the moderate length of the period in which the trend of $\tilde{c}$ is expected to change. We chose 18 months which accounts for the generational change in mining hardware. Figure 1 illustrates how the LOWESS curve algorithm makes the mildly changing curve, the blue curve, from the noisy time series data, the red plot.

We call the estimate of $\tilde{c}$ obtained in this method the hash cost indicator. We emphasize that calculating the indicator still takes only the Bitcoin prices and the difficulty parameters alone on input.

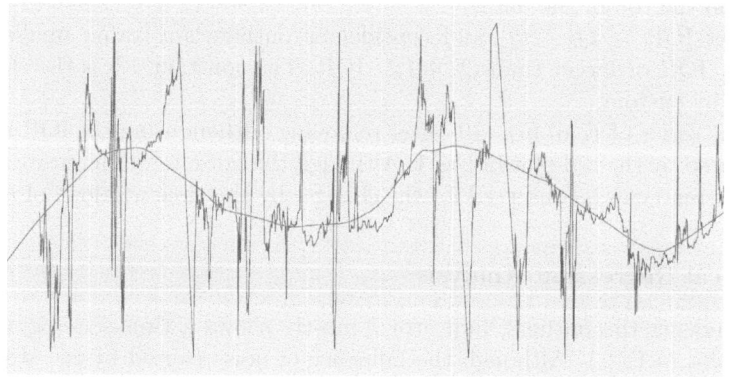

Fig. 1. Local regression analysis by the LOWESS curve.

4 Test-Driving the Production Cost Estimator

4.1 The Estimated Production Cost Tracks the Energy Cost

Using the miners' decisions model and data processing methods, we developed a new indicator that estimates the marginal cost of hash computation. It assumes that many Miners behave rationally according to the von Neumann-Morgenstern expected utility model. We test-drive the indicator using historical data to investigate whether the indicator is related to the known index of the energy cost of Bitcoin production.

One of the standard indexes commonly accepted in studies of the energy consumption of Bitcoin networks is the Cambridge Bitcoin Electricity Consumption Index (CBECI). The CBECI is unique because it provides up-to-date information on the energy consumption of the entire Bitcoin network and is publicly available and updated daily. We use the CBECI for our energy cost estimation.

The CBECI provides several metrics, including estimated, maximum, and minimum network-wide power demand and annualized power consumption. We use the estimated power demand, the "power, GUESS" column from the CSV data downloaded from the website [3], applying a 7-day moving average. We use the revised version released in August 2023.

The following formula gives the estimated energy cost to produce one Bitcoin on a particular day:

$$x = \frac{\text{PowerDemand} \cdot 1\,\text{day} \cdot \text{ElectricityPrice}}{\text{BlockReward} \cdot \text{BlockCount}}, \quad (12)$$

where BlockReward is 6.25BTC as of 2023, BlockCount is the number of blocks mined on the day, and ElectricityPrice is 0.05USD/kWh, following the assumptions used in the calculation of the CBECI.

Next, we estimate the production cost of Bitcoin using the hash cost indicator $\tilde{c}$. The expected production cost for one Bitcoin is estimated as

$$y = \frac{\tau \tilde{c} D}{\text{BlockReward}}. \quad (13)$$

Our implementation uses the lowess function provided in the Statsmodels module in Python. We follow the module's default behavior and use residual-based reweightings.

We use ten years of daily data from August 2013 to August 2023 of the Bitcoin price and the difficulty parameter applied to Eq. (10). Our data source is Blockchair.com [2]. We use $d = 35$ days fixed. We chose this d because the period must be short enough that the amount of capital does not change, yet difficulty adjustments must occur. We note that changing d does not change the trend of the result.

Figure 2 shows the scatter plot of the time series of the estimated energy cost by the CBECI and the estimated production cost by the hash cost indicator $\tilde{c}$. It is visually confirmed that there is a clear correlation between the energy cost and the estimated production cost by the proposed cost estimator throughout history. The regression line is shown in the figure. The line indicates a correlation with $R^2 = 0.855$, and we can also confirm that the correlation persists when the value of d changes. The R^2 scores for a varying d are shown in Table 1.

It is worth noting that the samples on the scatter plot in Fig. 2 lie within the acute triangle, evidencing that hash cost indicator $\tilde{c}$ tracks the energy cost for a hash computation estimated with the CBECI over the years. The graph in Fig. 3

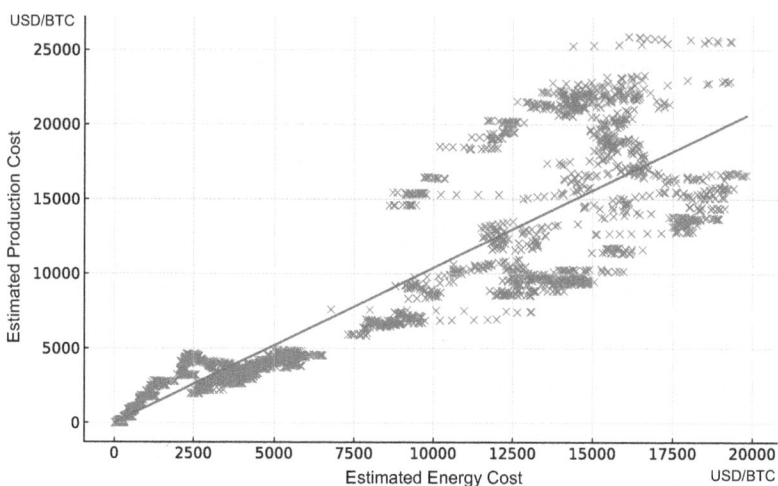

Fig. 2. Correlation of energy cost and estimated production cost.

Table 1. Regression lines and R^2 scores for varying d.

d (days)	Regression Line		R^2
	Slope	Intercept	
7	1.009	67.253	0.815
21	0.949	144.820	0.804
35	1.040	−0.641	0.855
49	1.086	−133.264	0.859
63	1.180	−270.717	0.888
77	1.183	−236.520	0.886
91	1.071	−132.395	0.921
105	1.100	-290.088	0.911

shows that the hash cost indicator (blue curve) has been consistently tracking the energy cost per hash estimated with the CBECI (red plot) since September 2014, while lower than the break-even cost per hash (black plot). This indicates that Bitcoin miners behave rationally, as theoretical analysis predicted.

4.2 Historical Correlation of Production Costs and Energy Costs

Observing the scatter plot in Fig. 2, one can see that the samples deviate from the regression line in some particular different ways at different periods. To analyze these trends in deviations quantitatively, we analyze the residuals of the regression analysis. We examine that the residuals are not random but have an apparent trend, changing over periods of years. It suggests that the presented

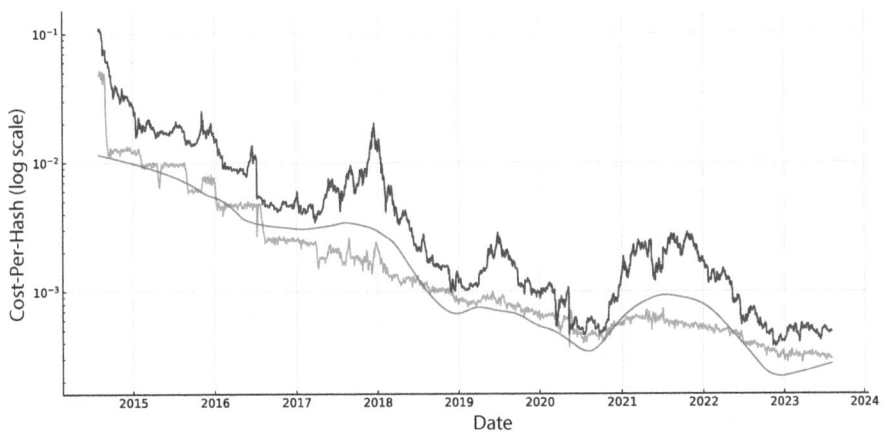

Fig. 3. Estimated hash cost and energy cost per hash.

estimation of production cost from the behavior of the Miners has more information than the energy cost estimation calculated from the CBECI.

We analyze the historical trends in the residuals by the ratio. Since the decade of historical data on Bitcoin mining shows prices and costs that vary by 100 times or more, we need to compare the size of the residuals by the ratio. When x_i is the time series of the energy cost, and y_i is the production cost, let $\hat{y}_i = ax_i + b$, where $y = ax + b$ is the regression line. We can then calculate the residual ratio, i.e.

$$\rho_i = \frac{y_i - \hat{y}_i}{\hat{y}_i}. \tag{14}$$

The time series graph of ρ_i is shown in Fig. 4. We can observe a trend that varies from a few months to years. If production costs are explained by energy costs alone, then this time-series graph of residual ratio should be random. Therefore, the trend suggests that factors other than energy costs affect production costs.

To quantitatively identify the trend, let us divide the ten years into several periods by clustering the time series of residual ratios. Figure 5 shows the frequency of residual ratios. It has several peaks and can be well approximated by the sum of four weighted Gaussian distributions. Such a model is called the Gaussian Mixture Model (GMM). We can cluster the time series data of ten years using the points of crossovers of adjacent Gaussian distributions as the thresholds. We also performed a smoothing process to eliminate extremely short clusters. The residual ratio's time series graph is thus color-coded in Fig. 4.

Figure 6 shows the scatter plot color-coded according to the clusters. Table 2 shows the regression analysis for the samples in each cluster.

According to our findings, while energy remains a primary expense in the mining business, the minor shifts in miners' behavior suggest that more complex factors influence their decision-making processes. Notably, the evolution in

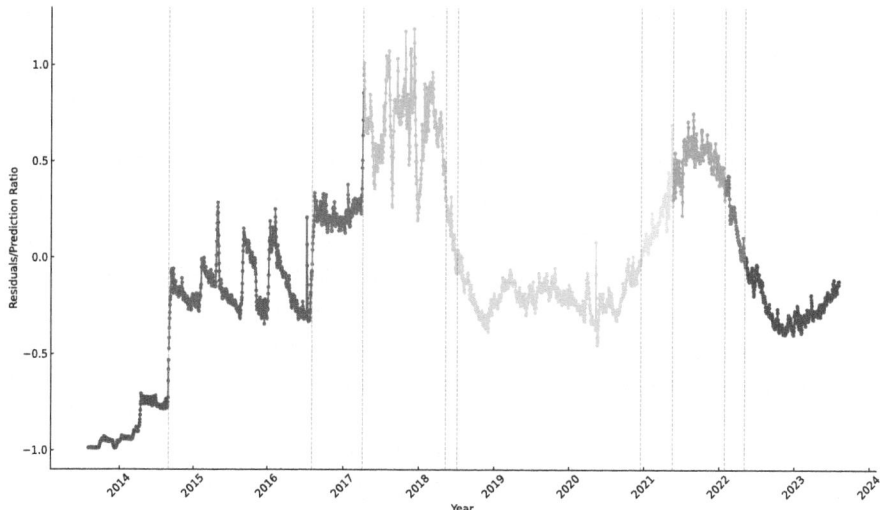

Fig. 4. Time series of residual ratio with clusters.

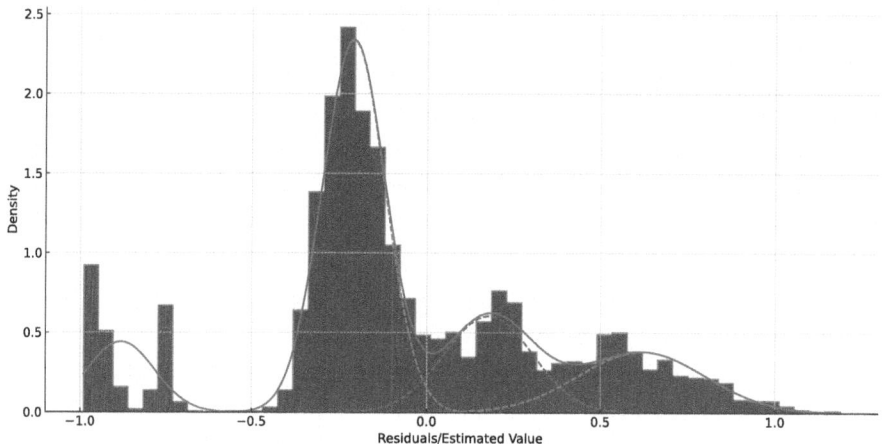

Fig. 5. Histogram of residual ratio.

miners' cost considerations seems to align with key historical milestones in the Bitcoin landscape. Around December 2020, a discernible shift towards incorporating higher non-energy costs was observed. May 2021 marked a transition to another cost structure, enduring for nearly ten months. In February 2022, we observed a temporary decoupling of miners' decisions from energy costs. This phenomenon persisted for about three months before settling into a new cost structure by May 2022. These patterns could reflect adaptive strategies responding to market price changes, regulatory changes, or other financial triggers. Further investigation into how these shifts correspond with the broader narrative of

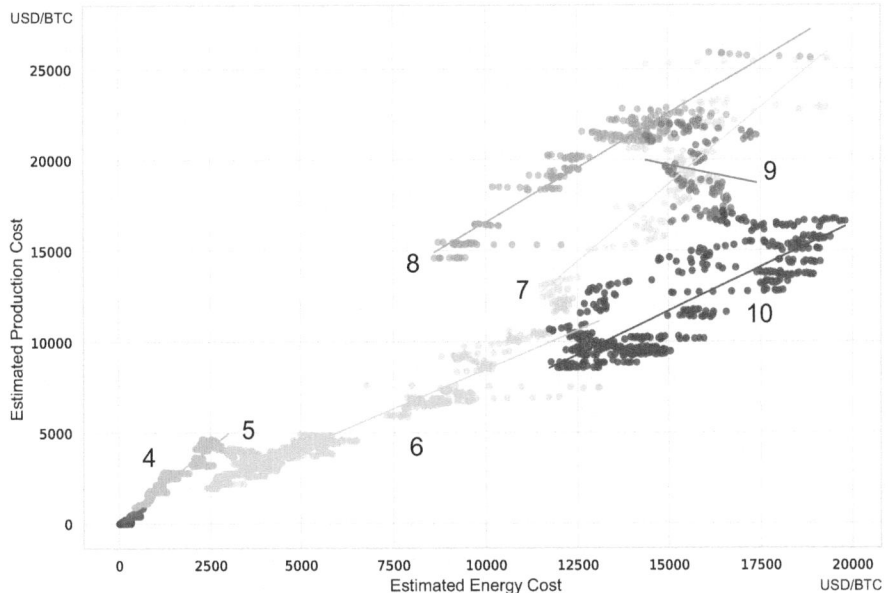

Fig. 6. Clustered correlations of energy cost and estimated production cost.

Table 2. Summary of clusters with regression lines and R^2 scores.

Cluster	Start Date	Duration (day)	Regression Line Slope	Intercept	R^2
1	2013-08-01	397	0.1977	−5.073	0.555
2	2014-09-03	701	0.7214	23.735	0.890
3	2016-08-05	245	1.3841	−46.418	0.940
4	2017-04-08	398	1.5893	195.259	0.931
5	2018-05-12	55	−0.0969	4184.826	0.055
6	2018-07-07	894	0.8626	−163.732	0.926
7	2020-12-18	154	1.6965	−6808.121	0.739
8	2021-05-22	253	1.1927	4640.815	0.903
9	2022-01-31	94	−0.4116	25884.272	0.024
10	2022-05-06	456	0.9621	−2745.904	0.696

Bitcoin's history could reveal insights into how the mining businesses adapted to the changes.

5 Conclusion

Starting from the rationality of risk preference as defined by the von Neumann-Morgenstern expected utility model, we applied an equation to derive miners' preferred hash rates given the Bitcoin prices and production costs. We theoretically showed that the production costs can be estimated from the Bitcoin prices and the difficulty parameters. This estimation method appears to work well when applied to historical data. The cost estimation, using only miners' behavior as input, was found to track the energy cost of the miners, suggesting that Bitcoin miners generally behave according to rational risk preferences.

The new method of estimating mining costs provides an independent source of information in addition to traditional energy cost estimations. This method allows for instant and easy calculation of Bitcoin production costs. We hope it will make a valuable tool for stakeholders interested in Bitcoin's stability, environmental impact, sustainability, and the fundamental value of cryptoassets.

The estimated production costs appear to offer more insight into changes in production costs compared to conventional energy cost estimations. The quantitative analysis of the correlation between the two reveals historical fluctuations over periods ranging from a few months to a few years. These fluctuations may reflect changes in the cost structure of production, including energy costs, throughout the history of Bitcoin mining.

References

1. Bevand, M.: Electricity consumption of Bitcoin: a market-based and technical analysis. mrb's blog (2017). http://blog.zorinaq.com/bitcoin-electricity-consumption
2. Blockchair.com. https://blockchair.com/bitcoin/
3. Cambridge Bitcoin Electricity Consumption Index. https://ccaf.io/cbnsi/cbeci
4. Cleveland, W.S.: Robust locally weighted regression and smoothing scatterplots. J. Am. Stat. Assoc. **74**(368), 829–836 (1979)
5. Hayes, A.S.: Bitcoin price and its marginal cost of production: support for a fundamental value. Appl. Econ. Lett. **26**(7), 554–560 (2019)
6. Skobelev, K.: Bitcoin Production Cost: Demystifying the Mining Industry. Available at SSRN 4005400 (2021)
7. Song, Y.-D., and Aste, T.: The Cost of Bitcoin Mining Has Never Really Increased. Frontiers in Blockchain 3 (2020)
8. Yamamoto, G.: An intrinsic mechanism deciding hash rates from Bitcoin Price. In FC 2023. LNCS, vol. 13953 (2024). https://doi.org/10.1007/978-3-031-48806-1_12

Ethereum Proof-of-Stake Consensus Layer: Participation and Decentralization

Dominic Grandjean, Lioba Heimbach[(✉)][iD], and Roger Wattenhofer[iD]

ETH Zurich, Zurich, Switzerland
research@grandjean.ch, {hlioba,wattenhofer}@ethz.ch

Abstract. In September 2022, Ethereum transitioned from *Proof-of-Work (PoW)* to *Proof-of-Stake (PoS)* during "the merge"—making it the largest PoS cryptocurrency in terms of market capitalization. With this work, we present a comprehensive measurement study of the current state of the Ethereum PoS consensus layer on the *beacon chain*. We perform a longitudinal study of the history of the beacon chain. Our work finds that all dips in network participation are caused by network upgrades, issues with major consensus clients, or issues with service operators controlling a large number of validators. Further, our longitudinal staking power decentralization analysis reveals that Ethereum PoS fairs similarly to its PoW counterpart in terms of decentralization and exhibits the immense impact of (liquid) staking services – a cornerstone of *decentralized finance (DeFi)* – on staking power decentralization. Finally, we highlight the heightened security concerns in Ethereum PoS caused by high degrees of centralization.

Keywords: Ethereum · Proof-of-Stake · consensus layer · decentralization

1 Introduction

The global market capitalization of cryptocurrencies currently exceeds a staggering US\$ 1T [21]. This value is secured by nodes in various open *peer-to-peer (P2P)* networks. These nodes follow the consensus protocol to record and verify transactions. The *decentralization*, i.e., fragmentation of control, of the node network is fundamental. Decentralization ensures that a small number of entities cannot manipulate the blockchain's records. Moreover, enhancing the decentralization of the consensus layer enhances censorship resistance, as no single party can exert significant control over the inclusion of transactions on the ledger.

To safeguard the distributed network from Sybil attacks, where a party tries to gain an advantage by creating numerous nodes, most blockchains employ either *Proof-of-Work (PoW)* or *Proof-of-Stake (PoS)* mechanisms. In PoW *miners* solve computational puzzles, while in PoS *validators* must stake (lock) the cryptocurrency's native token. In September 2022, Ethereum switched from PoW to PoS during "the merge". Ethereum is the second biggest cryptocurrency by market capitalization [21] and the largest PoS cryptocurrency. With its move from PoW to PoS, Ethereum aimed to reduce energy usage but also increase decentralization by lowering the entry barriers for network participants [15].

In Ethereum PoS, network participants wishing to partake in the consensus—be a validator—must deposit 32 ETH. Additionally, (liquid) staking services give participants easier access to Ethereum statking. Importantly, PoS requires continuous active participation of more than two-thirds of the validators for the blockchain to make progress. Therefore, for a PoS blockchain, it is not only essential that the consensus layer is decentralized but also crucial that its validators participate actively even when it is not their turn to propose a block.

Additionally, the switch from PoW to PoS introduced additional consensus layer security concerns. *Maximal extractable value (MEV)*, which refers to the maximum value that can be extracted through including, excluding, and re-ordering the transactions in a block, was prevalent in Ethereum PoW with more than US\$ 675M extracted value before the merge [14]. Thus, MEV poses consensus layer security concerns, as it incentivizes rational miners to fork the blockchain [40]. Not only does MEV remain a concern in Ethereum PoS, but there are also new types of MEV opportunities, e.g., *multi-block MEV*, that arise as a result of knowing the block proposer minutes in advance [38].

Contributions. In this work, we present the first comprehensive measurement study on the participation level and decentralization of the Ethereum PoS consensus layer. We summarise our contributions as follows:

- We study the participation level of validators in the Ethereum PoS and find that the participation levels are very high—exceeding 98%. Dips in participation levels generally coincide with network upgrades or bugs in one or more consensus clients. Additionally, we only find very few slashable offenses, i.e., instances of equivocation by a validator.
- To investigate the decentralization of the validator landscape, we cluster Ethereum validators into entities to find that the level of decentralization of the Ethereum consensus layer has not significantly increased since the merge.
- We highlight the challenges of increasing consensus layer decentralization, i.e., incentivizing users to bypass large staking services but to run their own validators. Large entities do not only receive higher consensus layer rewards, as their participation levels are higher, but they also have the unique opportunity to extract multi-block MEV and thereby are expected to also have higher execution layer rewards.

2 Ethereum Proof-of-Stake

During the merge on 15 September 2022 [20], Ethereum transitioned from PoW to PoS as Sybil resistance. Ethereum now runs two layers: the execution and consensus layer. The execution layer, resembling the previous PoW protocol, retains the responsibility of validating and executing transactions. On the other hand, the consensus layer, constructed atop the beacon chain, focuses on achieving consensus among validators. Importantly, in the PoS paradigm, participants known as validators have replaced traditional miners. Validators are responsible for proposing and validating blocks in the Ethereum network. To become a validator, one must *stake* (i.e., lock) 32 ETH into the designated deposit contract.

2.1 Block Generation

In contrast to PoW, where the timing of blocks is dictated by mining difficulty, PoS operates with a fixed tempo for block generation. To be precise, time is split into epochs. An epoch represents a fixed period in the Ethereum network, consisting of 32 slots. Each slot, in turn, is a time interval during which a single block can be proposed and validated. The duration of a slot is fixed at 12 s [35], i.e., block production is synchronous.

As previously mentioned, there is a chance for a single block to be added to the blockchain in every slot. As used to be the case with PoW Ethereum, a block contains a collection of transactions [43]. In each slot, a validator is selected pseudo-randomly as the block proposer. If a slot's proposer fails to propose a block within the allotted time, the slot remains empty. We note here that the probability of a validator being chosen as a proposer is inversely proportional to the number of active validators in the network at the time of selection [6]. In addition to being tasked with block proposals, validators are also assigned to committees to validate newly proposed blocks. We note here that validators chosen to propose or validate blocks are determined at least one epoch and at most two epochs in advance [22]. Finally, validators participate in sync committees to allow light clients to determine the head of the beacon chain.

2.2 Validator Duties

In the following, we detail the tasks performed by Ethereum PoS validators. Besides having to deposit 32 ETH, a validator must also operate three distinct software components: an execution client, a consensus client, and a validator client. Following the deposit, users enter an activation queue, which serves to control the influx of new validators joining the network. Once a validator joins the network, they are assigned three primary tasks:

Block Proposal. Validators are sporadically selected as a block's proposer, which involves proposing new blocks and making them available for attestation. A pseudo-random selection process for block proposers ensures a fair distribution of block proposal opportunities among all validators. At the present state of the network, an individual validator typically gets an opportunity to propose a block approximately every 2.5 months.

Block Attestation. Attestation involves validators confirming the validity and accuracy of the data contained within a block. Validators are expected to attest to their view of the head of the beacon chain, the most recent fully validated block, once per epoch. During each epoch, every validator submits an attestation to indicate their opinion on the head of the chain. Note that occasionally, validators are assigned the task of aggregating attestations from other validators in the same committee.

Sync Committee Participation. Sync committees have a duration of 27 h and validators are pseudo-randomly selected to participate in a sync committee [2]. A sync committee creates signatures to attest to the chain's head that can be used by light clients to determine the head of the beacon chain.

2.3 Validator Rewards and Penalties

Validators receive rewards for the previously outlined tasks. Their rewards can be divided into consensus and execution layer rewards. Note that consensus layer rewards were received by validators since the start of the beacon chain in December 2020, while execution layer rewards only became available to validators after the merge, i.e., when PoS replaced PoW on Ethereum.

Consensus Layer Rewards. Validators receive rewards for block proposal, attestation (i.e., attesting to the source epoch, target epoch, and chain head), and participation in sync committees [2]. Additionally, validators receive whistleblowing rewards for providing evidence of dishonest validators. Consensus layer rewards decrease on an individual validator basis as more validators join the network. Currently, a validator receives approximately 0.04 ETH for a successful proposal and 0.00001 ETH for a successful attestation [28].

Execution Layer Rewards. A block proposer also receives rewards from priority fees and direct user payments. These rewards are consensus layer rewards, which were introduced after the merge. On average, the execution layer reward of a proposal is around 0.1 ETH per block [45].

Penalties and Slashing. To incentivize network participation and honest behavior, validators receive penalties for missing target and source votes. These penalties are equal in amount to the rewards received for successful attestation. Additionally, validators can also be slashed for serious offenses (e.g., proposing and signing two different blocks for the same slot). Slashing removes at least 1/32 of a validator's staked Ether.

2.4 Staking Services

Staking services give users easier access to Ethereum staking. Generally, staking services are either *custodial*, where the service holds the user's keys, or *non-custodial*, where the user retains control of the keys. Liquid staking further offers tokenized representations of staked assets and has established itself as a DeFi cornerstone.

Custodial Staking Services. Custodial staking services, e.g., Binance, Bitcoin Suisse, Coinbase, and Kraken, hold the user's private keys and manage the technical aspects of staking. Users gain convenience, but besides paying a fee, they must also place trust in the service provider to safeguard their assets.

Further, custodial staking services such as Lido and Rocket Pool are staking pools governed by on-chain communities. In Lido, 30 permissioned companies provide staking services to the protocol, while Rocket Pool employs over 2,500 permissionless node operators for staking user funds.

Non-custodial Staking Services. Non-custodial staking services, such as Stakefish and Staked, provide the infrastructure for staking but allow users to keep control of their assets. The service runs the validator nodes, but users interact directly with smart contracts to stake their assets.

3 Data Collection

We collect Ethereum execution and consensus layer data by running a Lighthouse consensus client and an Erigon execution client. Our consensus layer data set covers the period from the genesis of the beacon chain on 1 December 2020 (i.e., slot 0) through 15 May 2023 (i.e., slot 6,447,598). Notice that the beacon chain launched well in advance of the merge. In the time before the merge, the beacon chain was reaching consensus on its state without processing mainnet transactions [20]. Additionally, our execution layer data covers the period from the genesis of Ethereum on 30 July 2015 through 15 Mai 2023 (i.e., block 17,268,587). We further enhance our data set with validator and address labels from the Rated Network API [17], `beaconcha.in` [5], and Etherscan [8] to allow for validator clustering. Appendix A provides a detailed overview of the data collection.

4 Beacon Chain Participation

We commence the analysis by providing an overview of the size of the network as well as the participation level of the validators in the consensus.

4.1 Number of Validators

Figure 1a displays the total number of validators on the beacon chain. Notice the consistent increase in the number of validators over time. In part, this growth

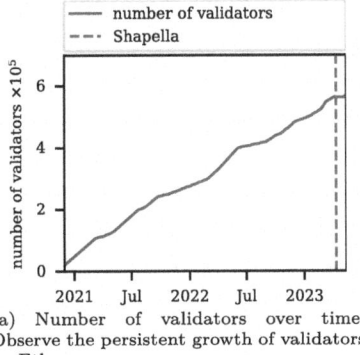
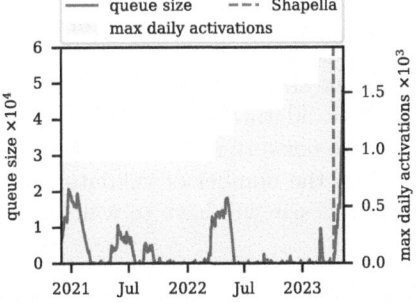

(a) Number of validators over time. Observe the persistent growth of validators on Ethereum.

(b) Number of validators in the queue waiting to join the network along with the maximum number of validators that can be activated each day.

Fig. 1. Number of validators (cf. Figure 1a) and number of validators in the queue (cf. Figure 1b) over time. We mark the Shapella upgrade by the purple dashed line.

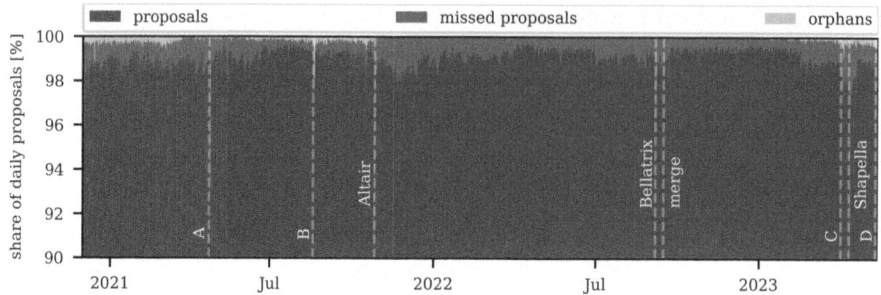

Fig. 2. Daily share of successful (shown in blue), missed (shown in red), and orphaned proposals (shown in yellow). We indicate major upgrades/events that had a noticeable impact on the network participation by white dashed lines. The Altair upgrade heavily reduced the number of orphaned blocks. Also highlighted are incidents A, B, and D. In all three cases bugs in the Prysm and Teku consensus clients resulted in increased numbers of missed/orphaned proposals. Incident C marks an attack on MEV-Boost. (Color figure online)

is due to withdrawals only becoming possible after the Shapella upgrade [19] on 12 April 2023. After the Shapella upgrade, the number of validators remained constant, as both the activation queue (i.e., the queue for validators joining the network) and the exit queue (i.e., the queue for validators exiting the network) were filled and the number of validators that can enter/leave the network is limited. Therefore, the in- and out-flow to the network was constant. Then, almost a month later, on 8 May 2023, the in-flow overtakes the out-flow again, and the number of validators starts to increase again. As of 15 May 2023, there are 572,497 active validators. Each has staked at least 32 ETH on the beacon chain, equivalent to 15.23% of all Ether in circulation.

We further plot the size of the activation queue in Fig. 1b along with the maximum number of daily activations, which depend on the network size. Post beacon chain launch, an initial rise in the queue size is observable. Subsequent significant increases are noted in mid-2021 and March 2022, which coincide with periods of high Ethereum prices. We observe the most significant and still persistent queue size increase after the Shapella upgrade. As of 15 May 2023, there are 48,903 validators in the queue waiting to join the network, while only 1,800 can join the network each day (yellow area in Fig. 1b). Thus, given these limits imposed on the number of validators joining the network, validators entering a queue of this size will have to wait more than 26 d to become activated.

4.2 Proposals

We commence our analysis of the level of network participation of Ethereum with a longitudinal study of the daily share of successful, missed, and orphaned proposals. In Fig. 2, we visualize the daily share of successful proposals in blue, while we show missed proposals in red and orphaned ones in yellow. The daily number of successful proposals is high throughout the entire history of the beacon chain, with an average success rate of 98.95%. Some days stand out with significantly lower success rates. Incidents A [26] and B [27] indicate two bugs in the dominant consensus layer (Prysm) that led to an increased missed and orphaned proposals. In particular, incident B was primarily triggered by a service degradation issue with a Lido operator who controlled roughly 2% of all validators. An existing Prysm bug then exacerbated the situation.

The next sharp increase in the proportion of missed proposals coincides with the Altair upgrade [19], which was the first beacon chain upgrade. While the missed proposals reached about 9% on the day of the upgrade (likely due to operators not updating their clients in time), the proportion of orphaned blocks almost dropped to zero after the update. From then on, the proposal success rate remained relatively stable for almost a year. The Bellatrix upgrade [19], which was the second beacon chain upgrade in preparation for the merge, only increased the number of missed proposals on the day of the upgrade. Further, there is no noticeable drop in the proportion of successful proposals during the merge.

After the merge, we observe a slight increase in the daily share of proposals. Potentially a consequence of the added execution layer rewards received by proposers after the merge—making block proposals significantly more profitable. However, this trend starts to change in early 2023, with both the share of orphans and missed proposals increasing. In particular, the attack by a validator on MEV-Boost [39] (event C) had a lasting impact on the number of missed proposals. After the attack, the timing requirements for validators using MEV-Boost were tightened, which might explain the persistent increase in missed proposals. Shapella [19], the third beacon chain upgrade, again increases the number of missed proposals in its immediate aftermath due to validators not updating their clients in time. The final sharp increase in the number of missed proposals during our data collection coincides with the finality issues experienced by Ethereum on 11 and 12 May 2023 [13] as a result of a bug in the Prysm and Teku consensus clients (event D).

We conclude that throughout the entire beacon chain history, proposal participation was very high. Noticeably, the most significant losses in participation, with the exception of upgrades, are at least in part a consequence of bugs in one or more consensus clients.

4.3 Attestations

We continue by analyzing the network's participation level for attestations. While lower participation in the block proposals reduces the blockchain's throughput, low participation (i.e., less than two-thirds) in attestation can stall the blockchain's finality. Finality indicates that a block is considered irreversible and permanently added to the blockchain, i.e., it cannot be removed or altered without burning one-third of staked Ether. Thus, high network participation for attestations might even be more crucial than for proposals.

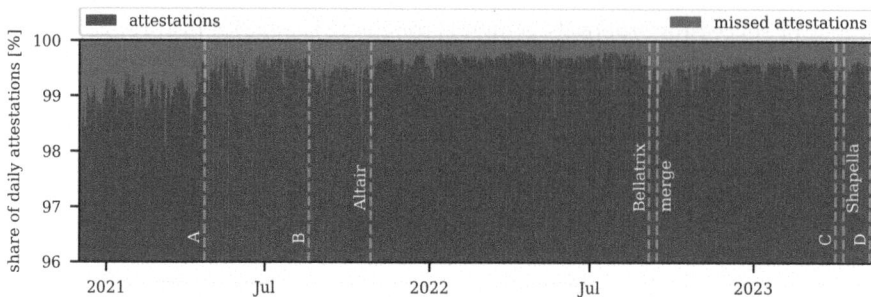

Fig. 3. Daily attestation success rate over time. We indicate major upgrades with a noticeable impact on the network participation by white dashed lines. Incidents A, B, and D, are bugs in the Prysm and Teku consensus clients that resulted in more missed/orphaned proposals. Further incident C marks an attack on MEV-Boost.

In Fig. 3, we plot the daily share of successful and missed attestations. First, we note that similar to what we previously saw with proposals, the overall participation for attestations is high. On average, 99.46% attestations are successful each day—even higher than for proposals. Further, we observe an overall increasing trend in the daily share of successful attestations. By looking at Fig. 3 in detail, we notice that incidents A, B, and D, which all mark bugs in one or more consensus clients, are not or less noticeable in the attestation participation levels. All three beacon chain upgrades (i.e., Altair, Bellatrix, and Shapella) and the merge led to short-term increases in the number of missed attestations. In the aftermath of Bellatrix and the merge, the daily share of missed attestations further stays higher than the previous level and only decreases slowly. Importantly, the drop in participation as a result of incident D led to a non-finalizing state. Incident C, the attack of a validator on MEV-Boost, does not appear to have caused a prolonged increase in missed attestations. This is likely because the tightened timing requirements imposed on MEV-Boost validators do not directly affect the attestation procedure.

4.4 Slashing

Until now, we focused on network participation. As mentioned previously, validators who do not fulfill their duties will only face minor penalties. To explore the prevalence of serious misbehavior, we examine all slashings—punishments for serious offenses. Figure 4 plots all slashings for attestation violations (i.e., attesting to a block that "surrounds" another or engaging in "double voting" by attesting to two candidates for the same block) and for proposal violations (i.e., proposing and signing two different blocks in the same block) from the inception of the beacon chain until 15 May 2023. The Y axis indicates the delay, the number of slots between the slashing, and the offense of the slashing. We find that there are a total of 248 slashings that have taken place: 230 for attestation violations and 18 for proposal violations. Thus, there are only very few (identified) violations in

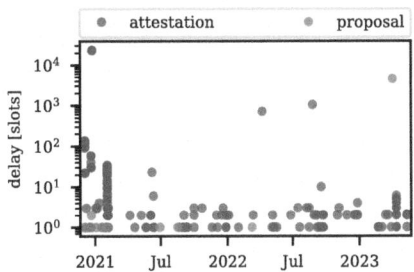

Fig. 4. Slashings for attestation violations (shown in blue) and proposal violations (shown in red) over time. We observe a total of 230 attestation violations and a total of 18 proposal violations. The Y axis indicates the delay of the slashing in comparison to the time of the offense. (Color figure online)

Fig. 5. Distribution of the number of validators in an entity. 7,855 entities are made up of a single validator (top left), while the largest entity consists of 81,165 validators (bottom right). Entity size follows a power-law distribution as demonstrated by the fitted curve.

the history of the beacon chain. Additionally, we observe that the vast majority of violations (81.45%) are identified within ten slots.

5 Validator Landscape

Although every validator starts with an equal initial stake of 32 ETH, a single entity can control multiple validators, thereby increasing their *staking power*. In the subsequent analysis, we group validators into entities and examine the level of (de)centralization within the validator landscape by assessing the distribution of staking power amongst entities. We detail our validator clustering procedure in Appendix B. Importantly, for liquid staking services where validators are operated by separate entities (i.e., Lido, Stakewise, Swell, and RocketPool), we do not cluster all validators into one entity. Instead, we only cluster validators belonging to staking services into one entity if they are run by the same operator. For example, Lido validators are run by 30 different operators and we thus cluster them by operator in the following. Importantly, it is ambiguous whether the validators associated with a staking service should be classified as a single entity or multiple distinct entities, as we will detail in Sect. 5.2. Thus, the following analysis is an *optimistic* analysis of the staking power decentralization, we also present a *pessimistic* analysis in Sect. 5.2.

5.1 Staking Power (De)centralization Optimistic Vantage Point

We proceed by analyzing the validator distribution across entities and assess the level of decentralization in staking power over time. To commence, Fig. 5 illustrates the distribution of the entity size—the number of validators belonging

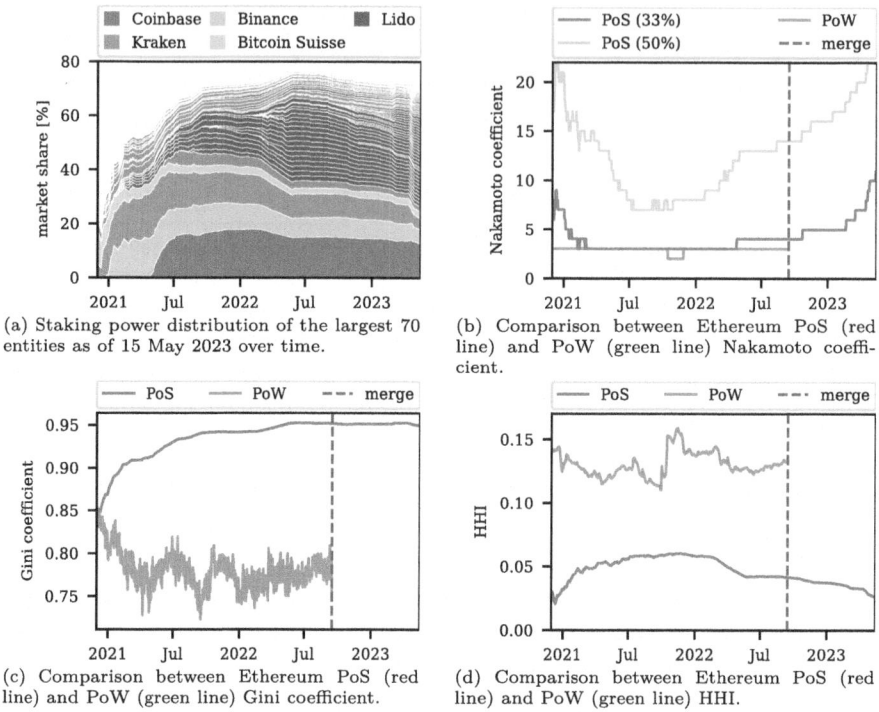

Fig. 6. Decentralization analysis for Ethereum PoS in comparison to Ethereum PoW.

to an entity. We observe that there are many small entities, e.g., nearly 7,855 entities only count a single validator and a few very large entities. The largest entity we identify is Coinbase, with 81,165 validators under their control. There are a couple of entities with the exact same size of around 6,000. These entities are all Lido operators, which are capped in size (cf. Appendix E). In short, we find that the entity size follows a power law distribution as demonstrated by the fitted curve (number of entities $\propto$ entity size$^{-\alpha}$).

We continue by analyzing the (de)centralization of staking power over time. In Fig. 6a, we plot the market share of the biggest 70 entities and highlight the biggest four entities (i.e., Coinbase, Binance, Kraken, and Bitcoin Suisse) as well as the 30 Lido operators. Remarkably, the biggest three entities hold more than 33% of the staking power from early 2021 until mid-2022. We further note that the combined market share of the 30 Lido operators sits at 32.75% and all 30 Lido operators are amongst the biggest 70 entities as of 15 May 2023.

To assess the decentralization of the staking power we utilize three measures: *Nakamoto coefficient*, *Gini coefficient*, and *Herfindahl-Hirschman Index (HHI)*, which we provide definitions for in Appendix C.

To start off, the Nakamoto coefficient determines the number of entities that need to be compromised for an adversary to disrupt the blockchain's network [44]. For Ethereum PoW the adversary requires $> 50\%$ to disrupt the system, while in Ethereum PoS the requirement is $> 33.\bar{3}\%$ to stall the system and $> 50\%$ to break the safety properties [9]). A high Nakamoto coefficient signifies greater decentralization, as it requires a larger number of nodes to be compromised to control the network. Figure 6b visualizes the Nakamoto coefficient of Ethereum over time. For Ethereum PoS, we show the Nakamoto coefficient with a $33.\bar{3}\%$ threshold and a 50%. We further show the Nakamoto coefficient for Ethereum PoW for comparison. Throughout we calculate the decentralization measures for Ethereum PoS based on the staking power and for Ethereum PoW based on a seven-day rolling average of block miners, i.e., mining power.

The Nakamoto coefficient of Ethereum PoW is between two and three from the beginning of the beacon chain to the merge. We notice that for Ethereum PoS, regardless of the threshold, the Nakamoto coefficient is at its highest during the initial phase of the beacon chain and reaches a low point by late 2021. In particular, with the $> 33.\bar{3}\%$ threshold the Nakamoto coefficient is equal to that of Ethereum PoW for approximately a year. However, the Ethereum PoS Nakamoto coefficient begins to rise again from 2022 onwards and reaches seven ($> 33.\bar{3}\%$) and 20 ($> 50\%$) respectively.

We continue by analyzing the Gini coefficient of Ethereum PoS and comparing it to that of Ethereum PoW (cf. Figure 6c). The Gini coefficient is an inequality measure [32] whose values range from 0 which indicates perfect equality to 1 which indicates maximal inequality. Interestingly, at the launch of the beacon chain in late 2020, the Gini coefficient of Ethereum PoS and PoW were almost equal at 0.85—indicating significant inequality. From then on the Gini coefficients diverge, while that of Ethereum PoW decreases to around 0.77 that of Ethereum PoS increases to 0.95. Thus, the inequality of the Ethereum PoS staking power is significant and even more so exceeds that of Ethereum PoW by a noticeable margin by the time of the merge.

Finally, we calculate the *Herfindahl-Hirschman Index (HHI)* [41]. The HHI is used for assessing market concentration, i.e., centralization, in economics. Similar to the Gini coefficient, the HHI ranges between 0, indicating a competitive market, and 1, representing a monopolized market with a single dominant firm. Thus, a low HHI value indicates a more decentralized network with numerous independent validators, while a high HHI value points to a more concentrated network, possibly making the system more vulnerable to attacks. Importantly, HHI measures concentration, while the Gini coefficient measures inequality. For example, the Gini coefficient would not distinguish between a single entity with 100% of the staking power and one with a thousand equal-sized validators. In both cases, the Gini coefficient would be 0 signaling perfect equality. The HHI, on the other hand, is 1 in the first case and 0.001 in the second case.

Figure 6d plots the HHI of the Ethereum staking power over time and compares it to that of the Ethereum mining power during the PoW era. The green line indicates the HHI of the mining power, which hovers around 0.13 from the beacon chain launch until the merge. For Ethereum PoS, the HHI is significantly lower than that of its PoW counterpart and ranges from 0.02 to 0.06, i.e., Ethereum PoS is less concentrated. The HHI increases initially and then from early 2022 starts to decrease again. The average staking power HHI is 0.046, which from an HHI perspective is equivalent to an industry with 21 equal-sized firms. Thus, while the HHI of 0.046 indicates perfect competition in economics, it is unclear whether such an HHI value is also sufficient to regard the staking power distribution as "perfectly" decentralized with 21 equal-sized validators.

We conclude that the decentralization of the staking power of Ethereum is slightly above that of the mining power during PoW times. While Ethereum PoS trails its PoW counterpart in terms of inequality (i.e., Gini coefficient), it fares better in our other decentralization measures (i.e., HHI and Nakamoto coefficient). Recall, that the preceding analysis is an optimistic view as we treat validators associated with the same liquid staking protocol as multiple entities separated by operators. Next, we discuss the validity and impact of this decision.

5.2 Staking Power (De)centralization Pessimistic Vantage Point

To minimize the risk of operator misbehavior or misconfiguration, multiple liquid staking protocols utilize a permissioned or permissionless set of operators to run the pool's validators instead of putting a single entity in charge of operating all validators. However, while the nodes of liquid staking pools such as Lido are operated by independent operators, there are common incentives and points of failure shared by all validators belonging to the same staking pool. For instance, the smart contracts that operate and govern the liquid staking protocols represent a single point of failure. Flaws in the governance smart contracts could allow an attacker to take over the protocol; similar to the Tornado Cash hack in May of 2023 [23]. Importantly, this risk is not easily overcome by having users stake across multiple differing implementations of the protocol logic. Not only could these implementations repeat the same mistakes if one does not know where they are in the first place, but the logic itself might also be flawed [24]. On a different note, governance could be susceptible to additional attacks and the node operators share common incentives. A liquid staking pool that exceeds consensus thresholds can achieve outsized profits in comparison to solo-stakers, for instance through (multi-block) MEV extraction or censorship, and presents an incentive for a liquid staking pool to cartelize the block space [1].

To summarise, there are valid reasons to view the validators associated with a liquid staking protocol as a single entity. Thus, we take this pessimistic view and repeat the staking power decentralization analysis to observe the impact thereof. We compute both the Nakamoto coefficient and the HHI for the Ethereum PoS staking power from this vantage point over time and compare it to that of the mining power distribution of Ethereum PoW (cf. Fig. 7). In both decentralization measures Ethereum PoS initially fares better than its PoW counterpart. However, with time the centralization of the staking power increases and overtakes that of the mining power which stays relatively constant. Interestingly, during the merge, the staking power Nakamoto coefficient with the 50% threshold equals that of the mining power, i.e., for both mere three entities hold more than 50%, while the staking power Nakamoto coefficient with the $33.\bar{3}$% threshold is two. Further, during the execution of the merge, the HHI of staking and mining power

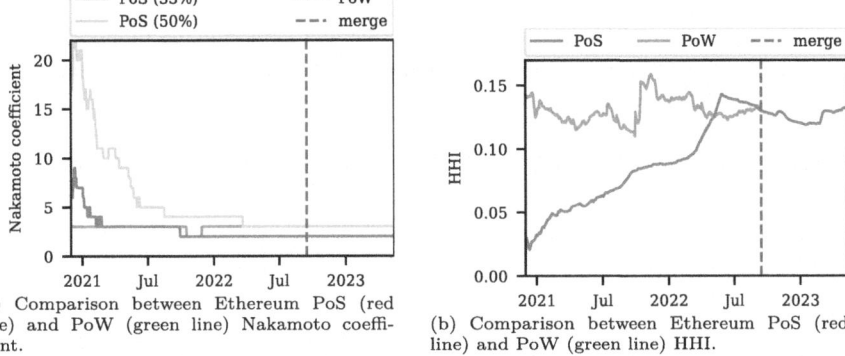

Fig. 7. Decentralization, i.e., Nakamoto coefficient (cf. Figure 7a) and HHI (cf. Figure 7b) of Ethereum PoS and PoW.

were almost equal at around 0.13. From then on, the HHI of the staking power stays relatively stable and sits at 0.13 as of 15 May 2023—equivalent to a landscape with eight equal-sized validators. We further note that in the pessimistic case, we do not consider the Gini coefficient in detail as the results are similar to the optimistic case.

Our analysis reveals that the approach to clustering liquid staking pool validators into entities heavily impacts the decentralization of the consensus layer. From the optimistic vantage point, i.e., clustering only validators run by the same operator, the staking power decentralization appears improved in comparison to that of the mining power (cf. Sect. 5). However, from the pessimistic viewpoint, i.e., clustering validators from the same liquid staking pool, the staking power appears as centralized as the mining power used to be. We further point out that even though we take both viewpoints for multiple liquid staking protocols (i.e., Lido, Stakewise, Swell, and RocketPool), Lido is responsible for the vast difference in the staking power decentralization from both vantages. Lido is the largest liquid staking protocol, and its staking power market share has increased to 32.75% as of 15 May 2023. Thus, Lido almost controls a third of all validators: the fraction of validators required to stall Ethereum PoS. Given Lido's significant influence on the network's health, we further provide a detailed discussion of the centralization within Lido in Appendix E.

5.3 Impacts of High Centralization

We continue by discussing the impacts of high centralization. Proposal assignments are known at least one epoch in advance. Thus, entities know ahead of time that they control a continuous sequence of blocks. This peculiarity of Ethereum PoS opens the door to what is known as *multi-block MEV*: value extraction through transaction order manipulation across multiple consecutive blocks. One example of multi-block MEV is oracle manipulation, which becomes cheaper when one is certain to be in control of at least two consecutive blocks [38].

To understand the threat of such attacks, we study the occurrences of uninterrupted block proposal sequences from the optimistic and pessimistic vantage points. An entity only controls a single block in a row in more than 90% of sequences. Sequences of length two and three both occur multiple times a day—more frequently from the pessimistic vantage point. Startlingly, regardless of the vantage point, all sequences of length four and longer were controlled by a mere five entities: Kraken, Binance, Bitcoin Suisse, Coinbase, and Lido (solely when considered as one entity). Further, when considered as one entity Lido controls all but one of all sequences of length eight or longer with the longest sequences being of length 13. The certainty for entities to control long sequences opens up additional security concerns for Ethereum PoS that were not present in the same form in Ethereum PoW and exemplify the threats posed by a lack of decentralization in the consensus layer. Further, given the novelty of this attack vector, the possible ramifications are yet to be quantified.

Table 1. Occurrences of continuous proposal sequences by the same entity.

sequence length	1	2	3	4	5	6	7	8	9	10	11	12	13
occurrences (optimistic)	5,885,903	232,377	26,469	3,618	498	79	13	1	0	0	0	0	0
occurrences (pessimistic)	5,345,711	388,036	73,893	17,115	4,490	1,336	382	116	35	18	4	2	1

5.4 Performance Advantages of Large Entities

Our preceding analysis demonstrates a dominance of staking services in the validator landscape. Reasons individuals might choose to partake in staking services as opposed to being solo-stakers, could include not only the ease but also the

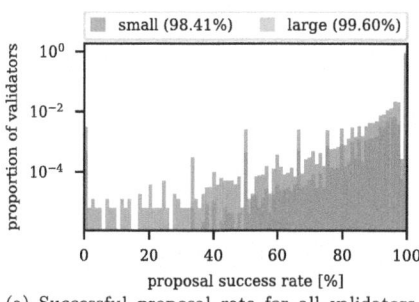
(a) Successful proposal rate for all validators. On average, the success rate of validators affiliated with large entities is elevated by 1.1%.

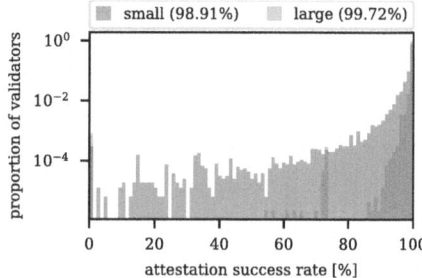
(b) Attestation success rate across all validators. On average, the success rate of validators affiliated with large entities is elevated by 0.9%.

Fig. 8. Proposal (cf. Fig. 8a) and attestation (cf. Fig. 8b) success rate of all validators split by entity size. We consider all entities with less than 1,000 validators as small entities, and all entities with at least 1,000 validators as large entities.

potential of higher returns given the specialized operators. Thus, we investigate whether we observe performance (i.e., the proportion of successful attestations and proposals) differences between small and large entities. In the following, we consider a validator to belong to a small entity if the entity size is smaller than 1,000, else we consider the validator to be part of a large entity. In Fig. 8 we visualize the proposal (cf. Fig. 8a) and attestation (cf. Fig. 8b) success rates of validators by their size.

Notice that overall validators, regardless of their entity size, exhibit very high proposal and attestation success rates with 99.52% on average for proposals and 99.30% on average for attestations, i.e., participation is very high regardless of entity size. Still, we observe noticeably higher participation from validators belonging to large entities. This difference in success rates could stem from larger entities being able to afford to use better hardware, having better network connectivity, and having faster emergency response times. We infer that large entities have a small advantage in terms of performance and further note that we provide a more detailed analysis of the performance of large known entities in Appendix D.

6 Related Work

Decentralization. One of the fundamental design principles and objectives of a permissionless blockchain is decentralization. Gencer et al. [31] were the first to investigate the decentralization of the blockchain consensus layer. Their research revealed that the mining processes of Bitcoin and Ethereum exhibit a significant level of centralization. Subsequent studies by Kiffer et al. [36] and Lin et al. [37] for Ethereum PoW also reach the same conclusion. In contrast to these works, we are, to the best of our knowledge, the first to study the decentralization of the staking power in Ethereum PoS.

Censorship. In light of the recent imposition of cryptocurrency mixer sanctions by the U.S. Office of Foreign Assets Control, the censorship resilience of Ethereum has come under scrutiny. Wahrstätter et al. [47] conducted a study on the security impact of blockchain censorship. Their findings indicate an 85% increase in the inclusion delay of sanctioned transactions and highlight the associated security concerns. Wang et al. [49] specifically focused on the security implications of censoring for validators. While these works focus on the security implications of censorship on the Ethereum blockchain, we measure the consensus layer decentralization of Ethereum. Higher decentralization in the consensus layer is expected to improve censorship resistance.

Maximal Extractable Value. MEV is a security concern to the Ethereum consensus [40]. Daian et al. [25] and Eskandari et al. [29] provide an early description of MEV. Measurement studies of MEV presented by Torres et al. [30] and Qin et al. [40] reveal the immense presence and value of MEV. Further, they outline the resulting security risks presented to the consensus layer of a permissionless blockchain. In comparison to these Ethereum PoW studies, we analyze Ethereum PoS and highlight the heightened security risk posed by MEV in PoS.

Proposer-Builder Separation. PBS was designed to decentralize the the consensus layer [16] and its adoption dramatically rose to more than 90% [34, 48, 50] since the merge. Recently, multiple works have emerged that study the PBS landscape [33, 34, 42, 48, 50]. These works highlight the increasing trends to centralization of block building under PBS. In this work, we focus on the decentralization of the consensus layer as opposed to block building.

7 Concluding Discussion

Active participation in and high decentralization of the Ethereum consensus layer are key to the health and security of Ethereum. Thus, understanding the network participation levels in the consensus and the decentralization thereof is essential.

Network Participation Levels. Our longitudinal analysis of the consensus participation levels demonstrates the incredibly high participation rates of validators. On average, 99.00% of blocks are proposed successfully, and 99.53% of attestations are received. Most dips in participation are during network upgrades or due to problems with consensus clients or large entities. While the vast majority of these temporary drops had no bigger impact on network consensus, the dips in participation level in May 2023, due to bugs in the Prsym and Teku consensus clients, prevented the network from reaching finality for a couple of epochs.

Decentralization. In our work, we analyze the decentralization of the Ethereum PoS consensus layer. We analyze the decentralization both from an optimistic vantage point, i.e., clustering only validators run by the same operator, and from a pessimistic vantage point, i.e., clustering validators from the same liquid staking pool. Our optimistic analysis demonstrates that the decentralization of the Ethereum staking power exceeds that of the past mining power. However, this does not hold for the pessimistic viewpoint, there the decentralization is approximately equal to that of a landscape with eight equal-sized validators. Lido's growing staking power represents a worry in particular; its staking power is approaching one-third at which point Lido alone could stall the Ethereum network. The Ethereum community is aware of this problem but cannot yet counteract this trend. Even though Ethereum ensures that the hardware requirements for running a validator are low [15], too many people choose the easier route by utilizing staking services instead of running their own validators, i.e., solo staking. Thus, these liquid staking services – a DeFi cornerstone – are threatening the decentralization of the consensus layer. As we demonstrate, large entities exhibit better performance compared to small entities, which is likely to cause a disproportionate growth of large entities. Further, staking services utilize the same hardware to run multiple validators and can thus amortize their hardware costs. Finally, the congestion in the activation queue means that it might be too big of a sacrifice for solo-stakers to wait weeks for activation, while the rewards with staking services would be almost immediate. Thus, incentivizing more solo staking is an open problem and it is unclear whether (liquid) staking services

Security Implications. We comment on the security implications of concentration in the consensus layer—these go beyond a single party exceeding the consensus threshold in size. MEV is very prevalent on Ethereum and a known risk to the consensus layer, the possibility of multi-block MEV in Ethereum PoS only adds to this. The larger an entity, the higher the chance that it will control multiple consecutive blocks and thereby profit from multi-block MEV. Thus, multi-block MEV could lead to their market share increasing due to higher rewards.

To conclude, we provide an overview of the Ethereum PoS consensus layer and underwrite the need and desire for increased decentralization—especially in light of the security concerns posed by heightened consensus layer centralization.

A Data Collection

In the following, we provide a detailed overview of our data collection. We collect beacon chain data (cf. Appendix A.1) by running a Lighthouse node, obtain data to cluster validators from various data sources (cf. Appendix A.2), and collect Ethereum PoW data (cf. Appendix A.3) by running an Erigon node.

A.1 Beacon Chain Data

We collect the majority of our data from the beacon chain with our Lighthouse client and provide an overview of the data collected in the following.

Validator Data. For each validator that was in the network at some time during our data collection period, we query our Lighthouse client to collect the epoch in which they became eligible for activation (i.e. when they staked 32 ETH in the beacon chain deposit contract), their activation epoch (i.e., when they joined the network), and where applicable the exit epoch (i.e., when they left the network).

Attestations and Proposals. We collect all attestations and proposals assigned to each validator. Then, we record the success status of each. For proposals, we collect data on all validators responsible for a proposal and the success or failure of each block proposal. We further differentiate between missed blocks and orphaned blocks. Orphaned blocks are valid blocks that were proposed but not included in the main chain, as they were outcompeted by another block at the same height. This can occur due to near-simultaneous block proposals, causing temporary chain splits. We use the API provided by `beaconcha.in` to classify missed proposals [5]. Regarding attestations, we gather information on all epoch committees and block attestations. In total, our data set encompasses 62,951,944,703 attestations and 6,447,599 proposals. Out of the 64,385 missed proposals, we identify 6,584 as orphaned.

Slashing. We analyze all beacon chain blocks to identify any slashings for proposer and attestation violations. For each, we record the slashed validator, the slot in which the slashable offense took place, and the slot in which the proposer was slashed.

A.2 Validator Clustering Data

As of slot 6,447,598, we have identified 625,193 validators who have participated in at least one attestation duty. For each validator, we collect additional metrics such as labels, deposit addresses, and fee recipient addresses. This information aids us in clustering these validators into distinct entities in subsequent analysis steps.

Deposit Addresses. Deposit addresses are those that provide the 32 ETH required to fund a validator. Note that a validator can be associated with multiple deposit addresses. We collect all such addresses by monitoring the logs from the beacon chain deposit contract. In total, we identified 99,711 distinct deposit addresses in our dataset.

Fee Recipient Addresses. A fee recipient address is an Ethereum address specified by the validator to collect the execution layer rewards for their block proposals. Validators sharing the same fee recipient address are likely to represent the same entity. To identify these addresses, we extract the fee recipient field for each block from our Erigon client. If a block is not created through *proposer-builder separation (PBS)* [16], this address corresponds to the validator's fee recipient address. Otherwise, it belongs to the block builder. Since a significant number of blocks are constructed via PBS, we also inspect the last transaction in each block. If the block was built through PBS, the builder transfers the fees to the validator in this transaction [11]. Hence, if no such transaction exists, we record the block's fee recipient address as the validator's fee recipient address. If such a transaction is present, we record the receiver of the ETH in the last transaction as the validator's fee recipient address. Our dataset identifies 11,515 unique fee recipient addresses.

Validator Labels. A validator label is a name that associates a validator with an entity, e.g., staking pools, staking-as-a-service providers, centralized exchanges, or institutional validators. Not all validators have an associated label, as some operators may choose not to disclose their identity or affiliation. We obtain and combine validator labels from the Rated Network API [17], through scraping data from `beaconcha.in` [5] and through manual identification of deposit patterns for Coinbase (cf. Appendix B.1).

Address Labels. We further obtain address labels for deposit addresses through data scraping from Etherscan [8]. Specifically, we collect *Ethereum Name Service (ENS)* domain names, i.e., web3 usernames [7]. We will utilize address labels in addition to validator labels to identify and label entities.

Etherclust Data Set. We cluster Ethereum addresses through the reused centralized exchange deposit addresses method introduced by Victor [46]. To be precise, we cluster together addresses that utilize the same exchange deposit address. The clustering compresses 6,788,215 addresses into 1,410,523 entities with more than one address – representing approximately 2.93% of the 231,625,425 unique Ethereum addresses as of 15 Mai 2023 [10].

A.3 Ethereum Proof-of-Work Miners

We amend our analysis of the Ethereum PoS consensus (de)centralization by comparing it to the former PoW consensus. Thus, we collect the miners for each block from the first block of the Ethereum blockchain on 30 July 2015 to block 15,537,392 (i.e., the last block before the merge on 15 September 2022) from our Erigon client. Additionally, we obtain labels for the miner addresses from Etherscan [4].

B Entity Clustering

We provide a detailed overview of our entity clustering procedure in the following. Our clustering relies on the data set described in Sect. A.2. Barring exceptions, which we detail in Appendix B.2, the clustering process is executed in four steps:

1. Validators sharing the same label (i.e., validator labels obtained from Rated Network API and `beaconcha.in`) are grouped into a single entity.
2. Entities or individual validators with at least one common *deposit address* (i.e., the address(es) used to stake the 32 ETH) are merged into the same entity.
3. Entities or individual validators sharing at least one *fee recipient address* are consolidated into the same entity if at least one of the entities does not have a label yet and has consistently used the same *fee recipient address*. This is a conservative approach that reduces the risk of incorrect clustering.
4. Entities or individual validators whose *deposit address(es)* belong to the same entity, as per the Etherclust data set, are combined.

We note that the inherent complexities and nuances to consider during entity clustering, especially given the variety of strategies and structures present in the Ethereum staking landscape, necessitate some manual adjustments and informed exceptions to our clustering process. Throughout, we always opt for the conservative route to maintain the integrity of our analysis. We detail our Coinbase validator identification process (cf. Sect. B.1) and all clustering exceptions (cf. Sect. B.2) next.

B.1 Coinbase Validator Labels

We undertake an additional identification process for Coinbase validators, as especially recent ones have not been labeled by our data sources, i.e., Rated Network API [17] and beaconcha.in [5]. Coinbase adheres to a unique and easily identifiable pattern when rolling out new validators, allowing a straightforward detection of their validators. In particular, the following properties hold for any Coinbase validator:

1. Each validator employs a unique deposit address.
2. The Ether sent to the deposit address originates from a Coinbase address.
3. Post-deployment, the surplus Ether is redirected back to a Coinbase address.
4. A small nominal amount of Ether, typically around 0.0006 ETH, is left in the deposit address.

Thus, we run through all unlabeled validators and label those for which all of the above properties hold as Coinbase. In doing so, we label an additional 3,222 validators as Coinbase. Note that we obtain a list of all Coinbase addresses from Etherscan [3].

B.2 Entity Clustering Exceptions

In the following, we detail the primary challenges and the corresponding adjustments we make during entity clustering. These exceptions allow us to mitigate any unnecessary over-clustering.

Validator Label Exclusion. Our data set includes labels for companies providing only the hardware and software for staking, with the staker controlling the deposit and fee recipient addresses—*non-custodial staking*. In such cases, we aim to sidestep clustering a validator with the company providing the underlying resources.

Instead, we strive to cluster it with other validators controlled by the same staker. The distinction between custodial and non-custodial staking services is not always apparent and some providers even changed over time. We do not cluster an entity by its validator label, if all three of the following criteria are met: (1) the service permits non-custodial staking, (2) the staker knows their exact validator ID, and (3) upon clustering all labels of this entity together, the entity exhibits numerous used deposit addresses and at least one of these deposit addresses is associated with an unrelated address label (ENS name), suggesting user control over this address.

We remove these validator labels for non-custodial staking services that meet all our previously outlined criteria. Namely, these non-custodial staking services are *Staked.us*, *Stakefish*, and *Bloxstaking*.

Validator Label-only Clustering. Liquid staking protocols such as *Lido* and *StakeWise*, multiple different operators run the protocol's validators. The validator labels we obtain from the Rated Network API allow us to identify which validators are run by which operator. Given all validators belonging to these protocols, regardless of the operator running them, they typically share the same deposit addresses. Our standard clustering method would cluster all validators belonging to such a liquid staking protocol as one entity.

To retain the higher resolution provided by the validator labels obtained from the Rated Network API, we modify our approach for validators from *Lido* and *StakeWise* and only focus on their validator labels during the clustering process. Throughout our analysis we will, at times, analyze the impact of viewing all validators belonging to a liquid staking service as one entity as opposed to multiple entities depending on the operators in control of the validators.

Fee Recipient Address Exclusion. Node operators participating in non-custodial staking services (e.g., Rocket Pool), have the option to designate a communal smoothing pool address as their fee recipient address. This shared pool is designed to even out the potentially fluctuating MEV rewards, which can be particularly beneficial for smaller node operators. However, this setup causes all Rocket Pool nodes that join the smoothing pool to be clustered as a single entity, even though they are controlled by multiple different operators.

To counteract this, we exclude certain fee recipient addresses from our clustering process. These include fee recipient addresses associated with *Stakefish*, *Staked.us*, *Ethpool Staking*, *Ankr*, and the *Rocket Pool smoothing pool*. A complete list of these excluded addresses can be found in Table 2.

Etherclust Exceptions. In step four of our clustering procedure (cf. Appendix B), we further manually ensure that entities unlikely to belong to the same entity are not further merged. To be precise, we refrain from clustering well-known entities with any other entity. We make this exception on five separate occasions: (1) multiple LIDO operators, (2) multiple Rocket Pool operators, (2) Bitfinex, Binance, and Whale 0xEAB8, (3) Coinbase and zachrellim.eth, and (4) Stakely.io and StaFi.

Table 2. Fee recipient addresses which we exclude during clustering and which entity they are associated with. These addresses would lead to unwanted linking of entities.

	fee recipient address
Stakefish	0xffee087852cb4898e6c3532e776e68bc68b1143b
	0x54cd0e6771b6487c721ec620c4de1240d3b07696
	0x5caf7c1b096cf684b09ece3d3a142db0d46fc58e
	0xe94f1fa4f27d9d288ffea234bb62e1fbc086ca0c
Rocket Pool Smoothing Pool	0xd4e96ef8eee8678dbff4d535e033ed1a4f7605b7
Ethpool	0xb364e75b1189dcbbf7f0c856456c1ba8e4d6481b
MEV Builder	0xac7ea48093b61f2e217b9d077d69d9d55ca1b106
Ankr	0x3bef77233e52d23969958587127d99ec2367c2bd
	0x90b0c836a19a74195d45fad2d2d3895a7a3eab08
	0x6a0db4cef1ce2a5f81c8e6322862439f71aca29d

C Decentralization Measures

In the following, we provide definitions of the three decentralization measures used in our analysis. **Nakamoto Coefficient.** The Nakamoto coefficient is a measure used to assess the decentralization of blockchain. In more detail, the Nakamoto coefficient represents the number of independent entities needed to disrupt the blockchain. For PoW blockchain, generally >50% of the mining power is required to disrupt the network. Thus, the Nakamoto coefficient is the minimum number of independent entities that hold >50% of the mining power together. For Ethereum PoS > 33.3̄% of the staking power is required to stall the network. While this causes problems for the network, it can recover from this by slashing inactive validators. With more than > 50%, on the other hand, the attacker can dominate the fork choice algorithm and honest validators would eventually follow suit [9].

Gini Coefficient. The *Gini coefficient* is an inequality measure. Mathematically, the Gini coefficient is calculated as follows

$$G = \frac{\sum_{i=1}^{n}\sum_{j=1}^{n}|x_i - x_j|}{2n^2\bar{x}}$$

where n is the number of entities, and x_i denotes the wealth of person i. A value of 0 indicates perfect equality, whereas a value of 1 indicates complete inequality. Note that in the context of Ethereum, we take a validator's market share as their wealth. A low Gini coefficient then indicates that the wealth is equally distributed amongst validators.

Herfindahl-Hirschman Index. The *Herfindahl-Hirschman Index (HHI)* is used for assessing market concentration and competition in economics. Mathematically, it is expressed as

$$HHI = \sum_{i=1}^{n} s_i^2,$$

where n is the number of entities in the market, and s_i denotes the market share of entity i as a fraction. Thus, the HHI ranges between 0, indicating low concentration, and 1, representing a concentrated market. In the context of Ethereum and staking, we apply the HHI to analyze validator concentration and potential centralization risks. For us, n is the number of entities, and s_i is the proportion of staking power controlled by entity i. A low HHI value indicates a more decentralized network with numerous independent validators, while a high HHI value points to a more concentrated network, possibly making the system more vulnerable to attacks.

D Entity Performance

In the following, we take an in-depth look at the participation rate of the five biggest entities (Lido, Coinbase, Kraken, Binance, and Bitcoin Suisse) in Table 3.

Note that, here, we consider Lido as one entity but provide an overview of the performance of the 30 individual operators in Appendix D.1. From Table 3, we can see that all big operators have very high and similar participation rates for attestations (higher than 99.80% for all) and proposals (higher than 99.44% for all). Further, it is not clear which of the five biggest entities has the highest participation rate. While Coinbase has the highest attestation success rate, Lido has the highest proposal success rate.

Table 3. Attestation and proposal success rate for the five biggest entities.

	attestation success rate [%]	proposal success rate [%]
Lido	99.858	99.755
Coinbase	99.891	99.485
Binance	99.877	99.448
Kraken	99.821	99.587
Bitcoin Suisse	99.810	99.529

D.1 Lido Operator Performance Comparison

We further take an in-depth look at the participation metrics across all 30 Lido staking operators in Table 4. A pattern of consistently high performance emerges throughout their operational history. However, RockLogic GmbH and Chorus One stand out with a comparatively lower performance. The dip in performance for RockLogic GmbH might be attributed to a slashing incident that occurred on 13 April 2023. The incident was triggered by the inadvertent duplication of validator keys across two active clusters, which resulted in a double vote and consequent slashing of eleven validators [12]. As for Chorus One, an extended downtime event in October 2021 might be the origin of this reduced performance. The downtime was accidental and was the result of complications during node migrations [18].

E Lido (De)centralization

As the dominant liquid staking protocol with a significant influence on the network's health, Lido merits a closer look. In the following, we provide an in-depth analysis of the distribution of power within Lido. As of the time of writing, Lido operates through 30 permissioned node operator companies tasked with performing the staking. Figure 9a visualizes the Lido staking power distribution across these operators. We notice that the number of operators is increasing with time and that at the end of our data collection window, the 30 operators are almost all of the same size with around 6,000 validators each.

Table 4. The 30 Lido staking operators exhibit consistently high performances in both attestation and proposal success rates.

	attestation success rate [%]	proposal success rate [%]
Allnodes Lido	99.981	99.932
Kukis Global Lido	99.973	99.971
Sigma Prime Lido	99.967	99.911
Attestant Lido	99.964	99.865
Everstake Lido	99.955	99.829
Blockdaemon Lido	99.952	99.806
ChainLayer Lido	99.952	99.915
RockX Lido	99.951	99.822
P2P.ORG - P2P Validator Lido	99.945	99.754
HashQuark Lido	99.943	99.856
Stakely Lido	99.943	99.892
InfStones Lido	99.942	99.660
CryptoManufaktur Lido	99.932	99.942
Staking Facilities Lido	99.925	99.860
Prysmatic Labs Lido	99.912	99.768
Blockscape Lido	99.905	99.882
Anyblock Analytics Lido	99.897	99.824
Nethermind Lido	99.894	99.718
Kiln Lido	99.886	99.705
Simply Staking Lido	99.852	99.728
Figment Lido	99.835	99.842
ConsenSys Codefi Lido	99.822	99.791
Stakefish Lido	99.803	99.833
DSRV Lido	99.784	99.914
Stakin Lido	99.776	99.813
Certus One Lido	99.765	99.430
ChainSafe Lido	99.750	99.768
BridgeTower Lido	99.697	99.788
Chorus One Lido	99.489	99.050
RockLogic GmbH Lido	99.396	98.820

Importantly, those operators alone do not have the power to arbitrarily change the protocol. Currently, Lido's operations on Ethereum are governed by LDO token holders through an Aragon DAO. This governance encompasses a wide range of aspects, including the Lido treasury, staking withdrawal keys, the registry of node and oracle operators, DAO Access Control List permissions, and

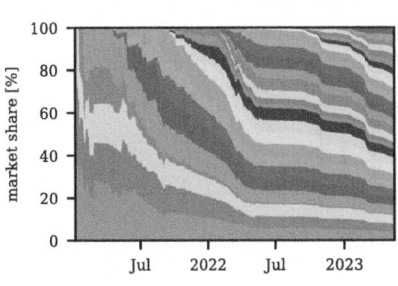 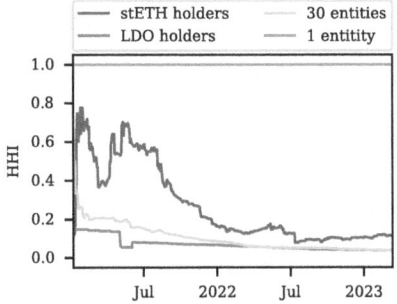

(a) Lido staking power distribution across Lido operators over time.

(b) Concentration (HHI) of Lido's stETH tokens, LDO tokens, and the 30 Lido staking operator entities included in our data set.

Fig. 9. Decentralization analysis (i.e., staking power distribution (cf. Fig. 9a) and HHI of staking power distribution (cf. Fig. 9b)) for Lido over time.

the execution of EVM scripts. In effect, LDO holders have root access to the Lido protocol. Proposals are being considered to circumscribe the DAO's authority by enabling stETH holders having the power to veto certain decisions. However, a wide and diverse distribution of the LDO and stETH tokens is indispensable for a healthy protocol.

Figure 9b visually represents the concentration trends among LDO and stETH holders over time, as measured by the HHI. It is encouraging to observe a progressive decentralization, with stETH holders' HHI approximating 0.1 and LDO holders' HHI around 0.034 towards the end of the observed period. Similarly, Lido's staking operators exhibit an ongoing dispersion trend with a current HHI of 0.036. Overall, the concentration has been on a decline for the past two years. Nonetheless, it is imperative to recognize and address risks the current Lido dominance poses to the Ethereum network, as for instance, the Lido smart contracts could be a single point of failure.

F Ethereum Proof-of-Work (De)centralization

In the following, we provide some additional insight regarding the network (de)centralization fluctuations during Ethereum's PoW era. Figures 10a and 10b illustrate an early surge in network decentralization following Ethereum's launch. However, this level of decentralization quickly diminished and largely maintained steady levels until the end of PoW.

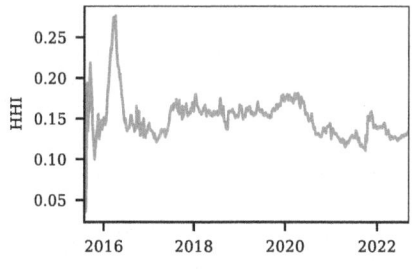
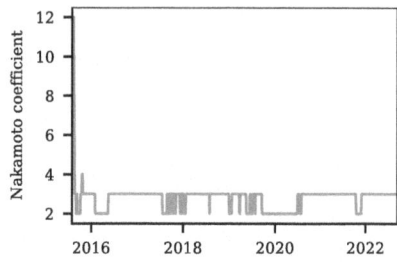

(a) HHI, i.e., concentration, of Ethereum PoW consensus from Ethereum genesis until the merge.

(b) Nakamoto coefficient of Ethereum PoW consensus from Ethereum genesis until the merge.

Fig. 10. Decentralization, i.e., HHI (cf. Fig. 10a) and Nakamoto coefficient (cf. Fig. 10b) of Ethereum PoW.

References

1. The Risks of LSD (2022). https://notes.ethereum.org/@djrtwo/risks-of-lsd
2. Upgrading Ethereum: One Page Annotated Spec (2022). https://eth2book.info/capella/annotated-spec/
3. Accounts: Coinbase (2023). https://etherscan.io/accounts/label/coinbase
4. Accounts: Mining (2023). https://etherscan.io/accounts/label/mining
5. Beacon Chain: Open Source Ethereum Explorer (2023). https://beaconcha.in/
6. Consecutive Block Proposals on Ethereum (2023). https://research.numeus.xyz/p/consecutive-blocks-ethereum
7. ENS: Decentralised naming for wallets, websites, & more (2023). https://ens.domains/
8. Etherescan: The Ethereum Blockchain Explorer (2023). https://etherscan.io/
9. Ethereum Proof-Of-Stake Attack and Defense (2023). https://ethereum.org/en/developers/docs/consensus-mechanisms/pos/attack-and-defense/
10. Ethereum Unique Addresses Chart (2023). https://etherscan.io/chart/address
11. MEV-Boost Github (2023). https://github.com/flashbots/mev-boost
12. Post Mortem: Lido on Ethereum RockLogic GmbH Slashing Incident (2023). https://blog.lido.fi/loe-rocklogic-gmbh-slashing-incident/
13. Post-Mortem Report: Ethereum Mainnet Finality (05/11/2023) (2023). https://offchain.medium.com/post-mortem-report-ethereum-mainnet-finality-05-11-2023-95e271dfd8b2
14. Pre-merge Data: December 14, 2019 - September 15, 2022 (2023). https://explore.flashbots.net/
15. Proof-Of-Stake vs Proof-Of-Work (2023). https://ethereum.org/en/developers/docs/consensus-mechanisms/pos/pos-vs-pow/
16. Proposer-Builder Separation (2023). https://ethereum.org/nl/roadmap/pbs/
17. Rated Network Explorer (2023). https://www.rated.network/
18. Reimbursement for Chorus One October 2021 Downtime (2023). https://research.lido.fi/t/reimbursement-for-chorus-one-october-2021-downtime/1456
19. The History of Ethereum (2023). https://ethereum.org/en/history/
20. The Merge (2023). https://ethereum.org/en/roadmap/merge/
21. Today's Cryptocurrency Prices by Market Cap (2023). https://coinmarketcap.com/

22. Buterin, V.: Vitalik's Annotated Ethereum 2.0 Spec (2020). https://github.com/ethereum/annotated-spec/blob/master/phase0/beacon-chain.md#aside-randao-seeds-and-committee-generation
23. Crawley, J., Malwa, S.: Attacker Takes Over Tornado Cash DAO With Vote Fraud, Token Slumps 40% (May 2023). https://www.coindesk.com/tech/2023/05/21/attacker-takes-over-tornado-cash-dao-with-vote-fraud-token-slumps-40/
24. Crawley, J., Malwa, S.: Euler DeFi Protocol Exploited for Nearly 200M (Mar 2023). https://www.coindesk.com/business/2023/03/13/euler-defi-protocol-exploited-for-nearly-185m/
25. Daian, P., et al.: Flash Boys 2.0: frontrunning in decentralized exchanges, miner extractable value, and consensus instability. In: 2020 IEEE Symposium on Security and Privacy (SP), pp. 910–927. IEEE, San Francisco, CA, USA (May 2020)
26. Edgington, B.: What's New in Eth2 - 24 April 2021 (2021). https://hackmd.io/@benjaminion/eth2_news/https%3A%2F%2Fhackmd.io%2F%40benjaminion%2Fwnie2_210424
27. Edgington, B.: What's New in Eth2 - 27 August 2021 (2021). https://hackmd.io/@benjaminion/eth2_news/https%3A%2F%2Fhackmd.io%2F%40benjaminion%2Fwnie2_210827
28. Edgington, B.: Part 2: Technical Overview The Incentive Layer (2023). https://eth2book.info/altair/part2/incentives/rewards/
29. Eskandari, S., Moosavi, S., Clark, J.: SoK: transparent dishonesty: front-running attacks on blockchain. In: Bracciali, A., Clark, J., Pintore, F., Rønne, P.B., Sala, M. (eds.) FC 2019. LNCS, vol. 11599, pp. 170–189. Springer, Cham (2020). https://doi.org/10.1007/978-3-030-43725-1_13
30. Ferreira Torres, C., Camino, R., State, R.: frontrunner jones and the raiders of the dark forest: an empirical study of frontrunning on the ethereum blockchain. In: 30th USENIX Security Symposium (USENIX Security 2021), pp. 1343–1359. USENIX Association, Virtual Event (Aug 2021)
31. Gencer, A.E., Basu, S., Eyal, I., Van Renesse, R., Sirer, E.G.: Decentralization in bitcoin and ethereum networks. In: Financial Cryptography and Data Security, vol. 10957, pp. 439–457. Springer Berlin Heidelberg, Curaçao (2018). https://doi.org/10.1007/978-3-031-48806-1_12
32. Gini, C.: Measurement of inequality of incomes. Econ. J. **31**(121), 124 (1921)
33. Gupta, T., Pai, M.M., Resnick, M.: The centralizing effects of private order flow on proposer-builder separation (2023). https://arxiv.org/abs/2305.19150
34. Heimbach, L., Kiffer, L., Torres, C.F., Wattenhofer, R.: Ethereum's Proposer-Builder Separation: Promises and Realities (2023). https://arxiv.org/abs/2305.19037
35. Kashyap, B.: Proof-of-stake (PoS) (2023). https://ethereum.org/en/developers/docs/consensus-mechanisms/pos/
36. Kiffer, L., Salman, A., Levin, D., Mislove, A., Nita-Rotaru, C.: Under the hood of the ethereum gossip protocol. In: Borisov, N., Diaz, C. (eds) FC 2021. LNCS, vol. 12675, pp. 437–456. Springer, Heidelberg (2021). https://doi.org/10.1007/978-3-662-64331-0_23
37. Lin, Q., Li, C., Zhao, X., Chen, X.: Measuring decentralization in bitcoin and ethereum using multiple metrics and granularities. In: 2021 IEEE 37th International Conference on Data Engineering Workshops (ICDEW), pp. 80–87. IEEE, Chania, Greece (4 2021)
38. Mackinga, T., Nadahalli, T., Wattenhofer, R.: TWAP Oracle attacks: easier done than said? In: 2022 IEEE International Conference on Blockchain and Cryptocurrency (ICBC), pp. 1–8. IEEE, Shanghai, China (May 2022)

39. Miller, R.: Post Mortem: April 3rd, 2023 Mev-Boost Relay Incident and Related Timing Issue (2023). https://collective.flashbots.net/t/post-mortem-april-3rd-2023-mev-boost-relay-incident-and-related-timing-issue/1540
40. Qin, K., Zhou, L., Gervais, A.: Quantifying blockchain extractable value: how dark is the forest? In: 2022 IEEE Symposium on Security and Privacy (SP), pp. 198–214. IEEE, San Francisco, CA, USA (May 2022)
41. Rhoades, S.A.: The Herfindahl-Hirschman-Index (1993)
42. Schwarz-Schilling, C., Saleh, F., Thiery, T., Pan, J., Shah, N., Monnot, B.: Time is Money: Strategic Timing Games in Proof-of-Stake Protocols (2023). https://arxiv.org/abs/2305.09032
43. Smith, C.: Blocks (2023). https://ethereum.org/en/developers/docs/blocks/
44. Srinivasan, B.S., Lee, L.: Quantifying Decentralization (July 2017). https://news.earn.com/quantifying-decentralization-e39db233c28e
45. Thalman, B.: Ethereum: a deep dive into new ETH rewards dynamics (2023). https://figment.io/ethereum-a-deep-dive-into-new-eth-rewards-dynamicsethereum-a-deep-dive-into-new-eth-rewards-dynamics/
46. Victor, F.: Address clustering heuristics for ethereum. In: Bonneau, J., Heninger, N. (eds.) FC 2020. LNCS, vol. 12059, pp. 617–633. Springer, Cham (2020). https://doi.org/10.1007/978-3-030-51280-4_33
47. . Wahrstätter, A., et al.: Blockchain Censorship (2023). https://arxiv.org/abs/2305.18545
48. Wahrstätter, A., Zhou, L., Qin, K., Svetinovic, D., Gervais, A.: Time to Bribe: Measuring Block Construction Market (2023). https://arxiv.org/abs/2305.16468
49. Wang, Z., Xiong, X., Knottenbelt, W.J.: Blockchain Transaction Censorship: (In)secure and (In) efficient? (2023). https://ia.cr/2023/786
50. Yang, S., Zhang, F., Huang, K., Chen, X., Yang, Y., Zhu, F.: SoK: MEV Countermeasures: Theory and Practice (2022). https://arxiv.org/abs/2212.05111

Short Paper: The PoW Landscape in the Aftermath of The Merge

Lucianna Kiffer⍟, Sophia Skorik, Yann Vonlanthen(✉)⍟, and Roger Wattenhofer⍟

ETH Zurich, Zürich, Switzerland
{lkiffer,yvonlanthen,wattenhofer}@ethz.ch,
sophia.skorik@inf.ethz.ch

Abstract. On 15th September 2022, The Merge marked the Ethereum network's transition from computation-hardness-based consensus (proof-of-work) to a committee-based consensus mechanism (proof-of-stake). As a result, all the specialized hardware and GPUs that were being used by miners ceased to be profitable in the main Ethereum network. Miners were then left with the decision of how to re-purpose their hardware. One such choice was to try and make a profit mining another existing PoW system. In this study, we explore this choice by analyzing the hashrate increase in the top PoW networks following the merge. Our findings reveal that the peak increase in hashrate to other PoW networks following The Merge represents an adoption of at least 41% of the hashrate that was present in Ethereum, with 30% thereof remaining over 5 months later. Though we measure a drastic decrease in profitability by almost an order of magnitude, the continued presence of miners halts claims that power consumption was instantly addressed by Ethereum's switch to PoS.

Keywords: blockchain · proof-of-work · mining · Ethereum · measurements

1 Introduction

Proof-of-work (PoW) was first introduced as a way to prevent spam emails and denial-of-service attacks [4,18]. By requiring users to spend resources solving computationally hard cryptographic challenges, it is possible to put a price on bot and spam activity. Soon after, the first applications making use of PoW for digital money were introduced by Hal Finney [27] and Nick Szabo [62]. Ultimately, circumventing the need for a central entity using PoW, Satoshi Nakamoto built the first permissionless digital currency [52]. Bitcoin's meteoric rise starting in 2008 truly brought PoW into the spotlight and made mining a highly lucrative venture [63].

Thus began a never-ending race of producing the most computation with the fewest resources [32]. As a consequence, many PoW algorithms quickly became profitable to mine only using application-specific integrated circuits (ASICs) [63]. At the same time, numerous cryptocurrencies emerged, many introducing their flavors of PoW [36,39,46,51]. Some of which designed algorithms to be resistant to ASICs [10] in a bid to lower the barrier to entry and improve democratization and decentralization [32]. These currencies make use of memory-hard mining algorithms that can be most efficiently run on consumer-grade graphical processing units (GPUs) [32,47].

The rise of Ethereum [6] starting in 2015 stands out, not just for its memory-hard PoW algorithm called Ethash, but also for allowing for not just money transfer but universal computing across untrusted participants. Its rapidly growing popularity was felt throughout the entire GPU industry [33], as Ethereum miners alone are estimated to have bought at least 10% of all produced GPUs between October of 2020 and March of 2022 [34]. Spiking prices, longer wait times, and chronically low supply have been the result for years [19].

Amidst growing concerns regarding PoW's tremendous energy consumption [69] in the advent of the climate crisis, Ethereum considered PoW as a temporary solution, with the goal to move its Sybil resistance mechanism to proof-of-stake (PoS) [7]. PoS prevents Sybils, by giving the voting power to the system's stakeholders [45]. After years of development and numerous delays, Ethereum finally switched to PoS on 15th September 2022, an event referred to as The Merge [30].

In this work, we explore the consequences of this long-anticipated switch. To this end, we perform a longitudinal study to quantitatively measure how much GPU mining power remains in the space after The Merge, the profitability of the ongoing mining business, as well as miner distribution. Based on this data, we analyze the impact of The Merge on energy expenditure, the decentralization of other currencies, as well as the consequences for miners, mining pools, users, and manufacturers. Our **contributions** are the following:

1. We collect an extensive dataset containing blockchain, market, and miner data for the main currencies employing memory-hard PoW. By additionally scraping GPU performance data we homogenize the different PoW algorithms to allow their comparison.
2. We measure that at least 12% of Ethereum's mining power remained active months after The Merge even though mining profitability has drastically reduced by almost an order of magnitude (87.7%). This provides a more nuanced perspective to claims which say The Merge reduced energy consumption by 99.95% instantaneously [30].
3. We explore which mining pools remained active across the different emerging forks such as Ethereum PoW [23] and Ethereum Fair [25], as well as other currencies. We show that surprisingly, in most cases, decentralization wasn't negatively impacted.
4. Finally, we discuss the effects of The Merge on the major stakeholders, such as miners and GPU manufacturers.

2 Data Collection

Our first goal is to determine which cryptocurrencies absorbed the bulk of the Ethereum mining power or *hashrate*. To do this we first look up the top 100 by marketcap [15] PoW currencies' hashrates on a popular miner website [2]

Table 1. Computation of ethash factor based on GPU hashrates

Algorithm	Nvidia GTX 1080	Nvidia RTX 3090	Nvidia RTX 2080	Nvidia RTX A5000	Nvidia GTX 1080Ti	Nvidia RTX 3060Ti	AMD RX 6800	AMD Radeon VII	AMD RX 5700XT	AMD RX 6600XT	AMD RX 6900XT	AMD RX 480	median
EtcHash	1.01	1	1	1	**1.14**	1.01	1	1	1	1	1	1	1
Autolykos	1.72	2.27	1.95	2.20	2.16	**2.45**	1.83	2.23	1.81	1.82	1.81	1.94	1.94
KawPow	0.46	0.41	**0.69**	0.41	0.56	0.50	0.52	0.37	0.45	0.50	0.52	0.41	0.48

on the days surrounding the merge. We make a list of all that had a *visually noticeable increase* in their system hashrates (i.e., what we see in Fig. 1) as we want to distinguish those likely directly impacted by The Merge, from other ongoing trends[1]. In doing so, it is possible we miss some hashrate that was less noticeably absorbed by other systems. We also include two new forks that split from Ethereum following The Merge; Ethereum Fair [25] and Ethereum PoW [23]. From these initial candidates, we want to gather which networks absorbed the majority of the Ethash computing power. Since these blockchains run different mining algorithms, we need to convert each network's hashrate to their Ethash equivalent.

Ethash Conversion Factors. The hashrates generated by different GPUs for a specific algorithm may vary due to differences in their design and processing capabilities. To account for this, we take 12 of the top Nvidia and AMD GPUs recommended for Ethereum mining in 2022 [5,8,71]. For each GPU we determine the hashrate per algorithm and calculate its factor in relation to Ethash hashrate[2]. Since different mining sites report slightly different values for a given GPU-algorithm combination, we gather multiple values from various sources and take the median factor across them [1,48,49,70].

We take the median and maximum of these values to get an Ethash factor to convert each mining algorithm hashrate to Ethashes. We show these values for Etchash [12], Autokylos [10], and KawPow [26] in Table 1, with the maximum factors in bold. Due to some variance in values, we use the maximum factor to give us a lower bound of the Ethash in each system, assuming the optimal GPUs went to the respective systems. Using this conversion factor, we get a list of the top 20 coins whose hashrates were impacted by The Merge (cf. Table 2). We see that a peak of a minimum of 41% (median of 48%) of the Ethash from Ethereum went into the top 20 GPU-minable PoW coins. Note that other top PoW coins like Bitcoin, Dogecoin, and Litecoin do not show up on our list likely as they are primarily profitable to mine via ASICs mining and thus did not have noticeable gains in hashrate at the time of The Merge. We see that Ethereum Classic, Ergo, EthereumPoW, Ravencoin, and Ethereum Fair jointly absorbed 98% (97%) of the peak of the minimum (median) noticeable Ethash hashrate increase. Thus we choose to focus on these systems for the remainder of our analysis.

---

[1] Note in Table 2 increases of 2x to 5x their relative hashrates.

[2] Though the use of ASICs was not prominent for Ethash, we do conservatively capture their hashing power as ASICs would suit only Ethereum forks at factor 1.

Table 2. Hashrate Increase for top 20 GPU-minable coins affected by The Merge.

Coin	Algorithm	Network Hashrate (7th Sep)	Network Hashrate (15th Sep)	Median Increase (Ethash TH/s)	Minimum Increase (Ethash TH/s)
Ethereum	Ethash	873.930 TH/s	–	–	–
EthereumClassic	EtcHash	49.67 TH/s	307.99 TH/s	258.32	226.60
Ergo	Autolykos	26.13 TH/s	149.39 TH/s	63.53	50.31
EthereumPOW	Ethash	-	46.16 TH/s	46.16	46.16
Ravencoin	KawPow	3.83 TH/s	18.82 TH/s	31.23	21.72
Ethereum Fair	Ethash	-	5.93 TH/s	5.93	5.93
Neoxa	KawPow	1.91 TH/s	3.75 TH/s	3.83	2.67
Conflux	Octopus	.84 TH/s	2.53 TH/s	4.46	1.32
Kaspa	kHeavyHash	75.20 TH/s	95.22 TH/s	2.21	1.32
Firo	FiroPow	91.86 GH/s	435.00 GH/s	.76	.59
EtherGem	Ethash	2.25 GH/s	448.78 GH/s	.45	.45
Sero	ProgPow	49.82 GH/s	182.88 GH/s	.33	.25
Expanse	Ethash	25.63 GH/s	264.73 GH/s	.24	.24
Nimiq	Argon2d-NIM	1.90 GH/s	3.97 GH/s	.21	.21
Vertcoin	Verthash	1.54 GH/s	3.57 GH/s	.20	.10
Etho	Ethash	4.95 GH/s	84.45 GH/s	.08	.08
Ubiq	Ubqhash	17.45 GH/s	83.06 GH/s	.07	.07
Quarkchain	Ethash	24.71 GH/s	82.76 GH/s	.06	.06
Callisto	Ethash	71.38 GH/s	102.22 GH/s	.03	.03
Zano	ProgPowZ	6.89 GH/s	16.77 GH/s	.03	.02
Total				**418.13**	**358.13**

Block Data. In lieu of running clients in all 6 systems to collect blockchain data, we rely on block explorers [17,22,56] to get all blocks of each system for the days surrounding The Merge and several months following. In total, we scrape block data from 1st September 2022 to 1st March 2023. In the block data, we get the block height, timestamp, miner ID, block reward plus transaction fees, and block difficulty. We also collect mining pool labels (if a miner address is associated with a particular mining pool) by cross-referencing additional block explorers [24,60].

Market Data. We scrape hourly price data for each coin from CoinGecko [14].

3 Analysis

3.1 Mining Power Redistribution

We begin by recomputing the network hashrates for each of the systems. The mining *difficulty* parameter in each block is set such that blocks are found in *expectation* at a rate determined by the *block rate*. Dividing the difficulty by the expected block rate gives us the *expected network hashrate* of the system, this is generally what popular mining statistics sites plot [2]. Usually, the *actual effective hashrate* of the system matches closely with the expectation, however,

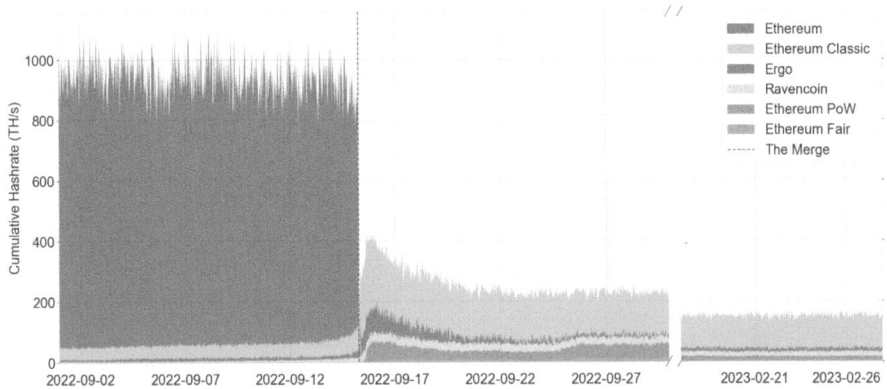

Fig. 1. Cumulative minimum Ethash equivalent hashrate in each of the systems.

during times of sudden increase/decrease in hashrate, this is not the case. To capture such fluctuations, we divide the difficulty by the *actual block rate*.

Due to the stochastic nature of mining, we additionally take the running average of the difficulty over the previous hour (3600 s) such that the computed hashrate H at time t is

$$H_{network}(t) = \sum_{b \in blocks(t-3600,t)} \text{diff}(b)/3600 * \text{factor}_{network}$$

We use diff(b) to denote the difficulty of a block b, and factor$_{network}$ the Ethash conversion factor computed in Sect. 2, for the remainder of the paper we use the maximum factor. We plot the cumulative hashrate across the studied systems in Fig. 1, note a break in the x-axis during a period of steady decrease.

Prior to The Merge, each system had a relatively stable hashrate, Ethereum's hashrate being just 18.6% from its all-time high a few months earlier [1]. The end of Ethereum's mining meant a sudden and brief spike in the hashrate of all networks, reaching 41% of Ethereum's hashrate. Within a few days, this spike leveled off and remained stable with a gradual decrease over the following five months. By the end of our measurement period, these five networks collectively still hold over 3x their pre-Merge hashrate, this increase is 30% of the peak of the 15th of September and accounts for a minimum of 12% (median of 14%) of the pre-Merge Ethereum hashrate still remaining in these systems. In other words, at most 88% of Ethereum's hashrate has left the ecosystem.

3.2 Miner Distribution

We group the hashrate data by the top miner addresses in each system, including those addresses for which we have labeled as belonging to a mining pool. We plot the distributions in miner hashrate for Ethereum Classic and Ethereum Fair in Fig. 2. We observe that most systems look very similar to what we see with Ethereum Classic, where most mining pools keep operating post-Merge with a growth in hashrate. Ethereum Fair on the other hand, from the onset, is under the control of a single large miner. We compute the Herfindahl-Hirschman Index for mining pool block share for each system in Fig. 3 and further see that The Merge has little to no impact on the concentration of miners.

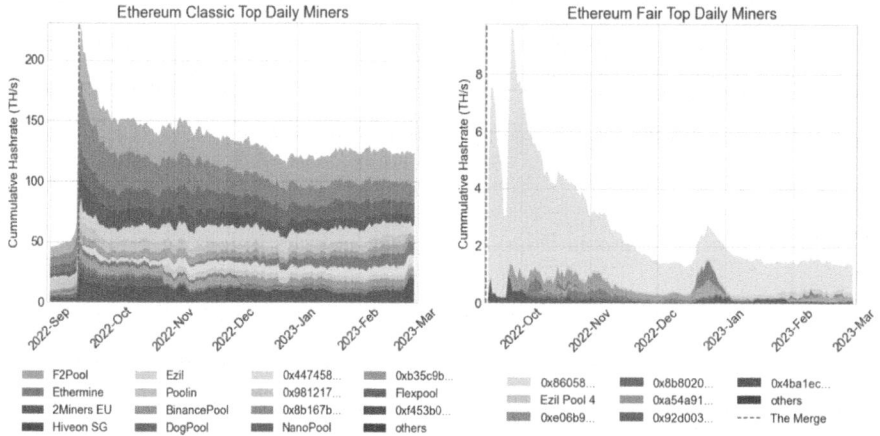

Fig. 2. Mining Pool Distributions for Ethereum Classic and Ethereum Fair.

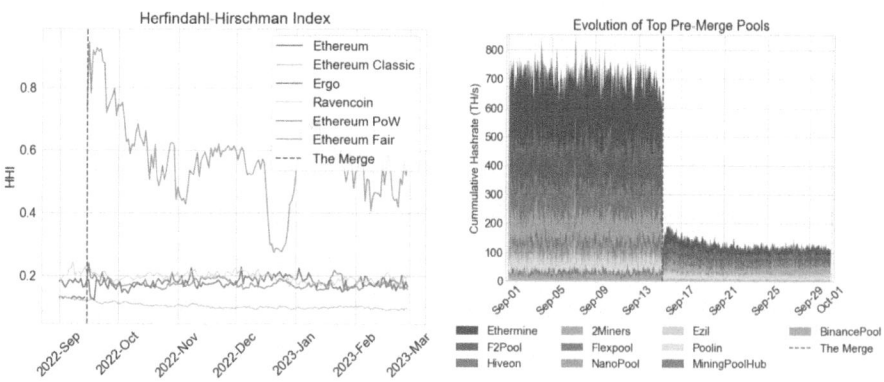

Fig. 3. HHI for mining pool share distributions (left) and the cumulative hashrates of the top pre-Merge mining pools before and after The Merge (right).

By taking common miner labels in all networks, we are also able to track a large portion of the pools following The Merge. Figure 3 plots the cummulative hashrate of the largest mining pools over all systems before The Merge. We believe that for monetary reasons (switching between most profitable currencies)

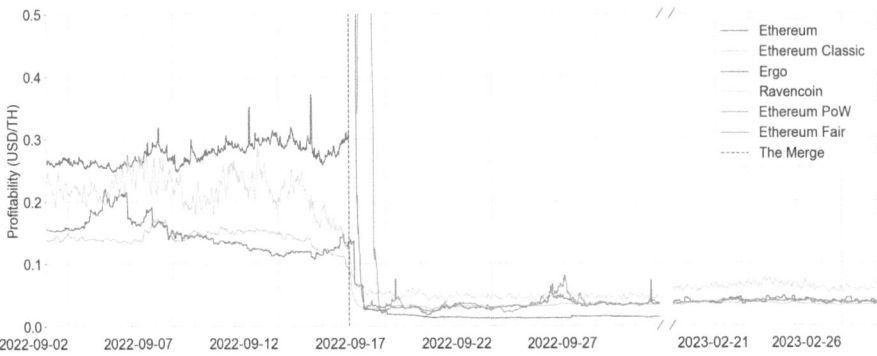

Fig. 4. Expected US dollar reward per Tera-Ethash of computation.

and for security reasons [9] most pools were already active across all platforms. Surprisingly, they make up a much lower portion of the total hashrate after the Merge. This could indicate more well-thought-out strategies from these pools.

3.3 Mining Profitability

We measure the block rewards and transaction fees that were collected by miners. Using the ensuing matching market price of a network's coin and the Ethash equivalent hashrate $H(t)$, we obtain the profitability $P(t)$, a metric describing the total US-dollar rewards per Ethash of computation done.[3]

$$P_{network}(t) = \frac{\left(\sum_{b \in blocks(t-3600,t)} \text{reward}(b) + \text{fees}(b)\right) * \text{price}_{network}(t)}{H_{network}(t) * 3600}$$

Figure 4 reveals that a large decrease in profitability across all coins occurred after The Merge. Interestingly, the initial peaks in profitability for Ethereum Fair and Ethereum PoW are due to very few entities mining at an extremely low difficulty for 2 and 25 h respectively. Conversely, Ergo suffered from its difficulty shooting up as large miners joined the network to reap profits. Due to the slowly adjusting difficulty function, this made Ergo block production excessively unprofitable for long periods. Eventually, EIP37 and the associated Hard Fork mitigated the issue [21], raising Ergo's profitability. These spotlight the instability period that follows such a drastic fork. Still, five months after The Merge, the profitability of each coins has converged to a value about 1/8th of what Ethereum's profitability used to be.

---

[3] In practice, profitability can also be impacted by block stale, reject, or orphan rates and associated rewards or penalties. We do not consider these differences.

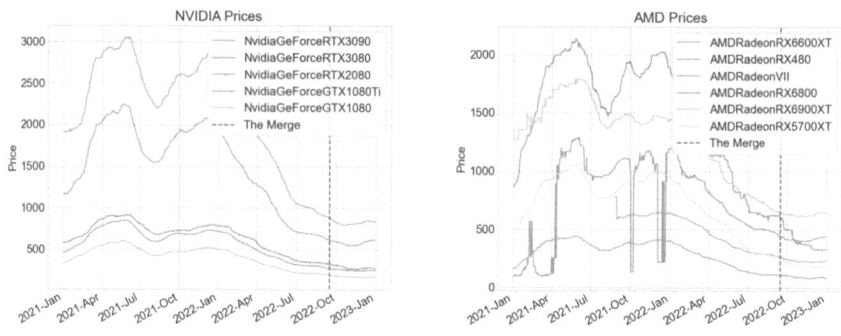

Fig. 5. Resale value of Nvidia and AMD GPUs taken from [58].

4 Discussion

Environmental Impact. One of the big promises of moving to PoS was the 30,000× decrease in energy [29]. Compared to the 1st of September 2022, on the 1st of March 2023, we see an excess hashrate of 116 THs (over a 2× increase) for the remaining systems. This increase has happened even though the profitability of mining is almost an order of magnitude lower. In other words, at least 12% of the original mining power of Ethereum is still operating, dampening the immediate environmental benefits of Ethereum's switch to PoS.

Impact on Miners. As evidenced by the trends in resale value of the GPUs considered in this study (cf. Fig. 5), the demand for GPUs went down leading up to The Merge[4]. Nonetheless, the reason for the excess mining power even through unprofitability can at least partially be explained through the behavior of private miners. We have found anecdotal evidence in discussion forums that some miners kept mining for i) speculative reasons, ii) to utilize heat for personal use, and iii) due to personal conviction (e.g., [50]). Others are opting to rent their GPUs on decentralized marketplaces [65]. On the other hand, Hut8 and HIVE, two large mining companies, have been public about their strategies following The Merge, extending their ASIC mining operations and re-purposing their GPUs for AI and High-Performance Computing (HPC). Both companies, however, report major losses [11, 31, 54, 55, 57].

Impact on the GPU Market. The GPU manufacturers themselves were initially predicted to have a bleak future as late as mid-2022 [13, 53] and experienced year-low stock prices [3]. The situation has very quickly turned on its head thanks to the recent disruption in AI and its equally insatiable hunger for GPUs [64]. As for the blockchain space, the use of GPUs is far from over, as (zero-knowledge) proofs of knowledge are becoming a pillar of Layer-2 technologies [37].

---

[4] This generally follows previously observed GPU usage cycles of miners [20].

5 Related Work

Previous work on the Ethereum Classic fork of 2016 [42], at the time the first persistent fork of its kind, studied its impact on the two systems including their profitability and mining pool distributions. They also showed a vulnerability caused by the shared history and code of the two systems which subsequently caused Chain-ids to be made standard in future forks. Social aspects of forks have also been studied including a case analysis of the Bitcoin Cash fork [38], and the ethics of planned forks [44]. Another line of work characterizes broadly the kinds of forks that exist [61], including the characterization of velvet forks [41] and their prominence and impact in Bitcoin and other networks [73]. There is a rich body of work on the dynamics of mining pools, including a breakdown of the market share of pools in Ethereum [43] and Bitcoin [68], as well as work on the incentives for miners to join different kinds of pools [16,28,59]. While we focus on the impact of The Merge on the general PoW ecosystems, others have studied its impact solely on the Ethereum system [35,40,66,67,72].

References

1. 2CryptoCalc: What is the most profitable gpu or asic? https://2cryptocalc.com/most-profitable-gpu. Accessed 2023
2. 2miners: Coin hashrate. https://2miners.com/coin-network-hashrate. Accessed 2023
3. AnalyticsIndiaMag: The merge is killing nvidia gpu prices (2022). https://analyticsindiamag.com/the-merge-is-killing-nvidia-gpu-prices/
4. Back, A., et al.: Hashcash-a denial of service counter-measure (2002)
5. Bitcoins: Ethereum mining hardware reviews & comparison (2022). https://99bitcoins.com/ethereum/ethereum-mining/hardware/
6. Buterin, V.: Ethereum: a next-generation smart contract and decentralized application platform (2013). https://github.com/ethereum/wiki/wiki/White-Paper
7. Buterin, V.: A Proof of Stake Design Philosophy. https://vitalik.ca/general/2016/12/29/pos_design.html. Accessed 2023
8. Changelly: Best gpu for mining: How to choose the best mining gpu (2022). https://changelly.com/blog/best-graphics-cards-for-crypto-mining-how-to-choose-the-best-mining-gpu
9. Chatzigiannis, P., Baldimtsi, F., Griva, I., Li, J.: Diversification across mining pools: optimal mining strategies under pow. J. Cybersecur. 8(1), tyab027 (2022)
10. Chepurnoy, A., Kharin, V., Meshkov, D.: Autolykos: the ergo platform pow puzzle (2019)
11. Chmiel, D.: Hut 8 loss deepens despite higher mining rate (2022). https://www.financemagnates.com/cryptocurrency/hut-8-loss-deepens-despiite-higher-mining-rate/
12. Classic, E.: Etchash. https://github.com/eth-classic/etchash. Accessed 2023
13. CoinDesk: Morgan stanley: Gpu demand likely to slow if ethereum moves to proof-of-stake (2022). https://www.coindesk.com/business/2022/06/27/morgan-stanley-gpu-demand-likely-to-slow-if-ethereum-moves-to-proof-of-stake/
14. CoinGecko: Cryptocurrency Prices by Market Cap. https://www.coingecko.com. Accessed 2023

15. Coinmarketcap: Today's cryptocurrency prices by market cap. https://coinmarketcap.com/. Accessed 2023
16. Cong, L.W., He, Z., Li, J.: Decentralized mining in centralized pools. Rev. Finan. Stud. **34**(3), 1191–1235 (2021)
17. Cryptoscope: Solus ravencoin explorer. https://rvn.cryptoscope.io. Accessed 2023
18. Dwork, C., Naor, M.: Pricing via processing or combatting junk mail. In: Brickell, E.F. (ed.) CRYPTO 1992. LNCS, vol. 740, pp. 139–147. Springer, Heidelberg (1993). https://doi.org/10.1007/3-540-48071-4_10
19. Economist, T.: Crypto-miners are probably to blame for the graphics-chip shortage (2021). https://www.economist.com/graphic-detail/2021/06/19/crypto-miners-are-probably-to-blame-for-the-graphics-chip-shortage
20. Eghbali, A., Wattenhofer, R.: 12 angry miners. In: Data Privacy Management, Cryptocurrencies and Blockchain Technology: ESORICS 2019 International Workshops, DPM 2019 and CBT 2019, Luxembourg, 26–27 September 2019, Proceedings 14, pp. 391–398. Springer, Heidelberg (2019)
21. Ergo: Eip37 hard fork. https://ergoplatform.org/en/blog/EIP37%20Hard%20Fork/. Accessed 2023
22. Ergo: Ergo explorer. https://explorer.ergoplatform.com. Accessed 2023
23. EthereumPoW: EthereumPoW - The Original Ethereum Blockchain powered by Proof of Work. https://ethereumpow.org/. Accessed 2023
24. Etherscan: The ethereum blockchain explorer. https://etherscan.io. Accessed 2023
25. Fair, E.: A fork of Ethereum that keeps POW. https://etherfair.org/. Accessed 2023
26. Fenton, B., Black, T.: Ravencoin: a peer to peer electronic system for the creation and transfer of assets (2018)
27. Finney, H.: Rpow-reusable proofs of work (2004). https://nakamotoinstitute.org/finney/rpow/index.html
28. Fisch, B., Pass, R., Shelat, A.: Socially optimal mining pools. In: Devanur, N.R., Lu, P. (eds.) WINE 2017. LNCS, vol. 10660, pp. 205–218. Springer, Cham (2017). https://doi.org/10.1007/978-3-319-71924-5_15
29. Foundation, E.: Ethereum's energy expenditure. https://ethereum.org/en/energy-consumption/. Accessed 2023
30. Foundation, E.: The Merge. https://ethereum.org/en/roadmap/merge/. Accessed 2023
31. Gkritsi, E.: Crypto miner hive blockchain posts q3 loss as ethereum merge cuts revenue, mining margin (2023). https://www.coindesk.com/business/2023/02/21/crypto-miner-hive-blockchains-posts-q3-loss-as-ethereum-merge-cuts-revenue-mining-margin/
32. Han, R., Foutris, N., Kotselidis, C.: Demystifying crypto-mining: analysis and optimizations of memory-hard pow algorithms. In: 2019 IEEE International Symposium on Performance Analysis of Systems and Software (ISPASS), pp. 22–33. IEEE (2019)
33. Hardware, T.: Gpu shortages will worsen thanks to coin miners (2020). https://www.tomshardware.com/news/gpu-shortages-worsen-cryptocurrency-coin-miners-ethereum
34. Hardware, T.: Ethereum miners spent $15 billion on gpus alone during latest cryptocraze (2022). https://www.tomshardware.com/news/ethereum-miners-have-spent-15-billion-on-gpus
35. Heimbach, L., Kiffer, L., Torres, C.F., Wattenhofer, R.: Ethereum's proposer-builder separation: promises and realities. arXiv preprint arXiv:2305.19037 (2023)

36. Hopwood, D., Bowe, S., Hornby, T., Wilcox, N., et al.: Zcash protocol specification. GitHub **4**(220), 32 (2016)
37. Ingonyama: The merge is killing nvidia gpu prices. Hardware Review: GPUs ,FPGAs and Zero Knowledge Proofs (2023)
38. Islam, N., Mäntymäki, M., Turunen, M.: Understanding the role of actor heterogeneity in blockchain splits: an actor-network perspective of bitcoin forks (2019)
39. Kalodner, H.A., Carlsten, M., Ellenbogen, P.M., Bonneau, J., Narayanan, A.: An empirical study of namecoin and lessons for decentralized namespace design. In: WEIS, vol. 1, pp. 1–23 (2015)
40. Kapengut, E., Mizrach, B.: An event study of the ethereum transition to proof-of-stake. Commodities **2**(2), 96–110 (2023)
41. Kiayias, A., Miller, A., Zindros, D.: Non-interactive proofs of proof-of-work. In: Bonneau, J., Heninger, N. (eds.) FC 2020. LNCS, vol. 12059, pp. 505–522. Springer, Cham (2020). https://doi.org/10.1007/978-3-030-51280-4_27
42. Kiffer, L., Levin, D., Mislove, A.: Stick a fork in it: analyzing the ethereum network partition. In: Proceedings of the 16th ACM Workshop on Hot Topics in Networks, pp. 94–100 (2017)
43. Kiffer, L., Salman, A., Levin, D., Mislove, A., Nita-Rotaru, C.: Under the hood of the ethereum gossip protocol. In: Borisov, N., Diaz, C. (eds.) FC 2021. LNCS, vol. 12675, pp. 437–456. Springer, Heidelberg (2021). https://doi.org/10.1007/978-3-662-64331-0_23
44. Kim, T.W., Zetlin-Jones, A.: The ethics of contentious hard forks in blockchain networks with fixed features. Front. Blockchain **2**, 9 (2019)
45. King, S., Nadal, S.: Ppcoin: peer-to-peer crypto-currency with proof-of-stake. Self-Pub. Paper **19**(1) (2012)
46. Litecoin: The Future Of Money. https://litecoin.com/en/. Accessed 2023
47. Meneghetti, A., Sala, M., Taufer, D.: A survey on pow-based consensus. In: Annals of Emerging Technologies in Computing (AETiC), Print ISSN, pp. 2516–0281 (2020)
48. Minerbay, T.: Gpu ranking (2022). https://theminerbay.org
49. Minerstat: Gpu mining: Best gpus by profitability and hashrates. https://minerstat.com/hardware/gpus. Accessed 2023
50. @MoarWhisky: Gpu mining for profit is dead right now. that doesn't mean it's dead forever, but not all of us mine for pure profit. i heat my shop with rigs in the winter time. my gpus have all paid for themselves. i'll be bringing them all online this winter for nothing other than cheap heat. even at negative profit it's cheaper to use as a heat source than propane. it's also a lot more fun! i personally love maintaining the rigs and tweaking things when needed. i'll probably add more cards as prices plummet (2022). https://www.reddit.com/r/gpumining/comments/xl6cgm/whats_the_state_of_gpu_mining_now_will_pools/
51. Monero: Monero Means Money. https://www.getmonero.org/. Accessed 2023
52. Nakamoto, S.: Bitcoin: a peer-to-peer electronic cash system (2009). http://www.bitcoin.org/bitcoin.pdf
53. Nasdaq: What will the ethereum protocol changes do for nvidia's gpu sales? (2021). https://www.nasdaq.com/articles/what-will-the-ethereum-protocol-changes-do-for-nvidias-gpu-sales-2021-03-12
54. News, C.: Hive blockchain to mine other crypto assets after merge (2022). https://bitcoinist.com/hive-blockchain-to-mine-crypto-assets-after-merge/
55. Newswire, P.: Hut 8 partners with zenlayer (2022). https://ai-techpark.com/hut-8-partners-with-zenlayer/

56. OKLink: Intelligent web3 data platform. https://www.oklink.com/. Accessed 2023
57. Pan, D.: Crypto miners pivoting to ai cloud services may face an uphill battle. https://www.bnnbloomberg.ca/crypto-miners-pivoting-to-ai-cloud-services-may-face-an-uphill-battle-1.1922515
58. Pan, D.: Price history. https://howmuch.one/gpus
59. Qin, R., Yuan, Y., Wang, F.Y.: Research on the selection strategies of blockchain mining pools. IEEE Trans. Comput. Social Syst. **5**(3), 748–757 (2018)
60. Ravencoin: Ravencoin block explorer. https://api.ravencoin.org. Accessed 2023
61. Schär, F.: Blockchain forks: a formal classification framework and persistency analysis. Sing. Econ. Rev. 1–11 (2020)
62. Szabo, N.: Bit gold (2008). https://www.difotech.it/immagini_articolo/Nick-Szabo/Unenumerated_Bit_gold_inglese.pdf
63. Taylor, M.B.: The evolution of bitcoin hardware. Computer **50**(9), 58–66 (2017)
64. Times, F.: Nvidia shares touch all-time high on back of ai boom (2022). https://www.ft.com/content/4197702a-9749-4eca-912b-07cc4880c336
65. Vast.ai: Global gpu market. https://vast.ai/. Accessed 2023
66. Wahrstätter, A., et al.: Blockchain censorship. arXiv preprint arXiv:2305.18545 (2023)
67. Wahrstätter, A., Zhou, L., Qin, K., Svetinovic, D., Gervais, A.: Time to bribe: measuring block construction market. arXiv preprint arXiv:2305.16468 (2023)
68. Wang, C., Chu, X., Qin, Y.: Measurement and analysis of the bitcoin networks: a view from mining pools. In: 2020 6th International Conference on Big Data Computing and Communications (BIGCOM), pp. 180–188. IEEE (2020)
69. Wendl, M., Doan, M.H., Sassen, R.: The environmental impact of cryptocurrencies using proof of work and proof of stake consensus algorithms: a systematic review. J. Environ. Manag. **326**, 116530 (2023)
70. WhatToMine: Gpu profitability ranking. https://whattomine.com/gpus. Accessed 2023
71. WindowsCentral: Best mining gpu 2022: The best graphics card for bitcoin and ethereum (2022). https://www.windowscentral.com/best-gpus-crypto-mining
72. Woitschig, P., Uddin, G.S., Xie, T., Härdle, W.K.: The energy consumption of the ethereum-ecosystem. SSRN 4526732 (2023)
73. Zamyatin, A., Stifter, N., Judmayer, A., Schindler, P., Weippl, E., Knottenbelt, W.J.: A wild velvet fork appears! inclusive blockchain protocol changes in practice. In: Zohar, A., et al. (eds.) FC 2018. LNCS, vol. 10958, pp. 31–42. Springer, Heidelberg (2019). https://doi.org/10.1007/978-3-662-58820-8_3

Accountable Wallet: A Comprehensive Framework for Proving the Multifaceted Legitimacy of Wallet

Masato Yamanaka[1,2(✉)], Mitchell Travers[3], and Ken Katayama[4]

[1] Georgetown University, Washington, D.C., USA
masato.yamanaka@ruri.waseda.jp
[2] Sumitomo Mitsui Trust Bank, Ltd., Tokyo, Japan
[3] Soulbis, Sydney, Australia
[4] Nomura Research Institute, Ltd., Tokyo, Japan

Abstract. This paper introduces the concept of an 'Accountable Wallet' to establish trust in decentralized finance. Our methodology reverses the traditional approaches, which primarily focus on preventing and penalizing illicit activities; we propose a framework where legitimate wallets actively prove their legitimacy to the counterparty before the transactions. Key elements of the proposed framework include proof of the legitimacy of wallet holders, wallet conducts, and crypto asset provenances. The paper explores and summarizes the implementation of this methodology to issue these proofs. The paper outlines comprehensive methods to ensure transaction legitimacy, including Chained Credentials for crypto asset provenance and approaches for evaluating wallet trustworthiness. The methodology cultivates an economy where transactions are exclusive to wallets that can prove their legitimacy. Consequently, illicit wallets in decentralized finance will face substantially restricted liquidity compared to legitimate investors. This restriction is a realistic punitive measure for malicious actors who have eluded penalization by traditional approaches. The proposed methods transcend jurisdictional limitations, offering a comprehensive framework for legitimacy verification.

Keywords: Blockchain · Decentralized Finance · Compliance · Credentials

1 Introduction

1.1 Motivations and Contributions

Mitigating illicit transactions in crypto assets presents formidable challenges, primarily due to inherent difficulties in intercepting or nullifying transactions linked to illicit wallet addresses. Unique to crypto assets is the possibility of operating wallets without stringent Know Your Customer (KYC) processes, enabling transactions without disclosing the actual wallet holder's identity. Furthermore, smart contracts allow transactions without pre-assessment of counterparty creditworthiness. While central to their appeal, the inherent anonymity and trustless nature of crypto assets can inadvertently lead well-intentioned investors to become careless, potentially unintentionally assisting in money laundering. Even if laws are applied to prohibit engaging with illicit entities, individual investors cannot typically discern the legitimacy of their counterparties. This limitation raises critical questions about the practicality and efficacy of applying stringent regulations without adequate technological support. Furthermore, the stringent regulations may inadvertently drive service providers and investors towards less regulated jurisdictions, potentially escalating risks to the broader populace.

This paper suggests a paradigm shift in tackling illicit transactions in crypto assets. The focus shifts from attempting to halt illicit transactions to creating mechanisms that encourage and facilitate transactions exclusively between legitimate investors. While subtle, this distinction is significant in enhancing transaction security and mitigating risks associated with anonymity. Dealings with wallets that actively demonstrate their legitimacy are inherently significantly safer than those with wallets that do not. Recent technological advancements show promise, such as issuing Verifiable Credentials and Soulbound Tokens (hereinafter collectively referred to as Credentials) to trusted wallets and using zero-knowledge-proof technology. By isolating illicit wallets, these technologies could potentially hinder the conversion of illicitly obtained crypto assets into monetary value. However, the effectiveness of this solution hinges on the widespread adoption of credentialing in wallets. Why are credentials seemingly valuable for proving legitimacy not widely adopted today? While the adoption lag can partially be attributed to the time required to integrate new technologies, a more crucial aspect, as hypothesized in this paper, lies in the unresolved issues surrounding using credentials for legitimacy proof. In the following sections, we comprehensively outline these significant challenges and detail the solutions proposed by this paper to address each one.

Defining Legitimacy in Decentralized Finance. The core objective of using credentials within decentralized finance is to prove one's legitimacy, conforming to the jurisdictional regulations and compliance rules relevant to the counterparty. However, the heterogeneity of legitimate frameworks across various jurisdictions presents a formidable challenge to this endeavor. Issuing a universally legitimate credential that aligns with every jurisdiction and compliance regulation is, in reality, an unattainable goal. Consequently, current credentials often serve as a service-specific license, exemplified by initiatives like Project Guardian [14], and are not universally applicable. This limitation arises from the diverse legitimate specifications under which these credentials are issued, complicating the establishment of a universally recognized compliance framework. The traditional approach to this challenge has been fragmented and jurisdiction-specific, lacking a cohesive methodology.

This paper proposes a novel approach to defining investor legitimacy in the decentralized finance ecosystem that transcends jurisdictional and service-specific constraints. It aims to construct an adaptable yet robust definition to uphold the principles of legitimacy and compliance universally. This endeavor necessitates a deep dive into the intricate balance of regulatory diversity and the overarching need for a standardized legitimacy framework in decentralized finance.

Methods for Proving the Legitimacy of Indirect Transactions. A pivotal aspect of establishing trust in decentralized finance is evaluating counterparties' trustworthiness through credentials. However, this alone is insufficient. The complexity of decentralized finance, where any investor may control multiple wallets, necessitates thoroughly examining direct and indirect transaction histories. Given the vast number of potential transactions, a comprehensive verification of all wallet interactions is theoretically infinite and practically unfeasible.

The paper proposes introducing a 'Chained Credential' system to circumvent this challenge. These credentials demonstrate that the crypto assets have been acquired through legitimate channels, such as compliant VASPs. Remarkably, if a legitimate investor can prove they are only engaging in transactions with counterparties who also possess such credentials, it establishes a chain of crypto asset provenance. This method essentially acts like mathematical induction, ensuring the legitimacy of all transaction routes and revolutionizing the verification process by obviating the need for complicated blockchain legitimacy checks.

Trustworthiness Evaluation Method for Wallets. This paper introduces a novel method for assessing wallet trustworthiness, named the 'Trust Score.' This score, derived from credentials and blockchain information, is designed to be a fixed, objective scalar value consistent across all evaluations. The rationale behind this uniform scoring method is threefold:

Privacy Protection. While this paper recommends using zero-knowledge techniques for verifying the trustworthiness of investors using credentials, it acknowledges a critical limitation. Even the most meticulously designed zero-knowledge proofs will inadvertently disclose some personal information. A unified Trust Score reduces the need to scrutinize various investor attributes, thereby minimizing the risk of personal information infringement.

Continuity of Transactions. If different parties use varied formulas, a transaction deemed legitimate under one scoring system might be considered illegitimate under another. This discrepancy can inadvertently damage an investor's credibility. The paper recommends a standardized trust score calculation formula to avoid inconsistencies. This uniform approach would ensure consistency and reliability in assessing the legitimacy of transactions across different parties within the crypto-asset ecosystem.

Self-sovereignty. To prevent arbitrary manipulation, the scoring formula must remain unchanged by any single entity. This guards against the unwarranted devaluation of a wallet's trustworthiness.

While acknowledging that no scoring system is infallible, the proposed Trust Score is conceptualized as a motivational tool. It encourages lawful behavior among investors, as illicit actions would detrimentally affect their score.

Enhancing the Distribution and Credibility of Credentials. This paper emphasizes the paramount importance of credentials in decentralized finance, notably as inputs for legitimacy-proof protocols. The accuracy of these credentials is critical; even the most stringent protocols will falter if based on flawed credentials. Therefore, the reliability of credential issuers is a cornerstone of this system. Prior studies often presuppose the reliability of credentials or the existence of a singular issuer, overlooking the benefits of multiple issuances by diverse entities.

The paper advocates for a decentralized model of credential issuers, ideally independent from the DeFi systems they support, to enhance credibility and reliability. However, the current landscape predominantly features issuers with financial ties to DeFi platforms, driven by the necessity of ensuring issuer viability. This necessitates discussing their business models to encourage the emergence of diverse, financially independent credential issuers. While this may seem akin to a commercial discourse, the system of appropriately rewarding trust guarantors is crucial, as evidenced by the Bitcoin ecosystem. In summary, this paper aims to provide a comprehensive framework addressing the aspects above of credential dissemination and reliability in the decentralized finance arena.

1.2 Related Work

Studies [10] and [11] delineate specific mechanisms hackers employ for money laundering using crypto assets, underscoring the necessity of robust KYC technologies. Works [1, 4], and [5] offer comprehensive insights into the efficacy of KYC in cleansing economic systems. Study [3] introduces a technique for validating investor attributes, aligning with this paper's focus on attribute suitability in P2P transactions. The discussion extends to the economic aspects of credentials, where [4] highlights the risks associated with centralized issuance and [7] demonstrates how credentials can augment financial service convenience. The importance of privacy in credential issuance is critically evaluated in [8] and [9], with caution against the residual risks of privacy breaches despite advanced anonymity technologies. Study [2] proposes a mixing methodology to balance transaction privacy and ethical investor engagement. This paper contributes to this discourse by suggesting a wallet reliability evaluation method as a tool for constructing practical association sets. Lastly, [6] proposes integrating KYC data with reputation scores, while this paper advances a comprehensive evaluation method considering wallet holders, transaction behaviors, and crypto asset acquisition routes.

2 The Framework

2.1 Tripartite Legitimacy Verification

This paper aims to establish a robust proof mechanism for certifying the legitimacy of wallets in decentralized finance and develop methods to validate these proofs. To achieve this objective, a nuanced understanding of the requirements for legitimate wallets to substantiate their authenticity to counterparties is essential. This involves thoroughly analyzing the criteria and evidence needed to establish transaction legitimacy. We have concluded that crypto asset crimes can be categorized into three primary groups: scams involving wallet owners, illicit transactions, and questionable methods of obtaining crypto assets. Therefore, legitimate wallets must prove and verify three aspects to each other: Legitimacy of Wallet Holders, Legitimacy of Wallet Conducts, and Legitimacy of Crypto Asset Provenances (Table 1).

Legitimacy of Wallet Holders. Legitimate service providers and investors must refrain from engaging with wallets associated with terrorists and other illicit entities. A critical aspect of this principle is that transactions should be avoided with them, regardless of their apparent legitimacy in blockchain activities. Conservatively, anonymous wallets, whose holders are unidentified, might potentially be controlled by illicit entities, thus posing a risk. However, revealing personal information like names or physical addresses to prove the legitimacy of wallet holders is undesirable. Instead, a method is required to confirm that an investor's attribute information aligns with counterparties' compliance standards without disclosing personal information. The methodology example for this proof is detailed in Sect. 2.

Legitimacy of Wallet Conducts. Legitimate investors must refrain from engaging with wallets in illicit activities in decentralized finance, regardless of their KYC status. It's crucial to distinguish fraud linked to the wallet holder from that associated with the wallet's actions. Proving a wallet's historical non-involvement in fraud is challenging, akin to a 'devil's proof.' One approach is to mark wallets involved in illicit activities, but this is not feasible with credentials alone due to the potential for either credentials or wallets to be abandoned. We propose using Oracle Chains to inform legitimate investors about illicit wallets. The specifics of this proof method are discussed in Sect. 3.

Table 1. Examples of factors for proving legitimacy

Required Proofs	Technologies	VASPs (Custodial Wallet Address)	DeFi (Smart Contract Address)	Investors (Self-Custodial Wallet Address)
Legitimacy of Wallet Holders	Verifiable Credentials, Soulbound tokens, etc.	- Business license - Place of business	- Complied with respective jurisdiction's laws - Source code security audit certificate	- Physical address - Not a person or entity on the sanctions list - Meets institutional investor criteria
Legitimacy of Wallet Conducts	Oracle Chains	- Never sent crypto assets to sanctioned addresses	- Not designated as sanctioned - Keeping sanctioned addresses out of the liquidity pool	- Never sent crypto to sanctioned addresses - Never accessed sanctioned DeFi
Legitimacy of Crypto Asset Provenances	Chined Credentials (described later)	- Never accepted crypto assets from illicit wallets directly or indirectly	- Never accepted crypto assets from illicit wallets directly or indirectly	- Never accepted crypto assets from illicit wallets directly or indirectly

Legitimacy of Crypto Asset Provenances. A wallet not controlled by a sanctioned entity and not engaged in illicit activities might still inadvertently receive illicit crypto assets from such sources. Legitimate investors should avoid transactions with wallets that are recipients of such assets. The crypto assets receivers must be able to verify the crypto assets' legitimacy without receiving the originators' sensitive information. To achieve this, we propose the chained credentials, enabling any wallet to verify the legitimacy of the source of crypto assets. There's also a need to address scenarios where illicit crypto assets are sent to a wallet involuntarily. The methodology for this proof will be elaborated in Sect. 4.

2.2 Accountable Wallets and Trust Scores

We introduce the concept of an "Accountable Wallet" as a wallet capable of proving three critical aspects: the legitimacy of the wallet holder, wallet conducts, and crypto asset provenances. A wallet that cannot demonstrate these facts, even if it is legitimate, is not regarded as an accountable wallet. This paper proposes three distinct proofs to affirm a wallet's compatibility. Accountable wallets are expected to actively verify the accountability of counterparties before engaging in transactions to maintain their credit. Furthermore, introducing a trustworthiness measuring mechanism, termed the 'Trust Score,' incentivizes wallet holders to adhere to legitimate standards. The Trust Score is computed based on the information derived from these three proofs, ensuring that wallet holders are motivated to maintain high levels of legitimate compliance. The methodology and implications of the Trust Score will be elaborated in subsequent sections.

Our methodology is not designed for any specific blockchain. Credentials management is expected to occur on a separate system layer from blockchains for financial transactions. Since legitimate investors face the potential consequence of reduced trust scores when transacting with parties of unverified legitimacy, the system's design negates the need for direct enforcement to decide the permissibility of transactions. Additionally, this methodology can promote compliance across diverse wallets and blockchains by not being restricted to a particular blockchain, broadening its applicability and enhancing cross-chain compliance.

The anticipated outcome of this methodology is the creation of an economy where legitimate investors conduct transactions exclusively among themselves. This exclusivity is expected to effectively marginalize illicit wallets, thereby impeding their capacity to launder illicit crypto assets through legitimate assets, reducing the circulation of illicitly obtained crypto assets. This approach enables the implementation of actionable and realistic countermeasures on illicit wallets that have been immune to any form of penalties within the traditional approaches.

3 Legitimacy of Wallet Holders

3.1 Navigating KYC in Decentralized Finance

Before transacting, wallet owners must prove to their counterparties and DeFi platforms that they are not illicit persons or entities. The absence of a globally standardized KYC process complicates matters further. Merely completing KYC does not unequivocally establish the legitimacy of the transaction. The KYC and subsequent transaction monitoring should be tailored to the unique context of each financial institution, including customer profiles, financial products, and specific transaction details (Risk-Based Approach).

In the DeFi sector, the decentralized nature of service providers complicates the implementation of KYC. An external entity often conducts KYC and then issues credentials proving KYC completion. This separation between the KYC process and financial services may lead to blurred lines of responsibility, especially in cases of overlooked illicit transactions or breaches of the suitability principle, complicating the application of a risk-based approach.

3.2 Attribution Credentials

To design DeFi as an entity implementing the risk-based approach, credential issuers must maintain neutrality in investment decisions, focusing instead on providing objective facts about the credential holders. Credential issuers must focus exclusively on issuing credentials that verify specific investor information rather than serving as qualifications for token ownership or granting access to DeFi services (Fig. 1). To underscore this distinction, credentials pertinent to investors' information will be termed 'attribution credentials,' highlighting that the credentials issued by credential issuers are fundamentally oriented towards identity verification rather than investment authorization. For effective functioning, industry-standard rules are needed to transform investor attribute information into credentials and a protocol for determining transaction feasibility based on these credentials and the Predetermined Compliance Rules (Fig. 2). Standardizing credentials is crucial for decentralizing credential issuing authority. If credentials are not standardized, DeFi providers may only trust credentials issued by specific authorities, leading to a concentration of issuing power and potential threats to the rights of credential holders.

The primary challenge is the potential requirement for investors to disclose personal information through credential presentation. To mitigate this, investors must issue proof demonstrating compliance with regulatory norms without revealing sensitive data. However, creating a universal proof for all transaction types is unfeasible, necessitating tailored technological architectures for specific scenarios. As an illustrative example, the subsequent section details a methodology using attribution credentials to certify non-inclusion on sanction lists.

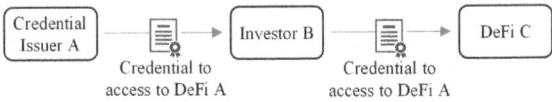

Fig. 1. Credential use cases where DeFi cannot take a risk-based approach

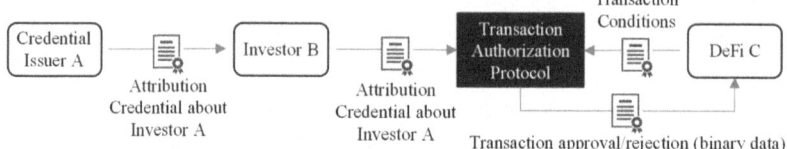

Fig. 2. Enabling a risk-based approach of DeFi using attribution credentials

3.3 Decentralized Sanctions Screening Protocol

In the realm of decentralized finance, it's essential to verify compliance while safeguarding privacy. A pertinent example of this is the implementation of sanctions screening. This process verifies that transactions do not involve individuals or entities on sanction lists managed by individual jurisdictions. Traditional financial systems require each jurisdiction to maintain its own sanctions list, with financial institutions referencing multiple lists for international operations (Fig. 3). Nodes in decentralized finance updating these lists should be incentivized for accuracy and honesty, akin to the Oracle chain's economic model. Upon presenting their attribution credentials, investors would receive a non-listing certification from the Sanctions List Oracle while maintaining privacy (Fig. 4).

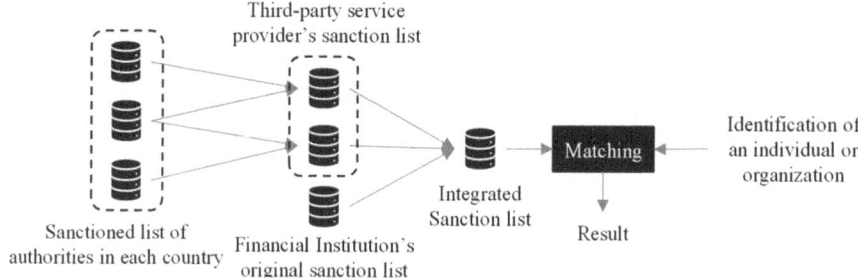

Fig. 3. Traditional Sanctions Screening

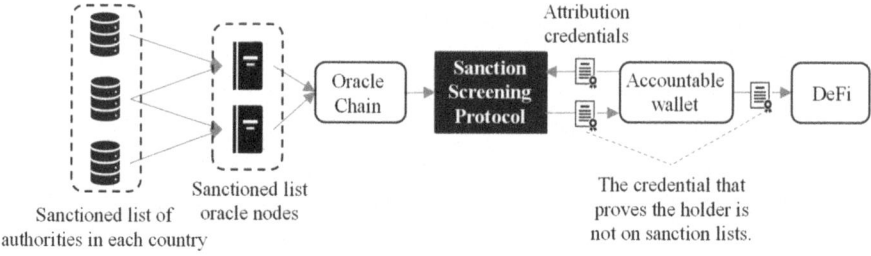

Fig. 4. Image of decentralized sanctions screening

The sanction list includes DeFi (contract addresses). Also, an essential protocol requirement is the verifier's ability to determine which country's sanctions list to apply.

For instance, U.S. authorities have prohibited U.S. residents from using Tornado Cash. Consequently, U.S. residents are restricted from receiving crypto assets from wallets associated with such services. In these scenarios, the verifier requests proof from the prover to issue a proof of compliance that the prover never used the Tornado Cash. This mechanism ensures adherence to international regulatory standards while maintaining the privacy and security inherent in decentralized finance.

3.4 Encouraging Attribution Credential Issuers

The discussion of compensating attribution credential issuers for their integrity is vital. Financial incentives are necessary for the system's sustainability. Direct fees for attribution credential issuance could be a revenue source. Another model involves allocating a small transaction fee to issuers, ensuring ongoing revenue, but raises practical concerns about continual fees despite one-time issuance involvement. A viable solution to the identified concern lies in the strategic design of attribution credentials (Fig. 5). Encrypting these attribution credentials and using them in compliance checking protocols contingent upon a minimal gas fee ensures enhanced security and controlled access. It is justified as a reasonable business expense for DeFi.

Also, the profitability of attribution credentials is anticipated to reduce entry barriers for potential issuers, leading to a diversified market of credential issuers. However, each issuer will inherently possess varying levels of trust, which impacts the credibility of the credentials they issue (as further discussed in Sect. 5). This dynamic creates a natural incentive for issuers to uphold honest practices. The diversified market is expected to gravitate towards a sustainable equilibrium, balancing reward and administrative precision to ensure long-term viability.

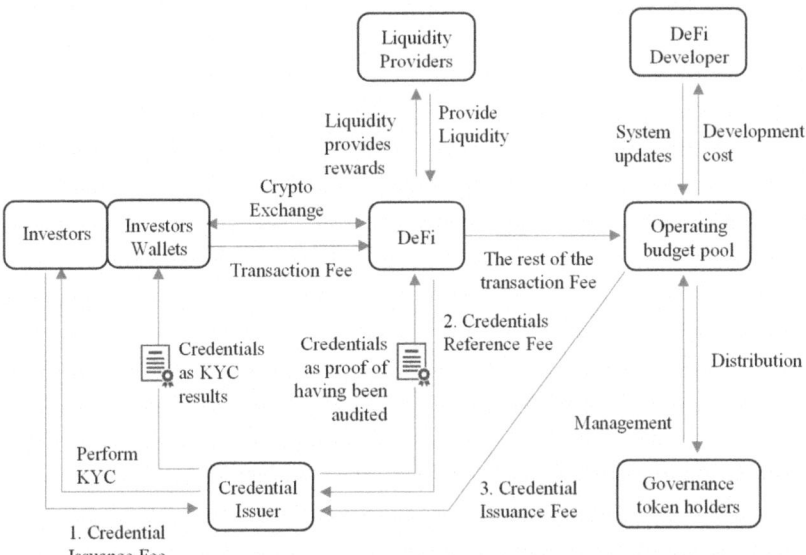

Fig. 5. Cash flow of attribution credential issuance

4 Legitimacy of Wallet Conducts

4.1 Approach

This section outlines the methodology for generating proofs, ensuring a wallet has not historically been involved in illicit activities. The essence of this proof lies in demonstrating that the wallet address is not on a sanction list designated by authorities and has no association with any such addresses. In many cases, it is possible to identify addresses involved in illicit activities like hacking or price manipulation. However, blockchain's inherent anonymity and self-sovereignty principles protect the wallet owner's identity. Therefore, the primary strategy for regulators, regulated VASPs, and legitimate investors is to abstain from transactions with these identified addresses. The ultimate goal is to sever all avenues through which criminals can convert illicit crypto assets into other forms of value.

4.2 Decentralized Sanctions Screening Protocol

We propose developing a consensus algorithm that accurately and rapidly identifies sanctioned addresses in a decentralized manner. The protocol aims to integrate off-chain regulator-designated sanctioned address information into the on-chain environment. This structure is essentially a specialized sanctioned-address-maintain version of the Oracle chain; the operating model is expected to resemble Chainlink (Fig. 6). The data's validity is then collectively verified by the nodes. Like Chainlink, ensuring this system's integrity is paramount, requiring carefully designed incentives for nodes to act honestly. If a node uploads arbitrary or false sanction list data, severe consequences, such as confiscating their staked assets, are necessary to maintain system integrity and trust.

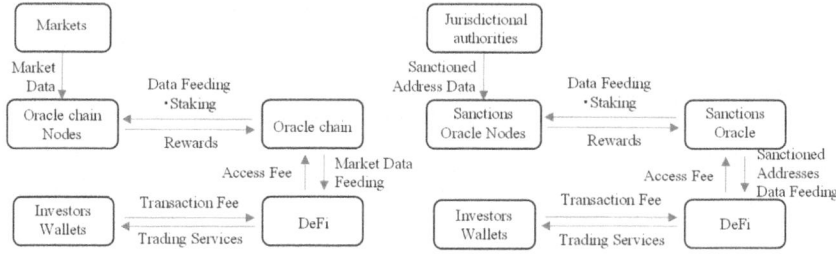

Fig. 6. Oracle chain for market data feeding (left) and Oracle chain for sanctioned address data feeding (right)

4.3 Prohibition of Transactions with Sanctioned Addresses

The prohibition of transactions with sanctioned addresses necessitates stringent measures. If a sanctioned wallet attempts to transfer crypto assets to another wallet, the receiving address must also be sanctioned, regardless of affiliation with the original illicit wallet. Consequently, investors must verify that their transaction counterpart is not a sanctioned address before every transaction.

However, there are some exceptions. A criterion to be sanctioned is the judgment of fault. An exemption applies if the receiving wallet is not sanctioned for accepting assets from a wallet that becomes a sanctioned wallet due to actions taken after the transaction. In such scenarios, the receiver should not be sanctioned and is not obligated to return or dispose of the received assets. However, if the originator was not sanctioned at the time of the transaction but was later found to have committed fraud and added to the sanction list, the judgment becomes more complex. Sanctioning the receiver in such cases could unfairly penalize legitimate investors. Yet, not sanctioning them might allow illicit wallets to transfer assets before being sanctioned. Here, the relationship between the receiver and the originator becomes crucial. Attribution credentials can be used to establish non-affiliation.

4.4 Suspect Designation

The exemption to be sanctioned poses a significant challenge. Due to this exemption, criminals can quickly transfer illicit crypto to another wallet within one block before being sanctioned, attempting to launder money. To counteract this, the sanction list oracle should possess a function allowing oracle nodes to preliminarily register addresses as "suspect" at an early stage, thereby necessitating the swift sanctioning of illicit addresses. Incentivizing early reporting is essential to this approach (Fig. 7).

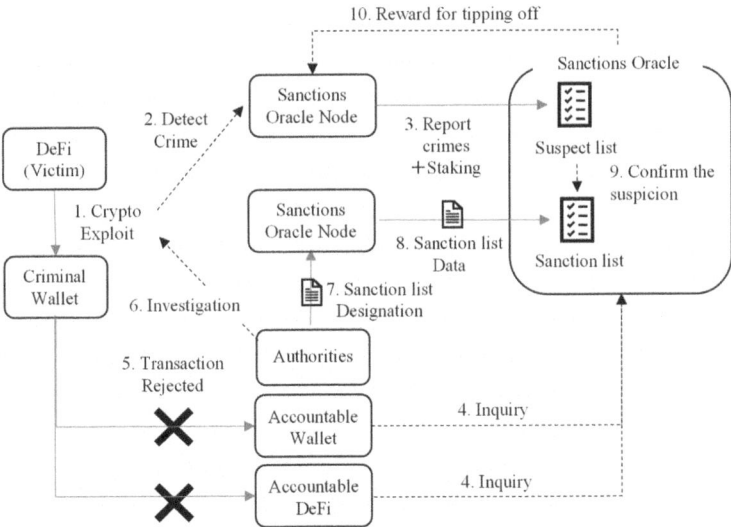

Fig. 7. Suspect designation Flow

Ideally, credential issuers should have binding agreements allowing them to disclose the personal information of credential holders only when escalated from a suspect list to an official sanction list. This process should be governed cryptographically. This protocol enables the disclosure of a wallet administrator's identity in the event of criminal activities, allowing for legitimately sound prosecution based on irrefutable on-chain evidence. This ensures that transactions conducted with wallets holding credentials from such issuers are considered highly trustworthy.

5 Legitimacy of Crypto Asset Provenances

5.1 Approach

To mitigate fraud risk, we must avoid trading with wallets controlled by illicit wallet holders and with wallets that have done illicit conduct, as we illustrated. However, these measures alone are not sufficient. It's also necessary to ascertain whether the counterparty has adhered to these rules. If your prospective counterparty has previously engaged in transactions without following these guidelines, you may unintentionally cooperate in illicit crypto asset laundering.

5.2 Chained Credentials

We propose the 'Chained Credentials,' a credential system that validates the legitimacy of currently held crypto assets. If possessing these credentials proves that a wallet engages only in transactions with other similarly credentialed wallets, the holder can inductively

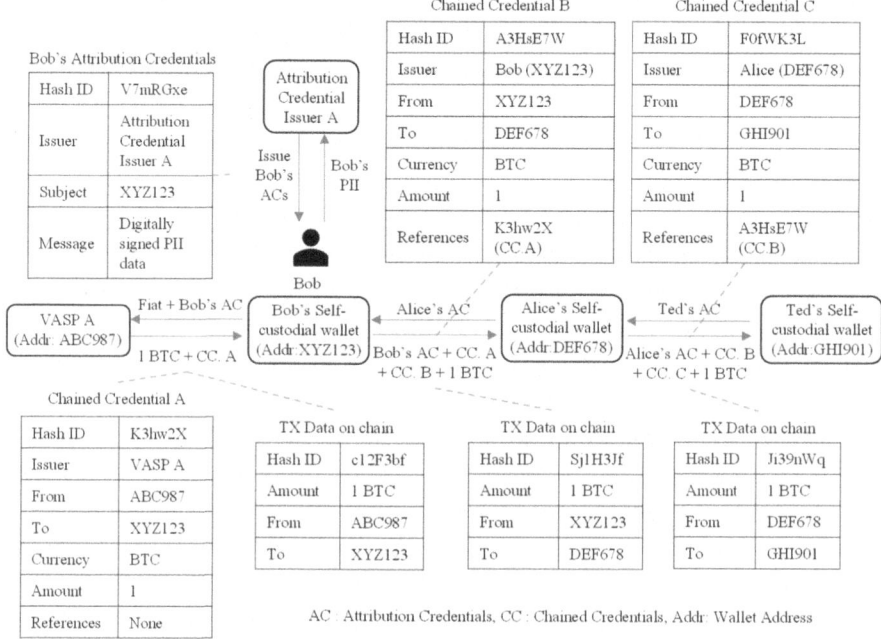

Fig. 8. Data flow image of Chained Credentials

demonstrate that the crypto assets have been transferred legitimately along all transaction routes (Fig. 8). Thus, recipients of crypto assets will no longer need to scrutinize the originator's past transactions on the blockchain. Chained Credentials function akin to blockchains, signifying a trust chain. Newly generated credentials incorporate information from previously referred credentials. If a wallet fails to receive the correct chained credentials in a past transaction, it cannot generate new ones, preventing trade with legitimate investors using those assets. Chained Credentials should be non-transferable independently and can only be passed along with the associated assets. VASPs are expected to have the authority to generate original chained credentials.

5.3 Unintentional Receipt

Since native tokens like Bitcoin and Ether cannot be intercepted, receivers cannot refuse incoming crypto assets. For example, a common phenomenon known as 'dusting' involves the unsolicited airdropping of scam tokens to various addresses. Penalizing receivers for involuntarily receiving illicit crypto assets would be unreasonable. However, discerning the receiver's intentions based solely on on-chain data is challenging. We suggest that wallet applications should detect receipts from non-accountable wallets and take actions like automatic returns. Only if no action is taken should the receiving wallet be sanctioned. The wallet's trust score should be contingent on the proportion of

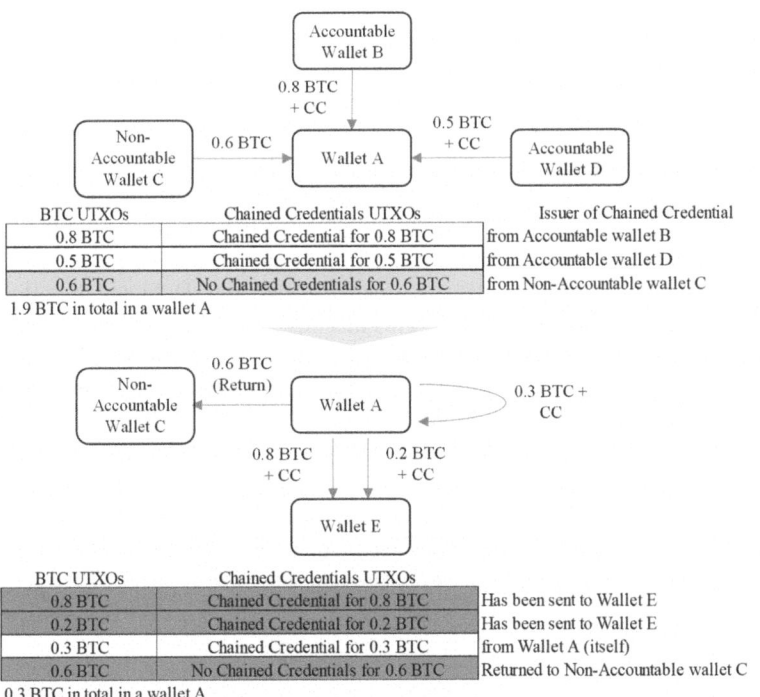

Fig. 9. A wallet where crypto assets are partially accountable

assets received with chained credentials (Fig. 9). Improving this score by taking appropriate actions for assets without credentials is vital; failure to do so risks temporary transaction restrictions with VASPs and other accountable wallets.

A phenomenon known as 'dusting' involves the unsolicited airdropping of scam tokens to various addresses. It is suggested that within the framework of accountable wallet compliance, there should be a provision to exempt these tokens from provenance checks. This adjustment acknowledges the need for practical measures to differentiate between legitimate transactions and superficial activities that could unduly influence compliance assessments.

6 Trust Score

6.1 Wallet Trust Score System

It is essential to establish robust incentives for legitimate investors to use this method and abstain from engaging in transactions with wallets that cannot prove their legitimacy with this method. A strategy is implementing Wallet's Trust Score system. This system equips investors with the capability to estimate a transaction's legitimacy based on proof provided by the counterparty. This scoring system enables informed investment decision-making in the context of transactional legitimacy. This trust scoring system extends to VASPs' custodial wallets as well. In this framework, if a custodial wallet frequently receives crypto assets from wallets with low trust scores, it reduces its trust score. Investors could interpret this erosion as a heightened risk of incurring a sanction from regulatory bodies to the VASP, encompassing penalties or suspension of operations. Such a perception might deter investors from engaging with the VASP, posing a significant threat to the sustainability of the VASP's business. This scenario compels VASPs to be wary of accepting deposits from low-scoring wallets. Conversely, a low trust score of a self-custodial wallet might impede the holder's ability to convert crypto assets into fiat currency through VASPs. Thus, wallet holders are motivated to avoid transactions with non-accountable or low-scoring wallets. The same behavioral model is expected to be formed similarly for DeFi. Trust scores are assigned to DeFi and are affected by interactions with low-trust sore wallets. This incentivizes DeFi platforms to verify self-custodial wallet eligibility before providing services. This system would likely lead to wallets with higher trust scores receiving more favorable transaction conditions, further encouraging investors to maintain high scores.

This paper acknowledges the absence of a definitive formula for calculating the Trust Score in decentralized finance. It presents an example formula rooted in the principle that the Trust Score should reflect the wallet's expected trustworthiness. This methodological framework aims to provide a theoretical basis for practical implementations of Trust Score calculations in the decentralized finance landscape.

6.2 Formula

We define the trust score as the wallet's expected credibility. Legitimacy here is defined in opposition to illegitimacy, which encompasses being controlled by sanctioned individuals or organizations, engaging in illicit activities, or receiving crypto assets from wallets meeting the former criteria. A wallet is deemed illicit if it meets any of these conditions.

Therefore, if an event set that a holder of wallet W is illicit is w_1, an event set that wallet W has ever engaged in illicit activity is w_2 and an event set that a wallet W has ever received crypto assets from those wallets is w_3, since the events of a wallet being legitimate are the complementary events of the union of these events, wallet W's trust score $T(W)$ is expressed as follows.

$$T(W) = P\left(\overline{w_1 \cup w_2 \cup w_3}\right) \tag{1}$$

When any of $P(w_1), P(w_2)$ or $P(w_3)$ is close to 1, $T(W)$ can be approximated as follows.

$$T(W) \cong 1 - Max(P(w_1), P(w_2), P(w_3)) \tag{2}$$

The specific calculation examples for $P(w_1)$, $P(w_2)$ and $P(w_3)$ are proposed in the Appendices. The formula lowers a wallet's trust score if the wallet managed by sanctioned person or involved in fraudulent transactions. Additionally, engaging in transactions with low-trust-score wallets further reduces an investor's own score. This system creates a strong incentive for investors to avoid trading with low-scoring counterparts. Practically, the implementation of this trust score calculation and the establishment of minimum trust score standards for transaction partners would need to be integrated into wallet applications.

7 Conclusion and Future Research

This paper has comprehensively analyzed the distinguishing factors between legitimate and illicit wallets. Implementing the unified wallet reliability evaluation method, the trust score incentivizes investors to avoid transactions with wallets that fail to prove their legitimacy to protect their trust scores, forming an economy where only verifiably legitimate wallets engage with each other. Those unable to prove their legitimacy will be constrained to transact within a separate economy of similarly unverified wallets. Consequently, it is anticipated that the liquidity accessible to illicit wallets in decentralized markets will be considerably less than that for legitimate wallets, substantially diminishing their asset values. This outcome is anticipated to serve as a deterrent against criminal activities, effectively functioning as a punitive measure within the decentralized finance.

Looking ahead, future research tasks entail the selection and integration of various elemental technologies essential for implementing the proposed framework. This includes addressing technical implementation challenges and exploring the economic principles that emerge upon the framework's introduction. We need to assess the method's potential to limit the liquidity of assets in wallets involved in fraudulent transactions, thereby devaluing such illicit assets. Quantifying this effectiveness is vital for providing concrete evidence to regulators and VASPs to support the adoption and recommendation of this method. Additionally, it is crucial to explore how individual investors can benefit financially, such as through preferential trading conditions, by enhancing their trust scores via credential ownership. This multifaceted approach underscores the necessity of comprehensively evaluating the framework's economic and technological dimensions.

A Appendices

A.1 Terminologies

We summarize the terminologies used in this paper in Table 2.

Table 2. Terminologies

Notation	Description
DeFi	An abbreviation for decentralized finance, yet the abbreviation and the original term are used distinctively in this paper. The 'DeFi' refers explicitly to the decentralized financial services, including decentralized vertical asset exchanges and the associated smart contract addresses facilitating these services. Conversely, 'decentralized finance,' in its unabbreviated form, denotes a broader financial ecosystem that uses blockchain technology, delineating it from traditional financial systems
Verifiable Credentials	A digital form of certification or attestation, a concept proposed by the W3C, allows a verifier to prove information about the issuer and holder cryptographically
Soulbound Tokens	Tokens are defined as non-transferable NFTs on the blockchain. Due to this property, it is believed that SBTs can be used as Verifiable Credentials on Blockchain

A.2 Probability of Legitimacy of Wallet Holders

A wallet holder can be trusted with the complementary event that the holder is involved in an illicit person or organization. The primary tool for this assessment is the Decentralized Sanctions Screening Protocol. In this tool, the probability of a wallet holder not being a sanctioned individual increases with the comprehensiveness of their attribution credentials. Consider the probability of a randomly chosen wallet holder being sanctioned as $P(A_{Criminals})$. If a wallet holder can possess a set of attribution credentials A_k, with $n(A_k)$ representing the number of holders with these attribution credentials, the probability of them being trustworthy, $P(w_1)$, can be expressed as follows.

$$P(w_1) = (1 - P(A_{Criminals}))^{n(A_1 \cap A_2 \cap \cdots \cap A_k)} \tag{3}$$

This formula assumes criminals are unlikely to hold incriminating attribution credentials. For instance, no one would be willing to possess attribution credentials proving residency in FATF-sanctioned jurisdictions. When calculating this probability, the independence of each event must be considered. For example, residing in New York is a subset of residing in the U.S., and the latter does not narrow down the candidates.

Let's apply this with an example. Assuming the world population is 8 billion, with 800,000 individuals sanctioned. If the number of people holding attribution credentials A_1 to A_k is estimated at 2, the probability of either being a sanctioned individual is approximately $1 - (1 - 0.0001)^2 \approx 0.02\%$. This probability increases to around $1 - (1 - 0.0001)^{10} \approx 0.18\%$ if only ten people can be narrowed down. It is approximately 1% for 100 people and approximately 9.52% for 1,000 people. This shows that more attribution credentials lead to a higher degree of trust. For instance, if a wallet holder has attribution credentials for their country of residence and date of birth, a rough calculation narrows it down to $8B \times \left(\frac{1}{190}\right) \times \left(\frac{1}{365 \times 80}\right) \approx 1{,}441$ individuals, making the chance of them being sanctioned 13.42%, rendering $P(w_1) = 86.58\%$. For a more precise calculation, the formula can become more complex.

A.3 Probability of Legitimacy of Wallet Conducts

The legitimacy of wallet conducts is contingent upon their association with unlawful endeavors. The primary concern addressed is the indirect financing of sanctioned addresses. Wallets transacting with sanctioned addresses are implicitly implicated in supporting criminal activities. The scenario posits that if an accountable investor, 'the originator,' transfers crypto assets to the non-accountable wallet, which subsequently transacts with a sanctioned address, the originator incurs indirect culpability. While direct legitimate accountability may not be enforceable for non-accountable wallets, the initial transfer of assets to the non-accountable wallet represents a lapse in due diligence. Therefore, the originator is regarded as engaging in these transactions and bears indirect liability for any illicit funds channeled to sanctioned addresses. The impact on the originator $P(w_2)$ is thus determined by the extent of their involvement, direct or indirect, in the flow of crypto assets to sanctioned addresses.

Let's consider a formula to quantify the erosion of trustworthiness in wallets indirectly engaged in illicit activities. Wallet A, depicted in Fig. 10, made an indirect transfer of 0.8 BTC from Wallet B to Wallet C, with an attributable fraction of $0.8 \times \frac{1.3}{2.8} \approx 0.371$ BTC. Before the transaction, Wallet A held 1.5 BTC and transferred 1.3 BTC to Wallet B. Consequently, Wallet A's involvement in the illicit transfer equates to $\frac{0.371}{1.5} \approx 24.7\%$ of its total crypto assets, with the remaining 75.2% constituting Wallet A's Probability of Legitimacy $P(w_2)$.

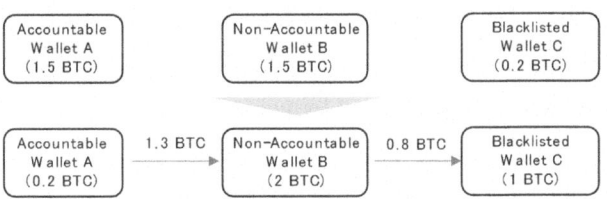

Fig. 10. Indirect illicit transaction

It is pertinent to note the variance in this measure under different initial conditions. For example, if Wallet B initially holds no funds, the trustworthiness of Wallet A would decrease more significantly, calculated as $1 - \frac{0.8 \times 1.3}{1.3} \times \frac{1}{1.5} \approx 46.7\%$. Similarly, if Wallet A directly transfers 0.8 BTC to Wallet C, the decrease in trustworthiness is identical, computed as $1 - \frac{0.8}{1.5} \approx 46.7\%$. This outcome illustrates that transferring crypto assets to an empty wallet, thereby assuming entire liability, is tantamount to direct involvement in the transaction. From these observations, we derive a generalized formula to estimate the wallets' reliability in crypto assets transactions.

$$P(w_2) = \frac{1}{AUM(W_0)} \sum_{k=1}^{n(Blacklisted)} AMT(B_k) \prod_{i=1}^{n(Intermediary)} \frac{AMT(I_i)}{AUM(I_i)} \quad (4)$$

$AUM(W_0)$: The amount of crypto assets the wallet originally had.
$AMT(B_k)$: The amount of crypto assets sent to the sanctioned address.
$AMT(I_i)$: The amount of crypto assets sent by the intermediary address.
$AUM(I_i)$: The amount of crypto assets the intermediary address originally had.

A.4 Probability of Legitimacy of Crypto Asset Provenances

The trustworthiness of currently held crypto assets is calculated as the weighted average of the trust scores of its sources, determined via Chained Credentials. Your trust score diminishes if you receive crypto assets from a sanctioned address or a wallet lacking proper credentials. To restore a reduced trust score, the receiver must either return the crypto assets to the sender or forward them to an authority-designated seizure address.

Let's calculate the Probability of Legitimacy $P(w_3)$ for a wallet receiving crypto assets from various sources with differing levels of trustworthiness, as illustrated in Fig. 11.

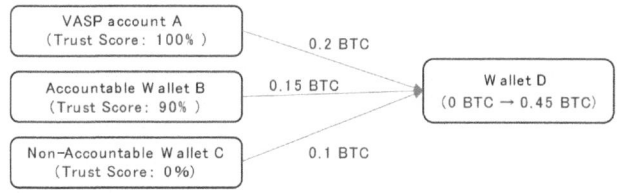

Fig. 11. Inflow of crypto assets with different trust scores

The methodology for estimating the expected trustworthiness of received crypto assets involves calculating the amounts of assets received from each respective wallet multiplied by the sender's trust score. Applying this formula, the Probability of Legitimacy $P(w_3)$ for Wallet D is determined to be $\frac{0.2 \times 100\% + 0.15 \times 90\% + 0.1 \times 0\%}{0.2 + 0.15 + 0.1} \fallingdotseq 74.4\%$. This calculation can be expressed as a general formula as follows.

$$P(w_3) = \frac{\sum_k^n C_k TS_k}{\sum_k^n C_k} \quad (5)$$

C_k : Amount received k-th. TS_k : Trust score of the kth remitter.

Wallet D can either return the crypto assets to wallet C or transfer them to the designated authority's address to restore its trust score. However, from a practical standpoint, likely, Wallet D has already provided some form of monetary value to Wallet C, and forfeiting the funds represents a financial setback for Wallet D. This underscores that Wallet D should have assessed Wallet C's trust score before the. By this mechanism, the proposed model advocates for responsible investment practices, encouraging entities to transact primarily with counterparts that maintain high standards of trustworthiness.

A.5 Trustworthiness of Attribution Credential Issuers

The credibility of a credential hinges on the trustworthiness of its issuer. Thus, the trust level conferred by a credential cannot exceed the trust score of its issuer. One approach to bolster issuer trustworthiness is through a licensing system from authoritative bodies, where the license becomes a credential. However, this might pose implementation challenges. An alternative could involve a feedback system from credential recipients to issuers. When the attribution credential issuer is not 100% trustworthy, the formula for calculating $P(w_1)$ is transformed and defined by the credential issuer i trust score a_i who is the issuer of the credential A_i as follows.

$$P(w_1) = (1 - P(A_{Criminals}))^{n(A_1 \cap A_2 \cap \cdots \cap A_k) + \sum_i^k \frac{1}{a_i}} \tag{6}$$

If a holder possesses credentials verifying the same proof from multiple issuers, the highest trust level among these issuers is used for each a_i.

References

1. Hannan, M.A., Shahriar, M.A., Ferdous, M.S., Chowdhury, M.J.M., Rahman, M.S.: A systematic literature review of blockchain-based e-KYC systems. Computing **105**, 2089–2118 (2023)
2. Buterin, V., Illum, J., Nadler, M., Schär, F., Soleimani, A.: Blockchain Privacy and Regulatory Compliance: Towards a Practical Equilibrium.SSRN (2023)
3. Sun, N., Zhang, Y., Liu, Y.: A privacy-preserving KYC-compliant identity scheme for accounts on all public blockchains. Sustainability **14**, 14584 (2022)
4. Schlatt, V., Sedlmeir, J., Feulner, S., Urbach, N.: Designing a framework for digital KYC processes built on blockchain-based self-sovereign identity. Inf. Manag. 59, 103553 (2021)
5. Malhotra, D., Saini, P., Kumar, A.: Singh how blockchain can automate KYC: systematic review. Wireless Pers. Commun. **122**, 1987–2021 (2021)
6. Rajyashree, U.A., Doulani, S., Pareek, S.: Blockchain-enabled e-KYC system. Int. J. Comput. Vision 137–143 (2019)
7. Khaqqi, K.N., Sikorski, J.J., Hadinoto, K., Kraft, M.: Incorporating seller/buyer reputation-based system in blockchain-enabled emission trading application. Appl. Energy **209**, 8–19 (2018)
8. Pfitzmann, A., Hansen, M.: A terminology for discussing privacy by data minimization: anonymity, unlinkability, undetectability, unobservability, pseudonymity, and identity management. TU Dresden (2010)
9. Beardsley, E.L.: Privacy: autonomy and selective disclosure. Privacy Pers. 56–70 (2017)

10. TRM Labs. Inside North Korea's Crypto Heists: $200M in Crypto Stolen in 2023; Over $2B in the Last Five Years, August 2023. https://www.trmlabs.com/post/inside-north-koreas-crypto-heists. Accessed 21 Aug 2023
11. U.S. Department of the Treasury. Illicit Finance Risk Assessment of Decentralized Finance, April 2023. https://home.treasury.gov/system/files/136/DeFi-Risk-Full-Review.pdf. Accessed 10 Apr 2023
12. Damgård, I., Ganesh, C., Khoshakhlagh, H., Orlandi, C., Siniscalchi, L.: Balancing privacy and accountability in blockchain identity management. In: Paterson, K.G. (eds.) CT-RSA 2021. LNCS, vol. 12704, pp. 552–576. Springer, Cham (2021). https://doi.org/10.1007/978-3-030-75539-3_23
13. Zetzsche, D.A., Buckley, R.P., Arner, D.W., van Ek, M.C.: Remaining regulatory challenges in digital finance and cryptoassets after MiCA. Study Report requested by the ECON Committee. PE 740.083 (2023)
14. Monetary Authority of Singapore, Project Guardian, June, 2023. https://www.mas.gov.sg/-/media/mas-media-library/development/fintech/project-guardian/project-guardian-open-interoperable-network.pdf. Accessed 2 Aug 2023
15. Kakebayashi, M., Beverley, J.: Soulbound Tokens (SBTs) Study Report, Blockchain Governance Initiative Network, BGIN SR 008 (2023)
16. Weyl, E.G., Ohlhaver, P., Buterin, V.: Decentralized Society: Finding Web3's Soul, SSRN (2022)
17. Financial Action Task Force. Targeted Update on Implementation of the FATF Standards on Virtual Assets and Virtual Asset Service Providers, June 2023. https://www.fatf-gafi.org/content/dam/fatf-gafi/guidance/June2023-Targeted-Update-VA-VASP.pdf.coredownload.inline.pdf. Accessed 3 July 2023
18. Bhaskaran, K., et al.: Double-blind consent-driven data sharing on blockchain. In: IEEE International Conference on Cloud Engineering (IC2E), pp. 385–391. IEEE (2018)
19. QUNIE CORPORATION. [Research on understanding the actual situation using on-chain/off-chain data in decentralized financial systems] Bunsangatakinyu System ni okeru On-chain/Off-chain data wo katsuyo shita jittai haaku ni kansuru kenkyu (in Japanese), Japan Financial Services Agency Blockchain International Joint Research Project, June 2023. https://www.fsa.go.jp/policy/bgin/ResearchPaper_qunie2_ja.pdf. Accessed 3 July 2023
20. Heiss, J., Muth, R., Pallas, F., Tai, S.: Non-disclosing credential on-chaining for blockchain-based decentralized applications. In: Troya, J., Medjahed, B., Piattini, M., Yao, L., Fernández, P., Ruiz-Cortés, A. (eds.) ICSOC 2022. LNCS, vol. 13740, pp. 351–368. Springer, Cham (2022). https://doi.org/10.1007/978-3-031-20984-0_25
21. Sundareswaran, N., Sasirekha, S., Paul, I.J.L., Balakrishnan, S., Swaminathan, G.: Optimised KYC blockchain system. In: International Conference on Innovative Trends in Information Technology (ICITIIT), pp. 1–6. IEEE (2020)
22. Bünz, B., et al.: Bulletproofs: short proofs for confidential transactions and more. IEEE Secur. Priv. (2018)
23. Shostack, A.: Threat Modeling: Designing for Security. Wiley, Hoboken (2014)

Reconstitution of NFTs Based on a Game Theory Model

Jiahui Shao[1], Maochao Xu[2], Rui Fang[3], Xiaoxiao Hu[1], Weidong Shi[4], and Dana Alsagheer[4(✉)]

[1] School of Mathematics and Statistics, Lanzhou University, Lanzhou, China
[2] Department of Mathematics, Illinois State University, Normal, USA
mxu2@ilstu.edu
[3] Department of Mathematics, Shantou University, Shantou, China
[4] Department of Computer Science, University Of Houston, Houston, USA
dralsagh@gmail.com

Abstract. Fractional non-fungible tokens (NFTs) represent a transformative innovation within the NFT landscape, potentially reshaping the foundational architecture of NFTs and unlocking novel opportunities for investors. Despite the promise of this innovation, a considerable challenge arises in the context of NFT ownership. This study introduces an innovative Bayesian Stackelberg game model designed to reconstitute NFTs. A penalty mechanism is also introduced to encourage the reconstitution. We establish the existence of a distinctive Stackelberg equilibrium, providing explicit solutions for computing equilibrium prices. To illustrate the application of our model, we present numerical examples to offer practical insights into its implementation.

Keywords: Discount factors · Fractional NFTs · leave-one-out strategy · Private information

1 Introduction and Motivation

Non-fungible tokens (NFTs) are cryptographic tokens that uniquely represent non-fungible assets, whether digital or real-world [7]. NFTs serve as unequivocal proof of authenticity and ownership within blockchain networks. The NFT market has witnessed explosive growth in recent years due to its distinctive attributes and potential for substantial investment gains. According to Statista[1], NFT market revenue is projected to reach $1,601 million in 2023, with an expected annual growth rate of 18.55% by 2027. Additionally, the average revenue per user in the NFT market is anticipated to be $114.80 in 2023. OpenSea, the largest NFT marketplace, boasts over 250,000 monthly active users, according to Metav.RS[2]. Highly valuable NFTs have garnered considerable attention, with examples like "The First 5000 Days" selling for $69.3 million in February 2021

---

[1] https://www.statista.com/outlook/dmo/fintech/digital-assets/nft.
[2] https://metav.rs/blog/nft-market-statistics-2021-2023/.

and "The Clock" fetching $52.7 million in February 2022[3]. However, liquidity concerns have arisen around such costly NFTs, leading to the innovative concept of fractional NFTs, which has the potential to redefine the core structure of non-fungible tokens and open doors for investors. A fractional NFT represents a whole NFT divided into smaller units, enabling multiple investors to hold partial ownership of a high-value NFT. Smart contracts can be employed to issue several ERC-20 tokens associated with an indivisible ERC-721 NFT. The original NFT is securely stored in a vault, while a limited supply of fungible tokens is issued to represent ownership of that NFT. These fungible tokens are accessible on fractional NFT platforms like *fractional.art* and *Unic.ly* and can also be traded on secondary markets such as *Uniswap*. For example, the NFT "The Merge" was auctioned for $91.8 million on the Nifty Gateway marketplace in December 2021. It was divided into 312,686 pieces and distributed among 28,983 investors.

While fractional NFTs offer a solution to the liquidity challenge posed by high-value NFTs, they introduce various risks related to ownership, regulation, and security [1]. Among these challenges, the most significant one faced by fractional NFTs is reconstitution. Coordinating the agreement and consent of multiple fractional owners can be a substantial hurdle. Unfortunately, research on reconstitution remains scarce in the literature, and solutions are still emerging. One notable contribution is by Chen et al. [3], where they propose a reconstitution protocol for participants who own a portion of an NFT to acquire complete ownership. Their protocol triggers the reconstitution process when a participant holds more than half of the fractional NFT units. To achieve reconstitution, all fractions of an NFT must be acquired, and the participant is required to sell all fractions if the reconstitution attempt fails. Several works in fractional NFTs have explored practical implementations and economic aspects without employing formal mathematical modeling techniques. For instance, Choi et al. [4] delve into implementing fractional NFTs, specifically evaluating their associated gas costs. The authors propose adopting ERC standards to implement fractional NFTs, emphasizing their potential for minimizing long-term gas expenses. In a complementary vein, Makori [6] provides insights into the concepts surrounding fractional NFTs, explores various purchase platforms, and addresses challenges associated with the reconstitution of fractional NFTs. Furthermore, Ko et al. [5] contribute to the economic discourse surrounding fractional NFTs, investigating their value proposition. Their findings suggest that investors can enhance the diversification of traditional asset-based portfolios by incorporating fractional NFTs into their investment baskets.

In this study, we introduce a novel model for the reconstitution of NFT ownership, presenting a distinctive approach in the literature by formulating the process as a Bayesian Stackelberg game [9]. Unlike existing works, our proposed model allows a participant who possesses at least half of the fractional NFTs to initiate the reconstitution procedure without necessitating the sale of all fractions in the event of reconstitution failure. This departure from the conventional

---

[3] https://www.coingecko.com/research/publications/10-most-expensive-nfts-ever-sold.

requirement of acquiring all fractional NFTs for reconstitution [3] introduces a trading model. Our model facilitates reconstitution with a minimum of k fractions from a total of M fractions, engaging at least q sellers, thus providing a motivational framework for owners to consider selling their shares. Furthermore, our model embraces the privacy of individual evaluations of fractional NFTs as private information, introducing an element of randomness to the bidding process. These key features collectively distinguish our proposed model, marking a significant departure from existing approaches in the domain of NFT ownership reconstitution.

The rest of the paper is organized as follows. Section 2 introduces the proposed model. Section 3 presents a detailed discussion of the game model with three players. Section 4 extends the model to include multiple players. The last section concludes the current work and presents some discussion.

2 Model Description

Assume a whole NFT is divided into M fractional NFTs, and owned by $n+1$ participants, namely, $S = \{S_0, \cdots, S_n\}$. Suppose that the ith participant S_i owns m_i fractional NFTs, and $\sum_{i=0}^{n} m_i = M$.

The reconstitution of the ownership can be triggered by only one participant who must own at least half of fractional NFTs. Without loss of generality, assume S_0 is the buyer who owns $m_0 \geq M/2$ pieces and send the bid price s_0 to the smart contract. The rest of the participants acting as sellers send their bids $(s_1, \ldots, s_n)$ to the smart contract. The purchase price is set at the average of the buyer's and seller's prices, which strikes a balance that ensures fairness and discourages any party from wielding excessive influence. For example, if the buyer successfully acquires the fractions from the seller S_i, the deal price for each unit is $(s_0 + s_i)/2$. To avoid malicious bidders, a predetermined range of deal prices can be set in the smart contract, namely, $[c, a]$. After the buyer acquires at least k fractions from at least q sellers, the buyer becomes the owner of the whole NFT. However, to be fair to other participants who do not sell their shares, the rest of the fractions are sold to the buyer by the smart contract at a discounted price. For instance, if participant S_j has the bid price s_j but fails to sell the shares, then S_j will be paid at a price $(r * s_j + s_0)/2$, where r is the discount factor.

We formulate the reconstitution as a Bayesian Stackelberg game, described as follows.

- *Players.* The players in our game are $\{S_0, \ldots, S_n\}$, where S_0 is the buyer and the other players are sellers. $\{S_1, \ldots, S_n\}$ acts as the leader, and S_0 acts as the follower.
- *Actions.* The sellers send their bids to the smart contract. The buyer who owns at least half of fractional NFTs determines whether to purchase shares and from which sellers. Note that the buyer needs to purchase all the shares from a single seller if the purchase decision is made. Similarly, a seller is required to sell all the shares.

Table 1. Summary of main notations.

S	Player set $S = \{S_0, \cdots, S_n\}$
M	Total number of fractional NFT
m_i	Number of fractional NFTs owned by each player S_i, $\sum_{i=0}^{n} m_i = M$
k	Minimum number of fractions to reconstitute the ownership
s_i	Bid provided by $S_i, i = 0, \cdots, n$, $s_i \sim U[c, a]$
v_i	$S_i's$ value estimate for each fractional NFT, $v_i \sim U[c, a]$
r	Discount factor for price
r_0	S_0's evaluation discount factor
q	Minimum number of sellers required to reconstitute the NFT
l	Total number of reconstitution strategies
A_j^q	The jth strategy-making method includes a set of at least q players
$\mathcal{A}_q$	The set of all strategies $\mathcal{A}_q = \{A_1, A_2, \ldots, A_l\}$

- *Private information.* Assume v_i is the S_i's value estimate for one unit of fractional NFTs, which is private information, only available to S_i. This is simply because different people have different valuations of fractional NFTs. We assume that v_i independently follows a uniform distribution $[c, a]$, and the bid s_i also independently follows the uniform distribution $[c, a]$, $i = 0, 1, \ldots, n$. We assume the bids s_is are only available to the buyer S_0.
- *Public information.* The information of shares $(m_0, \ldots, m_n)$ is recorded on the blockchain and public to all the players. The discount factor r and reconstitution number k are also public. After acquiring the ownership, we assume S_0's evaluation v_0 is discounted with a factor r_0.

Table 1 summarizes the main notations used in this paper.

3 Reconstitution Stackelberg Game with Three Players

In this section, we study the reconstitution of three players in the game. Specifically, assume that S_0 owns more than half of fractional NFTs and launches the reconstitution procedure with the other two players $S_i, i = 1, 2$. To explore the optimal bidding strategy for players, we model the reconstitution process as a two-stage game:

- *Stage I.* S_1 and S_2 act as the leader to send their bids s_1 and s_2 to the smart contract.
- *Stage II.* S_0 acts as the follower and decides the optimal strategy. The strategy set is $A_{S_0} \in \{NB, BS_1, BS_2, BA\}$, where NB represents S_0 does not purchase any fractional NFTs, BS_i represents S_0 purchases fractional NFTs from S_i, $i = 1, 2$, and BA presents S_0 purchases all the fractional NFTs from all the sellers.

We study several scenarios based on the number of shares. Without loss of generality, we assume $m_1 > m_2$ in the subsequent discussion, and the case of $m_1 \leq m_2$ can be similarly discussed.

3.1 Scenario 1: $m_0 + m_1 \geq k$ and $m_0 + m_2 \geq k$

In this scenario, the utility functions of S_0 in terms of payoffs in different strategies are

$$U_{S_0}(BS_1) = \left(v_0 - \frac{s_0 + s_1}{2}\right) m_1 - \left(\frac{s_0 + rs_2}{2} - r_0 v_0\right) m_2,$$

$$U_{S_0}(BS_2) = \left(v_0 - \frac{s_0 + s_2}{2}\right) m_2 - \left(\frac{s_0 + rs_1}{2} - r_0 v_0\right) m_1,$$

and $U_{S_0}(NB) = 0$, where $0 < r < 1$ is the discount factor of v_0 after becoming the owner of the NFT. Note that after acquiring shares from one of the players (e.g., S_1), S_0's evaluation v_0 can undergo a change, and therefore, we introduce a discount factor r_0. This scenario essentially constitutes a multiple-leader Stackelberg game [2]. To streamline the analysis for practical implementation, we convert this problem into a single-leader game by determining the maximum expected utility. Assume that BS_t can lead to the maximum expected utility, then we have

$$t = \arg\max E\left(U_{S_0}(BS_i(s_0, S_i))\right), i = 1, 2,$$

where

$$E\left(U_{S_0}(BS_1(s_0, S_1))\right) = \frac{-(a+c)(m_1 + m_2 r) - 2(m_1 + m_2)s_0 + 4(m_1 + m_2 r_0)v_0}{4}, \quad (1)$$

$$E\left(U_{S_0}(BS_2(s_0, S_2))\right) = \frac{-(a+c)(m_2 + m_1 r) - 2(m_1 + m_2)s_0 + 4(m_2 + m_1 r_0)v_0}{4}. \quad (2)$$

Given bids s_1, s_2 provided by S_1 and S_2, S_0 decides the optimal strategy $A^*_{S_0}(v_0, s_1, s_2)$ to maximize the utility.

Lemma 3.1. *In the two-stage Stackelberg reconstitution game, if BS_t leads to the maximum expected utility, the optimal strategy of S_0 given bids s_1 and s_2 is*

$$A^*_{S_0}(v_0, s_1^*, s_2^*) = \begin{cases} BS_t, & \text{if } v_0 > c_t, \\ NB, & o/w, \end{cases} \quad (3)$$

where c_1, c_2 are defined in Eqs. (4), (5), respectively.

Proof. For S_0, the utility should be positive if the purchase decision is made. Therefore, we have $U_{S_0}(BS_1) > 0$, i.e.,

$$v_0 > \frac{s_0(m_1 + m_2) + s_1 m_1 + rs_2 m_2}{2(m_1 + r_0 m_2)} = c_1, \quad (4)$$

and also $U_{S_0}(BS_2) > 0$ implies

$$v_0 > \frac{s_0(m_1 + m_2) + s_2 m_2 + rs_1 m_1}{2(m_2 + r_0 m_1)} = c_2. \quad (5)$$

The required result follows. □

Now, let us discuss the optimal strategies for S_1 and S_2, given the optimal strategy of S_0. The detailed proof can be found in the Appendix.

Lemma 3.2. *In the two-stage Stackelberg game for the reconstitution process, given the optimal strategy of S_0, the optimal bidding strategy for S_1 and S_2 is*

$$s_i^* = \begin{cases} \tilde{s}_i, & \text{if } c \leq \tilde{s}_i \leq a, \\ a, & \text{if } \tilde{s}_i > a, \\ c, & \text{if } \tilde{s}_i < c, \end{cases}$$

where $\tilde{s}_1$ is defined in Eq. (21) for $t = 1$, and defined in Eq. (27) for $t = 2$, respectively; $\tilde{s}_2$ is defined in Eq. (23) for $t = 1$, and defined in Eq. (29) for $t = 2$, respectively.

In the following, we present an example for illustration.

Example 3.3. Assuming the presence of three participants, denoted as S_0, S_1, and S_2, with individual valuations for fractional NFTs per unit represented as $(v_0, v_1, v_2) = (187, 140, 130)$, it is noteworthy that the valuation information is treated as private and follows a uniform distribution over the interval $[120, 200]$. The aggregate count of fractional NFTs stands at 100, with S_0 holding $m_0 = 70$ fractions, S_1 possessing $m_1 = 17$, and S_2 having $m_2 = 13$ fractions. The smart contract's policy dictates that ownership acquisition necessitates obtaining at least $k = 80$ fractions. Additionally, post-ownership acquisition, S_0 employs a discount factor of $r_0 = 0.55$, while a discount factor of $r = 0.8$ is applied to the selling price after the reconstitution.

For S_0, the expected utilities of purchasing different strategies when $s_0 = 187$ are

$$\begin{cases} E\left(U_{S_0}(BS_1)\right) = 224.05, \\ E\left(U_{S_0}(BS_2)\right) = -48.55. \end{cases}$$

The strategy corresponding to the maximum expected utility of S_0 is

$$A_{S_0} = BS_1.$$

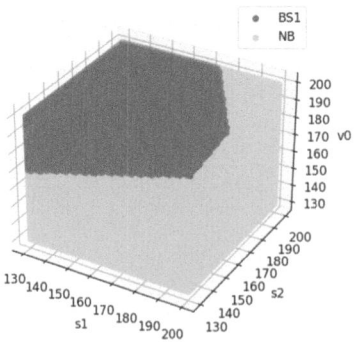

Fig. 1. The strategy of S_0.

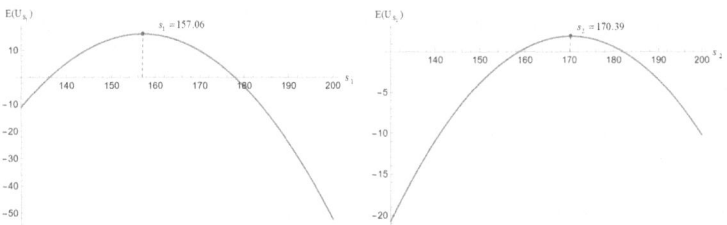

(a) Expected utility function of S_1. (b) Expected utility function of S_2

Fig. 2. Expected utility functions with optimal bids.

According to Eq. (3), $A_{S_0}(v_0, s_1, s_2)$ is a function related to v_0, s_1 and s_2. Figure 1 shows the strategies made by S_0 under different values. The gray area indicates the purchase of S_1, and the blue area indicates no purchase.

For S_1, Fig. 2a shows the expected utility of S_1 as a function of s_1, and we observe that when the expected utility is maximized, the optimal bid of S_1 based on Eq. (21) is

$$s_1^* = 157.06.$$

For S_2, Fig. 2b shows the expected utility of S_2 as a function of s_2, and it is seen that when the expected utility is maximized, the optimal bid for S_2 based on Eq. (23) is

$$s_2^* = 170.385.$$

Given the optimal bids of S_i, according to Eq. (4), we have $c_1 = 177.018$ and $v_0 > c_1$, therefore, S_0 makes the purchase decision which leads to

$$U_{S_0}(BS_1) = 243.67.$$

3.2 Scenario 2: $m_0 + m_1 \geq k$ and $m_0 + m_2 < k$

In this scenario, the strategies for S_0 are only BS_1 and NB, as the other strategies have fewer utility values which are easy to verify. Given bids s_1, s_2 provided by S_1 and S_2, S_0 decides the optimal strategy $A_{S_0}^*(v_0, s_1, s_2)$ to maximize the utility. We have the following lemma.

Lemma 3.4. *In the two-stage Stackelberg reconstitution game, the optimal strategy of S_0 given bids s_1 and s_2 is*

$$A_{S_0}^*(v_0, s_1^*, s_2^*) = \begin{cases} BS_1, & \text{if } v_0 > c_1, \\ NB, & o/w, \end{cases} \quad (6)$$

where c_1 is given in Eq. (4).

Now, let us discuss the optimal strategies for S_1 and S_2, given the optimal strategy of S_0.

Lemma 3.5. *In the two-stage Stackelberg game for the reconstitution process, given the optimal strategy of S_0, the optimal bidding strategy for S_1 and S_2 is*

$$s_i^* = \begin{cases} \tilde{s}_i, & \text{if } c \leq \tilde{s}_i \leq a, \\ a, & \text{if } \tilde{s}_i > a, \\ c, & \text{if } \tilde{s}_i < c, \end{cases}$$

where $\tilde{s}_1, \tilde{s}_2$ are defined in Eqs. (21) and (23), respectively.

In the following, we present an example for illustration.

Example 3.6. Assuming the presence of three participants, denoted as S_0, S_1, and S_2, with individual valuations for fractional NFTs per unit represented as $(v_0, v_1, v_2) = (195, 134, 132)$, it is noteworthy that the valuation information is treated as private and follows a uniform distribution over the interval $[130, 200]$. The aggregate count of fractional NFTs stands at 100, with S_0 holding $m_0 = 70$ fractions, S_1 possessing $m_1 = 18$, and S_2 having $m_2 = 12$ fractions. The smart contract's policy dictates that ownership acquisition necessitates obtaining at least $k = 85$ fractions. Additionally, post-ownership acquisition, S_0 employs a discount factor of $r_0 = 0.75$, while a discount factor of $r = 0.85$ is applied to the selling price after the reconstitution.

According to Eq. (7), $A_{S_0}(v_0, s_1, s_2)$ is a function related to v_0, s_1 and s_2. Figure 3 shows the strategies made by S_0 under different values. The gray area indicates the purchase of S_1, and the blue area indicates no purchase.

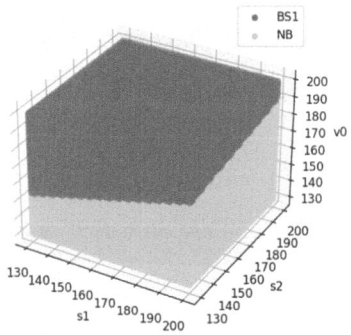

Fig. 3. The strategy of S_0

For S_1, Fig. 4a shows the expected utility of S_1 as a function of s_1, and we observe that when the expected utility is maximized, the optimal bid of S_1 based on Eq. (21) is

$$s_1^* = 167.25.$$

For S_2, Fig. 4b shows the expected utility of S_2 as a function of s_2. It is seen that when the expected utility is maximized, the optimal bid for S_2 based on Eq. (23) is

$$s_2^* = 199.41.$$

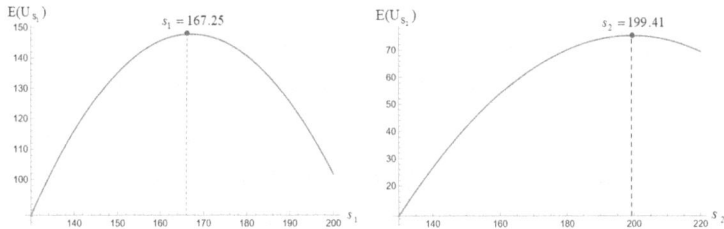

(a) Expected utility function of S_1. (b) Expected utility function of S_2.

Fig. 4. Expected utility functions with optimal bids.

For S_0, according to Eq. (4), we have $c_1 = 178.97$ when $s_0 = 154$, since $v_0 = 195 > c_1$, therefore, S_0 makes the purchase decision which leads to

$$U_{S_0}(BS_1) = 672.51.$$

Scenario 3: $m_0 + m_1 < k$ and $m_0 + m_2 \geq k$. In this scenario, the strategies for S_0 are only BS_2 and NB. We have the following similar results.

Lemma 3.7. *In the two-stage Stackelberg reconstitution game, the optimal strategy of S_0 given bids s_1 and s_2 is*

$$A^*_{S_0}(v_0, s_1^*, s_2^*) = \begin{cases} BS_2, \text{ if } v_0 > c_2, \\ NB, \text{ o/w}, \end{cases} \quad (7)$$

where c_2 is given in Eq. (5).

Lemma 3.8. *In the two-stage Stackelberg game for the reconstitution process, given the optimal strategy of S_0, the optimal bidding strategy for S_1 and S_2 is*

$$s_i^* = \begin{cases} \tilde{s}_i, \text{ if } c \leq \tilde{s}_i \leq a, \\ a, \text{ if } \tilde{s}_i > a, \\ c, \text{ if } \tilde{s}_i < c, \end{cases}$$

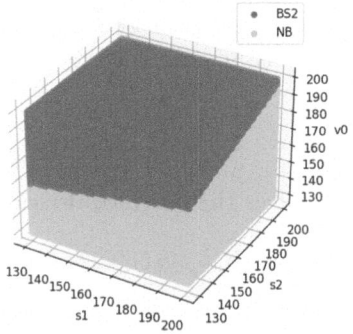

Fig. 5. The strategy of S_0.

where $\tilde{s}_1$, $\tilde{s}_2$ are defined in Eqs. (27) and (29), respectively.

Example 3.9. Assuming the presence of three participants, denoted as S_0, S_1, and S_2, with individual valuations for fractional NFTs per unit represented as $(v_0, v_1, v_2) = (197, 147, 132)$, it is noteworthy that the valuation information is treated as private and follows a uniform distribution over the interval $[130, 200]$. The aggregate count of fractional NFTs stands at 100, with S_0 holding $m_0 = 70$ fractions, S_1 possessing $m_1 = 12$, and S_2 having $m_2 = 18$ fractions. The smart contract's policy dictates that ownership acquisition necessitates obtaining at least $k = 85$ fractions. Additionally, post-ownership acquisition, S_0 employs a discount factor of $r_0 = 0.7$, while a discount factor of $r = 0.9$ is applied to the selling price after the reconstitution.

According to Eq. (7), $A_{S_0}(v_0, s_1, s_2)$ is a function related to v_0, s_1 and s_2. Figure 5 shows the strategies made by S_0 under different values. The gray area indicates the purchase of S_2, and the blue area indicates no purchase.

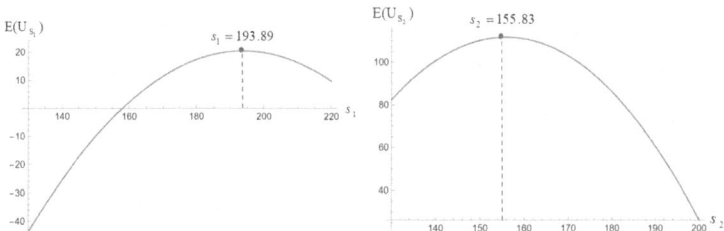

(a) Expected utility function of S_1. (b) Expected utility function of S_1

Fig. 6. Expected utility functions with optimal bids.

For S_1, Fig. 6a shows the expected utility of S_1 as a function of s_1, and we observe that when the expected utility is maximized, the optimal bid of S_1 based on Eq. (27) is
$$s_1^* = 193.89.$$

For S_2, Fig. 6b shows the expected utility of S_2 as a function of s_2. It is seen that when the expected utility is maximized, the optimal bid for S_2 based on Eq. (29) is
$$s_2^* = 155.83.$$

For S_0, according to Eq. (5), we have $c_2 = 180.28$ when $s_0 = 154$, since $v_0 = 197 > c_2$, therefore, S_0 makes the purchase decision which leads to
$$U_{S_0}(BS_2) = 509.22.$$

Scenario 4: $m_0 + m_1 < k$ and $m_0 + m_2 < k$. In this case, the buyer can only reconstitute the ownership of the NFT via purchasing all the fractional NFTs. The utility function of S_0 the strategy of BA is

$$U_{S_0}(BA) = \left(v_0 - \frac{s_0 + s_1}{2}\right)m_1 + \left(v_0 - \frac{s_0 + s_2}{2}\right)m_2.$$

Given the bid s_1, s_2 provided by S_1 and S_2, S_0 decides the optimal strategy $A^*_{S_0}(v_0, s_1, s_2)$ to maximize the utility.

Lemma 3.10. *In the two-stage Stackelberg reconstitution game, the optimal strategy of S_0 given bids s_1 and s_2 is*

$$A^*_{S_0}(v_0, s^*_1, s^*_2) = \begin{cases} BA, & \text{if } v_0 > c_3, \\ NB, & o/w, \end{cases} \quad (8)$$

where c_3 is defined in Eq. (9)

Proof. For S_0, the utility should be positive if the purchase decision is made. Therefore, we have $U_{S_0}(BA) > 0$, i.e.,

$$v_0 > \frac{s_0(m_1 + m_2) + s_1 m_1 + s_2 m_2}{2(m_1 + m_2)} = c_3. \quad (9)$$

The required result follows. □

Now, let us discuss the optimal strategies for S_1 and S_2, given the optimal strategy of S_0.

Lemma 3.11. *In the two-stage Stackelberg game for the reconstitution process, given the optimal strategy of S_0, the optimal bidding strategy for S_1 and S_2 is*

$$s^*_i = \begin{cases} \tilde{s}_i, & \text{if } c \leq \tilde{s}_i \leq a, \\ a, & \text{if } \tilde{s}_i > a, \\ c, & \text{if } \tilde{s}_i < c, \end{cases}$$

where $\tilde{s}_1, \tilde{s}_2$ are defined in Eqs. (11) and (13), respectively.

Proof. Under the optimal strategy of S_0, the utility functions of S_i, $i = 1, 2$, in terms of payoff is

$$U_{S_i}(v_i, A_{S_0}(v_0, s_1, s_2), s_i) = \begin{cases} \left(\frac{s_0 + s_i}{2} - v_i\right)m_i, & \text{if } v_0 > c_3, \\ 0, & o/w. \end{cases} \quad (10)$$

For S_1, the expected utility function is

$$E[U_{S_1}(v_1, A_{S_0}, s_1)] = \int_c^a \int_c^a \int_c^a U_{S_1}(v_1, A_{S_0}, s_1) F(v_0) F(s_0) F(s_2)$$

$$= \int_c^a \int_c^a \int_{c_3}^a \left(\frac{s_0 + s_1}{2} - v_1\right) m_1 F(v_0) F(s_0) F(s_2)$$

$$= \frac{m_1^2 * h_9 + m_1 m_2 * h_{10}}{48(a - c)(m_1 + m_2)},$$

where
$$h_9 = 4[2a^2 - c^2 + a(2c + 3s_1 - 9v_1) - 3s_1(s_1 - 2v_1) - 3c(s_1 - v_1)],$$
$$h_{10} = (a - c)[5a + 7c + 12(s_1 - 2v_1)].$$

Taking the first order and setting it equal to 0
$$\frac{\partial E\left[U_{S_1}(v_1, A_{S_0}, s_1)\right]}{\partial s_1} = 0,$$
leads to the following solution
$$\tilde{s}_1 = \frac{(a-c)(m_1 + m_2)}{2m_1} + v_1. \tag{11}$$

The second derivative of $E\left[U_{S_1}(v_1, A_{S_0}, s_1)\right]$ has the following form, i.e.,
$$\frac{\partial^2 E\left[U_{S_1}(v_1, A_{S_0}, s_1)\right]}{\partial s_1^2} = -\frac{m_1^2}{2(a-c)(m_1 + m_2)}, \tag{12}$$
which is negative.

For S_2, the expected utility functions is
$$E\left[U_{S_2}(v_2, A_{S_0}, s_2)\right] = \int_c^a \int_c^a \int_c^a U_{S_2}(v_2, A_{S_0}, s_2) F(v_0)F(s_0)F(s_1)$$
$$= \int_c^a \int_c^a \int_{c_3}^a \left(\frac{s_0 + s_2}{2} - v_2\right) m_2 F(v_0)F(s_0)F(s_1)$$
$$= \frac{m_1 m_2 * h_{11} + m_2^2 * h_{12}}{48(a-c)(m_1 + m_2)},$$
where
$$h_{11} = (a-c)[5a + 7c + 12(s_2 - 2v_2)],$$
$$h_{12} = 4[2a^2 - c^2 + a(2c + 3s_2 - 9v_2) - 3(s_2 + c)(s_2 - 2v_2)].$$

We take the first derivative and set it equal to 0
$$\frac{\partial E\left[U_{S_2}(v_2, A_{S_0}, s_2)\right]}{\partial s_2} = 0,$$
leads to the following solution
$$\tilde{s}_2 = \frac{(a-c)(m_1 + m_2)}{2m_2} + v_2. \tag{13}$$

The second derivative takes the following form
$$\frac{\partial^2 E\left[U_{S_2}(v_2, A_{S_0}, s_2)\right]}{\partial s_2^2} = -\frac{m_2^2}{2(a-c)(m_1 + m_2)},$$
which is negative. □

Combining the aforementioned analysis, we have the following result.

Theorem 3.12. *Under the three-player reconstitution Stackelberg game, there exists a unique Stackelberg equilibrium.*

4 Reconstitution Stackelberg Game with n Players

Within the framework of the n-player reconstitution Stackelberg game, we posit the requirement that the buyer must acquire ownership of at least k fractions from a minimum of q sellers, where $1 \leq q \leq n$, to reconstruct complete ownership effectively. Our consideration encompasses l reconstitution strategies, denoted as A_j^q, each strategy j involving the participation of at least q sellers within the game, with j spanning from 1 to l. The comprehensive set of all strategies is denoted by $\mathcal{A}_q$, articulated as $\mathcal{A}_q = \{A_1^q, A_2^q, \ldots, A_l^q\}$. When $q = n - 1$, it is named as the *leave-one-out* strategy, signifying that S_0 has the flexibility to refrain from purchasing from a single seller-an approach readily adaptable in practical scenarios.

Note that S_0 can use the strategy of A_j^q to reconstitute the ownership of the NFT (denoted by BA_j^q), and the utility function of S_0 in terms of payoff can be represented as, $j = 1, \ldots, l$,

$$U_{S_0}\left(BA_j^q(s_0, S_1, \ldots, S_n)\right)$$
$$= \sum_{s_e \in A_j^q}\left(v_0 - \frac{s_0 + s_e}{2}\right)m_e - \sum_{s_f \in (A_j^q)^c}\left(\frac{s_0 + rs_f}{2} - r_0 v_0\right)m_f, \quad (14)$$

and $U_{S_0}(NB) = 0$, where $s_f \in (A_j^q)^c$ represents that seller S_f's fractions of NFTs are sold at a discount price executed automatically by the smart contract. In practice, it is necessary to know which A_j^q can lead to the maximum utility. Assume that A_t^q can lead to the maximum expected utility, then we have

$$t = \arg\max_{1 \leq j \leq n} E\left(U_{S_0}\left(BA_j^q(s_0, S_1, \ldots, S_n)\right)\right),$$

where

$$E\left(U_{S_0}\left(BA_j^q(s_0, S_1, \ldots, S_n)\right)\right)$$
$$= \sum_{S_e \in A_j^q}\left(v_0 - \frac{s_0 + E(S_e)}{2}\right)m_e - \sum_{s_f \in (A_j^q)^c}\left(\frac{s_0 + rE(S_f)}{2} - r_0 v_0\right)m_f$$
$$= \left(v_0 - \frac{a+c}{4}\right)\sum_{s_e \in A_j^q} m_e + \left(v_0 r_0 - \frac{(a+c)r}{4}\right)\sum_{s_f \in (A_j^q)^c} m_f$$
$$- \frac{1}{2}s_0(M - m_0). \quad (15)$$

Now, given bids $s_e \in A_t^q$ and $s_f \in (A_t^q)^c$, we decide the optimal strategy given, $A_{S_0}^*(v_0, s_1, \ldots, s_n)$ to maximize the utility.

Lemma 4.1. *In the two-stage Stackelberg reconstitution game, if BA_t^q leads to the maximum expected utility of Eq. (15), the optimal strategy of S_0 given bids s_i, $i = 1, \ldots, n$, is*

$$A_{S_0}^*(v_0, s_1^*, \cdots, s_n^*) = \begin{cases} BA_t^q, & \text{if } v_0 > c_4, \\ NB, & o/w, \end{cases} \quad (16)$$

where c_4 is defined in Eq. (17).

326   J. Shao et al.

Proof. If the purchase decision is made, the maximum utility should be positive. Therefore, we have $U_{S_0}(BA_t^q) > 0$, i.e.,

$$v_0 > \frac{s_0(M - m_0) + \sum_{s_a \in A_t^q} m_a s_a + r \sum_{s_b \in (A_t^q)^c} m_b s_b}{h_{13}} = c_4, \quad (17)$$

where

$$h_{13} = 2\left(\sum_{s_e \in A_t^q} m_e + r_0 \sum_{s_f \in (A_t^q)^c} m_f\right). \quad (18)$$

The required result follows. □

Now, let us discuss the optimal strategies for S_i, $i = 1, \cdots, n$, given the optimal strategy of S_0. The detailed proof can be found in the Appendix.

Lemma 4.2. *In the two-stage Stackelberg game for the reconstitution process, given the optimal strategy of S_0, the optimal bidding strategy for $S_1, \cdots, S_n$ is*

$$s_i^* = \begin{cases} \tilde{s}_i, & \text{if } c \leq \tilde{s}_i \leq a, \\ a, & \text{if } \tilde{s}_i > a, \\ c, & \text{if } \tilde{s}_i < c, \end{cases}$$

where $\tilde{s}_e$, $\tilde{s}_f$ are defined in Eqs. (33) and (35), respectively.

Based on the above analysis, we have the following result.

Theorem 4.3. *Under the n-player reconstitution Stackelberg game, a unique Stackelberg equilibrium exists.*

In the following, we present an example for illustration.

Example 4.4. Assuming the presence of 5 participants, the buyer S_0 and sellers $S = (S_1, \cdots, S_4)$, the buyer needs to obtain NFT ownership from a minimum of 3 individuals, i.e., $q = 3$. This is the leave-one-out scenario. And the individual valuations for fractional NFTs per unit are represented as

$$(v_0, v_1, v_2, v_3, v_4) = (187, 140, 141, 143, 140),$$

the valuations follow a uniform distribution on $[a, c] = [140, 190]$. The fraction owned by a participant is denoted by

$$(m_0, m_1, m_2, m_3, m_4) = (76, 8, 6, 4, 6).$$

The smart contract's policy dictates that ownership acquisition necessitates obtaining at least $k = 96$ fractions. Additionally, post-ownership acquisition, S_0 employs a discount factor of $r_0 = 0.55$, while a discount factor of $r = 0.6$ is applied to the selling price after the reconstitution.

Note that the set of all strategies is

$$\mathcal{A}_3 = \{A_1^3, A_2^3, A_3^3, A_4^3\},$$

where $A_j^3 = \boldsymbol{S}/S_j$, $j = 1, \ldots, 4$.

For $\check{S}_0$, the expected utilities of purchasing different strategies when $s_0 = 160$ are

$$\begin{cases} E\left[U_{S_0}\left(BA_1^3\right)\right] = 178.8, \\ E\left[U_{S_0}\left(BA_2^3\right)\right] = 281.1, \\ E\left[U_{S_0}\left(BA_3^3\right)\right] = 383.4, \\ E\left[U_{S_0}\left(BA_4^3\right)\right] = 281.1. \end{cases}$$

The strategy corresponding to the maximum expected utility of S_0 is

$$A_{S_0} = BA_3^3 = \{BS_1, BS_2, BS_4\}.$$

For $S_e \in A_3^3$, $e = 1, 2, 4$, Fig. 7a, 7b and 7d show the expected utility of S_e as a function of s_e. We observe that when the expected utility is maximized, the optimal bids of S_e based on Eq. (33) are

$$\begin{cases} \tilde{s}_1 = 188.75, \\ \tilde{s}_2 = 206.00, \\ \tilde{s}_4 = 205.00. \end{cases}$$

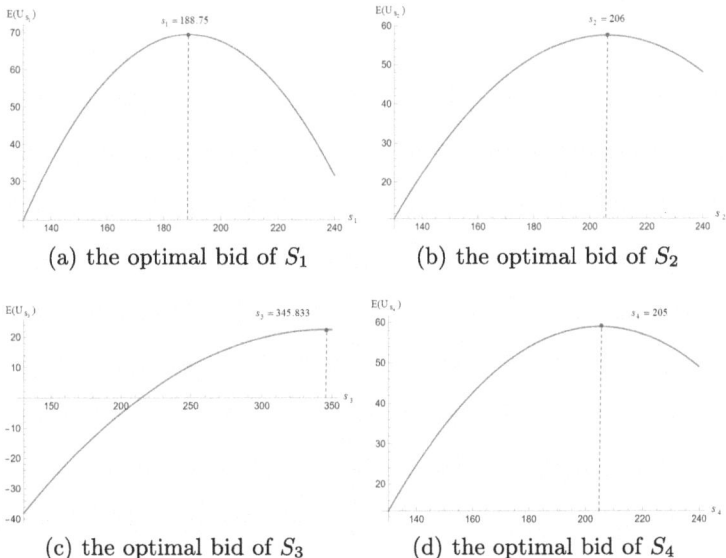

(a) the optimal bid of S_1

(b) the optimal bid of S_2

(c) the optimal bid of S_3

(d) the optimal bid of S_4

Fig. 7. Expected utility functions with optimal bids.

Since s_i, $i = 1, \cdots, 4$, follows the uniform distribution on $[140, 190]$ (i.e., the maximum selling price is 190), we have

$$\begin{cases} s_1^* = 188.75, \\ s_2^* = 190.00, \\ s_4^* = 190.00. \end{cases}$$

For $S_3 \in (A_3^3)^c$, Fig. 7c shows the expected utility of S_3 as a function of s_3, and we observe that when the expected utility is maximized, the optimal bid of S_3 based on Eq. (35) is

$$\tilde{s}_3 = 345.833.$$

Again, since the maximum selling price is 190, we have $s_3^* = 190$. Given the optimal bids of S_i, according to Eq. (17), we have $c_4 = 182.12$ and $v_0 > c_4$, therefore, S_0 makes the purchase decision which leads to

$$U_{S_0}\left(BA_3^3\right) = 108.4.$$

5 Conclusion and Discussion

This study contributes a Bayesian Stackelberg game model tailored to reconstitute fractional NFT ownership. Our analysis of optimal bidding strategies, within the framework of a two-stage game where sellers assume leadership roles and the buyer acts as a follower, sheds light on a distinctive aspect of our approach. A noteworthy feature is the flexibility we introduce in the reconstitution process, requiring ownership acquisition of at least k fractions from a minimum of q sellers. Unlike traditional models mandating the acquisition of all fractional NFTs, our approach employs a penalized mechanism for sellers unable to sell their fractions initially, fostering active participation among fractional NFT owners. This innovation is complemented by the provision of closed-form solutions for calculating optimal bids. Significantly, our proposed model, particularly the practical *leave-one-out* strategy, is well-suited for implementation via smart contracts.

The effective reconstitution of NFT ownership remains a prominent challenge in the blockchain domain, and this work constitutes an initial step toward addressing this issue. Future research avenues could extend our model to account for probabilistic owner participation, broadening its applicability. However, practical implementation may encounter challenges, given that owner participation is not mandatory. It is important to highlight that, despite sellers assuming leadership roles in our model, we streamline the problem into a single leader context by maximizing the expected utility. There is potential for further refinement by formulating the model as a multi-leader-follower game [8], where sellers act as leaders in pursuit of optimal solutions. Despite these potential challenges, our work lays a foundation for further exploration and refinement of models to enhance the efficiency and fairness of fractional NFT ownership reconstitution.

A Appendix

Proof of Lemma 3.2: Under the optimal strategy of S_0, we discuss the following scenarios.

Case I: If $t = 1$, we have

$$U_{S_1}(v_1, A_{S_0}(v_0, s_1, s_2), s_1) = \begin{cases} \left(\dfrac{s_0 + s_1}{2} - v_1\right) m_1, & \text{if } v_0 > c_1, \\ 0, & o/w, \end{cases} \quad (19)$$

and

$$U_{S_2}(v_2, A_{S_0}(v_0, s_1, s_2), s_2) = \begin{cases} \left(\dfrac{s_0 + rs_2}{2} - v_2\right) m_2, & \text{if } v_0 > c_1, \\ 0, & o/w. \end{cases} \quad (20)$$

The optimal strategy for S_i is to maximize the expected utility function. For S_1, the expected utility function is

$$E\left[U_{S_1}(v_1, A_{S_0}, s_1)\right] = \int_c^a \int_c^a \int_c^a U_{S_1}(v_1, A_{S_0}, s_1) F(v_0) F(s_0) F(s_2)$$

$$= \int_c^a \int_c^a \int_{c_1}^a \left(\dfrac{s_0 + s_1}{2} - v_1\right) m_1 F(v_0) F(s_0) F(s_2)$$

$$= \dfrac{m_1^2 * h_1 + m_1 m_2 * h_2}{48(a - c)(m_1 + m_2 r_0)},$$

where

$$h_1 = 8a^2 + 8ac - 4c^2 + 12a(s_1 - 3v_1) - 12s_1(s_1 - 2v_1) - 12c(s_1 - v_1),$$
$$h_2 = -(a^2 + c^2)(4 + 3r) + 2ac(-2 - 3r + 6r_0) + 12a^2 r_0 - 6[(a+c)(1+r) + 4ar_0](s_1 - 2v_1).$$

Taking the first derivative of $E\left[U_{S_1}(v_1, A_{S_0}, s_1)\right]$ and setting it equal to 0

$$\dfrac{\partial E\left[U_{S_1}(v_1, A_{S_0}, s_1)\right]}{\partial s_1} = 0,$$

leads to the following solution

$$\tilde{s}_1 = -\dfrac{m_1(-2a + 2c - 4v_1) + m_2(c + cr + a(1 + r - 4r_0))}{4m_1}. \quad (21)$$

The second derivative of $E\left[U_{S_1}(v_1, A_{S_0}, s_1)\right]$ has the following form, i.e.,

$$\dfrac{\partial^2 E\left[U_{S_1}(v_1, A_{S_0}, s_1)\right]}{\partial s_1^2} = -\dfrac{m_1^2}{2(a - c)(m_1 + m_2 r_0)},$$

which is negative.

For S_2, the expected utility functions are

$$E[U_{S_2}(v_2, A_{S_0}, s_2)] = \int_c^a \int_c^a \int_c^a U_{S_2}(v_2, A_{S_0}, s_2) F(v_0)F(s_0)F(s_1)$$

$$= \int_c^a \int_c^a \int_{c_1}^a \left(\frac{s_0 + rs_2}{2} - v_2\right) m_2 F(v_0)F(s_0)F(s_1)$$

$$= \frac{m_1 m_2 * h_3 + m_2^2 * h_4}{48(a-c)(m_1 + m_2 r_0)}, \quad (22)$$

where

$h_3 = (a-c)(5a + 7c + 12rs_2 - 24v_2),$
$h_4 = -4\left[a^2 + ac + c^2 - 3ar_0(a+c) + 3r(a+c-2ar_0)s_2 + 3r^2 s_2^2\right]$
$\quad + 12(a + c - 4ar_0 + 2rs_2)v_2.$

We take the first derivative and set it equal to 0

$$\frac{\partial E[U_{S_2}(v_2, A_{S_0}, s_2)]}{\partial s_2} = 0,$$

which leads us to the following solution

$$\tilde{s}_2 = \frac{(a-c)m_1 + m_2[-c - a(1 - 2r_0) + 2v_2]}{2rm_2}. \quad (23)$$

The second derivative takes the following form

$$\frac{\partial^2 E[U_{S_2}(v_2, A_{S_0}, s_2)]}{\partial s_2^2} = -\frac{m_2^2 r^2}{2(a-c)(m_1 + m_2 r_0)},$$

which is negative.

Case II: If $t = 2$, we have

$$U_{S_1}(v_1, A_{S_0}(v_0, s_1, s_2), s_1) = \begin{cases} \left(\frac{s_0 + rs_1}{2} - v_1\right) m_1, & \text{if } v_0 > c_2, \\ 0, & o/w, \end{cases} \quad (24)$$

and

$$U_{S_2}(v_2, A_{S_0}(v_0, s_1, s_2), s_2) = \begin{cases} \left(\frac{s_0 + s_2}{2} - v_2\right) m_2, & \text{if } v_0 > c_2, \\ 0, & o/w. \end{cases} \quad (25)$$

The optimal strategy for S_i is to maximize the expected utility function. For S_1, the expected utility function is

$$E[U_{S_1}(v_1, A_{S_0}, s_1)] = \int_c^a \int_c^a \int_c^a U_{S_1}(v_1, A_{S_0}, s_1) F(v_0)F(s_0)F(s_2)$$

$$= \int_c^a \int_c^a \int_{c_2}^a \left(\frac{s_0 + rs_1}{2} - v_1\right) m_1 F(v_0)F(s_0)F(s_2)$$

$$= \frac{m_1^2 * h_5 + m_1 m_2 * h_6}{48(a-c)(m_2 + m_1 r_0)}, \quad (26)$$

where

$$h_5 = -4[a^2 + ac + c^2 - 3a^2r_0 - 3acr_0 + 3ars_1 + 3crs_1 - 6arr_0s_1 + 3r^2s_1^2$$
$$-3(a + c - 4ar_0 + 2rs_1)v_1],$$
$$h_6 = (a - c)(5a + 7c + 12rs_1 - 24v_1).$$

Taking the first order and setting it equal to 0,

$$\frac{\partial E\left[U_{S_1}\left(v_1, A_{S_0}, s_1\right)\right]}{\partial s_1} = 0,$$

leads to the following solution

$$\tilde{s}_1 = \frac{(a-c)m_2 + m_1(-c + a(-1+2r_0) + 2v_1)}{2rm_1}. \quad (27)$$

The second derivative takes the following form

$$\frac{\partial^2 E\left[U_{S_1}\left(v_1, A_{S_0}, s_1\right)\right]}{\partial s_1^2} = -\frac{m_1^2 r^2}{2(a-c)(m_2 + m_1 r_0)},$$

which is negative.

For S_2, the expected utility function is

$$E\left[U_{S_2}(v_2, A_{S_0}, s_2)\right] = \int_c^a \int_c^a \int_c^a U_{S_2}(v_2, A_{S_0}, s_2) F(v_0) F(s_0) F(s_1)$$
$$c^a \int_c^a \int_{c_2}^a \left(\frac{s_0 + s_2}{2} - v_2\right) m_2 F(v_0) F(s_0) F(s_1)$$
$$m_1 m_2 * h_7 + m_2^2 * h_8 48(a-c)(m_2 + m_1 r_0), \quad (28)$$

where

$$h_7 = a^2(-4 - 3r + 12r_0) - c[c(4 + 3r) + 6(1 + r)(s_2 - 2v_2)] - 2a[c(2 + 3r - 6r_0)$$
$$+3(1 + r - 4r_0)(s_2 - 2v_2)],$$
$$8 = -4[2a^2 - c^2 + a(2c + 3s_2 - 9v_2) - 3s_2(s_2 - 2v_2) - 3c(s_2 - v_2))].$$

We take the first derivative and set it equal to 0

$$\frac{\partial E\left[U_{S_2}(v_2, A_{S_0}, s_2)\right]}{\partial s_2} = 0,$$

which leads us to the following solution

$$\tilde{s}_2 = \frac{m_1[-c - cr - a(1 + r - 4r_0)] + m_2(2a - 2c + 4v_2)}{4m_2}. \quad (29)$$

The second derivative takes the following form

$$\frac{\partial^2 E\left[U_{S_2}(v_2, A_{S_0}, s_2)\right]}{\partial s_2^2} = -\frac{m_2^2}{2(a-c)(m_1 r_0 + m_2)},$$

Which is negative.

Proof of Lemma 4.2: Under the optimal strategy of S_0, the utility functions of $S_e \in A_t^q$ and $S_f \in (A_t^q)^c$ in terms of payoffs in different strategies are

$$U_{S_e}(v_e, A_{S_0}(v_0, s_1, \cdots, s_n), s_e) = \begin{cases} \left(\frac{s_0 + s_e}{2} - v_e\right) m_e, & \text{if } v_0 \geq c_4, \\ 0, & o/w, \end{cases} \quad (30)$$

and

$$U_{S_f}(v_f, A_{S_0}(v_0, s_1, \cdots, s_n), s_f) = \begin{cases} \left(\frac{s_0 + r s_f}{2} - v_f\right) m_f, & \text{if } v_0 \geq c_4, \\ 0, & o/w. \end{cases} \quad (31)$$

The expected utility function of $S_e \in A_t^q$ is

$$E\left[U_{S_e}(v_e, A_{S_0}, s_e)\right]$$
$$= \int_c^a \cdots \int_c^a \int_c^a U_{S_e}(v_e, A_{S_0}, s_e) F(v_0) F(s_0) \cdots F(s_{e-1}) F(s_{e+1}) \cdots F(s_n)$$
$$= \int_c^a \cdots \int_c^a \int_{c_4}^a \left(\frac{s_0 + s_e}{2} - v_e\right) m_e F(v_0) F(s_0)) \cdots F(s_{e-1}) F(s_{e+1}) \cdots F(s_n)$$
$$= \left(\frac{1}{a-c}\right)^{n+1} m_e \int_c^a \cdots \int_c^a \int_{c_4}^a \left(\frac{s_0 + s_e}{2} - v_e\right) v_0 s_0 \cdots s_{e-1} s_{e+1} \cdots s_n$$
$$= \frac{m_e}{24(a-c) h_{13}} \{6 a h_{13}(a + c + 2 s_e - 4 v_e) - 3 h_{14}(a+c)(a + c + 2 s_e - 4 v_e)$$
$$+ (M - m_0)[-4(a^2 + ac + c^2) - 6(a+c)(s_e - 2 v_e)] - 6 m_e s_e (a + c + 2 s_e - 4 v_e)\},$$

where

$$h_{14} = \sum_{s_a \in (A_t^q - s_e)} m_a + r \sum_{s_b \in (A_t^q)^c} m_b. \quad (32)$$

We take the first derivative and set it equal to 0

$$\frac{\partial E\left[U_{S_e}(v_e, A_{S_0}, s_e)\right]}{\partial s_e} = 0,$$

leads to the following solution

$$\tilde{s}_e = \frac{2 a h_{13} - [h_{14} + (M - m_0)](a+c) - m_e(a + c - 4 v_e)}{4 m_e}. \quad (33)$$

The second derivative takes the following form

$$\frac{\partial^2 E\left[U_{S_2}\left(v_2, A^*_{S_0}, s_2\right)\right]}{\partial s_2^2} = -\frac{m_e^2}{h_{13}(a-c)},$$

which is negative.

The expected utility function of $S_f \in (A_t^q)^c$ is

$$E\left[U_{S_f}\left(v_f, A_{S_0}, s_f\right)\right]$$

$$= \int_c^a \cdots \int_c^a \int_c^a U_{S_f}\left(v_f, A_{S_0}, s_f\right) F(v_0)F(s_0)\cdots F(s_{f-1})F(s_{f+1})\cdots F(s_n)$$

$$= \int_c^a \cdots \int_c^a \int_{c_4}^a \left(\frac{s_0 + rs_f}{2} - v_f\right) m_f F(v_0)F(s_0)\cdots F(s_{f-1})F(s_{f+1})\cdots F(s_n)$$

$$= \left(\frac{1}{a-c}\right)^{n+1} m_f \int_c^a \cdots \int_c^a \int_{c_4}^a \left(\frac{s_0 + rs_f}{2} - v_f\right) v_0 s_0 \cdots s_{f-1} s_{f+1} \cdots s_n$$

$$= \frac{m_f}{24 h_{13}(a-c)} \{h_{13}[6a(a+c) + 12ars_f - 24av_f] - 6rm_f s_f[(a+c) + 2(rs_f - 2v_f)]$$

$$+ (M - m_0)[-4(a^2 + ac + c^2) - 6(a+c)rs_f + 12(a+c)v_f]$$

$$+ h_{15}[-3(a+c)^2 - 6(a+c)(rs_f - 2v_f)]\},$$

where

$$h_{15} = \sum_{s_a \in A_t^q} m_a + r \sum_{s_b \in ((A_t^q)^c - s_f)} m_b. \tag{34}$$

We take the first derivative and set it equal to 0

$$\frac{\partial E\left[U_{S_f}\left(v_f, A_{S_0}, s_f\right)\right]}{\partial s_f} = 0,$$

leads to the following solution

$$\tilde{s}_f = \frac{2ah_{13} - [(M - m_0) + h_{15}](a+c) - m_f(a + c - 4v_f)}{4rm_f}. \tag{35}$$

The second derivative takes the following form

$$\frac{\partial^2 E\left[U_{S_2}\left(v_2, A_{S_0}, s_2\right)\right]}{\partial s_2^2} = -\frac{r^2 m_f^2}{h_{13}(a-c)},$$

which is negative.

References

1. Ali, O., Momin, M., Shrestha, A., Das, R., Alhajj, F., Dwivedi, Y.K.: A review of the key challenges of non-fungible tokens. Technol. Forecast. Social Change **187**, 122248 (2023)
2. Aussel, D., Svensson, A.: A short state of the art on multi-leader-follower games. In: Dempe, S., Zemkoho, A. (eds.) Bilevel Optimization. SOIA, vol. 161, pp. 53–76. Springer, Cham (2020). https://doi.org/10.1007/978-3-030-52119-6_3
3. Chen, H., Cheng, Y., Deng, X., Huang, W., Rong, L.: Absnft: securitization and repurchase scheme for non-fungible tokens based on game theoretical analysis. In International Conference on Financial Cryptography and Data Security, pp. 407–425. Springer, Heidelberg (2022). https://doi.org/10.1007/978-3-031-18283-9_20
4. Choi, W., Woo, J., Hong, J.W.K.: Gas cost analysis of fractional nft on the ethereum blockchain. In: 2023 IEEE International Conference on Blockchain and Cryptocurrency (ICBC), pp. 1–6. IEEE (2023)
5. Ko, H., Son, B., Lee, Y., Jang, H., Lee, J.: The economic value of nft: evidence from a portfolio analysis using mean-variance framework. Finan. Res. Lett. **47**, 102784 (2022)
6. Makori, J.: What are fractional nfts, and where can you buy them? (2023)
7. Nadini, M., Alessandretti, L., Di Giacinto, F., Martino, M., Aiello, L.M., Baronchelli, A.: Mapping the NFT revolution: market trends, trade networks, and visual features. Sci. Rep. **11**(1), 20902 (2021)
8. Sherali, H.D.: A multiple leader stackelberg model and analysis. Oper. Res. **32**(2), 390–404 (1984)
9. Tadelis, S.: Game Theory: An Introduction. Princeton University Press, Princeton (2013)

Regulatory Implications of MEV Mitigations

Yan Ji[✉] and James Grimmelmann

Cornell Tech, New York, NY 10044, USA
{yj348,james.grimmelmann}@cornell.edu

Abstract. This paper examines the legal ramifications of Miner / Maximal Extractable Value (MEV), a phenomenon in which some entities (e.g., miners or validators) leverage their positional advantages to generate extra profits on blockchains. In previous work, Barczentewicz *et al.* argued that some MEV extraction techniques could constitute illegal market manipulation under United States securities law, depending on the *publicness* of the victim transactions. While their analysis applies to typical Ethereum and Flashbots implementations, we contend that the rapidly evolving blockchain ecosystem and the emergence of new MEV mitigation measures necessitate a revised test for market-manipulation liability. Our proposal focuses on the principle of respecting the initiating user's *intent*, rather than simply the network status of the transactions. We also identify new enforcement challenges that arise from the decentralization nature of blockchains. By offering a nuanced understanding of the MEV landscape and exploring the legal implications for manipulation liability, this paper contributes to the ongoing discussion on MEV regulation in blockchain ecosystems.

Keywords: Regulation · MEV · DeFi · Blockchain

1 Introduction

"Miner/Maximal Extractable Value (MEV)" is the potential extra profits some entities can make by leveraging their power to insert, omit, or reorder blockchain transactions. MEV concept was introduced in the paper "Flash Boys 2.0," by Daian *et al.* [38], and since then has been a topic of significant discussion and analysis in the blockchain communities given its substantial economic impact. Over $2 billion has been exploited through MEV strategies as of the time of this writing.[1] MEV exploitations result in revenue for validators but sometimes at the expense of ordinary users of these blockchain networks.

In recent work [14], Barczentewicz *et al.* made an initial attempt to analyze the potential legal liabilities associated with MEV extraction. In particular, they classified pending transactions by their publicness and discussed legal liability for extracting MEV from public and private transactions, respectively. They argued that (i) prosecuting cases involving MEV extraction from public transactions is

---

[1] More than $675 million worth of MEV were exploited in the two years leading up to the Merge on Ethereum [53] and $1.5 billion after the Merge [55].

likely to be a challenging endeavor, due to the difficulty in proving specific intent and demonstrating price artificiality (ii) for cases involving extracting MEV from private transactions, in contrast, there is greater potential for successful fraud-based manipulation charges, and the demonstration of a breach of trust or duty could offer a clear route towards establishing liability.

Given the nuance in transaction routing traces in practice and the significant differences in legal consequences, Barczentewicz *et al.* emphasized that whether a pending transaction is classified as public or private shouldn't be trivially determined by its purported routing. Instead, they proposed a standard for determining transaction publicness. Specifically, they defined a transaction as public if "an actor, who did not directly receive the transaction from the user who submitted it, can access it in an unencrypted state without undue delay and without any special arrangements with the node that initially received the transaction."

Barczentewicz *et al.*'s legal analysis aligns well with the particular Ethereum and Flashbots implementation they focus on. However, the rapidly evolving nature of the blockchain ecosystem, coupled with the emergence of new MEV extraction techniques and mitigation measures, presents new challenges in establishing liability for market manipulation. The multi-tiered, multi-entity MEV extraction supply chain introduced by Flashbots [50] and the increasing reliance on Trusted Execution Environments (TEEs) [80] introduce additional complexities to the liability landscape. In particular, a classification standard based only on transaction publicness is too simple. It overlooks potential fraud resulting from the abuse of public information and breaches of trust, and does not sufficiently address the complicated MEV landscape of today.

To resolve these issues, we propose a test that respects users' *intentions* rather than focusing solely on the *network status* of transactions. If an actor profits by routing a transaction contrary to the sender's intentions or by ordering transactions using information not intended for MEV extraction, there is likely to be liability of fraud-based manipulation. Recent MEV mitigation efforts also align in spirit with this shift in focus from transaction visibility to users' intent, as seen in slippage limits in Uniswap and intent specification in MEV-Share and SUAVE.

On the other hand, the complexities involved with multiple entities and the inherent permissionless and decentralized nature of blockchains introduce new challenges in enforcement. We note that the gap in meeting the prerequisites for establishing legal liability for MEV extraction largely hinges on the community's stance on whether to rely solely on technological solutions for MEV mitigation or to also embrace legal regulations as complementary measures. From a practical standpoint, the feasibility of implementing in-protocol accountability also significantly influences the challenges associated with prosecution.

In this paper, we first review existing attempts on mitigating MEV in Sect. 2. This backdrop illuminates the complexity of the current MEV landscape. In Sect. 3, we explore the regulatory framework for market manipulation, revisiting Barczentewicz *et al.*'s standard for determining the publicness of transactions and their analysis of market manipulation liability in MEV extraction. Next, we introduce our proposed modification of that standard, examine the challenges in pursuing liability under it, and discuss its implications for the community in Sect. 4. We conclude our discussion in Sect. 5.

We focus on United States law because of the exceptional global reach of U.S. financial regulation. U.S. authorities take the position that the U.S. has jurisdiction over transactions that pass through the U.S. financial system, even none of the end-user parties to the transaction have any other connection to the U.S. [43] But because so many transactions are denominated in dollars, pass through intermediary banks located in the U.S., and/or are cleared through U.S. financial institutions, a high proportion of all global payments are potentially subject to U.S. securities, sanctions, or other financial regulations. While there are limits on the degree to which some of these regimes apply to "foreign" transactions, [36] these are typically regime-specific and others apply broadly.

2 MEV Mitigation Attempts

Various efforts have been made to mitigate rampant MEV exploitation. In this section, we will discuss general-purpose approaches to mitigating MEV.[2] We specifically examine scenarios when these mitigation schemes have failed or may fail (due to design vulnerabilities or engineering bugs), to illustrate the complexity and difficulty in addressing this problem from a technical perspective and to shed light on when regulation may serve as a backup oversight.

2.1 Proposer-Builder Separation

Proposer-Builder Separation (PBS) [83], the increasingly popular design philosophy on Ethereum, aims to divide the tasks of block building and proposing - previously both dominated by validators - into separate stages. The primary motivation behind PBS is to prevent market monopolies, based on the view that MEV is an inherent aspect of DeFi and thus inevitable [37]. In Ethereum 2.0, which employs Proof-of-Stake, there is a risk that MEV exploitation could become dominated by a few validators with specialized expertise in extracting MEV. This could lead to a concentration of capital among these major validators in the long run, which is counter to blockchain decentralization and may introduce severe security issues.

Among various designs of PBS [21,81], the one in use today on Ethereum is MEV-boost [54], developed by Flashbots. MEV-boost introduces three new types of participants: MEV searchers, block builders, and relays. Any entity can participate as a searcher or builder, while there is a higher trust bar for relays. The workflow of MEV-boost is depicted in Fig. 1. Searchers scan the public

---

[2] We do not consider application-specific solutions [29,33,63,107,108] due to their limited scope [64]. A broad introduction to the prerequisite concepts of blockchains, smart contracts, decentralized finance and MEV is presented in Sect. A.

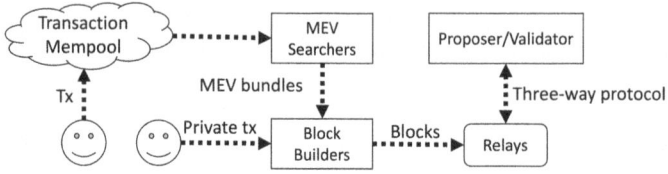

Fig. 1. MEV-boost workflow

mempool for MEV opportunities, create sandwiching bundles[3] and send those bundles to builders. Builders collect transactions from both the mempool and searchers, create blocks with transaction ordering that maximizes their profit, and send those blocks to relays. Next, relays engage in a three-way interactive protocol with the validator chosen to propose the next block. They first send the most profitable block header (without the actual transactions) to the validator. The validator selects the most profitable header, signs it, and sends the signature back to the corresponding relay. Upon receiving the signed block header, the relay broadcasts the full block, including transactions, to both the validator and the entire blockchain network. This allows validators to proceed with the Proof-of-Stake consensus protocol using the newly created block.

The three-way protocol between relays and validators is designed to prevent free-riding by validators. Without it, an adversarial validator who is less capable of exploiting MEV than searchers and builders could replace the sandwiching transactions with their own, following the same strategy developed by others. With relays revealing only the block header but not the transactions, the validator is unable to sandwich any transactions or learn the strategy of searchers and builders. After signing the block header, the validator is committed to proposing this particular block. If the validator deviates from this protocol and proposes a new block, it will be punished by the slashing rules [42], i.e., a proportion of their locked stake will be slashed. This strategy works as expected only if relays do not collude with validators or free ride by themselves, thus trust is needed in relays. In practice, relays are established by reputation [52]; Flashbots, for example, initially dominated the relay market, relaying over 80% of blocks in the early days [90]. This number has since decreased to around 30% [15], indicating a trend towards decentralization in the relays.

MEV-boost aims to abstract MEV extraction to a separate layer, providing all validators with equal opportunities to extract MEV and prevent market monopolies. Despite this goal, as previously mentioned, the dominant position of validators compared to other entities remains largely unchanged, with over 90% of profits eventually going to validators [12]. From another perspective, the situation might seem even worse for ordinary users due to the open MEV auctions. The total MEV extracted in the network depends on the capabilities of MEV seekers. Before the open auction market was introduced, validators had varying capabilities in extracting MEV, and the expected MEV was averaged

---

[3] Sandwiching is a common practice of extracting MEV by injecting one transaction before the victim one and another after it. For more details, see Sect. A.3.

out. With MEV-boost, however, the MEV extracted in each block is determined by the most skilled player in the network, not depending on the power distribution among validations. A study shows that validators earn more than two times the MEV than before [102]. Concerns have also been raised within the community regarding Flashbots' assumption that MEV is inevitable [87], as well as its overall impact on the ecosystem and alignment with the fundamental principles of decentralization and fairness [70].

MEV-boost was attacked in early April 2023 by an adversarial validator exploiting $20 million from MEV searchers and builders [76]. To mount the attack, the adversary sent several transactions that appeared to offer lucrative MEV opportunities to the public mempool. As anticipated, searchers and builders injected transactions to extract MEV from these transactions. The validator signed the block header from the relay and retrieved the transactions. However, instead of proceeding with the signed block in the consensus protocol, the adversary created a new block, extracting MEV from the injected transactions by MEV seekers, and proposed it to the network. The attack would not have been so smooth without a vulnerability in the Flashbots relay software [16]. Nevertheless, such an *equivocation* attack (equivocating the relayed block) remains possible in today's MEV-boost infrastructure, raising concerns about the effectiveness of the incentive mechanism aimed at enhancing security of Proof-of-Stake consensus in Ethereum 2.0 [84]. Typically, when the MEV opportunities are significant enough and exceed validators' stakes to be slashed for misconduct, there is evident motivation for validators to equivocate. In response to the attack, Flashbots not only patched the software bug, but also added a blacklist of adversarial validators [31]. However, the blacklist functionality was removed just a couple of days later [32]. This incident highlights potential vulnerabilities in the current MEV-boost infrastructure and challenges in PBS for the ecosystem.

2.2 Private Order Flow

To mitigate ordinary users' loss in MEV extraction, in contrast to the goal of PBS, one widely adopted strategy is private order flow (POF), by which users' transactions remain private at the POF provider before being committed on chain. Taking Flashbots Protect [51] as an example, users who prefer not to be a part of the MEV game can send their transactions to Flashbots. These transactions will not be publicly visible in the mempool; instead, they are secretly included in blocks created by Flashbots builders. Flashbots promises not to extract MEV from these transactions and not to disclose their information to any entity until they are included in a block signed by validators. Transactions that might fail and revert the state after execution are also excluded to save users' transaction fees. There are similar proposals for private order flows, such as the OFA design [60], which vary by privacy policies. However, transactions going through Flashbots Protect may experience delays; a higher proportion of Flashbots-built blocks results in shorter latency. Flashbots also does not protect privacy if the blockchain is forked, which is technically unavoidable. Furthermore, Flashbots Protect operates in a centralized manner due to its inherent privacy requirements, which leads to a lack of transparency. There is limited public information available regarding the statistics or details of its policy.[4]

An alternative implementation of POF without centralized trust uses Trusted Execution Environments (TEEs). This approach has been gaining traction, as TEEs offer integrity and privacy guarantees at the hardware level. TEEs are specially designed, isolated computing hardware enclaves that provide two key security guarantees, setting them apart from ordinary computers. First, TEEs ensure that program execution cannot be tampered with by adversaries. In the context of smart contract execution, for instance, users do not need to explicitly verify transactions, as the hardware manufacturer's attestations provide assurance of correct execution. Second, TEEs offer robust privacy protection, ensuring that the internal execution state remains invisible to external parties, including the operating system. To implement anonymous payments using TEEs, for example, users can encrypt transaction details, including sender, receiver and amount, before sending them to the TEEs. Transactions are then decrypted and executed inside the TEE enclaves without revealing any information to a third party. Intel's Software Guard Extensions (SGX) [80] is one example of a TEE that has been adopted for blockchain applications.

By employing TEEs to process POF, MEV exploitation can be mitigated. For instance, Secret Network [93] provides private smart contract execution and native MEV resistance by having validators order and execute transactions within SGX enclaves. Flashbots also recently released a builder implementation inside SGX [61], paving the way for a forthcoming plan for a more complex trustless order flow auction system called SUAVE [48]. The use of SGX in this context has the potential to address the transparency concerns associated with Flashbots Protect, as well as eliminate the need to trust Flashbots. Another recent academic proposal, called PROF [12], leverages SGX for private order flow while remaining compatible with the current MEV-boost infrastructure. PROF allows for seamless integration by providing economic incentives for all types of participants in the MEV ecosystem.

While the ideal security and privacy features of TEEs seem promising, incorporating them into real-world applications with the expected guarantees has proven to be challenging, and many issues can arise. For example, a recent study on Secret Network revealed that all the privacy guarantees it claimed were broken [68]. In particular, transaction details such as sender, receiver, and amount could be observed, leading to straightforward MEV exploitation. This attack could be mounted by any individual validator in the network independently, and it is not dependent on the TEE implementation (the underlying TEE remains intact). Secret Network froze validator registration before patch-

---

[4] To mitigate the need to trust a centralized entity not to abuse its non-public information, commit-reveal protocols [9,82,89] have been proposed to allow transactions to be ordered in their encrypted form first and then revealed for execution. These protocols trust among validators not to collude and decrypt transactions before the ordering is committed on chain. This strategy may introduce other concerns, such as spamming attacks, which are out of the scope of this paper.

ing the vulnerability. Aside from the intricacies of system deployment, several side-channel attacks[5] against SGX have also been demonstrated, including Spectre [77], Foreshadow [100], and AEPIC [59]. These attacks enable adversaries to breach TEE security guarantees and infer secret states within it.

2.3 Fair Ordering Protocols

Fair ordering protocols offer another possible approach to mitigating MEV extraction [72–74,78,106]. Unlike private order flow, which keeps transactions private from MEV extractors, fair ordering protocols aggregate different orderings from validators and produce an ordering that respects the majority of validators. This prevents a single validator who is responsible for proposing the next block from dictating the transaction ordering. Implementing these proposals requires fundamental changes to the underlying consensus protocol, making them more suitable for application-specific scenarios rather than general-purpose blockchains. For instance, Chainlink [69] is developing Fair Sequencing Service within its oracle network to fairly order transactions off-chain and send them in batches to the blockchain for DeFi applications, and Espresso Sequencer [94] is a shared fair sequencer for Layer 2 rollups.

On the other hand, the effectiveness of fair ordering protocols relies on the assumption that the majority of validators will follow the protocol and propose transaction orderings according to the public policy, e.g., based on a first-come, first-served basis. However, there is no inherent incentive for validators to adhere to the protocol, and accountability is not easily enforceable. If a validator misbehaves, holding them accountable for any unexpected outcomes is challenging. In the context of MEV resistance, when a significant MEV opportunity arises, there is no guarantee that the majority of validators will not collude and exploit it. This presents a potential risk to the effectiveness of fair ordering protocols, as their security is contingent on the assumption that the majority of validators will prioritize fairness[6] over personal gain. To address this issue, future research and development may focus on devising mechanisms to incentivize validators to adhere to fair ordering protocols, as well as creating methods to hold them accountable for any misbehavior.

3 Regulatory Framework

In this section, we describe the key U.S.[7] regulatory framework potentially applicable to MEV: the rules against market manipulation adopted by the two key agencies with jurisdiction over financial markets. We review Barczentewicz *et*

---

[5] Side-channel attacks are privacy attacks that probe secrets using side information outside the original security model, such as timing and resource consumption.

[6] This can be any predetermined ordering policy that promotes public good, such as first-come-first-served.

[7] As discussed in Sect. 1, we focus on U.S. law due to its exceptional global reach in financial regulation, and also for concreteness of discussions.

al.'s analysis of market-manipulation liability for MEV extractors, which argues that transaction publicness has significant regulatory implications.

3.1 Regulatory Agencies

The Securities and Exchange Commission (SEC) and the Commodity Futures Trading Commission (CFTC) serve as the two primary financial-markets regulatory bodies in the United States. They are charged with upholding the principles of market integrity, transparency, and investor protection. Though both agencies share the common goal of ensuring equitable and orderly markets, they focus on regulating different financial instruments. In particular, the SEC regulates *securities* (primarily stock and loans issued by companies to raise capital), while the CFTC regulates trading in *futures* (contracts for the future delivery of a commodity, like crude oil or aluminum) and similar contracts.[8]

The Mango Markets exploit [101] is an example case of crypto market manipulation. The attacker made purchases of MNGO on three digital exchanges that Mango Markets' price oracle depended on, in order to drive up the value of much larger MNGO-USDC swap contracts that he held. Both the SEC and the CFTC brought charges against the attacker, and he was criminally convicted. To be clear, the Mango Markets exploit is not an example of MEV extraction. It is closer in spirit to well-known illegal forms of manipulation in traditional financial markets, such as "banging the close" by submitting buy orders at the end of the trading day to drive up the reported closing price and increase the value of one's derivatives contracts based on that price. However, similar outcomes can be achieved with reduced risk by an MEV extractor who has significant control over transaction ordering [79]. They could employ the same strategy or even just freeride on the attacker's. The SEC and CFTC's action in the Mango Markets case send a signal that they believe that existing rules against market manipulation remain relevant for digital assets.

3.2 Price Manipulation

Both the SEC and CFTC have the power to address price manipulation. Section 9(a)(2) of the Securities Exchange Act (SEA) as amended (and codified at 15 U.S.C. §78i(a)(2)) prohibits price manipulation in securities, and Sect. 6(c)(3) of the Commodity Exchange Act (CEA) as amended (codified at 7 U.S.C. §9(3)) prohibits price manipulation in swaps and futures. Both these statutes have been held to require proof of two aspects: the existence of an artificial price and the specific intent of the defendant to manipulate the price.

CFTC Rule 180.2, 17 C.F.R. §180.2, which implements the CEA prohibition on price manipulation, makes it unlawful "for any person, directly or indirectly,

---

[8] The regulatory landscape for digital assets is still evolving. Both the SEC and CFTC have claimed jurisdiction over some digital assets, and both have taken numerous enforcement actions. The line between their respective jurisdictions is not firmly established, and several pending legislative efforts such as RFIA [4] may redraw it.

to manipulate or attempt to manipulate the price of any swap, or of any commodity in interstate commerce, or for future delivery on or subject to the rules of any registered entity." For the CFTC to apply Rule 180.2, it must satisfy the following four-part test [3]:

(1) the defendant possessed the ability to influence market prices; (2) an artificial price existed; (3) the defendant caused the artificial price; and (4) the defendant intended to do so.

This test creates two significant hurdles to an enforcement action. First, there are conceptual difficulties in element (2) in distinguishing between a legitimate market price and an "artificial" price that "does not reflect basic forces of supply and demand." The concept of "legitimacy with respect to supply and demand" remains ambiguous in both law and economics, making the artificial-price test circular unless the sole consideration is whether the forces were triggered by an unlawful act.

Second, the intent required under element (4) is the specific intent to cause an artificial price. Specific intent is the highest standard of culpable mental state used in law. It is not enough to prove that the defendant was negligent, or reckless, or even knew that a result would happen; specific intent is established only when the accused has a conscious desire to achieve a particular outcome. Sometimes, as in the case of an individual trader who brags about price manipulation on a logged chat platform, it is easy to prove. But in other cases, anomalous prices could also plausibly have resulted without a specific intent, and could be due to a software bug or a trading strategy gone awry.

3.3 Fraud-Based Manipulation

Given the difficulties with the price-manipulation theory, an alternate and often more viable enforcement strategy is fraud-based manipulation, which does not require proof of an artificial price or of specific intent. The SEC has traditionally used this approach under SEA §10(b) and its implementing rule, SEC Rule 10b-5. The CFTC originally had limited authority to pursue price manipulation liability. But following the financial crash of 2008, Congress enacted the Dodd-Frank Wall Street Reform and Consumer Protection Act in 2010, which gave the CFTC power to make rules against fraud-based manipulation. It promptly adopted Rule 180.1, 7 C.F.R. §180.1, which mirrors SEC Rule 10b-5.

Both SEC Rule 10b-5 and CFTC Rule 180.1 make it unlawful (1) "to intentionally or recklessly" (2) employ any manipulative or deceptive devices to defraud. This test departs from price manipulation in two important ways. First, the violation is complete the moment the defendant acts fraudulently; there is no requirement that the fraud resulted in an artificial price. Second, it is sufficient to demonstrate recklessness, which is defined as the accused acting in a highly unreasonable manner, to the extent that it seems implausible they were unaware of their actions [2], irrespective of whether they foresaw or intended the result [6]. This standard is generally easier to establish than specific intent.

What the fraud-manipulation theory does require is that there must be evidence of deceit or false statements. This could be a misleading signal of market price (as above), but it could also be any other traditional form of fraud, such as false statements about a company's financial condition. Similarly, insider trading is generally regarded as fraudulent behavior and can lead to allegations of fraud-based manipulation. The existence of fraud typically presumes some level of trust that was established and subsequently violated.

The typical actions of an MEV extractor—inserting and reordering transactions—look superficially like legitimate trading activity. This is analogous to open-market manipulation in traditional financial markets: the transactions are real, and are entered into with real counterparties making wholly aboveboard trades. Courts have split over whether open-market manipulation qualifies as fraud-based manipulation. The answer usually depends on whether the defendant disseminated false information. A subset of open-market manipulation, known as covered open-market manipulation, involves trading activity that creates heightened expectations of trust and honest dealing [14], and is usually considered illegal. For instance, in the Mango Markets exploit, the MNGO price oracle depended on the prices on other exchanges, a dependency that suggests a trust relationship.

3.4 Sandwiching Public and Private Order Flow

MEV extraction via sandwiching—unlike other strategies such as oracle manipulation or arbitrage—is an inherent characteristic of decentralized blockchains on which transactions are committed in batches. It causes the sandwiched user to trade at a worse price and is generally viewed as toxic MEV [13]. Thus, our analysis will focus specifically on its regulatory implications.

Barczentewicz *et al.* divide MEV sandwiching attacks into two types, based on whether the sandwiched transaction originates from a public or private order flow [14]. Under their proposed test, a transaction should be deemed public when "an actor, who did not directly receive the transaction from the user who submitted it, can access it in an unencrypted state without undue delay and without any special arrangements with the node that initially received the transaction." This standard captures the differing life cycles of transactions that are sent directly to the public mempool versus those that utilize a private order flow service like Flashbots Protect. In particular, when a transaction is in the public mempool, any network participant can access it via a straightforward in-protocol command. In contrast, for transactions sent through Flashbots Protect, only Flashbots can access the unencrypted transaction.

As Barczentewicz *et al.* argue, the act of sandwiching public transactions unlikely constitutes market manipulation. These are naked open-market trades, and it will be very difficult for prosecutors to prove the specific specific intent to create an artificial price that leads to price manipulation liability.

Recklessness may be somewhat easier to show for fraud-based manipulation, but there is another problem. Transaction sandwiching does not inherently involve misleading statements. Furthermore, no deceptive devices are utilized to mislead ordinary traders. It is common knowledge that MEV extraction is prevalent on blockchains. DEX operators, for example, allow traders to specify a slippage limit [97], indicating the maximum price deviation they are willing to accept. Moreover, the broader DeFi market is unlikely to be misdirected by sandwiching transactions, as an ordinary user's transaction can either benefit from the sandwiching or become a sandwiched transaction itself.

Despite these complexities, Barczentewicz et al. propose two arguments to support a potential fraud-based manipulation liability for sandwiching that relies on dominance in transaction ordering. These involve proving price artificiality via market power dominance or conflict of interest. However, both arguments assume highly moralized courts and regulators, and given the cost of investigation and prosecution, the certainty of their application remains unclear.

Sandwiching private transactions, in contrast, is much more likely to result in liability under SEC Rule 10b-5 or CFTC Rule 180.1, provided it can be established that "(1) the MEV extractor had a 'pre-existing duty' with the user from whom they received [the private order flow], and (2) the MEV extractor breached this duty in the process of either extracting MEV from the user's POF transactions or by 'tipping' the user's transaction to another who then extracts MEV from the user's transaction." [14] For example, Flashbots has explicitly promised users that their transactions will remain private until they are included in a proposed block (although the risk of being orphaned still exists) and are thus resistant to MEV extraction if sent via Flashbots Protect. Users who send their transactions through private order flow services such as Flashbots Protect do so for the purpose of avoiding MEV extraction, typically in exchange for paying an additional fee or accepting a longer latency for transaction settlement. In this context, there is explicit trust from users towards these private order flow service providers. Therefore, if these providers sandwich users' transactions or sell them to a third party for sandwiching, all entities involved in such misconduct could potentially be held liable for fraud-based manipulation, or more specifically, insider trading.

While the classification of public and private transactions and the ensuing discussions about market manipulation liability as formulated by Barczentewicz et al. are well-articulated within their specific context of how Flashbots and Ethereum normally operate today, we contend that this framework may not be exhaustive due to the overwhelming focus on transaction publicness. This is particularly true when considering the evolving landscape of MEV mitigation strategies, and even in the context of the earlier discussed MEV-boost equivocation attack. A crucial aspect overlooked in the framework is that a breach of trust leading to fraud-based manipulation does not necessarily involve possession of non-public information. Specifically, when a transaction transitions from being private to public before being confirmed on chain, there may still be a breach of trust when sandwiching it. Thus, manipulation liability may be found without using the moralized reasoning as Barczentewicz et al. proposed. Additionally, the publicness condition is not comprehensive, which may lead to ambiguity or unintended outcomes in practical scenarios. We delve deeper into these complexities and propose a solution in the next section.

4 Implications of MEV Mitigation Designs

In this section, we suggest switching from Barczentewicz et al.'s focus on transaction publicness to respecting users' intent. We argue that this change better accommodates the evolving landscape of MEV extraction and mitigation. We also discuss some of the enforcement challenges, particularly given the decentralized nature of blockchains and issues inherent to the mitigation technologies.

4.1 Issues of Publicness Standard and Proposed Fix

There are two main concerns associated with a standard based on publicness: (1) the publicness condition does not comprehensively cover all practical scenarios, and (2) breach of trust is only considered in cases involving non-public information, despite the possibility of breaches in public transactions. Given these issues, applying the publicness standard for analyzing the legal liability of MEV extraction could lead to either ambiguous or undesired outcomes.

First, the publicness definition does not properly capture all plausible scenarios in today's MEV landscape. On the one hand, the definition is ambiguous as applied to transactions that are neither fully private nor fully public. Some transactions are partially visible in practice; mitigation strategies such as MEV-share and SUAVE allow users to choose only certain transaction information to disclose to MEV seekers. On the other hand, the definition may lead to undesired outcomes. In TEE-based blockchains such as Secret Network, private transactions may not be divulged from the original receiving node. Instead, encrypted transactions are propagated throughout the peer-to-peer network by protocol, and each registered TEE can access the decrypted transactions in their plaintext form. An actor may be able to access transaction details by interacting with their own TEE, either by exploiting design flaws or through side channel attacks targeting TEEs, but without having any special arrangement with the node that originally received the transaction.

Second, a trust relationship may exist and be breached at any stage of a transaction lifecycle, not just the period when the transaction is private. For instance, in the case of the MEV-boost equivocation attack, the attacker manipulated transaction ordering by first signing a block header to trick the relay into releasing transaction data, and then subsequently proposing an equivocating block to extract MEV. In this situation, the transactions initially deemed private became public before on-chain settlement, and the attacker sandwiched them after they became public. According to Barczentewicz et al., the attacker targeted public transactions, so it would be hard to find market manipulation liability. However, we argue that even after users' transactions become public, it is still possible to identify fraud in such a case. In particular, if a relay provides blocks to validators only if they promise not to equivocate and extract MEV, that could suffice to establish a trust relationship between the relay and validators. Equivocation could be viewed as breach of that trust[9]. Similarly for fair ordering protocols, where transactions are publicly visible, validators are supposed to order transactions according to the pre-determined ordering policy (such as first-come-first-served) and not extract MEV. Here too it is possible to argue that there is beach of trust when validators sandwich public transactions.

Given these concerns, we propose a different rule for analyzing market manipulation liability of MEV extraction. Instead of focusing on the actual visibility of a transaction within the peer-to-peer network, we advocate for a perspective that respects *users' intent*. Specifically, if an actor profits from routing a user's transaction in a way contrary to the user's intentions or orders transactions using information not designated by the user for such purposes, this could lead to fraud-based manipulation liability. Since the prosecution bar is lower when pursuing fraud-based manipulation, the key questions are whether a trust relationship or duty exists between the sandwicher and the sandwichee, and whether that duty is breached. The focus of this approach is on the presence and potential breach of a trust relationship between MEV seekers and users. Our modification integrates Barczentewicz *et al.*'s concept of publicness by aligning it with the user's intended transaction routing, while also considering which aspects of transaction information the user consents to be used for ordering. The proposed rule not only upholds the liability analysis presented by Barczentewicz in specific cases they consider, but also extends its applicability to the more complex scenarios discussed in this paper. We delve into the challenges associated with proving fraud in the next two subsections.

4.2 Trust in the Decentralized Setting

As outlined by Barczentewicz *et al.*, holding MEV extractors liable under SEA §9(a)(2) or CFTC Rule 180.2 is a challenging proposition due to the difficulties in proving both the existence of an artificially manipulated price and the accused's specific intent. Fraud-based manipulation liability under SEC Rule 10b-5 and

---

[9] On May 15, 2024, as this article was going to press, the U.S. Department of Justice unsealed an indictment charging two defendants with wire fraud for the MEV-boost attack described in Sect. 2.1. Indictment, ECF No. 2, United States v. Peraire-Bueno, No. 1:24-cr-00293-UA (S.D.N.Y. filed May 8, 2024). The indictment alleges that the defendants made "material representations" by advertising lucrative "Lure Transactions" to attract transactions from MEV bots, and by transmitting a "False Signature" from a validator that they controlled (i.e., a signature that could not ultimately be validated for inclusion on the blockchain, but which would fool the relay into revealing private transaction data presented by the MEV bots to the relay).

The indictment's theories of falsity raise slightly different issues than we discuss. Lure transactions are best analyzed as a form of spoofing, which is already recognized as a form of manipulative conduct [91]. If the indictment is correct, the signature would be straightforwardly false, because it purports to be valid but is not. Our analysis of fraud-based manipulation applies to more general equivocation attacks. The indictment itself does not focus on the equivocation in the MEV-boost exploit, perhaps because these other theories of falsity were readily available.

CFTC Rule 180.1 emerges as a more feasible alternative, *if* a trust relationship between the users and the MEV extractor can be established. However, the concept of trust in a decentralized setting is complicated.

The trust relationship between users and a private order flow service provider such as Flashbots Protect is reasonably clear. Flashbots Protect makes specific claims about confidentiality, and users route transactions to it based on those representations. Violation of those claims, and misusing or disclosing users' transaction details other than as promised, could be a breach of trust.

However, it is empirically challenging to establish a trust relationship between blockchain users and a permissionless decentralized network of validators. Blockchains are fundamentally designed to inhibit misconduct via protocol enforcement; this is what makes them "trustless." For instance, most blockchains are constructed to be secure against a certain percentage of Byzantine participants who can deviate from the protocol at will. This design philosophy is followed by many new MEV mitigation strategies such as commit-reveal schemes and fair ordering protocols. Given the decentralized and Byzantine fault-tolerant nature of the protocol, anyone is theoretically capable of creating their own validator to participate. In the case of Ethereum, for example, there are multiple recommended implementations for validator software [45], yet only two contain explicit terms of use in their GitHub repositories [86,88], and none explicitly make any guarantees about avoiding MEV extraction.[10]

Instead of committing to running a specific version of software, an alternative may be to require validators, when joining the network or producing a block, to have a legally binding agreement on their alignment with the protocol specification. This requirement is not by itself in violation of decentralization, as validators can run any version of software, even one with their own modifications. However, given the current landscape and design philosophy of blockchains, establishing a legal commitment to MEV resistance for any validator may still be a difficult proposition, as shown in Flashbots' response to the MEV-boost equivocation attack. They initially added a blacklist of misbehaving validators, but subsequently removed it in pursuit of technical solutions [16]. This move could be attributed to concerns of potential censorship from the blockchain community, a point of contention that was earlier highlighted when Flashbots decided to comply with OFAC regulations [24].

Although the blockchain community has extensively debated whether to exclusively pursue technical solutions or to also embrace legal regulation, the absence of accountability in protocols for MEV resistance undeniably places extra strain on regulators. Even when fraud liability can be established, enforcement may prove challenging due to the decentralized and permissionless nature of validators. Hence, the incorporation of accountability within blockchain protocols is a pressing necessity for the evolution of the technology.

---

[10] There is a separate question of whether a blockchain user can rely on terms of use in a GitHub repository, but we leave that question for another day.

4.3 Failure Related to Trusted Execution Environment

Establishing fraud-based manipulation liability within TEE-based systems also presents challenges. In these systems, the trust relationship is not established between users and validators, but rather with the software development team and the underlying hardware it depends on. Thus whether a misbehaving validator can be held liable becomes questionable.

For instance, the Secret Network [93] promotes its confidential transaction execution and its resistance to MEV. However, a recent study [68] revealed substantial design flaws that entirely undermine the privacy assurances the network claims to provide. An actor operating as a validator, who has registered their own TEE within the Secret Network, can exploit these privacy vulnerabilities to access transaction details and subsequently extract MEV. To serve as a validator, an actor simply needs to download the source code and follow instructions to run it on suitable hardware with an embedded TEE. A TEE-based project typically has two types of code: trusted code and untrusted code. Trusted code is designed to run inside a TEE, providing guarantees of integrity and confidentiality. Additionally, the network can detect any modification to the trusted code, thanks to remote attestation. On the other hand, untrusted code operates outside the TEE and thus lacks such security guarantees. Its execution can be manipulated and its state can be probed. The Secret Network GitHub repository [92] clearly states that "the non-enclave code can be modified and ran on mainnet as long as there are no consensus-breaking changes." As the attack necessitates only modification of the untrusted code, the attacker does not breach any pre-existing trust or duties. In other words, it is a normal operation in the protocol and not a deceptive device. The standard fraud analysis applied to MEV extraction may not work in this scenario.

One may ask if bypassing the confidentiality of transactions inside a TEE using side-channel attacks could, alternatively, be seen as computer trespass under the Computer Fraud and Abuse Act (CFAA). Specifically, the use of a TEE establishes a code-based protective barrier, preventing external entities from accessing transaction details. On this theory, circumventing the protective function of a TEE might result in liability. However, given the Supreme Court's narrow interpretation of "unauthorized access" in *Van Buren v. United States* [1], courts are unlikely to find CFAA liability for side-channel attacks. These attacks rarely involve prohibited access as such; instead they are based on information inference from available resources.

5 Conclusion

In this paper, we have explored the current MEV landscape and existing mitigation strategies. We explored Barczentewicz et al.'s analysis, in which market manipulation liability for sandwiching transactions depends on those transactions' publicness, and identified limitations in that classification standard. We proposed a test for assessing manipulation liability that shifts the focus from network conditions to user intent. Our approach provides a more nuanced understanding of the dynamic lifecycle of transactions and accommodates the evolving landscape of MEV extraction strategies and mitigation measures, offering a more robust foundation for evaluating market manipulation liability.

We also described new enforcement challenges posed by the decentralized and permissionless nature of blockchain operations. Our research underscores the significant impact of the blockchain community's regulatory preferences and the crucial role of practical in-protocol accountability mechanisms in prosecuting MEV extraction. The recent equivocation attack incident highlights the inadequacy of Ethereum's incentive mechanisms, emphasizing the urgent need for accountable protocols and legal frameworks to reinforce the security and fairness of the ecosystem. By aligning technology with legal systems, we anticipate that MEV mitigation proposals can help illuminate the "dark forest" of the ecosystem.

Future research should continue to closely monitor the rapidly evolving MEV landscape. A comprehensive assessment of the harms and benefits of MEV, informed by well-defined metrics for user welfare, can significantly contribute to understanding its impact on the ecosystem.

A Technical Background

In this section, we will provide the essential technical background. First, we will introduce blockchain technology and its security features. Next, we will discuss smart contracts and demonstrate how they expand the range of potential applications on blockchains, with a focus on decentralized finance (DeFi). Finally, we will explain the concept of Miner/Maximal Extractable Value (MEV) and provide examples of how MEV can be exploited in practice.

A.1 Blockchain Technology

A blockchain is a public ledger composed of a linear chain of blocks,[11] each containing a series of sequentially ordered transactions submitted from users. These blocks are generated in a decentralized fashion by a group of validators, who are responsible for maintaining the integrity and security of the ledger. Blockchain technology offers security from several perspectives: (1) Immutability,[12] meaning that once a transaction is approved by validators, it will not be removed or

---

[11] There are a few exceptions, such as Avalanche and IOTA, that employ a DAG structure. The majority of blockchains in deployment today, however, are within the scope of discussion in this paper.

[12] There have been attempts in allowing mutability in history given validators' consensus on removal of certain illegal contents, but there is no such blockchain prevailing in the ecosystem yet.

altered, ensuring a temper-proof record; (2) Transparency,[13] allowing all participants in the network to verify if the execution result of all transactions included in the ledger is correct, promoting trust and accountability; (3) Decentralization, indicating that no single entity can take control of the system, enabling users who may not trust each other to transact reliably on the blockchain; and (4) Censorship-resistance, ensuring that even if a transaction is not favored by some entities, it will still be executed eventually as long as it is valid. Due to these features, blockchain technology offers a secure, transparent, and decentralized way to record and verify transactions, which fosters trust among users and enables various applications including asset management [28], supply chain tracking [10], digital identity management [66], and decentralized applications (dApps) [98].

A simplified depiction of the interactions between blockchain validators and users is presented in Fig. 2. In order to initiate a transaction, a user needs to send the transaction details to one or more validators. Validators, in turn, are responsible for disseminating valid transactions they receive to their peers, thereby creating a shared transaction mempool. A transaction is deemed valid if it satisfies specific criteria.[14] For example, the sender possesses an adequate amount of assets to be transferred to the recipient and the transaction is associated with a legitimate signature that confirms the asset owner's authenticity.

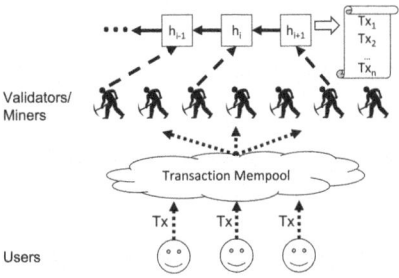

Fig. 2. Blockchain workflow.

The mempool serves as a temporary holding area for valid transactions awaiting execution and inclusion in the next block. In other words, transactions in the mempool do not have an immediate impact. Rather, they take effect-such as causing users' assets to be actually transferred-only after being incorporated into a block. Blocks are produced at a predetermined frequency, which may vary depending on the blockchain in question. For instance, the block interval of Bitcoin is roughly 10 min [18], while that of Ethereum is about 12 s [46].

---

[13] Transparency may vary in meaning for different blockchains, not necessarily requiring transactions to be publicly accessible. For example, there are rollups utilizing zero-knowledge proofs for public verification of the correct execution of transactions yet the transaction details are not needed.

[14] Another example: In account-based blockchains, users' sequential nonce also has to be incremental for preventing double executing the same transaction.

Valid transactions that enter the mempool during the corresponding interval have the potential to be included in the upcoming block. However, this inclusion is not guaranteed. Which transactions are selected for the next block can be impacted by several factors, such as network congestion, transaction fees, and the specific consensus mechanism at play. For instance, when the mempool holds more transactions than can be accommodated in a single block-due to each block having a block size limit, either measured by the size of transaction messages [17] or the computational resources for transaction execution as known as gas cost [56] - validators can only choose a subset of the pending transactions for the next block. The remaining transactions stay in the mempool until the network congestion subsides or they are eventually dropped. The block size limit arises from the fundamental trade-off between the scalability, security, and decentralization of blockchains [8], making it an unavoidable constraint. To encourage validators to prioritize the inclusion of their transactions, users can voluntarily offer transaction fees as an incentive [22]. By doing so, they increase the likelihood that their transactions will be processed more quickly, even during periods of high network congestion.

Validators rotate to take the responsibility of generating the next block and proposing it to the network for appendation to the blockchain. The selection of the block proposer depends on the underlying consensus protocol in use. In blockchains based on Proof-of-Work (PoW) [85], validators, commonly referred to as miners, consume substantial computational resources to compete in solving a cryptographically difficult puzzle. The winning miner who successfully solves the puzzle first earns the privilege to decide which transactions from the mempool to incorporate into the new block, and in return, is rewarded all the transaction fees associated with those transactions. On the other hand, Proof-of-Stake (PoS) blockchains [23,30] utilize a trustworthy source of randomness to appoint the validator responsible for proposing the next block [20]. The chosen validator is a member from a committee, each participant of which has previously committed a predetermined amount of assets as stake. In other words, a validator must lock up some native cryptocurrency as collateral and the chance of being selected to propose a new block is proportional to the validator's deposited stake. This approach contrasts with the resource-intensive nature of PoW, emphasizing the role of staked assets in securing the network, which is more energy efficient and environmentally friendly [67]. However, it is generally perceived as less secure than PoW [40]. To enhance security and accountability in practice, PoS blockchains are often facilitated with economic mechanisms to incentivize honest behavior among validators. For instance, one of the most commonly employed mechanisms is called slashing [42] - malicious validators are to be published by losing a portion of their staked assets, the proportion of which is determined by the type and severity of their misconduct.

As demonstrated above, although blockchains aim to promote decentralization in the long run, the generation of each block in most contemporary blockchains existing today is actually determined by a single validator. Consequently, decentralization does not have sufficient granularity at the individual block level, even though it is a fundamental aspect of the blockchain system as a whole. This key observation serves as the foundation for the discussion presented in this paper.

A.2 Smart Contracts and Decentralized Finance

While the most basic blockchain transactions are usually in the form of sending a specific amount of native cryptocurrency from one user to another,[15] many modern blockchains support more complex, Turing-complete[16] functionalities through the use of smart contracts. Smart contracts are essentially programmable scripts that reside on the blockchain and can be triggered by user transactions. They enable the automatic, atomic execution of functions with intricate logic, based on various conditions and corresponding actions. For example, consider the case of purchasing flight delay insurance [103]. Traditionally, claiming a refund from the insurance company could be time-consuming and require extensive paperwork. However, by utilizing a smart contract, the refund process can be automated, issuing the payout to the customer as soon as the flight delay is confirmed [105]. This eliminates the need for manual intervention, streamlining the entire process. Tornado Cash [99] is a more complex example of a smart contract application, which, although sanctioned by the OFAC, enables fully anonymous payments on the Ethereum blockchain.[17] Such a feature was not natively available on Ethereum without the use of smart contracts. By leveraging the power of smart contracts, Tornado Cash provides users with enhanced privacy in their transactions, while also raising concerns of being abused for illegal activities. In summary, smart contracts extend the capabilities of blockchains by incorporating programmable logic and automation, and enable various decentralized applications.

Decentralized Finance (DeFi) has been a rapidly growing sector in the industry largely due to the power of smart contracts. These trustless financial services circumvent traditional centralized intermediaries and foster transparency and accessibility, making DeFi increasingly appealing to traders.

Contrasting with traditional financial systems that depend on centralized operators such as Nasdaq or NYSE, DeFi features decentralized exchanges (DEXes) that operate using smart contracts. DEX users maintain full control of their assets at all times, and orders are settled directly and transparently on the blockchain without needing to trust an exchange operator or broker. In the early days, DEX users had to manually search for buy/sell orders and submit the bundled transaction on-chain for settlement [104]. However, modern DEXes, such as Uniswap v3 [96] - the largest DEX on Ethereum-now incorporate automated market makers (AMMs) [27] to streamline on-chain price discovery. This innovation enables traders to simply send their orders to the blockchain, which

---

[15] Bitcoin takes a slightly different semantic in the form of UTXO based.
[16] Although Turing-complete, the execution is guaranteed to halt due to the limit of gas.
[17] The anonymity comes from the mixer pool.

will be automatically settled by the exchange smart contract. Uniswap v3 boasts a 24-hour trading volume of around $290 million as of Sep 20, 2023 [34].

Another prominent application in DeFi is lending and borrowing platforms. These platforms allow users to lend their assets to earn interest or borrow assets by providing collateral. The process is managed by smart contracts, eliminating the need for users to place trust in a third party. Lending services contribute significantly to the DeFi ecosystem's efficiency by providing liquidity for all types of financial activities. The largest lending platforms, Aave [5] and JustLend [71], hold a combined total liquidity pool of over $9 billion in locked-up assets [39]. A unique innovation resulting from the atomic execution of smart contracts is the Flashloan [65], which enables borrowing without collateral. With Flashloans, a borrower can obtain a loan, utilize it, and return the assets to the lender all within a single atomic transaction. Since the smart contract guarantees full repayment (or the transaction reverts as if it never occurred), lenders face no risk in Flashloans.

Various types of assets can be represented and managed in DeFi with interoperability across multiple blockchains. For example, a user can trade Bitcoin for an equivalent amount of Wrapped Bitcoins (WBTCs) [95] on Ethereum using cross-chain bridging services, and then participate in diverse DeFi activities on Ethereum with WBTCs.

Gas tokens [57] serve as a unique example of a derivative contract on Ethereum, offering additional on-chain utility. Ethereum transaction fees are determined by computation and storage costs for validators, measured in units of gas. Each smart contract execution instruction incurs a predetermined gas cost, and the sender is required to pay a fee proportional to the gas usage by the transaction. However, gas prices can fluctuate due to network congestion. Storing data on a blockchain consumes gas, while deleting storage variables refunds gas. Users can mint gas tokens by storing data on-chain when the gas price is low (so is the transaction volume), then burning the storage and using the refunded gas to cover transaction fees when the price is high (usually due to network congestion or for the purpose of prioritizing an urgent transaction). Gas tokens can be viewed as futures contracts without expiration dates, and they played a significant role in the MEV game,[18] which we will discuss further in Sect. A.3.

In addition to digital assets and derivatives that are native to blockchains, smart contracts can tether off-chain assets with on-chain tokens for DeFi activities. Stablecoins [62], for instance, are backed by a reserve of assets, often in fiat currencies, at a 1:1 ratio to mitigate the volatility typically associated with cryptocurrencies. Another example is Non-fungible tokens (NFTs) which represent unique off-chain commodities that are not interchangeable, such as artwork [35], domain names [44], tickets and coupons [19]. Despite its non-fungible nature, an NFT can be converted to fungible assets by dividing the token into fractional shares and granting users partial ownership [58].

Overall, smart contracts facilitate a wide range of financial instruments and services, playing a crucial role in the expansion and development of the DeFi

---

[18] Gas token is now obsolete due to EIP-1559.

ecosystem. As the sector continues to evolve, it demonstrates the potential for a more accessible, transparent, and efficient financial landscape, underscoring the promising future of DeFi.

A.3 Miner/Maximal Extractable Value

Maximal Extractable Value (MEV), originally known as Miner Extractable Value, was introduced in a paper entitled "Flash Boys 2.0" by Daian et al. As previously mentioned, transactions are not settled in real-time but are first gathered in the mempool, which is publicly accessible. A validator then selects transactions and orders them in a block for execution. MEV exploitation refers to the practice of making profit through the strategic censorship, insertion and reordering of transactions within blocks. Validators used to be in the dominant position of determining what transactions are included in a block and how they are ordered, which is why the term was initially called Miner Extractable Value. This practice can have both positive and negative effects on the ecosystem, depending on how it is executed and the intentions of the actors involved.

DeFi is a complicated and interoperable ecosystem, so transactions from different users may have an impact on each other, and their execution results cannot be determined independently. Instead, they depend on their ordering. For example, an ordinary user wants to trade 40 WETHs for Example Dummy Tokens (EDTs) on Uniswap. Uniswap follows the rule $x \times y = k$ for a pair of exchange tokens [7], where x and y represent the amounts of WETH and EDT, respectively, and k is a predetermined constant. Let us assume $k = 1600$ and initially $x = y = 40$. After executing the user's transaction, we have $x = 80$ and $y = 20$, so the user receives 20 EDTs in return.

However, the execution result of this example transaction is not guaranteed. Once the transaction is sent to the public mempool, an MEV extractor can observe it and exploit the change in demand by creating a sandwiching transaction bundle for profit. In particular, the extractor first trades 120 WETHs for EDTs before the ordinary transaction. Based on the price invariant above, this frontrun transaction results in $x = 160$ and $y = 10$, with the extractor receiving 30 EDTs in return. Next, the sandwiched transaction is executed, leading to $x = 200$ and $y = 8$, with the ordinary user only getting 2 EDTs in return. At last, the extractor inserts a backrun transaction, trading the 30 EDTs for a profit of 38 WETHs, resulting in a loss of 18 EDTs for the ordinary user. As the saying goes in [12], "These two [inserted] transactions are the bread in the sandwich. [The ordinary user's] is the meat." It is worth noting that sandwiching attacks are not unique to Uniswap's price discovery mechanism, which was designed specifically for gas efficiency on blockchains. Sandwiching can also occur in traditional exchanges that employ limit order books [75]. In both cases, the sandwich attack takes advantage of the public nature of pending transactions to manipulate the order of trades and extract profits, potentially at the expense of other traders.

Because a transaction with potential MEV opportunity can only be sandwiched once, and anyone can create a sandwiching bundle upon an ordinary transaction in the public mempool, the MEV game is highly competitive. MEV extractors vie for the inclusion of their own sandwiching bundles by offering high transaction fees, incentivizing validators to prioritize their transactions. This leads to an implicit auction for transaction position within a block, which can be viewed as a scarce resource on blockchains. To win in the MEV auction, MEV extractors used to utilize gas tokens to save transaction fees while exploiting MEV, i.e., minting gas tokens when the gas price is low and then burning them to cover gas cost in transactions when the gas price is high. This was a common practice before Ethereum incorporated the EIP-1559 update [22], which introduced changes to the transaction fee mechanism. Nonetheless, the dynamics of MEV extraction has not changed significantly after a series of updates in Ethereum 2.0. While MEV exploitation has become more decentralized with a multi-stage, multi-entity MEV supply chain [49] introduced by Flashbots, the dominant position of validators in the game remains largely unchanged. Recent estimates suggest that over 90% of extracted MEV ultimately goes to validators, highlighting their continued influence in the ecosystem [12].

Sandwiching transactions is not the only way to extract MEV, and not all MEV exploitations are detrimental to the ecosystem. In fact, there exists "good MEV," which typically arises from arbitrage opportunities [47]. For instance, when a legitimate large trade is placed on one DEX, it may cause a significant price difference between that DEX and other DEXes for the same pair of tokens. An MEV extractor can take advantage of this price discrepancy by purchasing tokens at a lower price on one DEX and then selling them at a higher price on another DEX. In 2020, a savvy trader managed to generate a profit of $40K by exploiting the price discrepancy between two stable coins, USDC and USDT, leveraging the power of Flashloans for arbitrage opportunities [25]. This action does not harm any legitimate traders; instead, it helps to balance prices across DEXes, ensuring that they more accurately reflect the actual market price. MEV arbitrage is not considered price manipulation from a legal perspective because it does not create artificial prices. Instead, it plays a role in stabilizing markets and promoting price efficiency. Additionally, good MEV can contribute to the overall health of the ecosystem by reducing price discrepancies, fostering market equilibrium, and encouraging fair trading conditions for all participants.

Oracle manipulation presents yet another avenue for MEV extraction, offering potentially higher profits albeit with less frequent opportunities. DEXes and lending platforms often rely on price oracles to determine spot trading prices or collateral ratios [41]. Some on-chain oracles aggregate prices from multiple marketplaces and compute an average, which opens the door to arbitrage opportunities when prices on particular marketplaces are manipulated or do not accurately represent the actual market price. A notable instance of this strategy is the Mango Market exploit. Oracle manipulation can often yield higher profits than transaction sandwiching, as it does not require a counterparty and can be easily leveraged [11]. However, this form of MEV extraction can technically be more readily mitigated through improved oracle design [79] and risk monitoring measures implemented by exchanges - a lesson learned from the traditional financial market [26].

References

1. Van Buren v. United States, 141 S. Ct. 1648 (2021)
2. Drexel Burnham Lambert Inc. v. Commodity Futures Trading Commission, 850 F.2d 742 (D.C. Cir. 1988)
3. Commodity Futures Trading Commission v. Parnon Energy, 875 F. Supp. 2d (S.D.N.Y. 2012)
4. Lummis-Gillibrand Responsible Financial Innovation Act, S.__, 118th Cong. (2023)
5. Aave. Aave liquidity protocol (2023). https://web.archive.org/web/20230920221835/https://aave.com/. Accessed 20 Sept 2023
6. Abrantes-Metz, R.M., Rauterberg, G., Verstein, A.: Revolution in manipulation law: the new cftc rules and the urgent need for economic and empirical analyses. U. Pa. J. Bus. L. **15**, 357 (2012)
7. Adams, H., Zinsmeister, N., Salem, M., Keefer, R., Robinson, D.: Uniswap v3 core. Technical report, Uniswap (2021)
8. Altarawneh, A., Herschberg, T., Medury, S., Kandah, F., Skjellum, A.: Buterin's scalability trilemma viewed through a state-change-based classification for common consensus algorithms. In: 2020 10th Annual Computing and Communication Workshop and Conference (CCWC), pp. 0727–0736. IEEE (2020)
9. Asayag, A., et al.: A fair consensus protocol for transaction ordering. In: 2018 IEEE 26th International Conference on Network Protocols (ICNP), pp. 55–65. IEEE (2018)
10. AWS. Blockchain for Supply Chain: Track and Trace (2023). https://web.archive.org/web/20230920195444/https://aws.amazon.com/blockchain/blockchain-for-supply-chain-track-and-trace/. Accessed 20 Sept 2023
11. Babel, K., Daian, P., Kelkar, M., Juels, A.: Clockwork finance: automated analysis of economic security in smart contracts. In: 2023 IEEE Symposium on Security and Privacy (SP), pp. 2499–2516. IEEE (2023)
12. Babel, K., Ji, Y., Juels, A., Kelkar, M.: PROF: fair transaction-ordering in a profit-seeking world (2023). https://web.archive.org/web/20230920225103/https://initc3org.medium.com/prof-fair-transaction-ordering-in-a-profit-seeking-world-b6dadd71f086. Accessed 20 Sept 2023
13. Barczentewicz, M.: Mev on ethereum: a policy analysis. ICLE White Paper, pp. 01–23 (2023)
14. Barczentewicz, M., Sarch, A., Vasan, N.: Blockchain transaction ordering as market manipulation. Ohio St. Tech. Law J. **20**, 1 (2023)
15. beaconcha.in. Relay Overview - Open Source Ethereum Blockchain Explorer (2023). https://web.archive.org/web/20230920235153/https://beaconcha.in/relays. Accessed 20 Sept 2023
16. Bert. Post mortem: April 3rd, 2023 mev-boost relay incident and related timing issue (2023). https://web.archive.org/web/20230921001800/https://collective.flashbots.net/t/post-mortem-april-3rd-2023-mev-boost-relay-incident-and-related-timing-issue/1540. Accessed 20 Sept 2023
17. Bitcoin Magazine. What is the bitcoin block size limit (2020). https://web.archive.org/web/20230920212208/https://bitcoinmagazine.com/guides/what-is-the-bitcoin-block-size-limit. Accessed 20 Sept 2023
18. Bitcoin Wiki. Block intervals (2014). https://web.archive.org/web/20230920204907/https://en.bitcoin.it/wiki/Block_intervals. Accessed 20 Sept 2023

19. BloXmove. NFTicket (2023). https://web.archive.org/web/20230920224650/https://bloxmove.com/technology/nfticket. Accessed 20 Sept 2023
20. Brown-Cohen, J., Narayanan, A., Psomas, A., Weinberg, S.M.: Formal barriers to longest-chain proof-of-stake protocols. In: Proceedings of the 2019 ACM Conference on Economics and Computation, pp. 459–473 (2019)
21. Buterin, V.: Two-slot proposer/builder separation (2021). https://web.archive.org/web/20230807101311/https://ethresear.ch/t/two-slot-proposer-builder-separation/10980?u=barnabe. Accessed 07 Aug 2023
22. Buterin, V., Conner, E., Dudley, R., Slipper, M., Norden, I., Bakhta, A.: Eip-1559: Fee market change for eth 1.0 chain. Published online (2019)
23. Buterin, V., Griffith, V.: Casper the friendly finality gadget. arXiv preprint arXiv:1710.09437 (2017)
24. Carreras, T.: 51% of Ethereum Blocks Can Now Be Censored. It's Time for Flashbots to Shut Down (2022). https://web.archive.org/web/20230921020027/https://cryptobriefing.com/51-of-ethereum-blocks-can-now-be-censored-its-time-for-flashbots-to-shut-down/. Accessed 20 Sept 2023
25. Cawrey, D., Sinclair, S.: First Mover: How a DeFi Trader Made an 89% Profit in Minutes Slinging Stablecoins (2021). https://web.archive.org/web/20230920231351/https://www.coindesk.com/markets/2020/08/12/first-mover-how-a-defi-trader-made-an-89-profit-in-minutes-slinging-stablecoins/. Accessed 20 Sept 2023
26. CFTC. CFTC Market Surveillance Program (2023). https://web.archive.org/web/20230920232458/https://www.cftc.gov/IndustryOversight/MarketSurveillance/CFTCMarketSurveillanceProgram/index.htm. Accessed 20 Sept 2023
27. Chainlink. What Are Automated Market Makers (AMMs) (2021). https://web.archive.org/web/20230920220828/https://chain.link/education-hub/what-is-an-automated-market-maker-amm. Accessed 20 Sept 2023
28. Chainlink. The Future of Asset Management Using Smart Contracts and Blockchain Oracles (2023). https://web.archive.org/web/20230920195133/https://blog.chain.link/the-future-of-asset-management-using-smart-contracts-and-blockchain-oracles/. Accessed 20 Sept 2023
29. Chakravarty, M.M.T., Chapman, J., MacKenzie, K., Melkonian, O., Peyton Jones, M., Wadler, P.: The extended UTXO model. In: Bernhard, M., Bernhard, M., et al. (eds.) FC 2020. LNCS, vol. 12063, pp. 525–539. Springer, Cham (2020). https://doi.org/10.1007/978-3-030-54455-3_37
30. Chen, J., Micali, S.: Algorand. arXiv preprint arXiv:1607.01341 (2016)
31. Hager, C.: [@metachris]. flashbots/mev-boost-relay[commit: 84a9439] (2023). https://web.archive.org/web/20230921003137/https://github.com/flashbots/mev-boost-relay/commit/84a943925e62f20b812c60688b6e433fba8e0da7. Accessed 20 Sept 2023
32. Hager, C.: [@metachris]. flashbots/mev-boost-relay[pr: #338] (2023). https://web.archive.org/web/20230921003921/https://github.com/flashbots/mev-boost-relay/pull/338. Accessed 20 Sept 2023
33. Ciampi, M., Ishaq, M., Magdon-Ismail, M., Ostrovsky, R., Zikas, V.: Fairmm: a fast and frontrunning-resistant crypto market-maker. In: International Symposium on Cyber Security, Cryptology, and Machine Learning, pp. 428–446. Springer, Heidelberg (2022). https://doi.org/10.1007/978-3-031-07689-3_31
34. CoinGecko. Uniswap V3 (Ethereum) (2023). https://web.archive.org/web/20230920221522/https://www.coingecko.com/en/exchanges/uniswap-v3-ethereum. Accessed 20 Sept 2023

35. Coursera. What Is NFT Art? (How Does It Work) (2023). https://web.archive.org/web/20230920224409/https://www.coursera.org/articles/nft-art. Accessed 20 Sept 2023
36. U.S. Supreme Court. Morrison v. National Australia Bank Ltd. (2010)
37. Daian, P.: MEV... wat do (2021). https://web.archive.org/web/20221219142049/https://pdaian.com/blog/mev-wat-do/. Accessed 20 Sept 2023
38. Daian, P., et al.: Flash boys 2.0: frontrunning in decentralized exchanges, miner extractable value, and consensus instability. In 2020 IEEE Symposium on Security and Privacy (SP), pp. 910–927. IEEE (2020)
39. DefiLlama. All Protocols: Total Value Locked (2023). https://web.archive.org/web/20230920222250/https://defillama.com/. Accessed 20 Sept 2023
40. Deirmentzoglou, E., Papakyriakopoulos, G., Patsakis, C.: A survey on long-range attacks for proof of stake protocols. IEEE Access **7**, 28712–28725 (2019)
41. Dzyatkovskii, A.: The Strengths and Weaknesses of DeFi Price Oracles (2021). https://web.archive.org/web/20230920231609/https://hackernoon.com/the-strengths-and-weaknesses-of-defi-price-oracles-x7l35ui. Accessed 20 Sept 2023
42. Edgington, B.: Upgrading Ethereum: Slashing (2023). https://web.archive.org/web/20230920214103/https://eth2book.info/capella/part2/incentives/slashing/. Accessed 20 Sept 2023
43. Emmenegger, S., Zuber, F.: To infinity and beyond: U.S. dollar-based jurisdiction in the U.S. sanctions context. In: Swiss Review of Business and Financial Market Law, pp. 114–130 (2022)
44. ENS. Decentralised naming for wallets, websites, & more (2023). https://web.archive.org/web/20230920224534/https://ens.domains/. Accessed 20 Sept 2023
45. Ethereum. Staking Launchpad: Validator checklist (2023). https://web.archive.org/web/20230921020410/https://launchpad.ethereum.org/en/checklist. Accessed 20 Sept 2023
46. Etherscan. Ethereum Average Block Time Chart (2023). https://web.archive.org/web/20230920205201/https://etherscan.io/chart/blocktime. Accessed 20 Sept 2023
47. Finoa. The role of MEV in DEX arbitrage (2023). https://web.archive.org/web/20230920231201/https://www.finoa.io/blog/mev-arbitrage/. Accessed 20 Sept 2023
48. Flashbots. The Future of MEV is SUAVE (2022). https://web.archive.org/web/20230921005814/https://writings.flashbots.net/the-future-of-mev-is-suave/. Accessed 20 Sept 2023
49. Flashbots. The MEV Supply Chain: a peek into the future of this industry (2022). https://web.archive.org/web/20230920230907/https://flashbots.mirror.xyz/bqCakwfQZkMsq63b50vib-nibo5eKai0QuK7m-Dsxpo. Accessed 20 Sept 2023
50. Flashbots. Flashbots Doc (2023). https://web.archive.org/web/20230920194204/https://www.flashbots.net/. Accessed 20 Sept 2023
51. Flashbots. Flashbots Protect: Quick Start (2023). https://web.archive.org/web/20230920235910/https://docs.flashbots.net/flashbots-protect/quick-start. Accessed 20 Sept 2023
52. Flashbots. MEV-Boost Risks and Considerations (2023). https://web.archive.org/web/20230920234627/https://docs.flashbots.net/flashbots-mev-boost/architecture-overview/risks. Accessed 20 Sept 2023
53. Flashbots. MEV-Explore v1: Pre-merge Data (2023). https://web.archive.org/web/20230920184439/https://explore.flashbots.net/. Accessed 20 Sept 2023

54. Flashbots. What is MEV-Boost (2023). https://web.archive.org/web/20230920234424/https://docs.flashbots.net/flashbots-mev-boost/introduction. Accessed 20 Sept 2023
55. Flashbots. Flashbots Transparency Dashboard: REV activities since the Merge (2024). https://web.archive.org/web/20240510024731/https://transparency.flashbots.net/. Accessed 09 May 2024
56. Frankenfield, J.: Gas (Ethereum): How Gas Fees Work on the Ethereum Blockchain (2022). https://web.archive.org/web/20230920212352/https://www.investopedia.com/terms/g/gas-ethereum.asp. Accessed 20 Sept 2023
57. Breidenbach, L., Daian, P., Tramèr, F.: GasToken (2018). https://github.com/projectchicago/gastoken
58. Genç, E.: How Can You Share an NFT? Fractional NFTs Explained (2023). https://web.archive.org/web/20230920224744/https://www.coindesk.com/learn/how-can-you-share-an-nft-fractional-nfts-explained/. Accessed 20 Sept 2023
59. Goodin, D.: SGX, Intel's supposedly impregnable data fortress, has been breached yet again (2022). https://web.archive.org/web/20230921004825/https://arstechnica.com/information-technology/2022/08/architectural-bug-in-some-intel-cpus-is-more-bad-news-for-sgx-users/. Accessed 20 Sept 2023
60. Gosselin, S., Chiplunkar, A.: The Orderflow Auction Design Space (2023). https://web.archive.org/web/20230921001333/https://frontier.tech/the-orderflow-auction-design-space. Accessed 20 Sept 2023
61. Hager, C., Paape, F.: Block Building inside SGX (2023). https://web.archive.org/web/20230921004108/https://writings.flashbots.net/block-building-inside-sgx. Accessed 20 Sept 2023
62. Hayes, A.: Stablecoins: Definition, How They Work, and Types (2023). https://web.archive.org/web/20230920223845/https://www.investopedia.com/terms/s/stablecoin.asp. Accessed 20 Sept 2023
63. Heimbach, L., Wattenhofer, R.: Eliminating sandwich attacks with the help of game theory. In: Proceedings of the 2022 ACM on Asia Conference on Computer and Communications Security, pp. 153–167 (2022)
64. Lioba Heimbach and Roger Wattenhofer. Sok: Preventing transaction reordering manipulations in decentralized finance. arXiv preprint arXiv:2203.11520, 2022
65. Hertig, A.: What is a flash loan (2023). https://web.archive.org/web/20230920222954/https://www.coindesk.com/learn/what-is-a-flash-loan/. Accessed 20 Sept 2023
66. IBM. Blockchain for digital identity and credentials (2023). https://web.archive.org/web/20230920200735/https://www.ibm.com/blockchain-identity. Accessed 20 Sept 2023
67. Jain, A., Arora, S., Shukla, Y., Patil, T., Sawant-Patil, S.: Proof of stake with casper the friendly finality gadget protocol for fair validation consensus in ethereum. Int. J. Sci. Res. Comput. Sci. Eng. Inf. Technol. **3**(3), 291–298 (2018)
68. Jean-Louis, N., et al.: Sgxonerated: finding (and partially fixing) privacy flaws in tee-based smart contract platforms without breaking the tee. Cryptology ePrint Archive (2023)
69. Juels, A.: Fair Sequencing Services: Enabling a Provably Fair DeFi Ecosystem (2020). https://web.archive.org/web/20230921010521/https://blog.chain.link/chainlink-fair-sequencing-services-enabling-a-provably-fair-defi-ecosystem/. Accessed 20 Sept 2023

70. Juels, A., Eyal, I., Kelkar, M.: Miners, front-running-as-a-service is theft (2021). https://web.archive.org/web/20230920235654/https://www.coindesk.com/markets/2021/04/07/miners-front-running-as-a-service-is-theft/. Accessed 20 Sept 2023
71. JustLend. JustLend and Borrow in the Decentralized Platform (2023). https://web.archive.org/web/20230920222849/https://portal.justlend.org/. Accessed 20 Sept 2023
72. Kelkar, M., Deb, S., Kannan, S.: Order-fair consensus in the permissionless setting. In: Proceedings of the 9th ACM on ASIA Public-Key Cryptography Workshop, pp. 3–14 (2022)
73. Kelkar, M., Deb, S., Long, S., Juels, A., Kannan, S.: Themis: fast, strong order-fairness in byzantine consensus. In: Proceedings of the 2023 ACM SIGSAC Conference on Computer and Communications Security, pp. 475–489 (2023)
74. Kelkar, M., Zhang, F., Goldfeder, S., Juels, A.: Order-fairness for byzantine consensus. In: Micciancio, D., Ristenpart, T. (eds.) CRYPTO 2020. LNCS, vol. 12172, pp. 451–480. Springer, Cham (2020). https://doi.org/10.1007/978-3-030-56877-1_16
75. Kenton, W.: What is a limit order book? definition and data (2022). https://web.archive.org/web/20230920225847/https://www.investopedia.com/terms/l/limitorderbook.asp. Accessed 20 Sept 2023
76. Knight, O.: Ethereum Bot Gets Attacked for $20M as Validator Strikes Back (2023). https://web.archive.org/web/20230921001518/https://www.coindesk.com/business/2023/04/03/ethereum-mev-bot-gets-attacked-for-20m-as-validator-strikes-back/. Accessed 20 Sept 2023
77. Kocher, P., et al.: Spectre attacks: exploiting speculative execution. Commun. ACM **63**(7), 93–101 (2020)
78. Kursawe, K.: Wendy, the good little fairness widget: achieving order fairness for blockchains. In Proceedings of the 2nd ACM Conference on Advances in Financial Technologies, pp. 25–36 (2020)
79. Mackinga, T., Nadahalli, T., Wattenhofer, R.: Twap oracle attacks: easier done than said. In: 2022 IEEE International Conference on Blockchain and Cryptocurrency (ICBC), pp. 1–8. IEEE (2022)
80. McKeen, F., et al.: Intel® software guard extensions (intel® sgx) support for dynamic memory management inside an enclave. In: Proceedings of the Hardware and Architectural Support for Security and Privacy 2016, pp. 1–9 (2016)
81. Neuder, M.M., Drake, J.: Why enshrine Proposer-Builder Separation? A viable path to ePBS (2023). https://ethresear.ch/t/why-enshrine-proposer-builder-separation-a-viable-path-to-epbs/15710
82. Miller, A., Xia, Y., Croman, K., Shi, E., Song, D.: The honey badger of bft protocols. In: Proceedings of the 2016 ACM SIGSAC Conference on Computer and Communications Security, pp. 31–42 (2016)
83. Monnot, B.: Notes on Proposer-Builder Separation (PBS) (2022). https://web.archive.org/web/20230920234155/https://barnabe.substack.com/p/pbs. Accessed 20 Sept 2023
84. Gupta[@Mudit_Gupta], M.: That patch only patches a small bug but would've been irrelevant for the attack. The economic incentive is such that proposers will still manipulate the block. 25m profit for 1.8k slash. The vulnerability is in the design. X (2023). https://web.archive.org/web/20230921002806/https://twitter.com/Mudit_Gupta/status/1642873195475922946. Accessed 20 Sept 2023
85. Nakamoto, S.: Bitcoin whitepaper (2008). https://bitcoin.org/bitcoin.pdf. Accessed 17 July 2019

86. Nethermind[@NethermindEth]. Nethermind Ethereum client[version: aad88ee] (2023). https://web.archive.org/web/20230921021857/https://github.com/NethermindEth/nethermind. Accessed 20 Sept 2023
87. Pmcgoohan. MEV... do this (2021). https://web.archive.org/web/20230920235415/https://pmcgoohan.medium.com/mev-do-this-beb2754bca63. Accessed 20 Sept 2023
88. Prysm Ethereum Client[@prysmaticlabs]. Prysm: An Ethereum Consensus Implementation Written in Go[version: e76aedf] (2023). https://web.archive.org/web/20230921021611/https://github.com/prysmaticlabs/prysm. Accessed 20 Sept 2023
89. Reiter, M.K., Birman, K.P.: How to securely replicate services. ACM Trans. Program. Lang. Syst. (TOPLAS) **16**(3), 986–1009 (1994)
90. Sarkar, A.: Flashbots builds over 82% relay blocks, adding to Ethereum centralization (2022). https://web.archive.org/web/20230920234759/https://cointelegraph.com/news/flashbots-build-over-82-relay-blocks-adding-to-ethereum-centralization. Accessed 20 Sept 2023
91. Scopino, G.: Algo Bots and the Law: Technology, Automation, and the Regulation of Futures and Other Derivatives. Cambridge University Press, Cambridge (2020)
92. SCRT Labs[@scrtlabs]. Secret Network[version: f739659] (2023). https://web.archive.org/web/20230921021212/https://github.com/scrtlabs/SecretNetwork. Accessed 20 Sept 2023
93. Secret Network. Private Smart Contract on the Blockchain (2023). https://web.archive.org/web/20230921005955/https://scrt.network/about/about-secret-network. Accessed 20 Sept 2023
94. Espresso Systems. The espresso sequencer (2023). https://hackmd.io/@EspressoSystems/EspressoSequencer
95. Tran, K.C.: What is Wrapped Bitcoin (2022). https://web.archive.org/web/20230920223149/https://decrypt.co/resources/what-is-wbtc-explained-bitcoin-ethereum-defi. Accessed 20 Sept 2023
96. Uniswap. Introducing Uniswap v3 (2021). https://web.archive.org/web/20230920215730/https://blog.uniswap.org/uniswap-v3. Accessed 20 Sept 2023
97. Uniswap. Slippage Protection (2023). https://web.archive.org/web/20230921014544/https://uniswapv3book.com/docs/milestone_3/slippage-protection/. Accessed 20 Sept 2023
98. Upptic. Web3 Gaming (2023). https://web.archive.org/web/20230920201012/https://upptic.com/blog/web-3-gaming/. Accessed 20 Sept 2023
99. U.S. Department of the Treasury. U.S. Treasury Sanctions Notorious Virtual Currency Mixer Tornado Cash (2022). https://web.archive.org/web/20230920215017/https://home.treasury.gov/news/press-releases/jy0916. Accessed 20 Sept 2023
100. Van Bulck, J., et al.: Foreshadow: extracting the keys to the intel {SGX} kingdom with transient {Out-of-Order} execution. In: 27th USENIX Security Symposium (USENIX Security 18), pp. 991–1008 (2018)
101. Velasquez, F.: DeFi Exchange Mango's $114M Exploit Was 'Market Manipulation,' Not a Hack, Ex-FBI Special Agent Says (2022). https://web.archive.org/web/20230921011756/https://www.coindesk.com/tech/2022/10/20/defi-exchange-mangos-114m-exploit-was-market-manipulation-not-a-hack-ex-fbi-special-agent-says/. Accessed 20 Sept 2023
102. Weintraub, B., Torres, C.F., Nita-Rotaru, C., State, R.: A flash (bot) in the pan: measuring maximal extractable value in private pools. In: Proceedings of the 22nd ACM Internet Measurement Conference, pp. 458–471 (2022)

103. Whitmore, G.: Will You Purchase Blockchain Flight Delay Insurance (2022). https://web.archive.org/web/20230920214542/httsps://gum.criteo.com/syncframe?origin=publishertag&topUrl=www.forbes.com. Accessed 20 Sept 2023
104. Wikipedia. 0x (decentralized exchange infrastructure) (2023). https://web.archive.org/web/20230920215515/https://en.wikipedia.org/wiki/0x_%28decentralized_exchange_infrastructure%29. Accessed 20 Sept 2023
105. Zhang, F., Cecchetti, E., Croman, K., Juels, A., Shi, E.: Town crier: an authenticated data feed for smart contracts. In: Proceedings of the 2016 ACM SIGSAC Conference on Computer and Communications Security, pp. 270–282 (2016)
106. Zhang, Y., Setty, S., Chen, Q., Zhou, L., Alvisi, L.: Byzantine ordered consensus without byzantine oligarchy. In: 14th USENIX Symposium on Operating Systems Design and Implementation (OSDI 20), pp. 633–649 (2020)
107. Zhou, L., Qin, K., Gervais, A.: A2mm: mitigating frontrunning, transaction reordering and consensus instability in decentralized exchanges. arXiv preprint arXiv:2106.07371 (2021)
108. Züst, P., Nadahalli, T., Wattenhofer, Y.W.R.: Analyzing and preventing sandwich attacks in ethereum. ETH Zürich (2021)

Towards Regulation of Brazilian Blockchain Utilization

Marjori Klinczak[1]($\boxtimes$), Jose Simao de Paula Pinto[2], and Egon Wildauer[2]

[1] UFPR, Unifatec-PR, Mosaic Web, Curitiba, PR, Brazil
mnmk.lvseg@gmail.com
[2] UFPR, Curitiba, PR, Brazil

Abstract. Blockchain has seen significant growth in recent years, and although it is still related by many to Bitcoin, the growth of companies and other digital currencies is visible, which has led some countries to initiate a legislative approach in order to protect companies and consumers. Thus, some countries such as Switzerland have included cryptocurrencies within existing legislation with some adaptations, others such as Estonia have used blockchain in almost all of their public services, or already accept Bitcoin as a payment currency, such as El Salvador and Germany. However, little is discussed about the situation of emerging countries, such as Brazil, which has a vast territory and its particularities, mainly because it is still a developing country. The general objective of the work is to discuss the advances and challenges in regulating blockchain technology in general, focusing on Brazil, which, as it is still a developing country, has an even more uncertain scenario for the adoption of new and disruptive technologies., which can greatly help the country's growth and combat corruption.

Keywords: Blockchain · Brazil · challenges and opportunities

1 Introduction

According to Schwab (2016), Industry 4.0 has brought about a series of technological changes with a significant impact on everyday life, communication among people, businesses, and education. One of these changes is blockchain, which, despite being closely associated with cryptocurrencies and Bitcoin, has much broader applications across various sectors. It enables the creation of smart contracts, leading to the elimination of many intermediaries, such as banks and brokers.

Blockchain was introduced in 2008 as a new tool for data security and reliability, encrypting, recording, and making all transactions irreversible without the need for a regulatory authority (Nakamoto, 2008; Swan, 2015). According to Talwar (2015), all transactions are verified, and if applied, especially in the public sector, could reduce fraud, costs, and facilitate the processing of millions of daily transactions. Some countries, like Estonia, already have various systems and services operating on this technology (e-Identity, e-Health, e-Governance, e-Banking, among others), while others are still discussing how to implement or regulate it.

In Brazil, for instance, PIX was created as a way to transfer money almost instantly between individuals and businesses, and although it doesn't use blockchain architecture, it is based on it. The need (or not) for regulation is closely tied to the financial aspect involving decentralized finance and cryptocurrencies, where many believe that regulation would bring more security to the sector and the individuals involved in financial transactions.

The overall objective of this work is to discuss the advancements and challenges in the regulation of blockchain technology in general, with a focus on Brazil. Being a developing country, Brazil faces an even more uncertain scenario for the adoption of new and disruptive technologies that could significantly contribute to the country's growth and the fight against corruption.

The methodology applied to the research is bibliographic and exploratory, where, through the literature related to the already published theme and also on the official websites of the identified projects, we seek to investigate the initiatives that are being developed for the regulation of blockchain networks, along with their challenges and opportunities.

2 Blockchain

Blockchain is a decentralized architecture that can be applied in various sectors that require ensuring that transactions are executed, remain intact, and cannot be altered. Consequently, some of its applications can be found in storing medical data, citizen information, real estate and vehicle transactions, as well as in the financial sector through the creation of currencies or financial transactions, which were the initial purposes of its development, according to Khan and Byun. (2020).

With this, it can eliminate the intermediate parts of a series of transactions by creating a chain of blocks with reliable transactions, which are linked through hash values, ensuring that each block is not only unique, but that it has not been altered, as it contains the hash of the previous block.

This also means that a central authority is not necessary, as the entire network is responsible for validating these transactions, and it must be accepted by more than 51% of it to actually be executed (Khan and Byun, 2020).

According to Prux et al. (2021), blockchain can be divided into two major groups: public and private networks. Public networks have their own rules, and their operation does not depend on any legal aspect or regulation. On the other hand, private networks are generally used by companies and governments, thus needing to adhere to specific legislation.

The financial sector has also turned to the use of this technology, such as JP Morgan, which conducted its first international transactions on a public blockchain network in 2022 (Bloomberg, 2022). Many other institutions focused on decentralized finance have emerged, according to Prux et al. (2021).

Regarding the financial aspect, Makarov and Schoar (2022) mention that the 2008 financial crisis also contributed to a revolution in this sector, where the greatest focus of the new legislation that has been emerging is found. This is considered the most significant innovation in the sector in the last decade, with a focus on the ability to build decentralized and openly accessible platforms that reduce dependence on intermediaries.

As the financial sector has an impact on the entire economy, a significant portion of the regulatory discussion is focused on it, including the creation and provision of cryptocurrencies through exchanges. Another factor already under discussion is governance related to blockchain networks and the issue of data privacy, particularly in cases of potential money laundering.

3 Regulatory Frameworks

This section covers some of the initiatives aimed at regulating blockchain-based technologies, as well as the challenges and opportunities encountered in their use, first on a global scale and then with a focus on Brazil.

As a result, some countries with more advanced legislation on the subject include Canada, Estonia, Cyprus, Switzerland, Iceland, the United States, Japan, Malta, Germany, Australia, El Salvador, the United Kingdom, among others. In Europe, the Rue b portal (2023) provides information on the regulations of various European countries that have already adopted or are in the process of regulating the sector.

3.1 Switzerland

Switzerland has a project called 'Crypto Valley' in the Zug region, established in 2017 with legislation and tax incentives favorable to initiatives in the blockchain and crypto-assets market. One of the most attractive features is that gains from cryptocurrencies are treated as tax-exempt capital gains because cryptocurrencies and virtual currencies are classified as assets or properties. Mining is considered self-employment, and those engaged in the professional trading of cryptocurrencies or receiving them as salary need to declare them in their income tax. Since 2016, it has also been possible to use Bitcoin for tax payments.

The provision of cryptocurrency exchange and custody services is accepted and regulated by the Swiss Federal Tax Administration (SFTA) and the Swiss Financial Market Supervisory Authority (FINMA). Exchanges and virtual currency platforms are considered equivalent to financial institutions and, therefore, must comply with local anti-money laundering (AML), combating the financing of terrorism (CFT) obligations, and consumer protection, although some banking rules and limits are less burdensome (Rue a, 2023). To operate and list cryptocurrencies, Switzerland requires a license from the Swiss Financial Market Supervisory Authority (FINMA), and exchanges must inform their clients that their funds are not subject to protection if the company is supervised by FINMA.

Regarding cryptocurrency offerings (ICOs), they have been regulated since 2018 through a set of guidelines applying current financial legislation to proposals in various fields, such as securities trading banks and some collective investment schemes. In 2019, the Swiss government also approved a proposal requiring the Federal Council to adapt existing rules to include cryptocurrencies. In September 2020, the Swiss parliament approved the Blockchain Act, additionally determining the legality of cryptocurrency exchanges and cryptocurrency trading in Swiss law. The legislation requires compliance with local ICO, AML, and CFT requirements as soon as the token can be technically transferred to the blockchain infrastructure.

The country also has an extensive page with technical details of the mentioned legislation, security issues, and other rules, such as regulations against money laundering (AMLA) and necessary documents to start operations (Rue a, 2023).

3.2 Estonia

Estonia was one of the first countries to regulate cryptocurrencies in 2017 and has a portion of its public infrastructure built on blockchain, with initiatives such as e-Identity, e-Health, e-Governance, e-Banking, among others. For Estonia, virtual currencies have digital value and can be traded, distributed, or stored, but they are not considered legal tender.

In 2017, Estonia introduced a new law allowing entrepreneurs to apply for a license in two directions: virtual currency exchange for fiat/virtual currency and the provision of virtual currency wallet services (Rue d, 2023). The country is also aligned with anti-money laundering legislation. As an incentive, no annual license fees are charged, but a physical office on-site is required.

3.3 Other Countries

The United Kingdom has recently initiated plans to build an infrastructure for crypto assets, partially harmonized with the European Union, and has also adopted regulations regarding money laundering. Companies wishing to operate these assets in the country must register with the Financial Conduct Authority (FCA) to obtain part of the 4A license. Currently, it distinguishes between two categories of crypto assets – regulated tokens and unregulated tokens (Rue c, 2023).

In the United States, there is no consensus on blockchain and cryptocurrencies, with a mix of state and federal regulations. The Securities and Exchange Commission (SEC) regulates digital assets considered securities, while the Commodity Futures Trading Commission (CFTC) handles digital assets considered commodities.

Germany accepted Bitcoin as a means of payment equivalent to physical and legal currency in the country in 2018. It also has the Federal Financial Supervisory Authority of Germany (BaFin), responsible for enforcing national and EU regulations. As they are not yet fully harmonized, each case needs to be analyzed to identify which regulations will be applied (Rue e, 2023).

3.4 Brazil

Unlike the other countries mentioned, Brazil has much larger dimensions and is still in development, implying a different scenario for the regulation of blockchain and cryptocurrencies. The country still needs to address internal issues such as corruption, education, and other social problems, which are generally not as prevalent in already developed countries.

In 2017, a glossary was created with terms related to virtual currencies and forms of money laundering and corruption associated with them or other digital payment methods. In 2019, Brazil began issuing a warning through the Central Bank and the Securities and Exchange Commission (CVM) regarding the risk of investing in the crypto asset market. In the same year, through Normative Instruction No. 1,888, of May 2019 (IN 1888/19), the obligation to report cryptocurrency operations and capital gains in the income tax was established. This was due to a law from 2013 that aimed to regulate electronic payment systems, which did not include cryptocurrencies.

As an initial step in regulation, a CNAE class was created for crypto brokers or exchanges. This classification defines the activities provided by a company, defining them as 'legal entities involved in financial or non-financial activities that offer services related to crypto asset transactions, including brokerage, trading, or custody, and that can accept any means of payment, including other crypto assets.' It was only in 2020 that the use of blockchain in the public sector began to be considered.

Only at the end of 2022, Brazil established its legal framework for virtual assets (Law No. 14,478/22), which came into effect on June 20, 2023 (CMS, 2023). Its focus is to conceptualize the general principles of the area, and the Central Bank of Brazil has been designated as the competent authority to effectively regulate, authorize, and supervise virtual asset service providers ('VASPs') in Brazil, under Decree No. 11,563, of June 13, 2023. The rules are still under public discussion, and it is expected that they will come into effect in early 2024.

4 Opportunities and Challenges

As it is a technology that is not yet fully mature, there are numerous opportunities for applications, as well as challenges, given that it is an innovation and many aspects need testing. Consequently, some countries are betting on the greater growth of the technology, providing space for companies to operate there, while others do not view all the changes that its use can bring across various sectors of the economy as positively.

For example, the work by Trabalho and Prux et al. (2021) aimed to identify opportunities and challenges in the use of blockchain in the Brazilian government's accounts. They conducted a survey through a questionnaire with 94 professionals and found that 89.4% of the respondents believe that blockchain can be applied in financial transactions, auditing, and asset transfers. The main benefits identified include control, information security, and fraud prevention. However, 98.9% of the respondents believe that the biggest challenges in implementation are the lack of knowledge and the difficulty in adapting existing systems. In the context of Brazil, the country faces specific challenges in blockchain regulation, such as:

- Lack of regulatory awareness, as discussions about cryptocurrencies in the country began only with the rapid appreciation of Bitcoin. This lack of awareness could lead to legal complexity for companies and investors, such as barriers to accessing financial services for cryptocurrency exchanges.
- Complex tax framework for both employee payments and taxes, especially with the proposed current change in the union of some taxes, resulting in a VAT, as many

European countries already have. However, it is still unclear which taxes will be included and what their values will be.
- Need for regulatory education, as blockchain is still strongly associated with Bitcoin, potentially resulting in incorrect or outdated regulations. This point can also be impacted by the challenge in classifying digital assets, especially as new terms emerge and legislative capacity is not very agile.
- Implementation of digital identities, as it was possible until recently to have an identification document from each state in the country, and now there is integration between states and systems.
- Unequal internet access across the country, especially in more remote regions.
- Consumer protection with data privacy guarantees, as well as compliance with the General Data Protection Law (LGPD), similar to the General Data Protection Regulation in Europe (GDPR).
- Despite all this, some successful initiatives have emerged, such as the blockchain structure in the Commercial Registry Office of the State of Ceará, Brazil, aiming to protect company records, databases, combat fraud, and reduce the time spent validating documents (Biancolini et al., 2018).

The digital financial system is also running on a network similar to blockchain, known as PIX, a type of transaction that can be conducted 24 h a day, 7 days a week, where individuals or companies receive the amount almost immediately, unlike other types of transactions that must be conducted and executed within banking hours (Biancolini et al., 2018).

In 2020, the Federal Court of Accounts (TCU), the external control body of the federal government, published an extensive and detailed report on the adoption of blockchain and its technologies in public administration (TCU, 2020), with the primary goal of using the technology to oversee government spending in contracts and bids.

5 Conclusion

The blockchain has experienced significant growth, and its application is seen with great potential by many countries and sectors. Thus, it is important to define how to deal with the new technology and how to integrate it into the working methods of each nation to meet their needs.

Switzerland, for example, solved the issue of regulating cryptocurrencies within its existing legislation with some adaptations. Estonia extensively incorporated blockchain into its public sector. Some countries, such as Germany and Switzerland, allow payments and transactions to be made through cryptocurrencies. Overall, Europe appears to have a favorable scenario for blockchain, with several countries already aligned with the European Union and contributing to local legislations.

On the other hand, some countries are still uncertain about whether to adopt blockchain, but it is evident that this is the trend, and it will likely happen at some point. In Brazil, especially, a change in behavior is visible. In 2019, the focus was on warning the population that cryptocurrencies were unstable and could cause financial losses. Now, there is a discussion about greater regulation of exchanges, which are already allowed to operate in the country.

While many legislations focus on regulating the financial sector due to its significant impact on the entire economy, it is important to note that blockchain projects have an even broader application. New legislations may emerge to address this, or existing ones may undergo adaptations, as seen in the case of Switzerland. Therefore, this entire new market and new opportunities still lack regulation in many countries, as legal certainty is necessary in order to bring greater security to companies and consumers, in addition to preventing it from being used for fraud and crimes. With this, technology moves towards common regulatory objectives, bringing greater transparency to markets and focusing on the creation and distribution of new currencies, transaction taxation and governance.

As future work, a more comprehensive and in-depth comparative study is desired to analyze the scope of these regulations. This would enable a comparison between countries regarding the level of permissiveness in these regulations.

Disclosure of Interests. The authors have no competing interests to declare that are relevant to the content of this article.

References

Biancolini, A., Silva, F.C.D., Osti, J.R.: Como a tecnologia Blockchain vem impactando ou pode impactar nas estruturas administrativas estatais. Revista Jurídica da Escola Superior de Advocacia da OAB-PR (8) (2018)

Bloomberg. Portal Homepage. https://www.bloomberg.com/news/articles/2022-11-02/jpmorgan-executes-its-first-defi-trade-using-public-blockchain. Accessed 11 Dec 2023

Khan, P.W., Byun, Y.: A blockchain-based secure image encryption scheme for the industrial internet of things. Entropy **22**, 175 (2020). https://doi.org/10.3390/e22020175

Makarov, I., Schoar, A.: BIS Working Papers No 1061 Cryptocurrencies and Decentralized Finance, Monetary and Economic Department (2022)

Nakamoto, S.: Bitcoin: A (2008). https://bitcoin.org/bitcoin.pdf. Accessed 01 Dec 2023

Prux, C., Momo, F.D.S., Melati, C.: Opportunities and challenges of using blockchain technology in government accounting in Brazil. Special Issue on Blockchain, Cryptocurrencies and Distributed Organizations, vol. 18, no. Spe, Art. 4, e200109 (2021). https://doi.org/10.1590/1807-7692bar2021200109

RUE a, Switzerland Homepage. https://rue.ee/crypto-regulations/switzerland/. Accessed 08 Dec 2023

RUE b, Crypto Regulations. https://rue.ee/crypto-regulations/. Accessed 08 Dec 2023

RUE c, UK Homepage. https://rue.ee/crypto-regulations/uk/. Accessed 08 Dec 2023

RUE d, Estonia Homepage. https://rue.ee/crypto-regulations/estonia/. Accessed 08 Dec 2023

RUE e, Germany Homepage. https://rue.ee/crypto-regulations/germany/. Accessed 08 Dec 2023

Schwab, K.: A quarta revolução industrial. São Paulo: Edipro (2016)

Swan, M.: Blockchain: Blueprint for a New Economy. O'Reilly Media, Boston (2015)

Talwar, R.: The future of business: critical insights into a rapidly changing world from 60 future thinkers, 1st edn. Fast Future Publishing, London (2015)

TCU Blockchain Homepage. https://portal.tcu.gov.br/data/files/59/02/40/6E/C4854710A7AE4547E18818A8/Blockchain_sumario_executivo.pdf. Accessed 08 Dec 2023

An Analysis and Proposal on Standardization and R&D Strategies to Promote Responsible Development of Digital Asset

Takaya Sugino[✉], Masato Yamanaka[✉], and Carole House[✉]

Georgetown University, Washington, DC, USA
{ts1433,my601}@georgetown.edu, carole.n.house@gmail.com

Abstract. The use of digital assets in financial services introduces new and controversial challenges associated with the use of new blockchain-based technologies. To promote the mass adoption of digital assets for financial services, it is essential to standardize systems and mechanisms that enable efficient operations of service providers while mitigating associated risks. In contrast to traditional finance, the standardization of digital asset finance by standards-setting bodies has made limited progress. As an initial step towards promoting standardization in digital asset financial services, we have summarized technical, operational, and regulatory requirements that need standardization and presented the current status of standardization efforts in each requirement.

Keywords: Standardization · Standard · Regulation · Distributed Ledger · Blockchain · Digital Asset

1 Introduction

1.1 Background

This document outlines the requirements for standardization in the field of digital assets and ultimately aims to contribute to their development. In this context, digital assets are defined as any digital representation of value recorded on a cryptographically secured distributed ledger or similar technology [54]. Standardization is generally a process of reduction, simplification, and rationalization, supporting faster implementation of new technology and providing a mechanism for various stakeholders to objectively evaluate products and services in areas of quality and security. Standardization efforts are intended to bring together multiple stakeholders in an international forum to bring together their expertise to discuss the best standards for the entire ecosystem and to shape standards for new technology. Standardization of financial products and services is also meant to ensure the reliability of systems and interoperability among systems and to improve the operational efficiency of financial institutions. It also aims to ensure the safety and convenience of financial products and services provided to customers, reduce and control unfair activities and financial crimes, and stabilize the whole financial system.

For example, the International Organization for Standardization's Technical Committee 68 (ISO TC 68) [13] is responsible for coordinating the development of international standards in financial services. Message formats for transmitting transaction information, the development of coding systems, and encryption schemes are currently significant areas of standards research in financial services, with many standards currently under development, including proposal stage and working stage standards, as well as standards awaiting committee approval. Regarding regulation, international standards-setting bodies (the Financial Stability Board (FSB)"", International Organization of Securities Commissions (IOSCO), Financial Action Task Force (FATF), etc.) have also established standards for regulators and financial institutions. Standardized requirements include operational ones, including customer asset management, information disclosure, fraud, and crime control, and prudential ones, including setting capital and liquidity buffers. In traditional finance, standardization efforts have been successful due to the contributions of many international communities and organizations.

1.2 Our Contribution

In contrast to the success of standardization efforts in traditional finance, the digital asset industry is still in its infancy, with many operators building their own systems and operations without any discussion of technology and, operational standardization and compliance with regulations. However, standardization is eventually necessary to expand the scale of financial products and services in digital assets, just as in digital finance. On the other hand, since the industry is still immature and has emerging risks and challenges, it is unclear what specific requirements should be standardized among technologies supporting digital asset-related financial services, the operation of these services, and the regulations applied to them. This document provides a comprehensive list of technology, operational, and regulatory requirements for financial services in the field of digital assets that may need to be standardized. This work should be significantly valuable because it identifies which requirements can be addressed by applying existing standards for traditional finance or newly recommended standards by standards-setting bodies and which requirements will need further standardization efforts. By helping the industry have an overall picture of what organizations should be responsible for standardizing requirements, this paper significantly contributes to the efficient development of standardization efforts in the industry.

2 Categories of Requirements

In the following sections, the requirements are divided into three categories - technical, operational, and regulatory -, each of which is discussed later in detail. Such categorization has multiple implications. First, because there are numerous requirements for financial services in the field of digital assets, without such an axis, an exhaustive list would be very difficult to compile and complicated to understand. Second, the organizations that should lead the standardization efforts differ in each category. In standardization, the perspectives of technology developers and academia will be critical for technical requirements, the perspectives of service providers will be for operational requirements, and the perspectives of regulators and regulations will be for regulatory requirements. Then, discussions among all of the stakeholders will be necessary for each requirement under the responsible standards-setting bodies. This categorization will make it more efficient to determine who is responsible for future standardization efforts and to promote discussions among all of the stakeholders under the responsible party.

3 Requirements and Current Status

This section summarizes a description of each requirement in the field of digital assets and the current status of standardization for each requirement. The main categories of requirements include technology, operational, and regulatory requirements.

3.1 Technology Requirements

Technical requirements are divided into two categories: Technology and Operation. The Technology category encompasses requirements for cryptographic technology and the hardware and software technical specifications that underpin the digital asset mechanism. The Operation category includes requirements for operational mechanisms and organizational structures to ensure the security and integrity of these technologies. The distinction in this document between Operational Requirements and Operation as a subcategory of Technical Requirements is that operations contributing to improving and maintaining the technology (e.g., safety, interoperability) are included in Technical Requirements, while other requirements for the operations of digital asset finance are defined as Operational Requirements.

3.1.1 Technology Technology itself is an essential part of requirements that can be standardized for secure digital asset mechanisms.

Cryptographic Techniques: This category encompasses cryptographic methods essential for blockchain and distributed ledger technology, including encryption algorithms, digital signature schemes, key management protocols, authentication protocols, and hash functions. These techniques must adhere to the provable security paradigm, which entails rigorous mathematical security proofs based on challenging mathematical problems and secure key management assumptions. The validation of these security proofs is primarily conducted through academic processes, notably through a rigorous peer-review process at academic conferences organized by the International Association for Cryptologic Research (IACR), the Institute of Electrical and Electronics Engineers

(IEEE), and the Association for Computing Machinery (ACM), among others. This peer-review process is fundamental to establishing the trustworthiness and correctness of security proofs. Additionally, the standardization process at the National Institute of Standards and Technology (NIST), which includes cryptographic algorithm competitions such as the Advanced Encryption Standard (AES) [49], the Secure Hash Algorithm 3 (SHA-3) [46], and the Post-Quantum Cryptography (PQC) [47] competitions, applies a similar academic reviewing methodology. The ISO/IEC JTC 1 [6], which oversees the international standardization process through SC27/WG2, relies on academic evaluation results for its standardization activities, even though the organization itself lacks the capability to conduct security evaluations. Annex A of ISO/IEC 18033-1 [4] outlines a list of qualified academic conferences and journals and the processes for initiating standardization.

Backbone Protocol: This category encompasses the fundamental protocols that ensure the distributed nature and security of blockchain backbone systems, including peer-to-peer (P2P) protocols, consensus mechanisms such as Proof of Work (PoW) and Proof of Stake (PoS), and structures like Merkle Trees. The security of these protocols is validated through a rigorous academic review process, similar to that of cryptographic techniques. Although numerous academic papers have been published on the security of these protocols, there is currently no organization or entity dedicated to validating the correctness of these academic publications. Beyond security, other crucial factors such as interoperability and decentralization must also be assessed. The consensus protocol is further discussed in the Transaction Processing section of the Operational Requirements.

Application Protocol: This category includes protocols specific to individual applications. While not all applications require privacy protection, many blockchain-based applications, such as stablecoins, necessitate some privacy protection mechanisms. A common type of application protocol is secure transactions, such as those realized by the original Bitcoin protocol. Privacy protection mechanisms, known as Privacy Enhancing Technologies (PETs), are crucial in this context. The security of PETs is typically evaluated through rigorous academic review processes, similar to those used for cryptographic technologies. Some PETs have already been standardized by ISO/IEC SC27/WG2. For other types of protocols, numerous academic papers discussing their security have been published, yet there is no organization or entity dedicated to validating the correctness of these academic publications.

Application Logic: This category includes the protocols and software logic required to develop applications and businesses based on blockchain technologies. The security of such application logic is generally ensured under the Information Security Management System (ISMS), standardized by the ISO/IEC 27000 [8] series. Since no system is completely secure against all types of attacks, security controls are derived from risk management practices. Actual security assessments involve code reviews, penetration tests, bug bounty programs, formal analyses, and similar methodologies. Secure coding guidelines also play a crucial role in enhancing the security level of application logic.

Implementation: This category focuses on the security assurance of software and hardware that implement all cryptographic techniques, backbone protocols, application protocols, and application logic. The security level of these implementations is evaluated using common criteria, standardized as ISO/IEC 15408 [1]. The implementation must be secure at all points within a system. User wallets, in particular, represent a critical point of failure since they are often managed by individuals who may lack sufficient skill and literacy. Therefore, a user-friendly and secure standard for wallet software and hardware is essential. Ideally, protection profiles and security target documents that align with ISO/IEC 15408 should be developed, though these are currently lacking. Many wallets are implemented on smartphones, utilizing Hardware Security Modules (HSM) such as Trusted Execution Environments (TEE) and Secure Elements (SE). However, the functionality of HSMs is currently limited and not flexible enough to accommodate newly developed cryptographic algorithms and protocols aimed at enhancing security and privacy protection. Furthermore, the specifications of HSMs are controlled by a small number of companies, highlighting the need for open standards and fair governance of secure wallets. Additionally, supply chain management of software and hardware is crucial for ensuring implementation security. A standardized framework to enable public verifiability and provenance of implementation is also necessary.

3.1.2 Operation This category contains all operations related to security mechanisms and organizational operations. The security of this category is generally generated under the Information Security Management System (ISMS), which is standardized as ISO/IEC 27000 series.

Cryptographic Key Management: For digital asset mechanisms, the major part of operation is cryptographic key management on both the server (service provider) side and the user side. NIST issues special publications on cryptographic key management such as NIST SP800-57 [51].

Cryptogographic Agility Maintainance: Blockchain and digital asset mechanisms that require long-term security should consider cryptographic agility. Cryptographic agility is a concept to safely replace weak cryptographic algorithms/protocols to secure one when a compromise of cryptographic mechanisms happens. Cryptographic agility has been extensively discussed at IETF, but the process of transition varies according to the use cases of cryptographic techniques. Moreover, for digital assets, the system needs to ensure very long-term security. Because there is no current standard to ensure the long-term (or eternal) security of underlying cryptography, we need to establish a mechanism for cryptographic agility. It is essential in the era of Quantum Computing which breaks modern public key cryptography.

Audit and Inspection: Regarding the requirements mentioned in the Technology subsection, it may be necessary to standardize specific requirements for system audits to establish a cycle of regularly identifying vulnerabilities and enhancing system robustness. Naturally, if such standards are to be created, they will need to be updated regularly. The section on regulatory requirements mentions that service providers should standardize the conduct of system audits.

System Backup: Backing up the system in the event of a cyber attack or major system failure is one of the key requirements in this category. There may be a need to standardize specific technical methods for system backup. This requirement is also related to Incident Response, which will be discussed later as one of the operational requirements, as well as governance structure and contingency planning as regulatory requirements.

3.2 Operational Requirements

This document defines operational requirements as requirements related to the management of information and data needed for proper regulatory compliance and customer service.

Transaction Validation: This category includes requirements for procedures and mechanisms used to validate digital asset transactions. First, the requirements include consensus mechanisms (Proof of Work, Proof of Stake, etc.) adopted for validating transactions on blockchain technology. This requirement can be considered a technical requirement given that it is already embedded in the technology. While each consensus mechanism has strengths and weaknesses, each aims to exceed a certain level for security, accessibility, scalability, sustainability, and decentralization. The industry is currently working to overcome the shortcomings of consensus mechanisms. The NIST provides several guidelines focusing on consensus mechanisms and algorithms. NISTIR8202 [50] discusses different consensus mechanisms, highlighting their operational principles and security aspects. ISO TC 307 also aims to provide a reliable framework for selecting and implementing consensus mechanisms that best fit specific use cases and performance requirements in blockchain technology [12].

The requirements also include validating the legitimacy of the counterparty to prevent crimes, including Anti Money Laundering (AML)/Combating the Financing of Terrorism (CFT). This involves checking whether the counterparty may have been involved in criminal activity in the past or may be designated on blacklists. This requirement can be categorized as a regulatory requirement. Regarding this requirement, the Travel Rule [23] is a standardized rule that obliges service providers to check the validity of counterparty service providers and wallets involved in digital asset transactions. It also recommends reporting suspicious transactions to regulatory authorities in each jurisdiction. However, there are still various challenges: difference in the degree of compliance with the rule among service providers [26], the limited traceability of a wallet's criminal involvement, and the inapplicability for transactions that occur with self custodial wallets. Solutions such as issuing Verifiable Credentials to wallets are discussed to address these issues. Currently, DID/SSI and Verifiable Credential mechanisms are standardized at W3C [56] [?] [55]. However, these standardization efforts are on the fundamental framework, system model, and protocols. They are not financial application-specific. There are several existing trials to combine DID and VC mechanisms with AML/KYC functionality.

Customer Verification: This category includes requirements related to the identification of users by service providers. The requirements include both authentication and authorization. Authentication is the process of collecting, maintaining, and evaluating digital identity information, while authorization is the process of authorizing user access to services. In traditional finance, Open Authorization (OAuth) [34] has established a widely-used standard for user authorization, and OpenID Foundation has created a common standard for user authentication called OpenID Connect [35]. The Fast Identity Online (FIDO) Alliance has also developed standards for biometrics and secure keys in authentication, such as FIDO UAF (Universal Authentication Framework) [15] and FIDO U2F (Universal 2nd Factor) [14]. It is noteworthy how these existing standards or new ones for authentication and authorization will be applied to the field of digital asset finance. Conducting KYC in transactions is a regulatory standard by the FATF [24].

Privacy Protection: This category includes requirements related to protecting customer privacy information. While restricted access to private information can hinder criminal investigations, there exist various anonymization technologies in the field of digital assets, such as privacy coins and mixing services. With the ongoing development of many technologies, the standardization of privacy protection process remains a long-term goal. However, to balance the prevention of financial crime and privacy protection, it is ideal for multi-stakeholders in regulation, law, and technology to develop a common understanding of privacy protection and standardize appropriate processes. ISO 27701 [11] provides guidelines for a Privacy Information Management System, which can serve as a foundation for these efforts.

Consideration of privacy protection is crucial when designing widely-used digital asset systems. Standardizing privacy requirements is challenging because the concept and requirements of privacy vary according to community, region, and nation. While privacy is universally recognized as essential, there is no consensus on which privacy-enhancing technologies (PETs) and their combinations meet specific privacy requirements. Numerous efforts are underway to integrate PETs with blockchain technology, which may offer promising solutions. However, there is no common framework for evaluating the adequacy of specific PETs for specific use cases. Therefore, a series of common documents on PETs is needed to establish this understanding.

Data Integrity: This category includes data formats such as message structure, data types, message flows, and message versions, and a robust framework containing systems and procedures for accurate and timely collection, protection, and reporting of data. The use of standardized data formats ensures consistent and reliable data management.

Due to the global and cross-border nature of Internet technology, one of the main purposes of international standards is to ensure interoperability. ISO TC68 has been already working on identifiers of digital assets and identifiers of users. In the future, international standards regarding data formats are needed. ISO 20022 is an international standard for electronic data interchange between financial institutions. It includes the Legal Entity Identifier (LWI) [2,3], which uniquely identify participants in financial transactions; the Financial Instrument Short Name (FISN) [5], a data format of the issuer's short name and the abbreviated characteristics of the financial instrument for use in trading and administration of financial securities; and the Digital Token Identifier (DTI [7]), which defines the assignment and generation of unique, fixed-length identifiers for digital tokens. Several digital assets comply with the ISO 20022 standard, and the list of compliant assets is continuously expanding. ISO 20022 is periodically updated to include new additions. We should assume a situation in which different nations rely on different trust models for underlying technology, for example, different DLTs and consensus algorithms. In that case, we need to evaluate the level of trust for each specific transaction data. A framework to indicate such a level of trust and its provenance is needed.

Although it is rather a regulatory requirement, with respect to data collection, protection, and reporting, the FSB [28] and IOSCO [36] have published analyses of the types of data needed for the purposes of criminal investigation and prudential risk assessment. The FSB recommends that digital asset service providers have a framework for timely and accurate data management to fulfill their regulatory and supervisory mandates, and that regulators have access to such data.

Cooperation Among Authorities and Businesses: This category includes requirements of cooperation among digital asset service providers, between service providers and regulatory authorities, and among regulatory authorities in the process of risk management and criminal investigation. Due to the technical characteristics of distributed ledgers, unlike traditional finance, it is easier to provide financial services through digital assets both domestically and internationally. While on-chain data is generally publicly accessible regardless of location, there is often off-chain information and other data needed in the course of risk management and criminal investigation. It is essential that service providers and regulatory authorities cooperate with counterparts that adhere to similar standards of risk management and criminal investigation. Standardizing cooperation arrangements and mechanisms with other service providers and regulatory authorities should enhance the efficiency of their operations. While the FSB, IOSCO, and FATF have published recommendations for international cooperation among service providers and regulatory authorities, they do not provide specific cooperation arrangements or mechanisms [25,29,37]. No standardization efforts on such arrangements or mechanisms have been made yet.

Incident Response:: This requirement refers to rapid and appropriate post-incident response in the event of a serious cybersecurity incident. The NIST Cybersecurity Framework [48], ISO/IEC 27001 [9], and ISO/IEC 27035 [10] provide comprehensive guidelines for cybersecurity but are not explicitly limited to digital assets. The Information Sharing and Analysis Center (CryptoISAC) [21] aims to strengthen the cybersecurity posture of the digital asset industry by providing information sharing, threat intelligence, and best practices. Digital asset-related service providers often have opaque and inadequate cybersecurity systems, making the standardization of incident response in the industry a necessity.

Accounting and Reporting: Accounting and reporting requirements for digital asset services are subject to the evolving regulatory landscape and vary across jurisdictions. The International Accounting Standards Board (IASB) [20] and the Financial Accounting Standards Board (FASB) [19] have generally established traditional accounting standards such as IFRS and GAPP. Specific guidance on the trading, holding, and valuation of digital assets has been recently addressed in the core IASB and FASB standards [19].

3.3 Regulatory Requirements

Regulatory requirements are defined as those related to management actions and other actions that service providers are obligated to take by the laws of each jurisdiction. These requirements directly serve three objectives: protecting customers and investors, preventing unfairness and financial crime, and ensuring the stability of the financial system. In this section, this document organizes regulatory requirements according to these three objectives. While most requirements serve multiple objectives, this categorization is intended to provide clarity.

3.3.1 Protection of Stakeholders

Responsibility Identification: This category aims to clarify where the responsibility lies to apply regulations to digital asset service providers. The locus of responsibility is evident for centralized service providers but not for decentralized service providers. A number of international institutions tend to build new regulatory frameworks upon the principle of "Same Activity, Same Risk, Same Regulation." This principle means that decentralized service providers also have a locus of responsibility somewhere and should be subject to the same regulations as centralized service providers after identifying it. The IOSCO has recently published the Final Report with Policy Recommendations on Decentralized Finance (DeFi) [43], stating that "a regulator should aim to identify the persons and entities of a purported DeFi arrangement that could be subject to its applicable regulatory framework." It also provides a list of facts and circumstances that could be examined to determine a "Responsible Person(s)," although more detailed analysis to identify "Responsible Person(s)" might be needed if this approach is widely used. On the other hand, there are also studies that explain the need to accept the absence of a responsible party through "true decentralization." These studies provide an evaluation framework for decentralization and recommend regulatory frameworks for embracing decentralization [22,44,53].

Governance Structure: This section addresses the governance structures and procedures of digital asset service providers, emphasizing the necessity for external oversight mechanisms. In traditional finance, the Basel Committee on Banking Supervision (BCBS) has issued the Corporate Governance Principles for Banks [16], which traditional financial institutions are incentivized to follow. These principles address corporate governance risks specific to financial services, as well as general governance principles applicable to other industries. Similarly, centralized digital asset service providers face governance risks, such as conflicts of interest arising from third-party contracts and the operation of multiple services. Additionally, decentralized finance (DeFi) encounters issues like governance opacity (e.g., decentralization of control and conflicts of interest among market participants) and implementation risks (e.g., hacking and consensus difficulties).

To address these specific risks in digital asset services, international standards-setting bodies have established regulatory standards. The Financial Stability Board (FSB) [30] and the International Organization of Securities Commissions (IOSCO) [38] have set standards concerning relationships with third-party operators, including measures to protect client assets (redemption and withdrawals) in the event of issues with third-party operators and outsourcing arrangements. The FSB has also published a consultation paper [27] analyzing combinations of functions that could exacerbate vulnerabilities, including conflicts of interest. This paper discusses the standardization of these governance aspects. Regarding DeFi, the IOSCO DeFi paper recommends identifying and disclosing risks related to DeFi governance. It is crucial to detail these risks comprehensively and standardize specific risk identification methods.

Information Disclosure: This category encompasses the transparent disclosure of information about the products, services, and management of digital asset service providers to investors. In traditional finance, it is mandatory to disclose information necessary for investors to make informed investment decisions. Such information includes details about governance structures, operational procedures, and technical specifications. Standards for information disclosure, tailored to specific financial risks, are established by bodies such as the IFRS, FSB, BCBS, and IOSCO. Similarly, digital asset financial services require disclosure standards based on the identification of their unique risks.

For centralized digital asset service providers, the IOSCO and FSB [31] have already published papers outlining the specific information that needs to be disclosed to users and investors. The IOSCO [39] recommendations include disclosures about new digital asset projects when a provider begins handling a new digital asset. However, there is no standardized method for disclosing technical specifications and associated risks in a manner that is easily comprehensible to investors and users. Furthermore, for decentralized finance (DeFi), there is a need for standardized information disclosure based on the identification of risks specific to DeFi. Nonetheless, no standards-setting bodies have successfully provided a comprehensive identification of these risks. In relation to the section on Responsibility Identification, it is also essential to define what constitutes a digital asset service provider.

Asset Custody and Storage: This category encompasses procedures related to the business records, accounts, and reconciliation of customer assets, alongside policies to mitigate the risk of inaccessibility of customer assets. It includes guidelines for protecting customers in the event of theft or loss of customer assets, legal arrangements for the transfer of rights in custody and staking, and procedures for the holding and redemption of customer assets by stablecoin issuers. Additionally, it involves requirements for private key management for centralized custody service providers.

IOSCO [39] has already issued recommendations covering most items in this category for centralized service providers. These recommendations establish specific standards for maintaining up-to-date client asset records and accounts, conducting regular client asset reconciliations, and implementing processes to mitigate the risks of loss, theft, and inaccessibility. The FSB has also published a paper outlining standards for similar requirements for stablecoins in the context of financial system stability [33]. However, regulatory challenges persist for some aspects, such as the legal arrangements related to property rights in custody and staking. Regarding decentralized finance (DeFi), IOSCO recommends in the DeFi paper that decentralized financial service providers comply with its standards for centralized service providers. Nevertheless, it remains to be seen whether regulatory authorities in each jurisdiction will widely adopt and enforce the standards set forth in the IOSCO DeFi paper.

Marketing and Sales: This category includes requirements for evaluating and disclosing to customers the adequacy and appropriateness of digital asset products and services, the assessment of marketing materials and advertisements, and mechanisms for responding to customer inquiries and complaints. It also involves disclosing information about the project when marketing new digital assets handled by the service provider. Furthermore, this category addresses the adequacy of customer solicitation methods through referral programs, affiliation programs, social media, etc., known as reverse solicitation.

The requirements for this category have been largely standardized by the IOSCO [39]. Standards are established for clear, concise, non-technical disclosures of critical features and risks related to digital assets and services, as well as the evaluation of such disclosures. Additionally, there are standards for establishing efficient mechanisms to address customer complaints and prevent misinterpretation during the marketing and advertisement process. However, regarding reverse solicitation [52], although the associated risks have been discussed, no monitoring method has been established, resulting in an absence of standards, including within traditional finance. In the context of decentralized finance

(DeFi), decentralized service providers often do not comply with the standards due to a lack of regulation in various jurisdictions.

3.3.2 Prevention of Unfairness and Financial Crimes

Transaction Processing: This category pertains to the policies and procedures designed to ensure fair trading practices for customers and to prevent and enforce actions against criminal activities, including fraud and market abuse. It includes procedures for properly managing non-public information, systems and policies to ensure the fair and prompt execution of customer orders, market surveillance, and Anti-Money Laundering/Countering the Financing of Terrorism (AML/CFT) requirements. Regulatory standards for these requirements have already been recommended by the IOSCO and FATF [30].

For crime prevention and AML/CFT requirements, the FATF recommends standardizing compliance with the travel rule and the implementation of customer verification. However, as noted in the operational requirements, there is no detailed standardization of practical methods for complying with these specific regulatory standards. The lack of standardization in operational requirements, including data integrity and cooperation among service providers and regulatory authorities, complicates compliance with these regulatory standards. Regarding fairness in customer order processing, the IOSCO has recommended arrangements for routing client orders and other trade processing services, as well as surveillance and corrective action requirements to detect and prevent market abuse [40]. However, specific methodologies remain unclear. For example, Maximal Extractable Value (MEV) extractors engage in manipulative practices. Although technical and preventive measures are being discussed, unfair trading practices are currently unregulated. It remains to be seen whether the standardization of market surveillance and AML/CFT requirements will be effective not only for decentralized service providers but also for centralized service providers.

System Monitoring: This category includes risk management practices that monitor and assess all significant sources of risk related to technical flaws and cyber attacks. There are many different types of cyber attacks, and technical countermeasures against these attacks have been primarily discussed in academic circles. As mentioned in the section on technical standards, developing technical standards for countermeasures is effective. However, risk management also requires the monitoring and evaluation of technology, necessitating the standardization of risk management frameworks for personnel, processes, and systems. The IOSCO standardizes requirements for service providers to implement a risk management framework. [41] It also mandates that service providers review their risk management framework at least annually, conduct frequent normative audits, and undertake at least one independent audit per year. However, specific details on what constitutes adequate risk management to mitigate all risks-including ransomware, Sybil attacks, exploitation of smart contract vulnerabilities, exploitation of single points of failure such as Oracles and Bridges, and wallet-related hacking-are not provided. For standardization purposes, it is necessary to reconsider what constitutes an adequate risk management framework that addresses all these risks. While it is impossible to manage all risks because new vulnerabilities are continuously discovered, standardizing operational requirements for post-response to cybersecurity incidents is also crucial.

Information Disclosure: This category includes risk management procedures to disclose significant sources of risk, such as technical flaws or cyber attacks, to investors and customers in a clear and non-technical manner. While it is essential to have in place and disclose procedures to adequately protect clients and investors after a technical flaw or attack has occurred, the disclosure of technical risk and security information must be made in advance as well. The IOSCO has standardized the requirement to disclose information regarding these technical risks [42].

3.3.3 Stability of Financial System ***Contingency Plan:*** This category encompasses requirements related to governance arrangements for managing contingencies, ensuring effective managerial decision-making in the face of risks. The requirements include a business recovery and continuity plan, human intervention when necessary, and compliance and internal audit systems during contingencies. It is important to note that cyber security incident response is classified as an operational requirement and is not included in this classification. The Financial Stability Board (FSB) has already published high-level recommendations for this category for centralized digital asset service providers. However, there remain outstanding issues, such as the legal treatment of client assets during contingencies [32]. No recommendations exist for decentralized finance in this category, but numerous issues pertain to designing incentives for business continuity and the decision-making process when human intervention is required. The governance mechanisms in decentralized financial service providers face challenges in functioning effectively during contingencies, where prompt and adequate decision-making is essential.

Prudential Management: This category includes measures to mitigate the adverse impact of digital asset service operators on the broader financial system. Such spillover effects may result from their interconnections and dependencies with the broader financial system. This category encompasses appropriate measures to identify these interconnections and supervise and mitigate associated risks. Examples include procedures, disclosures, and capital and liquidity requirements regarding backed assets to ensure the stability of stablecoin value. The requirements also include capital and liquidity standards for lending services. For decentralized service providers, prudential risks also encompass "staking" requirements, which integrate one token type into another algorithm, as well as leverage and liquid staking requirements that could create asset bubbles.

The standardization of prudential requirements has been progressing, as evidenced by the FSB's publication of detailed recommendations on stablecoin arrangements [33] following recent incidents involving stablecoins. Additionally, the Basel Committee on Banking Supervision (BCBS) has published its standard on the prudential treatment of banks' exposures to digital assets [17] and recently issued a public consultation on proposed amendments to its standard [18]. While the global banking system's direct exposure to digital assets remains relatively low, international standards-setting bodies have been adequately fleshing out their standards as exposures grow.

3.3.4 Others

Other requirements include those related to leveraged investments to prevent losses from exceeding what the investor can bear, as well as requirements for staking, liquid staking, and the structuring of derivative instruments. While none of these requirements have been standardized by standards-setting bodies, they have been analyzed and discussed for risk identification [45,52]. For leveraged investments, the potential standardization might involve specifying protocols to limit excessive leverage and introducing automated position-clearing systems. Regarding staking and liquid staking, there are complex and opaque risks related to governance, technology, and prudence that need to be addressed. In the case of derivatives, complex instruments such as perpetual swaps, synthetic assets, and options entail significant prudential risks. This list of requirements needs to be carefully reviewed regularly, as the industry is still evolving, and new requirements may emerge that involve unrecognized risks.

4 Further Research

The comprehensive list of requirements provided above outlines the standards that are expected to be standardized in the future, along with a description of the current standards or standardization efforts for each requirement. The findings suggest that standardization, particularly for technology and operational requirements, is not yet sufficiently advanced. There remains significant work to be done, especially in the realm of decentralized finance. Three main reasons account for the lack of standardization efforts for these requirements.

Firstly, while there is an argument for industry-led standardization, it remains unclear who is responsible for this process. Standards-setting bodies acknowledge the need for collaboration with other entities to determine responsibility for standardization, but such efforts are currently insufficient. Future research should aim to clarify which organizations should create the standards for the requirements identified as lacking standardization in this document. Secondly, the industry is still in its infancy, with emerging technologies being developed rapidly. Consequently, standardizing some requirements may be premature. Early standardization could potentially reduce operational efficiency and stifle innovation. Conversely, delaying standardization could hinder the mass adoption of digital assets or leave serious risks unaddressed. Standards-setting bodies need to carefully reconsider the appropriate balance between early standardization and allowing innovation to flourish. Thirdly, the risks associated with each requirement are not comprehensively recognized. It is likely that not all risks, particularly those related to decentralized finance, are fully understood by standards-setting bodies. Risks involved with many requirements are still under discussion by standardization bodies or self-regulatory organizations in the form of consultancy papers. Comprehensive risk identification should precede standardization efforts. Additionally, the list of risks and requirements should be reviewed regularly to account for new risks or requirements that may emerge. The list of standardization requirements developed in this document is significant as a first step in future research to overcome the three challenges identified as obstacles to standardization efforts.

5 Conclusion

Standardization of financial services in digital assets aims to ensure system reliability and interoperability, improve operational efficiency for service providers, ensure the security and convenience of financial products and services for customers, curb unfair practices and financial crimes, and stabilize the financial system. This document provides an exhaustive list of technical, operational, and regulatory requirements that need standardization and analyzes the current status of standardization for each requirement. Despite efforts by many standards-setting bodies to extend traditional finance standards to digital assets, many requirements remain unstandardized.

For technical and operational standards, achieving the objectives of standardization necessitates the involvement of academia, regulators, and operators in the standardization discussion. However, industry-wide movements toward standardization are limited, with each business operator adopting its own technical and operational approaches to address immediate issues and meet customer needs. While business operators should participate in discussions on regulatory standards, the adoption of technical and operational standards remains largely voluntary. Conversely, once regulatory frameworks are established by regulators in each jurisdiction, the adoption of regulatory standards by operators will be facilitated, as compliance becomes mandatory. Nonetheless, the standardization of regulatory requirements for decentralized finance, particularly the identification of responsible entities, remains contentious. Although IOSCO has recently set regulatory standards for DeFi, the response of national regulators to these standards needs to be monitored closely.

To promote standardization that achieves its original purposes without stifling innovation, it is essential to begin precisely identifying the risks associated with these requirements and establish the responsible entities for standardization, particularly for those requirements with little or no standardization efforts observed. This approach, based on the exhaustive list of requirements provided in this document, will help ensure that standardization supports the growth and stability of the digital asset finance industry.

References

1. ISO/IEC 15408. https://www.iso.org/standard/72891.html
2. ISO 17422. Iso 17442-1:2020 financial services, legal entity identifier (lei) part 1: Assignment. https://www.iso.org/standard/78829.html
3. ISO 17422. Iso 17442-2:2020 financial services, legal entity identifier (lei) part 2: Application in digital certificates. https://www.iso.org/standard/79917.html
4. ISO/IEC 18033-1. https://www.iso.org/standard/76156.html#lifecycle
5. ISO 18774. Iso 18774:2015 securities and related financial instruments, financial instrument short name (fisn). https://www.iso.org/standard/66153.html
6. ISO/IEC JTC 1/SC27. https://www.iso.org/committee/45306.html
7. ISO 24165. Iso 24163-1:2021 digital token identifier (dti), registration, assignment and structure part 1: Method for registration and assignment. https://www.iso.org/standard/80601.html
8. ISO/IEC 27000. https://www.iso.org/standard/73906.html
9. ISO/IEC 27001. Iso/iec 27001:2022 information security, cybersecurity and privacy protection, information security management systems, requirements. https://www.iso.org/standard/27001
10. ISO/IEC 27035. Iso/iec 27035:2023 information technology, information security incident management part 1: Principles and process. https://www.iso.org/standard/78973.html
11. ISO/IEC 27701. Iso/iec 27701:2019 security techniques, extension to iso/iec 27001 and iso/iec 27002 for privacy information management, requirements and guidelines. https://www.iso.org/standard/71670.html
12. ISO TC 307. https://www.iso.org/committee/6266604.html
13. ISO TC 68. https://www.iso.org/committee/49650.html
14. Fast Identity Online (FIDO) Alliance. Fido u2f overview. https://fidoalliance.org/specs/u2f-specs-master/fido-u2f-overview.html
15. Fast Identity Online (FIDO) Alliance. Fido uaf architectural overview. https://fidoalliance.org/specs/fido-uaf-v1.1-id-20170202/fido-uaf-overview-v1.1-id-20170202.html
16. BCBS Basel Committee on Banking Supervision. Corporate governance principles for banks (2015)
17. BCBS Basel Committee on Banking Supervision. Prudential treatment of cryptoasset exposures (2022)
18. BCBS Basel Committee on Banking Supervision. Consultative document cryptoaset standard amendments (2023)
19. Financial Accounting Standards Board. https://www.fasb.org/
20. International Accounting Standards Board. https://www.ifrs.org/groups/international-accounting-standards-board/
21. CryotoISAC. https://www.cryptoisac.org/
22. CCI Crypto Council for Innovation. Key elements of an effective defi framework (2023)
23. FATF Financial Action Task Force. Updated guidance for a risk-based approach for virtual assets and virtual asset service providers, pp. 82–06 (2021)
24. FATF Financial Action Task Force. Updated guidance for a risk-based approach for virtual assets and virtual asset service providers, pp. 78–87 (2021)
25. FATF Financial Action Task Force. Updated guidance for a risk-based approach for virtual assets and virtual asset service providers, pp. 102–107 (2021)

26. FATF Financial Action Task Force. Virtual assets: Targeted update on implementation of the fatf standards on virtual assets and virtual asset service providers (2023)
27. FSB Financial Stability Board. The financial stability implications for multifunction crypto-asset intermediaries (2023)
28. FSB Financial Stability Board. High-level recommendations for the regulation, supervision, and oversight of crypto-asset activities and markets, pp. 9–10 (2023)
29. FSB Financial Stability Board. High-level recommendations for the regulation, supervision, and oversight of crypto-asset activities and markets, p. 6 (2023)
30. FSB Financial Stability Board. High-level recommendations for the regulation, supervision, and oversight of crypto-asset activities and markets, p. 7 (2023)
31. FSB Financial Stability Board. High-level recommendations for the regulation, supervision, and oversight of crypto-asset activities and markets, p. 9 (2023)
32. FSB Financial Stability Board. High-level recommendations for the regulation, supervision, and oversight of crypto-asset activities and markets, p. 7 (2023)
33. FSB Financial Stability Board. High-level recommendations for the regulation, supervision and oversight of global stablecoin arrangements (2023)
34. Internet Engineering Task Force. https://datatracker.ietf.org/wg/oauth/documents/
35. OepnID Foundation. https://openid.net/developers/how-connect-works/
36. IOSCO International Organization of Securities Commissions. Policy recommendations for crypto and digital asset markets, p. 53 (2023)
37. IOSCO International Organization of Securities Commissions. Policy recommendations for crypto and digital asset markets, pp. 31–32 (2023)
38. IOSCO International Organization of Securities Commissions. Policy recommendations for crypto and digital asset markets, pp. 16–18, 22–25 (2023)
39. IOSCO International Organization of Securities Commissions. Policy recommendations for crypto and digital asset markets, pp. 19–21, 33–38, 41–43 (2023)
40. IOSCO International Organization of Securities Commissions. Policy recommendations for crypto and digital asset markets, pp. 26–30 (2023)
41. IOSCO International Organization of Securities Commissions. Policy recommendations for crypto and digital asset markets, p. 65 (2023)
42. IOSCO International Organization of Securities Commissions. Policy recommendations for crypto and digital asset markets, pp. 39–40 (2023)
43. IOSCO International Organization of Securities Commissions. Policy recommendations for decentralized finance (defi), pp. 22–23 (2023)
44. Schuler, F.S.K., Cloots, A.S.: On defi and on-chain cefi: How (not) to regulate decentralized finance (2024)
45. OECD. Why decentralized finance (defi) matters and the policy implications (2022)
46. National Institute of Standards and Technology. https://csrc.nist.gov/projects/hash-functions/sha-3-project
47. National Institute of Standards and Technology. https://csrc.nist.gov/projects/post-quantum-cryptography
48. National Institute of Standards and Technology. https://www.nist.gov/cyberframework
49. National Institute of Standards and Technology. Advanced encryption standard (aes) (2001)
50. National Institute of Standards and Technology. Nistir 8202 blockchain technology overview (2018)

51. National Institute of Standards and Technology. Recommendation for key management: Part1, general, recommendation for key management: Part 2, best practices for key management organizations, recommendation for key management, part3: Application, specific key management guidance (2020, 2019, 2015)
52. European Parliament. Remaining regulatory challenges in digital finance and crypto-assets after mica (2023)
53. Rettig, K.G.R., Mosier, M.: Genuine defi as critical infrastructure: a conceptual framework for combating illicit finance activity in decentralized finance (2024)
54. Internal Revenue Service. https://www.irs.gov/businesses/small-businesses-self-employed/digital-assets
55. W3C. Verifiable credentials data model v2.0. https://www.w3.org/TR/vc-data-model-2.0/
56. W3C World Wide Web Consortium. Decentralized identifiers (dids) v1.0 core architecture, data model, and representations (2023)

Author Index

A
Alsagheer, Dana 313

B
Bahrani, Maryam 85
Benedetti, Anto 207
Berens, Benjamin 33
Blom, Michelle 3

C
Conley, Trevor 225
Crapis, Davide 135

D
de Paula Pinto, Jose Simao 364
Diaz, Nilsso 225

E
Ek, Alexander 18
Espada, Diego 225
Estrada-Galiñanes, Vero 170

F
Fang, Rui 313
Felten, Edward W. 135
Ford, Bryan 170
Fu, Xiang 225

G
Garimidi, Pranav 85
Grandjean, Dominic 253
Grimmelmann, James 335

H
Haines, Thomas 50
Harrison, Max 50
Heimbach, Lioba 253
Henry, Tiphaine 207
Hilt, Tobias 33
House, Carole 371
Hu, Xiaoxiao 313

I
Igarashi, Taichi 189

J
Jamroga, Wojciech 66
Ji, Yan 335

K
Katayama, Ken 293
Kiffer, Lucianna 281
Kim, Yan 66
Klinczak, Marjori 364
Kuruvilla, Alvin 225

M
Mamageishvili, Akaki 135
Matsuura, Kanta 189
Mayne, Stenton 225
Melkonian, Orestis 150
Moallemi, Ciamac 105

N
Neumann, Stephan 33

P
Pai, Mallesh 128
Patange, Utkarsh 105

R
Resnick, Max 128
Roenne, Peter B. 66
Roughgarden, Tim 85
Ryan, Peter Y. A. 66

S
Schlegel, Christoph 91
Shao, Jiahui 313
Shi, Weidong 313
Skorik, Sophia 281
Stark, Philip B. 18
Stuckey, Peter J. 3, 18
Sugino, Takaya 371

T

Teague, Vanessa 3
Travers, Mitchell 293
Truderung, Tomasz 33
Tucci-Piergiovanni, Sara 207

U

Udovychenko, Margarita 33

V

Vinogradova, Polina 150
Volkamer, Melanie 33
Vonlanthen, Yann 281
Vukcevic, Damjan 3, 18

W

Wattenhofer, Roger 253, 281
Wildauer, Egon 364

X

Xu, Maochao 313

Y

Yamamoto, Go 240
Yamanaka, Masato 293, 371
Yeo, Michelle 170

Z

Zhang, Haoqian 170

SPRINGER NATURE

GPSR Compliance

The European Union's (EU) General Product Safety Regulation (GPSR) is a set of rules that requires consumer products to be safe and our obligations to ensure this.

If you have any concerns about our products, you can contact us on ProductSafety@springernature.com

In case Publisher is established outside the EU, the EU authorized representative is:

Springer Nature Customer Service Center GmbH
Europaplatz 3
69115 Heidelberg, Germany

The manufacturer's authorised representative in the EU is Springer Nature Customer Service Centre GmbH, Europaplatz 3, 69115 Heidelberg, Germany. If you have any concerns regarding our products, please contact ProductSafety@springernature.com

Printed and bound by CPI Group (UK) Ltd, Croydon, CR0 4YY

26/03/2026

02078933-0018